Dreams of the Hmong Kingdom

Dreams of the Hmong Kingdom

The Quest for Legitimation in French Indochina, 1850–1960

Mai Na M. Lee

THE UNIVERSITY OF WISCONSIN PRESS

Publication of this book has been possible, in part,
through support from the **Center for Southeast Asian Studies**
at the University of Wisconsin–Madison.

The University of Wisconsin Press
1930 Monroe Street, 3rd Floor
Madison, Wisconsin 53711-2059
uwpress.wisc.edu

3 Henrietta Street, Covent Garden
London WC2E 8LU, United Kingdom
eurospanbookstore.com

Printed in the United States of America

Library of Congress Cataloging-in-Publication Data

Lee, Mai Na M., author.
Dreams of the Hmong kingdom: the quest for legitimation in
French Indochina, 1850–1960 / Mai Na M. Lee.
pages   cm — (New perspectives in Southeast Asian studies)
Includes bibliographical references and index.
ISBN 978-0-299-29884-5 (pbk.: alk. paper)
ISBN 978-0-299-29883-8 (e-book)
1. Hmong (Asian people)—Indochina—History.   2. Ethnic conflict—Indochina.
3. Indochina—Ethnic relations.   4. Indochina—Politics and government.
I. Title.   II. Series: New perspectives in Southeast Asian studies.
DS509.5.H66L45   2015
959´.00495972—dc23
2014035663

For the two Niam Nkauj Zuag Paj in my life:

my mother, **Lia Vue,**

Mao Song Lyfoung

Contents

Part I. Hmong Messianism
The Mandate of Heaven

Part II. The Secular Political Tradition:
A Mandate by Proxy

Illustrations

Maps

Figures

Preface

This work is the culmination of twenty years of thinking, intellectualizing, and researching and a lifetime spent dreaming about the Hmong. This "slow" history is the journey to find myself, my place among my people, and to locate our place in human history.[1] I embarked on my first oral research for various term papers during my years as an undergraduate at Carleton College. My first primary informants were immediate family members like my mother, Lia Vue, my father, Lee Cha Yia, and my grandfather, Lee Nao Mai, a shaman and highly renowned Hmong ritual expert who was also a former assistant to Tasseng (sub-district leader) Lee Blia Tria in Muang Pha, Xieng Khouang, Laos. An eyewitness to Pa Chay's War, my grandfather was the last of his generation. He was born in about 1904 and passed away in 2006. He went from the horse-riding age to the age of automobiles, airplanes, and space exploration.

My first non-Hmong informant was Robert Anderson, then executive director and a founder of the Hmong American Partnership (HAP), a nonprofit organization in Saint Paul, Minnesota. He provided insight about the political divisions within the Twin Cities Hmong community in the 1990s—particularly about how HAP was being perceived as a threat to Lao Family Community, another nonprofit organization founded by General Vang Pao. Mr. Andersen lent me some books on the Hmong to read, books that I am ashamed to admit I still have to return to him. In short, I have been doing oral research since my undergraduate days, having interviewed hundreds of informants. Only those I quote directly appear in the bibliography.

The research here spans the globe. To balance the narrative and construct a historical chronology of the Hmong, whose history has primarily been depicted from the outside using external sources, I have woven together French archival sources, oral interviews, Hmong oral traditions, and secondary sources. The multiplicity of source types and the complexity of source materials present different challenges that I hope I have managed to transcend to an extent. Interviews were recorded and lasted between three and six hours, but sometimes they were spread over a period of several days. It was impossible to record everything, however. The most intriguing information often seeped through when the recorder was off and the subject was not on the spot and, therefore, was more relaxed, such as when the informant and I were just conversing during a meal or while we were looking at a collection of photographs or other mementos. The recording device presents its own limiting difficulties, which cannot be addressed here. So ethnographic observations, personal communications, and conversations also inform this work.

This book is about Hmong aspirations and why the Hmong ally themselves with different powers and states in the hope of achieving their most cherished dream. That coveted dream is sovereignty, but, as demonstrated here, they have settled for autonomy. In the midst of pursuing their dream, the Hmong face divisions along political, regional, and social lines. These divisions occur as the result of both conscious choices and the larger historical processes that lay beyond Hmong control. Division and competition are strong themes, but these issues should not be taken negatively as symptomatic of a "Hmong cancer" of some kind. Rather, this work should be taken as a demonstration of the dynamism and plurality of ideas in Hmong society. If there is a lesson to be learned, it is that consensus can be found, that in the midst of political struggles there is the larger picture of the Hmong as a group, a people. Individual ambitions should be, must be tempered by this larger consideration. Others who have developed great civilizations already know this fact. The Hmong seem to know it only subconsciously. This is the one big lesson that this work hopes to impart to the new generation of Hmong leaders emerging around the globe.

Doing Hmong Oral History as a Native Researcher and Member of the Lee [Ly] Clan

The need for the oral historian to justify his or her sources and methodology is a product of oral history's secondary position within a discipline that privileges written documents. Yet Paul Richard Thompson reminds us that oral history "was the *first* kind of history. And it is only quite recently that skill in handling oral evidence has ceased to be one of the marks of the great historian."[2] Thompson traces the recovery of oral history in the twentieth-century West, tying its earlier decline in prestige to the oral historian's loss of standing due to the development of literacy and the fecundity of print material in eighteenth-century Europe. The oral historian's knowledge of lineage and regional history was once recited in ritualized contexts where he or she was received with awe, but "the spread of documentation in literate societies made redundant such public moments of historical revelation . . . [and] now the document stands as the final authority, and the guarantee of transmission to the future." Oral evidence gradually became associated with "social groups of low prestige, such as children, the urban poor, or isolated country people."[3] With literacy and modernity almost synonymous, it is not a surprise that nonliterate groups such as the Hmong, as demonstrated throughout this book, have expressed a strong desire for literacy. The Hmong's longing for a writing system of their own can be contextualized amid western modernization.

By the eighteenth century, the preponderance of printed sources made it "possible for some historians at least to dispense with their own field-work, and rely on documents and oral evidence published by others."[4] Secondary works burgeoned in the following century to the extent that even great historians can avoid oral research. Meanwhile, the development of history as a profession "brought with it a more precise and conscious social standing," requiring that historians gain "some form of distinctive training." Documentary research was emphasized, reinforcing negative attitudes about engaging in fieldwork. "By cutting themselves off," Thompson concludes, "they could also pretend to an objective neutrality, and hence even come to believe that insulation from the social world was a positive professional virtue."[5]

Oral history has been revived with efforts taken in the twentieth century. Karl Marx was quite keen in observing the elitism of historians, writing in 1856, "I know the heroic struggles the English working class has gone through since the middle of the last century; struggles not the less glorious because they are shrouded in obscurity and burked by middle class historians."[6] In the early 1960s, the English historian E. P. Thompson pioneered new methods of historical writing through his famous history of the working classes in Britain. A labor historian and a Marxist, he aimed to rescue the masses from "the enormous condescension of posterity" by making them historical actors and paying attention to their conceptual universe.[7] More recently the Subaltern School of historians in India established similar trends by using voices from below to challenge the notion of Europe, the colonial homeland, as a hegemonic center, to say nothing of Maurice Halbwachs and all the recent writings on collective memory.[8]

The revival of oral history and proliferation of the use of oral sources since the 1960s has led to the emergence of studies in social memory, collective memory, and historical memory, all of which closely examine and critique the cognitive and social ways in which memory is retained in living informants as well as how historians use these sources. Critical inquiry into using subjects as sources has revealed that "human memory (mainly what neuroscientists call episodic memory) is filtered as much as constructed. It is selective; it leaves things out, whether as a result of the kind of trauma that makes it harder for men and women to reconcile their past experience with a continuous sense of self, or because what is remembered is framed—perhaps in unconscious ways—by social and political needs in the present."[9] The reliability of the human brain comes into question because what the subject recalls, which is also dependent on what questions the historian poses to him or her, is continuously influenced by conditions in the past as well as the present. Memory sources, therefore, have to be treated as different from written sources. "What emerges from research across quite divergent scholarly disciplines, including cognitive psychology and neuroscience, is that individual memory does not function like an archive of lived experiences deposited somewhere in the brain, but is rather constructed anew at each moment of recall."[10] Because memory is influenced by both the past and the present, it also needs to be "rehistoricized."[11] Some note that, in the recalling of memory, processes of "confabulation" often occur due to the psychological and social circumstances of the recall.[12]

The conclusion from cognitive studies done on human abilities to recall what they observe largely concludes that the human mind can be unreliable. Oral information, therefore, has to be taken as an individual's interpretation of what he or she observes and not as facts. On the other hand, studies have also shown that the minds of individuals like the Hmong who are immersed in an oral universe may be very different from those of westerners, especially those who are the subjects of cognitive research. These studies conclude that the brain is essentially a "technology of memory" so that "a mind that was trained to remember telephone numbers is rather different from one that was not, or is not anymore; [and] one that developed the capacity to perform long oral narratives is in important ways different from one that was trained to reproduce long written ones."[13] Would Hmong people who are primarily an oral people who exist in a cultural universe that requires them to recall everything, including legal disputes and settlements, from memory have better memories? The studies seem to hint at that, but no conclusive facts have been established. Certainly the abilities of Hmong men and women to memorize hundreds of ritual and courting songs that would take days to perform are quite mind-boggling. On the other hand, memorizing ritual verses with rhyming stanzas might be very different from recalling life events that are disjointed. Certainly, the incredible memory ability of individuals such as the Hmong who are from an oral society merits scientific study. My informant Mao Song Lyfoung had treasured photos (see the many examples in this book) with dates clearly established and written on the back by her father and brothers, which guided her memory. These photos bolster the credibility of her memories where the chronology is concerned.

Questions about the role of the oral historian and how she or he extracts and interprets from the oral sources is a topic of its own discussion. The problems of "slippage" can occur during the process of interpreting the data, some warn us. "When historians move unannounced between different meanings of memory in their prose, when they refer alternately to cognitive processes of remembering, social acts of commemoration and to meta-entities such as 'collective memory' without qualification, their arguments lack precision. In the process memory becomes reified—treated in other words as a thing, an essence, cut adrift from the worldly networks in which its operations and their social purchase are enmeshed. It is often imbued with agency in its own right."[14] The role of the historian, how she or he handles the sources, the sources themselves, and the circumstances that produced the sources—all have to be critically examined.

Where it concerns the Hmong who are spread across the globe, the role of the historian in selecting his or her subjects also comes into play. When I met Touxoua Lyfoung, the son of Touby Lyfoung, a Hmong leader during the French period, in France in July 2002, he immediately registered a complaint about how Jane Hamilton-Merritt had ignored the Lyfoungs while conducting interviews in France for her book *Tragic Mountains* during the late 1980s. "At the time," said Touxoua, "all the Lyfoung brothers, including my uncles Tougeu and Toulia, who had worked closely with my father, Touby, were still alive. Jane Hamilton-Merritt bypassed them to interview only individuals sympathetic to Vang Pao." Some scholars of Southeast Asia also cite *Tragic Mountains* as a one-sided "propaganda" piece that aims to deify Vang Pao.[15] Constructing Vang Pao as a historical leader, Hamilton-Merritt glosses over Touby's preeminent role during the time of the French. When addressing this earlier period of history, she relied on the perspectives of French officers to the exclusion of the Lyfoungs even though she aimed for her work to be "the Hmong *voice*."[16]

Cognizant of the critical inquiries into memory and history, and despite a research trip to Laos in March 2008, I am conscious that this work is derived largely from oral interviews with members of the Lyfoung family and with Hmong sympathetic to Touby and Vang Pao. This was not by choice but by the political circumstances of the Lao People's Democratic Republic (PDR) having been, before full diplomatic relations with the United States were restored in 2004, a closed country, especially to exiles like myself. My trip to Laos proved fruitful in the ways that it opened my eyes to the rewards enjoyed by the families of the Hmong leaders of the revolution. The families of Lo Fay Dang, Lo Nhia Vu, and Thao (Mr.) Tou Yang, the main Communist Hmong leaders, for example, enjoy incredible educational and political privileges. Many of their members have obtained degrees of higher education from Vietnam, the former

Soviet Union, and Western European countries. Some hold high posts in the government, as well as in the party leadership. Hmong serve at every level of the Lao government from village chiefs to subdistrict and district officers, provincial governors, and nationally elected statesmen and stateswomen. The Hmong comprise only about 10 percent of the population, but they occupy 16 percent of government positions in the Lao PDR according to Tongeu Thao, the current vice president of the Lao Front for National Reconstruction, a position formerly occupied by Fay Dang.[17] In addition, there are Hmong with ranks of colonels and generals in the Lao military. Some even have the distinction of being Mig 21 fighter pilots. Like the legendary T-28 pilots on the right during the Secret War, these Lao-Hmong pilots who command the sky possess a unique distinction; they are viewed with awe akin to how Americans beheld astronauts in the late 1960s.

I was also able to travel along Colonial Route 7 (CR7) and grasp firsthand the historical import of the region. Talking to Hmong along the road from Xieng Khouang to Nong Het made me realize even more the devastation of the war. The names and stories in this book are not known to those who currently occupy this stretch of land. Most inhabitants around here are newcomers. A substantial section of those who had pioneered the settlement of the region have been pushed to Long Cheng, southwest of the Plain of Jars (PDJ), then were transplanted by the war and beamed to America. When I stopped in Phak Khe near Touby's native village, for example, I asked people in the market if they knew the location of the grave sites of Ly Foung and Vang Pao's father, Neng Chue. No one knew these names. People in Nong Het told me they were originally from Vietnam and not native to Laos. The names of Hmong historical figures in the region did not resonate with them.

I arrived in the Lao PDR over a decade too late to interview either Fay Dang or Nhia Vu. I spoke with their family members in Vientiane, but I was not able to obtain much information. These family members had no one alive who was familiar with the events of the early twentieth century. My short, one-month stay did not permit me to explore beyond Lo family members. In a hotel in Vientiane, a woman of the Ly clan who married into the Lo family pointed me to Ger Lo, the grandson of Lo Bliayao, the French-appointed Hmong leader before Touby, and Jer Jalao Ly, saying that he was the keeper of the family history. Ger showed me a finished manuscript in Lao containing photographs, family trees, and other images, but he quickly turned off his computer after piquing my interest.[18] He was not ready to make the information public. He intends to publish it, he said, but must first obtain official permission from the government. Ger also was not interested in a formal interview and would not allow me to tape our session. Apart from telling me some anecdotes, he was more intrigued by what I had already gathered from the Lyfoungs. He seemed more interested in filling in the gaps in his own manuscript.

Within these limitations, the oral interviews in this work span three continents, Asia, Europe, and North America, and include the divergent views of the Hmong and non-Hmong who have struggled alongside Touby and some of those who are members of Fay Dang's family. I was very fortunate also to acquire the government-sanctioned biography of Thao Tou Yang, which discusses the formation of the Hmong Communist militia, the Pa Chay Company. Together, the book and my few oral sources collected on the left have enriched this work to an extent, but there remains a need to focus more exclusively on the history of the Hmong Communists in Laos and those in Vietnam. The irony of the victory of the Hmong Communists is that while the stories of Hmong Americans (the "running dogs of the imperialists") are beginning to be produced in some quantity, stories about the Hmong on the left are almost nonexistent. Moreover, as victors of the revolution, their voices have been absorbed into nationalist historiographies as Lao, Vietnamese, or members of the working class, not as Hmong.

For now, however, I must be content with the fact that Touby and Fang Dang were nephew and uncle, and that the story of the Lyfoungs, to a limited extent, is that of the Lobliayaos as well. Extending this parallel more broadly, the story of the Hmong on the right is also that of those on the left, for the Hmong on both sides have blood ties across the political divide. Mao Song Lyfoung, from whom much of my information came, definitely viewed the personal histories of her maternal great grandfather, Lo Pa Tsi, a Hmong leader in the mid-eighteenth century, and her grandfather, Blia Yao, as an integral part of her own family history. Although the political struggle was intense, Mao Song said, the love between the two families was never snuffed out completely. The sentiments on the other side, decades after egos have subsided, appear to have been the same. The deepest regrets of Fay Dang and Nhia Vu, said Zong Blong, the son of Nhia Vu, was that they allowed Touby to die in the seminar camps.[19]

Certainly, these oral accounts are affected by the workings of historical memories that have emerged during the last three decades. While the Lyfoungs may have highlighted elements that support their story, the version from the other side does not vary too drastically in detail. The Lyfoungs, in their own oral accounts, framed the political struggles with their Lo rivals in terms of merit. They triumphed because, possessing literacy and other skills, they were the more qualified bureaucrats. The story from the other side is framed in terms of inheritance and being cheated of their family legacy.[20] These versions are essentially two sides of the same coin, hence eliminating some questions about a one-sided explanation. Since oral accounts often revolve around the issue of individual interpretation, it cannot be argued, at least very convincingly, that different members of this extended family provided a more or less objective version. After all, life stories that include individual perspectives "can be equally read as true or as mythical."[21]

Finally, as an oral historian, my own place within the Hmong community cannot be ignored. I am a member of the Lee (Ly) clan, one of the most active players in modern Hmong politics. Since many of the events described in this book involve clan politics, this affiliation will undoubtedly generate questions about my own bias. This work is not a conscious attempt to justify or glorify the actions of the Lee clan as some readers are bound to conclude no matter what. I just happen to belong to this particular clan, which played a dominant role during the period under discussion. Studying a period dominated by my own clan has privileged me with access to certain viewpoints, data, and individuals perhaps not available to others. It is possible that it was easier for individuals whom I addressed as relatives to trust me with certain information. The rape of the Ly women discussed in chapter 7, for example, was a particularly shameful event that might not have been shared with just any researcher. Even as a member of the clan, however, I was not allowed to ask questions about which specific women were victims of this rape. Ly Na Jalao and Tougeu Lyfoung both refused to give me names, although Ly Na hinted very subtly that his mother was in the fields that day.

A second, highly guarded secret shared with me was the story of how the French and King Sisavangvong offered the province of Xieng Khouang to Touby Lyfoung as an autonomous Hmong zone in 1946. Colonel Nao Kao Lyfoung explained that this information had never been made public by the Lyfoung family for fear that the present-day Hmong, who are especially desirous of a homeland of their own, would blame the family for failing to take advantage of that opportunity over a half century ago. My position as a Lee clan member may have privileged me with access to certain information, but, as Paul Thompson reminds us again, "it is not necessarily true that an interviewer of the same sex, class, or race [and, in this case, clan] will obtain more accurate information. . . . Nor does increased intimacy always bring less inhibition."[22]

My clan affiliation also may have closed the door to other channels of information. During my meeting with Vang Pao, for example, I bravely pushed into the next era, not covered in this book. I asked General Vang Pao to relate his version of the alleged "Lee Coup" against him in 1966. He looked me in the eye and replied, with full cognizance that I am a member of the Lee clan, "Koj mus noog nej cov Hmoob Lis" (You go ask your own Lee clan). His emphasis on "your own Lee clan" made it clear that he felt his version of the event would be too offensive to me, a Lee clan member. Pushing him to reveal his true "liver" would have been going beyond the realm of what is culturally polite to both of us in our respective positions as Hmong Vang versus Hmong Lee, and as "wise elderly male leader" of the Hmong versus "young female graduate student" with little social status. Moreover, the general had already related his understanding of the event in Jane Hamilton-Merritt's work.[23] He chose to remain silent on the issue with me, a Hmong Lee, affirming what had already been communicated to Hamilton-Merritt, a non-Hmong.

My membership in the Lee clan also undoubtedly affected the manner in which information came to me. I am not the first researcher to encounter this difficulty nor is my situation unique. Oral historians have long noted that "alterations" have occurred between researcher and subject during the process of conducting oral interviews. Indicating the universality of such problems, Jan Vansina, the preeminent oral historian, writes: "The performer [subject] handles the interviewer [researcher] as an audience and dialogues with him. He structures his content so as to make points relevant to this situation. Thus when L. Haring was collecting accounts in Kisii (Kenya) in June 1971 his informants emphasized their positive feelings towards Europeans and tried to use the interviewer as an arbitrator who would agree with them about the superiority of the Kisii over their neighbors. The same accounts would hardly have been told in this manner in front of another audience."[24]

Although Vansina's point resonates with my own experience, my status as a Hmong writing about Hmong added dimensions beyond even the complex postcolonial encounter between European and African that he describes. Instead of the Kisii-neighbor European triangle that Haring encountered, I faced an almost infinite intersection of family, clan, cultural group, and national and ideological conflicts. Compounding my difficulties, I faced questions about my ultimate "objectivity" in mediating these conflicts that would never have troubled a European scholar like Haring, whose objectivity is, of course, assumed by Vansina and his readers. But, like all Hmong driven into exile, perhaps like all exiles, I know that present-day politics within the Hmong American community rests, above all, on competing interpretations of a movable past, always contested, always politicized. Yet I have passed through the same academy as Vansina, read no doubt many of the same texts, and share a similar commitment to scholarship. Confronted with all these tensions, I write, I submit, with a fuller knowledge of my positionality than Haring or Vansina could ever have imagined. Reconciliation of these competing claims, political and intellectual, may ultimately be impossible, but at least I have a fuller, if not a full, sense of my limitations as a scholar and am self-conscious in my compromises. In the end, I do not expect to escape the scrutiny of others, but I take some solace in Thompson's final words. "The merit of oral history," he writes, "is not that it entails this or that political stance, but that it leads historians to an awareness that their activity is inevitably pursued within a social context and with political implications."[25]

Acknowledgments

Nicholas Tapp, one of my reviewers, thought it important that I articulate my reasons for pursuing history. I do not have much space to do so, but will briefly provide a nontraditional acknowledgement here. My first instructors about life were my mother, Lia Vue (after naturalization, Lia B. Vue Lee), who passed away on January 4, 2014, and to whom I dedicate this work, and my father, Lee Cha Yia (after naturalization, Cha Topson). Grandmother and Grandfather Lee Nao Mai also aided in shaping my life outlook. My parents and grandparents introduced me to the oral power of Hmong society—the central thesis of this work—with their incredible storytelling. Many stories and *kwv txhiaj* or courting verses I mention in the work come from my parents and grandparents.

My earliest inspiration from my mother was the story of Maum Nyab Lwj, a man who accomplishes miraculous things through writing—again, another important element of this work. For my own sake, as a toddler listening to the story, I somehow managed to miss the crucial detail that Maum Nyab Lwj is a male. I assumed that because of his name, Maum, which translates as "female" in Hmong, he was a she. For this reason, I not only identified with him but aimed, having absolutely no doubts about my own abilities as a girl, to possess the very same literate power when I grew up. I shuddered to contemplate what I would have become had I listened better to my mother, who, looking back on the way she told the story, made his sex very explicit. Now that she has passed on, I can finally admit that my mother was right to have accused me of never listening to her (though perhaps for good reasons?).

My father fashioned me into a historian. If anyone is to be blamed, it is he. Others inspired and nudged me in this direction, but looking back on my life I know it was my conversations and dealings with my father that set me on this road. After arriving in the United States, I watched as my father struggled with loss of status as a former military officer and clan leader. While my mother went to work right away because she knew we needed feeding, my father, who no doubt suffered from posttraumatic stress syndrome and other social issues he faced as a Hmong male in America, "tos tuag lawm xwb," or was just waiting for death. It was during the several years in which he stayed home to babysit us that he and I were able to converse about Hmong politics and his military experiences, which, I learned in college, had not been included in the conventional histories. I listened intently because it seemed to do him a lot of good to talk about his past. I noted how his shoulders would straighten and his voice would reverberate with command and pride—a contrast to his usual depressed, sad self—and so I listened. When I was a bit older, I accompanied my mother and father to our seasonal summer jobs, cutting asparagus or picking tomatoes, cucumbers, and other crops for white farmers whose land surrounded the Twin Cities, where I grew up. I had ample opportunity again to listen to my father's military experiences as he drove us to and from work. I know I had to be the one to write all this down because he couldn't.

My first role model for academic achievement was my brother Nao Choua. I remember as a child too young to attend school in Pha Nok Kok, Laos, how I envied my brother in his crisp uniform of blue pants and white shirt. I hung around outside his school, which had one open wall, to listen and watch as my brother, the top student in the class, administered physical punishments to his classmates in accordance with Lao educational practices back then. I remember thinking to myself, "I'd better be the top student like him when I go to school!" The war and our subsequent refugee experience prevented my schooling in Laos and Thailand. After surviving four years at the base of Phou Bia following Vang Pao's exile in May 1975 and one year in the Thai refugee camp of Ban Vinai, my education commenced in September 1980 in Omro, Wisconsin. I was eleven or twelve when I held my first pencil and began accumulating ideas in a foreign language and environment.

At Carleton College, Professor Chang-t'ai Hung, Chinese intellectual historian extraordinaire, piqued my interest in history in his freshmen seminar, which was, if I remember it correctly, about the May Fourth movement. I continued taking Chinese history classes with him. One particular lecture on how Lu Xun stopped pursuing a career in medicine to become a writer in order to "expose the ills of his society" and "restore the spirit" of his people convinced me that I needed to abandon the very same pursuit so that I could give Hmong people a history. I was impressed by the historical consciousness of the Chinese as constructed by Hung. Then a young idealist, I attributed the great civilization of the Han Chinese to this historical consciousness. At the same time, Hung's lectures highlighted for me my own people's lack of a glorious civilization, which I tied directly to their lack of historical narratives. Now, however, as I see Hmong Americans and Hmong in Asia, both young and old, abandon their language and culture unconsciously or by choice for other ways of being and thinking, I often feel that I've come along too late to save Hmong civilization. At times the legends of the Hmong messianic figure Sin Sai, stories largely appropriated from the Lao, resonate well. Because Sin Sai overslept and awoke from his slumbers to find that all the land had been apportioned to others, he could not find a kingdom for his people, the Hmong.

I thank my four brothers, Nao Choua, Boua Chao, Ge, and Va Thai, for always considering me their brother, immersing me in their male universe, and instilling a love of adventure and the courage to question. Back in Laos, Nao Choua would take me with him on hunting and trapping trips around our village, instructing me in the skills of men. My brothers, along with my father, did such an excellent job of initiating me into their male universe that I became the one who crossed oceans and encircled the globe while my brothers remained home with Mom and Dad. Along similar lines, I thank my husband, Tsong Sou, and my children, Ntxhee Yees Stephanie, Athena Nkauj Zag, and Maximus Tsim Nyog, who have sacrificed the most. My husband, much like my father, has stood with me against the social strictures of Hmong society. Thank you for not always expecting me to be a proper wife. My family members, Cha Fong Yang, Maia Lee, and Ge and Ah Lee, who babysat the kids, also made this book possible.

Among my informants, I thank Mao Song Lyfoung, the Hmong oral historian extraordinaire, in whose debt I shall remain until the end of time. The Hmong say that when you want to know something important you must go ask the *maum phauj*, the "grand aunt." I have experienced firsthand the wisdom of this adage in aunty. More than once she patiently recounted to me the intricacies of her family history and the history of the Hmong of Nong Het. I am touched by her enthusiasm in finding me a willing disciple. Aunty explained that, kept at home as a *qhev* (slave), like the women of her time, she never enjoyed the privilege of an expensive education, as her celebrated brothers did, and so she remained nonliterate all her life. She is, in my heart, however, the indisputable Lyfoung intellectual. When I met her, it struck me that I was not the first to be intrigued by my people; I was not the first to realize the significance of possessing history. Aunty Mao Song was an inspirational role model to emulate. As poetic justice for her lack of access to education due to her sex, I, also a woman but with more opportunities, dedicate this work to her as well.

I thank Charles Vannier (Vaj Neeb), Aunty Mao Song's son, who consented to multiple interview sessions and mentioned me to General Vang Pao. As the "slave" who "used to carry Vang Pao's lunch," and the only Hmong to have graduated from the prestigious St. Cyr French military school, Vannier had the trust, as well as the respect, of the general and so was instrumental in providing me with access. Vannier paved the way while Txiv Laus Chue Chu Cha took me to my first meeting with Vang Pao. Thank you both.

Others I must thank by name among the Lyfoung family are Tougeu Lyfoung, his wife, Sisamone, and his daughter, May Joua (Joyce), who also took me to see Vang Pao. Colonel Nao Kao Lyfoung and his wife, Mee Kue, generously shared their insights. Yangsao Sayasith Lyfoung and his wife, May Blia Vang, have been kind in always including me in their life events. Yangsao, also a nephew of Thao Tou Yang, translated Thao Tou's biography from Lao into English for me. May Blia cooked for me many times. I met Uncle Tougeu in France during the setting sun of his days, after years of my own exhaustive schooling. Uncle's interest in my education and recollections of his thirst for knowledge ignited my passion to complete my educational journey and make this book. Uncle made me realize that the struggle to understand the Hmong is a worthy endeavor. I am fortunate to have been touched by him during his lifetime, and I await the publication of his memoir. With this work, I make no pretense to be able to trump the literate Lyfoungs, who are very capable of writing their own histories. Like many of my informants, the Lyfoung siblings I interviewed, Mao Song, Tougeu, and Nao Kao, have all passed away, but I hope this work gives life to some of their memories.

General Vang Pao and his wives, Song and Chia Moua, kindly welcomed me to their home in California. The general, who was always surrounded by people, was generous enough to meet with me twice. I am fortunate to have experienced the charisma described to me by both his superiors and his underlings. The general and his wives have since passed on, but it was a once in a lifetime encounter. *Ua tsaug ntau.*

I also owe a debt of gratitude to Vang Tsoua Yang and his father, Colonel Shoua Yang. In France in 2001, Vang Tsoua drove me to see Maurice Gauthier, Jean Sassi, Andre Chenivess, Dr. Coindat, Ly Na Jalao, and others. Vang Tsoua also helped digitized some of the images in this book. He played a role in bringing to fruition the Hmong dream of having history. Merci beaucoup! Colonel Shoua Yang was generous with his time both in France and while he was in the United States in 2005.

I also thank Uncle Ly Tsia Tou and my cousins in Paris, who hosted me and drove me around. Mr. and Madame Ly Na in Toulouse talked almost non-stop to me about history and politics. Finally, Colonel Ly Pao and his wife, Tsia Moua, in Alençon were most kind as well, despite the colonel's deteriorating health.

In Laos, Kaying Yang introduced me to Nou Lo, the granddaughter of Lo Blia Yao. After confirming my credentials as a member of the faculty at the University of Minnesota, Nou brought me to her father, Zong Blong Lo. I also thank Ger Lo for meeting with me. I look forward to the publication of his book on the Lo family, which will no doubt balance my work here. Kaying also introduced me to Ly Tou, the vice deputy minister of education, and his family at Dong Dok. Ly Tou brokered my interview with Tongeu Thao, the vice president of the Lao Front for National Reconstruction. Finally, I owe much to Pai Yang, her husband, and her son, Anousith, who toured me around Vientiane and surrounding areas, and to Mee Yang, who accompanied me on CR7 from Phonsavan to Nong Het.

At the University of Wisconsin, Alfred W. McCoy has been a tireless advocate of the dream and Michael Cullinane a cheerleader for over a decade now. Katherine Bowie and Thongchai Winichakul are mentors extraordinaire. Paul Hutchcroft and Marlys Macken provided comments years ago. *Aacaan* Bob Bickner, Patcharin, and Janpanit introduced me to Thai language and culture. Mary Jo Wilson did lots of things for me, but, most important, she listened. As for my editors, Gwen Walker and Sheila McMahon, and others, I can't even begin to imagine their patience with me. Thank you so much for helping to bring to fruition the Hmong dream!

At the University of Minnesota, MJ Maynes, Jo Lee, and Jigna Desai provided feedback on parts of this work in various formats. Jo Lee, Donna Gabaccia, Chris Isett, Lisa Park, and Ruth Karras have been strong supporters. Ann Waltner has been generous in supporting Hmong studies, granting me the use of her office for three years, and allowing her staff at the Institute for Advanced Study to help with the Hmong Across Borders conference in October 2013. Ann, MJ, Ted Farmer, and Erika Lee have been my believers. Hiromi Mizuno, Andy Gallia, Tracy Deutsch, and Saje Mathieu have provided good advice. Professor Robert Entenmann of St. Olaf College, who was also my instructor in Chinese and Japanese history when Hung left for Hong Kong back in the 1990s, has been a lifelong mentor whose own interest in Hmong history supplied energy to this work. Thank you for nurturing multiple generations of Hmong students. Entenmann also pointed out the sources on the Chinese concept of the Mandate of Heaven.

My blind reviewers provided invaluable feedback. Enthusiastic (my own interpretation) about my work, Nicholas Tapp revealed his identity to me and sent over fifty pages of detailed suggestions for revision. The current work may still need deeper contemplation. I also thank Jacques Lemoine for his views on Touby Lyfoung, Ly Teck, and Pa Chay. Jean Michaud provided information about the Hmong of Vietnam. Paul Hillmer, Ian Baird, Pa Der Vang, Gary Yia Lee when he was in the United States, Prasit Leepreecha, Yang Cheng Vang, and Dr. Yang Dao facilitated good conversations. Colonel Vang Geu in North Carolina clarified historical details and identified photos for me.

Carolyn Wong has been a source of inspiration and support for me. My Hmong students urged me to bring this book to fruition. Finally, I've never met him but a big shout out to James C. Scott for his interest in the highland zone, which helped to shape my own argument. Christian Culas and Geoffrey Gunn's studies of the Pa Chay and Hmong rebellions have been inspiring. Thanks also to Yia Lor for providing me with his undergraduate thesis that focused on interviews with the Lo clan. All mistakes and shortcomings are mine, but let the praise go out to mentors, friends, and family members.

Maps were done by members of the Department of Geography at the University of Wisconsin—Madison, and the photos were cleaned and brought to publication quality by my brother Boua Chao, who also created the graphic art. Financial support for this work was provided by fellowships and grants from multiple sources at the University of Wisconsin—Madison: the Center for Southeast Asian Studies, the chancellor and dean, and the Department of History. At the University of Minnesota, the McKnight Summer Research Fellowship and a Faculty Summer Research Fellowship supported the trip to Laos. The Association of American University Women's Dissertation Fellowship also provided aid.

Thaum kawg no, ua tsaug rau txhua txhia tus ntawm kuv haiv Hmoob ua qhib siab nrog kuv laug hnub laug hmo tham txog keeb kwm Hmoob raws li nej tej qhov muag tau pom thiab nej tej tes tau nqis raus los lawm. Yog tsis muaj nej ces yeej tsis muaj kuv. Kuv yuav nco ntsoov nej txiaj ntsim mus niaj txhiab ib txhis. Yog nej muaj dab tsi hu tsis txog los kuv tsis xav li cas, yog nej hu txog lawm, txawm kuv tsis muaj nyiaj muaj txiaj tuaj pab los kuv yuav nqa lub dag lub zog, nqa los lus txhawb siab tuaj mus txhawb nej kom tau li kuv muaj tsab peev xwm ua tau. Vam hias tias peb haiv Hmoob yuav sib hlub kom huaj vam mus lawm yav tom ntej. Phau ntawv no yog peb sawv daws txoj kev npau suav thiab txoj kev ntshaw kom Hmoob muaj keeb kwm. Yam twg yuav tawg paj txi txiv thov nej khaws cia, yam twg yuam kev thiab tsis zoo thov nej zam lub txim, muab pov tseg es peb mam li sib qhia dua. Sib hlub, sib pab, sib nqis tes, tuav rawv Hmoob txoj kev npau suav, tuav rawv peb lub npe Hmoob tsis txhob pub kom tuag mog. Ua tsaug ntau.

Dreams of the Hmong Kingdom

Introduction

Leadership and the Politics of Legitimation in Hmong Society

In spring 2004, after several months of maneuvering for an interview with General Vang Pao, I found myself sitting behind him in a minivan on a road in Westminster, California. Vang Pao, the former commander of the secret army in Laos and Hmong leader in exile, was sitting in the front passenger seat next to his most minor wife, Song Moua, who was driving. Sisamone Thammavong Lyfoung, the wife of Tougeu Lyfoung, the former director general of the Ministry of Justice of Laos, and Chia Moua, Vang Pao's other wife, were sitting in the middle two passenger seats. Reflecting our most junior status among the group, May Joua (Joyce) Lyfoung Vang and I sat in the backseat. May Joua is the daughter of Madame Lyfoung and the widow of Vang Pao's nephew, Geu Vang. The six of us had just eaten steaming bowls of *pho* at a Lao restaurant—"General Vang Pao's favorite eatery" according to Madame Song. As the general was a denizen of the diminutive shop, many in the community had begun to refer to it as "the general's restaurant." The Lao proprietor, who recognized Vang Pao, greeted him with a *wai* and held the door for us when we arrived and departed.[1]

"Now you have seen the famous place for yourself!" Madame Song said to me in a sarcastic tone, alluding to the modesty of the restaurant as we exited the place. From the moment I had met her, I could see why she was the general's favorite wife. Her exuberant air contrasted with the introspective reserve of Madame Chia, who was her senior in rank. Vang Pao's favoritism of his individual wives, which shifted along with his politics over time, provides a rare insight into his political psyche.[2] Other wives had been favorites when their clans were instrumental to his influence back in Laos, but by the 1990s only

Figure 1. *Left to right*: Chia Moua, Mai Na M. Lee, Song Moua, Vang Pao, and Sisamone Thammavong Lyfoung pose in the backyard of Vang Pao's California home with his wives' prolifically blooming flowers serving as a backdrop. I had to coax the more reserved Madame Chia into the picture by taking and holding her hand. Madame Song, meanwhile, enthusiastically instructed everyone where to stand. (Photo by May Joua Lyfoung Vang, April 2004, author's collection)

Madames Chia's and Song's fathers remained loyal field commanders and the vanguards of Vang's homeland politics in Thailand and Laos. For this reason, although Vang had not divorced his other wives in accordance with Hmong tradition, Chia and Song were the only two he had kept with him (see fig. 1).[3] During the early years of the Secret War (1960–75), Madame Chia was the favorite "field wife" who accompanied Vang Pao even to areas under bombardment.[4] Indicative of her privileged position at the time, Madame Chia's father, Moua Cher Pao, was the commander of Boum Loung, a strategic site that provided intelligence from behind enemy lines during the Secret War period.[5]

Where affection is concerned, however, Madame Chia had long been eclipsed by Madame Song, whose marriage to Vang Pao in February 1973 was a love match of some scandal in Long Cheng. Madame Song had been kidnapped for marriage by Lo Ma, but had orchestrated her own divorce in order to return and marry the general as his most minor wife.[6] She came to the United States as Vang Pao's legal spouse and displaced others as the public companion who presided at the general's side. Her presence beside him undoubtedly contributed to her being perceived as the leading wife despite being the most junior.[7]

Back in the van in Westminster, a silence pervaded the air as we headed toward the general's home. I took a moment to observe the irony of my situation as I recalled having once seen pictures in a newspaper article of Vang Pao with his many wives at a roadside market. The general was in exile in Thailand at the time and could enjoy the fleeting moment of a leisurely stroll with his women. If that was the last time the general had gone somewhere accompanied only by women, I thought, then I was participating in a unique historical moment indeed. On the other hand, the opportunity to converse with the general had reduced me to a member of his female entourage, quite the contradiction given my feminist sensibilities. Nevertheless, "going through the kitchen door" was the most convenient way to have alone time with the general, as he was often guarded by a cohort of jealous male rivals who, much like his many wives, competed for his affection.[8]

As we turned the corner toward his house, the general interrupted my thoughts. He was talking to Madame Lyfoung, addressing her as *niam tij*, an endearment accorded the wife of one's elder brother. By using the endearment, the general was invoking multiple, previous marriage ties between his own Vang family and the Lyfoungs.[9] Speaking in a loud voice to make sure I heard him in the back of the van, Vang Pao began describing what he called the "strangest" dream of his life. The previous night, he said, he dreamed that he was in a grand palace with all the past leaders from Laos, both Hmong and Lao. Everyone there was working rigorously like a bunch of *qhev* (slaves). Incredibly, as he looked around, he saw that a man who resembled him exactly had also been brought to this place as a drone. "He, too, was hard at work!" the general said as he laughed heartily. We all laughed with him.

Suddenly, the general continued, he felt desperately lost and wanted to flee, but he did not know which road to take. "I looked and looked and did not know which way to exit," he said. "I finally said to myself, 'Bah! I must take Road Number Seven. In this country of ours, there is only Road Number Seven!'" So indelibly had the road been ingrained in the general's memory that even after thirty years in exile he still recalled it during the most desperate moment of his nightmare.

Sitting on a plane departing from Los Angeles International Airport several days later, the confidence with which the general stated his choice — "only Road Number Seven!" — reverberated in my mind. The moment he had named his exit point, the doubt in his voice dissipated and his words rose again in a confident timbre. How suitable a device for a Hmong leader, I thought, for Colonial Route 7 (CR7) was indeed a defining element in every Hmong leader's career. This intrusive French colonial project deeply affected the lives of hill peoples, shaping Hmong political structure and history down to the present. Constructed in 1910, it took the Hmong fifteen years of grueling labor under the relentless sun to complete the road. Sanctified by the sweat of tribal men and women, CR7 meanders gracefully like a mythical serpent—an Asian dragon—from Vietnam through the hills of Xieng Khouang Province, bisecting the Plain of Jars, where ancient stone monuments stand as a mute testament to a human civilization long since gone. Indeed, like an intractable dragon, the road has lured Hmong men to glory as well as defeat.[10]

Colonial Route 7 provides the northern access to the Plain of Jars, the heart of modern Laos. As it meanders west, the road intersects CR13, which leads to the administrative capital of Vientiane before it curves northwest toward the royal capital of Luang Prabang. On the Plain of Jars, CR7 also intersects CR6, which runs north from the direction of Hanoi. East of the plain, the road connects with routes coming from the Vietnamese imperial city of Hue and the commercial city of Saigon, which made it possible for the French to rule landlocked Laos from the coast of Vietnam. Surrounded by lush mountainous jungles, the Plain of Jars forms the heart of Indochina in both the pictorial and the literal sense. The roads CR6, CR7, and CR13 are the arteries of this heart, which was so essential to the integrity of French Indochina (see map 1). As the Hmong inhabited the mountains surrounding the Plain of Jars and the regions along CR7 all the way to the border of Vietnam, they were essential to French rule, particularly over Laos.

Because of its strategic location and its power to make or break landlocked Laos, Hmong chiefs have risen and fallen by this road. Lo Blia Yao became the first paramount Hmong leader under the French when he collaborated in its construction in 1910. Lo Shong Ger, on the other hand, succeeded in becoming a rebel leader in 1920 because he stood against his uncle, Blia Yao, and fought against French conscription of Hmong workers to build the road. Shong Ger's efforts were not completely noble. According to informants, he was also driven to rebel because his uncle refused to share the proceeds from the road budget with him.[11]

Since the time of Blia Yao and Shong Ger, Hmong leaders have fought along the road on different sides of the political divide—protecting the road, using it, upgrading it, and even abandoning it, only to return to it, like General Vang Pao, in the darkest recesses of their minds. Indeed, CR7 has divided and oppressed the Hmong even as it shaped their identity and empowered several

Map 1. Indochina. (Map by University of Wisconsin Cartography Lab)

generations of their leaders in Laos. After Blia Yao, the preeminent postwar
Hmong leader, Touby Lyfoung, made his political debut as a guerrilla leader
intercepting Japanese convoys along the road in 1945. For this effort, he was the
first Hmong to be inducted as a Chevalier de la Légion d'honneur, a most
prestigious award bestowed by the French government. Touby's uncle and
political rival Lo Fay Dang, the son of Blia Yao, fought on the opposing side
along this strategic road also to win favor with outside patrons. Out of favor
with the French after the death of his father in 1935, Fay Dang emerged on the
fascist side of the political divide during the Japanese Occupation and denounced
Touby as a French collaborator. After the Japanese defeat, he rallied to the
Communists as a nationalist with an even stronger political platform against
Touby, who had aligned himself with the king and submitted to French rule,
perhaps as a means of saving his preeminent status as paramount chief. The ease
with which Fay Dang, the son of a French-legitimated alliance chief, switched
sides reveals the volatile nature of the struggle for national independence in
Laos.

By 1946 Fay Dang was fighting on the left and Touby was on the side of
the Lao monarchy and the French, who proclaimed him the "King of the
Hmong."[12] Fay Dang, for the time being, was chased across the border to
Vietnam. He would return to Laos to reap the ultimate reward of the revolution
following the Communist victory in Indochina in 1975, however. Touby, meanwhile, was denounced along with other "running dogs of the imperialists" and
sentenced to die of hard labor in the seminar camps along with his patron, the
last monarch of Laos, King Sisavang Vatthana. Fay Dang, on the other hand,
became vice president of the Lao Front for National Reconstruction in the Lao
PDR, a position he held until his death in 1986. Fay Dang appeared annually at
state events alongside Souphanouvong, Kaysone Phomvihane, and Sithon
Kommadan as one of the four leading figures of the Lao PDR. When I asked
Fay Dang's nephew, Ger Lo, how it was that his grandfather Blia Yao was a
French ally but his uncles, Fay Dang and Nhia Vu, were nationalist heroes,
Ger responded that his grandfather was "forced" to serve the French—an experience that heightened Lo family members' sensitivity to colonial oppression,
priming them to become leaders of the Communist revolutionary struggle.[13]
His statement reveals how even happenings in the remotest hills of Laos cannot
escape the intrusions of historical memory. As heroes of the Communist revolution, Lo descendants have reinterpreted their grandfather's collusion in the
colonial project as coercion.

While Fay Dang remained a leader on the left until his death in 1986,
Touby Lyfoung had been eclipsed in the early 1960s by his protégé, Vang Pao.

Vang Pao was a man fashioned by the tides of his generation, a time of war, violent postcolonial upheaval, and an era of emerging military authoritarianism in Asia. Unlike Touby, who was the most educated Lao Hmong of his generation when he became the Hmong leader at the tender age of twenty-one in 1939, Vang Pao proudly proclaimed—much like General Suharto of Indonesia— that he had only a third-grade education.[14] Touby had recommended Vang Pao's enrollment in the French colonial police (the gendarmerie) back in 1946, helping him launch a brilliant career in the army. Vang Pao's knack for military maneuvers during the Viet Minh push into Laos attracted French attention, defining his political climb. In March 1952, he became the first commissioned Hmong officer in the Royal Lao Army.[15] For his valiant efforts in the field, he was the second Lao Hmong to be inducted as a Chevalier de la Légion d'honneur by the French empire.[16] A decade later the American Central Intelligence Agency (CIA) fashioned him into the only Hmong general in the royal Lao government, CR7's latest guardian, and the new Hmong leader. Until the Communist seizure of power in 1975, Vang Pao's CIA-financed clandestine army stood between Hanoi and Vientiane. Among those sentenced to death by the Communists, Vang Pao, unlike the diplomatic Touby, who held a more neutral view, took no chances. He flew directly from Long Cheng to Thailand and then followed his American patrons to the West.

In 2008 my visit to the historic region of Nong Het reinforced to me how essential CR7 was to the rise and fall of the Hmong leaders of the twentieth century. The graves of Blia Yao (in Phak Lak), Fay Dang (in Nong Het), and Thao Tou Yang (in Nong Het), the military commander and the Vang Pao equivalent on the Communist side, are located along this road (see figs. 2–4). These national sites emphasize how CR7 was a vehicle of legitimation for Hmong leaders on both sides of the political divide, revealing the working relationships between the Hmong and the state. Today Lo and Yang descendants command the military post of Nong Het, the gateway between Vietnam and the Lao PDR.

It has been nearly six decades since the French left Indochina, but CR7 remains as a testament to state power in the hills of northeastern Laos—a physical reminder of the alliance between Hmong leaders and their French colonial masters. More than just a symbol of oppression, the road also signifies the deep yearning of Hmong leaders to be free of lowland constraints and liberated from their role as instruments of the state, indigenous and/or colonial. It represents the Hmong aspirations for a king and a kingdom. As Vang Pao's dream so accurately demonstrates, however, for a Hmong leader to have weight he must seek the legitimation of the state. Only when an outside authority—be

Figure 2. The grave monuments of Lo Nhia Vu (*left*) and Lo Blia Yao (*center*) and another Lo family member (*right*) are situated in front of Blia Yao's famous stone house in Phak Lak. Blia Yao relocated here following the defeat of Vue Pa Chay in 1921. According to his granddaughter, Mao Song Lyfoung, Blia Yao's Chinese geomantic advisers told him that he should have himself buried in front of the main entrance to his house so he could stand guard over his legacy and ensure that his descendants will be leaders of the Hmong in perpetuity. Other family members are buried to the right of and behind the house. (March 2008, author's collection)

Figure 3 (*top right*). The grave monument of Lo Fay Dang in Nong Het. Fay Dang chose not to be buried in Phak Lak with his father (see fig. 2) or at his house, which is located about a mile farther east on CR7. He asked instead to be buried beside Thao Tou Yang's house (*partial view above*). The Yangs say that the cement house is haunted, so they no longer occupy it. They built and reside in a wooden structure two hundred meters south of this grave site. (March 2008, author's collection)

Figure 4 (*bottom right*). (*Left to right*): The grave monuments of the revolutionary nationalist hero Thao Tou Yang; his nephew, Paseurt Yang; and his brother-in-law, Viet Xuan Hung, in Nong Het. Thao Tou's soldiers are buried in the unmarked graves in front of his monument. These monuments are on Thao Tou's land, about eight hundred meters east of Lo Fay Dang's grave (see fig. 3). (March 2008, author's collection)

it Lao, French, or, as for Vang Pao, American—anoints a Hmong man as a leader will he hold sway over his long conquered and much divided people. Perhaps it is because a Hmong leader often endures a crisis of personality—as a Hmong leader but also a "slave" of the state—that he yearns ever so deeply to lead a "free" people. Also, for this very reason, the Hmong still await their sovereign king, who, it is prophesied, will return when rocks sprout flowers and the rivers flow uphill.

The Structure and Reach of This Work

This book explores the relations among the Hmong, the French, and the emerging Lao state from 1850 to 1960. To an extent, at least where rebellions are concerned, the story also strays across the border to Vietnam and China. This work is about empire in the highlands, French colonial rule at the margins, and the reasons why an ethnic minority that has long aspired to sovereignty is both attracted to and repulsed by the state. I argue that, while the Hmong yearn for independence, the legitimacy of their leaders has rested largely on outside patronage. The desire to restore sovereignty is, therefore, the impetus behind the attraction, as well as the submission, to the state. The lack of clan consensus, linguistic and cultural group disparities, and geographic divisions (the reality of a mountainous existence) are serious barriers to the Hmong dream of a kingdom and broader political unity under a "king." There exist, therefore, in our historical period, no kings but only clan leaders who vie for outside legitimation. The competition has resulted in two types of chiefs, figures that weave in and out of the chronological time line: the prophet or messianic leader who rejects the state and proclaims the Mandate of Heaven; and the secular political broker who, with state backing, achieves paramountcy as the supreme chief or ethnic representative of the Hmong. The existence of these two types of leaders has caused Hmong history to alternate between cycles of violent resistance against and peaceful alliance with the state. A central aim in this work, therefore, is to explore how and why leaders have emerged in highland Hmong society, and to unveil how Hmong continuously negotiate for agency within the state.

Chapter 1 provides the context for Hmong interactions with the lowland Lao kingdoms along the Mekong River and the Phuan of Muang Phuan or Xieng Khouang, an important site of heavy Hmong concentration. It also provides the context for understanding the political condition of the lowland Lao and Phuan kingdoms in the period of high colonialism before French annexation in 1893. I demonstrate how during this early period the Lao and

Phuan kingdoms endured invasions and defeats by the Haw Chinese (Black Flag bandits) of southern China and the Thai of Bangkok. The weakened political condition of the Lao and Phuan allowed the Hmong to maintain autonomy in the highlands, an autonomy they continued to enjoy into the twentieth century. It also opened the way for Hmong to become influential in modern Lao politics. Hmong migrants had extensive military experience because of centuries of struggle against the Chinese Qing state. As a result, they were the very first to stand against French colonizing efforts in Laos in 1896. This early rebellion forced the French to cultivate close relations with the Hmong of Xieng Khouang, creating an alliance that lasted until the French defeat in 1954. Thus, although the Hmong were the first to oppose colonialism in Laos, their leaders were also co-opted into the colonial project subsequent to this uprising.

Following chapter 1, the book diverges into two parts. Part I, containing chapters 2 and 3, examines two revolts in Tonkin led by prophets who proclaimed the Mandate of Heaven in an attempt to reconsolidate the ancient Hmong kingdom. The complexity of and lack of an extant narrative about these two rebellions requires chapter 2 to be devoted to outlining the chronology of the revolts by Xiong Mi Chang in Ha Giang (1910–12) and by Vue Pa Chay in Dien Bien Phu, Lai Chau Province (1918–21). Chapter 3, on the other hand, contains an analysis of the revolts. Rather than emphasizing an economic perspective, as political economist Geoffrey C. Gun has done in excellent detail, I rely on translated testimony by Mi Chang and on Hmong oral traditions about Pa Chay to unveil the cultural rationale for the rebellions.[17] Far from being "insane," as they were depicted by the colonial authorities, Mi Chang and Pa Chay operated within a Hmong cultural mind-set. Both leaders struggled to recapture a divine mandate lost ages ago. As such, their rebellions can be characterized as proto-nationalist movements that failed in the face of western military superiority. The Hmong absorbed the locus of blame by constructing the failure of the revolts in moral terms, and by perpetuating the idea that Pa Chay, the divine avatar, lives. This interpretation has allowed the Hmong dream to persist, resulting in the subsequent emergence of other prophets in the late twentieth century.

Part II of the book, containing chapters 4–8, is devoted to chronicling the histories of various secular political brokers and their interactions with the state. Here I make the subtle but crucial point that, to understand Hmong political practices, the secular and messianic traditions cannot be analyzed separately. These two political strains have been and continue to be intricately intertwined with one another. I trace, therefore, the rise and fall of several generations of Hmong brokers in Muang Phuan, unveiling how the first paramount chief emerged under French patronage, and how this led to competition and divisions in highland Hmong society. I demonstrate how the quest for legitimation tied down multiple generations of Hmong leaders as administrators, or, in Vang Pao's words, "slaves," of the state, and ally chiefs in the colonial project. As Hmong leaders drew the resentment of large sectors of Hmong society, messianic rebellions enveloped the highlands. Other secular leaders who fell out of favor with the French also sought legitimation from competing authorities of the nationalist movements, complicating French imperial ambitions.

Chapter 4 highlights the early period under the French, examining how the first Hmong leaders emerged in Laos. I argue that these pioneer leaders have roots that can be traced to Tuam Tshoj, China. Arriving in Xov Tshoj, Indochina, in the mid-nineteenth century from various Chinese regions, these leaders reconstituted Hmong society by forming marriage alliances. Women became important elements in this process of societal formation. The most powerful clans, the Ly, Lo, Moua, and Yang, intermarried, securing preeminent authorities in the highlands of Muang Phuan. Until the arrival of the French, the leaders of these clans existed as equals with authority only over their kinsmen, however. The French changed the balance of power when they imposed centralization. In 1910 Lo Blia Yao was appointed supervisor of CR7 and the ethnic administrator of the Hmong. While French-sanctioned authority fashioned him into a legendary figure, it also created fractionalization in Hmong society as others competed for legitimation. French appointment of a supreme Hmong chief complicated their position in the highlands. At the edge of empire, the Hmong began to influence the direction of history.

Chapter 5 details the struggle for paramountcy in the highlands between Lo Blia Yao, Lo Shong Ger, and Ly Foung (also known as Ly Tsia Foung). Literate in Lao, Shong Ger and Ly Foung began as Blia Yao's secretaries. Ambition and political differences soon prevailed, however. Shong Ger joined Pa Chay's rebellion in an attempt to displace Blia Yao, while the more diplomatic Ly Foung, who was not a member of the Lo clan, kidnapped Blia Yao's favorite daughter, Mai, as a wife. Ly Foung aimed for an advantageous connection to the preeminent Hmong leader. The brasher Shong Ger failed in his quest and committed suicide while Ly Foung, also failing to form a cordial tie with Blia Yao, resorted to divide-and-conquer tactics by marrying another wife from another clan and forming a new alliance. The violent struggles between Blia Yao, Shong Ger, and Ly Foung highlight why the state is a vital source of political legitimation for the Hmong.

Chapter 6 examines the rise of the family Lyfoung, and unravels the political ascendancy of Touby as a preeminent Hmong leader. Although all the brothers Lyfoung achieved literacy and obtained education in the lowland, it was the charismatic Touby who rose to paramountcy as the *tasseng* of Keng Khoai, the position once held by his maternal grandfather, Blia Yao. Touby's prestige did not go unchallenged, however, as his uncle, Fay Dang, also contested for his right to inherit Blia Yao's position. As the two men struggled for supremacy, with Fay Dang being backed by the Court of Luang Prabang and Touby by the French, the Japanese usurped authority in Laos, becoming an important patron of Fay Dang for a few months. The dispute between uncle and nephew remained unresolved, however. Blood was spilled on both sides as World War II winded down.

Chapter 7 examines the competition between Touby and Fay Dang during the revolutionary period from 1941 to 1945. The arrival of the Japanese complicated the situation in the highlands, reigniting the struggle for paramountcy in Nong Het. Fay Dang saw his chance to obtain Japanese backing to displace Touby. Denouncing Touby as a French collaborator, he successfully orchestrated for Touby's arrest, and eventually forced Touby to flee to the jungle. The political competition turned violent, but it finds no conclusion as the global war turned against the Japanese. When Japan surrendered, Fay Dang was divested of a patron.

The struggles between Fay Dang and Touby continue in chapter 8. In the postwar era, Fay Dang and his cousin, Thao Tou Yang, allied with the Communists, radical nationalists who sought independence from colonial rule, while Touby sought legitimation from the Lao monarch and the French in a newly created Kingdom of Laos. Fay Dang and Touby each obtained recognition as the respective Hmong leader on the left and the right, causing continual division in Hmong society. Touby appeared triumphant until the French defeat in 1954. When Fay Dang's Communist patrons, the Pathet Lao and Viet Minh, gained ground in Laos and Vietnam, respectively, he reemerged as dominant. Global geopolitical events also turned the tide against Touby. When the Americans intervened in Laos in 1960, they bypassed him to cultivate Vang Pao as a Hmong leader on the right.

This work ends in 1960, but I reflect on the continuity of Hmong political interactions with the state (in Laos and in exile) in an epilogue. Although this section describes events that lie beyond the breadth of this work, the emergence of Vang Pao as a leader during the Secret War (1960–75) and the challenges to his authority on multiple fronts help to elucidate more clearly the cycle of rebellion and subjection to the state that I aim to demonstrate. The emergence of Yang Shong Lue, more popularly known as the "Mother of Writing," and his challenges to Vang Pao's power after 1967 are particularly enlightening for my central argument about the alternating cycles of two types of Hmong leaders through time. As Vang Pao bolstered his authority by conscripting Hmong men to defend Laos, the Mother of Writing became an attractive alternative for disillusioned Hmong who felt that Vang Pao was sacrificing too much for the state. Like messianic leaders before, Shong Lue alluded to a direct mandate, becoming a threat to Vang Pao, whose legitimacy rested on a mandate by proxy of the state. Shong Lue was assassinated in 1971 while Vang Pao, following communist victory in Indochina in 1975, was driven into exile. Over three decades later, Vang Pao's American patrons orchestrated for his arrest by having an ATF agent lure the aged general into an RV to examine weapons that he could buy and use to retake Laos in a sting called "Operation Popcorn."[18] Vang endured the humiliation of incarceration and house arrest before dying of pneumonia on January 6, 2011.

Hmong American Politics of Belonging

I open and close this book with Vang Pao, but its central focus remains on the French colonial era, the period before the general emerged as a leader of the Hmong. My rationale for starting and ending with Vang Pao is both strategic and necessary. First, this work lays the foundation for future projects. A second, more fundamental reason is that Hmong history and society are evolving at a pace that has outdistanced the documentary abilities of the few scholars in the field. The historical narrative has barely been sketched, but scholarship on the Hmong has already begun the leap into the poststructuralist era.[19] In other words, while the analysis is just emerging, deconstructive discourse has already penetrated the field. Hmong history and society trail, therefore, as a topic on the tail of the comet of shifting human theoretical perspectives. For this reason, I could not neatly confine myself to a single period or perspective. To adequately construct a "Hmong history," I had to combine the long historical past with the insights of the present while keeping an eye on the future. Moreover, I had to historicize five thousand years of history even though I mostly aimed to add just a few more stitches to the *paj ntaub* (embroidery). Maneuvering multiple challenges, I had to somehow, with a single stroke of the brush, lay the historical foundation while at the same time remaining sufficiently critical to engage in its deconstruction—a nearly insurmountable task. Undertaking this project about the Hmong and the state, I often found myself in the difficult position of time traveling; of reconciling past, present, and future; and of constructing a narrative and analyzing it while remaining mindful of competing perspectives.

The above challenges aside, opening and closing this book with Vang Pao needs more serious political consideration because it may have implications for the field. Since the publication of Jane Hamilton-Merritt's *Tragic Mountains*, Hmong and non-Hmong alike have begun to absorb and reproduce the perception that Hmong history begins and ends with the Secret War and Vang Pao's alliance with the United States. I exploited this perspective to make my book more accessible to non-experts, but I remain cognizant of the critical risk of reifying a problematic, emerging discourse centered on one historical period. I certainly do not want to perpetuate the idea that the Hmong entered history only when they were tossed into the debacle of the Secret War. I hope this work demonstrates the opposite, in effect, that the Hmong have a long history, including contact with foreign powers, that demands documentation and analysis.

A recent book by Paul Hillmer, *A People's History of the Hmong*, provides a more multifaceted analysis of the Secret War and its political aftermath as Hmong became exiles in the United States and Thailand and rebellious "bandits" in Laos.[20] Hillmer complicates the historical canvas much further by also referencing the Hmong Communists, the one-third on the other side of the political divide, and by discussing the post-1975 exile politics of the Chao Fa leader and former disciple of the Mother of Writing, Pa Kao Her, in Thailand. The Secret War and America's moral debt of gratitude to the Hmong remain, however, central in his work.

The Secret War and the Hmong American alliance have also been greatly broadcast by Hmong veterans' groups that have been demanding congressional recognition since the early 1990s. Vang Pao, the commander of these veterans, often took center stage despite the fact that some groups operated politically independent of and in silent opposition to him.[21] The Secret War, the Hmong veterans and their spouses who bore witness to the event, and Vang Pao have, therefore, become defining elements of Hmong American national identity. Annually, these veterans appear in army fatigues and their wives in colorful, traditional Hmong garb on state and national capitol grounds, justifying their materialization in America. The Secret War has become a powerful way for the Hmong to lay claim to American history and the American land—the justification for their right to be here as citizens. The narrative of Hmong Americans is one of blood sacrifice in Laos on behalf of Americans even before they set foot on US soil.[22] "They were American soldiers," Minnesota state senator Foung Hawj said, "before we were American."[23] This discourse bares continuity with the way Hmong defined themselves vis-à-vis the state. As their ancestors did back in China and Laos, Hmong Americans continue to deal with the state as an independent group, pushing the idea that they entered the nation through service and sacrifice. The Hmong, even in exile, exert a kind of sovereignty unique to their own political tradition.

Hmong Americans' demand for recognition during the last two decades has resulted in policy changes and in plaques and memorials being erected across the nation. The most significant policy change was the Hmong Veterans' Naturalization Act of 2000, which waived the English-language requirement for Hmong veterans, their spouses, and their widows, allowing many elders to pass the citizenship exam orally in their native tongue.[24] I would argue that this act changed the face of politics in densely populated Hmong areas such as the Twin Cities in Minnesota and Fresno, California. Minnesota state senator Mee Moua's triumphant election in 2002, for example, may have been decided by the Hmong vote. Careful not to alienate her non-Hmong constituents, Moua would only say she employed "nontraditional" methods in her campaign.[25] Similarly, in 2006 Blong Xiong was elected to the Fresno City Council—the first Hmong to serve at that level in California.[26] Moua's and Xiong's historic victories had major implications in these two regions. Politicians in these states have been forced to reckon with the margin of victory Hmong votes can provide in close, contentious elections. Today members of competing parties can be seen courting votes at Hmong New Year's Festivals and the Fourth of July Soccer Tournament in Saint Paul, Minnesota.

In addition, monuments commemorating the Hmong and the Secret War have been constructed, especially in areas with heavy Hmong concentrations.[27] A small plaque was erected at Arlington National Cemetery in 1997 by the Lao Veterans of America. The first massive tribute, however, was located on the shores of Lake Michigan in Sheboygan, Wisconsin. Unveiled in July 2006, the Lao, Hmong, and American Memorial was established by the Lao-Hmong Coalition, another veterans' organization.[28] The monument commemorates both Hmong and non-Hmong veterans of the Secret War. The coalition's accompanying documentary about the Secret War highlights Hmong sacrifices and America's debt of gratitude, generating funds for the memorial.[29] Gatherings at the site since the monument's unveiling are also designed to raise mainstream awareness of the Hmong.

Similar monuments broadcasting comparable messages have been built in California. The Lao Hmong American War Memorial in Fresno depicts two Hmong soldiers rescuing a downed American pilot. Vang Pao appeared at its unveiling in January 2006.[30] Since Vang Pao's passing in 2011, other commemoration sites have been established in his honor. A site at the Fresno fairgrounds, where the annual Hmong New Year's Festival takes place, features Vang Pao sitting on a stone jar, representing the Plain of Jars. A Vang Pao Elementary School was also established in 2012, and a six-foot statue of Vang Pao in military regalia also was erected in the city of Chico. These public spaces have established a discourse about the loyal Hmong allies who shed blood in Laos for American democracy. Vang Pao, the leader of the clandestine army, is an integral part of the discussion. Opening and closing my story with him, therefore, resonates with media and popular cultural portrayals of Hmong Americans and their official historical significance. By recentering my analysis on the colonial period, however, I aim to demonstrate that the Hmong possess a history that stretches deeply into the past, far beyond the Secret War and outside the reaches of the general's charisma. The happenings of the Secret War were mere extensions of the events in the preceding era under the leadership of Lo Blia Yao and Touby Lyfoung. Grappling with these facts will lay the foundation for a serious, critical inquiry into the field of Hmong history as well as into contemporary political deployments of that history.

The Hmong Kingdom:
Kingship and Hmong Political Geography

Just as Vang Pao envisioned escaping the royal palace in his nightmare, so the Hmong people dream of having their own sovereign lord. "The Miao [Hmong] await a liberator, a king, a *phao thay* [*fuab tais*], as the Jews await a Messiah," according to F. M. Savina. "As soon as a *phao thay* is announced somewhere, in China, in Tonkin, in Laos, they quickly take up arms and put themselves under his orders. What we call a revolt, they call *oa phao thay* [*ua fuab tais*], king-making."[31] Savina was a priest who proselytized among the Hmong and other minorities of southern China, Tonkin (northern Vietnam), and Laos from 1901 until his death in 1941 at the age of sixty-five.[32] Fluent in Hmong language and traditions, in 1917 he published a pioneering Hmong-French dictionary and in 1924 the first historical account of the Hmong, which provides a rare insight into Hmong political culture.[33]

The Hmong longing for independence is a constant theme amid the tragedy of continual defeat. Judging by the criteria of modern political theorists, however, the Hmong face serious barriers in their ethnonationalist quest. According to Anthony Smith, nationalist ideology is linked to the symbolic use of a "homeland," and ethnic minorities lacked a clear territorial unity to support this ideology.[34] The only notable exceptions among Southeast Asian minorities who possessed the criteria necessary for strong nationalist movements, scholars note, were the Karen and Chin.[35]

Compounding the Hmong's situation, being recent migrants to Southeast Asia, they could not build a reliable case of having a claim to any land. In another study, Smith adds that the most important criteria for achieving strong nationalist aspiration are bureaucratic authority, the myth of a common history, and the rise of a local intelligentsia.[36] The Hmong seem to know the importance of these criteria inherently. While they did possess very strong myths of a common history, the Hmong did not possess land and they lacked an intelligentsia—hence, the stories about the need to recover literacy. As will be seen in chapter 8, the primary reason why Touby rejected the offer of Xieng Khouang as a Hmong autonomous zone in 1946 was that he simply could not find enough literate Hmong with sufficient administrative experiences to help him make the dream come true.

Being a stateless people and, because of a very strong Confucian notion that government authorities have a divine, sacred origin, the Hmong's aspiration for sovereignty has centered on the leader rather than the land. As I will elaborate in chapter 1, Hmong share the Confucian notions of kingship and state government, mainly the idea that a divinely bestowed king is the precursor to the founding of the dynasty, which consolidates its rule over the state. The sacred king is essential in Hmong beliefs. It is fitting, therefore, that the study of Hmong history should begin with an analysis of their leadership system. My focus on leaders is far more than an attempt to create great men, however; it is an effort to understand the mass political culture that constitutes Hmong society. Investigating its leaders and leadership systems can reveal aspects of the complex structures that make up Hmong society and ethnic identity. We study the man, therefore, in order to understand the group, and we go about it this way because it is the group's construction of what constitutes a great man that reveals its political tradition. Finally, the focus on the leader is necessitated by the fact that the Hmong have been, for a long time, a stateless people. The leader, not the territorial state, is the thread that can be pinpointed across space and time to reveal the dynamic history of this highland group from the ancient era onward.

The emphasis on leaders necessitates a certain intellectual concession as well. The Hmong, perhaps until as late as the last decades of the twentieth century, had only a vague notion of territory, or "mapping," in their conception of the kingdom. Hence, when Hmong speak of a kingdom in the past, I believe they refer more to the notion of what individual leaders symbolized in their society and to what leadership meant to followers. For the Hmong, the leader or "king" is a rallying point for broader political unity; his appearance is a sign of divine mandate. He is not, therefore, so much the lord of a bounded territory, especially since there was no such conception until very recently. Only in the last few decades did Hmong nationalists, using oral traditions and history, begin to construct the notion of a Hmong homeland. Perhaps for this reason, there is no consensus about where the homeland is located. Some pinpoint northern China, the eastern reaches of the Yellow River, as the area of Hmong origin while others claim the regions around the Yangtze River where the Chinese made references to an ancient San-Miao kingdom.[37] Lately some Hmong Americans, while continuing to recognize their origins in China, have been promoting Laos as the homeland. Since 2000, for example, I have observed multiple funerals in St. Paul, Minnesota, where Hmong ritual masters instructed the souls of the deceased only to their native villages in Laos and no longer to northern China.

The lack of a notion of the "kingdom" as a temporal space until lately also reflects the Hmong's modern geographic reality. In twentieth-century China and Southeast Asia, the Hmong lived above certain elevations, scattered between different ethnic groups that occupied the lowlands. These pockets of Hmong on mountaintops formed isolated islands amid lower-lying oceans of other ethnicities. Going between settlements often entails border crossing. This physical reality impeded the conception of a kingdom as a contiguous, expansive territory. This is not to say, however, that the Hmong did not value land or that they had no notion of landownership. They were, after all, agrarian people who drew their living from the land. Stories of land seizure by the Han Chinese in the following chapter will reveal that the Hmong had a deep understanding that their survival as a people was tied to the soil. What I am saying here, however, is that they probably had a vague notion of land as a politicized space with delineated boundaries. When the Hmong took up arms in the past, therefore, it was to defend their families, their human pride, and their way of life, not so much to lay claim to specific plots.

The Hmong often speak nostalgically of "our land" (*yus teb yus chaw*), but they have been forced by economic and political circumstances of the modern era to become a migratory people. Especially after their arrival in Southeast Asia, swidden agricultural life forced families to move every few decades without much regret, according to F. M. Savina. Observing the relocation of whole villages, he writes, perhaps with poetic exaggeration: "When all is ready, a signal is given to depart and everybody leaves as if they were going to the market—true nomads—without showing the least sign of regret or emotion. No one, in moving away, stops to throw a last glance on the old home that saw him born, to say a last farewell to the tombs of elder relatives abandoned forever on the deserted mountain. . . . They would not comprehend the 'Brizeux' regretting their native village.[38]

Given the structural impediments faced by Hmong, it makes sense for them to imagine a kingdom that is not territorial but more cultural and psychological, and infused with dynastic notions of the family and the clan. We could argue, in effect, that the Hmong kingdom has to be cultural and psychological and tied to concepts of descent and lineages due to the lack of military and bureaucratic power to enforce any claim. The Hmong kingdom, therefore, can be defined as a cultural realm that exists beyond the temporal universe and includes a leader as the unifying element that transcends clan divisions. The Hmong kingdom is perhaps best expressed as the psychological condition of being liberated from outside constraints, with the freedom to practice one's livelihood on the hillsides as one sees fit, having cultural, linguistic, and political autonomy and ethnic solidarity.

The conception of what constitutes a Hmong kingdom in the recent past facilitated the creation of a "Virtual Hmong Nation" in cyberspace among exiled intellectuals over a decade ago.[39] Indeed, the Virtual Hmong Nation is not confined by geographic reality. As Teev Lis, a multimillionaire Hmong American businessman and the main proponent of such a nation, defines the concept, "a 'virtual nation' is a nation comprising people of a common ancestry, origin, ethnicity, culture, tradition, history and who, by free will, organize in a collective manner to form a border-less and territory-less nation on a global basis, without regard to where each constituent may physically reside, or to what nation-state or ideology he/she may hold allegiance."[40] This definition is reminiscent of the Hmong's territorial reality in Asia, as noted above, where they lived scattered on the hilltops without the benefit of a contiguous expanse of earth large enough to call "Hmongland." Since 1975 the Hmong have also experienced the additional physical barriers of oceans and national boundaries. This reality further necessitates Lis's definition of a virtual nation as a place that can only exist in cyberspace and in the cultural imaginations of Hmong exiles, as well as those in the homelands of China and Southeast Asia.

In the past this idyllic imagining only required Hmong leaders to maintain constant contact with lowlanders and the state authorities, whose primary aim was to incorporate the Hmong into their own cultural-linguistic milieu and to assume political control over them. To an extent, therefore, the Hmong leader was, in the capacity of a political mediator between Hmong society and the state, a protective shield against rapid, catastrophic assimilation. For this reason, the Hmong political broker is perceived to be a legitimate leader who serves the Hmong's desire to remain autonomous. The period covered in this work (1850–1960) saw major shifts in the Hmong's leadership structure, however. The transition from leaders like Lo Blia Yao, especially when he still played the traditional role of an alliance chief, to Touby Lyfoung, who was a bureaucrat of the state, had a fundamental impact on Hmong society. Touby was the first Hmong leader in Southeast Asia to be educated in the lowland from an early age. Rather than acting as a screen against rapid absorption, Touby and his educated brothers, who were culturally oriented toward the Lao and the French, became the bridge for Hmong integration into the modern nation-state. As noted, when a Hmong leader becomes too willing a participant in the state's assimilationist scheme, the Hmong view him with some ambivalence. It is no wonder, then, that messianic leaders also appeared during this period of dynamic shifts. Indeed, the desire for cultural, linguistic, and political autonomy may have been the main impetus behind the appointment of a paramount chief to represent Hmong society in the first place. When the paramount chief fails to maintain Hmong autonomy, however, the Hmong will reject him in favor of the prophet who vows to reconsolidate a sovereign kingdom.

If the Hmong do not conceptualize a kingdom in territorial terms in the modern era, however, their oral traditions are suffused with myths about having possessed such a space in the ancient past while still in China. These oral traditions speak of a Hmong kingdom and a king. One king, named Tswb Tshoj, was descended from the union of a Hmong woman and a boar. For this reason, messianic groups in the modern era worship the boar as an important symbol in their movements. Tswb Tshoj was undone by the clever ploys of the Chinese, according to some.[41] Another king, Vaj Yim Leej, who perhaps reigned subsequent to Tswb Tshoj, was a kung fu expert with a flying sword. "It is believed," Gary Yia Lee writes, "that whoever was to find this sword would become the next Hmong king."[42]

Other equally intriguing tales speak of the Han Chinese ambition to destroy the Hmong kingdom. One particular legend, perhaps also a sequel to the story of Tswb Tshoj, tells of a woman warrior named Nkauj Ntxuam (Lady of the Fan),[43] who led Hmong troops against these Chinese. A divine avatar, she was born as the Hmong king's daughter. She bore a magical standard that commanded the forces of lightning, wind, and rain to aid the Hmong in battle, defeating the legions of Chinese. As her name implies, when she led the troops she used her flag to "fan" away the weapons of the enemy, thereby protecting the soldiers under her guard.

Typifying a Hmong political tradition based on marriage alliances—a reality also highlighted throughout this work—the Hmong kingdom of historical legend was undone by a botched political union. The story concludes when the battle-scarred Hmong king is tricked into sealing a marriage alliance with the Chinese emperor. Against her will, the warrior princess is betrothed to the son of the emperor. She is tortured to death. Nkauj Ntxuam curses the Hmong before she leaves her mortal vessel. As the Hmong have betrayed her, she says, they will be doomed to endure a cycle of perpetual self-betrayal and continual disunity. Unable to amalgamate as a force against foreign enemies they will exist in virtual enslavement. Only when rocks sprout flowers and rivers run uphill will Nkauj Ntxuam return to lead the Hmong in a triumphant struggle to reconsolidate their kingdom.[44] The betrayal of the warrior princess cost the Hmong the Mandate of Heaven. No one in the kingdom could bear her standard, which had no protective force. The power they had witnessed was embedded in the divine person of Nkauj Ntxuam and not in her flag. Once she was gone, the Chinese led a concluding campaign to destroy the Hmong kingdom. The king was captured and executed, and his subjects were scattered in various directions.[45] The memory of this warrior princess was invoked in Hmong messianic movements of the twentieth century when young virgins carried a flag and led troops against foreign enemies.[46]

This legend of the loss of king and kingdom also includes a sequel, which led to the loss of a once flourishing literary tradition. After the destruction of the ancient kingdom and the death of the sovereign lord, the fleeing Hmong refugees were pursued to a river where they "ate" their books before crossing. According to an informant in Thailand, "'We Hmong were so afraid of our books getting wet . . . and we were hungry, so we ate them up. That is the reason why now we can only be clever inside, in our hearts and only remember in our hearts, not in books.'"[47] Today Hmong individuals possess incredible memorization skills because they had swallowed the books of knowledge. For this reason, when a person performs these oral rituals that were once contained in books, the Hmong say that he or she is singing from the stomach. The Hmong claim they memorize with their stomachs and hearts (*cwj cia hauv plab plaw*) or with their livers (*hauv nruab siab*).

Another account of the destruction of the Hmong kingdom and the loss of literacy is told in musical rhymes (*zaj qeeg*) through the bamboo instrument *rab qeej*. One song is passed down secretly among ritual masters, the main keepers of Hmong oral traditions. Yang Cheng Vang, who despite his young age now ranks as a top Hmong ritual expert around the globe, learned this song in 2010 while studying abroad in Thailand from eighty-year-old Ntsum Txiab Yaj, who lives in Chiang Mai and is considered the most knowledgeable master among the Hmong Thai.[48] This *qeej* version also includes a marriage alliance.

While in the preceding story Nkauj Ntxuam is sent to marry a Chinese prince, in this song the Chinese emperor sends his daughter to wed a Hmong prince. Her mission is to learn everything she can about Hmong civilization and to send reports back to her father. Once Hmong weaknesses are identified, the Han emperor sends his fourth son, Xwm Kav (Fourth Guardian), to destroy the Hmong kingdom.[49] The Hmong king is captured and killed along with many intellectuals. The Han emperor concludes that writing is the powerful element that makes Hmong civilization strong, so he orders all the books burned and outlaws writing. One Hmong scholar escapes the carnage with the Book, which contains the most important knowledge of Hmong society. He tucks the Book into his belt and carries it everywhere, but he has to farm to make a living. The Book is a continual hindrance to his work in the fields. One day he places it in the drainage ditch dug behind his house (*kwj tse*) while contemplating the best place to store it. A pig who loves to play in the mud chews off a chunk. Next the man places the Book by the threshold of the door while he thinks some more about a suitable place to hide it, and a cow bites off another portion. Finally, he takes what is left and places it in a wooden trunk in the bedroom. Years go by before he retrieves it for examination. The Book has been chewed to pieces by mice. The man realizes the script is almost gone. He aims to preserve the remaining characters. He picks up the few scraps of paper and asks his wife to sew the letters into her embroidery (*paj ntaub*). Thus, ever since Hmong women have played a role in passing along the Hmong writing system in their needlework. These characters are embedded in the intricate patterns of Hmong funeral clothes.[50]

Oral traditions about the loss of the kingdom, the king, and writing provide the rationale for the existence and acceptance of two kinds of leaders among the Hmong: the messianic or prophet leader who claims to be the Hmong king incarnate; and the secular political broker who is legitimated by the state, the foreign lords who rule over the Hmong. These legends also provide insight into why Hmong history has been characterized by alternating cycles of rebellion against and submission to the state. The oral traditions advance an explanation for the loss of a great civilization, articulating Hmong submission to the state as a loss of the Mandate of Heaven. Conversely and potently, these stories also articulate Hmong rebellions against the state as an effort to recapture the mandate.

During times of submission to the state, Hmong people accept the secular political broker as legitimate. The broker is a man who, by virtue of his knowledge, oratorical talents, and personal charisma, obtains a mandate by proxy from the state that has captured the divine right to rule as evidenced by its ability to defeat the Hmong. The state, with celestial mandate, appoints the broker as the paramount chief, or ethnic representative. The Hmong accept him as legitimate while awaiting the return of their true king. This continual waiting opens the door for the emergence of the messianic leader or prophet during junctures of economic and political distress. The appearance of the prophet signals that the time is ripe for the Hmong to struggle for sovereignty. The prophet is believed to be a divine avatar, much like the legendary Nkauj Ntxuam, sent to liberate the Hmong from oppression. He is, literally, to borrow from the Chinese, a "Son of Heaven" who is endowed with supernatural abilities.[51] He may also claim to possess a divine script, further proof of his genuineness. As the prophet claims the direct Mandate of Heaven, he does not submit to the state. He is, in the views of followers, the Hmong king incarnate who has returned to reconsolidate the kingdom.

I will further speculate on the ties between Hmong and Han Chinese political traditions in chapter 1, where I address the long historical contacts between Han and Hmong, and Han civilizational influence on Hmong identity. For now, I merely want to acknowledge that the jargons I am employing here are tied to, and may be derived from, this enduring contact. We do not know if Hmong prophets in China styled themselves as a "Son of Heaven," but the belief in the celestial origin of the messianic figure made it easy for Hmong of Southeast Asia to co-opt the Lao royal title *chao fa*, which can be translated as "Prince of Heaven," as a name for their movements.[52] As a "prince" who proclaims the Mandate of Heaven, the prophet seeks to restore Hmong civilization to its original glory. The promise of sovereignty makes him a tantalizing figure that emerges time and again when the secular broker fails to balance Hmong desire for autonomy with the extractive demands of the state. Thus, the prophet and the broker are intricately tied to one another in a cyclical history of submission and rebellion. Although scholars often study the phenomenon of messianism as separate from and, sometimes, an antithesis to rational, bureaucratic political systems, I am advancing the argument that we cannot fully grasp the Hmong's political culture or their relations with the state until we have woven together the two types of leaders and political traditions. Where it concerns the Hmong, the two systems and their leadership types weave in and out of one another in complicated entanglements.

Hmong Notions of Masculinity and Charisma: Understanding the Two Types of Leaders

Max Weber outlines three ideal types of authority: traditional, legal-rational, and charismatic. Traditional authority is validated by customary practices based on "an established belief in the sanctity of immemorial traditions and on the legitimacy of those exercising authority under them"; legal-rational authority by impersonal rules, in which "obedience is owed to the legally established impersonal order"; and charismatic authority by the extraordinary qualities of the person, or an authority based largely on "personal trust."[53] While the first two types are more concretely defined, the definition of the charismatic type is vague enough to have generated debates among western scholars, leading some to trace the history and origin of the word and its change in usages over time.[54] Modern psychologists even attempt to dissect the term by applying psychometric testing on allegedly "charismatic" leaders. They have found nothing extraordinary about them other than a much more exhibited trait of narcissism.[55] Weber provides his own definition of charisma: "The term 'charisma' will be applied to a certain quality of an individual personality by virtue of which he is considered extraordinary and treated as endowed with supernatural, superhuman, or at least specifically exceptional powers or qualities."[56] Charismatic authority will endure for as long as a leader can repeatedly demonstrate charismatic powers, so that his followers maintain their beliefs in his charisma.[57]

In Southeast Asia, from 1850 onward, we see Hmong society drawn to all three types of leaders. The Hmong chief/broker in the highlands of Laos is both a traditional and legal-rational authority figure insofar as he is legitimated by the state, but he may also possess charisma, as evident in his expertise in the oral traditions. Similarly, the messianic figure may also possess secular (legal-rational) authority even though he also claims to possess extraordinary powers. Leaders who emerge more by virtue of their education than by their traditional roles, on the other hand, are closer to Weber's definition of legal-rational authority, but they can also be highly charismatic, as in the case of Touby Lyfoung. Hence, the boundaries between these three ideal types as they apply to the Hmong blur into one another and may not be as solidly defined as in Weberian terms.

Although colonial observers often dismissed him as a "madman," the mundane qualities of a messianic figure appear similar to those of a secular broker. Moreover, both kinds of leaders possess traits representative of the epitome of traditional Hmong manhood. That is to say, in order to understand various types of Hmong political leaders, we need to understand notions of Hmong masculinities. This statement raises the immediate question of what exactly that means, of course. There exist some studies about Hmong women in the highland settings of Southeast Asia, as well as in the modern, metropolitan West, but no one has dared yet to venture an argument on the topic of Hmong manhood.[58] Because of the paucity of scholarly inquiries into the subject, it has been ignored in most historical characterizations over the ages to the extent that Hmong manhood is often associated with violence and warfare.[59] Centuries of struggle in China and the latest military conscriptions in the Indochina Wars also aided in fashioning the present image of the rifle-toting male as the Hmong ideal. This stereotype has been further commodified for conspicuous consumption by the genius of Hollywood in a sensationalized movie, *Gran Torino*, which depicts Hmong gang violence in the midwestern United States.[60] Another tragic event involving a deer-hunting incident in northern Wisconsin also irreparably burned the image of the rifle-toting Hmong man into the psyche of the American mainstream. While scouting for deer, Chai Vang, a sharpshooter veteran of the California National Guard, claimed he got lost and wandered accidentally onto private land owned by white hunters who threw racial slurs at him. As he tried to leave he claimed the white hunters shot at him and he responded by shooting back, killing six and injuring two individuals.[61]

Rare incidents such as that of Chai Vang coupled with a history of armed rebellions in China and engagements in the Indochina Wars certainly must have colored notions of Hmong masculinity, but what that impact means and how it translates into everyday gender performance remain to be studied. Martial valor certainly seems to be a quality found in Touby Lyfoung and especially in Vang Pao. Both men were military leaders—Touby during the time of the French and Vang Pao during the American period. The traditional qualities that define a Hmong man of worth seems to have little to do with the weapon-toting macho-man image, however. Oral traditions that preceded the warring periods of the Indochina Wars pinpoint oratorical talents and ritual knowledge as the foundation of Hmong masculinity. Other qualities valued in men are diligence, perhaps because it is the prerequisite for the accumulation of wealth in an agrarian society, and kindness because of the Hmong's group-oriented mentality. Thus, the archetypal Hmong folk hero is Yob Nraug Ntsuag, Yao the Orphan Boy, who wins the hand of the Dragon Princess, Niam Nkauj Zuag Paj.[62] Multiple versions of this story emphasize the industriousness and kindness of the Orphan Boy—qualities that inevitably impress a princess, who offers herself in marriage and bestows on the Orphan her father's wealth.[63]

In another story, of the same genre, the Orphan Boy, through his marriage to a princess, succeeds in becoming a king. After the Orphan obtains the hand of the princess whose beauty is renowned throughout, the King of Heaven comes to investigate. The king offers the Orphan Boy his kingdom in exchange for the princess. Much later, the Orphan's son, Maum Nyab Lwj, reunites his mother and father through extraordinary literary feats. This folktale also associates literacy, a topic of importance in this work, with kingly powers.[64]

Although the story of Yob Nraug Ntsuag and his marriage to a princess is useful for the discussions of Hmong marriage politics as noted in subsequent chapters, he is not as much of a winsome champion as Nuj Toog Nuj Nplhaib Zag (henceforth, Nuj Nplhaib), the ultimate Hmong hero, who rescues his beloved, Ntxawm, from a tiger. Nuj Nplhaib is undoubtedly the Rama (of the *Ramayana*) of Hmong society. His mastery of the *qeej*, the bamboo reed, is unsurpassed, as told in the story. So are his talents in wielding the sword and shooting the bow and arrow, which are of less significance. Nuj Nplhaib's mastery of the *qeej* makes him the most eligible bachelor of his age, winning for him the love of Ntxawm, the most beautiful woman of the period. The tiger also covets the lovely maiden. He gets his chance to steal her soul when he overhears the young lovers arranging an evening tryst under a giant tree. The tiger uses his supernatural powers to delay Nuj Nplhaib while he disguises himself in human form to await the unsuspecting Ntxawm. Arriving promptly at the appointed hour, Ntxawm runs to embrace what she thinks is her lover standing in the shadow of the tree. Just as she reaches him the clouds lift and the moonlight reveals a monstrous face. Ntxawm retreats in horror, but her soul has already been stolen. To the villagers she becomes ill and dies, but in reality the tiger uses his supernatural power to disguise a dead goat as her replacement while he kidnaps the real Ntxawm as his bride. Nuj Nplhaib, renowned for his musical talent, is invited to play the *qeej* at her funeral. Only then does he realize that the body is not that of his beloved maiden. He immediately sharpens his sword and takes his bow and arrow to pursue the kidnapper. He succeeds in killing the tiger and takes Ntxawm home to be his wife.[65]

Of all the Hmong folktales, the act of Nuj Nplhaib killing the tiger comes the closest to revealing violence, which is committed during the rescue of a loved one, as a cultural element of Hmong manhood. The tiger, however, holds its own special significance in Hmong society as a wild, even demonic being that hinders Hmong physical and spiritual health. Also, the tiger symbolizes more of Hmong man's conquest of the wilderness in their constant migration as opposed to violence against other humans. Thus, although a violent act is portrayed in the story, further analysis of its significance needs to be considered before drawing a conclusion. As noted above, Nuj Nplhaib's talent in playing the bamboo reed—his oratorical skill—is emphasized above all else in the story.

Outsiders are rarely privy to the oratorical powers so valued in Hmong men. For this reason, associating oral performance talents with Hmong notions of manhood has escaped scholarly observation. While the verbal talents of women are often displayed publicly during ball-tossing games at the New

Year's Festival when they sing *kwv txhiaj*, poetic rhyming ballads, as Patricia
Symonds notes in her work, it is usually only on formal, private occasions, such
as during a funeral, a marriage ceremony, or a dispute case, that the oral mastery
of men is fully on display.[66] At these closed events Hmong men exhibit uninhib-
ited charisma, intelligence, and wit, revealing skills that make them rock stars
in the traditional context. Because of this, in every generation, in different
locales, there is a particular Hmong man who is esteemed above all others for
his mastery of the *qeej* or for his ability to sing *zaj tshoob txiv xaiv* (marriage
and funeral songs).[67] These men are sought out as mentors by youths. Although
Hmong often share courting rhymes, the ritual songs memorized by men are
usually maintained within the family and passed only from father to son precisely
because of the prestige associated with them.[68]

There are plenty of additional folktales that emphasize oratorical talent as a
hallmark of Hmong manhood. It is logical, therefore, that the messianic leader
and political broker also should possess this highly valued trait, this "X-factor"
that may be the source of their mysterious charisma.[69] A leader of either type
begins as a lineage or clan leader who has distinguished himself above others in
a certain locale as a result of his charisma; his oratorical knowledge, which is
acquired through rigorous apprenticeship under a master from an early age;
and his acquired wealth. Much like the folk hero Nuj Nplhaib, such a leader
exhibits mastery in the traditions involving funeral, marriage, and healing
practices. He may be a master of the *qeej* or possess talents in reciting marriage
and funeral songs and be familiar with the rituals involved in these important
life events. He may also be a shaman and have expertise in other arts of healing
such as herbal medicine or reciting magical incantations (*khawv koob*). Healing
and ritual knowledge, in particular, would also make him an expert in Hmong
customary laws (*kab lig kev cai*) and the "flowery," formal language (*paj lug*)
and mannerisms used to perform and discuss such laws.

Knowledge of Hmong ritual traditions that are intricately tied to customary
laws opens the way for the clan leader to become an adjudicator of disputes
involving thievery, murder, divorces, adultery, and other major conflicts and
social happenings that occur between individuals or clans. When external clans
seek his expertise, he may begin to acquire legitimacy as a paramount leader in
a particular locale, becoming to some extent, a regional chief whose authority
transcends his own clan. As will be demonstrated in chapters 4 and 5, Lo Blia
Yao and Ly Foung were primary examples of such men of skill. Within the
context of highland society, absent of the executive authority of the state, the
adjudicator/regional chief must also come from a dominant clan massive
enough to back his authority. His large group provides the executive power

necessary to enforce his rulings, coercing others to obey his pronouncements. Vang Pao aptly observed, "If you want to be a leader you have to have lots of kinsmen . . . [for] other clans . . . would not come to your aid."[70] Because numbers translate into power, Hmong "feel proud and honored when they have many relatives."[71] It would be hard, though not impossible, for a man from a small clan to achieve paramount status in Hmong society. He may become an ethnic leader if he can muster the support of affinal kinsmen with whom he has social ties through matrimonial alliances. For this reason, he has to engage in strategic marriages to women of the most authoritative clans. Vang Pao serves as the perfect example of this kind of leader. His six wives came from the three most powerful clans, the Ly, Lo, and Moua, in Laos. To extend his legitimacy beyond Hmong society, Vang also married one Lao Phuan woman from a prominent family in Xieng Khouang.[72]

The Hmong leader must also possess the required capital to maintain his position in the patron-client dyad. "The role of a Hmong chief [as a patron] is to lead, to demonstrate Hmong values, and to provide for and look after those who follow [his clients]. This last required wealth," Jane Hamilton-Merritt writes. Noting that Vang Pao lacked material resources, she continues, "Vang Pao was not a wealthy man; he had been a soldier all his life." So the American CIA had to provide Vang with a "contingency fund to carry out his dual functions of military and tribal leader."[73] Colonel William "Bill" Lair said there was no such fund, but he employed creative ways to obtain US dollars to bolster Vang's status. Before the CIA, Vang had depended on his wives' families.[74]

Affluent leaders like Touby Lyfoung used their families' wealth to build a clientele. "A leader does not necessarily need wealth in silver," said Mao Song Lyfoung, "but he must have material bounties such as food and domestic live-stock that could be slaughtered to nourish the constant trail of dignitaries and others." The modest salary of a bureaucrat was not sufficient to maintain guests who come to seek adjudication, advice, or other things. Absent of hired servants, the leader also must possess a large household full of members who can care for visitors. For this reason, Hmong leaders have multiple wives and many children who act as unpaid servants. Mao Song, Touby's sister, described herself as the primary "slave" in her father's household. She was held back as a cook and servant while her brothers obtained educations in the lowlands. Her brothers became leaders in various capacities while she was a nonliterate housewife all her life.[75]

A clan chief might become a paramount political broker or prophet leader depending on the historical situation and whether he accepts the mandate of the state. The leader who submits to the state competes with others to become paramount. Knowledge of the state language is a determining factor in this competition. The Han scholar Yan Ruyi (1759-1826), who was famous for his treatise on how to defeat the "Miao," writes about how knowledge of Chinese contributed to the rise and fall of leaders in the society.[76]

> [Among] the raw Miao . . . there are tribes, but no chiefs. . . . In a stockade a dozen or even several dozen fathers and sons, elder and younger brothers, vie for supremacy. If someone's able to speak to the officials in Chinese, then everyone in the stockade stands in awe of him and selects him a head of the stockade. If there are other households or individuals of this type in the stockade, they each form a faction. Therefore, one stockade may have one chief, or it may have several chiefs waxing and waning or strengthening and weakening in their turn. They cannot be like other tribes that have chiefs overseeing affairs on a hereditary basis.[77]

Literacy is also essential, enhancing his ambition to become the ethnic representative. Just as he parleys verbal contracts between different clans in Hmong society, so the broker negotiates agreements between the Hmong and the state. This role makes him indispensable as a peacekeeper, forcing the state to provide him with a title and a seal. On the other hand, state legitimation allows his authority to transcend clan, cultural group, and regional categories in the secular political context to influence what might be called Hmong identity and destiny. He becomes, in essence, the "King of the Hmong." When the state legitimates a Hmong man, he becomes, in Weberian terms, a legal-rational authority. Because the state enforces his authority, he has an interest in maintaining the connection to the state. Depending on how extractive the state is, he may come to feel, as Vang Pao did in his dream, that he is a slave. His Hmong clientele may also view him in a similar fashion and turn to the prophet who envisions sovereignty.

The Hmong accept the broker as a paramount chief because of their desire to be free—an ironic but logical contradiction. Socially segmented into clans and cultural-linguistic groups, Hmong society is wracked with division. Certain clans, by virtue of their manpower and their skill in building alliances, may obtain deference in specific locales, but they still compete for the paramount spot. For this reason, the state serves a useful purpose in imposing a political hierarchy, complete with a bureaucratic system. When the state legitimates a clan leader as supreme it ends, at least for the moment, the constant power wrangling. The state can fashion a clan leader into an ethnic representative. Thus, insofar as it fulfills the Hmong desire for ethnic unity—the precursor to finding a kingdom—the state is appealing when it provides a cogent hierarchy of leaders with an umbrella figure at the top. The Hmong, in effect, co-opts the state as a tool for "kingmaking"—especially during peacetime. Should the broker become more of an instrument of the state, doing its bidding as opposed to being a shelter for Hmong autonomy, however, the Hmong will replace him. The challenge for the broker is, therefore, to balance Hmong aspirations to be free and the state's desire to extract goods and services as well as impose assimilation. When a conflict arises between these opposing objectives, the political broker faces a dilemma. Should he lean toward his patron, becoming a tool of state control, the Hmong will abandon him for competing leaders waiting in the wings. Under extreme duress, and if there are no more appealing secular figures, some may turn to the prophet, who claims to possess the Mandate of Heaven. Those who follow the prophet will reject the authority of the state altogether. They seek divine legitimation and attempt to establish sovereignty. The prophet leads them in that endeavor.

As noted earlier, the prophet also has his beginning as a distinguished clan leader in a certain locale. He also possesses charisma and oratorical power. Much like the broker, he is skilled in the rituals associated with marriage, funerals, and healing practices. He may also possess the language and literacy of the state. Where the Hmong prophet diverges from the political broker is in his rejection of state legitimation. Unlike the secular political broker, whose title and seal come from the state, the prophet seeks the direct Mandate of Heaven. His title, which is revealed to him in a vision or dream, comes from above. He may also claim to possess objects of divine origin: Vue Pa Chay had a thirteen-shot rifle while Yang Shong Lue of the 1960s had a book and pen.[78] The Hmong prophet possesses the general characteristics described by Michael Adas, whose work focuses on millenarian movements in lowland Southeast Asia and Africa:

> A prophet is a person who believes and is able to convince others that he or she has special contacts with supernatural forces by means of dreams, visions, and special revelations. The prophet's followers are convinced that he or she possesses superhuman powers, which are frequently displayed in predictive or healing abilities. In some cases the prophet may claim to be or may be regarded by the faithful as an incarnation of the divine. . . . [Moreover] a prophet promises followers salvation expressed through millenarian visions, which vary according to the cultural idiom in which he works.[79]

Legitimated by Heaven, the prophet chief must succeed in unifying the Hmong for political action to reconsolidate the kingdom, as Nkauj Ntxuam stipulates in the legend described above. "Hmong messianic leaders," Christian

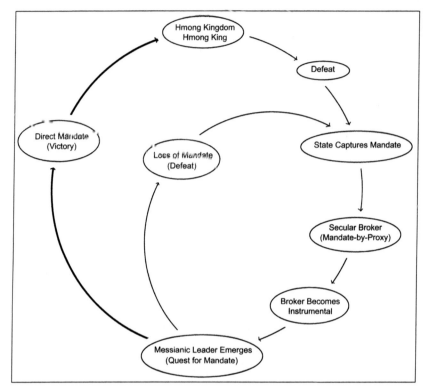

Figure 5. Since the defeat of the Hmong kingdom (*starting at the top*), the Hmong have been caught in a cycle of rebellion and defeat followed by subjection to the state, with the state appointing a secular broker as leader (*inner circle*). The Hmong dream is for the messianic leader to succeed in his quest to acquire the Mandate of Heaven (*arrow to the left of the larger circle*) and free them from this cycle of rebellion and subjection. Victory would allow the reconsolidation of the sovereign Hmong kingdom (*top*). (Graphic by Boua Chao Lee)

Culas writes, "combining oratory capacities with miracles, particularly of healing . . . [must] succeed in making their message regarding the necessity to rediscover the Unity of the Hmong understood. In messianic ideology, this Unity is presented as the keystone to the re-establishment of Hmong domination over their neighbors."[80] I do not think the Hmong aim for domination. They certainly desire self-rule and equality. Hmong political action has primarily centered on obtaining independence, not depriving others of freedom.

In the modern era, the existence of two kinds of leaders has caused Hmong society to shift dramatically between overt resistance against and a tenuous alliance with the state. When the Hmong broker becomes instrumental, advancing the interests of the state at the expense of the Hmong desire for autonomy, the Hmong rally to the prophet who promises liberation from onerous taxes, corvée duties, and other social injustices implicit in the state. Should the state succeed in eliminating the prophet, however, the Hmong interpret the loss as a failure to capture the Mandate of Heaven. Defeat also signifies the state's supreme mandate. These twin reasons compel the rebels to submit to state control and accord legitimacy to the Hmong broker. Despite its victory, the state is coerced into reckoning with the lessons of excessive extraction. The state reassesses and loosens its grip, generating the image of a benevolent patron again. Submission to the state is almost always temporary, however. Over time extraction, corruption, and onerous demands combined with the state's ambition to impose cultural and linguistic assimilation inevitably lead once again to a volcanic eruption of revolt. Thus, the Hmong cycle of history is characterized by periods of state extraction followed by messianic rebellions, which end with the state modifying its policies and legitimating a broker as paramount (see fig. 5).

Although the Hmong dream of capturing the mandate and establishing a sovereign kingdom, the path represented by the outer circle in figure 5, the reality is that they have not succeeded in extracting themselves from the cycle of rebellion, reconquest, and ultimate subjection. Hence, they have been caught in the path represented by the inner, smaller circle in figure 5. Hmong messianic leaders have suffered constant defeat, leaving the people subjugated. Rebellion has become, therefore, more of a means of negotiating with the state to loosen its policies, not necessarily an attempt to escape its control, as James C. Scott argues.[81] This is because just as the Hmong have been important in shaping the state, so the state has been important in the fashioning of Hmong leaders, both messianic and secular.

Nkauj Ntxuam's Curse: Segmentation of Hmong Society and the Quest for Bureaucratic Solidarity

Hmong Ethnic Identity and Its Limitations

It is a historical contradiction that while the Hmong yearn for sovereignty they accept leaders legitimated by outsiders. The clue to understanding this paradox lies in their social structure, which reflects the geographic divisions discussed above. There are divergent views about Hmong identity and unity. Some argue for a strong ethnic solidarity among the Hmong while others say Hmong ethnicity is shallow and segmented by the clan and does not translate into political consciousness. William R. Geddes, who studied the Hmong of Thailand in the 1960s, was impressed by their ethnic cohesion across space and time. He writes, "The preservation by the Miao of their ethnic identity for such a long time despite their being split into many small groups surrounded by different alien peoples and scattered over a vast geographical area is an outstanding record paralleling in some ways that of the Jews but more remarkable because they lacked the unifying forces of literacy and a doctrinal religion and because the cultural features they preserved seem to be more numerous."[82] The authenticity of this shared identity, Geddes continues, manifests itself in the ways Hmong interacted with one another on a day-to-day basis. "Miao may visit Miao anywhere and expect to be received with courtesy," he writes, "not as strangers but as belonging to the same brand of humankind."[83]

F. M. Savina, who lived among the Hmong of Vietnam and Laos decades before Geddes arrived in Thailand, made similar observations. "When a Hmong does not have anything to eat," he writes, "he would travel to the homes of his more fortunate neighbors and sit at his table as if he were family."[84] Generosity was a basic courtesy extended to non-Hmong as well, however. Though a Frenchman from half a world away, Savina experienced Hmong kindness firsthand. He writes, "The traveler who leaves the hospitable mountains of the Hmong would repeat the beautiful speeches made by Louis Veuillot while taking his leave of the Chartreuse of the Alps: 'Often would my heart return there . . . it's there that I received hospitality for the first time.'"[85]

The Hmong do not disagree with outside observers on the issue of their keen sense of identity, which is often expressed through a show of hospitality. Some supply more concrete examples from their own experiences to demonstrate the point further. The Australian Hmong anthropologist Gary Yia Lee writes, "The Hmong like to see themselves as an in-group called 'peb Hmoob' (Us Hmong) in contrast to outsiders who are seen as 'mab sua' (strangers). . . . This collective image is represented by certain very distinct social values and material objects. The most commonly cited value is that 'Hmong have to look after their own' (Hmoob yuav tsum hlub Hmoob)."[86] The Australian medical practitioner Pao Saykao Thao observes that the Hmong "have an inborn feeling of belonging and bonding toward one another, no matter what country they live [in]. . . . When I was traveling through the USA and was lost in a small town, I just called someone with my clan name from the telephone directory. In a few minutes, many had come to meet me despite [the fact that] we had never met nor known each other before."[87] I believe Pao Saykao has pinpointed the crucial distinction here. Hmong hospitality is a common thing, and Hmong identity is a sure reality, but he had to rummage through the telephone book to the *T* section containing the names of members of his Thao clan before he could call someone. Therein lies the contradiction of Hmong identity. The unity found in clan diversity prevents formation of the political consciousness necessary for building the kingdom.

Against a backdrop of general hospitality and a deep sense of ethnic identity, there are real issues associated with the lack of more comprehensive political identity and loyalty beyond clan and marriage groups or personal ties. Given the Hmong preoccupation with maintaining social and linguistic divisions, perhaps the claim to ethnic unity is more wishful thinking by the erudite few than an actual practice of the nonliterate majority—especially in the traditional societies of China and Southeast Asia. This reality has been observed in more recent scholarship on the Hmong. Jean Michaud and Christian Culas write: "The Hmong have a kinship-based society. They are related to each other primarily through blood ties and alliances, not through geographical proximity or political affinities. A Hmong from the province of Guizhou in southern China who belongs to the same patronymic clan as a Hmong from Laos is sure to get shelter and assistance from his kin. On the other hand, two Hmong from neigbouring villages in the same country, who belong to different clans, will not feel any obligation whatsoever to provide each other with help and support."[88] The lack of obligation to those who are not of one's clan drives Hmong to react in relatively predictable ways. A Hmong seeking assistance will go first and foremost to his or her own clanmates. Should we be surprised, therefore, that when he was lost in the United States Pao Saykao rummaged through the telephone book, bypassing the alphabetical listings of other Hmong clans such as the Cha, Kang, Lee, and Moua, and went to his own clan first?

Going beyond clan divisions, Long Yu-xiao, a professor of anthropology and law at Guizhou University, argues that the Hmong are enamored of continuously dividing into smaller, more distinctive segments. Hmong identity is characterized by branching while Han society is characterized by the snowball effect. The Han absorb diverse cultural elements to form an ever increasing snowball, but the Hmong make ever more detailed distinctions among themselves like a branching tree.[89] Indeed, Hmong identity does tend to lean toward division. Formerly, the Hmong identified themselves in terms of their cultural or dialectic groups, clans, and lineages. Divisions in these social categories were exacerbated by the realities of life in the highlands, where Hmong villages, composed mainly of a single clan, were scattered above the settlements of other ethnic groups. In the modern age, regional and national borders and religious conversion further challenged an already segmented mentality. The Hmong seem to be, indeed, branching into ever smaller groups.[90]

Hmong Cultural Groups, Clans, and Lineages

For the purposes of this study, which covers primarily the French colonial period, the traditional categories—cultural/dialectic groups, clans, and lineages—apply. Cultural groups are hard to define. Few agree as to their validity, and they are as "imagined" as clan and lineage categories, but their political implications are real. The Chinese distinguished five "Miao" groups, classified according to the color of the women's skirts: White, Black, Green, Red, and Hua Miao.[91] Similarly, the Vietnamese also recognized five Hmong groups in Indochina: the White, Flowered, Red, Black, and "Mong Sua" Hmong.[92] There is no correspondence in colors among those identified in China and Vietnam. In a study carried out in northern Laos, Jacques Lemoine mentions the White Hmong, Green Hmong, and Armband Hmong, who spoke the White Hmong dialect.[93] Robert G. Cooper and Nusit Chindarsi identified similar groups in northern Thailand, but they note that less prominent groups were being absorbed into the White Hmong linguistic category.[94] Such observations indicate an evolving, dynamic culture in the making.

The Hmong also distinguished themselves by clan, the single most significant social unit in the society. Their origin myth tells how the clans were derived from a brother-sister union.[95] The number of unique clans ranges between eighteen and twenty-one.[96] Membership in a clan is bestowed through birth or adoption. Those who belong to the same patrilineal clan are considered "brothers" (*kwv tij*) and "sisters" (*nus muag*). They do not marry each other even if an actual blood relation cannot be established.[97] The clan incest taboo extends across cultural groups as well. A White Hmong would not marry a Green Hmong of the same clan and vice versa. Men and women carry their clan names for life, but women are subsumed under the ritual practices of their husbands' clans after marriage.

Each clan is further segmented into lineages known in Hmong as "ceremonial households" (*ib tug dab qhuas*), whose members can "die in each other's houses" (*tug tuag tug tsev*). Two important rituals establish lineage ties: the Door Ceremony (Dab Roog) and the Ox Ceremony (Nyuj Dab). The Door Ceremony is the offering of a pig to the spirit of the southern door, asking for the protection of the family's wealth and domestic animals.[98] The Ox Ceremony, which requires a cow sacrifice, is performed when a major illness or misfortune signals that a deceased parent needs nourishment.[99] Of the two, the Door Ceremony defines lineage ties. Depending on the lineage, the cooked portions of the pig are placed on nine, seven, or five platters on the table.[100] These numbers are lineage markers within a single clan.

It is generally taken for granted that Hmong society is patriarchal, so scholars ignore how the Door Ceremony, first performed by the mother, according to myths, expresses bilateralism in Hmong society, articulating the matrilineal lineages within particular clans. The platters on the table commemorate the number of sons borne by each of the original matriarchs. In the Lee clan, for example, those who set out nine platters (*cuaj txim*) on the table say they are descendants of the First Wife, who had nine sons. When she performed the very first Door Ceremony, she prepared only nine plates of meat for her nine sons. The sons of the second wife were invited but allowed only to observe the feast. Similarly, those who set out five platters (*tsib txim*) are descendants of the Second Wife, who had five sons. The seven platters (*xya txim*) of the Lee clan are a variation acquired later, when a daughter and son-in-law of the Second Wife came for a visit and were included in the meal. According to the clan myth, the Second Wife prepared an additional two plates for them. Although the Lee five and seven *txim* are acknowledged as the sons of the Second Wife, however, they consider themselves to be two different lineages and are not close enough to "die in each other's houses."[101] Other clans in Hmong society have myths about three matriarchs, accounting neatly for the three lineages.[102] Some clans have only two lineages, characterized by an elder and a younger brother.[103]

To be considered *ib tug dab qhua* (part of the same ceremonial household) and able to "die in one another's houses," those of the same lineage (same mother) must share one more element: funeral practices. The details of funeral practices vary by lineage within a single clan, but important elements include whether the body of the deceased is exposed (*tshwm tshav*) or not exposed (*pos*) to the sun before burial and what kind of grave construction is required. A Hmong-style grave requires heaping a pile of dirt on top to form a mound while a Chinese-style grave is covered with a mound of rocks.[104] The Ox Ceremony, Door Ceremony, and funeral practices are the basic elements Hmong use to determine lineage ties, but the rules can be relaxed depending on the subjective circumstances. When a man is perceived to be of benefit to the lineage, subtle differences in ritual practices are overlooked. On the other hand, if the elders perceive him as a liability, they will reject him despite similarities.[105] Every Hmong person must seek membership in a clan and a lineage in Hmong society.

Cultural groups have political implications, but the clan is the most important social unit in Hmong society. One's physical and metaphysical needs are met in the clan. Geddes writes that without a clan a Hmong "will be an outsider in ceremonial life, be insecure in the spiritual world, and lack a reliable group of allies in the worldly competition and crises."[106] As the clan is prominent in Hmong sociopolitical maneuverings, so a popular Hmong origin myth — the Great Flood — opens with its founding and not, as in the Judeo-Christian tradition, with the fashioning of man by his creator.[107] The myth of the Great Flood tells how the clans emerged from an incestuous brother-sister union. The siblings survive by taking shelter in the hollow of a wooden funeral drum. When the flood recedes, the brother tricks his sister into marrying him. The siblings produce an amorphous, round object that they, at the behest of the god, Saub, cut into pieces and scatter around their home. Each piece forms a unique clan whose name rhymes with the spot where it fell.[108]

The Great Flood story serves as the dividing line between the rest of humanity and "Hmong-hood." With subtle irony, Hmong-hood is defined by the distinctiveness of the clan and is expressed in the strict prohibitions against clan endogamy. Robert Cooper writes: "The incest taboo is extended to the classificatory *kua ti* [*kwv tij*] and is, in certain circumstances, far more rigid between members of the same clan classification than actual blood relations. Thus, the preferred spouse is the mother's brother's daughter [cross cousins]. Sexual and marital relations with the father's sister's lineage are permitted because a woman changes her clan after marriage."[109]

F. M. Savina thought the flood myth was unique to the Hmong, and he used it to link them to biblical traditions and the ancient land of Mesopotamia, but we now know that flood myths exist among various groups across the globe. One study collected three hundred accounts in Southeast Asia alone. The author argues that the versions of the Hmong "belong to later forms," and have been adapted to reflect elements essential to their cultural repertoire.[110] As Hmong identity is deeply entrenched in the clan, so the Hmong's Great Flood story zeros in on the primordial origin of their clans with nuanced paradoxes. Despite portraying themselves as originating from an incestuous union, for example, the Hmong observe the incest taboo seriously and consider a marriage between individuals of the same clan to be a "crime."[111]

The Clan as a Barrier to Political Unity: The Testimonial Experiences of Hmong Leaders

The stone baby represents a time when the Hmong were one amorphous mass, but it is with the separation of this unified body that the Hmong as a people emerges in the form of distinct clans. Hmong group identity, therefore, seems to hinge on the separation of the clans, and therein lies the paradox, the challenge that Hmong leaders have had to contend with from time immemorial.

Clan division is the political nemesis of every Hmong leader. Toulia Lyfoung, the first elected National Assembly representative from Xieng Khouang Province in 1946 and the half brother of Hmong leader Touby Lyfoung, summarized the challenge of being a Hmong leader thus. "I'll tell you this story. You go down to the valley and cut down a fully grown pine tree. You got [*sic*] hold of the top of the tree and you pull that pine tree up the next mountain. When you manage to pull that tree to reach the top of the mountain, you have all the qualities of a Hmong leader!"[112] If the Hmong are the pine tree, then the branches that provide friction against the uphill drag are the clans. The Hmong leader certainly faces a colossal challenge. Hmong myths and proverbs drill Hmong boys about clan loyalty, drawing them psychologically away from broader, supraclan associations. A popular Hmong adage states that "one should only go bear hunting with brothers of the same womb." Back when the Hmong only had flintlock rifles, which took some time to reload, a single shot was usually not enough to kill a bear. The moral of the story is that only a true brother will stand to defend one from a wounded, angry bear. When it is a matter of life and death, one can only count on a blood brother.

I once asked Tougeu Lyfoung why the Lee clan dominated the civilian and military administrations under both Touby and Vang Pao. He looked at me intently and replied, "When it comes to pressing matters, only one's clanmates would come to one's rescue."[113] The Lee clan, Tougeu explained, were *kwv tij* (brothers) of Touby. They were the only ones who willingly offered their lives during the life and death struggle against the Japanese and the Communists. Understandably, Lee clan members were the first to gain military and civilian ranks during the time of the French. By a process of promotion, they continued to dominate the top echelons of Vang Pao's military and civilian administrations in the 1960s.

General Vang Pao agreed with Tougeu. The Lees were the first ones drawn by clan association to engage in the struggle with Touby: "That is the norm because at that time [when Touby was leader] there was war in the land, so those who were not his relatives did not follow him." Moreover, Vang continued, Hmong people only orient themselves to the clan because their leadership system had long been disrupted, affecting their sense of ethnic identity and political consciousness. A leader's clan members are his strongest supporters in any endeavor: "If you want to be a leader, you have to have lots of kinsmen. As for other clans, they would not come to your aid because, from the time of their migration from China, the Hmong have always considered the clan as paramount. Everyone respects only his clan, and everyone gravitates only to his [clan] leader since there had long been a break in the Hmong leadership structure. The problem is that there is no confidence [in a leader from another clan]."[114]

Asked how he was able to draw different clans to him as a Hmong leader, Vang Pao said he did it by distributing civilian and military titles to the clan leaders. He then called on these leaders to mobilize their kinsmen in support of his cause. He stated, "Later, when I was in charge, I tossed leadership titles to everyone. Whatever they wanted, I would make recommendations to the king, who would just sign. Whatever Hmong wanted they got, so it was not hard at all."[115] Vang Pao may have bought the confidence of the clan leaders by bestowing honorifics on them, but it was the state—the king—who legitimated these titles and the CIA who provided the salaries for the positions. The clan leaders, accorded with symbolic and material recognition, rallied their kinsmen behind Vang Pao, forming his secret army. Outside patrons, the Lao king and the CIA, fashioned Vang Pao's legitimacy as a supreme Hmong leader from 1960 to 1975.

Embedded in the underlying ideologies regarding Hmong unity are competing elements—cultural groups, clans, and lineages—that have plagued Hmong society since, to put it in mythic terms, the dawn of history. For the Hmong, the state was a useful means of surmounting social segmentation when it provided the bureaucratic rationale for ethnic unity. The Hmong submitted to the state—viewing it as possessing celestial mandate—so long as it served this purpose. The relation between the Hmong and the state, however, was tenuous and the balance easily broken, hence the repeated appearances of prophets through time. Analyzing how the Hmong secular political broker and prophet interacted in complicated entanglements with one another and with the state provides insight into Hmong political tradition as well as allows a critical inquiry of the working mechanisms of the state.

Hmong in the Context of Zomia Studies and Highland Political Systems

Hmong social organization, which impedes broader political unity, is reminiscent of Edmund R. Leach's classic study of the Kachin in highland Burma. Leach found that some villages among the Kachin had hereditary chiefs while others maintained a democratic form of social organization. The chiefly villages were attempting to imitate their Shan neighbors, who had social rankings and a king, by forming an "autocratic" society, but these systems were unstable and constantly breaking down and becoming egalitarian again. Assassination of ambitious chiefs forms an integral aspect of Kachin political disintegration.[116]

Spinning off Leach and others and relying on secondary sources, James C. Scott has written an anarchist history of highland Southeast Asia in *The Art of Not Being Governed*. Scott frames his anarchist theory in the context of "Zomia" studies, a concept of space first advanced in 2002 by Willem van Schendel.[117] Geographically, Zomia is the area that encompasses the highland regions located in the middle of four subregions—Central or Inner Asia, South Asia, East Asia, and Southeast Asia—but does not easily fit into any of them. According to Jean Michaud, the original areas comprised "all the highlands of Asia, from the western Himalayan Range through the Tibetan Plateau and all the way to the lower end of the peninsular Southeast Asian highlands," but the space has since been redefined and was enlarged in 2007 to also include "southern Qinghai and Xinjiang within China, as well as a fair portion of Central Asia, encompassing the highlands of Pakistan, Afghanistan, Tajikistan, and Kyrgyzstan."[118] Zomia is an isolated, sparsely populated region about the size of Europe, but with unimaginably more diversity in languages and cultures. The area measures 2.5 million square kilometers with elevations roughly above 300 meters, and has a population of over 100 million.[119]

Scott compares Zomia to Fernand Braudel's Mediterranean Sea or Anthony Reid's Sunda Shelf, seeing it as a mercantile space where trade and cultural exchanges have occurred over the ages, but Jean Michaud notes that this highland region is "less easily travelled than bodies of water" and so it would be "more productive to compare Zomia to other highlands, the Andes and the Alps for instance."[120] Using the state as a focal point of analysis, Scott defines Zomia as a "*nonstate space*" where, "owing largely to geographical obstacles [the "friction of height," for example], the state has particular difficulty in establishing and maintaining its authority."[121] The inhabitants of this *nonstate space* are "state evaders," people who adapt every aspect of their socioeconomic, political, and cultural systems to evade state control. Runaway techniques range from specializing in high-altitude crops such as opium and maize; consciously remaining nonliterate, since literacy is a product of state coercion; and maintaining acephalous, egalitarian social systems that impede group cohesion and, hence, state control. The irony embedded in Scott's argument is not lost on critics. "Scott sees virtually all highland behavior . . . through the prism of lowland state oppression. . . . But this means that ecological and cultural conditions that were intrinsic to the hills and that were substantially or completely divorced from the valleys receive little or no attention. Therein lies a certain irony. Scott implicitly applauds the uplanders' urge to freedom from valley domination. But in tightly tethering hill society to a lowland-centered dynamic, he robs that society of functional independence."[122] Moreover, Scott's thought-provoking thesis assumes that Zomians possess no dreams of their own, a central premise of my own work here. They are noble anarchists who simply exist in reaction to the state, and this is despite the fact that Scott has shown that a few Zomians have succeeded in establishing their own states. Scott, of course, does not view these as states in their own right; they are merely "imitative" states.[123] One wonders, however, whether Scott would so casually cast lowland Hindu-Buddhist states such as Pagan, Ayutthaya, or Sinicized Dai Viet just to name a few of the precolonial states—that had also appropriated their statecrafts from neighboring civilizations in the same light.

Scott's work has generated responses from multiple fronts, both serious and humorous. Taking the cue from the "slow food" movement, an antithesis to the abundance of fast food businesses in American society that is contributing to a growing health epidemic, Hjorleifur Jonsson advocates for a "slow anthropology" with practical applications. Jonsson ranks Scott's work among the orientalist projects that reflect more about the mindset of the author and his society (readers) than the subjects discussed. *The Art of Not Being Governed*

> is for the exclusive benefit of Scott's readers, who have come to rely on his books to situate themselves in the world through notions of peasants, moral economies, hegemony and resistance, weapons of the weak, state simplifications, and now state evasion. . . . Who would have thought that what looked so ethnic, traditional, un-modern, and Oriental (-ist) was, in fact, quite the opposite and anarchist . . . strategies of acquiring the freedom and egalitarianisms that we ourselves so value and desire in the Occident? . . . Who and what we think are the highland peoples of mainland Southeast Asia has quite a lot to do with how we imagine ourselves in the world.[124]

Jonsson closes with deft humor about his own role in all the "fuss":

> after various conference panels and workshops and symposia [on] Zomia . . . I felt like the member of some Buddy Holly tribute band who now got gigs after years of laboring in obscurity, because the master had delivered another brilliant album and everybody was excited about the sound and some also wanted to know what they should make of it . . . (and he has published at least two other books since, on other things). . . . We got Southeast Asia wrong, systematically, because of certain things that are systematically wrong or mistaken elsewhere.[125]

The critiques of Scott's work have diverged in several channels, each linked to the other. Perhaps because Scott milked his thesis primarily from anthropological sources, it has stimulated self-reflective analysis about the field as well as a scrambling of efforts to deconstruct assumptions and remedy the issues Scott ignored, which include: (1) Scott's basic premise that there is a static, unitary "state" that imposes a uniform rule on "nonstate" spaces and peoples at the margins, (2) his disregard for the role of highland minorities in the processes of state-formation, (3) his categorizing the multiplicity of highland minorities under the rubric "state-evaders" without regard for their historical and cultural differences, (3) his acknowledgement that economic exchanges have existed between highlanders and lowland states, but then (4) ignoring relations between highlanders themselves — relations that have been, at various points, contentiously exploitative.

Those of the field who engaged in self-reflection suggest alternative methods of approaching highland or Zomian studies. Jonsson demands a paradigm shift in the thinkings of researchers who should realize that what they do affect real lives, but for the most part, not always in practical or positive ways. These researchers, like Scott, mine their data from or situate their subjects within colonial studies analytical frameworks that often rob them of functional independence. A primary example, says Jonsson, is the problematic way Eric Wolf, in *Europe and the Peoples without History*, absorbed the Hmong and others into his capitalist world systems analysis:

> Over the last five hundred years, all the various supposedly isolated and traditional peoples [such as the Hmong] who have fascinated ethnographers have not only suffered from the impact of capitalist expansion, but they have also become agents of furthering its process, according to Wolf. [This] particular theory of history . . . enables Wolf to assemble a range of materials to illustrate his big-picture view of capitalism's people. The theory lends sense to the data as it inspires its collection. Once Wolf had come up with his premise, the various peoples of ethnography were slipped into identities and narratives that manifested the plot structure that had, by then, disappeared into its own designs.
>
> This anthropology, widely lauded as giving us a handle on history in our varied ethnographic fields, does symbolic violence. *Depriving peoples such as the Meo (Hmong, Mong, Miao) of their own histories and identities in ways that enable us to get a grasp on the world over the last five hundred years is an act of dispossession. The theory behind this deprivation or dispossession removes Wolf and his appreciative readers from the act of symbolic violence;* it is theory history, ontology, and narrative in an inextricable bundle that pretends to convey to us the world as it is.[126]

In closing Jonsson writes: "Cultural anthropology may wish to do better than just give the educated bourgeois Western readers of academic books some history and a place to stand by depriving others of theirs."[127] His own work exemplifies an interdisciplinary approach that combines feminist studies and postcolonial frameworks to arrive at a new definition of culture as "what can happen among people across difference, and not [just] what distinguishes one group from another."[128] The process of interaction across difference includes "a long trail of political negotiation within as much as between or among hill and valley peoples." This fact is often ignored, however, leading scholars to blindly "reproduce the rhetorical framework not only of colonial rule, but also that of subsequent chauvinist nationalist authorities from within the region . . . [and] endorsement of the impossibility of negotiated diversity or of equality in multi-ethnic settings."[129]

A special volume in the *Journal of Global History* also responds to Scott's work. In the editorial piece to the volume, Jean Michaud also advocates for an interdisciplinary approach. He notes the long-standing divide between history, which is preoccupied with sweeping changes over time, and anthropology, which is "miniaturist" and concerned with the "feel" of the immediate, but he advocates for a method that combines both disciplines to arrive at "micro-history," a field that "is becoming a leading historical paradigm." Of course, this means that historians will have to overcome what Scott refers to as the "friction of terrain" and venture up the mountains to collect the oral histories. Until now, "mainstream historians have been noticeably less inclined to tread the upland trails than their colleagues from neighbouring disciplines."[130] Lack of language knowledge and the fact that highlanders are scattered across the boundaries of different nation-states become serious challenges for the historian to overcome. Trapped by the discourse embedded in regional and nation-state studies, highland scholars often ignore populations of the same groups spread just a few hundred kilometers across the border from their field sites.

The lack of historicity of the state, how it is portrayed as static and its rule as uniform across space and time, has been another major issue of critique. The runaway analysis requires some upstreaming analysis whereby the authoritarian and imposing modern nation-state in Southeast Asia (Burma, Scott's area of specialty, is a primary example of one of these modern authoritarian states) is projected backward to the precolonial and colonial eras to advance the argument that the state exerts considerable hold upon the upland areas and its people. Jonsson argues that the state's rule was not uniform and its shape changed over time.[131] For this reason, incorporating a historical framework that accounts for changes and continuities over time is necessary.

Other studies examine the role of minorities in the emergence of the state itself. In another study, Hjorleifur Jonsson argues that the categories Lawa and Mien (Yao) emerged during the process of state formation and that these categories, important for a particular ruler's consolidation of authority, originally functioned as social rankings. Thus, ethnic identity and the process of ethnogenesis occur simultaneously with the establishment of the state and are integral to and part of the process of state formation: "The fixing of an ethnic label on highland peoples in northern Thai regions emerged from a cultural project that naturalized political control over the social landscape through the allocation of identities (ethnic, rank, and so on) as within or outside the state."[132] Similarly, Yao as a category emerged along with the state in China. "The making of the Yao," Jonsson writes, "concerned the outside of the state, a process of boundary-making that joined ecological, social, political, and ethnic categories as it established the landscape of history. The state was reproduced through the distribution of rank and through the control over trade and social relations. The Yao were framed as nonsubjects in the wilderness, physically and socially separate from the civilized domain."[133] In other words, the state is intricately tied to the shaping and reshaping of ethnic identities.

As the state defines and shapes ethnicity, so ethnic minorities also shape the state and bring it into existence through negotiated processes. Bernard Formoso argues that the highlanders of Southeast Asia are neither Zomians who evade state control nor Zombies who are unable to adapt: "Hill societies of the interstate Southeast Asian Massif were likely to become as much nation-state–shaping as state-repelling and state-preventing societies. . . . Hill peoples not only offered a foundation and a refuge to nationalist insurgents but that they also formed contingents of fighters for the advent of 'popular democracies,' and at the ideational level they served as models or anti-models for defining the criteria of citizenship."[134] Ethnic minorities, agents of history who must maneuver within the operational powers of the state, continually adopt creative methods to advance their agenda.[135]

Of course, the whole point of conjuring Zomia as a concept in the first place was to urge scholars to move away from the discourse embedded in bounded geographical territories. C. Patterson Giersch warns about the dangers of seeing Zomia only as a physical space and not as a concept:

> [Zomia] is designed to challenge institutionalized regional studies configurations. Such a proposal is exciting, although the creation of a new region, if implemented without nuance, may lead to simplifications mirroring past Orientalist writing about South or East Asian civilizations. . . . [Since] the spatial configurations of power, culture, and economy are not fixed, and are instead produced through historical processes [with human spillages across

regions,] . . . one way to deal with spillover is to analyse things and people in motion, although this is a major undertaking because people on the move might not record their motion; or their records may reside in different places.

To transcend Orientalist discourses in his article, Girsh "employs 'process geography' methodologies to reconstruct trading networks through the mountains and river valleys of nineteenth and early twentieth-century Inner Asia's Kham, East Asia's Sichuan and Yunnan Provinces, and Southeast Asia. In doing so, [he] reveals who traded commodities, on what scales they operated, and how their increasingly complex networks were imbricated with state and local power."[136]

Against the grain of all the fuss about the state, postcolonial scholars who examine the processes of globalization are moving toward the idea that the state is becoming obsolete as a category of analysis. According to a leading cultural theorist, Arjun Appadurai, the impact of mass migrations and mediations in electronic and audiovisual images offers new perspectives, promoting new images of the collective self. Minority ethnic identities, which traditionally gravitated around art, myth, and rituals, are now vastly expanded to include globalized concepts available to them through modern technologies and concepts.[137] The new method for doing ethnographic work should, therefore, focus on the concept of social spaces and the production of locality.

My work here advances the notion of dreams and aspirations for highlanders — how highlanders manipulate and appropriate the powers of the state. While I agree that the Hmong eschew state control — they abhor the taxes, labor conscription, and other exactions — I argue that it is precisely because of the nature of their segmented kinship system, coupled with their socioeconomic and political reality as hill dwellers who were scattered among other ethnic groups, that their leaders have found the state to be a useful means of consolidating power internally. As Jonsson demonstrates about the Lawa and the Yao, for the Hmong the state is attractive insofar as it facilitates ethnic cohesion and produces ethnicity, which, in the Hmong view, is the necessary ingredient for state formation. As the state defines and consolidates authority over its space, it helps to define Hmong as a category. When the state absorbs the Hmong into its bureaucratic system, it further establishes political stratification and hierarchy in Hmong society; it creates a paramount chief whose position rises above those of clan leaders. The state facilitates supraclan authority and identity. As observed by Yan Riyu, in the eighteenth-century Chinese context, when the "Miao" could not come to a consensus on appointing a paramount chief, they would subject themselves to a state-appointed leader.[138]

Thus, insofar as it facilitates Hmong aspiration, the state is attractive. Even when it instigates rebellion the state serves a unifying purpose. This process is not one directional, however. As ethnic minorities are shaped by the state, so they in return also shape the state. As the state legitimates Hmong leaders, these leaders also rally the Hmong to legitimate the state. Hence, in the post-1945 period, the Hmong became essential to the Lao king, helping to bolster his authority against competing forces. When Toulia Lyfoung marched to Luang Praban to rescue him from being placed under house arrest by the forces of the Lao Issara, for example, he helped to execute the king's authority as a legitimate force in Lao. Hmong on the communist sides, especially Thao Tou Yang, serve the same purpose for Prince Souphanouvong as the commander of one of the first two Pathet Lao battalions. In return for their loyalty, Hmong on both sides received recognition as citizens of Laos. This work examines how the Hmong or, more specifically, how Hmong leaders, resist and ally with the state in order to achieve autonomy, a step in the direction of their desire for sovereignty.

Hmong Alliance and Rebellion within the State (1850–1900)

The Han Chinese Influence on Hmong Identity

The Hmong, over the course of their history, have demonstrated a strong desire for sovereignty, but they have been continually subjected to state control. China and various states in Southeast Asia have been important in shaping Hmong identity over time and space. Hmong oral traditions tell of violent struggles against the Suav (pronounced *Shu-a*), the Han Chinese who molded Hmong identity from the earliest periods.[1] Relations between the Hmong and Suav predate the first dynasties, according to Long Yu-xiao, a professor of anthropology and law at Guizhou University. *Suav* is an elision of *Xia* and *Hua*, the terms used separately or together to refer to the Chinese before the Qin period (200 BCE–200 CE),[2] and it has been retained by Hmong speakers to refer to the Chinese. This linguistic evidence suggests prolonged historical ties between Hmong and Han.[3]

The Hmong of Southeast Asia still retain oral traditions about their close connections to the Han. Hmong informants in Thailand told Nicholas Tapp a story about a Hmong man who visits his parents' graves annually only to find another man, a Han Chinese, at the grave site. Further inquiries reveal that the Han is his elder brother.[4] Such traditions speak to the Hmong belief in a shared Hmong-Han origin. Hmong-Han relations have endured for such an extended time that, despite violence at various junctures, they were virtual brothers of the same womb who sprang from the same spot on Earth. Like the Han, the Hmong believe that they originated in the Yellow River region. Today Hmong ritual masters in Southeast Asia as well as in the diaspora still

50

instruct the souls of their deceased to go to this place to convene with the ancestors. This identification with the Chinese, the Chinese state, and China helped the Hmong of Thailand to rebuff Thai cultural assimilation and evade the lure of modernity, according to Tapp. "So the Hmong Village of Nomya . . . regard themselves as the outpost of a Chinese civilization long since dead and vanished. The sense seemed to prevail among [these Hmong] . . . of belonging to a much wider community, or 'great tradition,' even though that community and tradition — of late imperial China — had long since disappeared." For this reason, they "continued to define their ethnic and cultural identity in terms of a series of radical negative *oppositions* to that of the Han Chinese."[5]

While Hmong oral traditions reflect the Hmong desire to pull Han material civilization close, however, they also demonstrate the wish to rebuff Han assimilation. As the story above suggests, the Han and Hmong are brothers. Both visit the graves of the parents, but the parentage is ambiguous or lost, as evidenced by the lack of conscious memory between the two bloodlines. Depicted in this way, the Han Chinese state represents a tantalizing civilization — indeed, the lost sibling — that the Hmong dream of emulating but not being consumed by. The Han and Hmong, the story indicates, share the same but unrecognized origin.

Long contact and the struggle to free themselves from Han control have been essential in the formation of Hmong ethnic identity and political traditions. The Suav are the Other in the Hmong construction of themselves. Despite not wanting to be subsumed, the Hmong admired almost every aspect of Suav civilization, including its superior military technologies, which led to their defeat. The Hmong, much like other peoples on the fringe of Han civilization, acquiesce to the idea that the Suav are superior in looks and more advanced in material culture. Hmong deference to the higher cultural development of the Han is found in their everyday speech, courting and ritual songs, proverbs, and folklore, and even in the borrowing of Han proverbs and language to explain their laws and ceremonies.[6] Among the Hmong masters in America there were a few who, despite being generations removed from China, could still sing the "Txiv Xaiv" (Teachings of the Father) or "Foom Kom" (Funeral Blessings) in a Chinese dialect.[7]

Han superiority has been reinforced for the Hmong through centuries of political domination. The Han Chinese, throughout history, have consistently depicted the Hmong and other minority peoples as uncivilized "barbarians." Han hegemony has also made it hard for minorities like the Hmong to contest this perception. Modern Hmong ballads sung by flirtatious girls and boys at the New Year's Festival, for example, still praise Han material superiority while putting the Hmong down. A self-deprecating *kwv txhiaj* verse expresses a girl's humble origins to a suitor: "Nkauj Sua rau khau *paj*, nkauj Hmoob xib taw *daj*" (Chinese lady wears flowered shoes, Hmong lady is barefoot). Similarly, when a Hmong talks about physical beauty, he or she often references the Han, saying, for example, "zoo nkauj cuag nkauj Sua" (beautiful as a Han lady) or "zoo nraug cuag nraug Suav" (handsome as a Han gentleman). Hmong children, both boys and girls, are named Suav to reflect that they are unobtainably attractive. Even after three decades in exile, Hmong parents continue to give this name to their American-born children.[8] Finally, a Hmong proverb affirms the desirability of Han women, equating the difficulty of obtaining a Han wife with the patience needed to acquire a political appointment: "Zoo nraug thiaj tau nkauj *Sua*, siab ntev thiaj tau nom *ua*" (Only the handsome man obtains a Han lady, only the man with a long liver [patience] obtains a title). The saying also stresses the most important criteria for leadership, patience, a quality as rare, and almost as unobtainable, as a Han lady. As we shall see in chapter 3, oral accounts about the messianic leader Vue Pa Chay pinpoint impatience as the primary reason for his defeat and the loss of the dream of finding a Hmong kingdom.

The Hmong admired, but equally feared, this ancient foe they called Suav. The memory of the historical violence of the Han Chinese state resurfaces periodically. During the Japanese Occupation in World War II, the news of impending conquest reached the Hmong living in Laos. Although they were generations removed from China, these Lao Hmong thought the Japanese were "Suav *phais tsib*" (gallbladder-eviscerating Han). In the past they had only heard of Han invading armies. "We thought the Suav had come to kill us," said Lee Cha Yia, who was a young boy in 1945. "Of course, the Japanese invaded from China, too, so we appropriately thought they were Chinese. Our ancestors had spoken of the notorious ways of the Suav, who would kill you and then take out your organs as you breathe your last breath. The gallbladder was especially valued by the Han for its medicinal purpose. Our ancestors say they would take gallbladders from Hmong victims. These stories made us fear the Suav *phais tsib*."[9]

Hmong oral traditions speak of how the Chinese, so vastly more sophisticated in the arts of trickery and fraud, used their cunning to wrest away Hmong possessions.[10] Chinese observers, exhibiting typical Han chauvinism, indirectly confirm this claim by remarking that "uncivilized" non-Han minorities are "easily duped" and "slow-witted."[11] In his treatise on the largest Yao rebellion of all time, the Han scholar Wei Yuan assigned blame on the Yao but confirmed Chinese exploitation: "The Yao are stupid and violent by nature. . . . The Chinese take advantage of their stupidity by wresting things from them by force, by stealing from them, and by raiding and insulting them. The officials are prompt to assist wicked people to bind them fast (in this condition). The Yao accumulate malice and hatred and then rebel, and events (tribal rebellions) have ever followed this course."[12] The Yao are another minority people of southwest China who are linguistically linked to the Hmong and have also endured Chinese rule for thousands of years. Perceived in similar light by the Chinese, they endured common exploitation with the Hmong.

Stories of trickery and fraud remain fresh in the Hmong's oral memory. One tale I heard tells of how the Hmong were duped out of their land. As my mother told it, a Chinese comes and asks the Hmong to sell him some land.[13] They reply that they do not have much land so cannot sell him any. "I only want land the size of my palm," he says. Seeing that he asks for so little, the Hmong relent only to find that the Chinese then takes out a piece of leather the size of his palm and cuts it into a thin strip that stretches thousands of meters long. Then he uses it to measure the land that the Hmong had "sold" to him. By the time he finishes stretching the string cut from that piece of leather the size of his palm, its length had encompassed all the land owned by the Hmong. "But you saw it for yourself. It is only the size of my palm as I've told you," said the Chinese. The Hmong were at a loss for an argument against such a clever ploy. The Chinese took their land.

Such stories of Chinese employing clever tricks to seize Hmong land and possessions are formally incorporated into warnings in the "Qhuab Ke" (Teachings of the Way),[14] the most important Hmong ritual ballad, which is memorized and passed orally among masters from generation to generation. The similarity of the meanings, words, and themes of the song across space and time impress anthropologists, who have compared different versions possessed by Hmong groups from various parts of the world in different time periods.[15] The song is sung to the deceased, instructing its soul how to return to the ancestors in China. The "Qhuab Ke" warns the dead at various junctures to be wary of being tricked out of his or her worldly possessions or being captured by the Mab Suav (Han and others), who enforce Chinese imperial rule. On the way from Southeast Asia to the ancestors in northern China, taxes and tolls are owed to Chinese officials who guard the roads.[16] The deceased's coffin is literally and symbolically packed with money (burned spiritual papers) and possessions (clothes, shoes, blankets, etc.), which he or she is instructed to use to bribe these officials and other guardian spirits so as to be allowed to pass successive checkpoints undisturbed.

Before proceeding with the song, some ritualists cut the beautifully embroidered clothes of the deceased to make them resemble poor rags so the

Mab Suav will not covet them and take them away. The "Qhuab Ke" warns that the Mab Suav will attempt to steal the deceased's worldly possessions, including the animals that accompany him or her on the journey, by posing as ancestors. The deceased is told how to identify the true ancestors. They are the ones wearing hemp clothing, not the ones wearing beautiful silk; those are Mab Suav. They are the ones with dirty faces, who do not smile or embrace the deceased; the ones who are clean, who smile with open arms and embrace the deceased, are Mab Suav. They have houses made of thatch that are located along the mountains; the wealthy ones who live in houses of bricks are the Chinese. If lingering doubts remain, the rooster of the deceased will accurately identify the ancestors: "If your rooster crows and theirs answer, those are your ancestors."[17] Otherwise, the roosters of the Chinese will continually entice the deceased's rooster by crowing first. These foreigners only aim to trick and dispossess the deceased.

The Hmong ancestors are portrayed in the "Qhuab Ke" as most abject in every manner, and so the deceased is instructed to embrace this abjectness by always taking the middle path "full of cattle droppings." These instructions are quite revealing of the Hmong's conception of themselves vis-à-vis the Han, of their concession to the material and political superiority of the Han. They also highlight the long historical subjection and powerlessness of the Hmong, who often must pay taxes and bribes to officials when alive and to spirits when dead. Of the "Qhuab Ke," Nicholas Tapp writes:

> The song speaks of an inexorable sense of historical marginalisation, a left-overness, an inevitable supplementarity, which the Hmong take for their own and by which they tend to identify themselves. There is a huge humility here, particularly in relations to other people (the "Mab-Suav") . . . a recognition of tragedy in such humility which is not self-piteous, but more realistic, for that indeed is, and continues to be seen as the course of "history," however defined. The poor dead one must always take the very worst path, since those other fine ones leading unambiguously uphill or downhill are already reserved for more fortunate people; it is the rotten little narrow path in the middle full of cattle droppings which is the path for him. . . . And so, the implication is, it is actually a kind of luckiness, fortune, that the (deceased) Hmong have managed to survive at all, despite the very odds of all the powers historically pitted against them and their survival.[18]

I would also argue that this important song reveals the Hmong's acceptance of their historical defeat by and subjection to the Chinese state. They have been fortunate just to survive because they, as also encapsulated in the legends of Nkauj Ntxuam and Tswb Tshoj, have committed wrongs that cost them the Mandate of Heaven, a concept I will address shortly. They are a conquered people in the present era and are without a direct mandate. They should be grateful for what little is accorded to them by Heaven. They should accept a mandate by proxy via the Chinese, who have captured the moral high ground, as evidenced by Heaven's bestowal on them of a higher civilization, one that includes a writing system, a kingdom, and a king. This Hmong interpretation of the processes of history, revealed and retained in this most important of all the ritual songs, fully encapsulates the rationale for alliance with and rebellion against the state. Although the Mandate of Heaven was lost, there is an underlying message that it can also be recaptured. Alliance with the state is an expedient, temporary condition. When the state fails to rule with benevolence, it is a sign that the mandate is up for grabs. Should a prophet show up with writing and supernatural powers—proof of Heaven's forgiveness—the struggle for the mandate resumes. Therein lies the power and persistence of the latent Hmong dream. This hope is encapsulated in the "Qhuab Ke," and hence, as Tapp aptly observes, there is no self-pity even in recognition of the subordination. Rather, the message is one of hope and patient endurance while awaiting the opportunity to restore what was lost, what was once a golden age.

The Hmong view the Chinese with a mix of awe, fear, and contempt, while the Chinese—the literati, in particular—perceive all the "barbarian" tribes as "bestial aliens who had to be bound by the leash of Chinese moral superiority." For this reason, they append an animal—"dog" or "insect"—radical to the names of non-Han people, a practice that can be traced back as far as the Zhou period (ca. IIII-249 BCE).[19] The "Miao Albums" depict "Miao" women as loose and licentious, clad in scanty clothes with suggestive overtones. "Miao" men, on the other hand, were "fierce" and "warlike" and constantly making trouble while refusing to come to the fold of Han civilization.[20] These depictions did not prevent individual Hmong and Han from forming lasting, complex relationships that benefited both sides, however.[21] Indeed, it would be erroneous to bolster the image that all Hmong view all Han as cunning and corrupt, or as people to fear and avoid, because many Hmong lineages claim Han origin. Vang Say Pao, an important Hmong leader from the Long Cheng area and one of the first White Hmong Christian converts, told me, for example, that his Vang lineage is descended from a Han ancestor who fled into Southeast Asia with the influx of Hmong refugees in the mid-nineteenth century.[22] Say Pao's ancestor had acquired Hmong language and customs through prolonged contact with Hmong in China and Laos. He chose to marry a Hmong woman and lived among the Hmong in the Lao highlands. His descendants assimilated into Hmong society but preserved memories of their Han origin. For this reason, they and the Hmong they lived with maintained a distinction between the Han Vang and Hmong Vang lineages and would sometimes intermarry, breaking the Hmong taboo against marrying those who shared one's clan name. When Vang Pao arrived at Long Cheng from the region of Nong Het in the 1960s, however, he was horrified by what he perceived to be clan incest. Also a member of the Vang clan, Vang Pao felt deeply ashamed by the intermarriages that had been occurring between the Han Vangs and Hmong Vangs. He held a meeting and told Say Pao, "Even if you were Han before, you have adopted Hmong ways and have become Hmong. You must observe Hmong marriage taboos and stop marrying those of the same clan name." Vang Pao took the drastic step of forcing those Vang couples who had recently married but not yet borne children to divorce. "Then, Vang Pao threatened to use T-28 strikes against any Vang clan members, Hmong or Han origin, who disobeyed him and continued to intermarry amongst themselves from that day onward," said Say Pao. "This is why we Han Vang and Hmong Vang stopped intermarrying."[23]

In 2002 Ly Na Jalao and his wife in Toulouse, France, told me that they had recently gone to southern China to reconnect with each of their respective paternal kinsmen. Ly Na said he saw the grave of his ancestor, Joua Xa, a renowned and wealthy Hmong leader of the Ly clan. He learned from his Ly relatives in China that they were originally descended on the paternal side from a Han Chinese. Their family tree showed that from generation one to generation twelve, they were Han. Then, a paternal ancestor married a Hmong woman and became Hmong.[24] By that point, his ancestor had probably lived long enough among the Hmong so as to have adopted Hmong language and culture. Ly Na's story is not easily dismissed by the historical evidence, which points to Han Chinese often being rewarded with tribal chief positions. Richard Cushman provides one example of a Chinese named Wang Ch'ing from Kansu Province. Wang had participated in the suppression of a rebellion by a Chuang leader named Nung Chi-kao. As a reward he was granted hereditary rights over a territory then under native chieftain administration. Later, the Ming installed Wang's descendant as a local tribal official.[25] Perhaps something similar happened to Ly Na's Han ancestor who assumed Hmong ethnic identity after marrying into the society.

Ly Na's wife had a similar tale about her own origin. Her grandfather, Lo Pa Tsi (not to be confused with Lo Blia Yao's father of the same name), of Han origin, had fled from China with the influx of Hmong after participating in a rebellion against the state. Because the Hmong had struggled with corrupt

Chinese officials before fleeing, many hated the Chinese. Pa Tsi had to conceal his identity. He married a Hmong, took on Hmong language and cultural practices, and instructed his descendants to hide their origin as well. While the Ly couple was in China, Madame Ly also looked up her paternal relatives. She had concealed her Han identity from Ly Na, but once they began looking into her family, she had to divulge her secret. The admission was easier once she learned of Ly Na's own Han origin. Coincidentally, her Lo relatives lived just across the mountain from the Lys. She found her father's name on her Han family tree. Her family was happy to learn that their relative had survived and borne descendants who became Hmong. "Your uncle was delighted with my secret," Madame Ly said to me. "He jokingly quipped, 'Why didn't you tell me I had married a Han lady? I must be handsome, indeed, as stated in our Hmong proverb.'"[26]

These are just a few of the many compelling examples of individual Hmong-Han relationships that endured despite mutual prejudices over time. Just as some Han became Hmong to survive in the highlands of Southeast Asia, many more Hmong became Han in China. These conquered Hmong who were brought under the yoke of Chinese civilization were called "cooked Hmong," according to Vwj Zoov Tsheej, because they submitted to Chinese rule.[27] Given recent policies that favor minorities in China, however, some Han are finding political incentives to become "Miao." The one-child policy, for example, does not apply to minorities like the "Miao."[28] This work will also demonstrate that individual Hmong and Suav have always maintained complex, symbiotic relationships with one another over the long historical period. Hmong leaders in Southeast Asia such as Lo Pa Tsi, Lo Blia Yao, and Ly Foung maintained close connections with their Han counterparts, some of whom lived with them as servants, bodyguards, friends, teachers, and advisers. Thus, general prejudice did not preclude mutual friendship between individual Han and Hmong. This common bond between poor and exploited Han and marginalized minorities such as the Hmong formed the basis for the founding of the People's Republic of China in 1949. The Communists had generated broad appeal by promising to reorganize Chinese society along class rather than racial, ethnic, gender, religious, or national lines. The depiction of history as a struggle between the dispossessed working poor and the wealthy bourgeoisie allowed the Communists to exploit Hmong oppression as part of their class struggle platform. Under this rubric, Hmong history in China was acceptably reinterpreted as the struggle of poor people against rich people and the common man against state authorities, rather than Hmong against Han. For this reason, many flocked to the umbrella of the Communists, who aptly rewarded the "Miao" in China by creating autonomous regions and granting self-government to these areas.

The Mandate of Heaven
as a Hmong Political Ideology

Given how much Chinese thought influenced Hmong identity over such an extended time period, it is not surprising that Chinese political ideologies have also percolated into Hmong society. At the base of Chinese Confucian precepts is the notion that Heaven is an "anthropomorphic divine ruler" and the "embodiment and generator of supreme virtues."[29] The Hmong also view *Ntuj* or Heaven in the same way. Heaven is the Supreme Being with all seeing eyes. Heaven sits in judgment of human actions and decides the fate of individuals. Equating this Hmong concept of Heaven with the Christian God, F. M. Savina writes:

> The Miao . . . recognize the absolute sovereignty of God in His place, in this world and in the other, and profess their dependence before Him. They believe that they cannot escape God, that they cannot hide anything from Him: "Tsam Ntuj pom," the Master of Heaven sees me; "Ntuj pom," Heaven sees me, they would say at each turn. They believe that God alone could give them the good that they desire and remove the ill that they fear. They guard themselves well, therefore, from offending Him voluntarily. They seek, on the contrary, in winning good graces from and in becoming close to Him, not out of love, but out of interest, out of fear, out of necessity, because they cannot do otherwise. They hold themselves before God as a slave vis-à-vis his master and act the same.[30]

Where it concerns the Chinese state, the concept of Heaven is intricately tied to Confucian notions of government and sacred kingship. Three measures were developed to bind the king to the moral principles that were required for maintaining constant harmony within the state: (1) the doctrine of the Mandate of Heaven, (2) reverence for ancestors and the preservation of ancient culture, and (3) the doctrine of removing the Mandate (*geming*) from an unworthy ruler. The first, the doctrine of the Mandate of Heaven, dictates that without the support of the spiritual and metaphysical Ultimate, no government could be legitimate. The people are of utmost importance in this concept because Confucians "identified the Mandate of heaven with the will of the people." As to the second measure, an emperor must demonstrate reverence for the ancestors "whose blessing, protection and approval were believed to be essential for his identity and legitimacy. Loyalty to the ancestors thus became not only a way to link him to his powerful ancestors but also a means by which the ruler engaged in self-examination and repentance of his faults in exchange for the ancestors' continual support." Finally, as to the concept of removing the mandate, "Under an immoral ruler people would complain to Heaven, and Heaven would then 'withdraw' its Mandate and give it to those of brilliant virtues." A virtuous king would not treat subjects cruelly and exploit people to unbearable degree, leading to conflict.[31]

The Mandate of Heaven is a political ideology that was first articulated in Chinese sources from the Shang Dynasty. The idea was conceptualized by the Shang to proclaim their legitimacy.[32] Possession of mandate comes with responsibilities, however. Once he has obtained the mandate, the ruler is bound to the Way of Heaven and obligated to enforce and maintain Heaven's moral, ethical principles. The sacred king, as a "Son of Heaven" (*tianzi*), has the "exclusive responsibility in carrying out the Mandate of Heaven. Heaven and the human world are connected by the king who speaks to Heaven above and governs for the people below. The Han Confucian Dong Zhongshu was caught up with this communion and explained that the character for king, *wang* (王), composite of three horizontal lines and one vertical line running through them at the center, is in fact a representation of how the three realms are related in the kingship; three horizontal lines represent respectively Heaven (above), Earth (below) and humans (in the middle), with the vertical line referring to the king who connects them."[33]

The king's authority as a transmitter of Heaven's will gives him "a position of life or death (over other men), and share with Heaven its transforming power."[34] This concept articulates the philosophical need for just war. "The Confucian doctrine of 'revolution' is essentially ethico-religious, based on the harmony between humanity and Heaven, and revolution is believed to be a dynamic process of great transformation, which recreates harmonious relationships and renews the human mission to carry out the Mandate of Heaven on earth by removing the primary source of chaos and disorder from society."[35] Dynastic rise and fall was, therefore, rationalized in moral terms. Heaven rewards the virtuous king, but takes away from the immoral ruler. Frederick Wakeman writes, "Moral retribution was the earliest significance attached to the notion of a dynastic cycle. . . . After defeating the Shang, the Chou rulers thus proclaimed that they had won because their enemy had lost the Mandate of Heaven (*t'ien-ming*) by ruling immorally."[36]

Similarly, the Zhou Dynasty was established because of the virtues of King Wen and the immorality of his enemies:

King Wen . . . was able to illustrate his virtue and be careful in the use of punishments. He did not dare to show any contempt to the widowers and widows. He employed the employable and revered the reverend; he was terrible to those who needed to be awed. . . . The fame of him ascended up the High God [*shangdi*], and God approved. Heaven gave a great charge to King Wen, to exterminate the great dynasty of Yin, and receive its great appointment, so that the various states belonging to it and their peoples were brought to an orderly condition.[37]

On the other hand, as the king is merely the executive manager of the Way of Heaven on earth, he must model himself on Heaven's moral principles and love the people. Heaven does not establish the people for kingship but establishes kingship for the people. "Heaven, to protect the people below, made for them rulers and made for them instructors. . . . Heaven compassionates the people. What the people desire, Heaven will be found to give effect to."[38] Within this design, Confucians take the family as a model for the state. The king is the patriarch of the state. Hence, rules that guard harmonious familial relations also apply to the state:

In Confucian context, a state (*guo*) is nothing other than an enlarged form of family (*jia*) and the relations between the ruler and the subjects, and those between those who govern and those who are governed are equivalent to the relations between parents and children. However, unlike in the family where children are held primarily responsible for dissolving conflict, in the state the chief responsibility for reducing tension and solving conflict is laid on those who rule and govern. It is a Confucian conviction that with a cruel and immoral ruler no state would be at peace, and only humane and virtuous rulers could bring the end to conflict and make the state prosperous and harmonious. . . . Only those who have love and affection in their heart are considered to have the right to rule. . . . Confucianism opposes the policies of ruling simply by legal or military punishments.[39]

A ruler's primary responsibility, as a patriarch of the state, is to rule with benevolence and compassion or face consequences. "To preserve the Mandate of Heaven, the king is required to conduct rituals and ceremonies correctly, to do administrative work appropriately, and to pray and offer sacrifices to Heaven and the ancestors sincerely. He is also expected to reduce rather than increase the hardship of the people, to be benevolent rather than cruel to the people, and to take care of those who are suffering. Failure to do this will cause the people to complain to Heaven and Heaven will in turn withdraw the Mandate."[40] The consequence for a corrupt king was removal from his position. His displacement was often quite violently achieved through the concept of "just war."

In chapters 2 and 3 where I discuss Hmong messianic rebellions against the state, the Confucian precepts of sacred kingship and the Mandate of Heaven as requirements of governmental rule are quite evident. Although the Hmong possess no written record that would allow us to trace the appropriation of Confucian concepts for achieving supraclan political action, we can detect clearly, in the actions and ideologies of Xiong Mi Chang and Vue Pa Chay, Han Chinese influence. This is very similar to the cases of other groups in both China and Southeast Asia who have appropriated Confucian and Buddhist millennial concepts to achieve supravillage action.[41] For the Hmong whose identity is tied to the loss of king and kingdom, the moral factor embedded in the concept of the Mandate of Heaven, which rationalizes their defeat, is especially relevant. Mi Chang and Pa Chay were the sacred kings, sent by Heaven to reestablish the Way of Harmony by removing the corrupt state authorities that oppressed the Hmong. They failed because the Hmong did not deserve celestial mandate.

What is most intriguing and perhaps uniquely Hmong and, therefore, deviating from the Confucian tendency to place blame on the king for dynastic shifts, is that the responsibility for the Hmong failure to find a kingdom is placed upon the shoulders of followers, not on Mi Chang and Pa Chay, who were, of course, divine beings. This particularly "Hmong" method of applying Han Chinese Confucian concepts helps us detect, to an extent, Hmong agency. Indeed, the politics of appropriation and its dangers have been discussed in radical feminist scholarships. Some have argued that by appropriating the masculine genre of New Left manifestos in the late 1960s and 1970s, radical feminists were able to raise awareness about women's liberation movements in the United States, but at the same time, they were forced into the rhetoric of the discourse of the patriarchy they opposed.[42] The Hmong, while using Confucian concepts to rebuff the Han state, avoided to a limited extent the dangers of being appropriated by expressing a desire for sovereignty rather than an ambition to rule over the Han. In this, they are also different from the Mongols and Manchus who, proclaiming celestial mandate, have ruled over the Han majority for extended periods, and who have been appropriated in return by the Han.

A Hmong Historical Chronology Constructed from the Chinese Records

Chinese historians also construct a narrative of long-standing contact between the ancestors of the Hmong and Han. According to Chinese sources, considered fabulous by some, the Hmong king, Txiv Yawg or Chiyou, battled the mythical Yellow Emperor, Huangdi, for control of the fertile basins of the Yellow River during the twenty-seventh century BCE.[43] Vwj Zoov Tsheej, a lecturer in the Ethnology Research Office of Jishou University, Hunan Province, compiled the first historical account, *Haiv Hmoob Liv Xwm* (Hmong history), which was translated into the Romanized Phonetic Alphabet (RPA) script in 1997.[44] The president of the Association of Ancient China in Hunan, Vwj is a distinguished scholar of classical Chinese studies. He identifies as a Hmong, and he speaks the Black Hmong dialect. According to Vwj, Chiyou's people—the ancestors of the Hmong—were known as the Juili (Cuaj Lig), or the "Nine Laws," because they were composed of nine tribes. Each of the tribes was further segmented into nine groups, for a total of eighty-one groups under Chiyou's authority. Chiyou founded the very first human civilization on earth, located north of the Yellow River region near present-day Beijing. His kingdom, the Nine Laws Heavenly Kingdom (Kuj Cuab Cuaj Lig Ntuj), was the very first kingdom in China, preceding kingdoms in India and other parts of the globe.[45] For this reason, Vwj writes, both the Hmong and classical sinologists concur that the Hmong are the elder brother and the Chinese the younger brother: "The Hmong are the owners [aboriginals] of China. They have existed in China since the beginning of time." As the First Peoples, the Hmong called the Han Chinese *Qhua Tshiab*, "New Guests."[46]

Chiyou's struggle, like those of subsequent Hmong kings, ended tragically; his subjects were either enslaved or forced to migrate south. A Hmong proverb, according to Yang Dao, fondly remembers the Yellow River, the region of their homeland: "Tsis pom Dej Dag siab tsis nqig" (one is not satisfied until one has seen the Yellow River). Moreover, writes Yang, Huangdi's triumphant defeat of the legendary Hmong king made such an impression that Hmong shamans in the present era still invoke his military might in healing rituals. When a shaman ascends the winged horse and goes into a trance to battle for the souls captured by Ntxwg Nyoog, he or she invokes the power of Faj Tim Huab Tais, the Yellow Emperor.[47] Their worship of the Yellow Emperor as a god also indicates the defeat and prolonged assimilation of the Hmong by Huangdi's people. Huangdi plays a role in Hmong religious belief similar to the current worship of the Chinese emperor's son, Xwm Kav, in every Hmong home, as discussed in the introduction to this book. The exploits of Chiyou and Huangdi are commemorated by the "Miao" in China today. In 1998 the Chinese government allowed the "Miao" to raise a statue of Chiyou in their autonomous region of Guizhou.[48]

From the Yellow River area, the ancestors of the Hmong were driven to the region of the Yangtze where, during the twenty-first century BCE, Chinese sources allude to a "San-Miao" kingdom. The "Miao" were blamed for a rebellion, a pretext for the Chinese to send punitive expeditions, driving the ancestors of the Hmong for a second time to the vicinity of the Poyang and Dongting lakes, located on the borders of modern-day Jiangxi, Hunan, Hubei, Guangdong, Guangxi, Sichuan, and Guizhou Provinces.[49] In the fifth century CE, there were reports of the existence of another kingdom around the Five Lakes region of Hubei and Hunan. By the seventh century the kingdom was enough of a threat that the Chinese launched military campaigns to crush it, scattering the Hmong ancestors once again.[50] There are speculations that the Hmong fought with the army of Nan Chao in expanding the kingdom and taking Hanoi in 866.[51] Little else is mentioned of the Hmong until the end of the Ming and Qing dynasties when records indicate that the ancestors of the Hmong were forced into the mountainous areas on the Yunnan-Guizhou Plateau, where many remain today.[52] In 1682 a Chinese general reported that the Hmong had ambushed him in southern China but spared his life in exchange for instruction in the use and manufacture of the musket he was carrying.[53]

Although there appears to be some continuity in the way the Middle Kingdom dealt with the "barbarians" to the south, perhaps what stimulated a string of rebellions by non-Han peoples like the "Miao" during the Qing period was greater efforts to draw minorities under Chinese administration as part of the country's mapping initiative in the face of the western threat. Jennifer Took outlines Chinese administrative policies for non-Han peoples from the earliest periods to the Qing. The *tusi* (native superintendency), formerly called "bridle and halter" prefectures (*jimizhou*), was established during the Tang (618–907), but it originated with the Qin (221–206 BCE), according to Took. As a broad ideology, "bridle and halter" can be traced back to the Zhou (ca. 1111–249 BCE). The *tusi* system incorporated native chieftains into China's central administration through the conferment of titles and rights of hereditary succession. The basic aim was to bring the "barbarian" tribes into the fold of Chinese civilization, but during the early historical periods, when various dynasties contended for control of China, Han rulers were content to utilize a much more restrained approach: "*Jimizhou* were in effect Chinese protectorates . . . regional satraps, which minimized China's military expense."[54]

Intensification of the *tusi* policy during the Ming and Qing ended in *gaitu guiliu* (reforming the native chieftaincies by replacing them with direct Han rule). Han administrators were sent to replace local chiefs in areas considered sufficiently assimilated into the Chinese cultural milieu. *Gaitu guiliu* was, in effect, a system designed to weaken the authority of native officials and to consolidate the native chieftaincies under Han control. The Ming even implemented rules to get rid of native chiefs, resulting in rancorous rebellions that forced policy reversals.[55] The Qing rulers were much more successful in applying *gaitu guilui*, inventing more reasons to remove the natives. In addition to Ming prohibitions against revolt, the commission of crimes, and dying without an lieii, Qing policies included moral reasons for dismissing native chiefs. Lacking benevolence, for example, was a legitimate pretext for removal. These coercive policies resulted in "Miao" rebellions in 1733–37 and 1795–1806.[56] A final, massive "Miao" uprising occurred in Guizhou in 1854–73 when the central government replaced local indigenous authorities with Han mandarins.[57] Qing political actions represented a dramatic shift from previous state policies that can be summed up in the saying "Cherish the feudal princes; win the distant people by kindness and restraint."[58] Western impingements that threatened Qing sovereignty drove it to consolidate its internal authorities by deploying policies that were much more intrusive than those of the previous dynasties.

In areas inhabited by the "Miao," minority officials were displaced or undermined by a higher order of Han administrators. Moreover, the government also encouraged Han migration into regions inhabited by ethnic minorities, a policy that generated competition over land. Increasingly, Han settlers confiscated "Miao" land by means of trickery and loan fraud, perhaps stimulating stories such as the ones passed down by my own ancestors described above. When cases of land dispute were brought before judges, Han courts favored Han settlers.[59] Before long many "Miao" became tenants in their own territories. I am not privy to the oral histories of those Hmong still in China, but the oral histories of those in Southeast Asia pinpoint Han expansion and land expropriation as the primary reasons for their migration south.

Hmong Migrations into Southeast Asia

The anthropologists Jean Michaud and Christian Culas posit an economic theory for the Hmong migration to mainland Southeast Asia. Applying "upstreaming" methods, they rely on research done in twentieth-century Southeast Asia to construct a causal theory of pre-twentieth-century Hmong migrations into Vietnam, Laos, and Thailand.[60] Referring to fieldwork done by William Geddes in Thailand, in particular, Culas and Michaud reconstruct how the economic and cultural demands of a seminomadic lifestyle forced the Hmong of China to relocate their villages every ten to fifteen years in order to find new fertile jungle. The Hmong, according to this upstreaming reconstruction, gradually left China in the nineteenth century to seek unexploited land for poppy and crop production.[61]

While the reasons for Hmong migration can be found in cultural and economic frameworks, as evidenced by the fact that different groups did enter Southeast Asia at various historical junctures, the explanations of Hmong individuals for their mass migration into Southeast Asia in the mid-nineteenth century has always emphasized political considerations. By this I mean that Hmong connect their migration directly to Han Chinese oppression, not to the nature of their shifting-cultivation agricultural practices or opium cultivation.[62] The oral sources highlight injustice, corruption, land expropriation, and violent clashes as the forces that drove them from their native soil. These oral accounts corroborate the works of sinologists and notable "Miao" experts such as Herold Wiens and Robert Jenks.[63] The Hmong say they sought new land in order to survive both physically and culturally. This history of subjugation forms an essential part of Hmong identity in China, Southeast Asia, and the West today.[64] Indeed, Hmong migrations resulting from depletion of the soil every few decades would have been more gradual and spread over the course of centuries. But the largest influx of Hmong entering Southeast Asia in the mid-nineteenth century coincides with the period of high colonialism. The greatest Hmong migrations occurred between 1835 and 1870, years of violent rebellion in China. The Hmong, being targets of persecution and land expropriation, were among those in southern China who rose in rebellion. Harold Wiens compares "Miao" land expropriation and population destruction by the Chinese state to what occurred between whites and American Indians in the United States around the same time.[65] This process of dislocation came full circle by the end of the twentieth century as the Hmong of Laos were coerced by global imperialism to become the newest invaders of the Americas. Native Indian tribes in the vicinity of Wausau, Eau Claire, and La Cross, Wisconsin, perhaps empathetic with their plight, held powwows to welcome the Hmong, but the descendants of the European invaders who caused the Hmong's appearance in these areas in the first place perceive the Hmong as unwelcome foreigners.[66]

Hmong migration from China to Southeast Asia, much like that from Southeast Asia to the West, was political in origin. Over the course of centuries the Hmong were pushed southward by the expanding Chinese empire. Their migration was accelerated by the high colonial project of the nineteenth century, which stimulated the Chinese and other Asian feudal states to delineate their territorial boundaries. Just as the reason for Hmong coming to the West was gradually skewed toward an economic explanation by the early 1990s, the political aspects of Hmong migrations into Southeast Asia have been down-played.[67] The economic explanation maintains the image of the Hmong as a primitive, nomadic, opium-cultivating people who have no land. The concept of land seizure cannot be applied to nomads. The states that rule over them, therefore, can continue to dispossess them at will. But the Hmong who migrated from China in the nineteenth century did so for political reasons having to do with their very survival as a people. This perspective guided their interactions with the states of Southeast Asia. The Hmong view their struggles against injustice under the French as an extension of their long struggle against the Chinese state.

Joakim Enwall describes the Hmong arrival in mainland Southeast Asia as having occurred in three waves, each coinciding with war and rebellion.[68] The first group came during the later part of the Ming dynasty in the seventeenth century. The second wave arrived in the Qing period between 1796 and 1820, coinciding with and subsequent to Wu Bayue's rebellion in Guizhou.[69] The last and perhaps largest influx of Hmong entered Tonkin in the 1870s following the Great Taiping (1850–64), the Great "Miao" (1854–73), and Panthay (1856–73) rebellions in which the Hmong of Guizhou, Yunnan, and Guangxi provinces participated and were pursued with extreme vigor.[70] Some of these refugees entered the Vietnamese frontier through the regions of Dong Van, Yen Minh, and Quan Ba, then turned toward Lao Cai, Sapa, and down along the border of Laos into Lai Chau and Dien Bien Phu (Muang Thaeng). The Vietnamese mandarins in the area who failed to stop them committed suicide in shame as the invaders marched to Phu Yen Binh in the vicinity of Hanoi, where they were halted only by a charge of elephants.[71]

The stories of the leading Hmong families from Laos highlight the struggles that forced them to seek new land. Mao Song Lyfoung, the daughter of Ly Foung and granddaughter of Lo Blia Yao, told the story of her maternal great-grandfather, Lo Pa Tsi, who was leader of the Lo clan in Nong Het in the mid-nineteenth century. Mao Song said she learned the history of Pa Tsi from Jer Jalao Ly, the favorite fourth wife of her grandfather, Blia Yao. Jer and Mao Song were members of the Ly [Lee] clan, so they were doubly close. Under the Hmong's classificatory kinship system, Jer and Mao Song's father, Ly Foung, belonged to the same generation as "brother and sister." Mao Song addressed Jer as an "aunt" (*phauj*).[72]

According to Mao Song, Pa Tsi was a seasoned rebel leader who had led persecuted Hmong against Qing troops when the Great "Miao" and Great Taiping rebellions swept southern China. The "Miao" Rebellion in Guizhou spread south while the Taiping Rebellion in Guangxi moved north toward the Yangtze River into the city of Nanjing. It is not known whether Pa Tsi had direct ties to either rebellion, but the commotion he stirred up contributed to the chaos that roiled the last decades of Qing rule. Like the leaders of the Taiping and "Miao" revolts, Pa Tsi was outnumbered by trained troops armed with more advanced weapons. He was forced to fight on the run, moving from one defensive post to another, abandoning the women and children and losing more men at each turn. Subsequently, Pa Tsi headed south toward Vietnam, closely pursued by Qing soldiers, who slaughtered his ragtag troops. Only Pa Tsi and his closest bodyguard, Yang Zong Cher, reached Tonkin alive. "Nothing more was heard of the women and children," said Mao Song.[73] They most probably died at the hands of Qing soldiers or from starvation or disease while evading capture.

The story of another leading family in Nong Het is told with equal vigor. According to Ly Na, his grandfather, Ja Lao, came to Southeast Asia with three elder brothers. Among the Ly brothers, Kaitong Ly Nhia Vu was third in the birth order, but he was the most intelligent and charismatic and so he became the leader of the clan. Their most influential ancestor, who had been given a title of recognition from the Chinese authorities, was Ly Joua Xa, whose massive grave mound remains in China today. Like Pa Tsi, Nhia Vu and his brothers had led unsuccessful battles against the Chinese in Sichuan Province. Nhia Vu's father was a Hmong leader of an autonomous region who fought Chinese encroachment into his land. When the revolt turned against him, Nhia Vu's father told him to lead his Ly kinsmen south.[74] Another reason for the Ly clan rebellion may have been that Joua Xa, who had no direct male heir, was a victim of Qing removal policies. "When members of the Ly clan from different regions of Laos, including Ly Joua Vang, Ly Neng Tong, and others, met in Long Cheng in the early 1960s to establish a family tree, it was revealed that Joua Xa actually had no male heirs. He had only a mute daughter," said Lee Cha Yia. "Nevertheless, since he was the wealthy and influential clan leader in China, everyone was urged to remember his name and claim that they were descended from his line."[75] Qing efforts to eliminate Joua Xa's prefectural title as a native chief and not appoint another clan member, such as a nephew, to his position may have stimulated the rebellion that forced the Lys south. The Ly brothers preceded Pa Tsi into Tonkin and lived there for some years before Pa Tsi arrived. Unlike the lone Pa Tsi, the Ly brothers headed a large clan. Their strength and influence lay in their numbers.[76] Hmong leaders of the twentieth century, including Pa Tsi, Blia Yao, and Vang Pao, capitalized on

Ly manpower by marrying their women and establishing matrimonial alliances with them. Touby Lyfoung, a member of the Ly clan, did not have to marry in to obtain Ly support.

I heard another story of war and military struggle by General Vang Pao's great-grandfather from Tsia Long Thao. Tsia Long came from the same clan as Vang Pao's mother and Vang Pao's first wife, Sia Thao. As such, Tsia Long was related to Vang Pao by multiple generations of marriages and was aware of the Vang family history. According to Tsia Long, Vang Pao's great-grandfather was a grand commander who led rebellions against the Chinese authorities in southern China. He was extremely wealthy and influential but was subsequently forced to migrate south like other Hmong leaders of the time. He met his end when he was lured into a financial venture by a Chinese merchant. The merchant convinced him to go on a trading expedition. He loaded his horses with silver ingots. When they came to a cavern, the Chinese pushed him into the cave and ran off with his money. Years later the Vang family was able to ascertain the location of his body. They went to the mouth of the cavern and saw the bones of Vang Pao's great-grandfather far below, but they could not retrieve his remains for burial. "General Vang Pao," said Tsia Long, "was descended from this great military line."[77]

Though less dramatic, the history of the Lyfoung family, whose ancestors left China several decades later than Ly Nhia Vu and Lo Pa Tsi, was no less tragic. In 1870 Touby Lyfoung's grandfather, Ly Dra Pao, was among the displaced Hmong who went south in search of new land on which to make a living. Dra Pao passed the history of his Ly clan orally down to his son, Ly Foung, who reiterated it to Touby. Touby penned the account in a written memoir that he gave to his sons before he was arrested by the Communists in 1975. According to Touby, the orphaned Dra Pao had been adopted by a Chinese couple as a child and grew up away from his Hmong kinsmen. When he reached adulthood, he chose not to marry the Chinese wife his adopted parents had selected for him and assimilate permanently into Han society. Instead, he returned to his native village to find his Ly clansmen, who were destitute and stripped of their land. Dra Pao's uncle told him how their relatives had been forced from their ancestral land by heavy taxation. He urged Dra Pao to follow those who had migrated south years earlier. Touby writes:

> Dra Pao's uncle said to him, "The country was in upheaval long before you were born. The Chinese mandarins forced heavy taxation on us. The Ly clan, who had been administrators of this land, could not collect the demanded tax, so they had to sell their land to the Xiong clan. Then they migrated south.

Those of us who remained had to gather our last dimes to pay off the Han administrators, becoming destitute in the process. Now we possessed only one paddy field each, just enough to keep us from starvation. . . . Twelve years ago your uncle Tong Kia and I heard that the southern country was sparsely populated. The land is new and unclaimed. We also heard that Aunty Mee, who had married into the southern region, has had a good life. Ten years ago, after hearing this news, your uncle Tong Kia left for the southern territories. I have not heard from him since. You are still young and vigorous. Go search for Aunty Mee and see how Uncle Tong Kia has been faring." Dra Pao took his uncle's advice and traveled south with a caravan of Chinese traders.[78]

A descendant of the Moua clan, another politically influential group in Laos, also writes about his family's battles with the Qing. Persecution and land seizure forced the Mouas into war and relocation in Southeast Asia. Chai Charles Moua writes, "My great-great-great grandfather, Leng Jou Chong, was chased by the Chinese and, like thousands of other Mong who escaped China, he and many others of the Moua clan leaders decided to leave as well." Moua also emphasized the martial skills of this ancestor in a military encounter with the state: "Leng Jou Chong was a warrior who was skillful in martial arts and no one dared come close to him. When people heard of his gong (beating drum), they stayed far away from him. He was a martial arts expert, a member of the Chinese military, and a leader of the Moua Zaagpaws clan."[79] Moua's testimony resonates with those quoted above. Oppression and rebellion were the reasons for his clan's southern migration.

War and competition for land were the major causes of the Hmong exodus into Southeast Asia. According to Nicholas Tapp, those "Miao" (A Hmao) who chose to stay in China attempted to play the western colonial powers against their indigenous overlords. Many converted to Christianity in the nineteenth century in order to gain British protection from state authorities, Han and non-Han alike: "Church membership . . . assured them of a number of privileges. Yi landlords were afraid to molest the Miao tenants as they had done formerly."[80] The temporal power of westerners inspired one of the largest mass conversions to Christianity in Asia. Samuel Pollard of the British Inland Mission became the personal protector of the "Miao." He established the first church at the village of Stone Gateway and devised a written script for the "Miao" language — the Pollard script — which is still in use today. He also established schools and health clinics, nurturing the first educated people among this group.[81] Over two hundred thousand converted to Christianity, abandoning their own religious beliefs and traditions.[82]

The Political Landscape
of Nineteenth-Century Mainland Southeast Asia

Western expansion exacerbated ethnic tensions not only in southern China but also in Southeast Asia. Colonialism can be traced to the spice trade in insular Southeast Asia in the sixteenth century. By the nineteenth century, the archipelagoes had been carved up by the Spanish (the Philippines), Dutch (present day Indonesia), British (Malaysia), and Portuguese (Timor), but the mainland kingdoms of Vietnam, Siam (Thailand), and Burma remained largely untouched by the western powers. These kingdoms fought for control of the Southeast Asian peninsula while also confronting colonialists who imposed European nation-state concepts.

Vietnam had endured over a millennium of direct Han Chinese rule in its early history and so had adopted the Han's centralized bureaucratic system with a Confucian mandarinate, but the other Southeast Asian kingdoms had adapted their forms of statecraft from India. These Hindu-Buddhist kingdoms are characterized as mandalas, "exemplary centers," or, in the words of Stanley Tambiah, "galactic polities."[83] Unlike the Chinese state, these Southeast Asian states were much more loosely organized with only a semblance of territorial consciousness. Tambiah uses the imagery of the galaxy, with a sun and the planetary systems that orbit it, to help us visualize how these states operated. The center or capital of the kingdom is where the locus of power exists, with autonomous principalities on the periphery. As the center's power waxes and wanes, its orbiting planets (smaller states) pull away from or are drawn toward its gravitational force.[84] In this manner, smaller states interact with the center in continuously dynamic ways, shifting and changing their political loyalty as other centers emerged to compete for control over them. In the nineteenth century, the remaining powerful centers competed for control of the Southeast Asian peninsula. Burmese political ambitions were arrested by the British in the early 1820s, when Burma became the first of the mainland kingdoms to fall under western colonialism. The Burmese monarchy crumbled by the end of the century.[85]

Siam and Vietnam remained the two dominant states on opposite sides of the Mekong River following British seizure of the Burmese delta. On the west bank, Chaophraya Mahakasatsuk assumed the throne of Siam as Rama I in 1782, founding the current Chakri dynasty. Over the course of the nineteenth century, the Chakri kings, who had consolidated a base of power at Bangkok, struggled to rebuff the British. Kings Mongkut (r. 1851–68) and Chulalongkorn (r. 1868–1910) are credited with cleverly pitting the western powers against one another in order to maintain political control, albeit under British economic domination. Much more sensitive to the evolving political situation, the Thai kings quickly adapted and applied western mapping systems to consolidate their territories, avoiding official colonization.[86] In the end, however, the British and the French exerted considerable influence on the geobody of Siam.

On the Vietnamese coast in the city of Hue, Nguyen Anh, with the help of French mercenaries, took the reign name Gia Long and established dominance as the founder of the Nguyen dynasty in 1802. During the course of the nineteenth century, the Thai and Vietnamese kingdoms gradually consolidated claims on the petty principalities along the Mekong, Ou, and Black rivers, forming a complex hierarchy of tributary states under their control. The dire situation of these vassal states was evidenced by their obligation to pay simultaneous tributes to both courts in order to maintain a semblance of existence.

In the Tonkin highlands of Vietnam, the Tai feudal lords, who had linguistic affinities with the Chakri rulers at Bangkok, controlled the Sip Song Chau Tai, or the Twelve Tai State.[87] This mountainous region served as a natural buffer between the two contesting empires of China and Vietnam, and the peoples inhabiting the area were subjected to invasions from both sides over the centuries. White Tai domination of this region dates back to at least the fifteenth century when the Deo clan first obtained recognition as hereditary rulers of the region from the Vietnamese emperor. Philippe Le Failler writes, "Between 1431 and 1432, Lê Lợi (Lê Thái Tổ, 1428-1433) the Đại Việt ruler who had just repelled an invasion by the Chinese Ming Dynasty, crossed the vast Hưng Hóa Province and led his troops to Muäng Lễ to seize a local chief, Đèo Cát Hãn. From then on the central power always maintained the Đèo as heads of counties, or *tri châu*."[88] At various historical junctures, however, the Tai river valley dwellers paid tribute to China and Burma, as well as Luang Prabang.[89] Deference to multiple lords allowed local Tai chiefs to retain their autonomy, but it presented these competing Asian empires with major problems as each struggled to claim this highland region in the face of western encroachment.

In the eighteenth century, the Vietnamese began imposing more direct rule over the areas under Tai administration. Jean Michaud writes, "The northern frontier and the peoples inhabiting it were—at least nominally—under the responsibility of the Vietnamese Ministry of the Armies (Binh Bô). The peripheral and mountainous districts they inhabited bore a specific name (*châu*) to differentiate them from the standard districts (*huyên*). In theory, both were administered by Kinh mandarins sent to live on location, called *tri-huyên* and *tri-châu*. In the northern region there were 44 such châu and 163 huyên."[90]

Centralization efforts lagged as competing imperial dynasties vied for control of Vietnam.

By the time of the Nguyen dynasty, the Deo clan still retained control over the Tonkin highlands. The head of the clan was Deo Van Seng, a Chinese merchant from Hanoi who had married the daughter of the Tai ruler and taken his clan name. Deo Van Seng and his sons worked hard to emerge as leaders of the White Tai by establishing marriage alliances with ruling families and by assigning family members to preside over surrounding districts.[91] The Deos also played the contending lowland states against one another while obtaining legitimation from all. The Tai leaders, for example, sent annual tributes to Hue while also paying homage to Siam indirectly through its Lao vassal prince in Luang Prabang. Historical events would soon force the Deo clan to sever its loyalty to Siam, however. In 1850, Deo Van Seng remained as leader in Muang Thaeng or Dien Bien Phu while his son and successor, Deo Van Tri, relocated his headquarters to Lai Châu, farther north and west of the Black River.[92]

Foreign incursions between 1861 and 1885 complicated the political situation in the Tonkin highlands. When Yellow Flag bandits attacked from China in 1872, the Deos resisted the invaders successfully and were rewarded by the Vietnamese emperor. Deo Van Seng was appointed head of prefecture (*tri phu*) of Muang Thaeng while his son, Deo Van Tri, became the head of county (*tri châu*) of Lai Châu.[93] The father and son pair became the paramount leaders of the Twelve Tai State. Vietnamese recognition enticed them to abandon their loyalty to Siam. In the 1880s, when Siam attempted to consolidate rule over this Tai-speaking region, it met with resistance from the Deos. As part of his mapping efforts, King Chulalongkorn had aimed to use the Black River as a natural territorial barrier against French advancement. The Thai monarch could not, however, induce Deo Van Tri to relocate back across the river into Muang Thaeng to bolster Siam's position against the French. Deo Vang Tri's father, Deo Van Seng, had passed away in 1885, leaving him as the paramount chief of the White Tai. Complicating the matter further, when Deo Van Tri relocated his capital to Lai Châu in 1850, he also severed his tributary ties to Luang Prabang while continuing to pay tribute to Hue. In 1885, thirty-five years later, when the Thais challenged French and Vietnamese claims to the Twelve Tai State, their attempt to employ legalisms similar to those used by the French was voided by Deo Van Tri's long-severed ties with their Lao vassal, Luang Prabang. When the Thai commander, the Phichai governor, arrived in this highland zone, he "encountered unexpected resistance from the Twelve Chuthai elite, none of whom professed allegiance to the Luang Phabang prince. . . . The prince himself told Neis in 1883 that he had no control over the

Twelve Chuthai towns, including [Muang] Thaeng, and could not interfere in the affairs of the Deo family. The Deo held themselves entirely independent of the Lao and looked upon the Lao princes as not only militarily weak but also culturally inferior to their own Sino-Vietnamese style."[94]

Auguste Pavie, the French strategist who single-handedly negotiated for the Tonkin highlands to come under French control, exploited these legalities to claim the region for France. When he visited the area in 1887, he "described the ancient feudal society, stating that he had no doubt whether the Sip Song Chau Tai were then dependent on Annam. It is thus fairly certain that not only the Tho in the Claire River (Sông Lô) area closer to the delta but also the Tai of the Black River valley were paying tribute to Hue."[95] Pavie argued that since France had taken power in Vietnam it had a rightful claim on the Twelve Tai State, which was a vassal of the Vietnamese emperor. The dispute over control of the Tonkin highlands shifted in France's favor when China ceded its claim to the territory following the Sino-French Treaty in June 1885. China, a strong competitor in the region, bolstered the French claim. French possession of the region was finalized only when Deo Van Tri surrendered to Pavie in 1890 in exchange for legitimation as the supreme overlord of the highlands. His authority was not absolute, however. Failler writes, "On January 28, 1893, Deo Van Tri was named Uplands Patrol Commissioner [Quản Đạo]. Even though he retained the title of Head of the Sip Song Châu Thai, only the six counties surrounding Lai Châu, including Phong Thổ, remained in his power."[96] Following his death in 1908, Deo Van Tri was succeeded by his son, Deo Van Khang (r. 1908–30). Khang, like his father, continually rebuffed French attempts to foist their rule on the Tonkin highlands. He controlled the region as a feudal lord, imposing his own system of justice, which led, in 1918, to the most widespread anticolonial rebellion by the Hmong, as will be discussed in chapters 2 and 3. To curb the power of the Deo family, the colonial authorities eliminated the title "marcher lord" following Deo Van Khang's death in 1930. They also remapped districts in order to dissipate Deo influence and assigned the Tai lords as administrators away from their home cantons. This policy of diffusing Deo power was retained until the end of the Japanese Occupation. During the period of postwar nationalist revolution, however, the French needed strong ethnic support in the highlands once again. Deo Van Long, the son of Deo Van Khang, was installed as ruler of a Tai Federation in 1948. Long remained in power until the French defeat in 1953, after which he and members of his family were forced into exile in France.[97]

South of the Twelve Tai State were the three Lao kingdoms that straddled the Mekong, Luang Prabang, Vientiane, and Champassak. These states had also been reduced to tributary vassals of Siam and Vietnam. By the nineteenth century, Vientiane had become the most powerful Lao kingdom. Anouvong, the reigning prince of Vientiane, was a vassal of the Vietnamese and Thai. For his loyalty, these two contending powers recognized him as the legitimate suzerain of Muang Phuan (Xieng Khouang), the principality located on the plateau to the northeast inhabited by the Phuan, a people culturally similar to the lowland Lao and other peoples of the greater Tai group, which includes the Shan, Lu, Muang, and Central Thai. Centuries before, the Phuan had established themselves as the rulers of the region known today as the Plain of Jars. Located on the traditional invasion route from Vietnam to Luang Prabang and Vientiane, Muang Phuan was a strategically important and highly contested area. The ruler of this disputed region was the legendary Noi, who had been arrested and imprisoned in Vientiane for a short time as a youth. Noi's riding skills impressed Anouvong enough to secure his release and, subsequently, to secure a marriage with Anouvong's younger sister. Perhaps because of this marriage alliance, Noi was installed as the last king of Muang Phuan. Unfortunately, history also records him as the traitor who handed Anouvong over to the Thai, a fact that his descendant, Saykham, vehemently disputes in a memoir.[98]

During Noi's reign and before Anouvong's rebellion in 1826, the Thai court exercised indirect authority over Muang Phuan via Vientiane. Through Luang Prabang the Thai also laid claim to the Twelve Tai State, situated on the upper Black River, as well as the principality of Huaphan (Sam Neua). Similarly, the Vietnamese court staked a direct claim on the Twelve Tai State, whose lord, Deo Van Tri, paid it an annual tribute. Because Anouvong was also its vassal prince, Vietnam also claimed Muang Phuan through Vientiane.[99] Squeezed by Thai and Vietnamese expansionism, these complex relations ultimately led to the elimination of various principalities along the Mekong. The Lao kingdom of Luang Prabang and the Khmer kingdom of Cambodia survived into the twentieth century largely due to the intervention of the French. In 1946 the Luang Prabang monarch was formally enthroned as the king of a newly created Kingdom of Laos. Saykham, the hereditary feudal prince of Muang Phuan, was reduced to a governor, and Boun Oum, a scion of Champassak, was appointed inspector general of Laos.

Meanwhile, over a century before the Kingdom of Laos came into existence, a more deadly fate had befallen Vientiane. In 1826 Anouvong, who claimed to be a direct descendant of King Fa Ngum, the founder of the kingdom of Lanxang in the fourteenth century, attempted to regain his independence from the Thai. Some claim that Anouvong sought to reconsolidate Lanxang, which, at its height, encompassed the northern and northeastern territories of modern

Thailand, as well as Luang Prabang and Champassak. As its principal over-lord, Anouvong's ambitions impacted the politics of Muang Phuan, causing drastic changes in the ethnic makeup of the region and affecting the Hmong as well. After a year of rebellion, Anouvong was defeated and forced to flee south down the Mekong and across the mountainous land pass into the protective skirts of Hue. In the winter of 1828, he returned with a contingent of Vietnam-ese escorts by way of the northeastern overland route followed by present-day CR7, which bisected Phuan land. The Vietnamese general dragged his feet at the Phuan capital of Xieng Khouang while the impatient Anouvong stormed Vientiane with his contingent of Lao troops, reoccupying the city for a brief time.

In early 1829, the Thai retaliated by recapturing and razing Vientiane, leaving only the That Luang Temple, which remains today. Anouvong escaped once more toward Xieng Khouang, where he hoped his Vietnamese reinforcements might yet remain. They had long deserted the Phuan town, however, leaving it unprotected. Some argue that Noi negotiated a pact to surrender Anouvong to the Thai in order to save his besieged realm.[100] Noi's grandson, Saykham, disputes this view in a memoir. The Vietnamese emperor, he writes, fabricated this story in order to discredit Noi.[101] Whatever the case, the consequence was devastating for both Noi and Anouvong. The Thai took Anouvong to Bangkok, where he was mercilessly tortured until he died in 1829. His death ended the ancient royal line of the kingdom of Vientiane.[102] The demise of Anouvong raised the status of Luang Prabang, setting the course for this royal line to rule the French-created Kingdom of Laos in 1946. Vientiane, much more accessible from Cambodia and Cochin China, was retained as the administrative seat while Luang Prabang, located further up the Mekong, became the royal capital.

Noi's fate shadowed closely that of Anouvong. Anouvong's death became the pretext for a Vietnamese invasion and annexation of Muang Phuan. The Vietnamese emperor sent a punitive expedition against Noi, who had dared to surrender his vassal prince to an enemy. Vietnamese soldiers stormed Xieng Khouang that spring, arresting Noi and his family, which included multiple concubines and five young sons, and marched them to Hue. Noi was executed, and his wives and children were held as captives in the royal city for nearly two decades. The Vietnamese, meanwhile, established direct rule over Muang Phuan by sending a mandarin to supervise a rival who was installed as governor.[103] Eighteen years passed before Noi's sons were allowed to return home. Po, the eldest, was established as governor of Xieng Khouang in 1850.[104] Because of this bitter history, Noi's great-grandson, Saykham, opposed the Vietnamese in the post-World War II era. Saykham grudgingly remembered what his father,

Sainyavong, had told him: "When my father, Chao Kham, and his brothers returned from Annam after twenty years' absence, they spoke Phuan with an Annamite [Vietnamese] accent. They never rid themselves of this mark of oppression, and they never forgot the crime committed by the emperor of Annam who, in order to clear himself, had put to death *Chao* Noi after discrediting him. So be wary of the Annamites."[105] Saykham sided with Touby Lyfoung and the French against the Viet Minh during the political debacle that followed the Japanese Occupation.

For the Hmong, the struggles for control of the Plain of Jars in the nineteenth century remain as vague legends recounted in oral histories. Not aware of his personal name, Noi is referred to as the legendary Vaj Ncuab Laug, which translates as "Old King." When I visited Mao Song Lyfoung, whose brothers Touby, Tougeu, and Toulia were schoolmates and close friends of Saykham, she often told me stories of Vaj Ncuab Laug. Ignorant of the history of Muang Phuan at the time and much more interested in the twentieth-century struggles of her own family, I glossed over Mao Song's references to the Old King, but my interest was piqued one day by her dramatic details about his ability to fly. I finally asked who Vaj Ncuab Laug was. "He was the old king of Xieng Khouang, the great-grandfather of Saykham, who was arrested and taken away by the Vietnamese," said Mao Song. "Vaj Ncuab Laug was so powerful that his defeat came only after the Chinese [Haw?] dug up and destroyed all the *mem toj* [mountain veins] in the surrounding hills of Xieng Khouang. When they severed these *mem toj*, blood spattered forth and flooded the plains below where the royal family lived. After the *mem toj* that had protected this land were destroyed the king, Vaj Ncuab Laug, lost his power. He was captured, marched on foot with his hands tied behind his back to Vietnam, and executed."[106] Until I began researching Phuan history, I was skeptical that Vaj Ncuab Laug was a historical figure, especially in light of the stories that were told with mythic overtones.

Tougeu Lyfoung also spoke about Vaj Ncuab Laug to me. "When I was a boy studying in Xieng Khouang, I often heard about the powers of Vaj Ncuab Laug," he said. "They said Vaj Ncuab Laug could fly. If you took the overland pass, which included going on a river raft at one point from Xieng Khouang down to Vientiane, by the time you reached your destination Vaj Ncuab Laug would be there already. It's the same thing when you made the return trip to Xieng Khouang. He would be back already when you arrived." Tougeu reflected on these legends about the Old King by saying, "Imbued with these stories of Vaj Ncuab Laug's power, I had always wondered as a boy if I were to become a powerful political figure would I also attain the ability of flight. When I was the director general of the Ministry of Justice of Laos with much more expansive authority than Vaj Ncuab Lauj, I was disheartened by the fact that I still could not fly."[107]

Myths of Vaj Ncuab Laug still abound in the Hmong American community among men who—unlike the historically conscious Lyfoung family members, who had close contact with Saykham—were far removed from the royalty of Muang Phuan. I was quite shocked to learn that the myths of the Old King had taken new twists in exile. In the imaginations of some Hmong belonging to the Congress of World Hmong People, a political association, Vaj Ncuab Laug has been transformed into a Hmong king. One elderly Hmong man of the association had claimed on the Minnesota Hmong Radio that Vaj Ncuab Laug, of the Vang clan, was one of the first two Hmong kings who ruled over the kingdom of Xieng Khouang. The other was Yaj Tseem Ceeb of the Yang clan.[108] Indeed, the word *vaj* (*vang* or *wang*) means "king" in Hmong, as it does in the original Chinese, and it is also used as a clan name—as in the name Vang Pao. This double usage perhaps allowed the elderly Hmong man to conclude that Vaj (King) Ncuab Laug must have been a Hmong king. The transformation of this historical Phuan figure into a Hmong king in the exile period in America is perhaps evidence of the genesis of the Hmong's attempt to claim the land once ruled by the Phuan for their fellow coethnics, who are still resisting communism in the region today.[109]

As an interesting sidenote, this double usage of the word *vang* was also capitalized on by Vang Pao, whom I interviewed in California in April 2004. After several hours of conversation, Vang Pao took out his copy of *The Wall Chart of World History*—a gift from a British scholar, he said—to prove to me that the Hmong had a long history of kingship in China. Perhaps more important in his view, these first kings were from his very own Vang clan. Using a pen to mark the pages, Vang Pao placed an *X* above the years 1200 and 200 BCE of the Chinese chronological timeline, the historical period identified in the chart as the "Tchou" dynasty. The first ruler was Vou Vang, and the last was Ngan Vang II.[110] Vang Pao spoke with great pride about the Hmong and his clan when he made the marks, believing in his mind that the word *vang* is a clan name rather than the Chinese word for "king."[111]

Such deviations aside, following the sack of Vientiane and the death of Anouvong in 1829, the Thai accorded Luang Prabang nominal authority over Muang Phuan, claiming it as an indirectly ruled principality. This claim may account for another twentieth-century historical tension between the Luang Prabang and Xieng Khouang royal lines.[112] The Thai, meanwhile, pressured the Phuan princes to move their people to the west bank of the Mekong. When they dragged their feet, the Thai took matters into their own hands. Between 1830 and 1880, as part of Siam's early efforts to create ethnic buffers along its borders, Thai armies raided and forcibly relocated three-quarters of the Phuan population to the west bank—the northeastern "Isan" region—where their descendants remain today.[113]

Complicating the Phuan troubles, between 1869 and 1874 the Haw, Chinese-speaking Muslims who inhabited the frontier regions of southern China, looted the states between the Mekong and Black rivers, also encroaching on Phuan land. They captured Xieng Khouang as a base from which they raided the Lao settlements along the Mekong, leading finally to the occupation of Vientiane and threatening Siam.[114] In 1875 the Thai dislodged the Haw from Vientiane, but they failed to cast them out of Phuan territory. The bandits dug in at Chiang Kham, a town located on the upper Ngum River, northwest of Xieng Khouang. By 1883 the raiders controlled most of the plateau. The reigning Phuan ruler, Prince Khanti, was driven from his capital and forced to take refuge in Ngan, on the southeastern corner of Phuan land, "where he lived virtually in exile." Installed by Siam as governor in 1877, Khanti made "appeasement payments" to the bandits and sent tribute to Vietnam while also "profess[ing] nominal allegiance to the Thai king."[115] The Hmong played a strategic role in the region as Phuan authority waned and the Phuan population decreased due to raiding and relocation across the Mekong.

Early Hmong Relations with the Tai in Tonkin

The Hmong encountered the complex tributary systems described above when they arrived in large numbers in the Southeast Asian peninsula in the early nineteenth century. As in China, they faced centralization policies initiated by the lowland courts that placed them at a disadvantage. These policies were further exacerbated, again as in the case of China, by the perceived threat of the western colonial powers—especially the French, who had designs on the region by midcentury. Under such tumultuous conditions, the Hmong negotiated for a workable position amid the multitude of ethnolinguistic groups. Lacking the language and literary ability to articulate their demands and devoid of the formal channels of access to petition the lowland courts directly, some Hmong adopted violent resistance as the last means of curbing lowland efforts to articulate an ethnic hierarchy that placed them at the bottom. Lowland discrimination, which resulted in extractive policies, heightened Hmong dissatisfaction. "For most Lao civil servants, the Meo [Hmong] were lower beings and species of gangsters," writes Saykham as late as 1940.[116] Drawing on memories of their revolts against China in the previous centuries, the Hmong opted for armed rebellion. Among the Hmong were seasoned rebel leaders whose authority stretched back to their homeland. These figures led the charge for justice when the repression of lowland feudal lords became intolerable. When the lowland authorities responded by granting the Hmong autonomy, however, Hmong leaders collaborated as loyal enforcers of the state, thereby becoming the tools for integration as the nation-states of mainland Southeast Asia came into being.

Used to the more temperate climate of the north, the Hmong of Tonkin preferred the mild, mountainous regions of the Twelve Tai State under the authority of the Deo family from Muang Thaeng. The foot of the highland zones dictated where the mass of Hmong migration was arrested on the Vietnamese mainland. Lacking immunity against mosquito-borne diseases, the Hmong feared the malaria-infested, humid lowlands, preferring the cool safety of the heights. Through the Tai overlords, they were only indirectly connected to the Vietnamese emperor based in Hue. It is not clear if the Nguyen emperor even recognized the Hmong as subjects in this early period. Recently installed in 1802, Emperor Gia Long was preoccupied with the problem of establishing his own celestial mandate. Still haunted by memories of the Le dynasty, based at Hanoi, and mindful of the French, whose superior firepower had just aided his rise to power, the Vietnamese emperor seemed content to leave the politics of the highlands to his vassals, the Tai overlords.

On their arrival in the Tonkin highlands, the Hmong struggled to establish themselves in the ethnic hierarchy. They clashed with the Yao and Tai of Dong Van in Ha Giang Province and drove some of them out of the region.[117] They were, however, obliged to reach a modus vivendi with the White Tai of the Black and the upper Song Ma rivers, as well as with the Black Tai of Muang Thaeng and Son La. The Hmong situated themselves politically between the Tai and the Khmu, descendants of the mainland aboriginals. While they recognized Tai hegemony, they were not averse to emulating the Tai example of exploiting the Khmu.[118] The Tai, river valley dwellers of Tonkin, paid tribute to the Vietnamese emperor, but the Hmong, who lived at higher elevations, had minimal contact with the imperial city of Hue. Jean Michaud writes, "The Hmong, . . . the Yao, . . . the Khmu, . . . and the Lolo—to name but a few of the principal upland dwellers on either side of the Red River—were largely ignored or left to themselves higher in the mountains."[119]

The Hmong of Tonkin paid tribute to their Tai overlords. Recent arrivals, they were victims of Tai exploitation. Failler writes, "The consistent policy of the Tai leaders, irrespective of clan, was to deny new arrivals all rights of political representation while at the same time demanding taxes and corvée labor from them. Better yet, this new possibility brought benefits. The Tai could authorize the transfer of a part of the fiscal burden otherwise borne by Tai farmers (peasants) onto the uplanders, thus reinforcing the power of Tai leaders Deo Van Tri and his sons used this opportunity systematically, often abusively. This policy of exploitation was a source of tension that constituted a risk of migrant revolt, which happened in 1918 with the Hmong."[120] Although a per-household tax of four piasters was levied on the Hmong, "Their semi-nomadic practices enabled the Hmong to avoid this fee. They favored a levy on goods, particularly opium, rather than one based on fixed (or land) property. The Khmu, the poorest group in the *muang*, paid only two *piastres* for their homes but provided wood, bamboo, and rattan for the construction of Tai homes."[121]

The imposition of taxes was arbitrary across the northern highlands under Tai administration. Hmong in the region of Ha Giang paid twice as much in taxes as the Hmong in Muang Thaeng. After his capture by the French in 1912, the Hmong messianic leader Xiong Mi Chang testified that his family of eight cultivated a plot of land in Meo Vac that they rented from a Tai for eight piasters per annum. In addition, they also paid half a piaster per annum in tax for this same plot of land, which was just large "enough to sow 84 Annamite liters of seed."[122] Admittedly, by Xiong's time in the early twentieth century, the situation under French colonial rule might have been different from that of the nineteenth century, but it appears that the Hmong paid rent as well as taxes to their overlords, the Tai and the French. That they felt doubly exploited is evidenced by several violent uprisings, which shall be addressed shortly.

Hmong-Phuan Relations
in Muang Phuan (Xieng Khouang) to 1893

Hmong migrations from Tonkin to modern-day Laos occurred during the first two decades of the nineteenth century.[123] The earliest migrants in Nong Het were members of the Vue clan, who had settled in the Fan Si Pan Mountains, ruled by White Tai feudal lords, west of the Red River. These Hmong were enticed into northeastern Laos by a Chinese trader named Ton Ma who spoke of uninhabited virgin forests and land aplenty. Kue Vue led an initial exploratory trip to confirm Ton Ma's stories. Then he led his kinsmen into Nong Het and established the first ten villages in the surrounding mountains.[124] After the arrival of the Vue clan, there followed the largest influx of migrants from Tonkin to Muang Phuan, led by Lo Pa Tsi and Ly Nhia Vu, the respective leaders of the Lo and Ly clans. The Lo and Ly clans had also settled in the Fan Si Pan

Mountains following struggles with the Qing government. After hearing that their affinal kinsmen, the Vue, had succeeded in establishing thriving villages, they followed them to Laos. The Lo and Ly clans arrived in 1856 and also founded villages in the mountains north of Nong Het. Farther west the Moua clan also settled in the Phou San Mountains located on the fringe of the Plain of Jars.[125] These Hmong pioneers, each led by their own clan leaders, came under the authority of the Phuan princes. The Phuan governed a conglomerate of villages located on the Xieng Khouang Plateau at elevations above one thousand meters. Beyond the Phuan settlements were mountainous ranges with relatively untouched forests. The fertile jungle and mild climate of the heights was ideal for swidden agriculture and opium cultivation. The Hmong settled at the highest elevations in these highlands and challenged the Khmu, who lived at the middle elevations, for the right to farm land. Their flintlock rifle gave them a decided advantage. The Khmu had to share their land with the new migrants.[126]

The Hmong arrived in large numbers in Xieng Khouang in the 1850s, just when the Phuan had been weakened by Thai and Vietnamese political encroachments. The Phuan kingdom, much like the Khmer kingdom downriver, was under incredible pressure to defend its existence. Unlike the Khmer, who commanded the Mekong Delta, a possible "backdoor to China," the Phuan possessed little that would lead the French to rescue their kingdom from extinction. Instead, the French authorities courted Luang Prabang, now the most crucial Lao state on the Mekong. The weakness of the Phuan state is evident in the 1889 census taken by the French. According to estimates, Muang Phuan contained a total population of 24,920, of which 49 percent were Phuan, 30 percent Hmong, 14.3 percent members of other hill tribes, and 6.7 percent immigrants from Lao towns. Of these, approximately half lived near Chiang Kham, and, of those, 55.7 percent were Hmong, 40.6 percent Phuan, and 3.7 percent other hill tribesmen.[127] The Hmong were the majority population around Chiang Kham, the second most important Phuan town. The large Hmong population in Muang Phuan made them influential political players in this strategic region well into the twentieth century.

Under the politically debilitated Phuan, the Hmong enjoyed a high level of autonomy. They reconstituted the social and political structures of their society, shattered by centuries of struggle with the Qing imperial state, by solidifying marriage ties between the different clans, which had migrated from various regions of southern China. Having endured indirect rule as stipulated by the Chinese "bridle and halter" or *tusi* systems, the Hmong rekindled the tradition of looking to the lowland for political organization. They formed connections with the Phuan princes by offering tribute, in return for which the most powerful clan leaders received titles of recognition. The fractured Hmong leadership system made the Phuan princes, recognized by the Hmong as the original owners of the land, important sources of legitimation. But the Phuan quickly learned the challenges of ruling the Hmong. The settlers had arrived in Southeast Asia as groups of autonomous clans with no single recognized paramount chief. They also came from different regions of southern China, each clan being guided by its own leader. Clan fragmentation was exacerbated by dialectic differences and cultural group divisions distinguished by the clothing of the women. The complex of competing regional variations, cultural/dialectic differences, and the egalitarian clan system resisted attempts by the Phuan to nominate one man as an ethnic representative. The clans vied for supremacy in the highlands as the leaders of the largest clans descended to the plains to place themselves under Phuan jurisdiction. Among them, the White Hmong cultural group dominated in Laos. Their clan leaders were accorded local administration, supervised by authorities in Muang Kham. A descendant of the Xieng Kouang Phuan aristocracy told Touby Lyfoung that his ancestors were content to respect the Hmong desire for clan autonomy by awarding the leaders of the largest clans honorary titles: "[The royal prince of Xieng Khouang] went to investigate [the Hmong situation in Nong Het] and realized that the Hmong were different from the Lao. They were divided into clans, each of which had its own head who possessed the material means to be a leader. When the royal prince attempted to choose one among them as the main chief, however, none of the other leaders agreed. He had no choice, but to accord each of the major clan leaders a title . . . calling them *kaitong*."[128]

Leaders of dominant clans such as the Lo [Lor], Ly [Lee], Yang, and Moua obtained the title *kaitong*,[129] an honorific equivalent to the current position of *tasseng* (subdistrict chief).[130] This designation, considered prestigious by the Hmong of the time, was not cheaply attained. Kaitong Ly Nhia Vu acquired his title in 1878 when he killed a white rhinoceros in the vicinity of Yeng Pha, located north of Nong Het, and presented its prized horn to the Phuan authorities at Xieng Khouang. Lo clan members followed suit and killed another rhinoceros, obtaining the coveted *kaitong* title for Lo Pa Tsi.[131] Gifts of ivory registered well with both the Vietnamese commissioner and the Phuan governor at Xieng Khouang as these commodities were an important element in the cultural repertoire of tributary exchanges between Vietnam and China and between the Lao and Thai kingdoms of the Mekong and the Chao Phraya Rivers.

Below the *kaitongs* were the heads of clans of lesser significance, who bore the titles *phutong, chongcha, chongkone,* and *xaophay,* which were signifiers of village chiefs.[132] In addition to the initial presentation of rhinoceros horns, Yang Dao writes, "Hmong officials had to pay the Phouan authorities regular tribute in the form of games (boars, deer, etc.), bear gall (highly prized in traditional medicine), elephant tusks and honey, as well as some of their small livestock (pigs, capons) and a few kilograms of opium."[133] There is little other historical evidence beyond these anecdotes that would allow us to critically examine the workings of the leadership system of the Hmong in precolonial times or their relations with the Phuan. How the Hmong governed themselves in Muang Phuan in the nineteenth century is also vague. According to the Phuan authority cited by Touby above, each clan leader governed only his kinsmen. As each clan was autonomous, the clan leader's power did not extend beyond his group. How, then, did the different clans gather the required items to be presented as tribute to the Phuan rulers? Did each clan contribute on a rotating basis or was each clan responsible for specific items to be presented? Moreover, how often were these exactions in kind demanded? Although Hmong men were reputed to be expert marksmen, game parts such as elephant tusks and rhinoceros horns could not have been easily obtained with the single-shot flintlock rifle. The challenge of obtaining these precious objects is reflected in the cultural esteem in which they were held. Hmong often praise elephant tusks and lion fangs in *kwv txhiaj,* poetic courting rhymes.

> Daj dee sib tau cia koj hnia kuv seb puas tsw kuv hnia koj seb puas *dhuav*
> Seb puas yuav zoo tam ntua txheej laus thaum ub cav kaus *ntxhuav*
> Daj dee sib tau cia kuv hnia koj seb puas dhuav koj hnia kuv seb puas *tsw*
> Seb Puas yuav zoo tam ntua txheej laus thaum wb cav kaus *ntxhw*

> [When we are married, kiss me until you're bored, I'll kiss you until I'm tired
> We'll see if the experience merits comparison with the way elders praise lion's fang.
> When we are married, I'll kiss you until I'm bored, you kiss me until you're tired
> We'll see if the experience compares to the way elders praise elephant's tusk.]

Given their rarity, it is hard to imagine how Hmong could present game parts as tribute on an annual basis as Yang Dao claims. Moreover, opium is a crop that requires intensive labor for minimum production.[134] The amount of labor required to maintain a hectare of poppy is much greater than that required for a hectare of rice or corn, although scholars concede that the return is also greater.[135] Nevertheless, given the hard labor involved in cultivating and harvesting this crop, its demand in kind as tribute may not have been looked upon lightly by the Hmong. The very first uprising in Muang Phuan in 1896 was stimulated by the demand for more opium by the French and the Phuan. Although we do not know exactly how this tributary system operated, how the Hmong perceived it is clearly articulated in such rebellions. The lack of revolts against the Phuan in the precolonial era (1800–1893) suggests that the tribute may have been a token of respect sent voluntarily by the Hmong on major state occasions such as the New Year's Festival, a holiday also observed by the Hmong. The Phuan seemed powerless to enforce a strict taxation system as they were preoccupied with their own survival in the face of Thai, Lao, Vietnamese, and Haw Chinese intrusions. Moreover, it also appears that the Hmong were left to decide what to send and in what quantities, and they sent what they could. This situation changed drastically under the French, whose bureaucracy was much more intrusive. The French kept registers of the population and demanded specific amounts of taxes per head and per household. These records were also used to conscript Hmong men for state projects, particularly for the construction of CR7, which bisected the region inhabited by the Hmong. Although it seems plausible that Hmong leaders may have successfully bypassed French recording systems and evaded taxes by undercounting, the intrusiveness of the French was enough to stimulate multiple rebellions, both messianic and secular in character.

French Colonial Advances and the Hmong: Renegotiating the Ethnic Hierarchy (1858–93)

French missionaries had been in Vietnam for over a century by the time the French government imposed colonial rule in the region. By the middle of the seventeenth century, Alexander de Rhodes had developed a romanized alphabet (*quoc ngu*) for the Vietnamese language. In the early twentieth century, after some debate, Vietnamese intellectuals chose to adopt it, replacing the Chinese *nom* script used by the literati in the previous era.[136]

As Hmong refugees were entering Tonkin in large numbers, the French conquest of Indochina began in 1858 with the annexation of Cochin China, the first five colonized provinces on the Mekong Delta. Late arrivals to Asia, the French initially cast their eyes on the Mekong as a potential "river road" to China. Cambodia was persuaded to come under French protection in 1860 in order to ensure that the Mekong remained in French hands. A two-year expedition up the river headed by Doudart de Lagrée and Francis Garnier in 1866 led the French into landlocked Laos. In April 1867, the explorers reached Luang

Prabang, where they observed that the population, docile and primitive but not without merit, would benefit from France's *mission civilisatrice*.[137] The expedition charged forward into China, where Lagrée succumbed to illness, died, and was buried in the city of Dongchuan. Garnier, his second in command, had pushed on alone to the Mekong's source with a few native guides. When Garnier returned, he ordered the exhumation of Lagrée's body and forced the expedition team to transport it back to be reinterred in the French colonial cemetery in Saigon, where it remained for over a century until the Socialist Republic of Vietnam announced its intention to reclaim the land for development in 1983. Lagrée's corpse was exhumed once again and shipped to France, at the expense of the French government, and finally entombed in his family mausoleum in Saint-Vincent-de-Mercuze.[138]

The Lagrée expedition found the Mekong unnavigable for steamships. The strong current was exacerbated by waterfalls above Cambodia and areas farther north. Garnier, undeterred by the physical challenges of the Mekong, proposed exploring the Red River as a new route to China, but the French government abandoned the waterway option in favor of construction of a railroad from Tonkin. Garnier did not go down in history as the discoverer of a back door to China; he made his mark in a more gruesome manner. Following the Mekong expedition, he was stationed at a garrison in Tonkin and charged with subduing the Haw Black Flags. During an attack in 1873, the overzealous Garnier raced ahead of his native troops and was ambushed and decapitated by Haw bandits. Although the French government was critical of his rash actions at first, his beheading provided the pretext for a French military buildup in the region a decade later. A protectorate government was set up in Annam and Tonkin by 1883, giving colonial officials legal claim to the Lao kingdoms straddling the Mekong River, which had been tributaries of Hue. Siam registered a protest, but historical developments provided the opportunity for France to wrest away the kingdom of Luang Prabang and the rest of modern Laos in 1887. The Thai, cognizant of the colonial threat, had been trying to convince Deo Van Tri to place himself under their authority for several decades without success. In desperation, the Thai commissioner sent to negotiate with the White Tai leader kidnapped several of his brothers in December 1886 and marched them to Bangkok. When dialogues for their return failed, Deo Van Tri attacked Siam's tributary vassal, Luang Prabang, on June 10, 1887. The Thai army avoided a confrontation by simply relocating across the Mekong, leaving Luang Prabang unprotected. The aged King Unkham was left to die in the burning royal palace. Auguste Pavie, the French liaison, rescued the king and fled with him downriver.[139] Pavie used the opportunity to persuade

Unkham to place himself under French protection. By 1893 the French navy had consolidated authority over the rest of Laos by using "gunboat diplomacy" to force Bangkok to accept the Mekong as a territorial boundary.[140]

Taking control of the Mekong River valley and delta regions was not the end of France's struggles. To map French Indochina, a region of diverse ethnic and political entities, the French made pacts with dominant ethnic groups. As the Hmong in Xieng Khouang rebelled early on, colonial officials were obliged to cultivate relations with their leaders, thereby effecting a close Hmong-French relation for the next seventy years. In Tonkin, where the White Tai dominated, however, the French ignored much of the Hmong population, stimulating rebellions.[141]

French efforts to map "Indochina" profoundly affected preexisting inter-ethnic relations between the highlands and lowlands, as well as among highland groups. For the mountain minorities, categorized under the general rubric *montagnards*, the French served as both protector and oppressor. Highlanders of the Central Plateau of Vietnam, for example, benefited from the French prohibition of Vietnamese immigration into the area.[142] Similarly, in north-western Tonkin, Auguste Pavie's 1889 treaty with Deo Van Tri, which granted him political hegemony over the Twelve Tai State, coincided with the White Tai leader's interest in remaining free of the Vietnamese.[143] Giving the White Tai paramount authority of the highlands did not bode well for the Hmong, however. They became a minority within a minority zone and were thus doubly exploited by a multitiered, multiethnic administration. Hmong subjects of the Phuan in Xieng Khouang and of the Tai in the Twelve Tai State of Tonkin had to renegotiate their positions within this complex ethnic hierarchy. The rebellions of the early twentieth century constituted this renegotiation process, whereupon the French changed policies to benefit Hmong in certain regions but reinforced Hmong subjection in others. French treatment determined the political allegiance of the Hmong in different locales during the revolutionary period. Those who found favor sided with the colonial masters while others, who were disaffected by French policies, joined forces with Ho Chi Minh's radical Communists, tipping the victory for the Viet Minh.[144] As a reward for those on the left, in 1955 Ho Chi Minh created the Tai-Meo Autonomous Zone, which included the provinces of Ha Giang, Lao Cai, and Lai Chau, sites of the two major anticolonial rebellions led by Xiong Mi Chang and Vue Pa Chay. For the next twenty years, while Ho was embroiled in the Second Indochina War with the United States, the Hmong and other minorities in these regions enjoyed political autonomy. After the Communists triumphed in 1975, however, loyal minorities in the zones found themselves under Vietnamese neocolonial rule. Autonomy was revoked as the process of collectivization was initiated. The Hmong who practiced swidden agriculture, which requires migration every ten to fifteen years, fared the worst under modern policies of land use and registration. They are allowed to maintain swidden fields but have no official land rights.[145]

For the duration of the French colonial period, indirect rule coupled with the opium monopoly, which aimed to generate income for the colonial administration, adversely affected the Hmong. Due to the small number of French administrators, indirect rule over minority groups on the periphery was fiscally sound. So effective was this method that in 1904 the French were able to hold the paid colonial staff in Laos to just seventy-two officials, "the smallest anywhere in the French Empire."[146] Moreover, indigenous authorities who interacted directly with the minorities absorbed the brunt of their resentment, deflecting much of the locus of blame from the French. For the Hmong, indigenous officials (Lao or Tai) who showed up to collect taxes were seen as corrupt while the French authorities that the Hmong rarely saw were often perceived as a benevolent outlet for redressing grievances. For this reason, some found it advantageous to obtain direct rule so as to eliminate the middle lowland administrators and avoid being doubly exploited. In Tonkin, however, the French did not accord the Hmong the privilege of direct contact. When the Hmong answered the call of prophets who promised a sovereign state, the Tai feudal lords who were the ruling whips of the French became the main targets of attack.[147]

The Hmong were also affected by colonial policies designed to extract opium to finance France's struggling administration. From the beginning of French rule, opium was essential to the financial solvency of Indochina. Only six months after the annexation of Saigon in 1862, French officials established an opium franchise. At this early juncture, without independent sources, the French relied on imported opium from India, which was taxed at 10 percent of its value and sold by licensed Chinese merchants.[148] By the 1880s, French authorities had founded opium monopolies in Indochina. Gradually, colonial officials could rely on the wealth generated by indigenously grown poppy to maintain the solvency of their colonies. By 1902 opium accounted for one-third of all colonial revenues, allowing the colonial government to experience a budget surplus for the first time.[149]

The opium monopoly had ample repercussions for the Hmong, who previously had autonomy under the patronage of the indigenous authorities. Although predominantly dry rice agriculturists, the Hmong grew opium as a cash crop to trade with Haw Chinese caravans for the iron they used to make tools, flintlock rifles, and cooking implements, and for the silver used to fashion jewelry.[150] Raw opium was also exchanged for bolts of silk and used as medicine. As the Hmong lived in a cool mountain climate, ideal for opium cultivation, they were the primary growers of the crop in French Indochina. For this reason, the French certainly had a stake in controlling this scattered highland population. Consolidating the Hmong was not an easy task, however. They lived in precipitous redoubts thousands of meters above sea level. As James C. Scott aptly observes, the authority of the state was arrested at five hundred meters.[151]

While the Phuan authorities were content to accept the Hmong's segmented social system by according titles to the major clan leaders, the French, particularly in response to the 1896 rebellion discussed below, aimed to impose a more centralized system of rule. Just as Auguste Pavie made Deo Van Tri lord of the Tonkin highlands, in Laos the colonial authorities consolidated the Hmong's independent clan structure. Clan leaders, in an effort to obtain legitimation as the paramount chief, rallied their extended kinsmen as subjects of the French colonial empire. As Hmong leaders became tax collectors and conscription supervisors on behalf of the French, becoming rich and influential in the process, they were perceived in the same light as the Lao and Tai magistrates. They, too, were seen as tools of oppression. "Pom tsov ces yuav tuag, pom nom ces yuav pluag" (See a tiger you will die, see an official you will be destitute) goes a Hmong proverb. Hmong leaders became colonial officials backed with the might of the colonial army. For the first time, Hmong men had executive power and did not have to rule through a consensus of the clans. Hmong leaders were feared but also beheld with awe because of their power over life and death.

The massive wealth Hmong leaders accumulated through trading and serving as opium brokers and tax collectors for the French empire led to some social stratification in Hmong society by the early decades of the twentieth century. By the time of the Japanese Occupation, there had emerged what constituted a tiny group of wealthy "elites" in the highlands of Laos. This group included the families of Ly Foung, Ly Nhia Vu, and Lo Blia Yao and members of the Moua clan located in Phou San. The brothers Lyfoung would soon outpace the others because their father had the foresight to send them on educational pilgrimages to the lowland, where they studied in Vientiane, Vinh, Saigon, and Hanoi. They were not only wealthy but also educated and literate in multiple languages. Existing in a society that has long understood the power of literacy, they were accorded honor and regarded with deep respect. These Lyfoung men would hold power and positions unheard of by Hmong leaders in previous eras.

The 1896 Kaitong Rebellion and
the Hmong-French Alliance in Muang Phuan

The first Hmong rebellion against the colonial authorities occurred in 1896, just three years after the French protectorate was established. The rebellion coincided with French efforts to implement administrative policies in the highland zone. The manipulation of opium prices and the imposition of a new, two-tiered tax system aroused the Hmong of Nong Het to revolt. Wanting to obtain a cheap source of raw opium, the French required the Hmong to pay a portion of the tax in opium at an assessed value far below the market price.[152] The colonial authorities charged the Phuan to press the Hmong *kaitongs* for due payments. The Phuan wanted to retain their share of the taxes that had been submitted dutifully by the Hmong before French colonization. The Hmong found themselves squeezed by two masters, the French, who dominated the newly established colonial hierarchy, and the Phuan lords, the owners of the land toward whom the Hmong felt a debt of gratitude for allowing them to cultivate the uninhabited heights. Ly Na, the grandson of Ly Ja Lao and grandnephew of Kaitong Ly Nhia Vu, explained how his ancestors responded to this double-tiered tax system:

> At the time, the French exacted one kip in tax from every individual Hmong, but when the Lao came to collect, they demanded four kip so that they could keep three kip for themselves. Our grandfathers were fully aware of this kind of business, so they refused to pay. When the Lao came to extort them—they have Hmong [flintlock] rifles, you know, so they have bullets powered by powder—they said [to the Lao], "The French only want one kip. How come you're demanding for four? If you want four, you just want it for yourself. In that case, we'll render only bullets for you to take back with you." When the Lao returned to the French they said the Hmong had refused to pay their taxes and sent only bullets as payment.[153]

The Franco-Lao authorities responded immediately by sending a contingent of *garde indigene* into the mountains to intimidate the Hmong. Encouraged by Prince Kham Huang, a descendent of the Xieng Khouang aristocracy, who held a deep-seated grudge against the colonial authorities for demoting his princely status to a governorship, the Hmong *kaitongs* organized an attack against the French troops at Ban Khang Phanieng, twenty kilometers west of Ban Ban. The Hmong did not take the fort, but their slight success encouraged them to attack the provincial capital of Xieng Khouang. Armed only with short-range flintlocks, they put up a brave fight but were subsequently over-powered by modern French rifles.[154]

The Ly clan of Nong Khiaw led the charge against the French from the direction of Nong Het, according to Ly Na. The commander of the group was Ly Tsong Na, the eldest son of Nhia Vu. The Ly and Lo clans had planned the attack together, but the Lo clan members dragged their feet on the day of the battle. Tsong Na's group was the first to arrive at the fort of Cha Pha Ngoi, near Ban Ban. They surprised the Lao authorities, killing many before with-drawing. Ly Na stated, "The Lo clan did not help the Lys. The Lys arrived first and suffered one dead and three wounded. The Lys lost and retreated. On the way they met the Lo clan members, who had not arrived in time to help but also retreated. That's how the Ly clan [members] lost their status and the Lo also lost their status along with the Ly. According to our parents—we did not see for ourselves, of course—but they said that Ly Tsong Na killed about seventy to eighty Lao."[155]

When the French authorities heard of the armed revolt, they demanded an armistice. The Hmong willingly negotiated for a peace settlement. Ly Nao Lue, the second-eldest son of Nhia Vu, told Touby Lyfoung that after mutual consultation the Hmong clan leaders selected the leader of the Moua clan to go and negotiate a peace settlement with the French in Xieng Khouang. Touby reiterates the words of Nao Lue in his memoir: "They [the Hmong *kaitongs*] stipulated that if Moua Kaitong could reach a peaceful settlement he would henceforth be recognized as their paramount chief."[156] Naturally, the other clan leaders had to entice Moua Kaitong with such a promise because descending the protective heights to meet the lowland authorities was a dangerous under-taking. Moua Kaitong could be arrested and summarily executed upon arrival. Moreover, the Hmong lacked immunity to the mosquito-borne diseases of the tropics, which the Hmong of the period understood only in superstitious terms. A common explanation for someone becoming sick after returning from the lowlands was that the Lao had cast a black magic spell on the person. For reasons real and imagined, the Hmong equated the lowlands with death.[157]

Moua Kaitong appeared at Xieng Khouang and was appointed the first Hmong *tasseng* (subdistrict leader), with authority over the Hmong of the region. French consultations with Moua Kaitong after this period strengthened his position vis-à-vis the Hmong, forcing them to regard him as the legitimate supreme authority figure for a time. French dealings with Moua Kaitong and subsequent Hmong leaders also reduced the authority of Lao intermediaries. The 1896 revolt, therefore, resulted in a close French-Hmong alliance that endured to the end of the colonial period. Cooperation with the French was advantageous for several reasons. The clan leader who was legitimated by the French obtained increased status as the supreme ethnic representative. For the Hmong, having a supreme leader who the French recognized and dealt with directly also meant bypassing rapacious lowland officials. A Hmong leader provided some protection from lowland corruption and injustice. There was both a personal incentive (for the Hmong leader) and a larger ethnic motivation (for the Hmong) to befriend the French. The alliance meant keeping a semblance of cultural, economic, and political autonomy, which allowed the Hmong to live in peace for a time.

After the 1896 revolt, Nhia Vu and Ja Lao, discredited and afraid of being imprisoned, relocated across the Vietnamese border to the village of Long Hu. Tsong Na, who could not be persuaded to move, remained in Nong Khiaw, where he was assassinated by a relative, Ly Joua Kao. Joua Kao was from another lineage of the Ly clan. The Lao authorities induced him to assassinate Tsong Na with the promise of an official appointment. Ly Na continued:

> There was a Ly clan member named Joua Kao Ly . . . who has descendants in Colorado today. . . . The Lao posted a notice that whoever killed Ly Tsong Na would be awarded the title of *tasseng*. Joua Kao wanted to be *tasseng*, so he went to see the Lao authorities. Then he came back and assassinated his relative, Tsong Na. . . . There were two assassins; . . . one came to converse with Tsong Na in his house [i.e., distracted him] while Joua Kao climbed onto the roof, opened a wooden panel in the ceiling, and shot him. After this, Joua Kao went to the Lao and said he had killed Tsong Na. The Lao responded, "We did not ask you to go kill anyone. There was no longer any war; the peace settlement had already been drawn." So he [Joua Kao] took out the wanted note and said, "You were the ones who wrote this order for me." The Lao took it and threw it in the fire. Then the Lao tried to assuage his anger by giving him a huge feast. They laced his food with the [poisonous] liver bile of the peacock, but he didn't know it. He had barely finished his meal when he was on the verge of death. The Lao gave him a horse to ride home. He climbed on it, but keeled over to the side and died. This is a lesson for us all about how others entice us to kill our own kind.[158]

Tsong Na's assassination by his kinsman highlights how divisions within the clan affect Hmong politics. Lineage leaders who vie for outside legitimation in order to dominate their own clan could be easy victims of lowland divide-and-conquer tactics. The assassination incident also emphasizes the important role of lowland authorities as a legitimating force for competing Hmong leaders. Joua Kao, a lineage leader, did not have influence over the diverse branches of his own Ly clan and needed the support of the Lao authorities to be recognized as a clan leader in his own right. This need for legitimation was a major incentive for Hmong leaders to compete for the favors of lowland patrons, drawing them to the state.

Another consequence of the 1896 revolt was the discrediting of the Ly and Lo clans, leading to the appointment of Moua Kaitong as an umbrella authority. For the first time we see some political centralization among the Hmong of Laos. Rather than disparate clan leaders of equal weight as before, the Hmong now had a political broker, legitimated by the French. The process of creating a paramount chief was not simply a matter of the French imposing a central figure on Hmong society, but historical events did force the acceptance of Moua Kaitong as a paramount chief. Centralization, which led to competitions in Hmong society, would complicate rather than facilitate French power at the margin of empire, however.

Part I

Hmong Messianism

The Mandate of Heaven

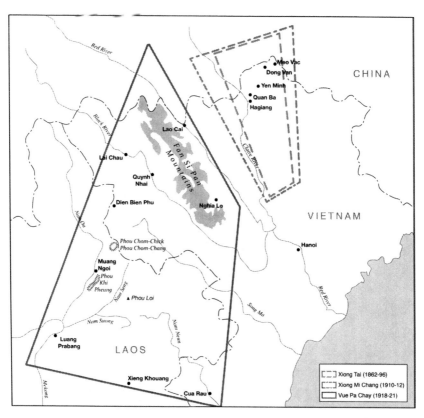

Map 2. Early Hmong rebellions in Indochina. (Map by University of Wisconsin Cartography Lab)

A Chronology of Two Rebellions (1910–1912 and 1918–1921)

The 1896 Kaitong Rebellion in Muang Phuan ushered forth a Hmong-French alliance and enabled some authority centralization in Hmong society. But the Hmong have their own tradition of authority consolidation, rooted in China, that rebuffs secular legitimation and is based on the Confucian concept of the Mandate of Heaven. Hmong chiefs who seek celestial legitimation to become universal monarchs attempt to reconsolidate a kingdom whereby they can deal with the state on equal terms and not just as subjects. These prophets style themselves as reincarnations of the mythical Hmong king and propose to liberate the Hmong from foreign oppression.

The inconsistency of colonial policies in Indochina provides insight into why Hmong messianic revolts erupted in Vietnam. French legitimation of local rulers was contingent upon which ethnic group best served their interests. The Tai, who were essential to French domination of Tonkin, were the preferential minority group. They were appointed lords of the Vietnamese highland zone. The French did have close alliances with several Hmong "kings," in Bac Ha in northeastern Lao Cai province and also in Sa Phin in Ha Giang Province, about which I will provide some detail in later chapters, but for the most part the Hmong of Vietnam were subjected to Tai authority through a system of indirect rule. In Muang Phuan (Laos), on the other hand, the Hmong captured French interest early by rebelling. For the duration of the colonial period, an economic incentive bound the Hmong in this region to the French. They provided tax revenues in opium, which offset Indochina's budget deficit, and they were conscripts for the construction of CR7, the road essential to the consolidation of French rule. The Hmong of Muang Phuan became, therefore, the group with which the French cultivated a special relationship. The Hmong-French alliance here, however, also complicated French political objectives. A group of Hmong in Xieng Khouang, unhappy with the French-appointed Hmong leader, Lo Blia Yao, rebelled after Vue Pa Chay arrived in the region in 1920.

I set the stage for discussing the Hmong of Laos in the previous chapter. I shall return to this close Hmong-French alliance in part II of this work. In part I, I examine two anticolonial rebellions in Tonkin. Due to the complex nature of the revolts and the difficulty of reconciling French archival sources with Hmong oral accounts, I lay out in this chapter the chronology of the rebellions as depicted by colonial sources. I will examine the Hmong rationale for rebellion in the following chapter, where I engage the extant Hmong testimonies of Pa Chay's War (1918–21). I have found no extant Hmong testimonies about Mi Chang's uprising (1910–12) among Hmong Americans or Lao Hmong, however, so I am forced to rely on Mi Chang's interrogation records kept by the French, in which he explained the origin and development of his movement.[1]

Xiong Mi Chang's Rebellion in Ha Giang, Vietnam (1910–12)

French favoritism of the Tai as feudal lords in Tonkin stimulated the emergence of prophets who led the Hmong population against their oppressors. Two large Hmong rebellions occurred in Tonkin in 1910 and 1918.[2] The 1918 rebellion, led by Vue Pa Chay of Dien Bien Phu, spread into Laos and found willing participants among the Hmong, who had become disenchanted with Blia Yao. The 1910 rebellion, led by Xiong Mi Chang, on the other hand, occurred in Ha Giang, on the northeastern frontiers of Vietnam and China. The insurgency spread back and forth across the border as Mi Chang attempted to evade capture by French and Chinese authorities (see map 2).

For the French, the more exotic elements of Mi Chang's rebellion stood out. Colonial sources concentrate on the manifestation of "hysterical displays" and dismiss him as insane and dangerous. As such the events that triggered French attention began with news of ominous stirrings in the hills surrounding the town of Dong Van. On September 17, 1910, Lieutenant Leonard, a French officer stationed at Dong Van, reported that a Hmong "madman" (*un fou*) in the village of Meo Vac, located in the mountains above Dong Van, had attracted a group of "admirers" with eccentric displays of physical prowess and flag-honoring ceremonies.[3] Leonard appeared on the scene several days later to find a group of "400 friendly" individuals. Other ethnic groups in the region, however, were quite nervous about the whole affair, he reported. The Tho, in particular, anxiously recalled the 1862 rebellion when Xiong Tai, another Hmong "madman," ravaged the region.[4] A Tho magistrate in the area claimed that the current madman, Mi Chang, had detailed his intention to incite a rebellion in a report addressed to him personally.[5] Furthermore, Mi Chang made explicit reference to the 1862 rebellion led by Tai, who had declared himself Thong Thien Chua, "Lord of the Heavens," and devastated the valley of the Claire River, an area inhabited by the Lolo, La Qua, Tho, and Vietnamese. Mi Chang was threatening to do the same by inciting his followers to dance all night, the Tho official continued. Even more alarming, Mi Chang had already begun distributing titles to his subjects, naming among them two chief generals, two generals of the army, and one chief of soldiers. There were an additional five civil functionaries, consisting of one governor and four *tri phu*.[6] The titles of the *phu* were He Who Penetrates Heaven, He Who Obeys Heaven, and several other names of lesser originality.

When Leonard showed up to investigate that September, however, Mi Chang's followers denied the existence of an impending uprising or a "king" in their midst. The recent unrest, they explained, was the result of invasions by Chinese bandits from the frontier. To demonstrate his good intentions, Mi Chang accompanied Leonard back to Dong Van, "not as a prisoner, on foot and tied up, but on horseback" and riding beside the officer as "an equal." Traveling with Mi Chang to the lowland was a man he later identified as a cousin.[7] Leonard detained Mi Chang at Dong Van for nearly three months before releasing him on December 28, 1910, whereupon Mi Chang immediately returned to the mountains to reassemble his followers. During Mi Chang's absence from Meo Vac, and perhaps because of it, the Hmong in the vicinity had already been incited to full revolt by his relative, Xiong Mao Chang, the *ma phai* of Luong Phin.

A little over a month after Mi Chang returned to the highlands, on February 9, 1911, alarming news came from another Tai magistrate that Mi Chang had proclaimed himself King of the Mountains and assembled six or seven hundred Hmong partisans armed with rifles and five or six trumpets. The trumpets, Mi Chang would explain after he was caught and interrogated, were used to generate noise and give the impression that he had more men than he did during battles.[8] Mi Chang's group had also begun digging trenches and conscripting neighboring inhabitants as soldiers, threatening to pillage the villages of those who shirked their duty.

Leonard was skeptical of the story of the magistrate, believing the report to be exaggerated. He was aware of the tensions between Hmong and Tai and of

Tai prejudices, which often stimulated false reports about the Hmong. Hoping to resolve the situation peacefully, Leonard twice went to assess the scene. On February 11, he went to the first group, assembled at Ngai Ban Sui. He saw four hundred individuals, "hair flowing freely without turban," among which a great number were carrying flintlock rifles.[9] (Hmong men of this period generally kept their hair neatly bundled in turbans or braided in queues in Chinese fashion. Letting their hair flow freely was a sign of discontent, a fact lost on Leonard.[10]) He asked these individuals to state their grievances. They responded that they no longer wanted to be under the Tho chiefs. When asked who they would like as chiefs, they refused to give names. In frustration Leonard told them to disperse, which they did peacefully, only to gather at Tao-Tsan-Luong several days later.[11]

On February 12, the *quan bao* of Bao Lac reported that Mi Chang's band, armed with three hundred rifles, had massacred a group of Yao. The following day he again reported that a band was threatening to massacre the Black Yao and others who did not join them. The reports did not make clear whether there were two different Hmong bands or whether the same band had molested two different groups of Yao. By mid-February the situation had become even more tense. According to French reports, Mi Chang not only handed out titles and ranks to his followers but also made them kneel before him while he breathed hallucinogenic incense on them, which caused them to see the image of two sorceresses "equipped with fans" on each side of him.[12] Undoubtedly, these sorceresses, purportedly heavenly beings, were proof to followers that Mi Chang had the Mandate of Heaven. Their presence probably allowed Mi Chang to accumulate more followers.

Meanwhile, Mi Chang had also begun appointing military and civil administrators for his kingdom. Here we can see how Mi Chang established a following by recruiting first from his own clan. The *binh dao* of Moi Su, Xiong Chinh Minh, was named a general while Xiong Tsan was named a commandant. After receiving their titles, the two men went to Sung Tiang to lead the group in that area and to recruit new members from the region. Still hoping for a peaceful dissolution of the group, Leonard went before those who had regrouped at Tao Tsan Luong and again talked to the relatives of Mi Chang, asking them to disperse. They promised they would, but when Leonard returned to see if they intended to keep their word no one would speak to him again.[13]

On February 25, the Hmong began digging trenches near Chang Poung. Lieutenant Colonel Mortreuil, who went to the mountains to investigate the matter personally, arrived at Pho Bang and was informed by the Hmong *chanh quan* and *chung cha* of Tsoung Lao that Hmong individuals had started arriving from China in groups of ten. The *chung cha* of Tsoung Lao had met two groups near Loung Cam, about three kilometers south of Pho Bang, and asked them where they were going. They said they were visiting relatives in the area but could name neither the relatives nor their whereabouts. They fled when pressed for details. Among them was Xiong Mi Kay, a Hmong Chinese and a relative of Mi Chang. He was from Siao Thien Pa in Quang Nam, where he had led and recruited rebels from the region. Literate in Chinese, he would later serve as Mi Chang's secretary.

Mortreuil found the reports of the two Hmong leaders in Pho Bang credible. He had also encountered strange behavior by Hmong villagers earlier. When he passed through the village of Phu Cao and asked the Hmong about their grievances, they said they had none. By evening, however, the village was deserted, and the *chung cha* who was summoned before Mortreuil would not supply information as to why. Everywhere the French officer went, there were ominous signs that the Hmong were consciously isolating themselves from the colonial authorities through passive noncompliance. After his conversations with the Hmong leaders from Pho Bang, Mortreuil continued on to Dong Van, the post commanded by Leonard. On the way he made a stop at Saphin, where the *chanh quan* lived. The brother of the *chung cha* of Luong Phin in Saphin informed Mortreuil that a contingent of armed Hmong had been spotted near the village, making their way toward Mo Rue.[14]

Full-scale rebellion erupted on February 26, 1911, several months after Leonard had released Mi Chang from the Dong Van prison. Around five o'clock that morning, Mi Chang's generals, Xiong Chinh Minh and Vang Van Sinh, led groups of two hundred and eight hundred, respectively, which simultaneously sacked the Tho village of Vinh Thon and the market of Mo Rue. The group of two hundred rebels from Vinh Thon made further preparations to move on to Yen Minh. At the same time, other Hmong rebel groups attacked the Hmong village of San Co Ping, located on the Yen-Minh pass, and pillaged and burned the village of Lung Cam, five kilometers south of Pho Bang. Two Chinese frontier posts, Ma Lin and Hou Tung, were also attacked early in the morning on the same day.[15]

The French responded quickly, deploying one company of Tonkinese *tirailleurs* and one section of *legionnaires*. On February 27, the commander of the territory convened the Hmong chiefs of Dong Van, who remained loyal to the French throughout the rebellion. The chiefs were apprised of the alarming situation and told that the revolt would be put down by force. Mi Chang, meanwhile, had confined himself to the mountains, leaving only his partisans to carry out military operations. The following day rebels led by one of Mi

Chang's generals charged the post of Yen Minh. They did not capture the village, however. A French sergeant named Alessandri had anticipated the move. He defended the town with reinforcements from the commander of territory and a section of *tirailleurs* returning from Dong Van.

Also on February 27 the Hmong of Duong Thuong, led by Vang Van Sinh and Vang Seu, pillaged the Tho village of Muang Cha (Du Gia) and attacked the Black Hmong of Lung Chung. During the 1862 revolt led by Xiong Tai, these Black Hmong, who "hated" the White Hmong, had taken up arms to defend other inhabitants. Mi Chang's group, composed of White Hmong, had aimed to avenge this long-standing grievance.[16] Clearly, the rebellion was complex, with Hmong on opposing sides.

The rebellion was not confined to Tonkin. Hmong troops operated back and forth across the Chinese border. On March 3 the Chinese mandarin at Chang Puong reported being attacked by a band of pirates from Tonkin. This group had killed a number of inhabitants of Ma Chang and Ma Leu, villages under Chinese jurisdiction. The mandarin was able to drive the band back into Tonkin. By this time, about three weeks into the rebellion, the situation was alarming enough that more French reinforcements were on the scene. The Hmong, according to Lieutenant Colonel Auguste Bonifacy, commander of the Third Military Territory, never encountered the colonial troops head on due to a lack of arms. Among the six to seven hundred rebels there were only several Winchesters and some modern rifles. The majority of the men had only flintlock rifles. In addition to territorial guards, troops deployed to quell the rebellion included companies from Bac Quang and Bao Lac, a section each of *tirailleurs* and *legionaires* from Cao Bang, and two companies from Yen Bay and Luc Yen Chau under Commandant Galland.

Meanwhile, Captain Cot was selected to lead negotiations at Meo Vac, the headquarters of the Hmong "king." The inhabitants informed him, however, that the king had retired to a hideout marked with a white flag in the mountains. Cot asked the Hmong to deliver a letter to Mi Chang in which he promised to ensure Mi Chang's safety if he surrendered. Cot "had *tirailleurs* and *legion-naires* with him," he wrote, "but would not fire a single shot if the Hmong did not fire first."[17]

On March 21, an emissary to Mi Chang's hideout returned without a response, even though Mi Chang had a literate Hmong Chinese secretary. The following day, in keeping with his threat, Captain Cot left for the mountains before sunrise to pursue Mi Chang. After a three-hour march, he reached Mi Chang's hideout. Only one Hmong presented himself before the captain, however. Mi Chang had left for the safety of the Chinese border, the man said.

Subsequently, the captain managed to capture three men and three women, among whom were the father, mother, and sister of Mi Chang. As Mi Chang and his subjects scattered, tranquility returned by April 10, 1911. Approximately ninety individuals had been killed, fifty-two of whom were Hmong. The Tho endured the second-highest casualty rate with twenty-nine deaths.[18]

During the following three months Mi Chang took refuge in China, going first to Na Sin, where his two wives and newborn son lived with his brother. He worked in the daytime to make a living and hid at night. French authorities reported having received two letters from him at this time, offering to surrender. The letters stated that during his three-month sojourn at Loung Koua, Hmong subjects had sent him gifts, asking for his protection. Also he was attacked by Chinese troops and had killed two men. After that, the letters attested further, he lived in Meo Sin for four months before the Hmong *chanh quan*, whose wives and sons Mi Chang had killed, attacked him. Mi Chang's wives and infant son died during this ambush. During an interrogation subsequent to his capture in April 1912, Mi Chang denied having written the incriminating letters, but he confirmed their contents.[19]

Mi Chang immediately attracted new followers among the White Hmong in China. He soon assembled a group of one hundred Hmong from the region of Ouen Tchay, south of La Pia. An additional twenty Hmong Chinese vowed to help him expel the Tho from Tonkin. With the backing of the Chang *binh dao* of Mo Sui and the Vang *ma phai*, Mi Chang's ragtag subjects showed up at Ma Su, a village on the Chinese frontier northwest of Dong Van, at the end of July.[20]

Events in Tonkin the previous month had already portended of Mi Chang's return. On June 28, 1911, after several months of relative quietude, things stirred once again in French territory. A group of Hmong began gathering at Luong Phin. Meanwhile, across the border in China, Mi Chang geared up once again to pursue his dream of a kingdom. On August 2 the French authorities learned that he had raised havoc at Ma Chan near Lung Ca in China. Seven days later he and a small band of rebels escaped to Tonkin. Mi Chang sneaked into Si Phai, the region of his birth. He went back to Ta San Mountain, his previous hideout near Meo Vac, to perform a ritual that he hoped would ensure a favorable outcome against the Chinese.[21] Then he left again for the Chinese frontier. Albeit brief, Mi Chang's return had major repercussions for the Hmong of Tonkin. News came quickly that several loyalists had resumed their sorcery at Meo Vac.

In mid-August the Chinese authorities suggested a coalition effort between French forces at Dong Van and Chinese frontier troops to attack the Hmong at Ma Chan. The French did not agree to an alliance, but they were convinced that drastic measures had to be taken. Leonard, now stationed at Pho Bang, believed reconciliation was no longer possible. He demanded reinforcements in order to capture the rebels.

The French also began to employ loyal Hmong chiefs in their pacification strategy. On September 11, the *binh dao* of the Chang clan and the *ma phai* of the Vang clan were sent to assess and negotiate for Mi Chang's surrender. They were not granted an audience but reported back that Mi Chang's troops—a group of about twenty men—were poorly equipped, with only one nine-shot, two seventy-four, and ten flintlock rifles. The Hmong chiefs concluded that these men would have to be captured in order to end the rebellion.

On September 16, the Chinese soldiers at the post of Tung Cam attempted in vain to capture Mi Chang near Ma Lin. The brigands of the region had grouped themselves around Mi Chang and threatened the post as well as neighboring villages. A group of three hundred Hmong retaliated against the Chinese post at Ma Lin on October 4. Unable to take the fort, they were forced to flee into Tonkin pursued by Chinese troops. On November 22, two of Mi Chang's men, detained at Dong Van and awaiting trial, escaped and fled to the highlands to join him.

Things settled down again. This time, however, the French did not wait for Mi Chang to regroup. They joined forces with Hmong partisans who held a grudge against Mi Chang. Obtaining Chinese permission, the youngest son of the *chanh quan* Hmong from Dong Van ambushed Mi Chang at his hideout inside Chinese territory. After the gunfire died down, they found the bodies of Mi Chang's two wives and his infant son. This attack had major repercussions for the movement since Mi Chang's followers believed that the infant son was the "true king."[22] After the infant died, the rebellion in the area dissipated to a trickle.

By the dawn of the new year, Mi Chang was in a desperate struggle to survive. His run-in with the Chinese and French authorities had cost him dearly in personal terms. The turning point of the rebellion came when Xiong Mi Kay, Mi Chang's secretary and second lieutenant, was captured and decapitated by the Chinese authorities in January 1912. Now alone, Mi Chang sent word to the authorities at Dong Van that he would surrender under certain conditions. Apparently, Mi Chang preferred to place his fate in the hands of the French rather than the repressive Chinese. The French only promised to spare his life. Now deprived of his family and his core of economic support in China, Mi Chang had no choice but to sneak back to Tonkin to live near his kinsmen. His plan was discovered by a Hmong informant and revealed to an indigenous official. On April 21, a Hmong informant told Nguyen Dinh Cuong, the brother of the chief of canton of Dong Van, that Mi Chang would come during the night to visit his family at Ma Pang, just a few kilometers from his birthplace, Si Phai. Cuong sent partisans to patrol the roads leading to Si Phai. On April 22, 1912, under the cloak of the early dawn, three shadowy figures—two armed with rifles—were spotted coming down the road. Mi Chang was arrested while his two companions fled. He was twenty-six years old.[23]

Mi Chang was sentenced to ten years of imprisonment. Because he was young and likely to survive that term, Bonifacy recommended that he be exiled instead to Poulo Condore, Algeria, or New Caledonia, where he would have no connection to the Hmong. Mi Chang's brother, Bonifacy added, who was equally culpable, should accompany him. Since Mi Chang suffered a deformity of the right hand that did not allow him to take care of himself, his brother could help him make a living. This exile, in Bonifacy's view, would be more merciful than turning Mi Chang over to either the Chinese or the Hmong, whom he had devastated during the rebellion. Bonifacy's recommendations went unheeded. On May 2, 1913, the governor general sentenced Mi Chang to hard labor at the Ile de la Table, a small island located on the coast of Vietnam.[24] He arrived there in January 1914 but remained only until the end of the month, when he and five prisoners were brought back to Quang Yen. Mi Chang was kept under surveillance in Quang Yen while the other five were transferred to prisons in the highlands.[25] As he had no relatives in the area, the resident superior asked that a monthly allowance of ten piasters be given to him for food. The governor general allotted the requested sum, but a telegram from Quang Yen indicated several months later that the money had never arrived.[26] These brief exchanges closed Mi Chang's case. It is unlikely that he survived his ten-year sentence. Meanwhile, in another locale west of Ha Giang, the legendary Vue Pa Chay was already gearing up to eclipse Mi Chang.

Pa Chay's War (1918–21)

From 1918 to 1921, a Hmong man named Pa Chay of the Vue clan led a rebellion that shook French Indochina to the core. The revolt, dismissed by the French with the demeaning epitaph "La Guerre du Fou" (The Madman's War) but known to the Hmong as "Rog Paj Cai" (Pa Chay's War), was notably the most expansive anticolonial struggle in Indochina, earning for Pa Chay a few laudatory lines in present-day Communist nationalist history.[27] Pa Chay's War also began in Tonkin, in the vicinity of Dien Bien Phu, where the Hmong were largely ignored by the French and forced under the rule of the White Tai. As had occurred in Ha Giang, Hmong interactions with the colonial state produced a prophet. Even more successful than Mi Chang, Pa Chay extended his movement into Xieng Khouang, where the Hmong had a more cordial alliance with the French.

Colonial sources on Pa Chay's rebellion are comprised of reports from the pacification campaigns. These reports contain information supplied mainly by those loyal to the French and reveal little about the source of Pa Chay's charisma and aspirations, but they do provide detailed accounts of military tactics and give insight into the material causes of the revolt. Broadly speaking, the revolt can be seen as an extension of the ethnic unrest that had plagued the borderlands between China and Southeast Asia since the eighteenth century, when expanding empires, Chinese and European, clashed and minority groups were caught in the grind. As an ethnic rebellion, Pa Chay's War can be seen in the context of the Great "Miao" (1855–76) and Panthay (1856–73) rebellions.[28] As a Hmong messianic uprising, it can be viewed as an extension of the rebellions led by Xiong Tai (1860–96) and Xiong Mi Chang (1910–12). The socioeconomic trigger for the revolt and the desire for celestial power are familiar. Allowing for some alterations, Pa Chay's War is a reemergence of the latent Hmong dream of a kingdom.

The incident that ignited Pa Chay's War originated in China. In January 1918, a Hmong man near the town of Muang Tinh, who had been paralyzed by an illness for several years, announced a miraculous recovery.[29] The Chinese authorities were cognizant of the implications of such an event. Eighty years earlier Hong Xiuquan, leader of the Taiping Rebellion, had experienced a similar cure before raising havoc in central China.[30] Although no records exist to connect Hong directly to Hmong pretenders to the throne, the process whereby ambitious Hmong men also emerged to pursue the Mandate of Heaven bears a striking resemblance to that of Hong. At the very least, we can argue that the Hmong, who had a long history of contact with the Han Chinese, operated within a shared cultural repertoire. If the district mandarin knew what the Hmong man's sudden recovery portended, he was not wise in his response. The official exacerbated an already untenable situation with his rash actions. The mandarin accused the Hmong man of sorcery and had him arrested and imprisoned. The man's family sought the aid of local Hmong leaders, who petitioned in vain for his release.[31]

Precedents in which greedy Chinese officials exploited such an incident involving the Hmong abound. By the nineteenth century, the Hmong of southern China had become milch cows for Han invaders. Zhiqiang Yang writes, "In the mid- and late-Qing periods, there was a popular saying 'no prosperity without Miao' ('*wu Miao bu fu*') among the Han immigrants (this means, without the Miao people, prosperity is not possible because there is no one to exploit)."[32] The ultimate fate of the man whose arrest ignited the rebellion is not known, but the Hmong leaders who petitioned for his release were thrown in jail. Each was set free only after he had paid a bribe in proportion to his own wealth. Incensed, the leaders returned to the mountains, quickly assembled a group, and went back to Muang Tinh. The corrupt mandarin had abandoned his post, however. Unable to avenge themselves on the mandarin, the Hmong burned Chinese properties around the city. After obtaining more weapons, they "showed signs of declaring themselves free."[33]

From Muang Tinh, the rebellion spread to Muang La and Dong Xuong on the Chinese side of the border. After capturing Dong Xuong on February 8, 1918, the rebels ransacked and burned the town center. The Chinese provincial authorities responded quickly. Chinese troops and Hmong engaged in sporadic combat throughout the month. The Chinese commanded Tai soldiers, hence the Tai also became the target of Hmong attacks and "suffered miserably." By the end of the month, the dissidents, who were armed with only flintlock rifles, threatened Na Phat and Muang La, but they were repulsed by trained infantrymen equipped with modern rifles. Now on the defensive, a mass exodus of Hmong women, old people, and children poured into Tonkin. The Chinese commanders were merciless in their pursuit, aiming to wipe out the rebels. Aware of clan and regional divisions in Hmong society and expert at divide-and-conquer tactics, the Chinese tried to recruit the Hmong of Lao Cai, Lai Chau, Sonla, and Yen Bay to their side. They, of course, found willing collaborators among the Tai in Tonkin. The fleeing Hmong refugees were "cruelly repressed."[34]

Already aggrieved by the corruption of Tai overlords, the Hmong of Tonkin joined the Hmong Chinese to declare their independence. The first manifestation of disorder occurred in Muang La and quickly spread to Lai Chau and Sonla, the areas of densest Hmong population, with over three thousand households. The Hmong of the region had close, regular contact with their coethnic neighbors. By June the Hmong of Quynh Nhai in the province of Lai Chau and those of Thuan District in Sonla Province were "unhappy." For decades the family of Deo Van Tri, the French-sanctioned lord of the highlands, had ruled these contiguous regions. After his death, the French appointed his eldest son, Deo Van Khang, as *quan dao* (county chief) of Lai Chau. Khang appointed his own family members to lower administrative posts, creating a political monopoly in the region.[35] The Hmong, who were ranked at the bottom of the ethnic hierarchy but controlled the lucrative opium economy, were the main target of Tai and French exploitation. While Tai peasants paid a modest amount of tribute to the French, the Hmong paid heavy taxes. The rationale for this unfair practice, explained the French, was that the Tai provided military services while the Hmong did not. Adding to the injustice, corrupt Tai officials, who considered the territory their personal fief, always collected tribute in excess of the taxes exacted by the French.[36] Doubly exploited, the Hmong of northwestern Tonkin were ripe for rebellion.

On June 17, 1918, a group of Hmong attacked the Tai in the region of Muang Dung between the district of Quynh Nhai and the canton of Luan. They killed or wounded several individuals and burned some houses before moving on. The Tai of Muang Dung and Bang Hot fled to Quynh Nhai to avoid the approaching Hmong band. The Hmong warned the chief of Luan that his village, Muang Moun, was the next to be attacked. At nightfall twenty Hmong appeared at the nearby village of Muang Bang, and the Tai inhabitants fled in disarray as the Hmong razed the village before moving on to Muang Moun. At Muang Moun the inhabitants sought shelter in the brick house of the canton chief when the attack ensued. The Hmong killed several of the resisting inhabitants. They attempted to burn the town but were prevented by Lieutenant Mariani, whose troops arrived on the scene. After a brief exchange of gunfire, the Hmong fled to the mountains. Exhausted by a long march through flooded rivers earlier that day, Mariani abandoned pursuit. Making his way across regions inhabited by Hmong, he had received promises of assistance from only one loyal group along the Meuck River.

By early June rumors of an impending revolt enveloped Thuan District. The Hmong who attacked from Quynh Nhai had launched a propaganda program aimed at rousing the populace to rebel. On June 11 news about the arrival of a Hmong "king" circulated in Thuan District, fanning the flames of revolt. Saint-Chaffray, charged with the investigation, writes: "It was announced [in Quynh Nhai] that Heaven had just produced a Hmong King, that all the Hmong must join him, and that it was useless to work the fields; that those who went to join the King needed but only a small amount of rice because, according to him, in eating just a little bit of a marvelous rice, [and] pushing aside all cares, one would be filled. . . . These idle gossips had great success. Numerous fields were left uncultivated or abandoned."[37] The news persuaded some families in Thuan to depart for Quyhn Nhai. They took with them horses, buffaloes, and rags but relinquished several rifles to the Hmong chiefs of the region.

By the end of June, the movement had become more complex, entangled in preexisting clan, cultural, and regional divisions. Messianic figures emerged simultaneously in different locales. A woman proclaimed herself "queen" in Thuan. The news of her appearance led believers to abandon their fields and houses. The queen, assisted by her sister, sat serenely on her throne, where she received homage from individuals who took a pledge as her subjects. There was no news of any attempt to set up an independent kingdom, but, like other messianic figures, the queen and her sister danced in trancelike reveries and had their followers imitate them. Since the group had not rebelled, the French were content to leave it alone for the moment. The colonial resident reinforced the regional military post and toured the area in July to instruct the group to maintain order. The queen's followers promised to remain tranquil and return to their fields. They assured the visiting resident that they had no complaints against the Tai or the mandarins in the region.[38] Far from showing compliance, however, the refusal to voice grievances against local authorities was an ominous sign of distrust and lack of confidence in the French authorities, who legitimated the Tai. The Hmong of Ha Giang had responded in a similarly silent fashion when Leonard ascended the mountains to speak to them. He had also taken the lack of complaints at face value—a grave mistake. These were crucial moments when colonial officials, to borrow a term from Michael Adas, "bungled" the opportunity to address the issue.[39]

The agitation in Quyhn Nhai now spread to Ta Phing. During May and June 1918, numerous families from China had passed through Quyhn Nhai toward Phuong Tho. These refugees settled in the village of Ta Phing, also under the jurisdiction of the Deo clan. Up until then, Ta Phing had been peaceful, but events developed following the arrival of the refugees. On June 13 a Hmong chief gathered the Hmong of the two tributaries of the Black River for an attack along the Ma River. These Hmong "raised havoc" and "terrorized" the Tai inhabitants into July. Events favored the French, who possessed superior firearms, however. On the defensive, the Hmong negotiated for a peace settlement. By the end of July, colonial officials reported that "talks had led to the Hmong of Ta Phing submitting definitively and handing over to the commander of the territory the weapons found in the possession of the Hmong Chinese. The sorcerers coming from China had to cross the frontier again."[40]

The Hmong of Quynh Nhai also abandoned their rebellion by the end of July. They agreed to reconstruct burned houses and pay restitution in kind to the Tai. The French, in return, promised to investigate grievances against Tai officials. According to the instigators of the movement, a "self-proclaimed king," a "Hmong chief," and a "sorcerer" were removed from Lai Chau. No information exists about the fate of these individuals. The Hmong demanded direct contact with the French. The commander of the Fourth Military Territory was amenable to the idea, but the Deo family refused the proposition for fear it would lose the lucre of Hmong opium. The French decided in favor of the Deos. No administrative changes were implemented, but Deo Van Na, the son of Tri Phu Cam Sang, who had organized a raid against Hmong villages, was arrested.[41] From the end of August to October, in the view of colonial officials, calm had returned to Lai Chau. But the stillness was just the deep breath before a much fiercer rebellion engulfed the Tonkin highlands.

The Arrival of Vue Pa Chay

On October 30, 1918, Vue Pa Chay led the Hmong of Dien Bien Phu in revolt. According to Colonel Angeli, Pa Chay, whose family had been imprisoned, began by spreading "dangerous propaganda." The Hmong of Sapa arrested him and brought him to the French at Lao Cai, but he was set free after an interrogation. Following his release, Pa Chay recruited numerous subjects and distributed pamphlets proclaiming himself the heir of a former Hmong king. It is not clear who this former king was, but, the report concludes, Pa Chay had "entered definitively against us."[42]

After razing the Tai village of Muang Phang, a group of three hundred Hmong pillaged other Tai hamlets around Dien Bien Phu. The French, who had declared the rebellion over several months earlier, now scrambled to reinforce their posts in Lai Chau with troops from Yen Bay, Bao Ha, and Than Uyen. The resident of Sonla immediately dispatched a detachment of forty men to Lai Chau. By November 11, the French had managed to obtain the submission of two Hmong chiefs and the surrender of several rifles. "But the definitive submission anticipated did not occur. Batchai [Pa Chay], despite rather long negotiations, proved implacable and finally, on December 5, the delegation from Dien Bien Phu [sent to negotiate with Pa Chay] was ambushed. Three under Sergeant François Feuillet's lead were hurt."[43] The Hmong were no longer just avenging themselves on the Tai; Pa Chay's men had gone against the French. Moreover, there were signs of agitation among the Hmong of Long He (in Thuan District), a town bordering Dien Bien Phu. Some in Long He talked about taking over the fertile paddy fields of the Tai.

On December 12, Pa Chay's "warriors" captured and fortified Ban Nam Ngham as a refuge for women, children, and elders. Pa Chay and his men could not hold the village for long, however. French troops, with modern weapons, inflicted serious casualties on the group. Pa Chay's men abandoned the post, leaving eight bodies in the bushes. The colonial troops suffered one dead and two injured. Pa Chay fled to Sonla, where he found shelter among the Hmong in rebellion in Thuan. At Dien Bien Phu, those who had not followed Pa Chay surrendered their weapons to the French.

Pa Chay's brazenness encouraged the Hmong in other areas to renew their revolts. On December 14, the Hmong of the Fourth Military Territory burned the village of Lu Pe in Lao Cai Province. Meanwhile, those from Phong Tho had a head-on encounter with the "pirates," who had taken refuge in the mountain village of Nam Dick Ho Tao. Several Hmong were killed, and two were arrested, but the rest fled. The French quickly established order. Two weeks later, on December 27, it was reported that twenty-seven weapons had been surrendered. Pa Chay and his loyal partisans took refuge at Long He, where a man named Cam Xu had also proclaimed himself king and led his followers in attacks on Tai villages in the vicinity. French retribution against Pa Chay and Cam Xu was extreme, but a flu virus that claimed the lives of two soldiers exhausted the reinforcements sent from Yen Bay under the command of an officer named Lafaye. Emboldened by the respite, the Hmong continued their rampage. On December 30, they attacked Ban Lieu, a small village located just ten kilometers from the administrative center of Sonla, where the French maintained a garrison. A company from Dien Bien Phu, commanded by Lieutenant Gautier, dislodged the Hmong from the village.

On January 2, 1919, shortly after the New Year's Festival, Gautier's troops encountered rebels in Ban Pu Veng, killing twenty Hmong. The French columns marched toward Long He, where Pa Chay and Cam Xu had merged their forces. Gautier's troops surprised Pa Chay's men, who were in the process of laying siege to the Tai village of Ban Lao. The Hmong, outgunned and outnumbered, fled once again, leaving behind one dead and several wounded. Gautier captured one prisoner, but Pa Chay and his men, equipped with only fifty flintlock rifles, fled into the more inaccessible parts of the region. On January 19, 1919, Gautier reached Long He, the headquarters of Cam Xu, located at an elevation of fifteen hundred meters. The village was taken, but with a heavy price. Cam Xu's men fled to a forest nearby, while Corporal Chiarri lay dead. Gautier and two indigenous guards were also wounded critically. Several days later colonial troops pursued the Hmong along the massif that surrounds Long He, forcing them to seek refuge in the mountains near Dien Bien Phu. By the end of the month, sixty-seven rifles had been surrendered to the French, but the fighting persisted as Cam Xu and Pa Chay led their groups in separate directions.[44]

The fate of Cam Xu remains unknown, but at the end of January 1920 Pa Chay led his followers down to the Phou Chom-Chick Phou Chom-Chang (henceforth Chom-Chick Chom-Chang) massif in Luang Prabang, fifty kilometers south of Dien Bien Phu in Lao territory (see map 2). The Hmong considered this region sacred. The uncharted Chom-Chick Chom-Chang had thick, vertical limestone escarpments covered in dense jungle forests that reduced vision to several meters. Thick fogs blanketed the rugged karsts year round.[45] Torrential rainfall fed the steep-sided river systems that flowed through the region, rendering them impassable during the monsoon season from May to October. The daunting landscape forced the Pavie survey team to skip the region altogether in the 1890s. When French officers scrambled to the archives to look for geographic details about this territory before embarking on their expedition against Pa Chay, they found nothing.[46]

At the center of Chom-Chick Chom-Chang was a plateau a thousand meters high with weather conditions ideal for crop cultivation. Pa Chay and his followers settled in this interior region, which is accessible only by deep, narrow gorges—ideal for the rock trap ambushes favored by the Hmong. The tapered trails that led into this area were virtually impassable to the colonial troops composed of Vietnamese and Tai infantrymen. Employing packhorses was also out of the question, so the French conscripted resentful Khmu coolies to carry provisions, compromising local support for their mission. The French felt they could rely on the Khmu because they were, according to colonial observers, "numerous and active but of a very timid temperament."[47]

From the confines of Chom-Chick Chom-Chang, Pa Chay's men harassed the surrounding villages. Pa Chay also began circulating propaganda pamphlets in the hope of persuading the Hmong in Xieng Khouang to join his cause. These written orders alarmed the French, who knew the significance of literacy for the Hmong. Pa Chay's writing, according to Dorey, was nothing but incomprehensible scribbles. Nevertheless, Dorey conceded that it boosted Pa Chay's prestige and added to his authority.[48] Writing has long been equated by Hmong with the Mandate of Heaven and a Hmong kingdom.[49]

Pa Chay relished his freedom for a season while the French called off the chase and waited out the monsoon. Reorganization of the colonial military was also deemed necessary before the 1920–21 winter campaign. Commandant Bochot, who had led the forces against Pa Chay, was to be replaced with Commandant Dorey of the Fourth Company of Tonkinese Tirailleurs. Bochot had been instrumental in crushing a loyal contingent of Pa Chay's followers on the Tran Ninh Plateau in Xieng Khouang during the previous winter, but the campaign had completely exhausted him.[50] He would not join the final expedition into Pa Chay's lair. Dorey departed from Hanoi on October 25, 1920, to assume command in Luang Prabang. He reached the post of Muang Ngoi on November 14 and immediately began assessing the situation. Concluding that the rebellion had economic causes, he placed a ban on the exportation of rice and livestock in the territory until matters between the rebels and the colonial administration had been resolved.

Dorey strategized an attack while awaiting the arrival of the Sixth Company of Tonkinese from Nong Het (in Xieng Khouang), located twenty days' walk away. He estimated that, given the time needed for the Sixth Company to reach Muang Ngoi and recuperate, the operation could commence on December 19, 1920. He had at his disposal five companies equipped with modern rifles, rapid-fire submachine guns, and grenade launchers. He knew that the battle against Pa Chay in the most rugged of terrains would not be easy. The rivers Ngoua and Ou formed a natural barrier west of the Chom-Chick Chom-Chang, so Dorey was confident that the Hmong, lacking the skills to fashion watercraft and fearful of rivers, would not flee in that direction.[51] Barricades only needed to be established to the north and east, using the Eleventh Company of the First Tonkinese Tirailleurs, stationed at Dien Bien Phu; the First Section of the Fifth Military Territory at Tay Chang, located at the source of the Ou River; and the Ninth Company of the Second Tonkinese Tirailleurs at Muang Son and Sam Neua. Once the escape routes were plugged, columns approached Chom-Chick Chom-Chang from the south in Luang Prabang. This invasion fell to three companies: the Eleventh Company of the First Annamite Tirailleurs, from Sen Chita; the Sixth Company of the Fourth Tonkinese Tirailleurs; and the Fourth Company of the First Annamite Tirailleurs from Muang Ngoi. The strategy was to penetrate Pa Chay's lair employing a pincer attack and force the Hmong rebels to flee toward the barricades north and east of the mountainous triangle that formed Chom-Chick Chom-Chang. Dorey estimated that should Pa Chay's men succeed in bypassing the barricades without being separated, it would take the strength of three companies to pursue them while two companies would be needed to occupy the Chom-Chick Chom-Chang to mop up and prevent continued rebel activities.[52]

Military operations commenced in December 1920 with the movement of the Fourth Company from Luang Prabang toward Muang Ngoi. The majority of Pa Chay's partisans were at the center of Chom-Chick Chom-Chang, but there was a small band taking sanctuary within the massif of Phou Khi Pheung, located between the Ou and Seng rivers. On the way to Muang Ngoi to join the Sixth Company for a concentrated advance into Chom-Chick Chom-Chang, the Fourth Company was charged with the task of crushing the rebels at Phou Khi Pheung. This region was secured quickly. The rebels had launched attacks on villages in the vicinity during the last several years, but they fled without much resistance when the colonial troops arrived. The French officers obtained oaths of loyalty from the Khmu and Lao, ensuring that Hmong rebels would not be allowed to reuse the region to attack them from behind. Then, on December 8, the Fourth Company marched to Muang Ngoi to capture Pa Chay.

After the Fourth Company left for Muang Ngoi, forty men of the Eleventh Company under the command of Lieutenant Padre at Sen Chita suffered an attack by a group of Hmong with an estimated sixty rifles. The Hmong, equipped with flintlocks and several modern rifles, forced the colonial troops to take cover for several hours. Daring feats by Padre's men finally persuaded the rebels to scurry back toward the mountains. Padre's group suffered three dead while the residents of Sen Chita took away several bodies and a number of wounded. This first strike made it evident that the Hmong would not be appeased by political negotiations alone. "To the orders of submission," Dorey writes, "of payment of taxes, of delivery of arms, they made only dilatory or ironic responses. The only representative who came to Muang Ngoi to whom one could attribute some credibility was found dead, arms in hand, during the course of one of the first battles. The use of force has become indispensable."[53]

The French concluded that the attack on Sen Chita was merely a diversion and the principal group of rebels had to be located much farther east near the village of Pa Chay and his top lieutenants, Sung Quan Lao Van and Kou. Dorey reassembled his troops at Muang Ngoi to launch a two-pronged attack into this rugged interior, with two detachments from three companies. The Eleventh Company, under Captain Limousine (Detachment Limousine), was to carry out attacks between the Heup and Bong, the left tributary of the Heup River. Meanwhile, the Sixth and Fourth Companies were combined in a single detachment, under the command of Captain Pesquidous (Detachment Pesquidous), responsible for operations east of the Bong. The principle objective was to capture the village of Sung Quan Lao Van, located at the heart of the rebellion and also believed to be the residence of Pa Chay.

On December 20, Detachment Pesquidous marched from Muang Ngoi toward the center of the rebel territory. The Hmong, more familiar with these mountainous surroundings, had already anticipated the direction of the attack. Two kilometers from the outermost village of Phya Cham, in an area surrounded by high terrain, they laid an ambush for the colonial troops, digging trenches, lacing the trail and the surrounding heights with booby traps made of spears and poisoned stakes, and setting log slides that could be released from the mountains above the trail. One hundred Hmong men sat behind this defensive perimeter, taunting the colonial troops to give a premature chase and render their traps more deadly. When the troops came within firing range of their archaic flintlocks, Hmong rebels began shooting. Fatigued by the long march and unused to the thin air at high altitude, the colonial troops responded in a dazed fashion — they were clearly at a disadvantage. Poisoned stakes and arrows that laced the ground prevented them from approaching the Hmong. The elevated terrain and heavy brush hindered their maneuverability while providing ideal cover for the rebels, who struck and then fell back, only to attack again from another direction. The exchange of fire went on for two and a half days with the Hmong holding the advantage of the high ground. The tenacity of the Hmong, armed with mostly flintlocks, while facing grenade launchers and rapid-fire submachine guns, was unexpected. On December 24, the Hmong were finally overpowered by the relentless bombardment of French artillery. They fled toward Phya Cham, where defenses had already been prepared on the outskirts of the village. As the Hmong warriors ran toward the narrow trail leading to the village, however, French submachine guns mowed them down. The dead and wounded were dragged away, but the puddles of blood that covered the two-mile trail were evidence of heavy casualties.

The defense of Phya Cham was concentrated around the perimeter of the village. Hmong troops dug in with tenacity and remained in their trenches for the rest of the day. Despite the difficulties of maneuvering, the two companies of Detachment Pesquidous penetrated the Hmong defense line as evening approached. At nine o'clock, two sections of the Sixth Company broke through to launch a full assault on the village. Thirty Hmong rebels fled in several directions as French troops marched into an empty village. An orderly evacuation of women and children had occurred undetected earlier in the day. The exit trail was littered with personal items that had been abandoned to hasten their flight. The last group of Hmong men must have remained in place only long enough to allow the villagers to escape. As before, the trail was drenched in blood, indicating serious casualties among the rebels. All the dead or injured had been carried away, however. The French had no means of measuring their effectiveness. The villages of Tham Tin and Li Thoeu, similarly fortified and defended, were taken next. When these major clashes (referred to as the Affairs of Phya Cham) were over, the colonial troops had suffered four dead and eighteen wounded. Among the wounded was one European sergeant who was evacuated to Luang Prabang.

While Detachment Pesquidous was engaged in the Affairs of Phya Cham, on the morning of December 23, Detachment Limousine set out from Muang

Ngoi toward the Heup and Bong rivers. News of the battle at Phya Cham had spread to the region, causing the population to disperse. Hmong burned their villages before taking flight. The colonial troops encountered no serious resistance until the next day, when Limousine approached the village of Lao Hou. Thirty men put up a strong show of force for several hours before superior French firepower forced a retreat into the sanctuary of the jungle. During the next few days, the rebels returned to harass the French at every turn, attempting to hinder the march toward the village of Phou Nhi, which Limousine reached on December 30. The Hmong made a last stand outside the village, engaging the colonial troops head on. As before, Hmong flintlocks were no match for modern French weapons. Long-distance artilleries relentlessly shelled the jungle where Hmong rebels had taken cover. After several hours of fighting, a group of fifty Hmong retreated to the crest of a hill behind the village, allowing the colonial troops to occupy Phou Nhi.

Outgunned, the Hmong reorganized themselves into mobile strike teams of six to eight men and began to engage in guerrilla warfare. They laid ambushes at advantageous points along the narrow trails and harassed the colonial troops at every juncture. Many of the Hmong's efforts aimed at undermining French morale by disrupting the line of communication between the troops and their headquarters and by attacking from behind and then retreating. Disconnection from headquarters caused a serious problem with provisions and reinforcements, forcing the French to slow their pursuit. The tenacity and courage of the Hmong revealed the seriousness of the struggle. Dorey reports: "The first information we obtained shows that we not only struggle against a band of eighty to one hundred rifles but against an entire population aroused and mobilized by Batchai [Pa Chay]. The operations have scarcely begun and our units have been attacked at each turn and distressed by loss. We have penetrated into a rebellious region whose inhabitants have given themselves up to daily guerrilla warfare, and if today we found them before us they would only attack us from behind later and take over our convoy of supplies."[54]

It became evident to Dorey that winning the fight would take more than overpowering the Hmong with modern weapons. Realizing that opium was a source of cash that had allowed these rebels to continue fighting for years, Dorey requested permission to systematically destroy poppy fields. French troops carried out a scorched earth policy of destroying not only poppy fields but also rice fields, houses, and everything in sight. Beasts of burdens and domestic animals found abandoned were slaughtered for provisions in order to deprive Hmong of the material means of prolonging the struggle. Systematic evacuations of inhabitants were also carried out to prevent the rebels from demanding supplies and conscripting men. Dorey deployed two more sections to aid Detachment Pesquidous—one from Luang Prabang and one from Phongsaly—under the command of Captain Henri Roux, the sworn brother of Hmong leader Lo Blia Yao and commander of the Fifth Military Territory.

From December 27 to December 31, 1920, Pesquidous evacuated and burned Hmong villages. He destroyed cultivated fields, opium, and crops that lay in the path of his troops. Employing these merciless tactics, Pesquidous succeeded in dislodging the Hmong from their encampments eight kilometers north of the trail. This last defense line broken, the colonial columns forced their way toward Pa Chay's home village. By the fourth day of the new year, a detachment of one hundred riflemen and sixty coolies captured Ta Deng and Ban Chie, the last two major villages on the route to Pa Chay. The French troops rested and feasted on livestock abandoned by the Hmong before the final strike. They vandalized cultivated fields in the surrounding area. Even clothes and personal items discovered in an abandoned cave were burned so as to deprive the Hmong of any means of continuing their resistance. The Hmong returned to ambush the colonial infantry now and then, but their attacks became less effective as the troops laid siege to key areas, gradually establishing military control over the region.

While Pesquidous made his way to Pa Chay, Detachment Limousine carried out mopping-up actions on the Heup and Bong rivers, using Phou Nhi as a base. On December 26, Limousine took over the home villages of Lao Yang, Lao Tso, and Tian Tao, lieutenants of Pa Chay. Several days later Limousine destroyed the villages of Lao Mang and Lao Ly, heavily defended by Hmong. After a brief rest, the colonial troops proceeded toward Sap Phai. The last two days of the month were spent battling over Ba Lac and Sac Phay, villages located on the route to Sap Phai, both of which were "rigorously defended" by Hmong. By day four of the new year, Limousine had gained control of the center of Phou Nhi. Hmong rebels stepped up their ambushes and "followed the company step by step." Despite a surprise attack on January 6, a reconnaissance team of three sections succeeded in gaining ground to the east of Sap Phai, where a brief firefight occurred, followed by the flight of Hmong in various directions. Thick fog and more night ambushes slowed the troops, but the surrender of the chief of Ba Lac became the turning point in the battle for Phou Nhi.

News of the success of the colonial troops came to Muang Ngoi, where, on January 6, the first of the influential Hmong chiefs in the region, Sung Quan Song, presented himself to the French authorities. Commander Dorey concluded that Sung Quan probably did not take up arms but offered his allegiance only when the battles of Phya Cham and Phou Nhi had conclusively established a French victory. Dorey aimed to use Sung Quan to build a pro-French base. "Through Sung Quan Song," he writes, "political action is initiated which can only bear fruit after the total defeat of Pa Chay and Sung Quan Lao Van, to whom all the villages in the region are definitively pledged."[55] Once the tide had turned against Pa Chay, the Hmong abandoned their villages for the forest. Camping in makeshift shelters, they avoided the river courses and built fires only at night. The colonial troops arrived at Hmong villages to be welcomed by only cattle and pigs, which provided nourishment for the exhausted men. Although the troops enjoyed victory after victory, they took no prisoners. The rebels always evacuated those who were hurt or killed. Only the odor of death, the sight of blood, and an occasional well-concealed grave indicated the repressiveness of French actions.

After Phou Nhi, Limousine and Pesquidous merged their forces on the heights for the final assault on the home villages of Pa Chay, Sung Quan Lao Van, and Lao Lou. It took the combined efforts of three companies to end two years of Hmong resistance. On January 9, 1921, at eight o'clock in the morning, the scouts of Pesquidous spotted bamboo spears, poisoned arrows, and log booby traps along the trail. As had occurred before, these traps slowed the advance of the troops, forcing them into areas where Hmong held the high ground. Evading these traps, the vanguard troops of Pesquidous found their way to the waiting rifles of Hmong warriors. The Hmong advantage did not endure in the face of the long-range weapons of the French, however. For three hours, French submachine guns strafed the Hmong lines, forcing them to take flight. At eleven o'clock, the colonial troops resumed their march. At the villages of Lao Hou and Phya Tong, French troops faced the rebels again, but their long-range weapons quickly dispersed the Hmong as before. The battle at Lao Hou was the last major stand of the Hmong. "Discouraged, without a doubt, by their repeated failure, and frightened by the appearance of a device [the machine gun] capable of reaching them at long distances," the Hmong retreated toward the village of Sung Quan Lao Van.[56] Ten native troops in the employment of the French were wounded, however. The number of Hmong in the ambushes surpassed one hundred, but no bodies were found, as usual. The Hmong had carried away their dead and wounded.

On January 11, 1921, a month after the French began their campaign, the villages of Pa Chay and Sung Quan Lao Van were occupied without a fight despite the heavy fortifications the Hmong had built to defend against attacks from all directions. Pesquidous approached from the east, where the heights allowed him to view the defenses on the perimeter of the village. Limousine attacked from the heights to the west, from the Bong River. The Hmong rebels burned their villages and dispersed as the French approached. This fertile region contained numerous hamlets surrounded by cultivated fields of opium, vegetables, corn, and rice—abundant harvests for the colonial troops and their coolies. Abandoned livestock also provisioned the troops as they prepared for the final chase. By January 12, the region was enveloped in a strange quietude. Pesquidous remained behind to assess the degree of French success and to reconnoiter the area while Limousine pursued the rebels toward Muang Heup. At the same time, Detachment Guinot, comprised of two sections of Company Frezouls, was dispatched to Phou Nhi to occupy this crucial center.

With Pa Chay's lair now penetrated, the surrender at Muang Ngoi began en masse. At first extremely fearful, each village sent only two or three delegates, who were notably "coolies or Hmong without influence or personal valor."[57] The French officers did their best to treat these individuals well before sending them home with orders for the more influential Hmong chiefs to present themselves. The Hmong chiefs appeared at Muang Ngoi in groups only after much delay. They conveyed resentment toward Pa Chay and Sung Quan Lao Van, who had wronged them. These chiefs provided no information about the strength or direction taken by Pa Chay's fragmented band, however.

From January to early February, the French blindly pursued Pa Chay. Vague intelligence indicated that the rebel band had gone in the direction of a village called Thong Man, located between Muang Heup and Muang Nha in Luang Prabang Province. Since there was no indication that Pa Chay had gone north, Limousine and Cadiou, who had formed a barricade southeast of Dien Bien Phu, were ordered to march toward Thong Man and to concentrate the hunt for Pa Chay at Soung Tia, another rugged, unfamiliar region located between Muang Nha and Muang Heup. The French could not find guides to lead the troops. Meanwhile, the indigenous soldiers, perhaps resenting the fact that they had to suffer another painful march, became openly defiant. The columns traveled blindly through unfamiliar territory and were often forced to turn back when they hit impenetrable areas. Limousine, on the trail connecting Kounot, Lao Ma, and Houei Tong, reported numerous horse accidents.

At Boum Kho, Limousine received instructions to return to Muang Heup to link up with Company Caidou, which had succeeded in reaching Lo Cao after enduring a harsh march. Though led astray by his guide at one point, Caidou finally had some success. During a reconnaissance conducted around Lo Cao on January 29-31, Caidou's soldiers captured two loyal subjects of Pa Chay. The following day inhabitants of the area captured and executed two other "bandits." These were hopeful indications to the French that members of Pa Chay's group had taken refuge in the area; Limousine could flush them out.

Other reconnaissance efforts by Frezouls at the sources of the Ma and Neun, where intelligence had indicated the presence of Pa Chay's partisans, brought no result. When the colonial troops approached the area, several Hmong villagers paid homage by offering provisions. According to reports, which reveal the extent of French neglect of the highlands, none of these Hmong had seen a European before. During the rest of February, Frezouls monitored the course of the Bong, but Pa Chay and his generals were nowhere in sight. At Muang Heup, efforts were made to involve the Hmong in intelligence gathering and capturing Pa Chay. An intelligence office had been created before incursions were launched into Chom-Chick Chom-Chang under the command of Captain Carboni, an assistant to Commander Dorey. After the dispersal of Pa Chay's group in January, Carboni was charged with organizing loyal Hmong guerrillas against Pa Chay. He was also to win over the local inhabitants. These efforts resulted in the Hmong of Ba Sing delivering the head of Chu Sao, the first lieutenant of Pa Chay, to the French at Muang Ngoi. The French cautiously confirmed Chu Sao's identity by showing his head to Hmong chiefs from different regions. The papers on Chu Sao's body, further proof of his identity, included identity cards of Lao victims and written proclamations in the Pa Chay script. "The illiterate Hmong," Dorey explained, "have no writing of their own, but Pa Chay, in order to increase his prestige, made a habit of scratching strange characters, without significance, and had these delivered to his correspondents. The messenger would convey the [real] communications of Pa Chay verbally. These correspondences carry various seals and the mark of a Mexican coin."[58]

The death of Chu Sao encouraged more Hmong to deliver the heads of Pa Chay's lesser-known lieutenants. In early February, five more heads were brought to Muang Heup and presented at Ban Houei Tong in return for supplies. On February 7 the chief of Tchang Tia Tao brought two more identified heads. They belonged to men who had been captured earlier but had escaped. Despite rumors that he was in Tchang Tia Tao, there was no evidence of Pa Chay. Limousine continued his reconnaissance efforts in the vicinity of Muang Heup. At various villages, the French officer noted the appearance of newly constructed houses, which he took as evidence that Pa Chay's followers were immersing themselves in the population. He did not force Hmong to turn in these new refugees, however. The Hmong promised to pay taxes, and they delivered a few rifles to show deference to French rule.

In mid-February Limousine arrived in Lo Cao to aid Caidou in the hunt for Pa Chay. A lack of Hmong interpreters made interrogations in Tai extremely laborious. The inhabitants seemed obedient, but the French officers had no doubt that Pa Chay's partisans must be among them, or living nearby. The village chiefs refused to say a word, but they brought the heads of the most prominent rebel leaders to the French. The French were careful to show these heads to different Hmong chiefs of the region, who unanimously identified them as belonging to Van Kou Yinn, Na Sao, and others loyal to Pa Chay. The inhabitants easily recognized the head of Van Kou Yinn, the celebrated "chef de guerre" of Pa Chay, who, according to Hmong informants, had assassinated Captain Vinet east of Dien Bien Phu in 1919.

The Hmong betrayed Pa Chay's closest lieutenants, but it was not long before they began to drag their feet. Eventually they declared that they could find no more rebels in their regions. Even the promise of financial reward could not entice the Hmong to continue their efforts. They soon declared, in effect, that they liked money less than the tranquility of their land, which had been disturbed by Pa Chay and the French. "After proof of activity in the beginning," Dorey writes, "it seems that their [Hmong] zeal dampened gradually, then died definitively."[59] Limousine's excursions in the area brought no better result. The last partisans of Pa Chay must have succeeded in camouflaging themselves among the population or they now lived hidden in the inaccessible forest, the French concluded. As for Pa Chay and Sung Quan Lao Van, there was no trace of them anywhere and no news of their whereabouts. These two leaders were probably accompanied by only a few of their most loyal subjects. Living in isolation in the deep recesses of the jungle forest, they probably passed through the territory undetected and would only be punished when one of their own betrayed them. "That day is far away perhaps," Dorey concludes, "because even though their prestige was ruined, it should be remembered that unless motivated by personal hatred 'a Hmong never betrays another Hmong.'"[60] In a footnote, however, Dorey states that at the very hour when he was typing his report the Hmong of Dien Bien Phu had betrayed Sung Quan Lao Van.

From mid-January on, not a single shot was heard anywhere in the country. The Hmong conceded defeat, and the colonial officials turned their attention to civil matters. Pa Chay evaded capture only to be killed by pro-French Khmu on November 17, 1922, in Muang Ngoi, Luang Prabang.[61] The Hmong say the French offered a huge bounty for Pa Chay's head and that these former followers, including a Hmong man, assassinated him for the silver. During our last conversation in Champlin, Minnesota, on July 3, 2004, Tougeu Lyfoung told me that in the 1940s, when he was studying in Hanoi, he saw a picture of a severed head identified as that of Pa Chay in a newspaper. Indeed, the French were uncannily meticulous in cataloging photographs of the decapitated heads of natives who stood against their imperial ambitions.[62]

Messianism as a Quest for the Mandate of Heaven

Colonial observers of Hmong messianic revolts emphasize the hysterics—the dancing, the acrobatic displays, the rumors of a coming New Age, and the appearance of a Hmong king—the elements they considered illogical, even "mad." The rationale of Mi Chang's and Pa Chay's actions emerges, however, when we place their movements within a Hmong cultural context and the cultural repertoires of other Asians, particularly those of imperial China, which influenced Hmong history and identity over the ages. Thus, one can easily detect the resemblances between these Hmong messianic movements and the Great Taiping rebellion, led by Hong Xiuquan.[1] By examining Mi Chang's and Pa Chay's backgrounds, and tracing their rise and fall, we gain insight into Hmong political tradition. The life histories of the two men reveal how their authority waxed and waned over time. As these men fit the Hmong ideal of a prophet, they were perceived as legitimate by Hmong. While French accounts emphasize the might of the colonial military (French power) and fantastical elements (Hmong irrationality), Hmong accounts construct the struggles of Mi Chang and Pa Chay as quests for the Mandate of Heaven. In the Hmong worldview, these two men were summoned to mete out divine justice and to liberate the Hmong from oppression.

The Origin and Background of Xiong Mi Chang

Mi Chang does not figure as much as Pa Chay in the oral history of Hmong Americans, probably because his rebellion occurred earlier and much too far away, in northeastern Vietnam, while Pa Chay's War spread into Laos to entangle the Hmong of Xieng Khouang, many of whose descendants ended up in the United States after 1975. Despite the lack of extant oral accounts, Mi Chang's rebellion was the first major Hmong revolt observed by the French. As such, colonial officials viewed the uprising with particular curiosity, noting meticulously the events that unfolded. Mi Chang was also the only messianic leader to be captured alive and interrogated. His testimony is precious to those who thirst for the faintest resonance of a Hmong voice from the murky past. The carbon transcriptions at the French archive in Aix en-Provence provide rare insight into the mind of a Hmong prophet. Mi Chang gave the economic rationale for his rebellion, and, more important to us, he laid out in concrete steps the processes through which he was able to establish legitimacy in the eyes of his followers. Personal charisma, physical appearance, and healing and predictive abilities were the evidence of his celestial mandate. Mi Chang also had the assistance of history. He came from the same clan as a previous prophet, Xiong Tai, who had emerged in the same region during the previous century.

Mi Chang was interrogated after his capture on April 22, 1912. Lieutenant Colonel Auguste Bonifacy, the commander of the Third Military Territory, led the proceedings, questioning him four times over the course of seven days. The French officer also enlisted the service of a Chinese interpreter. Mi Chang spoke in Chinese, and the man translated his words into French. The role of the Chinese interpreter is intriguing in light of the fact that the Hmong linked their oppression in part to their inability to communicate directly with the French. Lowland interpreters, Hmong often alleged, conveyed only what they wanted the French to hear.[2] Mi Chang's interpreted words appear matter-of-fact, however, corroborating much of what is already known about messianic rebellions in general. Nevertheless, the translation into French prevents a syntactic analysis of the meanings behind what Mi Chang may have tried to convey. Important elements of his words may have been lost in translation.

Mi Chang was twenty-six years old at the time of his capture. He was the son of Xiong Lao Lou and Hang Me Nhuong. He was born and raised in Si Phai in the canton of Quang Mau (Dong Van), province of Ha Giang. He had eight people in his household — his parents, an older and a younger brother aged twenty-eight and twenty-two, and his two wives. Together the Xiong family cultivated land they rented from a Tho, for which they paid eight piasters per annum. In addition, they paid half a piaster per annum in tax on the land, which was "just large enough to sow eighty-four Annamite liters of seed."[3] During the course of the interrogation, Mi Chang also made reference to a sister, but he did not describe her as a member of his household. She may have married, which explains why he excluded her from the household head count.

Mi Chang's first wife was probably sterile—the reason why he took a second wife. Hmong men of Mi Chang's time married between sixteen and eighteen years of age. At twenty-six Mi Chang should already have had several children by his first wife, but he did not. He probably realized that he could be the source of the problem, and so he waited until his relationship with his second wife proved fruitful before he was "forced" to marry her. The second wife gave birth to a son, who, along with Mi Chang's two wives and a brother, died during an ambush. At the end of the turmoil, with Mi Chang in prison, only a brother remained to care for the aged parents.

There was nothing terribly unusual about Mi Chang except that he had an accident as a child that left his right hand almost completely severed. Following the tragedy, Mi Chang became deeply "agitated . . . and people started to believe he was a king."[4] Whatever the circumstances that led to his deformed hand, it must have been traumatic enough to drastically affect the way people perceived him. The French were not meticulous about describing Mi Chang's other physical attributes. When asked why people recognized him as a king and sent him gifts, however, Mi Chang said, "Those who saw me have been struck by my sight." The gifts, he explained, were given in the hope that when he became powerful he would remember the donors. Intriguingly, Mi Chang said he believed himself to be nothing more than a "poor wretch."[5]

Mi Chang's statement does not shed light on any more unusual physical features, but the Hmong do associate extraordinary physical attributes with power. In "Qhuab Ke," the song that instructs the soul of the deceased how to return to its ancestors, the ritual master describes himself as the one with "ears the size of a fan and eyes the size of a cup" (*ntsej luaj ntxuam muag luaj nkhob*), implying that he is a powerful being.[6] This exaggerated physical description was meant to deter evil spirits from pursuing the soul of the ritualist, whose soul has made the crossover journey with the deceased and must now return to the world of the living. Bodily characteristics are also important elements in Hmong messianic traditions, as evidenced by the fact that Hmong readily attribute the physical characteristics of the Buddha to their prophets. Certain messianic leaders are said to possess extended earlobes that reach the shoulders and fingers and toes that are the same length.[7] Exaggerated body parts can, therefore, coincide with the ritual diagnoses of a shaman to transform ordinary individuals into superhumans. According to Mi Chang, he was not the only one who capitalized on his physical attributes as a source of power. "Born at Lung [Luong] Phin," he said, "was an infant who did not have the upper lips . . . and Xiong Mao Chang, profiting [from the incident], proclaimed himself the Thong Thien Chua (Lord of Heaven) . . . [and] had followers dance."[8]

Important here is the fact that the prophet did not have to possess the unique physical attribute; he merely had to claim its power.

Mi Chang's marked deformity and other aspects of his physical constitution seemed to strike Hmong observers with a sense of awe. Perhaps villagers had already perceived his survival of the horrible childhood accident as incredible. Imbued with this notion, it is not hard to see how they could, during periods of great economic and social distress, easily make a leap of the imagination to associate him with power and embrace him as the incarnation of the "Hmong king" who had returned to liberate them from foreign oppression. The French authorities, with a different worldview, saw Mi Chang's deformity merely as a debilitating handicap. They did not see Mi Chang as a terrible threat to internal security. His physical deformity may have been a contributing factor to the lack of severity of the sentence meted out to him. For inciting a rebellion that lasted two years, he was given a ten-year sentence. It should be stipulated here, however, that a prison sentence of that duration was a virtual death sentence, and Mi Chang did not survive his term.[9] Nonetheless, his treatment seems less severe than that of his cohorts. Shortly after he began to serve his sentence on Ile de la Table, Mi Chang was transferred back to Tonkin and allowed to mingle with the indigenous population while his fellow prisoners were sent to other places of incarceration. The main concern of the French was that he not be allowed to go back to the mountains. Mi Chang was also allotted money for food.[10] The French were not as lenient with Pa Chay.

To appreciate its full significance, we have to consider what Mi Chang's severed right hand meant in personal terms as well. The loss of an arm in an agrarian society where status was largely dependent on physical ability must have left psychological scars. A man who did not have full use of his body endures a serious handicap in that kind of society. No doubt social stigma and economic reality presented overwhelming challenges to Mi Chang from his earliest days. His "acting out" to convince others to perceive him as a "king" also can be understood as an extension of his desire to reclaim the vital limb necessary for wielding an ax, the mark of his masculinity. Robert G. Cooper notes in his study of the Hmong of Thailand that felling large trees is seen as a job for men and, for this reason, has symbolic psychological significance as a measure of manhood. Women, who also associate ax wielding with manhood, refuse to fell large trees. Cooper writes:

> Although Hmong men are taller and generally stronger than Hmong women, it is difficult to imagine that a woman who can work all day hoeing the opium fields in the hot sun, carry a heavy pack for nine hours up a mountain, and chop down thick undergrowth with a machete, could not cut down a tree with an

axe. However, she would never think of doing so. Hmong men and women both say that it is impossible for a woman to farm swidden alone because she could not clear the land. . . . (I could not persuade any woman to try cutting down a tree with an axe in spite of the fact that they were at the time chopping down heavy undergrowth with machetes.)[11]

For Mi Chang, the loss of a vital limb perhaps had an even more profound effect considering his strong personality and far-reaching ambitions. His leadership was clearly established in his small household. Though handicapped and second in the birth order, he was the dominant son with two wives. His position within his clan, and certainly within his own lineage, was also made clear by the way his Xiong relatives submitted to him during the rebellion. Among his appointed generals were many of his Xiong clansmen. Men from other clans also made up his entourage, evidence that he must have established himself in other important ways as well. We know, by his own testimony, that he had healing skills similar to those of a shaman and he could foretell the future. Did Mi Chang also possess oratory talents in marriage and funeral rituals? Knowledge of traditional rites would definitely distinguish him as a clan elder, an important figure in Hmong society to whom others must kowtow in times of trial and tribulation.[12] It would appear that his status within his clan and community had primed him to become an ethnic representative, a Hmong "king."

Although Mi Chang's accident and deformity may have played a role in his rise to influence, it must be noted that Hmong people do not automatically view physical deformities as special. The circumstances and the timing surrounding Mi Chang's life have to be considered in conjunction with his inborn charisma, his oratorical and other traditional skills, and the exploitative socioeconomic conditions in his community. Mi Chang's rise to influence had opportunities of both timing and chance. His physical malformation certainly added an aura of poetic nostalgia, however. The Hmong, who have endured oppression throughout history, could not have picked a more telling symbol than a deeply intelligent and ambitious man whose right hand had been rendered useless as a youth. Mi Chang was a perfect symbol for the historically battered Hmong.

The Call for Mi Chang to Serve
the Mandate of Heaven

Mi Chang's physical looks, which "struck" members of his community from an early age, converged with a dream revelation to win him loyal adherents in 1910. Like prophets around the globe, Mi Chang's authority came to him against his will.[13] He was called to obey and serve. His three-month illness and miraculous recovery were evidence of this calling. Mi Chang explained:

> In a dream, I saw a spirit who instructed me in lots of speeches in French, in Quah-hao, in lots of languages. It also imposed on me the title Lao Ling—I don't know what that means. I recounted my dream to my parents, who also did not know what it means. Then I was sick for three months. After this illness, I could say a bunch of things in spite of myself; I'm not responsible. During my sleep, I often saw a man, very tall, white, with very small eyes like those of a cock. I also saw twice some French officers who I've quarreled with. During my youth, I was always at Dong Van, at Tien Phong [Chang Phoung], or in surroundings where I acquired the influence that's attributed to me.[14]

Mi Chang's fantastic vision, in which he was nominated without his say, was evidence of his legitimacy. After all, a prophet is, much like a shaman, initiated against his resolve. Christian Culas points out, however, the crucial distinction between a messiah, who is a divine being born as a human, and a shaman, who is a mortal being endowed with divine powers.[15] In the retelling of the dream, Mi Chang was proclaiming that his actions arose not out of earthly ambition but because he was a receptor of a higher principle of justice. He was bestowed the title Lao Ling. The mysteriousness of the designation lent credence to its transcendental origin. Mi Chang did not know what it meant. By extension, neither could any other human be privy to its celestial definition. The enigma of the title infused it with godly power.

The dream itself, though crucial, was only the threshold of Mi Chang's legitimacy. What made it significant was that he was extremely sick for three months following the revelation. The Hmong believe that illness has a physical and/or spiritual cause.[16] Attempts to heal Mi Chang would have undoubtedly included herbal cures and shamanistic rituals. Evidently, Mi Chang's ailment responded to neither remedy, forcing him to seek alternative explanations. Prolonged illness had another meaning in Hmong society, critical to our analysis here. Mysterious, protracted sickness is a means whereby a higher power chooses human subjects to do its bidding. Shamans are often called in this manner. Dwight Conquergood writes, "This summoning is communicated through initiatory illness. . . . An experienced shaman is summoned to diagnose the source of the affliction. In this case the etiology is not simply a loss of soul but the desire of a previously deceased shaman's spirit-helpers to incarnate in the afflicted person."[17]

Mi Chang may have suspected that shamanistic spirits were plaguing him. If so, he would have tested his suspicions by seeking the diagnosis of a shaman, as Conquergood notes above, and found it not to have been the case. Mi Chang's condition was, therefore, a threatening enigma in the eyes of the indigenous authorities, who knew well the ominous implications of a miraculous cure. One indigenous official in his village accused Mi Chang of wanting to claim the throne. Mi Chang said, "After my first illness, Ma Phai Ou-La-Ou of Si Phai accused me of wanting to be king, so I was afraid and I hid, but I was never afraid of Lieutenant Leonard."[18] Of course Mi Chang had no fear of Leonard, who was ignorant of the larger implications of his sudden recovery. Mi Chang may also have wanted to demonstrate, postrebellion, that he trusted the French authorities more than the indigenous officials who were quick to accuse rather than render justice to a Hmong man such as himself.

When Mi Chang started to speak multiple languages, exhibit miraculous healing powers, and foretell future events, it became evident where he was heading. Arising from his physical stasis like a metamorphic butterfly, Mi Chang began to attract attention in Meo Vac. "I healed eight people in all," he said during his interrogation, "including my uncle, who is very old [and] whom I healed completely." Mi Chang did not mention what the illness of his uncle was, but he continued, "At Ma Pa, I healed a young girl with a large lump on the neck." He also claimed to be able to predict the future using his hand, stating, "I calculate with my good hand in order to predict [the future] by the means of cyclical numbers."[19] His supernatural powers made a deep impression on members of his predominantly animistic community. He had healing and predictive abilities, but he did not belong to the ordinary categories of Hmong medicine man, shaman, or fortune-teller. He had a much more powerful link to a higher power—which was, perhaps, a broker between Heaven and Earth and a vessel for the Mandate of Heaven?

Since ordinary humans lack the skills to determine whether someone is a prophet, it was up to Mi Chang to make the proclamation himself. He did that when personal difficulties converged with economic and political oppression to push him to the edge. Once he had proclaimed himself Lord of Heaven (Son of Heaven), Mi Chang's community interpreted his illness and dreams retrospectively to complete the picture. The signs had been there all along. Mi Chang's physical attributes, his unexplained illness, and his miraculous recovery, followed by demonstrations of language ability, healing powers, and predictive skills, were proof of his extraordinary status. Grand visions of a new and just world were not only appealing to the oppressed Hmong population but also further signs of Mi Chang's mandate.

Although Mi Chang was not a shaman, the shamans and sorceresses who gathered around him were the final evidence of his legitimacy. Savina writes that a king "must be recognized and named by the shamans. It is from them that he receives, so to speak, his power, and it is by them that he is advised for the duration of the operations."[20] Accordingly, two sorceresses "armed with fans" accompanied Mi Chang at his home base. French authorities understood these females to be mirages, generated by the use of hallucinogenic concoctions.[21] We could understand the female sorceresses in more concrete terms, however. These might well have been none other than Mi Chang's two wives, who were essential to his legitimacy. When the second wife had a son, he was believed to be the true king. And when this infant was killed along with the two wives during an ambush, people began to disassociate themselves from Mi Chang, ending his movement.[22] On the other hand, the sorceresses might also have been maidens chosen to legitimate Mi Chang as a messianic leader. During messianic rebellions, designated girls often led men in battle. Clearly, these young girls made up the entourage that surrounded Mi Chang. "Everyone, sorceresses and little girls gathered around me and did as I did," he said.[23] Females are essential symbols of legitimacy in Hmong messianic tradition. They were manifestations of the legendary Nkauj Ntxuam (Lady of the Fan) and precursors of the Hmong king and kingdom.

Mi Chang was not averse to seeking other religious symbols to boost his influence. Although he had initiated his claim to the throne with the fanfare of a shaman, over time he creatively incorporated Buddhist elements into his rebellion. After he fled to China, he checked himself into a monastery and shaved his head. During this period, the local population came bearing gifts, recognizing Mi Chang as their king. The trope of a Buddhist monk enhanced Mi Chang's prestige, and his followers began to shave their heads as well. This act contrasted with the "hairs flowing" described by the French at the beginning of the rebellion, but it contained the same underlying theme of nonconformance to worldly behavior.[24] Desecrating the hair or letting it flow disheveled must also be understood in the context of the queue and its political significance in Chinese society. According to Dorothy Ko, footbinding for women and hair fashion for men were the two subjects of contentious debates in the Chinese political arena during the nineteenth and twentieth centuries.[25] Hairstyles were mandated by the state, so the act of leaving one's hair loose or cutting it was a political statement.[26] Hmong messianic groups in the later part of the twentieth century have retained hairstyle as a political symbol. Chao Fa leader Pa Kao Her, who has led the messianic rebellions against the Lao PDR since 1975, explained in a 2001 interview that his men kept their hair long and disheveled to show their discontent with the state.[27] A former leader who resisted the Lao PDR at Phou Bia from 1975 to 1978 also said he kept his hair long and flowing because long hair had protective powers, a belief that originated among the Lao.[28]

Language ability was another source of legitimacy for Mi Chang and also an indicator that he was a local leader even before the rebellion. In the quote above, Mi Chang described having visions "during [his] sleep" in which he saw a strange heavenly being with "very small eyes like those of a cock" and French officers with whom he had "quarreled." Most important, he said, the "spirit . . . instructed me in lots of speeches in French, in Quah-hao, in lots of languages." Although it was not uncommon for Hmong to be multilingual, the crucial difference here was that Mi Chang was claiming that his language skills had been miraculously bestowed on him; it was not acquired through learning.

There is no confirmation of Mi Chang's language abilities, but the interrogation does make it clear that he was fluent in Chinese. Knowledge of Chinese had been an important means of legitimation for ethnic leaders back in China as described by Yan Riyu.[29] This may explain Mi Chang's influence among the Hmong Chinese who sheltered him for a time. If Mi Chang also spoke French, however, he did not reveal it. He may have possessed rudimentary phrases, but the need for a translator during the interrogation dismisses any notion of his fluency. It is difficult to imagine that Mi Chang, out of political or personal pride, would rather have an interpreter convey his grievances to the French. I would argue that it was the frustration of not being able to express his grievances to the colonial authorities directly that drove Mi Chang to rebel in the first place. Mi Chang had no alternative outlet for his grievances, as Michael Adas argues in his work about what instigated other prophets to rebel against European colonial powers.[30] Language barrier was probably Mi Chang's largest obstacle, and he may have felt that violence was his last, and perhaps only, resort. Whatever the case, knowledge of multiple Asian languages bolstered Mi Chang's image. Ultimately, Mi Chang obtained legitimacy within the bounds of Hmong cultural expectations.

Mi Chang's Claim to History

Mi Chang also established temporal legitimacy by capitalizing on his kinship ties to a previous prophet, Xiong Tai. According to the French, Mi Chang's rebellion was a direct extension of this movement. In 1860 Tai had led a revolt in Yen Minh to capture the Mandate of Heaven and establish himself as a sovereign king. Obtaining support from the four gods of the four corners of the world who reign supreme in Hmong cosmological belief, Tai proclaimed himself Lord of Heaven. The four gods would "plant beans and soldiers would sprout from them, [then] no one can conquer me," Tai said.[31] Tai excited the population with incredible acrobatic skills and demonstrations of invulnerability. He and his recruits ravaged the Tonkin highlands for over a dozen years before they succumbed to the humid lowland weather and Vietnamese mandarins frightened them with elephant troops. Tai was contained in the highlands of Quan Ba and Dong Quan, where he established a palace called Long Vei (Seat of the Dragon) on the mountain of Tang Chang, located between Yen Minh and Quan Ba. He ruled the region for over a decade and was recognized widely by numerous gift-bearing subjects. Tai was vicious toward his followers and other ethnic groups—acts that led to his ultimate downfall. He forced the surrender of the Nung and Yao, and instilled fear in the Tho. He was finally brought down by a botched marriage alliance. After he murdered his wife, his father-in-law hired Chinese assassins to kill him. Tai's reign came to an end in the mid-1870s.[32]

Colonial sources connected Mi Chang to Tai in intricate ways. Although the French authorities did not establish whether the two prophets were blood relatives, both bore the same clan name, and in Hmong society clan association transcends biological affiliation and geographic bounds. Hmong patrilineal society counts all members of the clan as kinsmen, born of the same primeval patriarch. For this reason, Mi Chang easily attracted the mass followings founded by Tai half a century earlier. Mi Chang recruited into his entourage Tai's lone surviving son and other adherents.

Before his death Tai had adopted as sons two youths of the Ly clan, Tsan Tsao and Tsan Pao. Following Tai's assassination, Tsan Tsao succeeded him as ruler at Yen Minh until he was dislodged from the area and forced to seek refuge in Meo Vac, the main site of Mi Chang's movement in 1910. From Meo Vac, Tsan Tsao led unsuccessful raids against enemies coming from China until he was finally killed near Xin Cai. Alone, Tsan Pao lacked the charisma to attract a mass following, so the movement trickled to a halt in 1896. Tai's subjects scattered, carefully nourishing the ember of hope for a sovereign kingdom in their hearts.

When Mi Chang declared his dream revelation in 1910, a sign of great significance to Tai's and Tsan Tsao's followers, Tsan Pao was still alive. He welcomed Mi Chang as the new leader of his adopted father's movement and received him at Tao Tsen Lung, near Meo Vac. Tsan Pao was initiated as one of Mi Chang's leading generals and brought his adherents into the movement.[33] Soon enough, other Hmong came from elsewhere to pay homage to Mi Chang as well. The dream of the Hmong kingdom was revived.

The Moral Failure of Mi Chang's Movement

Mi Chang's framing of the failure of his movement in moral terms makes it evident that he perceived his rebellion as a quest for the Mandate of Heaven. According to Mi Chang, the movement failed because his generals disobeyed his benevolent dictate by wreaking havoc and devastation on the populace. Xiong Chinh Minh, his leading general, was particularly cruel in pillaging and burning Tai villages. Heaven retaliated against every single instance of injustice committed by his men. Mi Chang's nonviolent decree extended even to animals. Every beast that was killed demanded the compensation of a human. Mi Chang stated: "Like the other generals, he was charged with advocating good-will between humans and animals. [But] Xiong Chinh Minh did not uphold my teachings. He killed a small pig and an infant died; then a big pig and an old woman died."[34]

Mi Chang vehemently denied personal involvement in the violence that had been precipitated during the previous two years. Throughout the interrogation, he maintained this nonviolent stance. He stated: "The goat had said, 'The sky covers the earth, the earth is covered by the sky. This year there will be lots of humans killed, but the honest people are unscathed.' A corn plant had said to a Chinese woman who complained of its lack of growth, 'We do not grow because your heart is not good and you are not worthy to eat us.' As far as those who are causing trouble are concerned, I am not with them."[35]

Finally, Mi Chang alluded to Koung-Am, the goddess of mercy, and he spoke of being a vegetarian, in accordance to Buddhist precept. "I told them [his subjects] that the spirits accorded them these ranks but they must harm neither humans nor animals. Killing too many animals upsets Koung-Am; that is why I only eat rice and water."[36] The ranks or titles that Mi Chang spoke of were also bestowed by Heaven. For this reason, the title holders were not to abuse their authority. Ignoring his orders, followers tainted the movement with bloodletting.

War was not his primary objective, according to Mi Chang. His Hmong Chinese subjects, however, felt oppressed by heavy taxation and the Qing prohibition against poppy cultivation. They aimed to find their own kingdom so they would no longer be subject to unjust Qing laws: "The inhabitants spoke of that [finding a kingdom in China] once; they wanted to ask the French government for weapons, [but] they did not dare to do so. . . . I said to be patient, and if the French authorities wanted to go to [attack] China, we would help them. The Hmong Chinese complained of the terrible salt [tax] and not being allowed to cultivate opium [to pay for it]. If we took China, they said, there would no longer be a world of paying taxes and performing corvée [labor], and their burden would lessen."[37]

Mi Chang denied having independent aspirations, but he did adopt the symbols of a modern nation-state. He had a white flag, which he insisted others borrowed for their own purposes—mainly to commit violence. "At my place," he said, "I had two white flags, so people imitated me and put white flags everywhere, but my people have not pillaged; it's the Hmong of Lung Phin [who did it]." Those who co-opted his symbols also invented emblems for their followers. "At my place there was no insignia, but those who went to pillage had a piece of white fabric as a badge," he said.

Mi Chang refused to say much about plundering the Tho. He persisted only on his innocence. "I like the Tho and the Hmong equally," he said. Then, contradicting his predominant role as a leader who directed the rebellion, he claimed others dictated to him. "I was told to go and pillage at Niem-Son, but I refused," he said. "I told my men not to do ill, but on the contrary to go and cultivate their fields in order to have things to eat. I said that every person loves life so they should not kill others." The *cha-chang* of Luang Po, Mi Chang admitted, had his home burned for making people pay too much tax, but "as to the other pillaging, I did not give the order." To the accusations of having raised havoc, he replied that on the contrary he "feared disorder."[38] Mi Chang claimed his movement aimed to reestablish order for society by removing corrupt officials. Through this testimony, we gain insight into his worldview—one organized by Confucian principles. According to Confucian notions of benevolence, the state and its officials were supposed to maintain a certain moral order. Both Chinese and French officials were corrupt and unjust, however. There were ample economic incentives for the rebellion. The Hmong were oppressed by the imposition of heavy taxes. At the same time, the prohibition against opium cultivation—the only cash crop available to Hmong—exacerbated the situation. Imposing heavy taxes without allowing the cultivation of poppy to pay for them incited rebellion. That was the situation across the Chinese border, where the revolt originated.

The Hmong in French territory joined the cause of those in China. The French had also imposed heavy taxation and failed to render justice. The state's lack of benevolence was a sign that the Mandate of Heaven was up for grabs. As explained earlier, Mi Chang was advancing both moral and temporal reasons for the insurrection. He was not responsible for its failure, however. The blind rampage of his followers caused the loss of celestial mandate. Intriguingly, Hmong subjects of messianic figures often gave this explanation as well. When a messianic revolt fails, the prophet is not faulted. Hmong pinpoint the failure on the unjust actions of the followers. As we shall see below, the rationale for the failure of Pa Chay's rebellion makes this point even more explicit.

Pa Chay's War (1918–21)

French reports construct the narrative of Pa Chay's rebellion in simple terms. Economic and political considerations aside, Pa Chay was an "epileptic" who employed sorcery to hypnotize the naive and force the unwilling into a death pact. He held power briefly, caused massive devastation among the common people, and was put down definitively by the might of the colonial army in March 1921. Modern historians who rely on colonial records have examined in excellent detail the socioeconomic causes of Pa Chay's rebellion.[39] To avoid redundancy, I neither reiterate nor dispute the logic of these landmark studies. What I highlight here are Hmong memories of Pa Chay's rebellion, which have been largely ignored by scholars. These accounts may provide crucial information from the Hmong perspective, informing a deeper understanding of this major highland revolt.[40] Much like Mi Chang's account of his own rebellion, Hmong accounts about Pa Chay construct his movement as a quest for the Mandate of Heaven.

Thanks to the meticulous efforts of Father Yves Bertrais (Txiv Plig Nyiaj Pov), one oral testimony of Pa Chay's War survives, providing us with a Hmong perspective. This account was dictated by Yaj Txooj Tsawb and transcribed and published by Bertrais in 1972. Txooj Tsawb claimed that his testimony came from his uncle, who had struggled with Pa Chay, but the complex manner in which Txooj Tsawb was able to relay events makes it evident that his account is a compilation of the memories of multiple individuals.[41] I would argue, therefore, that this version represents an assemblage of what constitutes Hmong memories of Pa Chay's revolt. Furthermore, unlike Mi Chang's interrogation, which was sifted through multiple languages, Txooj Tsawb's testimony in Hmong allows syntactic scrutiny of the activities that unfolded.

In Txooj Tsawb's account, Pa Chay's War emerges as a complete event operating on multidimensional levels: temporal, political, and above all spiritual. Pa Chay was a heavenly being sent to challenge the legitimacy of the colonial masters whose corruption had gone unchecked. For this reason, his appearance rendered the mandate of the French questionable, challenging it. Hence, Pa Chay's emergence signaled that the Hmong should struggle against the colonial state. In the end, Pa Chay was not defeated by the might of the colonial army; he was undone by followers who deviated from the moral dictates of Heaven.

The Hmong lost the quest, but Pa Chay, in a fundamental sense, lives on to be reincarnated in the distant future as another Hmong king. The dream of the Hmong kingdom remains alive.

One is struck by the almost complete absence of justifications for the rebellion in Txooj Tsawb's testimony. The intricacies of the corrupt colonial system receive no more than a paragraph in the text. Instead, almost the entire narrative focuses on the rise and fall of Pa Chay. Shadowing closely the trajectory of his defeat is the Hmong aspiration for, but failure to achieve, a sovereign state. The account details how Pa Chay obtained the Mandate of Heaven, how this mandate manifested itself before witnesses, and how Pa Chay lost it due to the moral transgressions of followers. The overarching aim is to explain why the Hmong have no kingdom and why they are continually subjected to foreign rule. Critical to the narrative is the notion of Hmong betraying Hmong that is encapsulated in the legend of Nkauj Ntxuam. Pa Chay was assassinated with the participation of a Hmong man. Intriguingly, this story of Hmong self-betrayal was published immediately following the assassination of another messianic figure, Yang Shong Lue, more popularly known as the Mother of Writing, because he had invented a unique script for the Hmong language.[42]

Txooj Tsawb's testimony can be divided into three parts, each establishing the evidence for Pa Chay's worthiness to assume the mantle of kingship. The similarity to Mi Chang's testimony is striking. The narrative begins with the call, through a vision, for Pa Chay to serve the will of Heaven by leading and instructing the Hmong in matters of civilization, or modernity. Here Pa Chay passes a series of moral tests to demonstrate his fitness to rule over an oppressed people. The second part of the account deals with the manifestation of Pa Chay's powers, which proved that he was the chosen one. Pa Chay's power is revealed to witnesses in the form of supernatural abilities, innovative knowledge, divine literacy, incredible acrobatic skills, and physical invulnerability. The final section of the testimony speaks to the loss of legitimacy and the moral failures of disobedient subjects who hindered the realization of the dream. This concluding part includes the assassination of the messiah, which occurred with his full knowledge and participation. The narrative reveals that Pa Chay did not die, and thus the dream of the Hmong kingdom is not gone but merely latent.

The Mystery of Pa Chay's Origin

Neither French military records nor Hmong oral accounts tell us much about Pa Chay's background. Out of sheer ignorance about it, both skip over what are, in almost any life, formative years and important family influences. The enigma of Pa Chay's origin may bolster his legitimacy as a messianic leader, however. His obscure background, including a questionable clan affiliation, fulfills the expectations of the mysterious provenance of prophets, who are thought to be divine beings, even sons of God or Heaven.[43] The Hmong debate today about what clan Pa Chay belonged to, with some claiming that he was of the Xiong and others that he was of the Vue. Affiliating Pa Chay with the Xiong clan is understandable. The two previous prophets, Tai and Mi Chang, who emerged in Ha Giang, were of that clan.

Some say that Xiong Pa Chay was an entirely different individual who must not be confused with Vue Pa Chay, the rebel leader who launched the uprising in Dien Bien Phu. While Vue Pa Chay came from Vietnam, Xiong Pa Chay was a native of Laos. He served under Vue Pa Chay, leading a rebel contingent in Xieng Khouang in 1920. "When the French captured Xiong Pa Chay," said Tsia Long Thao, "they beheaded him in Nong Het and then displayed his head at Xieng Khouang. The descendants of this Pa Chay presently live in St. Paul, Minnesota. The two Pa Chays were distinct individuals."[44] The debates about their identity add to the prophet Vue Pa Chay's mysteriousness, bolstering his prestige.

According to Hmong informants, Vue Pa Chay was the son of a notable family from the village of Na Ou in Dien Bien Phu (Muang Thaeng) District, where his uncle, Vue Shong Tou, was a village chief.[45] Orphaned at an early age, Pa Chay migrated from China as a teenager to join his relatives in Tonkin. Vue Txu Keu, a relative, adopted and raised Pa Chay with his four sons.[46] Despite his humble origins, Pa Chay apparently managed to become literate. The legends about him attest that, without ever having gone to school, he was able to read Chinese, Vietnamese, and Lao.[47] Multilingualism and literacy are important symbols of legitimacy in the Hmong conception of leadership, a significant fact that will be addressed more thoroughly later. Aside from these few details, we know little about Pa Chay's childhood. Never caught and interrogated at length like Mi Chang, Pa Chay's personal life, family history, and thinking elude us.

Even more intriguing is the complete lack of information about Pa Chay in the French colonial archives. This is especially surprising since his movement was far more costly for the French and over four times more expansive than that of Mi Chang. While Mi Chang's rebellion was confined to a few key villages in the mountains of Ha Giang, Pa Chay's War extended over forty thousand square kilometers from Dien Bien Phu, Vietnam, to Sam Neua, Luang Prabang, and Xieng Khouang, Laos (see map 2).[48] While it appears that painstaking

Figure 6. The execution of a group of Pa Chay rebels in Xieng Khouang, Laos, 1920/21. (Courtesy of Archives nationales d'outre-mer, FR ANOM, Aix-en-Provence, 16_8FI_524_V054N312)

efforts were devoted to researching Mi Chang's background, the colonial authorities who pursued Pa Chay from one defensive post to another for three years were content to dismiss him as an "epileptic sorcerer."[49] Extant army records focus primarily on military encounters and attack plans, providing little data that would allow us to understand Pa Chay as a visionary.

French information about Pa Chay is inversely proportional to the threat he represented to the colonial state. Perhaps his rebellion was so massive and dealt such a blow to the state that it forced the French to respond with haste to the neglect of collecting biographical or other background data. French records do indicate that Pa Chay was captured and interrogated before being released back into the mountains, but there is no extant transcript of this interrogation.[50] The extreme repression that followed his revolt indicates the degree of Pa Chay's threat, however. His top lieutenants were summarily executed, hence leaving no firsthand account of the movement (see fig. 6).[51] The merciless show of force by the French and their allies may have also served as an incentive for Hmong rebels to fight to the death, giving the French no chance for an interrogation. These scenarios shed light on the significance of the revolt and the difficulty entailed in analyzing it.

Also, the lack of information about Pa Chay from Hmong loyalists might be a reflection of widespread support for him. One French officer confirms: "We not only struggled against a band of 80 to 100 rifles, but against an entire population aroused and mobilized by Batchai [Pa Chay]."[52] By 1920, several years into the rebellion and after Pa Chay was already on the defensive, French teams sent to assemble intelligence about Pa Chay still encountered an uncooperative population. French neglect of the Hmong facilitated noncompliance. Another report states, "Unfortunately, it is difficult to play good politics with an enemy one scarcely knows."[53] Unlike Mi Chang, who was quickly betrayed to the French, few Hmong informed on Pa Chay—another reason for the paucity of evidence. It was only very late in the rebellion when some Hmong, perhaps to save their own skin, began to inform on Pa Chay.[54]

The dearth of information about Pa Chay can perhaps also be attributed to his humble origin as an orphan, which was, of course, crucial to his legitimacy as a prophet. Hmong oral tradition has a recurring theme about the Orphan Boy who plays a critical role in history, sometimes becoming a king.[55] The legend of Tswb Tshoj, for example, includes an oracular precursor about the first Hmong king, who was an orphan of ambiguous paternal lineage.[56] Orphanhood is "particularly important since it does to some extent allow him [the king] to transcend the bonds of affiliation to a particular clan, and represent the kind of political unity among the Hmong which is often seen as marred by clan divisions," Nicholas Tapp writes.[57] Hmong leaders such as Lo Blia Yao and Touby Lyfoung rank as notable orphans. Touby was descended from another orphan, Ly Dra Pao, whose kinsmen adopted him to a Chinese couple. Dra Pao returned to his relatives as an adult, but did not easily find a place among his kinsmen.[58]

How orphanhood impacted individual leaders remains an intriguing detail of Hmong history, adding an aura of grandeur to the mundane facts of individual biography. The Hmong's oppressed status vis-à-vis much more powerful Others facilitates their identification with the orphan. Tapp points out, in fact, that the Hmong perceive themselves as orphans with an ambiguous paternal line, and they define themselves structurally opposite the Han Chinese in this regard. He writes, "It is significant that where the Hmong has lost a father, the Chinese has lost a mother."[59] For multiple reasons, Pa Chay's orphan status and ambiguous clan affiliation may have helped him recruit a mass following.

Another explanation for the lack of data about Pa Chay, as evidenced in the oral accounts, is that he was a newcomer to Dien Bien Phu. According to Txooj Tsawb, Pa Chay appeared one day to court the daughter of Phe Cas, a man who lived near Dien Bien Phu. After much inquiry, the Hmong learned that Pa Chay had just arrived from China. Pa Chay later established himself in the community by marrying Phe Cas's daughter. A few years later he had his first vision, which led to the events that catapulted him into colonial history.[60]

Pa Chay's arrival as an adult of marriageable age also explains the claim that he knew how to read and write multiple languages without ever attending school. He had probably acquired these skills in China before migrating to Tonkin. Since fellow villagers did not witness his educational upbringing, they may have accepted his literacy was an extension of his mysterious power.

Finally, the lack of data on Pa Chay may simply be because not all French records have been unveiled yet. F. M. Savina was commissioned by the French government to negotiate a settlement with the Hmong, but according to him, he was bound by confidentiality.[61] Fluent in Hmong, Savina would have had easy access to Hmong perspectives. Also a meticulous person with vested interest in the Hmong, as evidenced by his pioneer publications, he very likely kept a journal that is awaiting discovery. Meanwhile, the scarcity of information about Pa Chay adds to his mysteriousness, making him even more of a symbol to the Hmong.

Pa Chay's Summons to Fulfill the Mandate of Heaven

Unlike the French sources, which highlight the irrational aspects of Pa Chay's rebellion, Txooj Tsawb's testimony delineates the spiritual and temporal dimensions to elucidate Pa Chay's legitimacy and its subsequent loss. Txooj Tsawb explains why followers believed Pa Chay was a prophet. The account focuses on Pa Chay's ascension to Heaven (the acquisition of legitimacy), his demonstrations of power to fellow villagers (proof of his legitimacy), and his failure to realize the Hmong dream (the loss of legitimacy). The mega explanation is that, through impatience and moral transgressions, followers failed Pa Chay.

The narrative begins with the ascension of Pa Chay in bodily form to Heaven. The story of Pa Chay's summons, closely resembling a shaman's initiation, contains cultural elements familiar to Hmong and, hence, would be taken as believable by the society.[62] Just as the shaman is called to serve against his will, so Pa Chay, like Mi Chang as well, was summoned without his say to lead and instruct the Hmong. According to Txooj Tsawb, several years after Pa Chay married the daughter of Phe Cas, he had a vision following an argument with his wife. Pa Chay was deeply wounded by her words of insult, so he strapped his baby boy to his back with a carrier and walked outside to appeal aloud to Heaven (*Ntuj*). Pa Chay's exact words of appeal are not known, nor do they seem to be important to the story. What is significant is the response he received. A neighbor named Xauv Tswb had a dog that had just given birth to a litter of three puppies. Hearing Pa Chay cry out to Heaven, the puppies responded in unison, referring to Pa Chay as Lwj Xeeb, which translates as "second in rank": "Lwj Xeeb, Lwj Xeeb, you are a good being who will rise to take charge of Heaven and Earth. Our owner does not feed us, our mother does not give us her breast milk; we are hungry. We beg food from you, Lwj Xeeb."[63] Pa Chay's personal name at this time was Xeeb Txoov, but for some reason he responded to the name the puppies called him by. The name Pa Chay did not come into play until much later when he was in full rebellion. Name changes of this sort are normal practices among the Hmong, done to mark life transitions or evade misfortune and illness.

Pa Chay was not alarmed that puppies spoke to him. He petted the puppies on the head and went inside. He brought back some rice, which he divided into three portions in three bowls for each of the puppies. After the puppies finished eating, they told Pa Chay to take his son inside and come back alone. Niag Neeg, the "Big Person," wanted to talk to him, they said, and would send a messenger to fetch him shortly.[64] Pa Chay did as he was told and returned to the doorway. Suddenly he felt a strong breeze, and then a man appeared out of nowhere. The man stood in front of Pa Chay's house holding the reins of a black and white horse. The individual spoke to Pa Chay, also referring to him as "second rank": "Lwj Xeeb, the Big Person, said the Big Person had allowed you to come to earth to instruct people about [proper] customs and behavior so that they wouldn't just eat and do whatever they wanted. But you have not taught them. Faj Tim [the Yellow Emperor] wants to give you instructions that you can bring back to teach the people."[65]

Pa Chay said he was only a "humble man," a *me neeg*, and would not go. One should understand Pa Chay's refusals here and elsewhere as demonstrations of humility and not willful disobedience because, although he verbally said no throughout the story, he subsequently obeyed and carried out, directly or indirectly, all the orders given to him. One could argue, in fact, that it was Pa Chay's compliance that allowed these strange events to transpire. His refusing was important, however, as evidence of his having been chosen against his will like all shamans and prophets.[66] More significant, thus far Pa Chay has revealed two essential qualities valued by the Hmong—kindness and humility. Although Hmong have been noted for their kindness to animals, the act of Pa Chay feeding the puppies in bowls was extraordinary—the reason why the detail was carefully retained in the retelling of the story by Txooj Tsawb.[67] Pa Chay also responded in the most humble manner, revealing a quality renowned in the legendary Orphan Boy.

After humbly refusing to go with the stranger, Pa Chay fainted. When he awoke, he was astride a black and white horse, heading for a cave in Heaven.

Passing two guardian tigers at the mouth of the cave, the horse went straight through into the darkness. When light returned, Pa Chay saw a palace of clay and marble that shone with the color of gold. He entered and saw six figures sitting on six chairs surrounding a table full of books. They invited him to join them at the table so that the Big Person, who was revealed to be none other than the legendary King Tswb Tshoj, could give him instructions. An important element is revealed here for the first time, as we now learn that Pa Chay, having been invited to sit with the six individuals at the table, is one of the seven Sons of Heaven. These seven, according to messianic tradition, rotated back and forth, being born and reborn as kings of oppressed peoples. Their significance is symbolized in the star with seven points on the flag of Yang Shong Lue's messianic group, known as the Chao Fa, which emerged during the Secret War period.[68] Thus, Pa Chay was a divine being.

After sitting for what seemed like hours, Pa Chay asked what it was they needed to instruct him about. The six told Pa Chay to be patient since it was not yet time for the Big Person to speak to him. After revealing that it was King Tswb Tshoj who wanted to talk to him, the six individuals went back to referring to the king as Niag Neeg, or the "Big Person," throughout the rest of the account. This name is perhaps meant to remind us of his humanity, as he had been born a king among humans before. It might also be an archaic Hmong or borrowed method of referring to a king. In Chinese tradition, for example, the king often refers to himself as "One Man."[69] Niag Neeg in Hmong can also be rendered as "Big Man." Even more significant, and revealing of Sinic influence, is that it is Faj Tim, the Yellow Emperor of Chinese history, who demands a session with Pa Chay.

Pa Chay waited patiently, thus demonstrating a third important quality possessed by a chosen leader.[70] Indeed, Pa Chay would continue to demonstrate his patient nature throughout the story. Later, when his uncle complained openly about the corruption of overlords and urged him to lead a rebellion, Pa Chay cautioned him to be patient and wait for directions from above. "Someone will come to instruct us," he said.[71] Thus, it appears that Pa Chay passed each of the tests presented to him, overtly exhibiting the qualities of kindness, humility, and patience and indirectly showing that he was willing to obey the will of Heaven.

After a long while, Txooj Tsawb continues, the Big Person came down from upstairs and greeted Pa Chay, saying, "Have you come, Lwj Xeeb?"[72] Then the Big Person reminded Pa Chay that, although he had been instructed to descend to earth to teach the Hmong to be pure and clean, so far he had not done so. That was why he had been summoned. The Big Person said to Pa Chay:

It seems that of those who live under Heaven our Hmong people are the ones who have not taken to good and clean ways. Children are ragged and disheveled. Parents do not carefully dress them. When you return, instruct all people under Heaven who are Hmong how to dress. At night they should pull blankets over themselves so that mosquitoes do not bite them; when they go into the forest, do not let bloodsuckers bite them. Heat water to wash the body so that the body will be warm and the blood can circulate well. This way everyone will be able to make a better life in the future. When a sow gives birth and there are dead piglets, tell people not to eat them. Tell them not to dig for *nas kos* [a wild rodent]. It is because people do not know how to abstain and eat the wrong things that they get sick and die. Tell the whole world this.[73]

Intriguingly, King Tswb Tshoj's lecture on personal hygiene echoes the lessons of Samuel Pollard, the British missionary who brought the Protestant faith to the "Miao" (A Hmao) in southern China during the early 1900s. Attributing the high infant mortality and death rates among the "Miao" to their unsanitary living conditions and lack of knowledge about communicative diseases such as syphilis, Pollard took pains to stress strict codes of moral behavior and cleanliness. According to R. Alison Lewis, who has studied the personal correspondence and diaries of Pollard, these hygienic efforts were serious enough that "cleanliness and health became associated with Christianity."[74] If missionary teachings found their way into Hmong messianic movements, it would not be surprising. Other Hmong messianic leaders have been known to borrow from outsiders. Mi Chang, as noted earlier, even went so far as to shave his head and proclaim a peaceful unity between man and beasts, thus echoing the precepts of Buddhism.[75]

Aside from its literal sense, the instruction has symbolic meaning as well. The reference to the Hmong's "disheveled" and "ragged" ways is perhaps an indirect allusion to their poverty and oppressed status. This observation is followed by the stricture that the Hmong must cover themselves with blankets at night and not let mosquitoes and bloodsuckers bite them—possibly a directive exhorting them to protect themselves and not to act like milch cows. Encoded in this instruction is a radical call to action. Pa Chay has been summoned to awaken the Hmong from their abject state and lead them to civilization.

Pa Chay again, in accordance with polite Hmong cultural practice, humbly refused to obey the dictates of the Big Person, saying that the world would not believe the words of an unworthy man such as himself. Pa Chay's refusal may have been the correct response, allowing him to pass yet another humility trial, because the Big Person did not press him further. Rather, the Big Person said it was all right if Pa Chay was not comfortable with conveying his words to the people. Instead, if on his way back to earth Pa Chay would take mouthfuls of water from the bowl that the Big Person had given him and spray the four corners of the world with it, that would be enough. This was not an unusual request, as spraying water from the mouth is a familiar practice carried out during certain Hmong healing rituals.[76] Water, once endowed with supernatural properties following the recitation of a spell, protects, heals, or purifies all that it touches. Another crucial point, however, is that Pa Chay eventually does pass the words of the Big Person on to humanity through the retelling of these events to witnesses. Thus, his refusal to do so when standing before the Big Person merely demonstrates humility, as noted above.

After being instructed about hygiene and eating taboos, Pa Chay was invested with three pens, one book, and a rifle that could fire thirteen shots.[77] The rifle is a unique symbol not found in other messianic legends, but here it serves as a foreshadowing of the military role assigned to Pa Chay. The number thirteen is also associated with the dead and is important in Hmong cosmological beliefs. In Hmong tradition, a family member goes halfway to the grave of the deceased to leave food for it for the last time on the thirteenth day. Moreover, in the "Qhuab Ke," the deceased ascends thirteen steps to the world of Ntxwg Nyoog, the god of the underworld.[78] The instruments of writing, the pens and book, are familiar symbols found in other messianic movements and serve as marks of a Hmong messiah's legitimacy. Writing is, after all, an essential aspect of Hmong history and identity and the precursor to the consolidation of the Hmong kingdom.[79] The French did not believe that Pa Chay actually possessed a writing system, saying only that papers covered with "scribbles" were found on the bodies of his lieutenants.[80] While Pa Chay's literacy cannot be conclusively established, Yang Shong Lue's *Phaj Hauj* script is widely used today.[81] Shong Lue, much like Pa Chay, was given a book and pen made of living tissue. Pa Kao Her, Shong Lue's first disciple, claimed that he had touched the pen and book, which were in the possession of Vang Chue Chi Vue, the religious figurehead of the Chao Fa, who remained in the jungles of the Lao PDR.[82]

Once the sacred relics were handed to Pa Chay, he was allowed to return home. The journey seemed to have taken only hours, but when he returned Pa Chay learned from his penitent wife that he had been gone for a day and night. She had searched in vain for him everywhere. Her inability to find him was, of course, subtle testimony that Pa Chay had ascended in bodily form to Heaven, that what he experienced was not just a vision or a dream like that of Mi Chang. Pa Chay said nothing about his journey at first. He merely told his wife he had been out on an errand. For the time being, he kept everything that had transpired to himself. Pa Chay's silence is the crucial testament of his sanity. Being of perfectly rational mind, so the story subtly attests, Pa Chay anticipated that such an incredible tale, if leaked to others incautiously, might brand him as a mere lunatic. The world would come to know the story of his ascension, but only after he had performed the deeds to prove it. In the retelling of this legend, the narrator, perhaps a believer, offers a deft personal testimony on behalf of Pa Chay.

The Manifestation of Pa Chay's Powers

The second part of Yaj Txooj Tsawb's testimony deals with the manifestation of Pa Chay's powers. This part carefully explains the reasons why Hmong were drawn to Pa Chay. It not only attests to Pa Chay's genuineness but also argues that neither he nor his followers were "mad" by normal standards. On returning from his conference with King Tswb Tshoj, Pa Chay resumed his normal life, keeping all that had transpired a secret. At the New Year's Festival, when villagers were gathered in groups, Pa Chay chose to reveal his power to the Hmong for the first time. That year, Txooj Tsawb continues, Pa Chay's uncle, who was the village chief, killed a pig to celebrate. As was customary, he invited all the elders in the village to the feast. At such times it was common for the Hmong to hold a *baci* ceremony in which the elders tied white yarn on the wrists of family members to wish them prosperity and long life. Once the elders had gathered, Pa Chay took the skein of yarn intended for this ceremony and wound part of it tightly into a ball. He threw the ball of yarn six yards away, and it exploded with a loud boom that frightened everyone. The explosion left a hole "big enough for a fully grown castrated pig to lie in."[83]

Pa Chay then challenged the villagers to do the same thing using the same yarn, and they said they could not do it. Pa Chay handed the skein of yarn to his uncle. Imitating Pa Chay's example, his uncle also wound a small ball of yarn and threw it a few feet away, but nothing happened. Pa Chay went to pick it up. The unbelieving onlookers asked him to demonstrate his power again by throwing the ball of yarn made by his uncle. Pa Chay threw it, and, as before, the ball of yarn exploded.[84] The Hmong were no strangers to trick explosions. The first ball of yarn, which Pa Chay had wound himself, could have contained explosives, but, in the eyes of the witnesses, certainly the second ball, wound and thrown first by his uncle, had to be real. Pa Chay had demonstrated one element of his extraordinary power—his military prowess, his possession of the art of war. Nevertheless, this was only preliminary evidence. Pa Chay, as before, said nothing about where he had acquired his power.

Exhibiting his power over explosives bears important symbolism for a leader who is bound to lead an armed rebellion. In Hmong tradition, the legacy of kingship is often tied to martial valor. Military prowess, however, must be combined with other elements, primarily literacy. Spontaneous acquisition of literacy was thus the next astonishing event surrounding Pa Chay. Following the explosions at the New Year's Festival, four adults of the clans Vang, Yang, and Lo became "mad" (*vwm*) with the knowledge of literacy. The use of the word *vwm* connotes the idea that they acquired literacy not through rigorous training but by mysterious means. These individuals wrote to Pa Chay, perhaps to test whether he was the true king. Sure enough, Pa Chay wrote back, asking them to teach the precepts that were dictated to him by the legendary King Tswb Choj. These four became the disciples who disseminated the oral orders given to Pa Chay. Hmong were told to adopt hygienic practices, avoid mosquito bites at night, and refrain from eating piglets born dead. They were also told to practice conservation and respect animals, which meant curtailing funeral expenditures by killing fewer cows. "For one's mother and father who one loves sincerely," he said, "kill only one cow."[85]

The last recommendation is understandable. The excess displayed in funeral practices, a means of displaying wealth and prestige to observers, has always been a major concern of the Hmong. It was not unheard of for families to become destitute after spending their life savings on a funeral. For this reason, Hmong leaders have often felt the need to tackle the issue. During the course of our conversations in 2004, for example, General Vang Pao, without any lead from me whatsoever, brought up the topic of lavish animal sacrifices during funerals. "This is one important tradition that we need to change," he said.[86] We can, therefore, interpret the dictate to sacrifice only one animal as an attempt by Pa Chay, as a leader, to transform certain practices in order to improve the economic well-being of followers.

Power over literacy allowed Pa Chay a means to gather disciples around him. During writing sessions, Pa Chay took the opportunity to demonstrate further his personal ties to Heaven. He had a nine-branched tree planted in front of his house. He went back and forth between Heaven and Earth through this tree. "When Pa Chay wanted to go meet the Big Person, he would climb this tree, and when he returned he would come down," said Txooj Tsawb.[87] How followers determined that Pa Chay went to Heaven and back is unclear. There is no testimony about his disappearing in bodily form once he climbed the tree as during his initial trip after feeding the talking puppies.

Embarking on the Rebellion

So far Pa Chay's actions appeared innocuous, but in essence he was raising new consciousness by speaking out about the Hmong's lack of progress. He was also gathering adherents and instructing them in literacy and the ways of modernity. For the Hmong, literacy was synonymous with sovereignty. Taking up pen and paper was a declaration of the aspiration for independence.[88] Sure enough, Pa Chay began to distribute functionary titles to clan leaders in the region and to embark on the first stages of rallying the Hmong to resist colonial rule. Loyal subjects acquiesced to Pa Chay's legitimacy by accepting the titles and roles he assigned them. There had been no talk of armed rebellion, however. Pa Chay's movement was still in a latent stage.[89]

The transition from peaceful civic action to armed resistance against the colonial order occurred at the behest of Pa Chay's impatient uncle. I will discuss this below when I examine Txooj Tsawb's explanation for the failure of the movement. Here I analyze further manifestations of Pa Chay's powers during battle. As before, Pa Chay proved his prowess in war to followers. Prior to every battle, he performed a flag-raising ceremony to summon Heaven's protection. Then he asked his assistant to chop his shoulder three times with his sword. Each time, the sword fell on Pa Chay's shoulder without drawing blood. Pa Chay's invulnerability was a sign that his men were protected and would be safe in battle. These exhibitions were instrumental in raising the morale of his men. For three years, Pa Chay was victorious in battle without suffering so much as a skin wound, said Txooj Tsawb.[90]

Pa Chay did not rely on prayers and showmanship alone to rally followers. He also exhibited knowledge of weaponry. He had a Hmong rifle maker forge a huge cannon, perhaps to his specifications. The cannon took six *las* of gunpowder to light and ejected thirty cartridges at a time.[91] This instrument of war could only be fired from the shoulder of the man who had been endowed with divine physical prowess. Each time it was fired, the weapon lurched with a backward kick strong enough to lodge it in the ground at a depth of over an arm's length. A team of men stood by, ready to dig the cannon out of the ground after each shot. A single shot could kill fourteen people.[92]

Pa Chay also surrounded himself with men gifted in the art of war. The account of the battle of Muang Thaeng (Dien Bien Phu), a major town, reveals Hmong military strategies. On the site was a French garrison in which four French officers commanded a contingent of Vietnamese soldiers. When the Hmong attacked, the French officers fled, leaving behind the indigenous soldiers. Pa Chay's forces could not capture the fort, so they laid siege and waited. The colonial troops had food and ammunition to last for days, but they had no water. They painstakingly excavated an underground tunnel to the river nearby. The Hmong countered by contaminating the river with a poisonous fruit (*txiv puab tawm*) that grew in the area. The colonial soldiers became sick with vomiting and diarrhea. As most lay dying and the remaining few fled, Vaj Tuam Thaij, Pa Chay's leading general, marched victorious into town.[93]

Txooj Tsawb's testimony does contain fantastic elements, but his discussions of the way Pa Chay awarded titles to clan leaders in order to attract support, his troops' usage of poison and special weapons, and their employment of various tactical strategies are revealing of rational actions by people with an agenda. Pa Chay's followers posed a challenge to the French. Each successive victory over a vastly superior opponent was also proof to followers that Pa Chay had the Mandate of Heaven.

Losing the Mandate of Heaven

Yaj Txooj Tsawb pinpoints the vicious behavior of Pa Chay's men as the reason why the Hmong lost the Mandate of Heaven and, consequently, the war against the French. Vaj Tuam Thaij's victory at Muang Thaeng was also the tragic turning point for Pa Chay. When the French soldiers fled, the female inhabitants of the town surrendered to Vaj Tuam Thaij. They begged for their lives. Vaj Tuam Thaij was merciless. He permitted his soldiers to rape the women and pillage the town. Xyooj Teev not only raped but also killed and dissected the women, extracting their uteruses for examination. Bodily desecration is strictly tabooed in Hmong society; it is the rationale behind the Hmong reluctance to undergo autopsies and surgeries in current times.[94] Pa Chay had forbidden even the skinning of cows during the butchering process for the reason that it was not humane. Aware that Pa Chay would not approve of these atrocious acts, Vaj Tuam Thaij prohibited his men from speaking about them.

The Hmong often say, "Neeg tsis pom los Ntuj pom" (People may not see, but Heaven will).[95] It was not long before Vaj Tuam Thaij's men had to confess their sins to Pa Chay. Vaj Tuam Thaij could not occupy Muang Thaeng indefinitely. The French launched an attack on the garrison from the three major towns nearby. Vaj Tuam Thaij resisted the siege for days but was finally driven to desperation. He dispatched messengers to Pa Chay. As usual, Pa Chay raised the flag and summoned Heaven's protective powers. When he had finished the ritual, he proceeded with the usual test of invulnerability. Txooj Tsawb states: "He took out his sword and handed it to Nkaj Suav's Yaj's kinsmen. Nkaj Suav's relative took the sword and struck Pa Chay's shoulder. Blood spurted forth! Pa Chay cried [in pain]. He said, 'You people, when you went to battle, you committed a shameful act against Heaven and Earth. Now we stand in shame before Heaven and Earth. Whoever has done wrong must confess before this altar. Will anyone come forth to confess?'"[96]

Lauj Tuam Thaij, one of the messengers, stepped forward to tell about the rape, murder, and dissection of the Lao and Hmong women at Muang Thaeng. He begged that Pa Chay render a final judgment on the troop. Should Pa Chay determine that they had sinned and no longer had the Mandate of Heaven, they would humbly abandon the movement and surrender to the oppressive colonial authorities. Pa Chay said they had broken the laws of Heaven and lost the mandate, indeed. It was useless to struggle further since they would not win. They must endure unconditional surrender to the French.

When the men reported Pa Chay's orders, Vaj Tuam Thaij did not agree to surrender. He insisted on going to battle in order to ascertain Pa Chay's claim. He stated proudly: "In the past, we won every battle. I carried the flag every day. Bullets hit my ears and forehead, bruising but not penetrating them. Don't be afraid! Ask him [Pa Chay] to plead [with Heaven]. Don't let him do that [abandon the cause] so quickly. Let me alone bear the burden of this battle. I will be the one who protects all of us. If I fail he can then allow his generals to surrender."[97]

Vaj Tuam Thaij's men went to plea once more with Pa Chay, subsequently persuading him to release the three thousand soldiers under his command to go and rescue the besieged forces at Muang Thaeng. Pa Chay stipulated, however, that his disciples and generals must remain behind and take the women and children to surrender to the French.

Vaj Tuam Thaij alone led Pa Chay's soldiers into battle. His men fired first, using Pa Chay's cannon. The explosion killed four Vietnamese soldiers. The return fire from the enemy, however, killed Lwv, the man endowed with the physical prowess to fire the cannon from his shoulder. Undeterred, Vaj Tuam Thaij took off his shirt and bared his chest defiantly. He snatched up the magic flag and summoned Heaven's protection. The enemy fired a single shot, killing him in his tracks. The bullet did not bounce off as before. Another man picked up the flag and waived it to summon Heaven's aid, but the enemy's next volley of machine-gun fire killed four more Hmong. Within minutes fourteen men lay dead. The Hmong were no longer invulnerable. They retreated in desperation, each fleeing for his life. The colonial soldiers chased and shot them down one by one.[98] Pa Chay's army was decimated that day. Back at his headquarters, Pa Chay's disciples and other generals prepared to surrender to the French. Pa Chay's war had come to an end.

Though tragic, this last part of the story is perhaps the most significant section of the narrative. Txooj Tsawb's testimony builds to this climactic point, with the primary purpose of explaining how the Hmong had lost the Mandate of Heaven. Other incidents had also portended the final fall. Unlike Pa Chay, so the narrative goes, followers failed to exercise kindness, humility, patience, and moral virtues. They were arrogant and disobedient even during earlier stages of the movement. The first breach of celestial mandate occurred when Pa Chay's uncle prematurely opened a mysterious flying chest. Shortly after Pa Chay had gathered his disciples together and before open rebellion ignited, a chest with written instructions flew into the house. Pa Chay read the instructions to the crowd: "They said that inside is something good, that we must set the chest in a good place, and patiently await the right moment to release its contents. When these things are released, wherever they go in the land, peace will reign."[99] While Pa Chay went to look for a secure place to store the chest in his bedroom, his uncle pried it open, filling the house with grasshoppers. Everyone attempted to put as many of the grasshoppers as they could capture back into the chest, but it was found to be empty three days later. "Everyone wants to find a country; how come they have such a disobedient, impatient heart?" Pa Chay asked. "Because of this the Big Person will not be able to help us in this important task."[100] The hope of victory was undermined early on.

The timing of the rebellion was also premature, again spurred on early by Pa Chay's impatient uncle. Long before the Hmong were ready, Pa Chay's uncle complained that the Lao were oppressing them, conscripting them to work as slaves in their paddy fields. The uncle insisted that Pa Chay take action to remedy this wrong. Pa Chay's response was to burn incense and ask for Heaven's deliverance from oppression. Then he returned to his uncle and, in line with his patient nature, told his uncle to wait six years to see how events developed. His uncle angrily replied that the Lao were not only corrupt but also disrespectful. Those who sought meetings to discuss grievances were forced to crawl and sit until their legs went numb only to be subjected to a verbal assault and dismissed without being heard. Pa Chay must lead the Hmong against these corrupt figures. As the uncle was complaining loudly, a Hmong loyalist overheard him. The man reported to the authorities that a Hmong uprising was brewing. Colonial troops were dispatched to investigate, resulting in the first head-on encounter.[101] The theme of Hmong betraying Hmong also appears for the first time here.

Ultimately, impatience was less significant compared to the rampant disregard for life by Vaj Tuam Thaij's men. The rape and murder of the women at Muang Thaeng betrayed a sacred Hmong belief concerning the sanctity of the body that must not be desecrated even in death. The crime was heinously in-humane. The failure to show pity for their captors made Hmong men unfit rulers. For many reasons, Heaven nullified its support for the Hmong.

Pa Chay Lives

The final segment of Txooj Tsawb's testimony focuses on the assassination of Pa Chay by a Hmong and four "Mab Daum" (Khmu) assassins, and his triumph over death.[102] After Pa Chay's army was decimated, he left his village and went with his wife to live in an isolated crop field he cultivated in a jungle. Although he had abandoned his pursuit of a Hmong kingdom, he carried with him the moral burdens of Hmong sinners. His death alone could compensate for the transgressions. Like other prophets, Pa Chay knew when and how he would die. Three days before his death, Pa Chay summoned his brother-in-law to the field and told him he would soon die at the hands of assassins. "Let me die to atone for this sin," Pa Chay said to his brother-in-law.[103] Pa Chay also told his wife about the forthcoming tragedy, to which he was resigned. He instructed her not to bury his body immediately. She was to arrange his corpse in a sitting position behind their house back at their home village until animals appeared to dig a hole in which to bury it. Pa Chay told his wife to return to their village while he remained alone to face his final ordeal. She would know of his death when thunder and rain announced it, he said.

Following the anticipated rainstorm, Pa Chay's headless body was found in the field and transported back to the village as he had instructed. Sure enough, during the night a tiger and an antelope (*tus kauv*) came to dig the hole for Pa Chay's corpse. The lion dug the area for the head and the antelope the area for the lower extremities. The next morning relatives interred Pa Chay's body in this sanctified ground. The act of predator and prey combining efforts to bury Pa Chay has literal and symbolic significance. Indeed, after the tide had turned against Pa Chay, the Hmong (the prey) who did not want to be punished for the rebellion hunted down Pa Chay's men, collected their heads, and brought them to the French (the predators) for bounty.[104] The French disposed of the decapitated heads while the relatives of the dead men buried the bodies. It is also believed that Hmong informants provided the French with the strategies to defeat Pa Chay.[105] The narrative of Hmong betraying Hmong is revealed again here through symbolic imagery.

Pa Chay's ordeal did not end with his death. The narrative concludes with Pa Chay transcending mortality. After the assassins took his head, they made for the Ma River, which flows toward Hanoi. The part of the river where people crossed back and forth was only knee-deep, but the rainstorm that had announced Pa Chay's death had caused a great flood. The assassins had to cross the river on a bamboo raft. They placed Pa Chay's head in a bag and tied it to the raft. Halfway across the river the bag fell into the water and was carried away by the current. The assassins searched for three days before they found the bag on top of a tree. They retrieved it, but the head inside was no longer that of Pa Chay. "Pa Chay was a charismatic (*muaj tsim*), handsome man," said Txooj Tsawb, "The Hmong conspirator [named Qhua Kuam] with the Khmu had a hairy face with a beard. Lo and behold, the head inside the bag had a hairy face with a beard, resembling exactly that of Qhua Kuam."[106]

The bounty hunters brought the head to the French anyway. To confirm its identity, the head was shown to a French officer who had previously seen Pa Chay. The officer said it was not the head of Pa Chay and accused the assassins of having murdered an innocent man just to collect five hundred silver coins. The killers insisted it was indeed the head of Pa Chay. They had also captured Pa Chay's rifle that had his name carved on it, so it boosted their credibility a bit. Nevertheless, the French only paid the assassins two hundred silver coins. They were told to come back for the rest of the reward when it was established conclusively that Pa Chay had died. The assassins had no choice but to agree.

On their way home, at the juncture where the road diverged to the Khmu's country, Qhua Kuam keeled over by the roadside. His Khmu comrades rushed to lift him up only to find a headless corpse. His head had been severed so long ago that the blood around the neck wound was cauterized and the neck rotten. Qhua Kuam's relatives who came to fetch his body suspected that his fellow assassins had killed and taken his head to be offered to the French as that of Pa Chay. They had to let the matter drop, however, because the two Hmong witnesses who had traveled with the group up the mountains corroborated the Khmu's story. "Some say they [the Khmu] were foreigners [*mab sua*]. He [Qhua Kuam] had betrayed his own king, however, so Heaven exacted restitution from him."[107] Hmong betraying Hmong and bearing the consequences of the betrayal has become a familiar metatext of messianic revolts. The head of disputed identity was buried on a mountain near a Buddhist temple, thus bringing to an end Pa Chay's War.

Modern historians tend to emphasize the economic and political causes of Pa Chay's revolt, but for the Hmong the moral elements are primary. The stories of the revelation, ascension to Heaven, incredible physical feats, and other superhuman abilities are taken as proof of Pa Chay's legitimacy. Overall, Txooj Tsawb's eloquent narrative—undoubtedly a compendium of multiple oral accounts—can be read as a collective memory of the rebellion retained by the Hmong. Although the account contains fantastic elements, Txooj Tsawj's testimony finds some coherence and meaning, when placed against the backdrop of Hmong cultural expectations. This testimony is the megaexplanation for the loss of the dream of the Hmong kingdom.

The Goals of the Rebellions

Although the colonial authorities conceded that Hmong rebellions were rooted on economic grounds, they glossed over these reasons to emphasize the irrational aspects of the movements. Even the more sensitive observers dismissed Hmong prophets as "madmen," thus negating the validity of their actions. There was no attempt to understand these uprisings from the indigenous perspective, as doing so would have required the colonial masters to step down from their privileged position and to venture well beyond their cultural comfort zone to empathize with their subjects—a step that was virtually impossible for many colonizers, who believed in the temporal and moral superiority of their own race.

We understand the rationale and aim of Mi Chang's and Pa Chay's rebellions more clearly by considering the sociocultural context in which they flourished. Mi Chang highlighted the difficult run-in with the colonial authorities as impetus for his revolt. His prolonged illness and miraculous healing, and the manifestations of his mastery over languages and other abilities, helped to convince his frustrated community that he was the long-awaited divine liberator, sent to free them from oppressors. Mi Chang's linguistic skills, perhaps both real and imagined, were the major lure for the Hmong. Language had often paved the way for Hmong men to become political brokers. The ability to communicate with state authorities allowed Mi Chang to become more than a messianic figure endowed with supernatural powers; he was also a legitimate political broker. He had connections to the divine as well as the higher authorities of the state, the Chinese, the French, and others.

Mi Chang's other statements provide insight into the political rationale that guided his actions—a logic based on Confucian concepts of the Mandate of Heaven. When asked if he intended to become a leader, he replied, "I cannot say if I want to or not; it is up to the higher powers to decide." The higher power in this case was Heaven. Mi Chang stuck to this rationale throughout his interrogation. Even the names, titles, and ranks he distributed to his followers came from the divine. For example, when asked about the distribution of names and titles, Mi Chang replied, "Xiong Chinh Minh . . . presented himself to me at Lung Vai. It is I who gave him this name [Chin Minh] because the spirits told me to."[108] Furthermore, "the spirits gave them their ranks."[109] Every act was dictated by "the spirits," gods, or Heaven. This claim reveals Mi Chang's understanding of his own behavior. He had submitted in total to the Mandate of Heaven. This argument indirectly challenged the French and Chinese authorities. Heaven had summoned him to rebellion, meaning that the Chinese and French authorities had lost the mandate to rule over the Hmong. Heaven was using him as a vessel through which to render justice in the face of state corruption. Naturally, the French had to dismiss his words as the "mad" babblings of a man who was now caught and looking to evade responsibility for his actions. To lend credence to Mi Chang's testimony was to concede that the state was, indeed, corrupt and inept in its rule.

As for Pa Chay's War, we have two divergent accounts. French reports focus on the rationale for defeating Pa Chay and the military and political strategies used to quell the rebellion. Like Mi Chang, Pa Chay was a "madman" wreaking havoc on the innocent population. Although the French conceded that economic and political exploitation had driven the Hmong to rebel, they were not interested in addressing these concerns. Their primary aim was to maintain show of force so as to obtain definitive submission.

For the Hmong, Pa Chay's movement, like that of Mi Chang, aimed to capture the Mandate of Heaven. Not only was it a political and economic movement, but it was also a moral and spiritual one. Pa Chay's appearance, accompanied by literacy and supernatural power, was taken as a sign that the Hmong had earned the right to be a sovereign people. Although economic exploitation drove the movement, it did not dominate the narrative — a sign that it was not a primary concern. In other words, the Hmong were not merely reactionary. They had an agenda, a dream they wanted to realize. The attainment of the kingdom was synonymous with achieving moral perfection. And it was because the Hmong had engaged in immoral behavior that they lost the ability to reconsolidate the kingdom. Pa Chay's triumph over death was, however, the signal that the dream had merely gone latent.

Part II

The Secular
Political Tradition

A Mandate by Proxy

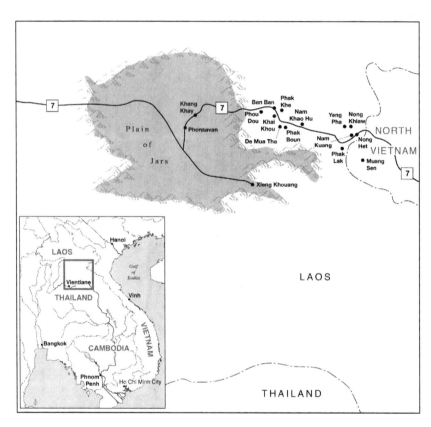

Map 3. Hmong villages in the Nong Het region. (Map by University of Wisconsin Cartography Lab)

The Creation of
a Supreme Hmong Chief
(1900–1935)

The Hmong of Southeast Asia came from multiple regions of China, led by different clan leaders who traced their legitimacy back to the Middle Kingdom. The leaders of the most dominant clans mention an ancestor who had been a tribal official with titles bestowed by the Qing state. As these clans migrated into Southeast Asia, they fought to maintain clan autonomy. By 1910, when the French began constructing CR7 and appointed Lo Blia Yao as the project supervisor, the lucre of the position only intensified clan competition. Blia Yao's control of the road budget and his refusal to share the bounty of his post aroused the envy of many. Ultimately, the colonial state's attempt to consolidate authority in a single paramount chief—done for the efficacy of control, or so they thought—backfired, setting into motion a tumultuous struggle for paramountcy in colonial Indochina. Thus, at the edge of empire, the natives affected the direction of historical events.

Once they had arrived en masse in Southeast Asia in the mid-nineteenth century, the main task of the Hmong was to reconstitute their society, which had been shattered by war and displacement. The clan elders who traced their leadership to China exhibited oratorical skills and distinguished themselves with wealth accumulation. Much like the lowland Lao aristocrats, the most influential clans forged marriage alliances with one another in order to consolidate authority over their clienteles.[1] The most ambitious men also obtained state legitimation as supreme chiefs in their respective regions. As noted in chapter 1, in Nong Het, the Ly and Lo clans were the first to acquire titles from the Phuan princes by offering rhinoceros horns as tribute. The Ly and Lo *kaitongs* were discredited after leading the 1896 rebellion, however. Moua

155

Kaitong dominated for several decades, but by the early twentieth century, Lo clan prestige was renewed through the political ingenuity of Lo Blia Yao, the son of Lo Pa Tsi. Blia Yao snared the support of multiple clans by orchestrating marriage alliances and obtaining French backing.

By 1910 Blia Yao was the paramount Hmong leader in Xieng Khouang. He was the *tasseng* of Keng Khoai and, signifying his legendary status, he was referred to as Lo Kaitong.[2] French backing contributed to Blia Yao being the most renowned Hmong *tasseng* in Laos. Perhaps because Blia Yao had infused his position with so much prestige, while other clan leaders also obtained this same bureaucratic title, the *tasseng* of Keng Khoai was perceived as the most distinguished one; he was the legitimate leader of the Hmong. Touby Lyfoung, Blia Yao's grandson and successor, writes, "The Hmong say the *tasseng* of Keng Khoai has authority and prestige far beyond the region of Nong Het. For this reason, every Hmong leader in the vicinity of Nong Het coveted the title, *tasseng* of Keng Khoai."[3] Understandably, the competition for Blia Yao's position after his death in 1935 was the origin of the Hmong division into leftist and rightist camps after World War II — the consequence resulting in driving half the Hmong population of Laos into exile across the globe. French creation of a "Hmong king" and the competition by Hmong to capture its authority had massive implications for Hmong history and society and, more important, also for the French colonial empire. The Hmong, embroiled in wars since 1945 and entangled in the struggle to survive culturally and linguistically in Southeast Asia, as well as in the West, since 1975, have yet to grasp fully the grave consequences of internal competitions for this position. We examine here the means whereby Blia Yao obtained Hmong and French legitimation to emerge as paramount in Xieng Khouang, formerly Muang Phuan.

Lo Pa Tsi and the China Legacy

The lack of studies about how Hmong leaders emerged and how leadership transitions occurred in highland society makes it difficult to generalize about Hmong political organization. The Hmong often say they have no leader — a sentiment expressed in the ancient tales about the lost kingdom and king. As noted earlier, outside observers like Yan Riyu claim that the "Miao" have no hereditary leadership.[4] I dispute this proposition, of course, in another work where I use marriage alliances and kinship structure to argue that Hmong leadership transition or inheritance, at least during the last century and a half in Southeast Asia, has occurred through women. Others, blinded by patriarchal lenses that anticipate direct male successions, miss this fact.[5] When we account for how women complicate Hmong politics and examine the oral sources of this period, there appears to be a continuity of leadership from China. Hmong chiefs in Southeast Asia trace their authorities to the ancient homeland, where their ancestors were legitimated by the Chinese state through its *tusi* (native superintendency) system.[6] These figureheads reconstituted their influence in Southeast Asia and passed their heritage on to succeeding generations. For this reason, the legacy of Blia Yao's family history played a large role in priming him for the preeminent position he came to occupy in 1910.

Blia Yao was the son of Pa Tsi, a first-generation migrant to Southeast Asia who made his mark early on as a clan leader and wealthy individual. Pa Tsi was a rebel leader who led Hmong troops against the Qing in the mid-nineteenth century. He was defeated and chased across the border into Vietnam, accompanied by his closest bodyguard, Yang Zong Cher.[7] Pa Tsi's leadership skills soon distinguished him among the Hmong in the Tonkin highlands, the area dominated by the White Tai. He became the recognized leader of the Lo clan before long. His political skill was evident in his ability to forge marriage alliances with the most powerful clans.

Sometime around the middle of the nineteenth century, Pa Tsi settled among the Hmong of the Fan Si Pan, a mountain range west of the Red River in Tonkin. Among the Hmong of this region was the Ly clan, headed by Nhia Vu, who had also led his large group in battles with the Qing and had preceded Pa Tsi into the region. Unlike Pa Tsi, Nhia Vu had two elder brothers and a younger brother, Ja Lao. Although they were junior in the birth order, Nhia Vu and Ja Lao were the leaders of the clan by virtue of their charisma and oratorical skills. The elder two brothers were not as knowledgeable about customary law and rituals, the mark of leadership in those days. Nhai Vu's widespread influence lay in his large clan.[8]

A brilliant tactician, Pa Tsi recognized the advantages of a marriage alliance with the Ly clan. Among the Lys was a first cousin of Nhia Vu named Ly Va Ger, whose sister was twice widowed and thus open to a third, more political marriage. The moment they marry, Hmong women are called "mother," "daughter-in-law," or "sister-in-law" or they are addressed only by their husbands' names (as in "the wife of so and so") or the name of their eldest child, "the mother of so and so." Over time they are completely subsumed by these forms of address; their personal names disappear and are forgotten forever. For this reason, many women go down in history without a name. Today the Ly woman Pa Tsi married is remembered only in terms of her relation to her brother. My informant in the Ly clan, Ly Na Jalao, calls her "the sister of Va Ger" or "our aunt." I will call her "the Ly woman."

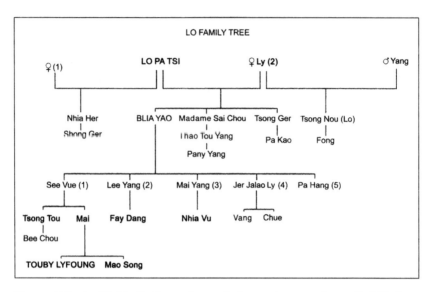

Figure 7. This simplified Lo family tree shows only the most important figures. Pa Tsi had two wives, and his second wife, the Ly woman, was formerly married to a Yang husband. Blia Yao, her son, was married to five women (the ordinal numbers represent the order in which they married Blia Yao), who bore him many children. Touby Lyfoung is a direct descendant of Blia Yao through his daughter Mai. (Graphic by Boua Chao Lee)

When the Ly woman's first husband, of the Yang clan, died suddenly, she married his younger brother in accordance with the Hmong's levirate tradition. During this second marriage, she gave birth to Tsong Nou. After her second husband also passed away, she was a widow with two young children, Shoua Long by her first marriage and Tsong Nu by her second. Pa Tsi took the Ly woman as a second wife, obtaining the strong backing of Nhia Vu's group.[9] This marriage alliance solidified two generations of collaboration between the Ly and Lo clans, maintaining the political support essential to Pa Tsi and his son by the Ly woman, Blia Yao (see Lo family tree, fig. 7).

As part of the negotiations between Pa Tsi and the Yang clan, the Ly woman was allowed to bring her infant son, Tsong Nu, into the Lo clan with her—a rare exception to Hmong customary practice—while her elder son remained in the Yang clan.[10] Hmong usually keep boys within their paternal clans, mostly awarding girls to the woman during a divorce or, as in this case, the marriage of a widow to a member of another clan. The reason for this exception may have been that Tsong Nu was still a nursing infant who would not have survived without his mother. Also, as I note below, Pa Tsi may have been a close affinal kinsman of the Ly woman's Yang husbands. Hence, Tsong Nu, who was of the Yang bloodline, was adopted into the Lo clan and became the grandfather of the renowned Lo Fong, whose education rivaled that of the Lyfoung brothers.[11]

The situation of Tsong Nu's adoption from the Yang into the Lo clan merits deeper analysis here because it is one of the multiple connections to this clan that Blia Yao, as well as his sons Fay Dang and Nhia Vu (he should not be confused with Ly Nhia Vu), exploited in order to boost his political influence. Hmong men like Tsong Nu who are adopted away from their paternal clan through marriage in traditional society may relinquish their clan name but not their loyalty to it. In other words, someone like Tsong Nu would have continued to maintain a tie with his Yang bloodline, and he would have strictly observed marriage taboos with both the Yang and Lo clans. This is especially true given that his brother by the same mother, Shoua Long, had been left in the Yang clan. Moreover, Blia Yao, Tsong Nu's half brother born to the same mother, would have also claimed Shoua Long and his Yang clan as relatives and potential allies even though he should not have observed the marriage taboo with the Yangs. Blia Yao's second and third wives were, indeed, from the Yang clan, although we do not know if they were of the same lineage as his half brothers, Tsong Nou and Shoua Long. Whatever the case, this early alliance made by Pa Tsi had political repercussions across multiple generations. It afforded Pa Tsi and his descendants not only alliances with the Ly clan but also with the Yang.

In addition to his adopted son Tsong Nu, Pa Tsi had three biological children with the Ly woman: Blia Yao; Madame Sai Chou Yang; and Tsong Ger, who was known as Tsong Ger the Blind (Txooj Ntxawg dig muag) because of his loss of sight. Blia Yao's sister, whose name we also do not know, married Sai Chou Yang, further tying Blia Yao to the Yang clan. Madame Sai Chou was the mother of the legendary Thao Tou Yang, the first Hmong colonel in the Pathet Lao army and the Vang Pao equivalent on the left until his untimely death in a car accident in 1961.[12] During the period of revolutionary struggle, Fay Dang recruited Thao Tou and his many brothers to the Communist side against Touby.[13] Thao Tou was the military commander of the Pa Chay Company, named after the anticolonial messianic leader and composed exclusively of Hmong soldiers. He enjoyed a brilliant military career on the Communist side as the commander who legitimated Fay Dang as a preeminent Hmong leader. After Thao Tou's death, his nephew Praseurt Yang, also a nationalist revolutionary hero in the Lao PDR, succeeded him as the commander of the Pa Chay Company and was also killed during the war (see Praseurt's grave monument in fig. 4).[14]

The Lo and Yang clans have maintained a close marriage alliance. Thao Tou's sister Mai married Vang, the half brother of Fay Dang and eldest son of Blia Yao's favorite fourth wife, Jer Jalao Ly.[15] In short the relationship between the Lo and Yang clans has been solidified in multifaceted ways across multiple generations from the time of Pa Tsi in the mid-nineteenth century down to the present. This alliance was instrumental in the political rise of the Lo family for three generations from Pa Tsi to Blia Yao and, finally, Fay Dang. Moreover, this alliance seems to have stretched back to China, long before their arrival in Southeast Asia, as evidenced by Pa Tsi and Zong Cher's close relationship as commander and bodyguard as noted earlier. Pa Tsi's marriage to the Yang widow, the Ly woman, may also have had something to do with a prior relationship between himself and the Yangs. Hmong usually prefer to have younger brothers or someone close enough to be perceived in that guise marry a widow of the clan. There are indications that Pa Tsi was closely related to the Yang husbands of this widow, as evidenced by the marriage and also the fact that the widow was allowed to bring her infant son into Pa Tsi's clan. We do not have the information to sketch out the relation, but these events indicate a prior alliance.

Pa Tsi's relationship with the Ly clan was also crucial to his family's politics across several generations. Not long after his marriage to the Ly woman, Pa Tsi and Ly Nhia Vu decided to take their clans and affinal relatives to Nong Het, just across the Vietnamese border in northeastern Laos. According to Keith Quincy's informants from the Vue clan, the first group of Hmong was drawn to the region on the advice of a Chinese opium merchant who told them that the lush jungle and fertile soil were ideal for growing this cash crop. These Vue clan members appear to have been the first migrants into Nong Het (Rhinoceros Lake).[16] Pa Tsi and Nhia Vu also heard of this promising land that was unoccupied and good for crop cultivation. At that time the Lao, Khmu, Yao, and others lived at lower elevations, but only wild animals inhabited the heights.[17] As evidenced by the historical struggles between Hmong and Tai in Tonkin, the decision to migrate across such a vast distance into Nong Het might have to do with the political tensions with Tai feudal lords as well. Pa Tsi and Nhia Vu, the leaders of their respective clans, may have deemed it better to relocate their families away from Tai domination. They chose to relocate to the eastern fringes of Muang Phuan. This mountainous highland zone kept them relatively isolated from the Phuan authorities.

The Ly and the Lo clans settled in the region the Hmong call Nong Het (see map 3), in Muang Kham. They founded the village of Yeng Pha (Yeej Phaj Pas Ntxhw, or Yeng Pha, "Elephant Lake"), located at the base of a large mountain called Tsua Ntuj (Heavenly Mountain). When they arrived in 1856, the lush jungle of the area enclosed a huge lake where elephants, rhinoceroses, monkeys, lions, tigers, and other wild creatures came daily to drink. Later the lake dried up due to use and deforestation, and many of the animals were hunted to extinction. While the Lo clan settled at Yeng Pha, the Ly clan subsequently relocated about seven kilometers away and founded the village of Nong Khiaw (Green Lake), whose settlers consisted exclusively of Nhia Vu's large clan.[18] This Ly lineage became widely known as the Lys of Nong Khiaw (Hmoob Lis Noom Khiam).

Although it is generally assumed that Hmong society is egalitarian, the oral sources reveal wealth as a distinguishing characteristic of men like Pa Tsi and Nhia Vu, priming them to become clan leaders and political brokers for the ethnic group. When the two leaders first arrived, according to Ly Na, Nhia Vu was the first to obtain recognition from the Phuan. The Ly family killed a rhinoceros and presented its horn to the Phuan, who invested Nhia Vu with the title *kaitong*. Pa Tsi followed suit when his own clan members killed a rhinoceros, and he also received the title, which was later passed down to Blia Yao in the twentieth century.[19] It can be imagined that Pa Tsi and Nhia Vu each had authority mainly over his own clansmen in the mid-nineteenth century, but once they had legitimation from the Phuan rulers, clans of lesser influence would have looked to them to settle disputes when no consensus could be reached among themselves. Thus, it could be expected that these two *kaitongs* played important roles as adjudicators in dispute cases involving thievery, divorce, murders, or other issues. As such, their authorities, legitimated by the state, rose above others. Their influence also lay in their large clans. The Lo and Ly clans were arguably the two most numerous groups in Nong Het.[20] With state authority weak in the heights, Hmong leaders who possessed the manpower became the executors of justice. Their large clans enforce their rulings. For this reason, Nhia Vu and Pa Tsi probably were looked up to as adjudicators of disputes by smaller clans. Intermarriages between their clan members also bound the two as preeminent allies.

We do not have much information about Nhia Vu's wealth, although his family's political influence in the modern era hints of it. Over a century later, Nhia Vu's descendants still ranked among the wealthiest Hmong of Xieng Khouang. Vang Pao's rise to power, according to Dia Yang, a granddaughter of Madame Sai Chou Yang, was aided by the wealth of Ly Nhia Long, the grandson of Nhia Vu. Before becoming Hmong leader in the 1960s, Vang Pao married Nhia Long's daughter, True, as a minor wife and obtained the financial and political support of the Ly clan.[21] On the other hand, the oral evidence about Pa Tsi's wealth is well established by the extant account surrounding the theft of his buried silver that resulted in his assassination in the mid-nineteenth century. Pa Tsi was reputedly the richest man in Nong Het. This may have been the primary reason for his influence during the period. He lived in Yeng Pha with members of his Lo clan and his trusted bodyguard, Zong Cher, who called him "father."[22]

When Pa Tsi first arrived in Nong Het, the Hmong leaders in the region, probably members of the Vue and Moua clans who preceded him to the area, were getting old and the clans were receptive to new leaders. Endowed with his leadership experience in China, Pa Tsi quickly distinguished himself through his business ingenuity and language skills. As the Hmong fled from China into Indochina, pursued closely by Chinese soldiers, a contingent of Haw Chinese merchants and rebels traveled with them. The merchants who were familiar with the territory and interacted with lowland officials through their business dealings may have been instrumental in guiding and perhaps even brokering relations between Hmong and non-Hmong as noted above in the story of Ton Ma, who first led the Vue clan into Nong Het. Despite the bloody revolt against Qing oppression, the Hmong leaders were receptive to alliances with these Haw merchants. A symbiotic relationship may have existed between them in China as well—perhaps indicative of the fluidity of ethnic relations during this early period, as Daniel McMahon notes in his work.[23] Evidently, personal ties and individual relations were more important than ethnicity—a supposition that perhaps sheds light on the multiethnic rebellions in China, even those that were attributed to specific ethnic groups like the "Miao."[24]

In the Southeast Asian highlands, the Haw merchants who circulated among the Hmong made up an essential component of their opium economy, exchanging silk, salt, and iron implements that they obtained in the humid lowlands for opium grown by Hmong in the cool highlands. In Nong Het these merchants established business relations with Pa Tsi, who was fluent in Chinese. Pa Tsi's rise to leadership resulted largely from his role as a middle-man, brokering opium deals between the Chinese merchants and the Hmong villagers. He became so rich as a result of these business dealings that he was able to maintain a small army.[25] He probably used this militia to ensure the safety of traders passing through his region, thereby making them loyal allies. A combination of business ingenuity and military experience allowed Pa Tsi to become rich and influential.

Hmong usually keep their wealth hidden so as not to arouse jealousy in others, but Pa Tsi could not conceal his affluence because his wealth stirred a legendary scandal that involved his assassination by Zong Cher, his trusted bodyguard and lone companion from China. The story is that Pa Tsi had buried silver treasure troves, which were inadvertently discovered by a member of the Moua clan, the elder brother of Pa Tsi's son-in-law, who dug them all up. Circumstances led Pa Tsi to accuse and torture Zong Cher, who afterward held a deep-seated grudge. When everyone least expected it, Zong Cher struck, assassinating Pa Tsi in his home in 1866.[26] Zong Cher ran away, but he was chased down and killed by Pa Tsi's relatives. The truth about the Moua family stealing Pa Tsi's wealth was unveiled years later, but that revelation involved yet another tragic scandal—one even more horrible in the eyes of the Hmong— the exhumation of Pa Tsi's body by the Yangs.[27]

The Hmong, who observe geomancy when choosing grave sites for their deceased, also hold strict views about grave desecration. They believe that disturbing a grave in any way can bring about unaccountable disasters for multiple generations of descendants. "To cause misfortune for descendants," said Tougeu Lyfoung while relaying Pa Tsi's story to me, "the Chinese have been known to dig up Hmong grave sites in the past. For this reason, some Hmong lineages started to conceal their identities by constructing Chinese-style graves for their deceased back in China, ultimately passing the practice down to their descendants today."[28] Due to Hmong beliefs about grave desecration, over the years the legends about the Moua family stealing Pa Tsi's wealth and his exhumation by the Yangs have become the theoretical launching pad, the megaexplanation, for the fall of Blia Yao's family from power in 1936.[29] I would argue the reverse, however, and say that this legend actually serves to solidify the reputation of Pa Tsi as a figure of unimagined wealth and influence. The legend was also the launching pad for Blia Yao's rise to power from 1910 to 1936 and his descendants' continued influence in the Lao PDR today. The incident made the family known for generations as Pa Tsi's name echoed through time.

When Pa Tsi was assassinated, his son Blia Yao was a mere toddler who had only begun to learn to "play bullfight" (*txawj ua nyuj sib nraus*) by holding two index fingers on either side of his temples and pretending to be a bull while butting heads with other children. Based on that description, Mao Song estimates that he was probably no more than three or four years old.[30] Over the decades, as he was growing up, the story of his father's exhumation, perhaps also infused with his personal charisma, established Blia Yao as a legendary figure in Nong Het, paving the way for the orphan to become the most renowned Hmong leader of all time.

The Rise of Lo Blia Yao (1910–35)

Some members of the Lo clan in exile argue that Blia Yao rose to power solely because of his willingness to act as an instrument of the French. He helped spearhead the construction of CR7, the major road that links northern Laos and Vietnam. In return for his complicity, the colonial masters installed him as the leader of the Hmong. These Lo clan members do not paint a positive picture of Blia Yao. They characterize him as willful and vindictive from his earliest days. Xai S. Lor states, "'As a young boy . . . he was the most mischievous person [and] no one dared argue with him. If he lost a rooster fight, he would sneak an attack on his opponent's rooster until he was satisfied with the injury he had inflicted.'"[31] Blia Yao was also an irresponsible youth with a gaming addiction, said Lor. He spent his days chasing and hunting down wild beasts rather than tending to his chores.

Admittedly, these opinions contain overtones of bias, perhaps influenced by political partisanship. Critical informants of the Lo clan were among those who had sided with Touby Lyfoung as well as Vang Pao to fight Blia Yao's Communist sons since the 1940s. They may also be descendants of Lo clan members who had sided with Lo Shong Ger during Pa Chay's War, and were punished or put to death. Obviously, these contemporary informants did not observe firsthand what Blia Yao was like as a child back in the nineteenth century. On the other hand, their opinions form portions of a historical memory about Blia Yao and also fashioned a powerful myth that bolstered his legendary status. For boys to possess bullylike qualities is not always perceived as negative in Hmong society. In fact, a strong will portends leadership qualities tantamount to what is characterized as an alpha male personality. Hmong believe that, geared in the right direction, boys with such willful tendencies often become great leaders—those who "can eat and speak" (*noj tau hais tau*), that is, those who are not afraid to act or take responsibility for what has to be done. Hence, what may seem like character defamation can also be interpreted as accolades for a worthy opponent. Such stories of unruly obstinacy and talents with a rifle, especially since the time of the Secret War when century-old stereotypes of the Hmong's martial valor have been revived, are essential components of the legends associated with Blia Yao.[32] Indeed, he possessed innate qualities and good pedigree, which allowed his ascension to power. This did not stop some from challenging his paramountcy, however. When he served more the interests of the colonial state, the Hmong turned to competing leaders.

The French were an important source of legitimacy for Blia Yao, but family legacy, personal charisma, wealth, and political foresight in arranging marriage alliances with multiple clans formed the foundation of his rise as well. The colonial masters were always keen on picking influential members from indigenous societies to do their bidding. Because Blia Yao was an extraordinary character, the French chose him as an instrument of their colonizing efforts, thereby raising his status above that of others. Blia Yao was the first Hmong leader in the fullest sense of the word, the political broker between the Hmong and the colonial state. As such, his authority transcended clan and cultural group boundaries, and he remains a towering character in the memory of the Hmong today.

As in the case of Pa Chay, orphanhood may have played a crucial role in fashioning Blia Yao into a legend. He was only a toddler when his father, Pa Tsi, was assassinated, but he inherited his father's wealth and status and became an influential leader. He also possessed unique qualities valued by the Hmong. According to Mao Song, he was a charismatic, sociable man who interacted easily with Hmong and non-Hmong alike. Tall and handsome, Blia Yao exuded a rare confidence and a strong presence (see fig. 8). From an early age, his social skills distinguished him from the crowd. "At that time," said Mao Song, "Hmong people viewed outsiders with a combination of fear and contempt. They often shut their doors when outsiders came into their villages. Grandfather Blia Yao was different. When non-Hmong officials showed up, he greeted them warmly and welcomed them into his home."[33]

Blia Yao was not without skills and learning either. Although I can no longer find living informants who could attest to his oratorical skills—his knowledge of the traditional rituals involving birth, marriage, and death—his distinction as a clan leader hint of such skills. Ritual knowledge was the requisite of a clan leader whose primary task was to adjudicate disputes between the living, and to ensure communication between humans and spirits, including ancestors. In traditional Hmong society, only ritual masters knew enough customary law to assume the role of being a judge. Thus, Blia Yao's distinction as a leader implies that he was the foremost ritual and genealogical expert of his clan. Furthermore, according to Henri Roux, the French military officer who was his sworn blood brother, Blia Yao was literate in Chinese.[34] In a society in which literacy was an important source of legitimacy, this would have had important ramifications. Blia Yao's ability to read Chinese distinguished him as unique among the multitude of clan and lineage leaders. It seems evident, then, that by the time the French came into contact with Blia Yao, he already stood out as a man of distinction. He had the skills to be a political broker for the Hmong.

Of course Blia Yao's wealth was also an important factor in his rise to power. Although some make the argument that Blia Yao became rich as a result

Figure 8. The last photograph of Lo Blia Yao, taken days before his death in January 1935. The writing below it is that of Touby Lyfoung, who, according to Tougeu Lyfoung, got the date of the photo (1925) wrong. Tougeu witnessed the taking of this photo in early 1935, he said. Note Blia Yao's Manchu hairstyle, with a shaven forehead and a queue (albeit not visible here) in the back. He also proudly displayed on his chest the medals awarded to him by the French. (Courtesy of Mao Song Lyfoung)

of skimming from the state budget allocated for the construction of CR7 and extorting money from rebels during Pa Chay's rebellion in 1920, it is evident that his wealth originated before that period.[35] As noted, Blia Yao inherited Pa Tsi's wealth, some of which he recovered from the Moua family, who had stolen it.[36] Henri Roux, who was also the French officer who oversaw the construction of CR7, attested to Blia Yao's wealth at the onset of the road construction. An anecdote related by Roux is quite telling. One day in 1914, the inspector of the Garde Indigene of Xieng Khouang offered to purchase Blia Yao's beautiful dapple-gray horse for four hundred piasters. The inspector was a great horseman who appreciated a fine breed. Far from being flattered, Blia Yao was insulted by the mere suggestion that he might sell his horse. Without saying a word, he showed the inspector some fifteen crates full of gold bars and silver jewelry, saying, "When I want to go to Xieng Khouang [a distance of 150 kilometers, which would take Blia Yao three days to travel], can your piasters be put on the road and can they transport me to the administrative center?" Roux further notes that a good horse at the time fetched about forty piasters.[37] Blia Yao was unimpressed by a sum ten times what the horse was worth because he had plenty of money.

Blia Yao was also not ashamed to show off his wealth. Part of his pride and joy was to dress his beautiful wives in it. The women of Blia Yao's household were never seen without heavy silver necklaces. Roux notes, however, that they never wore gold jewelry, of which Blia Yao possessed "some kilos'" worth. One day, communicating in Lao, Roux asked Blia Yao what was behind the Hmong fondness for these heavy necklaces so that even when his wives went about their chores they were never without them. Exhibiting a machismo attitude, Blia Yao replied, "It's very convenient because one can always tell what they're doing at night!" He was referring to the fact that the necklaces, which jingled at the slightest movement, functioned much like the bells tied around the necks of cattle. Upon hearing his remark, Blia Yao's fifth wife, Pa, who was not only "very young and pretty" but also "extremely smart," retorted, "That is why we are so fond of the handkerchiefs used for tying them and for preventing them from making any noise."[38]

Blia Yao was rich in material possessions as well. One thousand head of his cattle and numerous fowl roamed the mountains surrounding his village. When Roux learned of the declaration of war in Europe in 1914, he prepared to leave for France. Blia Yao, he noted, immediately sent him one hundred heads of cattle and a dozen capons to sustain him during the long trip. Blia Yao did not want him to waste time stocking up in the Vietnamese country. On September 7, 1914, Blia Yao accompanied Roux from the Keng Khoai Plateau in the midst of a rainstorm. Along came the hundred heads of cattle, the capons, and numerous horses that carried an ample supply of corn, all gifts from Blia Yao.[39] Roux's testimony attests to Blia Yao possessing great wealth even during the early days of their friendship. Undoubtedly, some of this wealth as well as Blia Yao's social standing was inherited from his father, Pa Tsi. Blia Yao also had a knack for cultivating close relations with outside authorities, giving him a decisive political advantage over other clan leaders.

Blia Yao's ingeniousness in arranging marriage alliances with the most powerful clans also contributed to his rise to power. He married five beautiful wives, chosen from the most influential clans in Xieng Khouang. These wives, symbols of his male potency and testaments to his wealth, were also the political links to other clans. The significance of the wives, albeit not fully understood given the lack of extant oral testaments, cannot be overemphasized. To understand the impact of Blia Yao's wives had on his political influence one has to understand how women and gender operate in Hmong society.

The important sphere Hmong women occupy in Hmong society is emphasized via folktales, which are recited again and again to children. As noted earlier, Hmong oral tradition often speaks of the plight of an orphan who becomes king by virtue of his wife's ingeniousness or her status as a princess, which brings him into alliance with her father, the king.[40] The Hmong often attribute a man's rise in position to his wife's diligence and intellect and to the political ties she brings to the marriage. The right woman makes a man, but, as the stories of Nkauj Nog and Niam Nkauj Zuag Paj remind us, foolishness in choosing the wrong woman or abandoning the right one can have dire consequences.[41] Because his wife can affect a man's wealth and standing, every Hmong man has to pay a hefty brideprice. Conversely, from the woman's perspective, a high brideprice reflects her appeal as a woman of value and often determines her social status within her husband's clan. Only the richest man can afford more than one wife, each of whom brings more resources into the family and increases his political ties, thereby expanding his influence.

For Blia Yao, the women in his life were crucial to his political influence. Perhaps the most prominent of his wives, the one that afforded him the strongest alliance, was his fourth wife, Jer Jalao Ly. Blia Yao's paramount authority was largely a result of his connections to Jer's clan, the Lys of Nong Khiaw. Of course, as noted earlier, Blia Yao was already tied to this clan, being descended from it on the maternal side. Blia Yao's mother was a Ly woman. Taking no chances, however, Blia Yao rekindled the Lo-Ly alliance by kidnapping Jer, the daughter of Ly Ja Lao and the niece of Kaitong Ly Nhia Vu, as a bride. The Lys of Nong Khiaw, because of their numbers, comprised a clan of considerable influence in Nong Het.[42] The leaders of the Ly "aristocrats," the brothers Nhia Vu and Ja Lao, traced their origins to southern China, where their family had reigned over an autonomous region from the days of the Ming dynasty.[43]

The Ly clan's influence was widespread in Xieng Khouang, stretching from Nong Khiaw north of Nong Het to the region of Khai Khu, located near the mountain chains surrounding Ban Ban, which was inhabited by Ly Tong Pao's group and to the southwest of the Plain of Jars, where Tasseng Lee Blia Tria was leader before 1945 and Tasseng Lee Za Lue was leader afterwards. Because the Hmong of Nong Het were later forced to migrate into this region south of the Plain of Jars, the Ly clan continued to exert considerable influence in Hmong politics into the Secret War period (1960–75), when Vang Pao presided as Hmong leader due to US backing. Having been drawn into politics by Touby Lyfoung during the colonial period and been rewarded by the French for their participation from early on, Ly clan members dominated the civil and military bureaucracies under both Touby and Vang Pao.

During the early twentieth century, Blia Yao's association with the Ly clan helped to secure his place as the most prominent leader in Nong Het. Among the first generation of Hmong born in Laos, he was still influenced by Chinese cultural traditions, however, as evidenced by the fact that he wore a Manchu style haircut (shaved his forehead and wore a queue) to the end of his life (see fig. 8). He was literate in Chinese, but not in Lao or French, the administrative languages of the region. Following French colonization in 1893, the dynamics of his family's literate power in Chinese changed. Blia Yao's fourth wife, Jer Jalao Ly (see fig. 9), would help make up for his shortcomings, however. She was the fairytale dragon princess who made the orphan, Blia Yao, a king. She not only facilitated the alliance with her large clan in Nong Khiaw but, according to Mao Song, she was also instrumental in strategizing Blia Yao's rise to power by cajoling Ly Foung, a fellow clan member, to be Blia Yao's secretary, expanding Blia Yao's authority. Mao Song stated:

> [Chaomuang] Neng Tong's aunt [Jer Jalao] was grandfather's [Blia Yao's] fourth wife. She and my father [Ly Foung] were brother and sister [first cousins], brother and sister but only relatives from China. [We] know that [we] are from the same clan only [i.e., don't know about actual blood ties]. So my father could read and speak Lao. My father knew how to speak, so grandfather constantly asked him to come over, and Neng Tong's aunt called my father, "dear uncle, dear uncle"—[in short,] expressing a lot of affection for my father. [She] expressed affection [for my father] because my father had speaking skills—knew how to discuss custom law, knew how to write and speak Lao and Chinese—so she was affectionate toward my father so that grandfather would be able to use him.[44]

Figure 9. A portrait of Blia Yao's family taken in Xieng Khouang in 1926. *Front, left to right*: Jer Jalao Ly; Choua Kue, third wife of Ly Foung; and Pa Hang, Blia Yao's fifth wife, who was famous for her beauty. *Back, left to right*: Mrs. Za Teng, Blia Yao's daughter-in-law; Lee Yang, Fay Dang's mother and Blia Yao's second wife; Blia Yao (in hat); and Za Teng, Blia Yao's son. (Courtesy of Mao Song Lyfoung)

Because Jer was instrumental in Blia Yao's rise to power, she herself exercised unusual influence and indirectly affected Hmong society in that time period. She often rendered judgments in disputes brought before Blia Yao. Being the favorite wife, Jer remained in the house to perform the domestic duties while the other wives worked in the fields, tending to the crops and animals. As she cooked and stirred the daily meals at the hearth, the men who came to seek Blia Yao's mediation in disputes would argue their cases nearby. Jer always kept a keen ear on the exchanges. After each group had testified, Blia Yao would turn to Jer and ask her how she would decide such a case. She would then recap the different arguments made by the men, weighing carefully all the evidence presented, and render her judgment accordingly. Mao Song continued, "After 'Madame Blia Jer' finished speaking, grandfather would turn to the men sitting before him and say, 'Do as Jer said.'"[45] Since Jer was an extremely intelligent woman, she often proved herself fair and reasonable, and Hmong tended to accept her judgments. Jer's influence over Blia Yao also allowed her to control his great wealth. When he died in 1935, she was left in charge of the whole sum of seven hundred silver bars, a huge fortune by the standards of the day.[46]

Jer's power arose from the fact that she was the daughter of Ja Lao and the niece of Nhia Vu, the leaders of the Ly clan. Deference to her judgment probably stemmed from the fact that her paternal Ly clan, as well as her husband's Lo clan, could and did enforce her decisions. Indeed, Jer's clan was the mainstay of Blia Yao's authority when his own clan turned against him in 1920. When Pa Chay's rebellion spread to Xieng Khouang, Blia Yao's nephew, Lo Shong Ger, sided with Pa Chay. The Ly clan saved Blia Yao from the rebels by hiding him in the nearby cave of Shila (Qhov Sislav).[47] The Ly clan also helped put down Shong Ger's rebellion. Reflecting their contribution, Ly clan members received three of the six French medals of commendation. According to Touby, those who got medals were Blia Yao, Ly Nhia Vu of Nong Khiaw, Ly Pa Yia of Nong Khiaw, Ly Vam Khue of Pha Kong Noi, Thao Saykao of Keng Khoai, and Kue Joua Kao of Phak Boun.[48]

Just as they were instrumental to Blia Yao's rise to power, members of Jer's Ly clan went on to play an influential role in Hmong history in the next half century. When the Ly clan sided with its own kinsman, Touby, and withdrew its support from Blia Yao's sons, the long history of the Lo influence came to an abrupt end. The support of the Lys was so essential to Hmong leaders of the period that when they started to back away from Vang Pao in the mid-1960s, he perceived them as a threat, alleging to the CIA that a Ly coup d'état was brewing in Military Region II.[49]

Undoubtedly, Blia Yao possessed the charisma, wealth, status, and political acumen to become a unique clan leader even before the arrival of the French. But because each Hmong clan operated autonomously, he needed outside legitimation in order to supersede the boundaries of the clan, in essence becoming a Hmong leader. The French who took possession of Indochina would provide Blia Yao the legitimacy he needed to achieve this end. During the first decade of the twentieth century, colonial officials began surveying the Nong Het region in order to construct a road linking the Lao kingdoms along the Mekong to Vietnam. The Hmong who lived in Nong Het anticipated correctly that a road would render their region vulnerable to the intrusion of the state. Many still retained memories of corrupt Chinese mandarins and were distrustful of outside authorities. Lowland officials were synonymous with corruption, extortion, and financial ruin. When they showed up in Hmong villages they had to be hosted with feasts and other luxuries befitting their standing, thereby becoming a huge burden on the population. Meanwhile, these authorities brought no perceivable benefit to Hmong society. If they ever showed up in Hmong villages, it was always to collect taxes, demand requisitions, or conscript laborers. The Hmong paid the highest tax of all, three or four times what lowland groups such as the Tai, Lao, and Vietnamese paid.[50] Those who could not pay were hauled off to lowland jails—a virtual death sentence in the eyes of the Hmong—until their relatives paid on their behalf. For what Hmong were exacted, they got nothing in return. There was no modern health and social programs, and the first school for Hmong children was not constructed until 1939.[51] Heavy taxes and harsh penalties for failure to pay were the major impetus behind Pa Chay's War in 1918.

Ambitious men were attracted to the colonial state, however. The state could provide the legitimation necessary to allow a man who faced a society segmented by clan and cultural divisions to become an influential political broker. In his position as the negotiator between the state and the Hmong, the broker could transcend social divisions to become, in essence, to borrow an apt Lao term, a Lord of Life (Chao Siwit) who dominates over the population. Outside legitimation gave Hmong leaders impetus to rise supreme. For this reason, the politically conscious clan leader found the state appealing.

Indeed, Lo clan members in the United States credit Blia Yao's rise to power to his close alliance with the colonial authorities. They tell of a chance opportunity that paved the way for Blia Yao to become the paramount Hmong leader of his time, displacing the Moua *kaitong* who had negotiated the peace settlement in 1896. When the French began surveying the Nong Het region to construct CR7, no Hmong leader would aid their efforts. They could not, however, overtly refuse to cooperate, so they conspired to lead the French through the most rugged mountains in hopes of discouraging them from building the road. French administrators were not oblivious to this clever scheme. They knew that Nong Het provided the best geographic setting for the road. Subsequently, they threatened to punish the Hmong if they did not cooperate. As no respectable Hmong leader wanted to play a part in constructing a road that would bring the Hmong more stringently under the French yoke, they all got together to formulate a plan that involved Blia Yao. Xai S. Lor puts it most succinctly: "The *kiatongs* and elders chose Bliayao [*sic*] to help the French since he was a trouble maker in the village and was not well respected. All he cared about was hunting so [they thought that] if the French were to kill him, it would not be a great loss to the Hmong community."[52]

The tone of Lor's remarks has to be tempered with his political partisan-ship as noted earlier. Evidence suggests that by the time the French came to survey the land for the construction of CR7, Blia Yao was already an established clan leader of some renown. As a descendant of the former Lo clan leader, Blia Yao could not have just been a nameless nobody in the early 1900s, but perhaps Lor's words can be understood in another way. Blia Yao may have also inherited his father Pa Tsi's propensity to take matters into his own hands—such as when Pa Tsi tortured the innocent Zong Cher, whom he suspected of having stolen his wealth—instead of consulting a group of leaders so as to reach a shared consensus about what to do, as was the tradition among the Hmong. Thus, it is likely that some Hmong resented Blia Yao's authoritarian ways. Lor's contention that Blia Yao was "a trouble maker" who was "not respected" could perhaps be a reflection of Blia Yao's dictatorial personality, which he often exhibited, prompt-ing even his own clan members to go against him. However people regarded Blia Yao, it is clear that his influence was the reason why he was singled out by the French. It is not the usual practice for colonial authorities to select those with no standing to represent them at the local level. Lor is extremely accurate, however, in pinpointing the significant impact Blia Yao's collaboration with the French had on his growing power as an ethnic representative in Nong Het.

In the backwoods of neglected Laos, where only a handful of colonial administrators with very limited resources had to forge a colony through alli-ances with indigenous leaders, cultivating personal relations had tremendous repercussions on both sides. On the indigenous side, Blia Yao's friendship with Henri Roux had major implications for his paramount authority. Blia Yao could not very well marry into Roux's family in accordance with Hmong tradi-tion, but he sealed their relation with a blood oath in 1914 after a two-year friendship. Roux was close to Blia Yao because Blia Yao had been instrumental in the road construction. When Blia Yao proposed that they become blood brothers, Roux agreed. He had come to admire Blia Yao and the Hmong for their martial skills, strength, and loyalty. In a ritual described by Roux, Blia Yao killed a chicken, mixed its blood with alcohol, and offered the drink to Roux after both had taken an oath of eternal friendship and fidelity. They promised to remain blood brothers for life.[53] This close alliance helped Blia Yao rise to power while facilitating Roux's effective role as an administrator in the region. The relationship was comparable to that between Auguste Pavie and Deo Van Tri in the Tonkin highlands several decades earlier. Just as Pavie was instrumental to the consolidation of French rule of the Vietnamese highlands, Roux played a similar role in Xieng Khouang by befriending Blia Yao.

Roux describes the blood pact with Blia Yao casually in his memoir without fully grasping how seriously Hmong men take the oath. As described by Hugo Adolf Bernatzik, the ritual involves summoning Heaven and the ancestors of both participants to witness the verbal promises made, which include the words "We are friends. If I become rich, you will too; if I become poor the same will happen to you." These words convey the idea that the brothers will share every human hardship against all odds. The vow is sealed with the drinking of the chicken blood mixed with alcohol. After that, "the two are regarded as brothers by others and share all their possessions with each other, [and] help and support each other in every way."[54] Whether or not Roux understood the seriousness of the oath, Blia Yao's loyalty to him and the French throughout his tenure in office can be traced back to this blood pact. I also did not fully grasp the seriousness of this oath of loyalty until April 2005, when Colonel Shoua Yang paid a visit to my home in Madison, Wisconsin, where he told me that he and other officers had partaken of this very ritual with General Vang Pao back in the 1960s. The colonel laughed heartily as he said, "We all took an oath never to part ways with Vang Pao, but I don't know why none of us who had parted ways with him after 1975 died or met with tragedy as we had promised. I guess the ritual oath lost its effectiveness in the West."[55] The colonel's quip provides us a unique insight into the differences between how Roux and Blia Yao may have perceived this ritual. Roux's view may have been tempered by his rational modernity, as evidenced by his casual description of the ritual, while Blia Yao, immersed in animist traditions like Colonel Yang, may have interpreted the pact between the two as a matter of life and death should the oath be broken. However different the two perceived the ritual, the oath was a sign to the Hmong of Blia Yao's legitimation by the French.

Blia Yao's preeminent role in the construction of CR7, his alliance with the colonial state, allowed him to centralize his authority, thereby becoming a paramount chief. He collected taxes and requisitions, and disseminated corvée labor orders to various clan leaders beneath him. Each village in the region of Nong Het was responsible for a certain section of the road. Ly Foung, Blia Yao's secretary, handled the paperwork required of Blia Yao's position. Families who could not provide labor had the option of converting their corvée obligation into cash payments that could be used to hire replacements.[56] The work was heavy, and people lost much time that could have been spent in their own fields cultivating their crops. Many Hmong moved away from the region to avoid conscription. Keith Quincy claims that Blia Yao was able to convince the French to increase wages, which served to stifle some protests, but he paid the Hmong the same wages as before and kept the additional portion of the funds, further increasing his wealth.[57] As Blia Yao grew in prestige and wealth through his association with the French, other ambitious Hmong men began to covet his position. Blia Yao's two literate secretaries, Shong Ger and Ly Foung, would exploit the general population's disillusionment to thwart Blia Yao's authority.

Vue Pa Chay Arrives in Laos (1920)

The close alliance with colonial authorities had fashioned Blia Yao into a much-feared figure in Xieng Khouang, but Pa Chay changed the state of things. Pa Chay's War and his defeat at the hands of the French bring to light the many contradictions of Blia Yao's leadership. The rebellion had the effect of bolstering Blia Yao's authority while at the same time serving to remove it. Pa Chay's appearance, signifying that the Mandate of Heaven was up for grabs, highlighted Blia Yao's role as an instrument of the French, but at the same time Pa Chay's subsequent defeat also attested to Blia Yao's legitimacy—in essence, Blia Yao's mandate. After the defeat of Pa Chay in 1921, Blia Yao was affirmed in his position as the paramount Hmong chief by the French. At the same time, however, the rebellion emboldened Blia Yao's underlings to wrest away his position. Blia Yao's cruel handling of the rebels following their defeat further alienated many, allowing his competitors to insert a wedge into his authority. As loyal as Blia Yao had been to the French colonial masters, their primary interest was to maintain peace in the backwaters of Laos, not to reward loyalty. For this, they willingly entertained the ambition of challengers.

At the end of 1919, Pa Chay's rebellion spread south from Dien Bien Phu into Luang Prabang and, ultimately, into Xieng Khouang, where the rebellion acquired an intensity of its own. Little is known about Pa Chay, but the movement in Laos sheds light on the grandeur of his vision. Pa Chay was an extraordinary character—purposeful, innovative, and a man with a vision far ahead of his time. As news of Pa Chay's successes against the French spread, providing proof of his heavenly mandate, the Hmong of Xieng Khouang who resented the corruption of the colonial authorities united behind him.

After fleeing from Dien Bien Phu in July 1919, Pa Chay went to Laos to recruit more followers to his cause. He found great appeal among those who were disillusioned with the French. Almost immediately the Hmong in the region of northern Luang Prabang, as well as those in western Sam Neua, rose in rebellion. Using Phou Loi as a citadel, they launched a first strike against the post of Muang Son, forcing the Lao of the Ou and upper Seng rivers to abandon their villages. Monsieur Barrelle, the commissioner of Luang Prabang, organized his troops for a quick response. On September 21, 1919, while en route to meet the Hmong head on, Barrelle's small column was "attacked from front and back" and suffered "heavy losses." Barrelle's troops were forced to return to Luang Prabang, carrying their wounded.[58] The Hmong were not to be underestimated.

Watching the Hmong of Luang Prabang and Sam Neua rise in revolt, the French desperately hoped that Pa Chay's call to arms would be less effective in Xieng Khouang, the province with the highest concentration of Hmong. The Phuan, who shared linguistic and cultural similarities with the Lao and Tai, were the recognized lords of Xieng Khouang, but a strong Hmong presence could already be felt in the region by the time of the French incursions in 1893. Throughout the nineteenth century, the Phuan state was victim to constant invasions from China, Vietnam, and Siam. The most devastating invasion by the Thai occurred in the 1870s when a substantial number of Phuan were permanently relocated to the west bank of the Mekong. The depopulation of the Phuan made the Hmong presence in the region noticeably more important. As early as 1899, a French census estimated that the Hmong comprised 30 percent of the population in Xieng Khouang. They dominated the second-most-important Phuan town, Chiang Kham, making up 55.7 percent of the population as opposed to 40.6 percent Phuan. The rest of the population was composed of other ethnic minorities.[59]

By the early 1920s, the Hmong were thirty thousand strong on the Keng Khoai Plateau alone.[60] This figure did not include the substantial population south and west of the Plain of Jars. The Hmong of the Keng Khoai Plateau, also known to the Hmong as the region of Nong Het, were of special concern. This group had settled in the area at the beginning of the nineteenth century. Their villages were more concentrated and well established, thereby making their mobilization en masse quick and easy. This group was also influential politically and economically, with a history of strong leadership stretching back to China. The French prayed that their contacts with the group since 1902 would be enough to prevent an outbreak of rebellion. "One can hope," Angeli writes, "that in this province [Xieng Khouang], where the Hmong have been in more contact with the Europeans, the rebellion will not easily gain ground."[61]

Blia Yao was the paramount leader of the Hmong of Nong Het. And, although it was true that the French had enjoyed good relations with him, the sworn blood brother of Henri Roux who would play an essential role in defeating Pa Chay, the French were hoping for too much. Blia Yao, having become complacent in his role as an instrumental political broker, had begun to exploit the Hmong—much like other colonial officials did. Over the years, Blia Yao's jars of silver and numerous herds of cattle had multiplied while the rest of the Hmong scraped up their last dimes to pay their taxes and satisfy the terms of their corvée conscription. The Hmong of Nong Het especially detested the construction work on CR7, the road that passed through their homeland.

As the French watched for signs of disturbance in Xieng Khouang, the situation in Luang Prabang and Sam Neua intensified. On November 5, 1919, the Eleventh Company Annamites had barely begun to establish the post of Muang Heup (Luang Prabang) as a staging garrison when the Hmong attacked the site. After a brief but vigorous encounter, the French were forced to evacuate the post. One European sergeant was killed in action, and seven indigenous soldiers were wounded. The disturbance reverberated on the east side of the Ou River on the western frontier of Luang Prabang among the Yao of Muang Sinh and the Chinese population, which had also registered its dissatisfaction with the colonial authorities. These two groups, a French report states, "seemed to indicate that they wanted to join the Hmong." There was also concern that the Thai and Chinese would take advantage of France's current vulnerability. Three companies and one detachment of 120 men were sent to Sam Neua, Muang Ngoi, Xieng Khouang, and Luang Prabang to reinforce the border and intercept any rebels coming from Muang Sinh.[62]

By the following month, the buildup of the Hmong in Sam Neua and Luang Prabang had reached alarming proportions, with a large group having convened at Muang Son. On December 12, Hao Mong suffered a concerted attack by Hmong rebels. The commissioner of Luang Prabang raised the alarm and called for reinforcements from Xieng Khouang. Commandant Thomas responded quickly. He left the garrison of Xieng Khouang to one section of machine gunners and led the rest of his company toward Tam La. The rebellion had not yet touched the Tran Ninh Plateau (Xieng Khouang), but there were already anxious reports coming from the area by December 16. Commandant Prevost dispatched a detachment of forty men to Ko Ngoua to survey the mountain ranges of Phou San, a potential rebel site west of the Plain of Jars dominated by the Moua clan. One Madame Nieville passed through Keng Khoai (near Nong Het) on December 16 and 17 and reported encountering no difficulties. Three days later, Colonel Angeli received news at Muang Sen, a town across the border in Vietnam, that the region was in rebellion. Angeli had just arrived from Hanoi and was on his way by land to take charge of the operations against Pa Chay in Luang Prabang. The Hmong, the report informed him, had "made common cause with the rebels and threatened their *kaitong* [Blia Yao]." Angeli was instructed to wait at Muang Sen for a military escort from Xieng Khouang.[63] What the French feared most had unfolded. The Hmong of Xieng Khouang had joined Pa Chay.

Lo Shong Ger's Revolt in Xieng Khouang (December 1919–March 1920)

According to oral informants now living in America, Shong Ger's rebellion against his uncle, Blia Yao, stemmed from both political and personal considerations. Broadly speaking, French colonialism was especially hard on the Hmong, who ranked near the bottom of the ethnic hierarchy and had no direct access to their colonial masters. Like the Tai overlords of Tonkin, Lao officials often exacted what they felt was their deserved share of taxes in addition to what the French stipulated. Under this system of indirect rule, the Hmong were doubly exploited. Since the French first set foot in Laos, there had been several uprisings against this double-tiered exploitation. As Blia Yao's prestige and power grew, he began to exhibit behavior similar to that of the Lao. During his lifetime, Blia Yao acquired his wealth from multiple sources. Some was inherited from his father, as noted above, but a substantial portion of his riches came from money skimmed from the budget for the construction of CR7—a budget left largely in Blia Yao's hands. As shall be discussed further below, another huge amount of wealth came from the indemnity exacted from rebels who joined Shong Ger in 1920. Also, being the recognized Hmong leader of Nong Het who was called on to settle lawsuits and disagreements between individuals and clans, there were ample other opportunities for Blia Yao to make money. He often settled disputes in his own favor against any notion of justice to the victims, according to some. Bribery was a major deciding factor as to which side would emerge triumphant.[64] This lack of ethics was partly the reason for Shong Ger to rebel against Blia Yao, his own uncle.

Hmong individuals were drawn to Shong Ger's side as a result of old grievances and new developments. As early as 1912, tensions mounted when the resident of Xieng Khouang became apprehensive about deforestation, which he attributed directly to Hmong swidden agricultural practices in the hills. The resident issued a decree that the Hmong must replant the acres of land cleared for cultivation or else leave the province. The Hmong agreed to replant.[65] Four years later, in 1916, as a result of the increasing funds needed to carry out the construction of roads in Laos, the French raised taxes. Not surprisingly, the opium-cultivating Hmong were forced to shoulder a heavier burden than the lowland Lao. The Hmong were required to pay two annual per capita taxes as well as a semiannual tax. Also, for the first time, taxes were levied on widows and adolescents. To ensure Hmong payment, the colonial militia accompanied tax collectors to Hmong villages. Those who could not pay were escorted to Xieng Khouang, where they were imprisoned until relatives paid on their behalf.[66] As the colonial agent who enforced these harsh policies, Blia Yao must have borne the brunt of Hmong resentment. That he himself was a Hmong who lived with the inhabitants made him an easy target. Lao or French officials came to collect taxes, but they left the heights for the safety of the lowlands once the job was done. The Hmong, who had a superstitious fear of the lowlands, were reluctant to pursue them.

Many Hmong were also subjected to exorbitant taxes and corvée conscriptions, which were tied directly to the colonial projects in Xieng Khouang. The construction of CR7, running from Vietnam to the Plain of Jars and beyond, began in earnest in 1910. Each village, depending on the number of taxable men, was assigned a certain length of the road to dig. Adult males were obliged to provide two weeks of free labor on road projects, losing valuable time that could be devoted to fieldwork. After the two weeks, workers were paid two kip per day. Conscripts had to bring their own provisions to the job sites, which were located at lower elevations far from home. The man in charge of enforcing tax payments and corvée work was Blia Yao. He made no effort to ease the burden on the Hmong. Instead, he capitalized on the situation for his own gain. He approached the colonial authorities with Hmong complaints. Quite influential, he succeeded in obtaining an increase in wages to three kip per day, but he kept the additional kip for himself and continued to pay the Hmong as before. When Hmong and Khmu workers protested, threatening to go to the French, Blia Yao threatened them with rifles.[67] The Hmong resented the work so much that many relocated west and south of the province, away from the construction site.[68] Facing worker shortages, the French were forced to hire paid labor. By 1920 the Hmong of Xieng Khouang had multiple reasons to follow Pa Chay.

Over time Blia Yao's accumulated wealth became a source of resentment for Hmong as well. He was so rich that after his death in 1935 his sons could not agree on how to divide his caches of silver and gold and his numerous herds of cattle.[69] The Hmong who watched Blia Yao live lavishly while they scraped for basic survival became disenchanted. Never before in their oral memory did they recall such a huge disparity in wealth between a leader and the general population. Some began to covet Blia Yao's lucrative position. His two closest associates, Ly Foung and Shong Ger, each laid out his own plans to seize it. Shong Ger joined Pa Chay's rebellion while the more cautious Ly Foung, as shall be seen in the following chapter, forged alliances among the powerful clans and set about educating his sons. Shong Ger's bid for a quick triumph ended up costing him his life, while Ly Foung's appreciation for delayed gratification paid off in the long run.

Pa Chay's call for rebellion reached Xieng Khouang in December 1919. From his entrenchment deep inside the Chom-Chick Chom-Chang mountain chain, Pa Chay sent word that the Heavenly Father and Mother were coming to liberate the Hmong from their oppressive overlords. At the time Shong Ger was also working as Blia Yao's secretary. He and Ly Foung supervised the construction of CR7 and collected taxes on Blia Yao's behalf. Shong Ger and Ly Foung were the only two Hmong of their generation to be literate in Lao.[70] Shong Ger, like Ly Foung, was instrumental in establishing Blia Yao's legitimacy. And, if there was anyone with inside knowledge of the true extent of Blia Yao's financial schemes, it was Shong Ger. Unlike Ly Foung, who was an outsider, Shong Ger was Blia Yao's trusted nephew and thus privy to his inside activities. Shong Ger's father, Nhia Her, was Blia Yao's elder half brother and one of the sons of Pa Tsi's first wife (see Lo family tree in fig. 7).[71] Blia Yao was the son of Pa Tsi's second wife, the Ly woman. Because the maternal line is recognized as important in Hmong rituals, this crucial origin may be at the heart of Shong Ger's willingness to challenge his uncle. Also, Pa Tsi had taken his second wife late in life, so, although Blia Yao and Shong Ger were uncle and nephew, they were virtually the same age.[72] The two probably grew up as playmates in the same village, creating a familiarity that undermined the respect Shong Ger should have exhibited toward an uncle who ranked above him on the generational tree.

Not much else is known about Shong Ger. Blia Yao exterminated the male lines of many of his rival kinsmen, but, according to Colonel Nao Kao, his father, Ly Foung, helped save Shong Ger's sons by hiding them. Shong Ger still has descendants in America today. His wives, who were sent back to their paternal relatives, survived long enough to relay bits and pieces of Shong Ger's history to Mao Song Lyfoung, who also heard other details from her father, Ly Foung. Shong Ger, she said, was from the same village as her father, a fact that Blia Yao later used to incriminate him, as shall be discussed in chapter five, so he was able to observe firsthand the beginning stages of the movement.

It appears that Shong Ger's initial dissatisfaction was more with the Lao authorities than with his uncle, Blia Yao. On receiving Pa Chay's call for liberation, Shong Ger began to recruit Hmong to his side. Soon these followers gathered en masse for daily discussions at Shong Ger's house, where dancing and praying accompanied reading and writing lessons—the telltale signs of a messianic revolt. Mao Song told us:

> There emerged a group who shook and quivered and clapped, [claiming that] the Heavenly Father and Mother were coming to help them. The Lao were oppressing them, imposing slavery upon them, so the Heavenly Mother and Father were coming to help them, King Faj Tim [Huangdi] was coming to help them. Then they cried and cried and cried, and they suddenly knew how to read and write and clapped their hands and stamped their feet. [When they] learned to read [they said,] "kaim kais kaim kais kaiv kais ves ves pob" [gibberish sounds] only. They opened books and clapped their hands and stamped their feet. [They kept] doing this, then they said the Lao were oppressing them, forcing them to be slaves, so they were going to go kill the Lao.[73]

The group danced around the village, recruiting individuals from house to house. Those who did not open their doors fast enough had their doors kicked in by streams of screaming men and women.

After many days of hysterical displays, Shong Ger finally led an attack on the Lao village near Ly Foung's home of De Mua Tha. When Blia Yao learned of the situation, he went and collected the rifles of Shong Ger's followers. Shong Ger demanded to be given the rifles back, but Blia Yao said no. Shong Ger next attacked a caravan of Lao traders on CR7, hoping to obtain their cargo of salt. With only a few weapons, he was unsuccessful, so he went back to Blia Yao and demanded the return of the rifles again. Blia Yao adamantly refused to hand them over.[74] He now became a target of Shong Ger's grievances.

Shong Ger had other reasons to resent Blia Yao as well. Despite being a hardworking secretary and a nephew, he was largely excluded from Blia Yao's financial gains. We do not have much information on Shong Ger's compensation, but Ly Foung's situation allows some insight into Shong Ger's grievances.

Blia Yao also refused to share the financial bounty of his administrative post with Ly Foung. Both Mao Song and Tougeu Lyfoung attested that their father drew no salary as a secretary. The only reward was having his annual tax and conscription services forgiven. When I asked Tougeu what the incentive for Ly Foung to remain in Blia Yao's house as a secretary was, he said he did not know. Mao Song, on the other hand, stipulated that Ly Foung's position as secretary allowed him to make money by other means. Ly Foung's creative financial ventures will be discussed fully in the next chapter, but, to put it succinctly here, Ly Foung was able to conduct trade between the Hmong and the Lao when he accompanied Blia Yao to deliver the annual taxes to the French at Xieng Khouang. After Ly Foung broke with Blia Yao in 1926 and was placed in charge of a section of CR7 by the French, he also ingeniously converted the road construction budget into cash for himself. He paid workers with his own family's opium and kept the French silver piasters meant to cover the cost of the road. As Hmong considered working on the road to be "slave labor" (*ua qhev*), Mao Song said, those who came to work were mainly addicts who happily took Ly Foung's opium as payment. As a teenager in the early 1930s, Mao Song cooked for her father in makeshift shelters along CR7 and helped weigh opium as payment for these workers.[75] In other words, it was not until he had broken from Blia Yao that Ly Foung finally found a niche where he also benefited as a road supervisor. Control of a portion of the state budget seems to be one of the multiple material incentives for capturing Blia Yao's position.

Blia Yao had his own lucrative financial schemes, which Shong Ger knew about. During the construction of CR7, wealthy Hmong families often paid off their conscription duties. The money was supposed to be used to hire replacements, but Blia Yao kept much of it for himself. Shong Ger caught on quickly and began to apply the same methods to the villagers under his charge. When workers came to pay off their conscription contracts, Shong Ger simply kept the money without hiring replacements. Blia Yao confronted him but was powerless to do a thing because Shong Ger alluded to his own corrupt practices, calling him a hypocrite and threatening to reveal his schemes to the French.[76] Blia Yao was helpless.

Adding to the grievance, when a dispute occurred between Shong Ger and one of his wives, Blia Yao resorted to his usual practice of extorting a handsome bribe from her. Blia Yao was an expert horseman who loved and possessed the finest breed of horses, as Henri Roux noted. Blia Yao coveted one of Shong Ger's stallions, so when Shong Ger's wife went to ask for a divorce, Blia Yao told her he would grant it if she brought him the stallion. Blia Yao was the clan leader who could authorize her divorce. Ly Na Jalao told us:

Shong Ger was Blia Yao's nephew, the son of his brother, but they both were the same age, working together on the officials' road [CR7]. At the time Blia Yao was also married to our aunt [Jer Jalao]. He's not very honest either. He extorted bribes from everyone, so when Shong Ger's wife—whose complaint [about her marriage] was very minor—went to Blia Yao, he said if she brought him Shong Ger's stallion he would grant her a divorce. The father-in-law said that to the daughter-in-law! So Shong Ger rose up in rebellion against Blia Yao.[77]

Promising to grant an easy divorce in exchange for Shong Ger's stallion was a betrayal. A Hmong wife is not cheaply obtained. She often comes with a huge brideprice, which takes a man's family multiple years to save up. For this reason, Hmong often haggle over the brideprice in divorce cases. Unless the woman's family repays the brideprice, she is often stuck in her marriage. Blia Yao, as the clan leader who was supposed to look after Shong Ger's interests, was offering an easy way out for Shong Ger's wife. Unfortunately for Blia Yao, the wife had second thoughts. She returned to Shong Ger and told him about Blia Yao's proposal. Shong Ger angrily broke with Blia Yao to form his own lineage. He took along with him Lo clansmen who were also disenchanted with Blia Yao.[78]

The theme of a disagreement over a woman is echoed by Henri Roux, Blia Yao's sworn blood brother. According to Roux, however, it was Shong Ger who coveted Blia Yao's most minor fifth wife, Pa Hang. Pa had the reputation of being the most beautiful maiden of her generation and is still talked about today as a sort of Hmong Helen of Troy (see fig. 9). Roux, who frequented Blia Yao's home, also mentioned that she was a stunning beauty. In 1920 Blia Yao kidnapped the thirteen-year-old as a trophy bride.[79] Shong Ger, Blia Yao told Roux, had wanted her for himself and was now trying to remove him in order to obtain her.[80] Perhaps it was that since Blia Yao had planned to allow Shong Ger's wife to divorce her husband behind his back without just compensation, Shong Ger now thought it appropriate that he should acquire Blia Yao's new wife as repayment. The Hmong practice intergenerational taboos when choosing a spouse, however. For a nephew to dare to articulate his designs on an uncle's wife was to break a taboo. If it is true, Shong Ger's articulation of this desire highlights how serious the break had been between uncle and nephew. To entertain designs on Pa, Shong Ger would have had to psychologically remove himself as a family member. Blia Yao only told Roux his side of the story and not about the prior incident involving Shong Ger's wife, but, whatever the case, both stories signified a deep conflict and highlighted the competition between Shong Ger and Blia Yao for bounties in cash and a woman.

Once he renounced his lineage affiliation, Shong Ger brazenly staged Blia Yao's assassination. The first attempt, by men with rifles one early morning, was botched due to humid weather. The misty fog did not allow the flintlocks to be fired. When Shong Ger's men had a clear shot later, they could not summon the courage to shoot Blia Yao. They feared the consequences of his death. Blia Yao was merciless and a man of tremendous presence. Over the years, his reputation had become legendary. He had the might of the French colonial army and the support of Ly Nhia Vu's powerful clan behind him. He also had the backing of the Yang and perhaps even the Moua clan because many of his sisters and daughters were married into that clan. Despite the promise of protection by higher powers from above by Pa Chay followers, Shong Ger's men cringed at the sight and sound of Blia Yao's approach. No one could summon the courage to shoot him. Xai S. Lor states, "When he [Blia Yao] coughed out loud, Shonger's men fled in fear."[81]

Frustrated, Shong Ger led a final attack on Blia Yao's house in the village of Yeng Pha. When he arrived, Shong Ger called out to Blia Yao, but Blia Yao refused to come out and face him. In the hope of enticing him out of the house, Shong Ger harassed Blia Yao's prized stallions in the barn and set his bulls to fighting with one another. Blia Yao loved these animals—especially his prized stallions—more than money itself, but he still did not come out. As the night wore on, Shong Ger and his men decided to wait for Blia Yao on the road that led from Yeng Pha to CR7. They anticipated correctly that he would flee into Vietnam to solicit French protection. Mao Song Lyfoung picked up the narrative.

> Shong Ger's minor wife told me about this [event]. [They watched Blia Yao's house all night, but they] could not kill him, so when daylight arrived they went to guard the main road [out of Yeng Pha]. When the sun rose and its rays became warm, grandfather *kaitong* [Blia Yao] saddled a horse and took with him a dried-up leather stick. He climbed onto the horse and beat that horse with it into a running gallop. As he approached, they each said, "You shoot him this time, you this time." Grandfather *kaitong* rode for his life, beating that horse into a running speed, and passed them into Vietnam. Everyone [then] shouted angrily, "I told you to kill him, why didn't you shoot?" "What about you? Why didn't you shoot?" They argued and argued.[82]

Shong Ger's men had lost their final opportunity to shoot Blia Yao. Shong Ger did not step up to the task either. The inability to act would have grave consequences for these men.

The Defeat of Shong Ger
and the Decline of Lo Power

After Blia Yao fled from Yeng Pha, he took refuge at the nearby Shila Cave. The Lys of Nong Khiaw, Blia Yao's maternal relatives and in-laws, supplied him with food and contacted the French on his behalf.[83] For the moment Shong Ger was triumphant, but fate intervened on Blia Yao's behalf soon enough. Part of the reason why Shong Ger was so brazen may have been that Blia Yao's patron, Henri Roux, had left nearly six years earlier to command troops in Europe during World War I. Just as Blia Yao was fleeing from Yeng Pha, Roux returned to Saigon via the *Porthos*. Knowledgeable about the Hmong, he had been ordered back to Indochina to quell Pa Chay's rebellion. Roux heard about the revolt in Xieng Khouang from General Puyperoux and his chief of staff, Colonel Pierlot. They were traveling on the same boat. The general was also on his way to lead the troops. Neither Roux nor Pierlot, who had also come to know the Hmong well, could believe they would rebel without just cause. Roux feared that Blia Yao, his sworn brother, was among the rebels.[84]

At Muang Sen, he learned from the Chinese that Blia Yao had been forced into hiding in a forest nearby by the dissident Hmong. Roux immediately dispatched a letter in Chinese characters to Blia Yao. He attached a photo of himself as proof that the letter came from him. Blia Yao replied three days later, saying that he would wait for Roux at Nong Het. Once reunited, Roux and Blia Yao renewed their blood oath. A rooster was killed, and droplets of its blood were added to a cup of water. Then both swore to be loyal to one another for life and sealed it by drinking from the same cup. Blia Yao had already gathered forty men, all armed with Hmong flintlock rifles. He was ready to fight Shong Ger.[85]

As soon as Blia Yao fled to Vietnam, Shong Ger and Lo Chai Vang, another rebel leader, prepared for his return. They cut down trees and gathered bat droppings from nearby caves—the ingredients for the powder used to power the flintlock rifle. They also fashioned cannons out of hollow tree and bamboo trunks. Then they built an armory where troops gathered for training exercises and gunsmiths could be forced to manufacture rifles and ammunition. While some prepared for war, others of Shong Ger's men went from village to village to recruit or coerce the population to join them. "Shong Ger ordered everyone to rebel, threatening to cut off the heads of those who refused. Every Hmong man fifteen and over who knew how to use a rifle was drawn into the rebellion."[86]

Women and children also participated in their own way. Virginal girls were chosen to lead the troops in battle, bearing the protective flags and playing the role of the legendary Nkauj Ntxuam, the mythical Hmong princess who had led Hmong men against the Chinese eons ago. At Xieng Khouang F. M. Savina watched as a young girl led twenty men in an attack on the town. She sang and waved her aprons—believed to deflect bullets—as she marched at the front of the column.[87] Savina also learned from Roux of a similar incident in which a young girl led a troop of two hundred men. Standing only several hundred meters from the French firing line, she ordered the men into formation and cheered them on while attempting to protect them with her flag.[88]

Those who were too young to bear arms prayed and lit incense at spirit temples constructed outside villages. It was widely believed that if one prayed at these temples, one could summon the tigers of the forest to come and help Pa Chay's men battle the French. Lee Nao Mai, who was born around 1904, was a teenager in 1920. He lived in the mountains south of Xieng Khouang in Pha Nok Kok, Muang (district of) Pha, near the village of Long Cheng, which became Vang Pao's military headquarters in 1962. One morning, when the sound of cannon fire announced an attack on Xieng Khouang, Nao Mai went to light incense to conduct the ceremony to summon the tigers to come and aid the Hmong in battle. He knelt and prayed to Heaven, asking the Heavenly Mother and Father to send tigers to help the Hmong. "As I finished and stood up to place the incense on a platform in the spirit temple, I saw a tiger just a few feet right opposite me. For an instant the tiger and I locked eyes, both shocked by the encounter. Then we each turned to run in the opposite direction," said Nao Mai, laughing. Reflecting on the situation nearly eighty years later, he believed the tiger had been attracted to the site by the smell of food and incense placed on the temple by worshippers. Such coincidences made the Hmong believe in Pa Chay's powers, however, said Nao Mai. He also reported that during this period women, without ever having been instructed, suddenly knew how to play the *qeej*, the bamboo instrument traditionally played by men. A master of the *qeej*, Nao Mai still recalled a line from one of their songs: "The Hmong will journey to the sky, the Hmong will march across the earth, they will free themselves from oppression."[89]

In January 1920, Blia Yao returned from Vietnam with the full force of the French colonial army. He established a base at the village of Phak Lak, where he would remain permanently after the rebellion. Blia Yao battled beside Henri Roux, the officer now in charge of pacifying Xieng Khouang. Blia Yao and several clans loyal to him guided the colonial troops against the rebels (see fig. 10). Shong Ger and his men put up a strong show of force, but the battle turned

Figure 10. Loyal Hmong guides posing with the French colonial troops that chased down Pa Chay's rebels in Xieng Khouang, Laos, 1920/21. (Courtesy of Archives nationales d'outre-mer, FR ANOM, Aix-en-Provence, 16_8FI_524_V054N315)

quickly in favor of the French. Though resourceful with what they had, Shong Ger and his men were no match for modern machine guns, which could reach long distances with deadly accuracy. By the end of February, Shong Ger's troops were running for their lives. Those who had not believed in the cause in the first place quickly surrendered to Blia Yao. In March Shong Ger left the region, escaping with just a few of his closest male relatives.

With a large portion of the population having surrendered, the French "convened tribunals consisting of three Hmong and three Lao in each *moung* [county] to estimate losses to be paid to the Lao." Hmong losses were not addressed by these tribunals. "The Meo chiefs are to decide among themselves on how much to compensate for losses incurred by the Meo." The telegram from Xieng Khouang to the resident superior in Vientiane ends by affirming that "the Meo had admitted they were crazy and possessed and they were now ready to pay."[90]

Figure 11. Captured Hmong rebels of Pa Chay's War in Xieng Khouang, Laos, awaiting their sentencing. Unfortunately, no one alive that I know can identify these men. (Courtesy of Archives nationales d'outre-mer, FR ANOM, Aix-en-Provence, 16_8FI_524_V056N330)

In Nong Het, Blia Yao began in earnest to punish those who had dared to rise up against him. Ly Foung was the secretary in charge of the paperwork. As Blia Yao pronounced the fate of those who surrendered, Ly Foung recorded their names, their crimes, and Blia Yao's sentence on paper. Mao Song noted:

> Those who guarded the roads and killed people were sentenced to life imprison-
> ment. Some were beheaded or taken to be shot at Xieng Khouang. Those who
> only bore arms were fined three silver bars—those over eighteen, that is. But
> the Hmong could bear arms at fifteen! [Laughs]. So my father was summoned
> to do the paperwork. So, [Blia Yao said,] "This one, Tsia Foung, this one has
> no crime, release him." Then my father did the paperwork and released him
> after he paid three silver bars to grandfather. My father said [that the rebels
> were] fined and fined and fined until the silver necklaces were stacked up in all
> the corners of the house looking like piled-up loops of dried rattan![91]

Blia Yao handed over some of these payments as indemnities to the French and Lao, but he kept a substantial portion for himself, said Mao Song. Blia Yao's wealth increased substantially after the rebellion. He built himself a stone house in Phak Lak and relocated there permanently. The stone structure of the house still stands today (see fig. 2). The French resident superior of Laos reported to the director of the Banque de l'Indochine that he had collected 376,745 kilograms of silver in bars and necklaces from the Hmong. The resident asked the director to determine the purity of the silver.[92]

Blia Yao next schemed to capture Shong Ger and the rebels who had followed him into hiding. Invoking the Hmong's custom of using outside clan intervention, Blia Yao asked the Lys of Nong Khiaw to go and negotiate with Shong Ger. He promised to spare Shong Ger's life if he returned to Nong Het. Shong Ger did not trust his uncle, but he trusted his uncle's words to the Ly clan. Believing that he would escape punishment, Shong Ger and his men surrendered. Ly Na Jalao stated: "Shong Ger was Blia Yao's nephew. So he asked my Ly relatives to negotiate for Shong Ger's surrender, saying that if he returned, he would not be killed—[Blia Yao] was the uncle. As soon as Shong Ger arrived, he arrested Shong Ger and sent him to Xieng [Khouang]."[93]

The men who surrendered with Shong Ger were publicly executed for the Hmong to see at Nong Het (see figs. 6 and 12). Larteguy and Yang write,

> The French authorities, once the rebellion had been put down, organized a grand festival to which all the inhabitants of the region were invited. Suspecting nothing, the Hmong, men, women and children, all dressed in their finest festival customs, descended on horseback, on foot, from the mountains. Toward five o'clock in the afternoon, a French officer marched a dozen of the rebels, including the brother of Lo Toua Thay [a rebel leader who had been executed earlier] from the prison. They [the rebels] were tied to a dozen posts. Three firing squads arranged themselves in front of the rebels and opened fire. Lo Blia Yao became the important grand chief of Tran Ninh [Xieng Khouang].[94]

The French wanted to send a clear message to the Hmong. "Even my mother went to watch and told me about it," said Ly Na.[95]

Blia Yao also ordered the execution of the male children of Shong Ger, Chai Vang, Soua Ger, and Toua Zeng—all members of the Lo clan—in an effort to wipe out their lineage "so as to prevent future revenge" against him. Lo clan members who did not want the clan weakened devised a scheme to save these boys. Yia Lor writes, "[Xaisoua Lor] asked the widows to disguise

Figure 12. A Hmong crowd watching an execution of Pa Chay rebels. The Hmong came dressed in their best clothes, accompanied by women and children, and having no idea what was to take place. (Courtesy of Archives nationales d'outre-mer, FR ANOM, Aix-en-Provence, 16_8FI_524_V054N314)

the boys in female clothes. . . . [Then he reported to Blia Yao,] 'Uncle, all the boys have been killed. . . . Only the widows and girls were [*sic*] left. I suggest you allow them to return to their maternal [paternal?] families.' Bliayao agreed. . . . Some of these disguised children would later support Touby Lyfoung against Faydang Lor (Kiatong Bliayao's son)."[96]

Shong Ger suffered a less heroic death then his kinsmen. Refusing to submit to a slow, miserable death in prison, he ingested a poisonous plant called *teeb nyug* and expired on his way to Xieng Khouang.[97] Because the Ly clan had negotiated for his return, it bore the blame for his death. The Lys did not appreciate that Blia Yao had made liars out of them, but they were powerless to intervene on Shong Ger's behalf. Blia Yao had the military might of the French colonial masters behind him. The Lys have borne the blame silently to this day. Ly Na concluded:

Later on the Lo clan was not happy with us Ly. They said we [Lys] of Nong Khiaw had murdered Shong Ger. It was not us who killed him. It was his uncle who collaborated with the French. He [Blia Yao] asked us, his maternal relatives, to bring Shong Ger to him and he would resolve everything then end it. When we took Shong Ger to him, he just had Shong Ger executed. It is not the Ly clan's fault. The Ly clan was only the middleman. Both of them were our kinsmen, so what do you expect us to do? We cannot say a thing about this event to this day. Our parents do talk about it, but we cannot defend ourselves because we have no witnesses [who heard Blia Yao's promise not to harm Shong Ger], so we say, it is all right. What has come to pass is in the past.[98]

Blia Yao emerged victorious and wealthier than ever after Pa Chay's rebellion. He had won, but his alliance with the French had also alienated a large sector of Hmong society. The execution of and extortion of money from the rebels did not aid his image either. Moreover, the killing of his own Lo kinsmen caused the Lo clan to decline in power. When Blia Yao's maternal Ly relatives sided with their clansman, Ly Foung, to usurp the leadership of Nong Het in 1939, Blia Yao's family suffered. Members of the Lo clan who sympathized with Shong Ger also took the side of the Lyfoungs.

As they did for Pa Chay, the Hmong invented explanations for Shong Ger's defeat. They said that his men had violated proper taboos by eating animal organs or sleeping with their wives before battles. As a result they lost the power of invulnerability.[99] Shong Ger was eliminated as a threat, but Blia Yao faced much fiercer competition from Ly Foung in the next decades.

The Struggle
for Paramountcy
(1921–1935)

In the remote highland zone, especially among groups like the Hmong, who have a segmented, mostly egalitarian social structure, the historical roles of individuals loom large. The mapping of Indochina required Frenchmen like Auguste Pavie and Henri Roux to negotiate and befriend ethnic leaders like Deo Van Tri and Lo Blia Yao. Depending on individuals to facilitate the demands of empire presented unique challenges, however. In the case of the Hmong, when the French created a paramount leader it had the adverse effect of making them dependent on him to enforce the colonial project. The Hmong leader, having obtained state legitimation, meanwhile, became an authoritarian figure, a source of clan disharmony. Lack of contact with the population prevented the French from fully grasping the situation. They may also have chosen to turn a blind eye to circumstances due to the sheer need for centralization. The lack of qualified administrators and other material factors, such as an absence of knowledge about local languages and customs, not to mention the friction of heights, made it virtually impossible for Frenchmen to administer the Hmong locally.

Creating a paramount chief for the purpose of control had a contradictory effect. The authoritarian chief himself often provoked Hmong resistance against the state. Even where rebellions were contained, the challenge of competing clan leaders was another major problem for the French, who were continually engaged in dispute settlement, leading only to the further disenchantment of those who fell out of favor with them. Creating a paramount authority inevitably led to trouble. The moment the French bestowed favoritism on a single chief, their empire-building efforts were undermined, if not also doomed.

Hence, what James C. Scott says about how the social structures of highlanders hinder state control has relevance here.[1]

The Orphan Ly Foung

Among Lo Blia Yao's most effective competitors was Ly Foung. A western biographer inclined to cite skill or talent as the impetus for an individual's climb to power would probably emphasize Ly Foung's literacy, multilingualism, and political acumen as the primary causes of his growing influence over the Hmong of the Tran Ninh Plateau during the 1920s. When Ly Foung's children narrate his life story, however, his political rise seems preordained and his success the unfolding of destiny. Structuring his life achievements after the Hmong tale of the Orphan Boy who marries a dragon princess and inherits her father's throne, Ly Foung's relatives describe his climb as effortless.[2] Even questionable factors such as Ly Foung's "lazy" nature, which had inadvertently led him to acquire literacy, the ultimate key to his power, seemed ordained by fate. It was as if his ancestors' graves were aligned correctly, as prescribed by Hmong geomancy, with the positive forces of the universe to gearing events in Ly Foung's favor.[3]

Intriguingly, the details of Ly Foung's early days as the "lazy" son of a rejected man bear a certain similarity to the biography of Lyndon B. Johnson, the thirty-sixth president of the United States. Johnson's biographer, Robert A. Caro, attributes his extraordinary ascent from the "bottom of the heap" in the ecological trap of the Edwards Plateau to leadership of the US Senate to his ability to persuade a crowd of "just the right size."[4] Whereas Ly Foung's children focus on the externalities of his fate, Caro takes a western approach and emphasizes Johnson's innate abilities and social conditioning. Perhaps one need not adhere too strongly to, or dismiss completely, either approach. Men and women often do not control the larger events that shape their lives, but the skills they possess do affect how these elements touch them. Accordingly, if we blend these two approaches judiciously, we can see that innate skills, luck, and historical contingency all accounted for Ly Foung's ascent to political power, as they may have for Johnson's as well.

Ly Foung's political triumph was to apply his literate talents to wresting the coveted position of *tasseng* from his patron, Blia Yao. Ly Foung was aided by Pa Chay's rebellion, which forced the French to address the inadequacy of their governance over the Hmong. Since the early 1900s, Blia Yao had been the uncontested Hmong leader in the region of Nong Het. Backed by the might of the French colonial army, Blia Yao's power reached its zenith with the defeat of Pa Chay in 1921. Administrative changes designed to redress Hmong grievances after the revolt, however, undermined Blia Yao while allowing Ly Foung to rise in importance.

In a sense it could be argued that the Hmong leaders of the twentieth century, ranging from Ly Foung to his son Touby and even to Vang Pao, owed much to Pa Chay. They could all be said, as Keith Quincy so adroitly observes, to be "harvesting Pa Chay's wheat."[5] Pa Chay's assassination in 1922 was, therefore, also a beheading of Blia Yao's paramount authority. Pa Chay's claim to the Mandate of Heaven greatly undermined the status of traditional leaders such as Blia Yao, who rose to the political heights by virtue of their prestige within powerful clans and their recognition by earthly patrons of the state. Although clan support remained essential, henceforth literate men who could serve the state as bureaucrats would take precedence. This changing political climate allowed Ly Foung, just as it would also allow Vang Pao in the 1960s, to become a major player despite his more humble standing as the son of a man who had been rejected by members of his own clan. Ly Foung's literacy paved the way for him to become rich and influential, eclipsing Blia Yao by 1930. Blia Yao's demise five years later would have brought a more decisive end to Lo clan power had it not been for the global power shift that initiated the decolonization process in the following decade.

Although he was born to a humble family, innate intelligence allowed Ly Foung to maximize his opportunities. Literacy had always been an important legitimating element, accounting for the rise of prophets in Hmong society.[6] Hmong prophets, as noted earlier, always claim to possess a divine script in the Hmong language. Intriguingly, according to Mao Song, Ly Foung also possessed knowledge of an ancient Hmong script called Ntawv Puaj Txwm, but how and if this skill boosted his legitimacy is not known.[7] More important is that the literacy of secular political leaders like Ly Foung, that is, men who were legitimated by the state, was in a foreign language. And, we do know how such skills affected Ly Foung's political climb. By coincidence Ly Foung acquired literacy in the language of the state during his youth. According to his children, his abhorrence of hard labor and preference for matters of the mind led him to reading and writing, accounting for his rise as a leader of distinction in Xieng Khouang. Ly Foung supplied the literate skills required by the French for the administration of the nonliterate Hmong, and in doing so he was able to obtain French backing to become an influential leader.

Ly Foung's drive to be noticed may have stemmed from a drive to move up in society. He was the third son of Ly Dra Pao, born to Dra Pao's second wife, a woman of the Thao clan who had eight children in all. Dra Pao's first wife, of

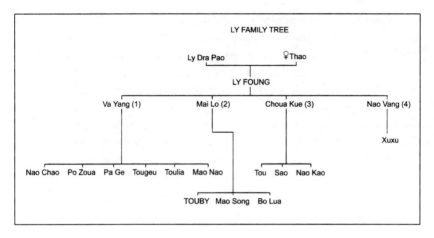

Figure 13. This simplified Ly family tree contains only the most important individuals. The numbers in parentheses represent the ordinal number of Ly Foung's wives by marriage. He had four wives in total but only two at any one time. After Mai died in 1921, he married Choua, and after Va died in 1929, he married Nao. After Ly Foung died in 1939, Nao remarried, but Choua remained the family matriarch all her life and died in exile in France in the 1980s. (Graphic by Boua Chao Lee)

the Yang clan, had six children (see the Ly family tree in fig. 13). Ly Foung was born in the village of Hav Quav Liab Huakhilees, in Muang Kham, or the region of Nong Het. This strategic area bordering Vietnam contained the largest concentration of Hmong with a population of thirty thousand in 1920.[8] Accordingly, most of the prominent Hmong military and civilian leaders of the twentieth century—Lo Blia Yao, Touby Lyfoung, General Vang Pao, and many of his top military officers—trace their roots to this region.

Ly Foung's birth date, albeit important for historical purposes, can be established only from intriguing anecdotes.[9] Tougeu Lyfoung said his non-literate mother, Ly Foung's first wife, Va Yang, told him once that his father was born during the year when the French silver coin with six circles came into circulation. While saying this to Tougeu, she drew in the dirt two groups of three circles stacked on top of one another. It was not until he had grown up and become literate that Tougeu realized his mother had been trying to convey to him that his father was born in 1888—the eights forming two groups of three circles stacked on top of one another. Today Ly Foung's children accept that date as their father's birth year.[10] As is the case with all the Hmong of these early generations, however, the date of Ly Foung's birth is but an approximation.[11]

When Ly Foung was fifteen years old, his father, Dra Pao, passed away while en route to Muang Sen, a town east of CR7, across the border in Vietnam, where he had gone to buy salt for the people of his village. While traveling in the lowlands, Dra Pao died tragically of unknown causes, though circumstances hint at his fate. A trip down the mountain during this period was highly dangerous for Hmong, who lacked immunity to the insect-borne diseases of the tropics.[12] Travelers often fell victim to thieves and robbers as well.[13]

Unable to survive alone, Dra Pao's widows took their children, including Ly Foung, to live with members of the Moua clan. The sister of Dra Pao's second wife had married into the Moua clan in De Mua Tha De Chaw Shia (Dej Muaj Ntab Dej Cawm Siav), a village distinguished by a river that ran beneath rocky karsts, above which huge honeycombs hung, hence its name, "River of Bees, River of Life."[14] It would have been ideal for the widows to seek out Dra Pao's clansmen, but the two powerful Ly lineages in Nong Het had rejected him years earlier, forcing him to relocate away from the region. The Lys in Hav Quav Liab Huakhilee, the subclan of Ly Tong Pao and Ly Sai Her, had accepted Dra Pao when he had first arrived from China in the 1860s but withdrew their welcome when ritual discrepancies between themselves and Dra Pao were discovered.[15] During their dispute about ritual differences, Kaitong Ly Nhia Vu, the leader of the Ly lineage in Nong Khiaw, realized that Dra Pao shared ritual similarities with him, which meant that Dra Pao might belong to his lineage and not to the Lys of Hav Quav Liab. But because Dra Pao had openly disputed with the Ly leaders in Hav Quav Liab, indicating a recalcitrant nature, Nhia Vu's brother, Ly Ja Lao, advised Nhia Vu not to inquire further about Dra Pao. Dra Pao, Ja Lao said, was a learned but arrogant man with a loose mouth—a potential liability for any clan leader who accepted him.[16] Moreover, as Nhia Vu's descendants explained years later, Dra Pao was from a different region of China and had worked as "a virtual slave for a hated Chinese" during his migration to Nong Het.[17] For these reasons, Nhia Vu's group did not accept Dra Pao, a fact that may have scarred Ly Foung and inspired him to prove his worth later on. The orphan Ly Foung thus grew up among his extended family in De Mua Tha, not among his paternal relatives as preferred by Hmong of the period.[18] Ly Foung began his adventures into the literate world of other cultures from this village.

In his memoir, Touby, the most prestigious of Ly Foung's sons, claims that his father learned to read and write Chinese from his grandfather, Dra Pao. As a child back in China, Dra Pao had been orphaned and adopted and educated by a Han Chinese couple. Dra Pao, Touby writes, later passed his knowledge on to Ly Foung.[19] Touby's sister, Mai Song Lyfoung, told a different story. She claimed that all her brothers, Touby included, went to the lowlands for school beginning in 1926. They did not begin to return until 1930. Touby himself returned just three months before his father died in a horseback-riding accident in October 1939. Mao Song, meanwhile, "was kept at home as a *qhev* (slave)" like other Hmong women of her time.[20] She was born in 1919. Starting when she was ten years old and continuing until she married her husband in 1936, she worked with her father as his cook while he was a supervisor on CR7. She and her father lived in makeshift shelters alongside the road and she personally handed out payments to the workers at times. She remained nonliterate all her life, but she did have ample opportunity to hear her father's life story from his own lips. She also witnessed and participated in some of the political events that occurred around this time. For this reason she was more familiar with her father's life history and the happenings of the events discussed here.[21]

According to Mao Song, it was Ly Foung's gambling habit that led him to acquire literacy. Touby, although he avoids tying Ly Foung's literacy to gambling, confirms Ly Foung's addiction in his memoir. According to Touby, Ly Foung finally realized he had hit rock bottom when a day of gambling left him deeply in debt and contemplating further wrongdoing by not repaying the Chinese friend who had lent him the money to gamble with in the first place. Having awakened to how deeply he had sunk, Ly Foung returned home, lit candles, and, in front of his wife, vowed to his ancestors, Heaven, and the Lord Buddha that he would never gamble again. Then he paid his friend back every cent. Ly Foung often recounted this story to his children, strictly prohibiting them from trying their hands at a quick game.[22]

Ly Foung's early life in colonial Laos, as narrated by Mao Song, bears a certain resemblance to Lyndon B. Johnson's Texas boyhood. Like Johnson, Ly Foung was an eccentric youth who did not have the physical constitution for the hard labor of swidden cultivation. He was light skinned and burned easily in the baking sun, a trait reminiscent of Johnson's days on a pick-and-shovel team, building roads beneath the burning Texas sun. Caro writes, "Such work was 'too heavy' for Johnson. He would come home at night . . . exhausted. His skin — that Bunton skin — refused to callus; blister formed on top of blister on his hands, which were often bleeding."[23] Johnson, who detested physical labor, submitted to the work only after having failed in his dream of becoming a lawyer. More fortunate, Ly Foung successfully avoided his menial chores as a youth. Was he, as Caro argues about Johnson, avoiding labor as a way to distinguish himself from the rest of his humble family, which had fallen to "the bottom of the heap"?

Ly Foung seemed unsuited to live in his time and society. Not only did he abhor agriculture work, but he also found the idea of animal husbandry repulsive. "My father could never stand the smell of chicken coops and pigpens," said

Tougeu.[24] This abhorrence for menial tasks may have led to his feigning "laziness." As a result, Ly Foung's primary responsibility as a young man was to stay home and watch over his siblings while his mother and other household members toiled in the fields. Because he remained at home, Mao Song continued, Ly Foung soon acquired a negative reputation among villagers. For that reason, he could not find a woman willing to marry him until he was thirty years old. "When my father wanted to marry the tall, beautiful niece of my grandmother, the niece replied, 'Oh, that Foung Dra Pao is too lazy!' She ran off and married another man," Mao Song said as she laughed.[25]

Undoubtedly, in an agrarian society that esteemed physical labor as a measure of individual worth, neighbors would have looked askance at such a youth. The judgmental eyes of his fellow villagers probably fell especially hard on Ly Foung, who was a third son. In the absence of a father, he would have been expected to actively contribute to the arduous work of clearing jungle land for planting. The physically demanding task of felling large trees, which Ly Foung would have none of, was reserved for men—indeed, it was the hallmark of Hmong manhood.[26]

Intriguingly, this negative portrayal of the young Ly Foung seems also to typically constitute the narrative structure of the rise of the great man in Hmong society—a coincidence that calls for a close, critical examination. The narrative of Ly Foung's early days as an irresponsible, lazy orphan resonates with those of Vue Pa Chay and Lo Blia Yao. Later Hmong leaders have also been portrayed in this fashion. Yang Shong Lue, the Mother of Writing, who led a messianic movement from 1959 to 1971, was characterized by his neighbors as an indolent man who spent his time doing nothing to the detriment of his neglected crops when he was secretly inventing his pathbreaking Hmong writing system.[27] Clearly, as cautioned earlier, there is a tendency for oral sources to frame Hmong leaders in the guise of the archetypal folk hero, the Orphan Boy. Adapting the historical figure to the image of the rejected orphan seems to be a narrative technique that foreshadows his rise to renown, raising him to legendary status. The humble characterization of Ly Foung during this early part of his life, even if true, serves to heighten the anticipation, among listeners to the family stories, of his redeemable qualities at the end.

On the other hand, it is also possible that men who achieve greatness in a particular society share similar characteristics within its cultural forms—hence their portrayal by diverse sources in the same unappealing early stages. Maybe these men were perceived and portrayed negatively by neighbors not so much because of their imperfect dispositions but because of their vision and unique, even eccentric qualities as human beings—the manifestation, perhaps, of a certain inborn genius. Judged by the standards of an agrarian society that emphasized diligence and earning a living by the sweat of one's brow, men like Blia Yao, Ly Foung, and Shong Lue, who engaged in intellectual pursuits, were out of character. They did not measure up to the standards of manhood of their time. It is no wonder that they were judged harshly. Their eccentric nature was, however, what subsequently distinguished them as pioneers. From this perspective, the awe conveyed by these oral narratives is maybe a mix of literary device and social reality.

Ly Foung's languid nature led him to unique life opportunities. He was lucky to exist during a time of transition when Hmong society was moving beyond a strictly agrarian base toward economic diversification as the opportunities of trade and French colonial service presented themselves to key individuals. As a youth, Ly Foung's avoidance of physical labor pushed him toward individuals with a similar nature, allowing him to become literate in Chinese and Lao and to acquire the business skills that generated wealth and social status. Several kilometers from Ly Foung's village of De Mua Tha was a village inhabited by the Haw, Chinese traders who also came from China. According to Keith Quincy's informants, it was a Haw merchant by the name of Ton Ma who led the first group of Hmong into Nong Het in the early 1800s.[28] When Ly Foung was a teenager in the 1900s, these traders were still operating among the Hmong, forming a symbiotic relationship with them. Familiar with lowland climates, they monopolized the crucial trade routes connecting highlands and lowlands, and made their living exchanging silk, salt, iron, and other goods for Hmong opium, rice, and precious game parts used in traditional healing practices.

The young Ly Foung, who stayed home every day, fell in with these "indigent" Chinese.[29] As his younger siblings grew up and took to the fields, Ly Foung became bored at home, so he went to try his luck at gambling in the village of the merchants. We can imagine that Ly Foung was inspired to learn one Chinese character at time while interacting with these Haws. A few years later he also acquired reading knowledge of Lao. When the Lao authorities began to take an interest in the Hmong of the Nong Het region, a man named Cha Ou came from Ban Ban to survey the Hmong population. Unlike the Hmong of his day, who usually shunned lowlanders, the desultory Ly Foung welcomed Cha Ou's company. From him Ly Foung learned to read and write Lao. Subsequently, he also picked up some knowledge of land surveying and mathematics, both of which would serve him well in the future as a trader and secretary to Blia Yao, in charge of apportioning sections of CR7's maintenance to nearby Hmong villages.[30]

Early on, then, Ly Foung's personal preferences and circumstances opened the door for him to become literate, multilingual, and multicultural. By the time he was in his twenties, he had acquired the skills necessary to distinguish himself as an emerging leader in the region of Nong Het. He was extremely sharp in utilizing his language skills as well, allowing for him to rise in esteem in the eyes of his fellow villagers. Touby writes: "Back at the time [early twentieth century], in the surrounding Hmong villages of Nong Het, no Hmong could read Lao, speak Lao, or knew Lao culture [and law] well. Ly Tsia Foung alone possessed those skills. Thus, Hmong relatives often came to depend on his aid when they had words to be conveyed to the Lao authorities. In this way, they all began to perceive him as an elder and to respect him like a teacher."[31] Like men of distinction before him, language and literacy skills were the foundation on which Ly Foung built his leadership. In time these skills would present Blia Yao with serious competition.

Ly Foung was quite accomplished in the oral tradition as well according to his family members. Thus, while acquiring the talents of a modern bureaucrat, he also did not neglect to cultivate the traditional oratorical skills so valued in Hmong men. According to Touby, Ly Foung's knowledge of oral rituals and his command of the *qeej*, bamboo reed, were reputedly equal to those of Lo Nhia Ma, one of the great masters of the period.[32] As shall be seen below, he was quite talented in singing *kwv txhiaj*, courting songs, as well, using his skills to entice Lo Mai, the daughter of Blia Yao. Skill in the ritual arts gave Ly Foung a solid footing in Hmong society, while literacy and language skills allowed him to penetrate the worlds of non-Hmong. He was, in essence, a shaman of cultures and social boundaries, well equipped to cross ethnic lines and become a political broker for the Hmong. Following Pa Chay's rebellion, officials beyond the Hmong villages would recognize his linguistic ability. Accordingly, Ly Foung rose in social status as his much-demanded skills were put to use by the colonial government.

Ly Foung the Trader

Ly Foung's acquisition of literacy may have occurred without much fore-thought, as Mao Song said, but that did not stop him from capitalizing on its potential to move up the social ladder. The story of how Ly Foung built his wealth, a source of his own legitimacy as a leader in Hmong society, also sheds light on the reasons why there was so much contention over the paramount position. The Hmong leader was in a position to generate great wealth for himself and his loyal clients or clan. Wealth can come from engaging in trading while one sends taxes from the highlands to the lowlands, or from more questionable means such as skimming taxes or manipulating the state construction budgets (such as the CR7 funds). Whatever the case, there were material incentives to being a Hmong leader.

During his gambling days, it is unlikely that the young Ly Foung was aware of how literacy could serve his needs. Yet command over reading and writing later allowed him to become a member of an emerging colonial elite. Once he realized this possibility, he forced literacy on his own sons by introducing them to formal education, a topic that will be dealt with more fully in the next chapter. As a secretary to Blia Yao, Ly Foung was presented with the opportunity to enrich himself through trading and, later, through manipulating the budget for the construction of CR7. Literacy opened the door to wealth, which in turn paved the way to strong marriage alliances with the preeminent Hmong leaders of Nong Het, most notably Blia Yao.

While associating with the Chinese and Lao, Ly Foung may have already realized the benefits of the merchant life. During his term of service to Blia Yao, he would capitalize on trading opportunities. Around 1910 Ly Foung married his first wife, Va Yang. By coincidence the French began constructing CR7 during this year. Every man eighteen to sixty years of age was assigned a specified length of the road to dig. Those who had the money paid migrant laborers to do the job on their behalf. Ranked among the less fortunate, Ly Foung had to fulfill his conscription orders firsthand. The burden of corvée labor led to a grand opportunity, allowing Ly Foung to rise quickly in prestige and social standing. While working on the road, his linguistic and surveying skills attracted the attention of Blia Yao, who noticed Ly Foung apportioning a section to each individual from his village, carefully writing down who had to dig which part. Blia Yao was impressed. Being a visionary who was quick to surround himself with men of knowledge in order to boost his own authority, Blia Yao befriended Ly Foung. Before Ly Foung had finished digging his section of the road, he was appointed Blia Yao's secretary.[33]

By 1910 Blia Yao was chief of canton in the subdistrict of Keng Khoai with nominal authority over the Hmong of Nong Het. He was a powerful man with intimate connections to the colonial authorities. Commanding both fear and respect, he was addressed only by his title and clan name, Lo Kaitong— indicating that his reputation was nearly legendary. Although Blia Yao read Chinese characters easily, he was not literate in Lao and could not prepare tax papers or update the annual birth and death registers as required by the

French.[34] Ly Foung joined Blia Yao's administrative team to carry out this task without pay, rewarded only by exemption from the annual head tax of eight kip and corvée conscription.[35]

Meanwhile, shortly after his marriage to Va, Ly Foung's first son, Nao Chao, was born, and other children followed in rapid succession. The demands of secretarial work forced Ly Foung to take up permanent residence at Blia Yao's house. Every month Ly Foung returned to his wife and children for only a few days at a time. Alone at home and with a brood of small children Ly Foung's wife could not work the fields. One year four fields were untended, forcing her to rely on her mother and other relatives. Va suffered miserably, and her children often went without so Ly Foung had to find a means of extracting a living from his job.[36]

Fortuitous circumstances seemed to favor Ly Foung. About the time he became a secretary to Blia Yao, the French authorities began to crack down on the Chinese merchants residing among the Hmong in the mountains. These merchants commanded profitable incomes by disregarding French monopoly law and illegally buying opium from Hmong. They were serious competitors of the colonial state, paying the Hmong higher prices for their opium. Moreover, since these merchants lived in mountain villages beyond the reach of the colonial authorities, they had been operating virtually tax free while evading corvée labor and other requisitions imposed on indigenous groups. In the eyes of the authorities, the merchants were noncontributors to colonial society.[37]

The French also believed the Chinese merchants were becoming a security risk. Many were staunchly opposed to the colonial government, their loyalty focused on their motherland, China. Just prior to the outbreak of World War I, a French officer noted that Chinese in the border regions of Laos and Vietnam were publishing propaganda pamphlets with pictures of soldiers in German uniforms.[38] The French, therefore, systematically forced the Chinese away from the Hmong villages as instability began to increase in Europe. Traders residing in Hmong villages were ordered to relocate to lowland towns where they could be supervised and their trading activities taxed. The evacuation of the Chinese merchants left the Hmong in dire need of basic necessities, particularly salt and cloth. No one emerged to fill the gap. Fear of disease, lack of language, cultural ignorance, and lowland prejudice made the Hmong of this period reluctant to go to the lowlands.[39] F. M. Savina, the French priest who circulated among the Hmong of Xieng Khouang and Tonkin during this period, wrote that the Hmong "all have the same fears of the plains, the humid lowlands which they call the land of buffaloes and leeches."[40]

Referring to the occasional interactions between Hmong and European courts, Maurice Abadie, a military officer who served in Tonkin in the early twentieth century, writes, "The Hmong dread European courts not because of the severity of the penalty laid down, but because these courts are most often located in towns situated at low altitudes where the Hmong cannot live. . . . At the announcement of sending them before the courts of the resident in Lao Kay (altitude of 90 meters), the culprits would throw themselves at our feet saying, 'Kill me right away because if you send me to Lao-kay, I will surely die there.'"[41] Henri Roux tells of a similar reaction by Blia Yao. When Roux left Nong Het to return to Europe on September 1914, Blia Yao accompanied him as far as the road that led to the lowland. Not wanting to appear disloyal but hoping that Roux would relieve him of the burden of going further, Blia Yao declared adamantly, "You know that I would, without a doubt fall sick [in the lowland], but I am prepared to accompany you all the same."[42] Roux, being a good blood brother, relieved Blia Yao of the burden of going further.

In addition to health considerations, the condescending attitudes and the alien cultures of the lowlanders were hard for the Hmong to comprehend. Savina describes the lowland perception of the Hmong: "Whoever has traveled among the Chinese, the Man, the Thai or the Annamites [Vietnamese], must have heard it said several times that the present Miao [Hmong] are still cave-dwellers and cannibals; that they are cruel, ferocious, traitors and thieves; that they eat raw meat and that they are ignorant of the usage of chopsticks and spoons; briefly, that they live secluded in their mountains as true savages, going about daily almost nude, and at night sleeping in the dirt, pell-mell, between niches like animals."[43]

This prejudice often resulted in discrimination. Perceiving the Hmong as intruders, lowlanders often subjected them to arbitrary rules. Speaking of the Lao in particular, one of Yang Dao's informants stated:

> In general the Lao were hostile toward the *montagnards*. They forbade them from passing through their villages or valleys with an ill person under the pretext that it would contaminate the region. They impose heavy fines upon Hmong who, through carelessness, pass through their land transporting a deer, a stag, or a wild boar. The Lao would claim that they have offended the protecting spirits of the soil, the Phi Moung. As a result, the culprit is fined a cow or a buffalo, which must be sacrificed to the spirits as sacrilegious reparation. The sacrifice would never occur, and the Hmong never understood much about these complicated histories of the *phi* that never remains in the same place.[44]

For a Hmong man, the lowland was a tantalizing, exotic mirage epitomized by the common phrase "The eyes see, but the feet do not reach" (*muag pom taw mus tsis txog*). So far removed was the lowland from his imagination that, in his mind, nothing less than the shedding of his mortal shape and his rebirth could persuade him to live there. This feeling persisted into the last decades of the twentieth century. Based on his fieldwork among the Hmong of Thailand, William Geddes writes, "In October 1970, I stood on top of Chiengdao Mountain with a Miao [Hmong] whose maize and opium field was just under the lip of the crater. As we looked down six thousand feet at the cars moving along the road to Chengmai he remarked that he would like to die and be born again so that he could live as a lowlander."[45]

In addition to the fear of death or unfair treatment, the majority of Hmong were simply not in the habit of trading for a living. As noted earlier, they viewed the Haw traders as lazy, dishonest indigents. Most Hmong cultivated opium for medicinal purposes and as a cash crop with which to pay their taxes, but they drew their livelihood primarily from swidden rice cultivation, not trade. Ly Foung was different. Disdaining hard labor and friendly with traders from his teenage years onward, he was not averse to the merchant life. He was also multilingual and multicultural and could easily traverse the ethnic lines even if the climate should still trouble him. He had already begun to trade on a small scale shortly after his marriage to Va, selling his first surplus rice harvest to the nearby merchants for a silver bar. He had an even better taste of profit when he sold wood he had gathered to build his house to a Chinese for forty kip, a nice sum in that day. Using this cash and two additional silver bars borrowed from his mother and grandmother, Ly Foung began small-scale trading.[46]

After the Chinese merchants were relocated to large towns around 1915, Ly Foung seized the opportunity to become a full-time trader. He was encouraged by the demands of the Hmong. Each year, as Ly Foung prepared to deliver the annual tax at Xieng Khouang, Hmong individuals approached him to ask that he bring back cloth and other necessities. Mao Song recalled:

> [The French made the Chinese go and] live in large towns, so that whoever engaged in trading would have to be registered and pay taxes. These Chinese had been trading and following the Hmong, selling things to the Hmong. When they made a profit, they only sent it to their wives and children in China. They were not requisitioned as coolies or corvéed to clear the jungle and dig the land for making roads. They [the French] chased those Chinese to town, to

Xieng Khouang. Thus, alas, no one remained to go and buy cloth and thread for the Hmong. Cloth and thread for making *paj ntaub* were nonexistent, so when my father went to Xieng Khouang, the Hmong would say, "Oh, this year we have no cloth or thread for making *paj ntaub* at all, no cloth for making clothes, but we cannot go [to Xieng Khouang]." It takes three days to get there [to go from Nong Het to Xieng Khouang on horseback]. . . . Three days! [So, the Hmong said,] "Since you can go, since you always go there with Kaitong [Blia Yao] to deliver the tax, you must buy [these things] for us so that we would have cloth to wear and use."[47]

Gradually, Ly Foung became the middleman in the region of Nong Het, exchanging goods between highlands and lowlands. He had the help of two opium-addicted Chinese brothers named Nai and Bo Han. Too poor to relocate, the brothers remained as servants in Ly Foung's household. Bo Han cared for the horses and helped Ly Foung in his trading business. When Ly Foung made the annual trip to Xieng Khouang, Bo Han came along to load the goods onto the horses. He saddled four horses for every trip, two for him and Ly Foung to ride and two to transport the goods back to Nong Het.

In Xieng Khouang, following the delivery of the taxes, Ly Foung was free to rummage through the local market stalls while Blia Yao and other indigenous leaders attended an oath of allegiance ceremony at the provincial *wat*, the Buddhist monastery. Ly Foung was exempt from the proceedings because he was only a secretary.[48] Mao Song continued: "So when they [the leaders] had gone to partake in the oath of allegiance ceremony, my father came to buy cloth, thread, shoes, hats, and all sorts of knick-knacks for that one [Bo Han] to package and saddle on the horses to take back home to stepmother [Va] so that stepmother could sell [them] and use the money to buy rice to feed her own children."[49]

Although Ly Foung had no salary working as a secretary, during these annual trips he capitalized on a very lucrative opportunity. According to Touby, he also traded in Vietnam, selling buffalo skins, deer antlers, and tiger and monkey bones at Muang Sen and buying cloth, salt, and other utensils to take back to his Hmong customers in Nong Het.[50] Among the important items that Ly Foung brought back were modern French medicines and Chinese herbal cures used to stave off common illnesses.[51] Over time Ly Foung became wealthy. He also became well known among the Hmong of the region who depended on his goods. Ly Foung's customers may have formed a political base, allowing him to become a potent rival of Blia Yao.

The Kidnapping of Lo Mai
and a Volatile Alliance with Blia Yao

Literacy, which brought Ly Foung to Blia Yao's house, also exposed him to the political requirements of a paramount Hmong leader. An ambitious man who did not hesitate when opportunities came along, Ly Foung seized the chance to become Blia Yao's political apprentice. Endowed with keen intelligence, he expertly adopted Blia Yao's skills for his own use. Just as Blia Yao's marriages to women of different clans had made him the paramount Hmong leader of Nong Het, so Ly Foung hoped to solidify an alliance with Blia Yao through his daughter, Lo Mai (see fig. 14). Ly Foung had been persuaded to remain at Blia Yao's house by Jer, Blia Yao's fourth wife, of the Ly clan, but he was not of the same lineage as her. In fact, her relatives had rejected Ly Foung's father, Dra Pao, decades earlier.[52] Ly Foung needed to forge a closer tie to Blia Yao, and he did that by marrying Mai.

When Ly Foung came to work for Blia Yao, Mai was a child. She was the daughter of Blia Yao's first wife, See Vue, and the full sister of Tsong Tou, Blia Yao's eldest son, who inherited his title in 1925. By 1917 Mai had matured into an attractive maiden. She had grown up around Ly Foung, but given their relationship it is doubtful he would have dared to flirt with her. According to the system of Hmong social reckoning, Ly Foung was a clan brother of Jer, Mai's stepmother, and, therefore, an "uncle" (*dab laug*) to Mai in the family tree. Given the generational difference, it would have been considered highly improper, though not completely impossible, for anything to develop between the two. As Prasit Leepreecha explains, the Hmong practice social etiquette to guard against intergenerational marriages: "Based on a former marriage between the two clans, marriage across generations is prohibited. For example, a man cannot marry any of his mother's sisters (*mi tub yuav niamtais*), or any of his sister's daughters (*dablaug yuav mi ntxhais*). However, if this situation does occur among the close relatives of two clans, the groom's side may be fined during the wedding ceremony, in order to adjust the generation system between members of both sides."[53]

The "fine" is the sacrifice of a pig, quite a hefty price in those days, in order to "twist the tongue" (*quav nplaig*) and remove the public scandal. "Twisting the tongue" refers to the idea that the relations of the groom (Ly Foung) and bride (Mai), the forms of addresses, have to be redefined. Specifically, in this case, Ly Foung was demoted in the family tree so that he would be of the same generation as Mai, becoming a cousin as opposed to being an uncle, before they could solemnize the marriage.

Figure 14. A rare image of Lo Mai (*right*) smiling for the camera next to one of Blia Yao's wives (*left*), who may or may not be her mother, See Vue. (Courtesy of Archives nationales d'outre-mer, FR ANOM, Aix-en-Provence, 16_8FI_524_V059N349)

Mai's kidnapping was also wrong on another level given that Ly Foung, for many years, had been a trusted member of her family and, in some ways, had become a true uncle to her even if his designs on her were not tabooed by actual blood tie. Moreover, because Ly Foung was a grown man well versed in Hmong ritual protocols, it is not inconceivable that Blia Yao would have considered the kidnapping of Mai to be a deliberate transgression against his authority. Ly Foung would have been expected to know better and to treat Blia Yao, a patron, with more respect. Blia Yao's grandson, Ger Lo, said indeed that Ly Foung was given explicit warnings by Blia Yao. "My grandfather, Blia

Yao, told Ly Foung to give up any designs on my aunt. He said he was against any contemplation of such a marriage."[54]

That Ly Foung resorted to kidnapping Mai confirms that he knew Blia Yao was against the marriage. Otherwise he would have sought a formal negotiation using marriage brokers. Hmong often avoid formal negotiations because it requires additional fees on top of the formal brideprice paid to the bride's clan and so is more expensive, but Ly Foung was a rich man who would have had no problem absorbing the supplementary costs. Kidnapping Mai was a way for Ly Foung to force Blia Yao's hand. Unless Blia Yao could put up with the resulting loss of face and a tarnished reputation for his kidnapped daughter he would have to allow Mai's wedding to proceed.

Ly Foung may have had his eye on Mai for some time, but he needed the right encouragement to make his move. The opportunity came during Tsong Tou's wedding celebration. When Tsong Tou brought his wife home there was a joyous celebration. Back then a wedding, especially one in a rich family like Blia Yao's, was incomplete without a formal feast accompanied by the ritual exchange of *kwv txhiaj*, a poetic singing contest between the most talented eligible maiden and the men. Married men were not excluded from singing because men could marry as many wives as their wealth and personal standing would allow. Married women, however, could only hope to participate vicariously through their grown daughters and nieces. Ly Foung, a virtual resident of Blia Yao's house, was among the guests. He was a gifted singer, able to create intricate rhymes extemporaneously.[55] Blia Yao's three minor wives, bursting with youthful spirits but tied down by the rules regarding married women, wanted to hear Ly Foung sing. They asked, and Ly Foung said, "I will sing only if Mai answers me."[56] Blia Yao's wives, who were about the same age as Mai, cajoled her until she agreed. Mai and Ly Foung exchanged flirtatious rhymes in this love court, a contest of wits. Perhaps the teenage Mai had innocently aimed only to appease her stepmothers, but her willingness to engage in verbal jousting opened the door for Ly Foung to redefine their relationship. She had changed her position from that of a niece to that of an eligible maiden, a potential match for Ly Foung.

Blia Yao was not oblivious to Ly Foung's ambition. After Tsong Tou's wedding, Blia Yao forbade Mai to go anywhere alone. But he could not monitor her every move. The exact circumstance that led to Mai becoming a captured bride remains unclear. Touby, Mai's son, says that the kidnapping took place on a day when Blia Yao was not home. Mai's sick mother asked her to go to a distant village and gather medicinal herbs to be made into a potion for her to drink. Mai could not find anyone to accompany her, so she went alone. Ly Foung, who had kept a watchful eye on her, recruited ten of his relatives to intercept her en route.[57] Mao Song, Mai's daughter, on the other hand, described a more elaborate plan, saying that Ly Foung conspired with the women of Mai's household. He had the women lure Mai to Blia Yao's crop fields in Naj Hais, located furthest away from Blia Yao's village, where he could kidnap her at will. Mao Song hinted that Jer, who lavished attention on Ly Foung as a clan brother so that he would serve Blia Yao, may have had a hand in the plot.[58] Alfred W. McCoy's sources confirmed the conspiracy, although they said it was an uncle who lured Mai away. He writes, "In 1918 Ly Foung decided to marry Lo Bliayao's favorite daughter, May [Mai], but instead of consulting with the father himself, Ly Foung reportedly paid the bride's uncle to arrange the abduction."[59] McCoy's version, it should be noted, seems to be about another one of Ly Foung's wives, Choua Kue, and not about Mai. Choua's kidnapping, as will be described below, was indeed orchestrated by her uncle and Ly Foung. Careful orchestration undoubtedly also played a part in Mai's capture as well. Arranging for ten men to carry off a bride could not have been done on the spur of the moment.

Blia Yao was furious at the audacity of Ly Foung. He refused to accept the negotiators sent to formalize the marriage, causing consternation among the clans. Blia Yao was a willful man who could not be easily persuaded. The elders of the Lo clan had to intercede with a united voice. Citing custom dictated by reciprocal actions between the clans, they argued that because Blia Yao had kidnapped Jer, a woman of the Ly clan, he had no grounds to contest Ly Foung's abduction of Mai.[60] Not allowing the wedding to go forward would have soured Blia Yao's relations with the Ly clan. Thus, he grudgingly allowed the wedding to proceed, but at the conclusion of the ceremony he expressed his disapproval once again by withholding Mai's dowry. He handed Mai her clothes and promised only that he would send her dowry when he judged that Ly Foung was a good husband. Touby chooses to interpret Blia Yao's withholding of the dowry as the beginning of what eventually led to Mai's suicide, writing, "How sad my mother must have been that she no longer wanted to live."[61] From the start, Mai was caught between the egos of her father and her husband. Moreover, Ly Foung had aimed to acquire an ally, but instead he aroused lasting enmity.

A minor wife is generally perceived as the one who commands the husband's love since her marriage is often the result of self-indulgence on the man's part.[62] It is not uncommon for Hmong men to marry the first woman their parents choose for them out of material interest; then, when they are financially established and can pay the brideprice on their own, they may marry another wife for what would be considered romantic reasons in the western tradition. Mai had witnessed her father treating his then most junior fourth wife, Jer, with great affection.[63] She provided him with political support but had his heart as well. While the senior wives did the backbreaking work of swidden cultivation, Jer did less demanding domestic tasks at home. She was Blia Yao's public wife, who received guests and oversaw every cent of Blia Yao's great wealth. She also exercised tremendous influence over Blia Yao, often being summoned, as noted earlier, to render judgment in disputes. The bad aura of Mai's wedding afforded her no favor as the most junior wife, however. Her marriage to Ly Foung was not out of love. Ly Foung had already married his first wife, against the advice of his mother, for that indulgent purpose.[64] Ly Foung married Mai for political advantage, but the marriage was marred by Blia Yao's public disapproval.

As a minor wife without status, Mai was the workhorse in Ly Foung's household. In effect she suffered the reverse fate of her stepmother Jer. While Ly Foung's first wife stayed home with her five children as the public wife, Mai worked in the fields. She bore her burden quietly at first, but bearing children added to Mai's hardship. Mao Song spoke of her mother's ordeal:

> In [19]17 my father kidnapped my mother. Then my mother had to bear the burden of transporting goods from the fields, of working in the fields. After my mother had died and I had grown up, I saw those fields myself. My mother went to work in the fields every day, to carry back the corn, a basket full of mustard leaves. After Nhia By [Touby] was born, when she went [to the fields] she carried him on her back, carried her basket in the front. When she returned and had gathered goods, she carried the basket on the back, [and] carried Nhia By in the front. This was the only way she could gather greenery for the pigs to eat and mustard leaves [for the family] to eat. Some days she carried corn. My mother did that all the time until all three of us were born. My father still went to work for grandfather as usual. My father was never home.[65]

Ly Foung's constant absences may have contributed to Mai's hardship. Without him to mediate the power dynamics of the home, the teenage Mai was under the control of the older, more mature first wife. Hard work did not drive Mai to suicide, however. Political complications between Ly Foung and her father did that.

French Administrative Changes (1921)

For two decades, Blia Yao had monopolized the power structure in the region of Nong Het. Close to colonial figures, he had the undisputed backing of the

French and ranked among those native officials who "brandished the scarecrow of the French bogeyman."[66] Hmong feared Blia Yao because of his French connections. This fear proved to be not unfounded when, in January 1920, several weeks after Shong Ger had chased Blia Yao from his home village of Yeng Pha, Blia Yao returned with the full force of the colonial army. Blia Yao was merciless in his victory, almost decimating completely the male lines of Shong Ger and his followers. The few boys who survived did so because their relatives dressed them as girls or hid them in baskets and had them carried off to live with their maternal relatives. By March 1921, the rest of Pa Chay's troops had been hunted down, and the rebellion that had begun in 1918 was finally brought to an end.

Blia Yao's merciless show of force was also the beginning of his gradual decline in power. Although Blia Yao was victorious, Pa Chay's rebellion had caused irreparable damage to his prestige. The way he extorted money from participants after the rebellion did little to help his image. Most important, Pa Chay had forced the French to recognize the need for qualified Hmong administrators and power sharing among the clans. Under these circumstances, Ly Foung's language skills became indispensable. Pa Chay's rebellion caused the French to recognize and reward Ly Foung for his abilities, an effort that led to a complete break between the two men.

Although the French dismissed Pa Chay as a "madman," the three-year rebellion that spread across forty thousand square miles was a testament, so some admitted, to the inadequacy of their administration. "An entire people does not become fanatical overnight," Savina writes, "without apparent reason, following the voices of the first sorcerers who came along; and mere neglect has never pushed to rebellion an entire group of people, composed of different tribes separated from each other by a hundred kilometers."[67] Colonial officials were forced to reckon to an extent the complex ethnic political situation under their charge.

R. Barthelemy, the commissioner at Xieng Khouang, was even more direct about French neglect of the population in the heights:

> Laos is apparently organized for administrative purposes as though it were populated solely by Laotians. The laws are Laotian and so are the officials who apply them; and the Provincial Council, the embryo of our future Consultative Chamber, has never included a single representative of the mountain races. Fixed in the valleys from the beginning because of logistic necessity, we have little by little centralized the indigenous administration into the hands of those who were nearest by. . . . The oversimplification, on the contrary, increases our

administrative difficulties because, to all those non-Buddhists who live in the mountains and are still illiterate, orders can only be transmitted verbally; they are ill-understood and often ill-transmitted.[68]

Addressing the Hmong situation specifically, another officer observes: "For twenty-five years we have been, in effect, in a country occupied by the Meo [Hmong] and we do not know a word of their language. We have neither interpreters, nor schools, nor troops, nor administrators in sufficient numbers . . . [and] no study exists on the social state of our subjects with which . . . we are not in direction relations. The Meo say, 'We do not see you.'"[69]

The new demand for qualified administrators who could deal directly with the Hmong made Ly Foung's language abilities indispensable. For over a decade, he had toiled quietly behind Blia Yao. As an insignificant secretary, he was not even included in the oath of allegiance ceremony that took place annually at Xieng Khouang. After Pa Chay's rebellion, however, Ly Foung's unique skills attracted French attention. He was among those whom the French envisioned as the next generation of qualified administrators.

Addressing the grievances of the Hmong included giving them access to the colonial government and establishing power sharing among the different clans. A redistricting of the cantons took place, and eight new *tasseng* (sub-district) positions were created: four in the region of the south, in Xieng Khouang; and four in the region of the north around Muang Heup (Luang Prabang). The Hmong were told to elect their own chiefs to occupy these positions, ending perhaps some of the complaints about being subjected to the authority of Lao officials. Savina, fluent in Hmong, served as the interpreter. He writes, "The Government of the Protectorate has decided that the Miao [Hmong] race will henceforth not be subordinated to any other race. The Miao will therefore govern themselves in the future, like the Laotians, the Tho, and the Annamites [Vietnamese], under the supervision of the Government of the Protectorate."[70]

Although a substantial number of Hmong had rallied to Pa Chay, the French decided that former Hmong village chiefs, with the exception of the *sung quan* of Phou Nhi, would be retained. The *sung quan* was demoted to punish him for his tardiness in surrendering. The French officer in charge of these negotiations believed that the Hmong could occupy positions beyond the subdistrict level, though only after they had proved themselves worthy, writing, "Election of a *quan* [county leader] Hmong will be undertaken later when the actions of the *tasseng* can be judged, and when one among them shows his loyalty and intelligence above those of his colleagues."[71] Although the Hmong held only subdistrict positions, they could now submit taxes directly to the French. Additional plans were drawn up for schools to be created to educate the sons of the Hmong chiefs, ending the need for non-Hmong interpreters, whom the Hmong distrusted. This educational provision, however, was not carried out until 1939.[72]

The French also agreed, as a final provision, not to intercede in Hmong social and cultural matters. The Hmong were to be governed under their customary laws; the French would intervene only as a court of last appeal when Hmong laws were deemed inadequate. The colonial authorities were positive that these measures would produce the desired effect of bringing the Hmong gently into the fold. A final colonial report states, "The commander of operations and the commissioner of government took away from these meetings the best impression and the certitude that calm has absolutely returned to these cantons where two months before the entire population, up in arms, had engaged our companies of *tirailleurs*."[73] Accordingly, the military columns were disbanded on March 21, 1921, and the troops sent back to their respective posts in Dien Bien Phu, Hua Phan, and Xieng Khouang. A single company of Vietnamese infantry was maintained temporarily in Luang Prabang, occupying the posts of Muang Heup, Hatsa, and Muang Ngoi. Additional *garde indigines* were kept at Nong Het and Sop Sang to discourage further rebellion in Xieng Khouang.[74]

Although they were meant to appease the Hmong, the new positions led to tension as competing clans vied to stake a claim to the titles being handed out. Most noticeable was the bitter rivalry generated between Ly Foung and Blia Yao, who had no intention of allowing anyone to emerge as an equal in the region of Nong Het. Blia Yao was even more determined to keep Ly Foung down when French efforts to make him the paramount chief in Xieng Khouang Province were blocked by other clan leaders. At the conclusion of Pa Chay's War, the commissioner delivered the order announcing their plans to fashion Blia Yao into a Hmong broker, the first ethnic representative. Ly Foung was charged with the task of disseminating the news orally to all the Hmong *tassengs*. According to Touby, three Hmong *tassengs* in the regions of Phukheb, Moos Moj, and Khookheej Moos Pej refused to be subjected to Blia Yao's authority. The *tasseng* of Moos Moj, Lo Chue, was of the same clan as Blia Yao. Ly Foung faced a dilemma. He was caught between fulfilling the duty of conveying these objections to the French or being loyal to his father-in-law, which meant keeping silent and allowing the French to proceed with their appointment. Ly Foung chose duty over loyalty. Touby explains: "Ly Tsia Foung got these double-edged-knife words [of objection] from the *tassengs* and became very despondent and stressed. He was unsure of the best course of action to take. If he did not publicize the objections [to the French] it would not be right, but if he did not keep these objections sealed, he would make enemies [especially of Blia Yao]. Ultimately, he conveyed every word to the French authorities and to Lo Blia Yao, who was his father-in-law."[75]

The Hmong were used to a more egalitarian system in which clan leaders enjoyed approximately equal status and a large degree of autonomy. It is not surprising that centralization efforts to nominate a paramount chief met with resistance. Due to their lack of knowledge about Hmong social structure, the French had opened the door to a potential squabble. They did not want to risk creating another ethnic situation since they had just emerged from a period of instability. They therefore recanted their promise to promote Blia Yao—an act that humiliated him. Touby contionues: "After the French commissioner received the news [about the objections] he did not make Lo Blia Yao a paramount leader as he had promised. He only made him a *naikong* [district chief] with authority over the Hmong *tasseng* in Muang Kham [Nong Het]. Lo Blia Yao declined the offer. He said that his title of *kaitong* was more prestigious than that of a mere *naikong*, and that a *naikong* was only a minor servant of the French."[76]

Understandably, Blia Yao felt insulted and perhaps even betrayed by the broken promise. This may be the reason why his grandson, Ger, told me in 2008 that their family later turned to struggle against the French because, by serving the French, they experienced firsthand the colonial yoke.[77] The French had not only embarrassed Blia Yao, but they had undermined his authority with their action. They had also signaled to the Hmong that there was room for other leaders to have a voice in the system and that Blia Yao did not enjoy their unconditional blessing. The message was certainly not lost on the perceptive Ly Foung. A united group of leaders could curtail Blia Yao's dictatorial influence with the French. Once he fell out of favor with Blia Yao, Ly Foung would apply this strategy to his own benefit.

Blia Yao perceived Ly Foung's reporting of the *tassengs'* objections to the French as an attempt to supplant his authority. As he understood it, perhaps accurately, the three nonliterate *tassengs* had little standing with the French, which led him to suspect that Ly Foung as a lone culprit had persuaded the French to renege on their promise. Blia Yao therefore held a grudge against Ly Foung.[78] French efforts to make Ly Foung a *tasseng* several months later seemed to confirm Blia Yao's suspicions. Unaware of Blia Yao's feelings, Ly Foung accompanied him to Xieng Khouang as usual when it was time to deliver the taxes in 1921. The trip was a quite a joyous occasion for Blia Yao because he had extorted a hoard of silver from the Hmong who had joined Shong Ger. In a celebratory mood, Blia Yao took along his minor wives and his daughter Mai, who carried Mao Song on her back. Blia Yao had no inkling of the incident that would radically change relations between himself and Ly Foung.

After the delivery of the taxes in Xieng Khouang, the French commissioner announced that Ly Foung would be assigned to one of the newly allotted *tasseng* positions, presiding over Blia Yao's subdistrict of Keng Khoai.[79] The French were recognizing Ly Foung's centrality to their administration. Since Ly Foung was his son-in-law, there was no reason to think that Blia Yao would object — revealing once again French ignorance of the complexity of Hmong social structure. A son-in-law was an ally but an outsider, not a family member. Unaware of what they were doing, the French had shown favor to the Ly clan, undermining Blia Yao's Lo clan. Blia Yao insisted that the new title must be given to his eldest son, Tsong Tou.[80] The commissioner did not want to create a fallout with Blia Yao, who had just helped him put down a rebellion. But the commissioner also did not want to appoint Tsong Tou to the position, as he was nonliterate and unqualified. At the end of the day the matter was quietly dropped. Neither Ly Foung nor Tsong Tou was named *tasseng*, and Blia Yao's group returned home in somber spirits.[81]

The Death of Lo Mai

Back in Nong Het, Ly Foung went to work for his father-in-law as before, but he did not forget what Blia Yao had done in Xieng Khouang. Ly Foung now realized that Blia Yao was determined to keep him from rising. His marriage to Mai had not solidified their alliance as he had hoped. Reflecting on the incident, Ly Foung felt ever more strongly that he should have been given the *tasseng* position since he already oversaw the daily operations (of the local administration. He was a *phutong* (assistant to the canton chief), but that was a minor honorary title that carried little weight within Hmong society. He felt used, but, in the position of a son-in-law and secretary, he was powerless to counter Blia Yao overtly. Ly Foung's frustrations grew until his dissatisfaction turned into bitterness and ill treatment of Mai. Although he maintained a respectful demeanor in front of Blia Yao, in his own home Ly Foung began to openly complain about the injustice of his father-in-law. He spoke incessantly to visitors about the incident that had occurred at Xieng Khouang. Mai was deeply embarrassed when Ly Foung attacked her father's name, but she bore the shame silently.[82]

As Ly Foung's bitterness grew, he began to neglect his role as household head, which required the fair treatment of Mai as a minor wife. Since her marriage in 1917, Mai had quietly borne major responsibility for the daily chores outside the home. The situation became worse when the first wife was allowed to isolate and exploit Mai without a word from Ly Foung. One day the first wife told Mai to grind some corn, using the heavy grindstone. Usually such work took a minimum of two persons—one to pull the handle that moved the grindstone and one to feed the corn into it. No one was sent with Mai, however. She went alone, carrying a basket of corn on one shoulder and her infant son, Bo Lua, on the other.[83] She attempted to grind the corn alone but found the task too much to bear and returned home to plead with Ly Foung. To her chagrin, Mai found Ly Foung and the first wife in a united front against her. Mao Song described the first of two major incidents that led to Mai's suicide.

> So my mother carried a baby and dragged a basket full of corn on one shoulder to go to the grindstone to be ground, but it was too heavy, and my mother could not grind [the corn], so she returned [home] and said, "Tsia Foung, when [Nao] Chao's mother [the first wife] goes to do the grinding, everyone goes along to help. When I go, I have to go alone. I can't grind it. It [the grindstone] is too heavy. I can't grind, so I won't." [She] said this, which made the first wife angry, so she cut in and an argument ensued.
>
> My father intervened, saying, "[If you] can't grind, then don't grind! Who is forcing you? Who is paying you? Who is insisting that you grind?" As my father said that, my mother talked back, so he hit her. . . . My father never allowed anyone to talk back. One can never talk back to my father. So my mother was beaten. Both of them, the first wife and my father, ganged up on my mother [verbally]. Then my father beat up my mother, and my mother cried and cried. Then she carried me, Bo Lua, and Nhia By [Touby], all three of us, to the house of my father's mother.[84]

After her beating, Mai ran to her mother-in-law's house to seek sanctuary with a female kin. At the time, Mai's mother-in-law was living with her elder son, who was married to Mai's maternal aunt, the sister of her mother.[85] Mai sought her aunt's protection and refused to return home. Ly Foung refused to invite her back either. This was a contest of wills, and neither side seemed willing to concede.

The final incident that led to Mai's suicide occurred several days later when the family slaughtered a cow for a feast. Since no one was available to fetch water or other things necessary for butchering and cooking the cow, Ly Foung's first wife sent her oldest daughter, Po Zoua, to ask Mai to return home. Mai had always been the one who did these outside chores, but she refused to come. Mai's mother-in-law advised that Mai should not be forced to return home given her unsettled state of mind. Po Zoua abided by her grandmother's advice and returned home alone, but she was immediately sent back to fetch Mai a second time. She barely succeeded in persuading Mai to return home, dragging and pulling on her clothes.

Sending Po Zoua to fetch Mai twice was as close to an apology as Mai would get from Ly Foung and the first wife, but Mai was not appeased. It would have been more respectful for Ly Foung or the first wife to fetch her instead of sending a child to do the job. As soon as Mai arrived home with her three children, Touby, Mai's eldest child, saw that they were butchering a cow. He had not eaten and was hungry, so he asked to eat some of the cooked meat. Still angry, Mai yelled at Touby, "Gluttonous maggot!"[86] Ly Foung knew the insult to his child was really aimed at him. It was perhaps an allusion to Ly Foung's seemingly unquenchable thirst for power that had led him to daily abuse Blia Yao's name to visitors. He beat Mai once more for her insolence, this time in front of everyone who had gathered to butcher the cow. Mai was deeply shamed. She went straight into the bedroom, slammed the door behind her, and swallowed a fatal dose of opium. For the whole day, Mai was left to sulk alone as everyone feasted.

As the day wore on, one of Ly Foung's sisters became concerned. She went to see what was up with Mai. When she learned that Mai had eaten opium, she went to inform Ly Foung's first wife, but the first wife responded with anger instead of empathy or concern. The sister left, not really knowing what to do since the first wife was mistress of the house. She returned a little while later to check on Mai's condition. Not wanting to offend the first wife, the sister came under the pretext of asking for one of Mai's hens. Through the bedroom door, Mai said the hen was roaming in the yard, and Ly Foung's sister should catch it on her own if she wanted it. Since Mai was able to answer her, the sister thought she was still lucid so there was no need to worry. The sister did nothing else and returned to her own home.[87]

As the sun set, Mai was inching closer and closer to death. Still, neither Ly Foung nor his first wife expressed concern about her condition. Neither of them went to inquire after Mai. Finally, realizing that she was going to die, Mai asked her son Touby to fetch Ly Foung so she might say her last few words to him. Ly Foung stubbornly refused to go to the bedroom. Later Touby was asked a second time to fetch his father only to provoke screaming rage in Ly Foung. Mao Song continued her narration:

> At the time, Tsia Ze Moua, who was my father's brother-in-law, was sleeping on the guest bed smoking opium. The first time summoned, my father did not

go [to my mother]. The second time [Touby] said [to my father], "My mother has eaten opium. Go so that she can have a word with you."

[My father replied] "Oh, she has not died yet? Add two more *lag* [of opium]. She has not died."

So the brother-in-law got up [from the guest bed] and went to raise my mother into a sitting position. He gave her water to drink. After he gave her water, he had two persons hold her on each arm and turn her in circles to induce vomiting. They'd only done two complete circles when my mother could not stand anymore. Her knees buckled under her, and she vomited until she died. Thus, I was left without a mother.[88]

Death by opium poisoning is excruciatingly slow as the person's lungs fill with bodily fluid until he or she is drowned. From her aunt's description, Mao Song felt that her father was determined not to save her mother. It took her mother all day to die, and he did nothing during that time. That was perhaps his final revenge on Blia Yao for having refused to allow the French to appoint him a *tasseng*. Allowing Mai to die signaled how deeply disillusioned Ly Foung had become with Blia Yao. Although Mao Song and Touby were innocent bystanders in this adult contest of wills, they were often told that they were responsible for their mother's death, perhaps to shift the blame away from the first wife, Ly Foung, and the many who stood idly by while Mai was dying. Mao Song recalled: "Later on they say—when we were little, that is—they told us that the reason our mother died was because we wanted to eat meat all the time, and no matter how much meat we were fed, it was not enough. We just wanted to eat more and more of it. No matter how much we ate, it was not enough, and that was why our mother died."[89]

A hoped-for alliance had developed into a chasm of bitter sentiment, culminating in Mai's tragic death. Unlike the fairy tale, the princess had not been able to put the rejected orphan, Ly Foung, on the throne after all. Through her son Touby, Mai did open the door for Ly Foung to stake a claim to Blia Yao's legacy, however. Touby emerged decades later as the most prestigious Hmong leader of the twentieth century. Meanwhile, shortly after Mai's death in 1921, Ly Foung sought another dragon princess to establish an alliance with another clan.

Divide and Conquer Politics: Ly Foung's Alliance with the Green Hmong

Mai's death, however tragic, freed Ly Foung from Blia Yao's shadow. As a son-in-law, Hmong decorum dictated that he not compete overtly with Blia

Yao. But now, after Mai's death, he had the independence to maneuver openly for power. Blia Yao was devastated by the death of his beloved daughter. He and his first wife, See, were not appeased by overtures of apology made by Ly Foung. See cursed Ly Foung loudly throughout the long days of the funeral and created a ruckus by banging on the walls of his home. For his part, Blia Yao demanded that Ly Foung relinquish Mao Song, Mai and Ly Foung's daughter, as compensation for the loss of his own daughter. Blia Yao would raise Mao Song as a wife for her cousin, Bee Chou, Tsong Tou's son and Blia Yao's grandson. Ly Foung agreed to an engagement but begged that he be allowed to raise Mao Song until she was sixteen. Blia Yao relented only when Ly Foung also agreed to pay a heavy fine of twenty-four *lag* of silver (two bars) for having driven Mai to suicide.[90] The betrothal of Mao Song to Bee Chou appeased Blia Yao a bit, but the marriage never took place. Blia Yao died before Mao Song turned sixteen, and since Ly Foung had no interest in furthering an already broken alliance he never mentioned the engagement again. As Ly Foung had ignored Blia Yao's explicit instructions not to kidnap Mai years earlier, he easily broke the promise of a marriage arrangement. Blia Yao's sons were probably powerless to pursue the matter. Mao Song eventually married into the Vang clan.[91]

Although McCoy claims that Blia Yao, "in a rage," fired Ly Foung and "severed all ties with the Ly clan" immediately after Mai's death, Mao Song insisted that her father worked with Blia Yao until 1926.[92] She supplied as proof a photo, taken that year, of Choua Kue, Ly Foung's third wife, posing with the Lo family (see fig. 9). Ly Foung married Choua after Mai had died. That year, he took Choua with the entourage to deliver taxes in Xieng Khouang, where she sat with Blia Yao's family for the portrait. Thus, it appears that despite the bitterness caused by Mai's death, Blia Yao continued to rely on Ly Foung to do paperwork. Blia Yao's persistent dependence underscores the power of literacy and foreshadows the later usurpation of his position by Ly Foung and his educated sons. As much as he may have wanted to, Blia Yao could not dismiss Ly Foung's practical role in bolstering his own prestige. Blia Yao may have also felt that he should watch Ly Foung closely, keeping him under surveillance to ensure that he did not rise to a position of significance.

For his part, Ly Foung continued to serve Blia Yao, maintaining a loyal image. Besides, he could not easily relinquish the financial opportunities offered by his position. So Ly Foung went to Blia Yao's house as usual, returning to his home in De Mua Tha only sporadically. He also continued to oversee the construction of CR7 on Blia Yao's behalf, registering and paying workers on a regular basis. Each year he accompanied Blia Yao to Xieng Khouang as before to deliver the taxes. From Xieng Khouang, he brought goods that his first wife sold to Hmong at a profit.[93] The unchanged pattern belied a torrent of emotion beneath the routine. It was only a matter of time before these sentiments erupted into open conflict.

While father and son-in-law feigned loyalty to one another, others were ready to exploit the raw emotions that lay beneath the calm. Perhaps Ly Foung was also contemplating his escape from under Blia Yao as well. He was open to a new marriage alliance, which he found quickly in the Green Hmong of Phak Boun, located southwest of CR7. As the White Hmong were the first group to migrate into Nong Het, they had long dominated the leadership of the region. For years the Green Hmong of Phak Boun, led by three half brothers of the Kue clan—Joua Kao, Cha Tsia, and Tsong Lia—had felt that a leader of their own cultural group would rule them more justly. Hoping to obtain a *tasseng* appointment, they had asked Ly Foung on several occasions to convey their wishes to the French. When he was hoping to advance via Blia Yao, Ly Foung had rejected their overtures. After Blia Yao had blocked his appointment by the French and following Mai's suicide, he no longer had illusions about his relationship with Blia Yao. In light of this, the Green Hmong became a viable and valuable ally.

Less than a year after Mai's death, Ly Foung kidnapped as a third wife Choua Kue, the daughter of Tsong Lia. The attractive sixteen-year-old Choua was engaged to another man with whom she was in love. Her brideprice had already been paid in full. All that remained was for the couple to celebrate the wedding feast. She could not have imagined marrying Ly Foung, an old man who had driven his second wife to suicide. Choua's uncle, Cha Tsia, wanted a convenient alliance with Ly Foung, however. Ly Foung was relatively wealthy, literate, and well positioned to help the Kue clan obtain a title from the French. When Choua made a final visit to her uncle's house before the celebration of her wedding, Cha Tsia asked if Ly Foung was interested in having her as a second wife. Cha Tsia promised to resolve the potentially explosive situation with Choua's intended husband so that Ly Foung would lose no more than three bars of silver, the brideprice already paid for Choua. Ly Foung was intrigued by the proposition. While Choua was swimming at the river with her cousins, he checked her out secretly. He brought his first wife, Va, along. Va saw that Choua was a decent young lady and gave Ly Foung permission to marry her. Choua was bitter about her kidnapping throughout her life. Strong willed and physically robust, she was not the long-suffering wife that Mai had been. She often took on the aging Ly Foung physically, pulling his shirt over his head to arrest his beating arms and letting him go only when he had promised not to lay a hand on her again.[94]

Several years after Ly Foung had solidified his alliance with the Green Hmong of Phak Boun, an incident finally gave him the pretext to make a clean break with Blia Yao. In 1925 the construction of CR7 was completed. The French authorities held a recognition ceremony the following year and invited the indigenous dignitaries to Xieng Khouang. The authorities wanted to recognize the contributions of the major clan leaders whose cooperation had made the road possible by bestowing on them medals of commendation. Since Ly Foung had been instrumental in the construction, supervising the actual work of the road, he ranked first among those expected to receive a medal. Instead, Blia Yao gave the medal intended for Ly Foung to his half brother, Tsong Nou. The French saw Ly Foung's worth, however, and they nominated him to be a *tasseng* once again, as in 1921. Blia Yao countered again, declaring that any open position should be given to his son Tsong Tou. The French dropped the matter as before, but on his return to Phak Lak, Blia Yao decided on his own to hold a *baci* ceremony.[95] There he publicly pronounced Tsong Tou as his replacement.[96] Blia Yao presented the smaller of his three rhinoceros horns to Tsong Tou during the ceremony. Ly Foung was sorely disappointed and immediately resigned as Blia Yao's secretary.[97]

The Green Hmong leader of the Kue clan did not miss the cue to capitalize on the break between Blia Yao and Ly Foung. Joua Kao went to Ly Foung for a third time, asking him to petition the French for a *tasseng* position. This time, in the position of a son-in-law, Ly Foung willingly obliged. He led an entourage of the Green Hmong down to Ban Ban to ask that Joua Kao be appointed a *tasseng* with authority over the Green Hmong of Phak Boun. As Blia Yao had feared back in 1921, Ly Foung proved influential. The Lao and French authorities granted his request by dividing Nong Het into two separate subdistricts, Phak Boun and Keng Khoai, and awarding Phak Boun to Joua Kao, leaving Blia Yao with authority only over Keng Khoai.[98] This division effectively broke Blia Yao's hold over the Hmong of Nong Het, opening the door for Ly Foung to stake a new claim to regional leadership. Ly Foung became Joua Kao's secretary, serving in the same capacity as he had under Blia Yao.

Naturally, when orders for the division were presented to Blia Yao he responded in kind. Not lacking in political wiles, he fired back by alleging that Ly Foung had committed three crimes. Appealing directly to the provincial authorities at Xieng Khouang, Blia Yao petitioned Commissioner R. Barthelemy, claiming that Ly Foung was the real ideologue behind the Hmong rebellion of 1920. Shong Ger had led the battles, Blia Yao alleged, but Ly Foung was behind the strategies. Second, Blia Yao said, Ly Foung had murdered Lia Nao Vang in 1921. Finally, Ly Foung was now conspiring to overthrow the newly appointed Tasseng Kue Joua Kao in order to take over the subdistrict of Phak Boun.[99]

These were serious allegations. Curiously, Shong Ger was from the same village as Ly Foung—a village that served as the center of activity throughout much of the resistance. Many of Ly Foung's relatives had joined Shong Ger.[100] Moreover, three years later, in 1929, Ly Foung did take over the administrative position of Joua Kao, which he then handed over to his oldest son, Nao Chao. Thus, perhaps not all charges were baseless, brought by an embittered man. The charges of murder and of Ly Foung being a rebel leader seemed to have stemmed primarily from a defensive response to Ly Foung's divide-and-conquer tactics, however. Blia Yao took his time in making the allegations, reporting them five years after the fact. In any event, the report of these crimes coincided too perfectly with Ly Foung's political maneuvers.

Of the three charges, the accusation of murder, which came from Lia Nao's wife, seemed most credible to the authorities. Ly Foung was jailed for six months primarily on this charge. The death of Lia Nao was a tragic and complicated event that had occurred in 1921 before the death of Mai. A noted black magic practitioner and an opium addict, Lia Nao had been arrested by his fellow villagers on allegations of witchcraft. They accused him of having set in motion an evil conspiracy that fed his addiction while driving some families into destitution. They claimed that Lia Nao was setting his malignant spirits loose in order to make people sick so that they would have to call on his services, for which they had to pay him liberally in opium. In this manner, neighbors argued, they were kept as virtual slaves to Lia Nao's opium habit. This was a serious charge in the eyes of both the animist Hmong and the Christian French, who had an even more notorious history of dealing with suspected witches.

After the Hmong arrested Lia Nao, they sent him to be sentenced by Blia Yao at Phak Lak. As these Hmong lived several days' walk from Phak Lak, they had only reached Ly Foung's village of De Mua Tha by nightfall. They asked for shelter at Ly Foung's house since he was the village chief and the secretary of Blia Yao. That evening, before everyone retired to bed, Lia Nao's wife arrived to deliver a ball of opium to Lia Nao and then returned to her home village. In the middle of the night Lia Nao was heard panting and moaning, on the verge of death. As it was taboo for a nonkinsman to die in one's house, Ly Foung had the men who accompanied Lia Nao carry him to a guest shelter.[101] Lia Nao expired shortly afterward, and the men took him away to be buried before they returned home. Lia Nao never saw a trial.

It is unclear exactly what transpired. Tougeu Lyfoung guessed that fear of being sentenced to death by Blia Yao, who was notorious for his merciless temper, and poor health must have done Lia Nao in. Opium addicts were relatively inactive people who lay in bed most of the time, said Tougeu. That day Lia Nao had been forced to march for miles with his hands tied behind his back at a pace set by the physically robust men who accompanied him. Moreover, he had gone a whole day without opium. Ultimately, a combination of ill health, fear, hunger, dehydration, and withdrawal may have contributed to Lia Nao's death.[102] Touby offers an equally plausible scenario. He suggests that while Lia Na was in the house, he may have overhead Ly Foung say that the French burned witches at the stake. Lia Nao chose instead the Hmong path of committing suicide by ingesting opium.[103] Whatever the case, Ly Foung had no apparent motive to kill Lia Nao. Moreover, Lia Nao's death had occurred years earlier. It was evident that Blia Yao exploited the situation only to take down Ly Foung, not because he had an interest in finding genuine justice for Lia Nao's family. Besides, Ly Foung had bloodied his hands by driving Mai to commit suicide that same year. He could not be tried for Mai's suicide under either Hmong customary or French law, but Lia Nao's death gave Blia Yao legal grounds to allege murder.

When the Lao official in Ban Ban came to pay Blia Yao an annual visit at Phak Lak, he had Lia Nao's wife come before them to accuse Ly Foung of having killed her husband. An interpreter spoke on her behalf. Her testimony was accompanied by a "physical tantrum" during which "she threw herself on the ground at Blia Yao's house, crying and kicking like a child." This show of sentiment moved the Lao official to petition the French authorities at Xieng Khouang to investigate the charge.[104] The French sent an order demanding that Ly Foung come to the provincial capital, which he did without hesitation. When he arrived, Commissioner Barthelemy had left for France on a six-month vacation leave. The minor administrators placed Ly Foung in jail for the duration to await Barthelemy's return. When a trial was finally held, Tasseng Joua Kao, Madame Lia Nao, and other influential Hmong leaders were called to testify. Ultimately, no evidence was found against Ly Foung. Madame Lia Nao also admitted that Blia Yao had persuaded her to make the accusation. Ly Foung was released with an apology.[105]

Although Blia Yao had succeeded in embarrassing Ly Foung, his heavy-handed efforts backfired. While in jail, Ly Foung came to realize the full potential of his literacy. Unlike the ignorant Hmong who, when faced with such circumstances, would most likely have perished quietly, Ly Foung took the opportunity to research French law. He learned that he was entitled to a hearing and petitioned the French resident superior in Vientiane, who ordered that a trial take place.[106] When the charges were shown to be unsubstantiated, the

French authorities in Xieng Khouang, perhaps embarrassed by their own incompetence, personally accompanied Ly Foung home on horseback. Realizing that these allegations were the result of a personal feud between Blia Yao and Ly Foung, the Hmong, Lao, and French authorities attempted to heal the wound with a *baci* ceremony.

Mao Song Lyfoung, who was seven at the time, recalled the details of her father's return and the feast.

> So the French authorities accompanied my father from Xieng [Khaoung] to De Mua Tha, my father's village. There were so many people who filled the whole house—Hmong, Lao, everyone came. The Lao liked my father, so they came to see my father, too. [They] said, "Ly Foung has returned!" So they all came. They also asked Thaan Kam Muv [the French commissioner] to bring Grandfather Kaitong Blia Yao from his stone house. Then they killed chickens, pigs, and a cow to call back my father's soul, and they tied [strings around] the wrists of Kaitong Blia Yao and my father, asking them to be father and son-in-law as before.[107]

Despite the efforts of the French and Lao authorities, no reconciliation took place between Ly Foung and Blia Yao. The damage was too great on both sides. The *baci* ceremony, attended by many Hmong leaders and the Lao and French administrators who accompanied Ly Foung home, made a great impression on the Hmong, however. Ly Foung's release and the apology of the French were more evidence of Blia Yao's waning authority, sending a clear message that he no longer had a monopoly on French influence. Ly Foung became, therefore, an alternative source of hope for survivors of the 1920 rebellion who resented Blia Yao.

Unable to forget what Blia Yao had done to him, Ly Foung bought a piece of land for two hundred thousand kip and relocated farther west, founding the village of Phak Khe in 1927. He took with him all his relatives from the Thao, Yang, and Moua clans. Touby describes this move away from Blia Yao in the most evasive but symbolic terms: "He [Ly Foung] moved far away so that he would be free to raise his cattle. Grandfather Kaitong Lo Blia Yao's many cattle and water buffaloes, which had continually come from Phak Lak to graze among those of my father in the vicinity of De Mua Tha, would no longer be able to reach Phak Khe."[108] Certainly, the cattle of Blia Yao and Ly Foung had competed for grazing in the same green valley for far too long. As these cattle multiplied over the years, the valley had become overcrowded. At Phak Khe, far from the scrutiny of Blia Yao, Ly Foung was free to concentrate on his plans, and to consolidate more allies.

From Phak Khe, Ly Foung now worked as a secretary to Tasseng Kue Joua Kao of Phak Boun. For money, he sought an additional job with the colonial government. Although CR7 had been largely completed, sections of the road needed to be upgraded, and drainage ditches had to be dug. During the monsoon season, parts of the road would be washed away, requiring constant repairs. The French needed individuals to oversee the continual maintenance of the road. They assigned Ly Foung to the task over a stretch of road that passed near Phak Khe.[109] Decades earlier Blia Yao had risen to power because he cooperated in the road's construction. Ly Foung now occupied a similar role.

Ly Foung was also becoming essential to the nonliterate Hmong village chiefs. On a daily basis, the Hmong *naiban* (village chiefs) in the region sought his aid with paperwork, making up the constant stream of visitors to his temporary shelters built along the one section of CR7 that he supervised. These *naiban* asked Ly Foung to do everything, from reading and translating orders to writing tax receipts and recording birth and death registers. Mao Song Lyfoung, who, as a teenager in 1931, lived in these makeshift shelters with her father, recalled:

> At the time, no one was literate. For every village, the *naiban* had to come register you. He had to come ask what the mother's name is, what the father's name is, how many children, and so forth. Each [*naiban*] only had to register [people in] his village. However many households, he would tell my father who, then write it down. My father lived alongside the road only. My father went and took charge of a section of the road, and whenever he got a chance to sit down, he would just work on those papers. After he did the paperwork for Grandfather Kue [Joua Kao] and the *naiban*, they then collected the taxes, and then my father would have to do the paperwork for the taxes. After they collected the taxes—the Hmong are really smart, however much money they collected, they just told my father orally. When it came time to deliver the taxes, my father went [to Xieng Khouang] with Grandfather Kue, too.[110]

In essence Ly Foung was doing the administrative work for a substantial portion of the region. Over time village leaders from far and wide who depended on him came to know and respect Ly Foung. Gradually, Ly Foung's far-reaching duties made it possible for both the Hmong and the French to accept him as a leader. Ly Foung was, after all, the only one capable of carrying out the bureaucratic duties required by the French.

Getting the colonial authorities to divide Keng Khoai into two subdistricts was a most strategic move in curtailing Blia Yao's authority. It turned out also to be beneficial for Ly Foung. A drought in 1929 that devastated the year's opium crop paved the way for Ly Foung to assume charge of the Phak Boun subdistrict. By that time, Joua Kao had died, passing his *tasseng* title to Cha Tsia, a younger brother. Because the drought had wiped out a substantial portion of the Hmong's opium fields, Cha Tsia suffered a tax shortfall of two hundred thousand kip — a huge sum of wealth. At a loss as to what to do, the *tasseng* consulted with Ly Foung. Over the years, through trading and working on CR7, Ly Foung had become an extremely wealthy man. According to Mao Song, by that time, her father's wealth in silver and livestock had surpassed that of Blia Yao. Ly Foung offered to make up the tax shortfall. "After my father paid the tax, Tasseng Cha Tsia simply moved away from the region, leaving the administrative position of Phak Boun unoccupied. I don't know why."[111]

In light of the difficulties the Green Hmong went through to obtain the position, it is curious that Cha Tsia abandoned it so easily. On the other hand, the colonial yoke may have proved to be too much for Cha Tsia, who now realized that the burden of being an administrator often outweighed the benefits and prestige. He may also have felt that Ly Foung should be left in charge since he made up the tax shortfall. Or, he may have actually taken off with a portion of the tax money and made an agreement for Ly Foung to make up for it. Whatever the case, some Hmong interpreted Ly Foung's act as a purchase of the *tasseng* position and confused this 1929 tax shortfall incident with the one in 1936 that involved Tsong Tou, the son and successor of Blia Yao. Like Cha Tsia, Tsong Tou also relinquished the subdistrict of Keng Khoai to the French after encountering tax problems and having to pay for it out of his family's pocket. The French then handed the position to Ly Foung as well. Mao Song wanted to set the record straight that these were similar but separate events that occurred years apart.[112]

Ly Foung had been the one in charge of the administrative work all along, so little changed for those who remained in Phak Boun. He presided over the vacant position until 1930, when his eldest son, Nao Chao, returned to Nong Het with a primary school degree. From 1930 to 1935, Nao Chao oversaw the administrative duties of Phak Boun without carrying the actual title of *tasseng*.[113] He did not assume the official title of the position until Blia Yao had passed away. This may have been a cautious move on the part of Ly Foung. Blia Yao had accused him of conspiring to take this position back in 1926. Now that the allegation had become reality, Ly Foung probably wanted to avoid trouble by allowing Blia Yao to retain the illusion of being the uncontested paramount leader and the only Hmong *tasseng* in Nong Het.

Meanwhile, in the subdistrict of Keng Khoai, Blia Yao had bequeathed his title to his eldest son, Tsong Tou, in 1925, but in actuality he continued to perform the daily administrative work. Tsong Tou had no opportunity to gain experience. Moreover, while Blia Yao was not literate in Lao, he was robustly charismatic and reliably consistent in his manner. By contrast, Tsong Tou was a quiet, even reclusive, individual. Chronic ill health had also forced him to become an opium addict. The Hmong may cultivate opium as a cash crop to pay taxes, trade, and use as medicine, but they stigmatize addicts. Tsong Tou, therefore, had neither the reputation nor the force of personality to command authority over the Hmong. He was sent to work in the fields while the aged Blia Yao continued with the drudgery of administrative work and engaged in the mediation of disputes brought before him. Blia Yao's action undermined Tsong Tou's credibility. Blia Yao's other sons by his minor wives were equally unprepared to assume his responsibilities. He indirectly expressed his disappointment in his own sons by bemoaning openly that Touby, his grandson by Mai, alone had inherited his disposition. "Only my [Tou]By is like me," he often said with a sigh.[114] Blia Yao's words of praise became a self-fulfilling prophecy. Personable and innately intelligent, it was not long before Touby proved himself worthy of Blia Yao's mantle.

On the second day of the first month in 1935, Blia Yao died suddenly. His death came as a shock to his family. He was in his seventies, but was still in robust health. Just days earlier, he had been seen by Tougeu Lyfoung arriving in Xieng Khouang, dressed in his mandarin tunic with his Manchu-style shaven forehead and long queue dangling neatly down his back. At the provincial capital, Blia Yao's first order of business was to sit down for a final portrait, a three-quarter headshot that now decorates the walls of many Hmong Americans (see fig. 8).[115] This beautifully crafted shot caught him looking away from the camera, revealing the intensity in his eyes that exuded the charisma and authority that made him a legend in the oral memories of the Hmong.

Blia Yao's sons were unprepared to assume his position of responsibility. Following his death, their primary obsession centered on dividing his massive estate. They squabbled over the thousands of cows, hundreds of fowl, and numerous caches of silver and gold while Ly Foung moved quickly to take charge of Nong Het. By the time Blia Yao's younger son, Fay Dang, awakened to the fact that his family had lost an important wealth-generating position, it was too late. Ly Foung easily thwarted the last desperate maneuvers of Fay Dang. For over a decade, he had worked hard to curry favor with the French and Lao administrators while also winning over the traditional clan leaders one by one. Within a year of Blia Yao's death, Ly Foung was asked by the French to take over Blia Yao's subdistrict of Keng Khoai. His son, Nao Chao, was already the *tasseng* of Phak Boun. Ly Foung now dominated the leadership of Nong

Het. The bitter struggles between Ly Foung and Lo Blia Yao, with Ly Foung triumphant because of French and lowland backing, highlight the essentiality of the state to the rise and fall of Hmong leaders in the highland zone of colonial Indochina.

The Emergence
of an Educated Hmong
Broker (1936–1940)

Lo Blia Yao and those before him were traditional leaders who rose to prominence by virtue of their oratorical talents. They were the ritual and genealogical
experts of their clans who knew Hmong custom law enough to serve as facili-
tators of peace between the clans in Hmong society. Ly Foung represented a
transitional figure within this development. He was, as a leader, still deeply
immersed in the oral cultures of the Hmong, being a grand master of the *qeej*,
or bamboo reed. What distinguished him from Blia Yao and previous leaders
was his literacy in Lao, the language of the state. The fact that Ly Foung was
an indispensable bureaucrat to both the French and Blia Yao emerged time
and again as the French attempted to nominate him to office multiple times
while Blia Yao blocked the appointments. The tenacity with which Blia Yao
refused French appointment of Ly Foung as a *tasseng* but insisted in keeping
him as a secretary highlights furthermore Ly Foung's indispensability.

Ly Foung, in some ways, was a visionary beyond his time. He knew the
power he had over Blia Yao, and he seemed to have anticipated the directional
development of the kinds of men the French would favor as Hmong leaders,
as brokers between the Hmong and the state. The new generation of Hmong
leaders would represent a break from Blia Yao and even Ly Foung. They would
not be ritual and genealogical masters, but educated men, literate in both the
colonial language and nationalist lingua franca. Ly Foung set his sons in this
direction by enrolling them in the colonial schools in the mid-1920s, right at
the height of his struggle with Blia Yao. Within a decade, his family had seized
power from the Lo clan. Of his sons, Ly Foung strategically aimed for Touby,
also the grandson of Blia Yao, to succeed Blia Yao. Using Touby rather than

one of his elder sons to usurp Blia Yao's title reveals Ly Foung's brilliance as a political strategist. While clan leaders may have objected to Ly Foung or any of his other sons taking over Blia Yao's position, Touby had just enough of the right breeding to assume it. The French, the final adjudicator of this Hmong dispute, agreed.

The Education of Ly Foung's Sons

Although literacy had paved the way for Ly Foung's political advancement, according to his family members, he was only awakened to its true power during his six-month confinement in 1926. Refusing to succumb quietly in the colonial bastille, Ly Foung asked his Lao friends about French colonial law and learned that he could not be imprisoned indefinitely without a trial. Bypassing the French authorities in Xieng Khouang, who were loyal to Blia Yao, he petitioned the resident superior in Vientiane in writing. A trial was ordered, and he was found innocent. Ly Foung's literacy had saved him, and he wanted to equip all of sons with this skill so that they also could defend themselves from the powerful Lo Kaitong. "My father educated all of us so that we would survive, so that we would not die," said Nao Kao Lyfoung.[1] Throughout his life, Ly Foung recounted the story of his incarceration to his sons, constantly reminding them of the importance of literacy.[2] All his sons were educated in the lowlands of Laos and Vietnam. Tougeu and Toulia were inspired to study law, with Tougeu serving as the director general of the Ministry of Justice in Laos before his exile to France in 1975. Blia Yao's merciless tactics had profound implications for the Lyfoung family. On the one hand, all of Ly Foung's educated sons became prominent in civilian and military positions, but, on the other, the power struggle for paramountcy also cost them a heavy price — death for Touby and permanent exile for his brothers.

The education of Ly Foung's sons, which was interrupted at several stages, began in the privacy of their home village. In 1925, even before his arrest, Ly Foung built a small hut next to his house in De Mua Tha and hired a Lao tutor, Thao Kham Pha, to instruct his sons in Lao and French. The following year, when Ly Foung was imprisoned in Xieng Khouang, Kham Pha returned to the lowlands. Following Ly Foung's release, and after he had relocated to the village of Phak Khe in 1927, he brought Kham Pha back to teach his sons. The year was barely over, however, when Kham Pha contracted a debilitating illness that forced him to leave again, this time for good. Ly Foung finally decided to send his young sons to the lowlands. Pa Ge, Touby, Tougeu, and Toulia attended the primary school at Xieng Khouang where they boarded

Figure 15. Ly Long Vakhue (*left*) and Nao Chao Lyfoung (*right*) were the first two Hmong graduates of the colonial primary school in Xieng Khouang. This photo was taken in 1927 to commemorate the occasion. (Courtesy of Mao Song Lyfoung)

with Samouty, a Phuan friend who owed Ly Foung money.[3] Ly Foung's eldest son, Nao Chao, had preceded them to Xieng Khouang. Nao Chao and Ly Long Vakhue, a grandson of Ly Nhia Vu, were the first two Hmong to graduate from the colonial primary school in 1927 (see fig. 15). Long, however, died prematurely and never had the opportunity to apply his studies to bureaucratic work.[4]

Living among lowlanders was not easy, but perseverance got the brothers Lyfoung through their studies. Tougeu recalled the hard days of his early education and his struggle to study by the light of vine sticks and oil lamps:

At first there was no lamp, so *hmab tua leeg* [muscle-inhibiting vines] that had been cut from the forest, [and] their resin extracted had to be used. A long time ago, when the French traders came, they brought these vines from France [or other overseas French colonies?] to be sold. Later the French traders abandoned these vines—about 100 to 200 kilos' worth of it were left. So he [Samouty] took these *hmab tua leeg* and burned them. Although not very bright, the light produced was enough to see [by] . . . [but the fumes] caused one's nose to turn black. When one blows one's nose, it was all black. After one or two months the vines were used up. Then there were these little lamps about the size of an egg that used kerosene fuel. The wick was very small and made of polyester ropes obtained from parachutes. This little lamp also produced just enough light for one to read.[5]

Cognizant of the tremendous financial sacrifice their father was making in order to send them to school and constantly reminded of their father's earlier persecution, the Lyfoung brothers studied diligently. In his memoir, Touby recalls reading late into the night and never taking a break even during vacation periods: "Every night I read my lessons by the light of a kerosene lamp or a lamp fueled by lard until eleven o'clock or midnight. Still, in the mornings I would get up very early, before dawn, to light my lamp again and read my lessons thoroughly once more before washing my face and packing my bag to go to school. During the warm seasons, from July to September according to the French calendar, I would hire private tutors to teach me. [In four years] I returned only once to visit my [step]mother and father."[6] On top of their academic work, the brothers helped Samouty's family work the paddy fields, sowing, weeding, and harvesting. At the end of the first year, Touby and his brothers moved in with a Vietnamese teacher, Nai [Mister] Loiy, from whom they learned to speak Vietnamese.

Living with others entailed doing chores that distracted Ly Foung's children from their schoolwork. So when Ly Foung delivered the annual tax to the French commissioner at Xieng Khouang in 1932, he asked that a sum of five hundred kip be allotted to build a dormitory for his sons. His request was in line with the agreement established between Hmong leaders and the French following Pa Chay's revolt. The French had promised to establish schools to educate Hmong children, thereby eventually eliminating the need for lowland interpreters. The next generation of Hmong leaders was to be drawn from among these educated youths, who would be equipped with the language skills required to gain direct access to the French. Since then, however, very little effort had been made to fulfill this promise. In 1926 the Hmong leaders reminded the French again that they had promised to establish a school and dispensary. The Hmong wanted their children to learn Lao and French. Again nothing was done.[7]

A French-sponsored school was finally built in the village of Pas Dej Poob Qho, Nam Khao Hu, in the early 1930s, but it was a failure. As Hmong villages were scattered about in the surrounding hills, not many families could afford to board their sons at the school. Only the richest families could feed and shelter their children throughout the long duration of study. Even Blia Yao's sons, Fay Dang and Za Teng, who attended the school, stayed for only a few months. Poor attendance eventually forced the school to close.[8]

Perceiving Ly Foung's request to be legitimate, the French commissioner allotted five hundred kip to pay for the dormitory. Ly Foung used the money to buy materials and hire Vietnamese workers to construct the modest building. When it was completed, Blia Yao also sent his younger sons and a grandson to Xieng Khouang to enroll in the school. Tougeu recalls: "My father obtained five hundred kip of the tax money to pay—obtained from the commissioner— to be used to hire Vietnamese workers to construct a dormitory for us. When we moved in, Kaitong's [Blia Yao's] children also came to live [in the dorm]. Nao Tou came too. Kaitong's sons who came were Vang Kaitong, the one who came to attack us and died at Nam Kuang, and Chue Kaitong and Tong Kaitong—all came to study with us. Nao Lue Kaitong had a son named Nou who came to live and study with us as well."[9]

It is doubtful that any of Blia Yao's sons obtained degrees of completion from the primary school. Ger Lo, the son of Chue, whom Tougeu mentioned above, confirmed that his uncles and father took their education for granted. "Fay Dang was supposed to be in school in Xieng Khouang," Ger said. "But instead he remained in Ban Ban, where he gambled all the time. When he ran out of money, he even had the audacity to sneak back to Phak Lak to steal my grandfather's cattle to sell for more money. My grandfather never knew he was in Ban Ban [and not in Xieng Khouang]."[10] Zong Blong Lo, the son of Nhia Vu, also stated that his father had a serious gambling problem and did not take his studies seriously. "It is true what they said about my father. My father told us he finally quit gambling when he lit a candle and vowed to the ancestors and the gods of the heavens that he would stop."[11] We do not know how Blia Yao felt about his sons' behavior, or about Fay Dang stealing his cattle, but his decision not to divide his wealth between them may indicate his silent disap- pointment. Moreover, in death Fay Dang has chosen not to be buried next to his father at the Lo family's historic stone house in Phak Lak like Blia Yao's other sons, Chue and Nhia Vu. Rather, he has asked to be buried next to Thao Tou Yang's house in Nong Het (see fig. 3). Can we find meaning in Fay Dang's choice?

Tougeu confirmed Ger and Zong Blong's testimonies. While the Lyfoung brothers studied, said Tougeu, Blia Yao's children preferred other activities:

> There was no school at Nong Het. At Xieng Khouang, where we were, Kaitong's sons came to live and study with us, but the small difference was that on Saturdays and Sundays we [the Lyfoung brothers] went to launder our clothes. Each of us had to wash our own clothes. I, for example, would wash my clothes then come and sit at a desk to write my lessons and do my homework, but Kaitong's sons would go chase *noog ncuas*. *Noog ncuas* is a kind of bird that cannot fly very far, so it takes flight from somewhere high, then glides down. They kept on chasing those birds. Because those birds did not have much strength, they actually succeeded in catching two or three every two or three days. When they're chasing birds, we were studying. At examination time, we passed while they remained in grammar school, so I don't know [*shrugs shoulders*].[12]

Touby made remarkable progress and emerged as Ly Foung's leading son. Within patrilineal Hmong society, his loyalty lay with Ly Foung rather than his maternal grandfather, Blia Yao. As Blia Yao watched Touby grow into a confident youth who attracted attention, he continued to remark nostalgically that only Touby possessed his charisma. Mao Song stated, "Grandfather [Blia Yao] would often say with a deep sigh, 'Oh, only my [Tou]By is like me.'"[13] Sociable, Touby easily befriended lowland elites like Saykham, a scion of the Phuan aristocracy and the future governor of Xieng Khouang. They became best friends and, later, allies in the struggle against communism.

In 1934 Touby and his elder brother, Pa Ge, graduated from primary school. Pa Ge remained in the provincial capital to work with the commissioner while Touby and a group of students from prestigious lowland families made the arduous overland trip to Vientiane to attend the Lycée Pavie. Among the group were Kham Fua, who was the son of the *chaomuang* (county leader) of Tha Thom, Saykham, Khan Hong Kingsada, Thao Mo, and one Vietnamese and one Lao student. Their journey to Vientiane was a dangerous seven-day trip across mountains and valleys and down river rapids on makeshift rafts. Particularly grueling was the trip down the rapids of the Tha Thom River to Paksane, which was accompanied by prayers and fervent appeals to the gods, according to Touby. When the group reached Paksane, Touby writes, they hurriedly telegraphed their families. Then "each person took a chicken, some candles, and some flowers to offer at the *wat* as recompense [to the gods] for the safe journey."[14] Embarking on a steamboat at Paksane the following day, the group made the two-day trip up the Mekong to Vientiane.

At the administrative capital, the group of eight, including Touby, stayed at the home of Madame Vanh Chanh, the daughter of the *chaomuang* of Tou-lakhom, who knew the Samouty family in Xieng Khouang. Several days later the hopeful eight passed an oral exam and received their primary school certificates, but they all failed the entrance exam for the Lycée Pavie. Only Touby and Kham Fua were good enough to be allowed to take preparatory classes, with the understanding that they could enroll the following year. The others returned to Xieng Khouang, their dreams of a middle school education dashed.

After Touby finished his preparatory classes, he asked and was given permission to live in the home of Prince Souvanna Phouma, the royal official in charge of the Electric and Public Works Department and, later, prime minister of Laos. Touby's first year as a registered student at the Lycée Pavie did not go smoothly, however. Among his main obstacles was the prejudice he faced from a young Lao who also resided in Souvanna's home. After three months of constant harassment, a violent fight broke out between the two. Touby conferred with a silent Souvanna, then he went to live with the Vietnamese couple that cared for the Ho Yia Pagoda. There Touby paid for his food and cleaned the temple grounds on Sundays and after school. Touby recalls his days with the couple nostalgically. "Come to think of it," he writes, "they cared for me and loved me very much. They followed the head monk's instructions, and did not ask me to do too many chores. The head monk had asked that they not divert too much of my time to work so that I could study and fulfill the hopes of my father, making it worth my father's money to send me there from so far away."[15] Despite his determination, Touby fell victim to beriberi disease. He returned to recuperate in Nong Het, ending his educational pursuit in Laos.

After Touby recovered from the beriberi attack, he decided to embark on further study in Vietnam. By this time his younger brother, Tougeu, had also completed primary school at Xieng Khouang. The Lyfoung brothers' pilgrimage to pursue literacy in the distant lowlands echoes those in Hmong myths and legends. Taking CR7, the two brothers walked to Vinh, the capital of Nge Anh Province, ignorant of what awaited them. They aimed to study in either Hanoi or Saigon. This was the journey of a lifetime, a rite of passage of the utmost importance. The brothers left as boys; they returned as leading Hmong figures.

In Vinh, Touby and Tougeu met a Frenchman named Legalle who was, coincidentally, the former official in charge of administering the annual primary school examination at Xieng Khouang. After an extended conversation with the Lyfoung brothers, he convinced them that the school in Vinh was the best. The students, he said, passed the annual examination every year, acquiring the coveted diploma that led to employment in the civil service. As a final appeal, he offered to write the brothers a letter of introduction to the school. Touby and Tougeu decided to remain in Vinh. Touby acquired his diploma four years later, in 1939, and then returned home to help his father with administrative duties.[16] Tougeu went on to Hanoi to obtain a postsecondary degree in agriculture, which ranked him among the half-dozen most educated elites with a French education in Laos by the mid-1940s.[17] Toulia had also completed primary school and was studying law in Vientiane when the Japanese invaded Indochina. After years of perseverance, the Lyfoung brothers had achieved educations comparable to those of the most privileged Lao scions from Xieng Khouang, Vientiane, Luang Prabang, and Champassak. Educational privilege allowed them to dominate Hmong politics and influenced Lao national affairs during the next quarter century.

Touby Lyfoung, *Tasseng* of Keng Khoai

Ly Foung's investment in his sons' education began paying off by the late 1930s when three of them returned to preside over administrative positions in Nong Het, including the Keng Khoai subdistrict position once held by Blia Yao. Ly Foung's political climb had begun with his takeover of the Phak Boun subdistrict in 1929.[18] After Blia Yao died in 1935, Ly Foung consolidated his influence over the two subdistricts, bringing them under the rule of one family again.

Meanwhile, events conspired against the Lo family after Blia Yao's death. Hmong elders knowledgeable in traditional beliefs link the fall of the Lo family directly to the exhumation of Pa Tsi's grave in the previous century.[19] Others felt that Heaven, with its all-seeing eyes, had simply corrected an injustice by bringing Blia Yao down. On the other hand, Sutdālā, a nephew and the biographer of Thao Tou Yang, pinpoints the fall on Ly Foung, saying that he aroused discord among the Lo brothers by applying his brilliant divide-and-conquer skills yet again. "In 1936," Sutdālā writes, "Ly Foung deceived Tsong Tou Lobliayao, who was Fay Dang's half brother with a different mother, by getting Tsong Tou into a dispute with Fay Dang on dividing money and properties inherited from their father, Kaitong Lo Blia Yao. Tsong Tou and Ly Foung's wife [Mai] were siblings of the same mother (Kaitong Blia Yao had many wives)."[20]

Whichever conclusion one reaches, Blia Yao's marriage alliances with women from multiple clans contained an inherent weakness as articulated in Hmong oral traditions. Hmong myths recognize that members of a single clan shared the same patriarch, but there were different mothers, which accounts for the existence of lineages that are not allowed to "die in each other's house." Blia Yao's sons were experiencing the effects of this myth in real time. Thus, while having multiple wives aided Blia Yao's rise to power by winning him the support of the most prominent clans in Nong Het, the loyalties of his sons were split along maternal lines. Fay Dang and Nhia Vu were the sons of Blia Yao's second and third wives, from the Yang clan.[21] Their maternal ties allowed the two half brothers to unite against Tsong Tou, whose mother was from the Vue clan. Fay Dang and Nhia Vu's gambling addiction exacerbated the dispute. Shortly after Blia Yao died, the Chinese and Vietnamese who lived in Blia Yao's village of Phak Lak devised a plan to expropriate his wealth. They established a casino in the village, tempting Blia Yao's sons to gamble away their father's riches. The Lo brothers squandered what they could of Blia Yao's estate and then bickered with Tsong Tou over what was left.[22]

Blia Yao's numerous cattle were another source of contention between his sons. Over the years, Blia Yao's herds had multiplied by the thousands, "occupying three mountains and three valleys."[23] When he died, much of his estate, including the livestock, was left in the charge of Tsong Tou, Blia Yao's eldest son, who had inherited his title in 1925. Although Tsong Tou's brothers did not hesitate to slaughter the cows for their own consumption, they did not help Tsong Tou care for them. The herd of cattle was left to wander untended in the hills surrounding the town of Nong Het, eating the crops of others un-checked. Hmong villagers complained to the French at the military garrison in Nong Het, and the French ordered the herd fenced. When Tsong Tou turned to his brothers, they refused to lift a hand to help him with the task. They seemed to prefer lives of leisure and ease. Tsong Tou was forced to work alone, cutting down huge trees in the surrounding mountains in order to build a fence large enough for the cattle. Tsong Tou became completely disillusioned with his brothers.[24]

Perhaps jealous that Tsong Tou had inherited their father's prestigious title, Fay Dang and Nhia Vu, the two brothers who had some education, did not help Tsong Tou administer the canton either—a hard task for any one man. Tsong Tou was left, therefore, with the duties of running his father's large household, which included five wives, many children, and a multitude of grandchildren, as well as the heavy burden of administration. Tsong Tou often found these tasks overwhelming, especially in light of a physical ailment, which many Hmong felt had been brought on by his own wrongdoing. When Blia Yao died, his sons had constructed a coffin that was too narrow for his frame. Blia Yao was a tall man with robust shoulders too wide for the coffin. "Tsong Tou, in frustration, stood on top of Blia Yao's chest and crammed him into the tight space," said Ly Na. "After the burial, Tsong Tou developed painful gout in his foot, rendering him incapable of much physical activity." [25] The gout in the very foot that had jammed Blia Yao into the small coffin was evidence to many Hmong that Tsong Tou had committed a grave sin against his father. Not surprisingly, he was unable to keep his father's title for long.

The event that led to the final fall of the Lo family began with the completion of the railroad connecting northern and southern Vietnam in 1936. To mark this major technological achievement, a huge celebration was held in Saigon. Ly Foung and Tsong Tou, the primary leaders of Nong Het, were invited to attend. Mao Song, Ly Foung's daughter, who was now a young maiden, and Choua, Ly Foung's third wife, went as part of a small entourage (see fig. 16). Before heading out, Tsong Tou collected the annual tax and left it in the care of the Lao *naikong* (district leader), Thao Suk Savang. Because of the disputes over Blia Yao's wealth and their gambling addiction, Tsong Tou did not trust his half brothers with the money. Discord between the Lo brothers ended up costing the family everything Blia Yao had worked his whole life to obtain. [26]

On his return from the celebration in Saigon, Tsong Tou discovered that Thao Suk Savang had run off to Thailand with the tax money. At a loss as to what to do, Tsong Tou showed up empty-handed in Xieng Khouang, where he learned that Thao Suk had written a note to the French, alleging that Tsong Tou had gambled the money away. [27] Because Tsong Tou was there to face the consequences, logic would suggest that he was innocent, but the French were not pleased with his incompetence. The nonliterate Tsong Tou did not even think to obtain a receipt and so could not produce one to back up his story. The French threatened to divest Tsong Tou of his title and throw him in prison. [28] Tsong Tou begged to be allowed to return to Nong Het to confer with his family. He promised to make up the taxes from his own pocket. Perhaps knowing that the amount owed was not beyond his family's means, the French released him.

At Nong Het, Tsong Tou went to Jer to beg for money. Jer had been left in charge of the bulk of Blia Yao's great wealth. Blia Yao was savvy enough to realize that his family's power depended on keeping his fortune intact and he had forbidden its division. "My grandfather left explicit instructions not to divide up the money," said Ger, the grandson of Blia Yao and Jer. [29] Blia Yao may have also aimed to keep his estate intact to force his sons to work together as a team. His sons lacked his political vision and knack for building alliances, however. They could not even unite among themselves. Nhia Vu and Fay Dang brokered a weak alliance against Tsong Tou.

Figure 16. Ly Foung and his companions in Saigon in March 1936 during the celebration commemorating the completion of the Trans-Indochinese railway, which connected Tonkin, Annam, and Cochinchina. *Left to right*: Ly Foung, with a medal; Lo Tsong Tou (*peeking from behind*); Choua Kue; Chue Yang Tsonglue (*behind*), an expert *qeej* player who attended to perform as a Hmong representative; Mao Song Lyfoung; an unidentified security guard; and Po Chi (Mrs. Blia Yang Vue). (Courtesy of Mao Song Lyfoung)

Despite the lavish spending of Blia Yao's wealth, there were still seven hundred silver bars left in the possession of Jer. Tsong Tou begged his step-mother to hand over three hundred bars to pay the tax. She was reluctant but relented under pressure from many who did not want to see Tsong Tou incarcerated. The family divided the remaining four hundred bars between the five wives and their sons, resolving the financial dispute. The rancor of personal jealousy was slightly abated, but this resolution seriously weakened the power of the Lo family. After paying the taxes, Tsong Tou resigned as *tasseng* of Keng Khoai without consulting his brothers. He handed the seal of office back to the French.[30] Disenchanted with his brothers, Tsong Tou rallied to his brother-in-law, Ly Foung.

Fate seemed to have intervened in favor of Ly Foung once again. With Tsong Tou's resignation and the Lao *naikong's* departure, there were two empty positions in Nong Het. At a loss as to who to appoint to take over the coveted position once held by Blia Yao, the French turned to Ly Foung. They asked him to help them find a new *tasseng*. Mao Song recalled the day that the

French officer at Nong Het, known to the Hmong as Thaan Kam Muv, came to call on her father.

> In [19]36, everything occurred as I've said earlier. Uncle Tsong Tou was working [as *tasseng*] and Thao Suk took the [tax] money away, and [uncle] had to use grandfather's money that he extorted [from the Hmong] during the Madmen's War to pay it off. In [19]36, [after Tsong Tou resigned] there was no one working anymore, so in the third month of [19]37, [the French] came to summon my father. Grandfather [Blia Yao] had died in [19]35, on the second day [of January]. My father had not been working [in Keng Khoai] for ten years. Thaan Kam Muv and Thaan Commissaire came in a car. I was home with my father. He [the commissioner] said, "Ly Foung, find someone to come with you to Nong Het." So my father told me to go ask . . . Chaomuang Tsia's grandfather, who was Phutong So Tsai [Thao]. He was my father's first [maternal] cousin.
>
> I went to call Uncle So . . . and he came . . . he was a *phutong* too. [Then] Thaan Kam Muv and Thaan Commissaire took both of them to Nong Het where they spent the night. When my father returned [the following day], he said, "They placed the region of Nong Het, the *tasseng* of Keng Khoai, under my charge because I used to work there."[31]

Over the years, members of the Lo family have come to view the loss of their position as usurpation by Ly Foung, but Mao Song and her brothers made the argument that the Lo resigned on their own. The Lyfoungs' argument is bolstered by Tsong Tou's alliance with Ly Foung and Touby. After 1945 Tsong Tou and his son Bee Chou relocated from the region of Nong Het to Xieng Khouang. Bee Chou fought the revolution on the side of Touby. It was not until the 1960s, after Touby was eclipsed as Hmong leader by Vang Pao, that he urged Bee Chou to return to be with Fay Dang in Nong Het. "There were rumors about Bee Chou being a Communist spy because he was related to Fay Dang," said Mee Kue, the wife of Nao Kao Lyfoung. "Uncle Touby was afraid that he would not be able to protect Bee Chou anymore, so he had soldiers accompany him back to Nong Het."[32] Fay Dang had no choice but to accept his nephew's return. During my conversations with different members of the Lo family in Vientiane in 2008, however, it was apparent that they viewed Tsong Tou and Bee Chou as "traitors" of the family.

Mao Song also disputed the usurpation argument by noting her father's reluctance to take over the position even after he was handed the seal of office for the canton of Keng Khoai. He delayed relocating there for another two years, she said. Whatever the case, Ly Foung now held Blia Yao's coveted position, and he resorted to every stratagem to make sure it remained in his family. Midway through 1936, his second-eldest son, Pa Ge, who had completed elementary school at Xieng Khouang with Touby several years earlier, returned to Nong Het. Since graduation Pa Ge had been working closely with the French commissioner during a tour of the countryside, serving as an interpreter and secretary. Because he was already well known to the French, Pa Ge was appointed as the new *naikong* of Nong Het, presiding over the position formerly occupied by Thao Suk Savang.[33] Pa Ge was the first Hmong *naikong*, a position the French had once dangled as a reward for Blia Yao in 1921 but retracted after some Hmong leaders protested. Meanwhile, Ly Foung delayed appointing anyone to the coveted position of *tasseng* of Keng Khoai. A united front of clan leaders in the region might have been enough to force him to appoint someone immediately, but, as each of them was vying for Ly Foung's favor so as to be nominated, they could not rush him. Their lack of consensus gave Ly Foung a strategic advantage. While the clan leaders bickered for the next several years, Ly Foung waited for his next eldest son, Touby, to complete his studies in Vinh.

Hmong attributed the fall of the Lo family to the desecration of Pa Tsi's grave without giving Ly Foung much credit or blame, but Ly Foung's political climb had as much to do with his political skills as it did with the Lo family's alleged curse. With careful orchestration and gentle patience over the years, Ly Foung's influence had reached its zenith even before Blia Yao passed away. Beginning in the 1930s, the French, ignorant of Hmong society and at a loss as to whom to appoint to various positions, were placing major decisions in Ly Foung's hands. Now, with Blia Yao finally eliminated by mortality, Ly Foung's grasp reached well beyond the region of Nong Het. Mao Song narrated how her father achieved paramountcy:

> My father was already overseeing the subdistrict of Phak Boun [since 1929], formerly under the authority of the *tasseng* of the Kue clan. Then the *tasseng* of the Vang clan, in Phu Sa Bouk, fell off a horse and was impaled in the mouth by bamboo, breaking all his teeth and rendering him unable to talk and, therefore, unable to carry out his administrative duties. His subdistrict was also placed in my father's care [in 1932]. My father was told to find someone qualified for the position. So my father was in charge of both of those subdistricts already. Now the subdistrict of Keng Khoai, that was going to be given to my father a long time ago [1921] and grandfather [Blia Yao] did not allow it—Uncle Tsong Tou had resigned so no one was overseeing it—was handed over to my father too.[34]

Although Ly Foung did not have the force of personality to become a legend in the oral memory of the Hmong, his authority reached well beyond that once held by Blia Yao. Perhaps realizing this, Fay Dang, the eldest son of Blia Yao's second wife, Lee Yang, suddenly felt threatened. He rebuked Ly Foung publicly for daring to take charge of what he felt was his father's personal fief.[35] Just as Tsong Tou had done, Fay Dang turned to Jer, Blia Yao's favorite wife, who had been left with the wealth and precious heirlooms of the Lo family, including two priceless rhinoceros horns. He used one of the horns to gain the favor of the Luang Prabang Court. Ly Foung had the support of the Phuan royalty in Xieng Khouang and the French, but the viceroy of Luang Prabang supported Fay Dang and the Lo clan. Prince Saykham observed a few years later, "The Lao [of Luang Prabang] supported the Lo who were the richest and the French the clan of Ly, which was more educated, i.e., more Frenchified. Because Viceroy Phetsarath supported the Lo, Touby could not be named head of the administrative service of Nong Het in place of his elder brother Pa Ge who had just died."[36] Saykham, a client of the Luang Prabang Court, was powerless to intervene but his family may have been on the side of the Lyfoungs due to their boyhood friendship. Before the arrival of the French, Saykham's family had awarded titles to the Hmong of Nong Het. Fay Dang had probably appealed to the Phuan first, in vain, before going to Luang Prabang.

Fay Dang's presentation of the rhinoceros horn to Prince Phetsarath in 1936 was an act steeped in tradition harking back to the early nineteenth century when great marksmen like Ly Nhia Vu and Lo Pa Tsi, Fay Dang's grandfather, had presented the priceless ivory to the lowland authorities in return for titles. Blia Yao was the only Hmong man who owned three rhinoceros horns. One had been given to Tsong Tou in 1925 when Blia Yao held a feast to appoint him as the *tasseng* of Keng Khoai. The other two were left in Jer's care. For a time, she had left one of the horns with her Ly family in Nong Khiaw, but she retrieved it when the Lo family was in dispute over Blia Yao's estate.[37] Jer had already given the horns to her sons, Vang and Chue. These half brothers were moved to support Fay Dang only when he vowed that they, too, would have a turn at being *tasseng* if they helped persuade the Lao authorities to return Keng Khoai to the Lo family. The brothers relinquished the smaller, white rhino horn to Fay Dang.[38]

Fay Dang made the 120-mile journey to Luang Prabang with the precious commodity. At the royal city, he presented the horn to Prince Phetsarath, the administrator of Laos, and asked that he intervene to appoint him the *tasseng* of Keng Khoai, a position he felt was rightly his to inherit. We do not have Fay Dang's version of Phetsarath's reaction, but, according to Touby, the prince immediately dispatched a letter to Ly Foung. In the most diplomatic language possible, the prince asked Ly Foung to assign Fay Dang to the position in dispute. Touby writes:

> Then Prince Phetsarath, who was in charge of the administrative affairs of the land on behalf of King Sisavangvong, wrote a letter to Ly Tsia Foung. He asked Ly Tsia Foung to assign Fay Dang a leadership position, to look after the descendants of Tasseng Lo Blia Yao, who had performed honorable services for the country, and to love Blia Yao's descendants in the manner that one loves one's closest relatives. After Ly Tsia Foung received Prince Phetsarath's letter, he asked Phiaxim Yaj Txoov Tuam to invite his brother-in-law [Fay Dang] to be the *phutong*, aiding Ly Foung in administering the villages. Fay Dang did not agree. He sent a message back, saying that if his brother-in-law [Ly Foung] did not appoint him but insisted on nominating another individual from another clan to be the *tasseng* of Keng Khoai, then it was his choice. He just wanted his brother-in-law to know that someday down the line he would return to take over the *tasseng* position once held by his father.[39]

Other sources suggest that Phetsarath went out of his way to work out an agreement whereby Ly Foung promised that Fay Dang would be given the position upon his death.[40] The Lyfoung siblings disputed this viewpoint, saying that Ly Foung had never assumed the title of *tasseng*, so it was not his to bargain away. He was merely charged with the task of appointing someone to the position. Ly Foung, therefore, could not have entered into such an agreement.[41] Moreover, it is highly unlikely that Phetsarath would have involved himself so deeply in Hmong affairs at that time. The lowland Lao kingdoms along the Mekong River valley had exercised only the most minimal of authority over the Hmong, who lived in the distant mountains to the east. In practice it was members of the Phuan royalty of Xieng Khouang that had dealt directly with the Hmong of Nong Het.[42] The French retained this practice of indirect rule through the indigenous Phuan authorities until Pa Chay's revolt encouraged a massive uprising in the region in 1920. The royal family of Luang Prabang had no precedent for dealing with the Hmong of Nong Het despite their strategic importance by the 1930s. It was not until after the Pacific War, when the French created the Kingdom of Laos and appointed the Luang Prabang monarch as its king, that Phetsarath began to recognize the tactical significance of the Hmong in the region. By that time Phetsarath and the king had parted ways, however. The king backed Touby while Phetsarath supported Fay Dang.

Moreover, if Phetsarath had hesitated to intervene directly in Hmong affairs, it was understandable. The prince's action reflected his own rudimentary conception of the Lao nation during this period. Although he was kind enough to entertain Fay Dang, he made no attempt to enforce the order sent in his letter to Ly Foung. Phetsarath was content to leave the job of adjudicating Hmong disputes to the French and the Phuan provincial authorities. Unfortunately, that meant that Fay Dang would be left out of the political process. His family had fallen out of favor with the French and the Phuan while Ly Foung had assiduously nurtured relations with both.

Despite Phetsarath's rather modest efforts on his behalf, Fay Dang did not take his gesture lightly. Phetsarath's letter to Ly Foung may have contributed to Fay Dang's decision to join the anti-French Pathet Lao Party led by Phetsarath's younger half brother, Prince Souphanouvong. Similarly, the letter may have helped push the Lyfoung family toward the French and King Sisavangvong, Phetsarath's political rivals. Fay Dang's trip to Luang Prabang, therefore, not only marked the moment when the Hmong moved down from the hills into lowland Lao national politics, but it also set the stage for the development of Hmong factions on the left and the right in the postwar era, when "whatever Touby's people do, Faydang's people will do the opposite."[43]

Over a decade earlier, Blia Yao had insisted on keeping Ly Foung in the lowly position of *phutong*, a village headman. Now Ly Foung seemed determined to keep Fay Dang in the same insignificant position. According to Ly Foung's children, his actions were not driven by a personal grudge. Fay Dang, being virtually nonliterate, was simply not a qualified individual. Ly Foung felt that anyone serving as a canton chief should be able to handle the bureaucratic work firsthand.[44] The dispute between Fay Dang and Ly Foung revolved around the issue of merit-based advancement versus inheritance. Fay Dang felt entitled to the position while Ly Foung felt it should go to someone with valid credentials. The French shared Ly Foung's sentiment.

The rise and fall of Hmong leaders was largely dependent on their relationships with colonial patrons. Blia Yao's power was intricately tied to his friendship with Henri Roux, the military officer who oversaw the region of Nong Het. Roux had long ago left for France at the end of his term of service, however. Without a personal patron to speak on their behalf, Blia Yao's less qualified sons were cast aside. Tsong Tou's incompetence the previous year had already forced the French commissioner to look to Ly Foung. Fay Dang's current attempt to bypass the colonial authorities and appeal directly to the indigenous prince reaffirmed the French sentiments against the Lo family. Still, the French may have made a strategic mistake by leaving Blia Yao's descendants out. They had incurred the wrath of those loyal to Blia Yao and opened the door to factionalism. With the Japanese Occupation looming on the horizon, the French also provided Touby with a strategic bargaining advantage. Once Fay Dang turned to the Viet Minh, the French had to give Touby more concessions in order to maintain his loyalty. Capitalizing on the quagmire the French had created, Touby became the most powerful Hmong leader of the twentieth century, playing a central role in Lao national politics.

Far from resolving the issue at hand, Prince Phetsarath's letter exacerbated the dispute between Fay Dang and Ly Foung. Outside legitimation was important for the Hmong, who were divided along clan and cultural group lines. Fay Dang had found an outside supporter in the prince and so was considered legitimate by those who were loyal to his father. He became bolder in his efforts to recoup his father's position. When the French authorities in Saigon announced a historic visit to Xieng Khouang in 1938 that included passing through the strategic Hmong area of Nong Het, Fay Dang made his move against Ly Foung. During such visits, it was traditional for the Hmong to construct an elaborate gate, decorated with flowers and plants, to honor and receive these authority figures. Ly Foung, who had remained in his home village of Phak Khe in the Phak Boun subdistrict, was now summoned to construct an official gate at the town of Nong Het in the Keng Khoai subdistrict. Mao Song recalled:

> In [19]38, Thaan Phub Nyawj was coming, so they asked my father to go and build a gate. It takes two days to travel from Phak Khe, Tiaj Tauj Tiaj Mooj, to there [Nong Het town]. My [first] husband [Tong Ger Vang] had just come to marry me during the first or second day of the second month . . . [when] my father went to construct the gate. He summoned the people, and many individuals came to plant flowers and trees—came to gather flowers for planting. All the *naiban* and the young maidens and young men came to receive [the officials] during the third month.[45]

By asking Ly Foung to build the gate, the French were recognizing him as the legitimate administrator of Keng Khoai, but Fay Dang was undeterred. He had his own message for Ly Foung and the French. He aimed to renew his family's prestige and deprive Ly Foung of full legitimacy by constructing a competing gate. Fay Dang ordered his relatives to construct another gate west of Nong Het, at the junction where CR7 crossed the footpath that departed for Yeng Pha, the village founded by Pa Tsi. During the time of Lo Kaitong, this crossroads was where gates were built to formally receive lowland officials. By erecting his gate there, Fay Dang was making an appeal to the Lo clan's leadership heritage and reminding the French of the debt of gratitude they owed his father, Blia Yao. Mao Song continued:

> Just as my father had gone to receive the officials, Uncle Fay Dang also went to construct his own gate at the junction departing to Lo Fong's village [of Yeng Pha]. I did not see it, but my [second] husband's [Ka Ge Vang's] first wife was among those who went to receive the officials [at that gate]. My husband's first wife was a woman of the Lo clan. My husband also went there. They were courting one another [at the time]. Fay Dang's people were not allowed to go to my father's gate. Fay Dang rode on horseback, chasing everyone, ordering them to come to his gate only.[46]

Once the French authorities had passed through the region, entering the gates of both Ly Foung and Fay Dang, the scramble for the *tasseng* position intensified once again, especially in light of Fay Dang's attempt to undermine Ly Foung. Large in number, Ly clan support was crucial. When Ly Nhia Vu's group had been the backbone of Blia Yao's authority he was supreme, but the Lys had become disillusioned with Blia Yao's heavy-handedness. During the rebellion of 1920, they had supported Blia Yao, but they did not approve of the mass executions or the extortion of money from rebel Hmong afterward. They felt especially exploited when they were used to lure Shong Ger to his death.[47]

By 1935, the Ly clan had silently withdrawn into the distance. Although the two Ly lineages in the region had rejected Ly Foung's father, Dra Pao, they now rallied behind Ly Foung. Much more diplomatic than his father, Ly Foung had proved to be quite influential. Ly Nhia Vu's group had considered Dra Pao a liability, but Ly Foung was a valuable asset. He was wealthy, owned a multitude of cattle, and had a large family. His first wife, Va Yang, had passed away in 1929, but he had since married Nao Vang, who was helping his third wife, Choua, manage his large estate. Moreover, his sons were educated, with two already serving in positions of distinction. It was no longer possible for neighbors to dismiss Ly Foung as the "lazy" orphan from whom young maidens ran away. By securing the backing of his own clan, Ly Foung made possible Touby's rise to paramountcy in 1939.

The two Ly lineages in the region were also competing with Fay Dang for the *tasseng* position. They each needed to be in Ly Foung's good graces. Ly Tong Pao, the emerging leader of the lineage in Tha Khu, and Ly Shoua Toua of Nong Khiaw were among the most determined candidates. Although each of the lineages coveted the *tasseng* title for its own member, neither wanted the Lo clan to reclaim it. They therefore banded together. The Lo family, they argued, had resigned of its own accord, so it was no longer qualified to compete for the position.[48] Not missing the cue, Ly Foung courted the leaders of the other two Ly lineages. He assigned Tong Pao and Shoua Toua positions of responsibility. Tong Pao was asked to relocate to the home of Naikong Pa Ge, becoming an apprentice of sorts. Despite his hopes, however, "Tong Pao was nonliterate and therefore as unqualified as Fay Dang. New to the scene, Tong Pao also had not yet captured the admiration of the masses."[49] Still, his support was essential if Touby was to win.

Unable to agree on one individual and lacking qualified candidates, the discussion in the hills dragged on. The powerful Moua clan of the Phou San mountain range west of Nong Het also supported Touby and the Ly clan even though it had generations of multiple marriage alliances with Blia Yao. Many of Blia Yao's sisters and daughters had married into the Moua clan. Blia Yao's son, Nhia Vu, was married to the daughter of Tasseng Nao Tou Moua.[50] For members of the Moua clan, support for Touby was based on another political consideration. They felt that the paramount leadership over the Hmong should alternate among the clans, not passed directly from father to son as in a primogeniture system. As they saw it, the paramount position had shifted between the Ly, Lo, and Moua clans since the mid-nineteenth century. Tong Pao Moua, a witness to these political struggles, stated, "The Moua has had their turn [at being a Hmong leader]. Blia Yao, from the Lo clan, has had his turn. So it was only fair for Touby from the Ly clan to succeed Blia Yao."[51] Perhaps for Tong Pao and other Moua clan members, supporting Fay Dang's claim to direct inheritance was less attractive because invoking the right of primogeniture or, in the case of Fay Dang, who was a younger son, ultimogeniture, was tantamount to an indefinite Lo clan monopoly on the leadership position. Supporting Fay Dang meant cutting themselves and other clans off permanently from the helm of power. Since the Moua, Ly, and Lo clans had a long history of intermarriages, passing the title along the female lines within their closed circle would allow the leadership position to alternate between these three powerful clans. Thus, Moua clan members like Tong Pao agreed that Touby should take over Blia Yao's position because, although he was a member of the Ly clan, he was Blia Yao's grandson. To curb the Lo political monopoly, they preferred Touby over Fay Dang.

Fay Dang would not be appeased with anything less than his appointment as the *tasseng* of Keng Khoai, however. When Ly Foung suggested that Keng Khoai be divided again, with Fay Dang in charge of his clan and extended relatives and another individual in charge of everyone else, Fay Dang refused to compromise. He would not have what he felt was his father's personal fief divided a second time. Fay Dang was wise enough in his own right to see through Ly Foung's clever ploy. Division would essentially mean that Fay Dang would rule over mainly his own Lo clan, thus, being only a clan leader and not a leader of paramount standing. Ly Foung, on the other hand, would not appoint Fay Dang as *tasseng*. What occurred was a repetition of the contest of wills in 1921 that had led to the death of Mai. This current struggle would also spill much blood before it was resolved in favor of the Lo clan in 1975.

The negotiations between Ly Foung and Fay Dang went back and forth until the middle of 1938 when Touby returned home for a ten-week vacation. The discussion quickly centered on the young man. Despite his inexperience and lack of standing as a clan leader, Touby's reputation as a pioneering Hmong who had excelled in his studies in the lowlands had reverberated throughout the mountains of Laos. He was the most educated Hmong in Laos, with a command of reading and speaking in Lao, French, Vietnamese, and Hmong. Furthermore, during his extended stay in the lowlands, Touby, with his easy manner and charismatic smile, had befriended elite families and solidified friendships that were burgeoning into rudimentary political alliances. Through Touby's association with lowlanders, he had gained extensive knowledge of their languages, cultures, and political systems. He had also acquired a Buddhist outlook on life, rendering him acceptable to the lowland elites.[52]

Touby was also appealing to the colonial masters because he was a Francophile and a living example of the success of France's *mission civilisatrice*. Intelligent, sociable, possessing a flawless command of French, and always dressed impeccably, Touby exuded a confidence not usually found among humble natives. Both the French and the Phuan authorities recommended his appointment. The Hmong, incredibly awed by Touby's educational attainments and multilingualism, and enamored of his friendly demeanor, concurred. Touby was blessed with his maternal grandfather's charismatic personality, but in the Hmong's patriarchal worldview he was of a different patrilineal lineage, and so he was not burdened with Blia Yao's reputation. In patrilineal, patriarchal Hmong society, Touby could appeal to the legendary aspects of Blia Yao's legacy as a grandson without the stigma of belonging to Blia Yao's clan—an additional advantage over Fay Dang.

Touby wisely refused the appointment, however. He had one more year of school left. He wanted to complete his education. Mao Song described her brother's position.

> [They] struggled with one another until the vacation period of [19]38, when Nhia By [Touby] returned. Then all the leaders said Nhia By should be appointed. Nhia By had completed his education at Xieng [Khouang] and then was sent to

Vientiane where he got sick and had to come back home. Then in [19]35, he was sent to Vietnam. So they pulled Nhia By into the position, but he refused. Nhia By said that Nhia By wanted to finish his education so that he could have a salaried position. The position of a *tasseng* did not come with chickens, pigs, or a monthly stipend. Nhia By did not agree at all. All the leaders, the French, everyone agreed that there was no one who knew the language, no one who could get close to the French authorities, and that Nhia By was the one who knew the leaders, knew the French, [and] the Hmong, so Nhia By should be appointed in order to bring peace to the region.[53]

Touby's decision not to accept the appointment at this time was strategically important. Completing his education would add to his status, making him competitive nationally. Touby, like Ly Foung, also knew the value of delayed gratification. In the long run, he would have it all.

When the next school term began, Touby returned to Vinh to finish his studies. Meanwhile, the discussion in the hills went on as usual to no avail. Ly Foung and Fay Dang could not come to a consensus. During an earlier discussion, when Touby's name was mentioned, Fay Dang had signaled that if it were Touby who was appointed to the position he might reconsider his stance on the issue. According to Mao Song, "Uncle Fay Dang said that he would not allow the position to go to anyone else, but if it were given to Touby who was the son of his sister, perhaps Touby would give him face."[54] Far from conceding his stance, Fay Dang was hoping Touby would invite him to preside over a position of more significance once he was appointed as *tasseng*. Those who heard it, however, saw Fay Dang's words as a concession and began to view Touby as the most logical compromise. He was the grandson of Blia Yao and the son of Ly Foung. Moreover, he was of the Ly clan and so was acceptable to Tong Pao and Shoua Toua, the two emerging Ly lineage leaders of the region. All hopes centered on the twenty-year-old youth as the means of resolving the long-standing dispute.

In 1939 Touby returned from Vinh, having completed his studies. He was the most educated Lao Hmong of the period. In light of the unimpressive educational achievements of lowland Lao students at this time, Touby was exceptional even by national standards.[55] That the Hmong admired him was understandable. Touby began his career by helping his father administer Keng Khoai. Within a few months of his return, however, Ly Foung had a tragic horseback-riding accident. He died in October 1939. Shortly afterward all the clan leaders gathered for a final decision as to who would be the *tasseng* of Keng Khoai.

There are competing accounts of what took place during this "election." McCoy's informants of the Ly clan said the French "barred" Fay Dang from the election. "Touby ran unopposed and won an overwhelming victory."[56] Nhia Vu, Fay Dang's brother, who left a video testimony, said Fay Dang did not run in the election because Touby had promised that he would assign Nhia Vu to the position once Touby had won. Yia S. Lor, who cites this testimony, did not explain why Touby made this promise or why Nhia Vu and Fay Dang would have believed him.[57] My informant, Ly Na Jalao, said both Touby and Fay Dang ran in the election and Touby won the majority vote because the Hmong leaders had become disenchanted with Blia Yao's authoritarian ways.[58] Touby's sister, Mao Song, doubted that there was an election. She said the French, with the consensus of the Hmong leaders, simply appointed Touby as the *tasseng* of Keng Khoai. Fay Dang was included in the discussions, and he consented because Touby was his nephew. Both Fay Dang and the Hmong leaders were in awe of Touby's educational achievements.[59]

Touby says the French refused to appoint Fay Dang to the position, confirming McCoy's finding about Fay Dang's exclusion from the election. Touby cites his education and being a grandson of Blia Yao as the primary reasons for his selection. Moreover, he had the support of Tsong Tou, the former *tasseng* of Keng Khoai. Touby writes:

> After much deliberation, the Hmong leaders agreed that I would become the *tasseng* [of Keng Khoai]. They said I was young but educated and had helped my father for four months prior to his passing away. They said, furthermore, that I belonged to both clans. My father was of the Ly clan, [and] my mother was the daughter of Kaitong Lo Blia Yao. If I were appointed as *tasseng*, the dispute would end. The French also held this view so they handed me the official seal. My uncle Lo Tsong Tou was happy for me. Only my uncle Fay Dang was unhappy about the situation.[60]

The state became the final judge of the dispute, making the decision for the squabbling Hmong leaders who could not come to a consensus. Again, the incident highlight why the Hmong were drawn to the state. It imposed a hierarchy, a political rationale that the Hmong could not create on their own. Touby won in the battle because he represented a balance of merit-based advancement and inheritance in this case. Furthermore, he was attractive to the French because, according to Gary Yia Lee, he was "the only Hmong who could speak and think like a French."[61] Moreover, McCoy, Read, and Adams write that the French "regarded Faydang's petition to the royal court two years before as an act of insubordination and were unwilling to entrust Faydang with any authority in the region."[62]

Touby Lyfoung became the *tasseng* of Keng Khoai, occupying the most coveted position in Nong Het in 1939. Tsong Tou's son, Bee Chou, and Fay Dang's half brother, Nhia Vu, were invited to help Touby with the administrative work.[63] For the moment, it seemed that the long political struggle that had begun with Blia Yao and Ly Foung had finally reached a conciliatory end. Balance seemed to have been restored in the person of Touby, a product of the two most powerful clans in the region. As in 1921, however, the calm on the surface belied the torrent of hidden emotions underneath. As long as Touby had the French on his side, he was perceived as the legitimate Hmong leader. But the arrival of the Japanese in the next few months would revive the dispute between uncle and nephew once again.

The Impact of
the Japanese Occupation on
the Highlands
(1941–1945)

Just as the Japanese Occupation of Indochina from 1940 to 1945 affected the structure of lowland Southeast Asian history, its impact in the highlands was equally significant. In 1939 the dispute over the canton of Keng Khoai and the fact that the French favored Touby Lyfoung over Lo Fay Dang had caused major discord in the region of Nong Het. The Occupation deepened the conflict between nephew and uncle while also dramatically redefining highland-lowland relations. Up to this moment, Hmong leaders such as Lo Blia Yao and Ly Foung had little bargaining power. With the exception of Blia Yao's brief military collaboration with the French against Lo Shong Ger in 1920, his main task as a Hmong political broker was to collect taxes, conscript workers for state projects, and enforce the opium monopoly in the highlands by keeping this lucrative product away from the Haw merchants. The arrival of the Japanese, a competing colonial power, would redefine relations between the Hmong broker and the state, affecting as well the population.

The Japanese gave Fay Dang an edge against the French and Touby, resuscitating the dispute over the *tasseng* of Keng Khoai. Fay Dang turned to the Japanese for legitimacy, affecting the dynamic of the relationship between Touby and the French. The chaos of the Occupation and the revolutionary period, complicated by the internal competition between the two men, had the effect of forcing Touby and Fay Dang to become a different breed of leader. They were no longer just tax collectors and corvée enforcers. Henceforth, their leadership also hinged on their ability to conscript manpower to advance the

252

agenda of the state. In return, competing colonial and nationalist groups legitimated Touby and Fay Dang as leaders on opposing sides, gradually shifting their role from brokers to being national leaders with the primary task of integrating the Hmong into the emerging Lao state, where the Hmong became, at least in theory, "Lao" nationals.

On the French side (later, the political right), Touby and his educated brothers, Tougeu and Toulia, played central roles in the creation of the Kingdom of Laos. The brothers Lyfoung helped to develop the concept that the Lao citizenry included ethnic minorities such as the Hmong. Using his influence with the French, Touby secured Hmong political representation at the provincial and national levels while attempting to retain a sense of autonomy, something the Hmong had sought throughout their long history. Fay Dang did the same thing on the opposing side of the nationalist divide by jumping on the bandwagon of the Communist platform of a multiethnic Lao nation with equal rights for all citizens. For the first time, both Touby and Fay Dang claimed Lao nationalism as their own. Different nationalist factions legitimated them in return.

Highland Feud during the Japanese Occupation: Touby versus Fay Dang

As the Hmong disputed in the highlands of northeastern Laos, their French colonial masters were fighting their own war in faraway Europe. It is hard to imagine that the Hmong of the period had the faintest conception of where Europe was. Aside from leaders like Ly Foung and Blia Yao, few Hmong had seen a Frenchman. None could have imagined the destructive power of the colonial master's modern technology. When Frenchmen parachuted into northern Laos to recolonize the land after World War II, the Hmong thought they were divine beings descending from Heaven. Colonel Jean Sassi, who led the Groupement de Commandos Mixtes Aéroportés (GCMA) in Xieng Khouang in 1951, recalled that Hmong individuals kowtowed before him as he landed, awestruck at the sight of his parachute.[1] As late as 1975, when Hmong exiles in Thailand were anticipating immigration to America, they still imagined that the land of the Americans was beyond the clouds, in another universe where white doctors ate brains.[2] In other words, after enduring six decades of colonization and over a decade more of struggle with the Americans, the Hmong of Laos still perceived whites as human-eating aliens from another world. For this reason, Hmong refugees at Ban Vinai had the highest no show rates for their mandatory exit interviews to immigrate abroad.[3] They did not want to go to the land of the "Nyav" (a word borrowed from the Lao term "Yak" or demons). Hmong perception of whites is an indication of the extent of French neglect of the highlands. Intriguingly, and to the benefit of the French, lack of white presence in Hmong villages had the ironic effect of making the Hmong feel that they were independent even though they were bounded stringently by the colonial yoke. The perception of autonomy facilitated the loyal alliance with the French during the revolutionary period.

The German invaders occupied France in May 1940. Following negotiations with their German ally, the Japanese entered Indochina to extract raw materials with which to wage war on China and other regions of Southeast Asia. Administrative responsibility for the colonies was left in the hands of the French. There was little change for Touby and the Hmong during most of the Occupation. Touby carried out his duties as a tax collector and enforcer of the French opium monopoly, thereby preventing this lucrative cash crop from falling into the hands of illegal traders. The Japanese also competed for opium, showing up in Hmong villages to purchase what they could from cultivators.[4]

Opium made the Hmong essential in the struggle for Indochina. Accordingly, the Japanese, the French, and the Viet Minh lured Hmong leaders to their side. The Japanese stay in Indochina was short and we do not have much information on their relationship with the Hmong either in Vietnam or Laos (although we do know they replaced Touby with Fay Dang as noted below), but both the French and the Viet Minh courted Hmong leaders to ensure a monopoly on opium, which they used to finance their war efforts. In Ha Giang, Vietnam, where Xiong Mi Chang led his rebellion in 1910, a Hmong "king," Vuong [Vang] Chinh Duc, was instrumental to French colonial rule and his son and successor, Vuong Chi Sinh (1886–1962), to Viet Minh victory. The "king," Duc, had been a wealthy opium warlord and a former mandarin of the Nguyen Dynasty in close alliance with the French. He generated enough riches to build a sixty-four-room "palace" in Sa Phin, guarded by a private army, which still stands as a tourist attraction today. During the revolutionary period, Duc was invited by Ho Chi Minh to join the Viet Minh. The aged mandarin sent his son, Sinh, to meet with Ho. A deal was struck where the Vuong family aided the revolution by channeling Hmong opium to the Viet Minh. For his role, Sinh was rewarded with a position in parliament.[5] Vuong family members continue to have educational and political privileges in Vietnam today. Unfortunately, we do not have the oral evidence to analyze how Duc, the "king," affected the rebellion of Mi Chang, or articulate further his and his son's special relationship with the French and the Viet Minh, but opium was the basis of Duc's political prominence as a colonial-administrator turned revolutionary-nationalist.

McCoy pinpoints Touby's preeminence in Laos during and subsequent to the Occupation period on his role as an opium broker as well. Months after defeating Fay Dang in the 1939 election, "Touby began an eight-year tenure as the only Hmong member of the opium purchasing board, providing valuable technical information on how to best expand Hmong production." Part of the strategy involved raising the annual head tax "from three piasters to an exorbitant eight piasters but [giving] the tribesmen the alternative of paying 3 kilograms of raw opium instead." The Hmong, who had no cash crop of any other kind and usually produced only one kilogram of opium per annum, were forced to grow three times the usual amount, precipitating "an opium boom in Nong Het." According to McCoy, Touby himself attested that "Laos's harvest more than doubled during this period, rising to as much as 30 or 40 tons a year. As one French colonial official put it, 'Opium used to be one of the nobles of the land; today it is king.'"[6] As shall be demonstrated in the following chapter, Touby's role as an opium broker would be even more crucial after the Japanese Occupation.

By the middle of 1943, the tide had turned against Germany in Europe. In Southeast Asia, the Japanese courted indigenous support by making political concessions to quasi-independent governments. Meanwhile, French efforts to launch a full-scale invasion of Indochina began in India in mid-1944 when the Free French collaborated with the British to train special commando teams to be parachuted into the Plain of Jars. Capturing this strategic area was seen as essential to retaking Indochina. The British, who also planned to recolonize Burma, had been successful in forming anti-Japanese militia units composed of highland minority groups like the Karen, Kachin, and Wa.[7] The French servicemen were in India to acquire the British insurgency techniques used to form these ethnic armies. They hoped to apply the skills of the British to the hardy mountaineers of Laos and Vietnam, including the Hmong.[8]

Among the first Frenchmen to parachute into Laos in January 1945, after six months of training, was Second Lieutenant Maurice Gauthier, whose family in France had been killed four years earlier during the bombing of his home village.[9] Gauthier first met with Moua Chong Toua, the *naiban* of Phou Dou, a village in the Phou San mountain range located east of the Plain of Jars. Chong Toua connected the French to Touby in Nong Het.[10] Chong Toua's alliance with the French in the 1940s sheds light on the complexity of his politics. He was the son of Vang Nhia Kao, a first cousin of General Vang Pao. Nhia Kao's father was the elder brother of Vang Pao's father, Neng Chue. Chong Toua was, according to the Hmong's classificatory system, Vang Pao's "nephew" by blood. He was sold as a child to Tong Ge, a wealthy man of the influential Moua clan, after his family had encountered financial difficulties.

Chong Toua's family was forced to pay restitution to villagers for causing a fire that burned down some homes.[11] As a child of twelve, Chong Toua had participated in Pa Chay's rebellion, for which he was sentenced to life imprisonment at Khang Khay. Precocious and charismatic, he impressed visiting French dignitaries with his sociable, friendly demeanor. Before they left, the dignitaries demanded his release on account of his young age. Chong Toua was freed after four months of incarceration.

The life of Chong Toua's wife, Lo Drou, is equally intriguing, allowing us glimpses into the ferocity of Blia Yao and the French in punishing the rebels of Pa Chay's War. Drou was the daughter of Lo Chai Vang, another important rebel leader in 1920. Chai Vang sided with Shong Ger against Blia Yao. Following the revolt, Chai Vang and his male line were exterminated by Blia Yao, leaving Drou as a lone survivor. Drou's mother had died years earlier, so she lived with a Lo kinsman who also sold her to the wealthy Tong Ge. Chong Toua and Drou grew up in the Moua household as brother and sister. A diligent woman, Drou was admired by a visiting relative who commented that should she marry the Moua family would lose a valuable asset. "Don't let her go to another clan," urged the visitor. The Mouas, who had raised her as a daughter, orchestrated a plan to keep Chong Toua and Drou in the family. Since he and Drou were from different clans, the Moua rationalized that it was acceptable for them to marry each other. Drou suddenly became a daughter-in-law.[12] In this way, the Moua family continued to exploit the young couple's economic value.

By the 1940s, Chong Toua had long ago left his youthful anti-French sentiments behind. He had, in fact, capitalized on a French connection to enrich himself. He found work on the farm of a French man named Hazé, a retired army officer who had married an indigenous woman. Having spent nearly a lifetime in Southeast Asia, Hazé had made Laos his home. He opted not to return to France when his term of service ended. Instead, he asked permission from Chong Toua to live at Phou Dou, where he maintained a large farm. Chong Toua's family became hired hands on the farm, helping to grow potatoes and vegetables to sell to the colonial troops stationed at Khang Khay. From Hazé, Chong Toua picked up enough French to communicate easily.[13] Knowledge of French allowed him to become the first important guide for the Free French commandos who parachuted into the Plain of Jars in 1945, establishing him as an important leader in highland Hmong society. During the Japanese Occupation, Chong Toua and his Moua kinsmen assisted in the retrieval and concealment of weapons and ammunition dropped in preparation for the anticipated French invasion, which never occurred.[14] The Moua clan also sheltered Touby and the French at Phou San when they were being hunted by the Japanese and Fay Dang. Following the Occupation, Touby rewarded Chong Toua by appointing him a *naikong* (district leader). Chong Toua's legacy allowed his son, Toulu, to rise to the rank of colonel and serve as the secretary of General Vang Pao's secret army in the 1960s.

In early 1945, while Chong Toua was in comfortable alliance with the French, the tide turned against Germany in Europe. The Japanese, anticipating their own difficulties, executed a preemptive strike against the French in Indochina. Japanese troops occupied Xieng Khouang for the first time in February 1945, a month before Free French agents had made contact with Touby. Touby tells how he was co-opted to aid the French recolonization efforts during this tumultuous time: "On March 4, Louis Doussineau, the chief officer of the Nong Het post, came to inform me at Nam Kuang that a very young French officer named Captain Ayrolles, who was accompanied by two lieutenants and some other soldiers, had arrived in Nong Het. They wanted to see me. This news distressed me tremendously. When your own boss wants to bring his friends to meet you, how can you say no? The polite thing is to welcome them into your home. So I invited them to come and have lunch with me on the sixth."[15]

Touby prepared a huge feast and invited other Hmong leaders to be present as well. After they ate, Ayrolles explained that the Japanese were losing the war in the Pacific. French commandos were staging an invasion of Indochina from India. They had been parachuting into the Plain of Jars along CR6 and CR7 to guard the passes between Sam Neua, Xieng Khouang, and Vietnam. He wanted Touby and the Hmong to conceal the commandos wherever they landed, and he also wanted several young men to act as guides to help retrieve ammunition and weapons that were being dropped during the cover of night. After Ayrolles departed, Touby consulted with the clan leaders. They made a decision to aid the French. Touby writes:

> The majority of us decided to help the French. Everyone said that since French colonization there had been many improvements. There is a school and a medic in Nong Het. There is a road that allows the Chinese to bring cloth, thread, goods, and salt to be sold to the Hmong in plenty. For many years now, the Hmong had no longer suffered for want of these products. The French had also recognized Kaitong Lo Blia Yao as a leader. The French seemed to have rendered justice. They also appointed the literate Hmong, Ly Pa Ge [Touby's brother], as the *naikong* of Nong Het, presiding over both the Hmong and the Lao *tassengs* in the Nong Het district. The most important thing was that there had been peace and liberty in the land so that the Hmong could earn a living.[16]

Touby presents the rationale for collaboration with the French as a united consensus made after discussions between the clan leaders. The justifications above, however, may very well have simply been his own persuasive speech to the leaders, who listened intently and then gave nods of agreement. This passage should be taken as revealing Touby's powers of persuasion rather than as historical reality. I doubt, for example, that the Hmong leaders would have been aware of the benefits of the medic in Nong Het since, as noted above, even as late as the 1970s the descendants of these very Hmong still believed that doctors consumed brains. Moreover, the Chinese had always circulated in the highlands of Laos, trading lowland products for Hmong opium. I also doubt that the construction of CR7, which did allow the French to scrutinize Chinese business dealings with the Hmong, improved the Hmong's situation as drastically as Touby depicts. Nevertheless, having obtained the consensual nod of the clan leaders, Touby agreed to aid the French. The next day he selected two Hmong guides to accompany Ayrolles back to the Plain of Jars.[17]

The Japanese *coup de force* occurred on the evening of March 9, 1945. In Laos, Japanese soldiers occupied the administrative capital of Vientiane while the Lao gathered to watch the arrest of the French and "contemplated in silence the march past [them] of the fallen gods."[18] Farther north the French who had evaded capture in Tonkin poured into Xieng Khouang. Others headed toward China, guided by the Hmong. Doussinneau, the commanding officer in Nong Het, waited a week for the fleeing Frenchmen and their families to cross to the Lao side before destroying all the bridges to slow down the Japanese convoys. He collected the weapons of the Lao and Vietnamese soldiers under his command, whom he had grown to distrust, and dismissed them. Then he handed fifteen rifles and ten boxes of ammunition to Touby. He asked Touby to hide the remaining supplies, weapons, ammunition, and silver piasters—remnants of tax and duty money. Touby's Ly kinsmen from Nong Khiaw provided the manpower to carry these supplies into the surrounding mountains while Ly Tong Pao, the lineage leader of Tha Khu, escorted the French officers and their families to the remote mountain ranges of Phou San east of the Plain of Jars. The Moua clan of Phou San provided food and shelter for the French. Touby and Tougeu remained in Nong Het to accommodate the Japanese.[19]

A column of three hundred Japanese soldiers entered Nong Het on March 24, 1945. Thirty of them remained at Nong Het while the rest marched toward the Plain of Jars. The captain of the group, a young officer, summoned Touby before him. He gave Touby a well-crafted speech about how the Japanese had come to liberate their Asian brothers from the grasp of white colonialists. Touby writes:

Speaking in Thai, he talked about the events that had occurred in Indochina. He said the Japanese were not there to colonize the land for themselves. They were only there to help the Lao, Vietnamese, and Cambodians liberate their country from the French. The Japanese would not remain fifty years like the French. When they have achieved independence for the Indochinese population they will leave. They will not remain to persecute the population like the White Man. . . . Then he asked me to fulfill my duties as *tasseng* and help him maintain tranquility in the region as I had done under the French. I agreed to do as he instructed.[20]

While the Japanese recognized Touby for the moment, the new power structure meant that Fay Dang had another patron to whom he could appeal for legitimation. Fay Dang capitalized on the opportunity to compete for his father's position once again. Before the Japanese entered Laos, he had witnessed Touby and the Ly clan taking French weapons, ammunition, and money into hiding. Full of hatred for the French, who had cast his family aside, and perhaps jealous that Touby had been left with many possessions, Fay Dang began to spread rumors about Touby. When an opportunity allowed him to go to Ban Ban, he reported to the local Japanese administrator that Touby was planning a rebellion. Touby's sister, Mao Song, gave us her version of the events:

Tong Pao of Tha Khu was the one who hid the French. Ly Na's relatives from Nong Khiaw were the ones who assisted in carrying the ammunition and weapons by the loads and loads to be scattered between the valleys and dried creeks of the hills. The French forced them to do that. The Vietnamese, Lao, and Fay Dang saw this, and they knew. They [Fay Dang's people] began to tell everyone that Uncle By [Touby] coveted the money and the things of the French so he killed the French in order to have those money and things. That was what they told the Hmong. The truth was that Tong Pao took those French into hiding. When the Japanese arrived at Toom [Ban Ban], they [Fay Dang's people] went to accuse [Touby], saying that Tasseng By had already assisted in hiding the weapons and ammunition of the French. If they [the Japanese] did not arrest him, Tasseng By would lead the Hmong of Nong Khiaw and Tha Khu in a war against the Japanese.[21]

Touby learned quickly the consequences of Fay Dang's action. A month after the Japanese entered Nong Het he received a letter from Thao Lek, the governor of Xieng Khouang, ordering him go to Ban Ban to consult with him and the *chaomuang* (county chief). Thao Lek, who had sided with the Japanese, also demanded that Touby bring with him the weapons, ammunition, and money left behind by the French. Sensing trouble, Touby opted to reply by letter alone, explaining that he had in his possession only five suitcases of clothes and fifteen rifles for maintaining peace and order in his canton. Three days later another letter from the governor ordered Touby once again to go down to Ban Ban. This time Touby complied and arrived in the town with five armed men. Only the *chaomuang* was there to take Touby to be interrogated by the presiding Japanese officer. Touby writes: "He [the *chaomuang*] took me to the Japanese officer in Ban Ban. I reiterated what I had said earlier [in the letter to the governor] to the officer. In the end the officer took away the five rifles of my traveling companions. He told me to go home and hand over the remaining ten rifles and cases of ammunition to the presiding [Japanese] officer at Nong Het. I returned home and did as he ordered. Several days later the Japanese officer of Nong Het came with ten soldiers to arrest me in Nam Kuang."[22]

Touby was detained and interrogated at Nong Het for three days. He admitted that he had been forced to hide the guns, ammunition, and money, but he pleaded ignorance of the whereabouts of the French. He only saw the French officers leave in the direction of Khang Khay, he said. As for the French women and children, they were sent to stay with the priest.[23] Then the Japanese officer inexplicably released him with an apology. Touby continues: "He interrogated me for three days and saw that it was useless, so he released me. Before I left the fort, he invited me to lunch. He apologized and said he arrested me because some important Hmong leaders had reported to his Japanese superiors and to the Lao authorities at Xieng Khouang that I was hiding French weapons and ammunition in preparation for a revolt against the Japanese."[24]

According to Jean Lartéguy and Yang Dao, Touby's release was thanks to the intervention of Father Mazoyer, the bishop of Vientiane, who had been stranded in Nong Het in the midst of the Japanese takeover. Mazoyer told the Japanese that any mistreatment of Touby would spark a rebellion by the Hmong who respected their leader.[25] The Japanese officer, having only thirty men under his command, made the wise decision to release Touby. The officer asked only that Touby relinquish the remaining French possessions that he had hidden. Touby told his sister Mao Song and her husband, Tong Ger Vang, to retrieve some of the possessions in order to appease the officer. Mao Song continued:

> After they imprisoned Uncle By, my husband, Tong Ger, went to visit him. The Ly clan did not even dare to go visit him anymore. [The Japanese] said if there is anything of the French left, to give it to them, so my husband Tong Ger and me, we carried the suitcases loaded with the clothes belonging to the

French women and children back to [Touby's] house. Then Uncle By took the Japanese to go get it. After that he asked the [Ly] relatives of Nong Khiaw to retrieve the weapons and ammunition thrown in the dry creek beds and to hand them over to the Japanese. Once that was done, the Japanese said, "Since you have given these things to us, go back and assume your administrative duties as before."[26]

On his release, Touby went into hiding in the jungle. He joined the French commandos at Phou Dou, who were being supplied by the Moua clan. Tougeu (see fig. 17), Touby's younger half brother, who had recently returned home after obtaining his baccalaureate degree at Hanoi in 1942, was left in charge of administrative duties in Nam Kuang. Several days later a group of Japanese soldiers, armed with rifles and swords, returned to arrest Touby again. They physically restrained Tougeu while soldiers ransacked the house and stole money from the bedroom. When Tougeu confronted the Japanese about the theft, he was threatened. Tougeu described this tense encounter:

Two or three days later the Japanese came back to arrest Touby [again] but did not succeed. They pointed their rifles at the window, waiting to shoot him in case he tried to jump out. [But] Touby was not home. I was home. The Japanese inquired where Touby was. I said Touby had gone to look for animals—cows and pigs—to feed the Japanese soldiers.

They said, "When Touby returns, you two need to come meet with the Japanese soldiers at the Nong Het fort."

I said, "Sure, when my elder brother returns, we will come."

"How many days will he be gone?"

"He'll be back in four days."

While this conversation was taking place, four or five soldiers ransacked the bedroom. Once things had relaxed a bit, I looked through the bedroom door. The dresser and the door lay broken in pieces. Twelve or thirteen thousand kip were gone, so I said the dresser and door had been broken and the money was gone. The Japanese [officer] stood up in front of me with his sword raised in [his] hand. "Are you accusing the Japanese soldiers of theft?"

I said, "I did not accuse the Japanese soldier of theft. I said my dresser is broken and some money is gone."

Just then he remembered that I had promised to come to Nong Het, so he relaxed a bit and put his sword back in its sheath. "When Touby gets back, you come with him to Nong Het."

I said, "Okay." Once he left, I was not going to stick around![27]

Figure 17. Tougeu Lyfoung in formal uniform. (Courtesy of Tougeu Lyfoung)

Tougeu also went into hiding. Intimidated by what had happened to the Lyfoung brothers, other clan leaders quietly remained out of sight in their home villages. Only the young, energetic, fourteen-year-old Vang Pao came daily to Touby's house. Touby had instructed him to collect intelligence while playing the part of a collaborator. Vang Pao requisitioned food for the Japanese while observing their every move. Being a teenager, he went back and forth easily between the villages and the jungle, reporting every Japanese movement to Touby.[28] Vang Pao's humble beginning as a protégé of Touby paid off tremendously in the long run. After the Japanese Occupation, Touby recommended him into the French colonial police, staging for him a triumphant career in the military. A quick study, Vang Pao acquired Touby's political skills easily. He applied these skills for his own benefit. Under American tutelage, he eclipsed Touby in the 1960s and dominated the next chapter of Hmong history.

Shortly after his escape from Nam Kuang, Touby learned that Fay Dang had claimed his administrative position. Touby writes, "I had fled from Nam Kuang for a mere seven days when Ly Tong Pao and Ly Shoua Toua arrived to report to me in the jungle that my uncle, Lo Fay Dang, had relocated to Nong Het and was now the *tasseng* of Keng Khoai."[29] True to his words to Ly Foung nearly a decade earlier, Fay Dang had reclaimed the position once held by his father, Blia Yao. Just as Blia Yao had used the French colonial army to pursue Shong Ger in 1920, Fay Dang used the Japanese to hunt down Touby. Fay Dang distributed written pamphlets, ordering the Hmong villagers to capture Touby dead or alive.[30] When all efforts to capture Touby failed, Fay Dang turned to the nearest targets—Touby's wives and children and the Ly clan. Perhaps, Fay Dang had not forgotten how the Lys sided with Touby during the struggle for Keng Khoai, tipping the scale in favor of Touby's appointment. Now that they were aiding Touby and the French, he forced them to pay in personal and financial terms.

According to Ly Na, before Fay Dang's extortions, the Lys of Nong Khiaw had been neutral in the personal dispute between Touby and Fay Dang. Ly Na points to the long history of marriage alliances between his clan and Blia Yao's family as the reason for their neutrality. Fay Dang himself was married to one of their Ly daughters, Gao Li.[31] Several incidents that turned the Lys of Nong Khiaw and Tha Khu decisively against Fay Dang occurred by accident as well as design. After Touby and Tougeu had fled, a Japanese platoon occupied Touby's home in Nam Kuang. Touby's wives, both about to give birth, went to live with Bee Chou, Lo Tsong Tou's son. After Touby's second wife gave birth to a son, Teng [Touxoua], Touby had his family relocated to his opium field in the mountains. Shortly afterward, in May 1945, the Japanese began a massive manhunt for them. Afraid they would be apprehended, Tougeu relocated Touby's wives a second time to the distant jungles south of CR7, near the crop fields of the Lys of Nong Khiaw. Tsai Saykao of the Thao clan farmed a plot of land nearby. He spotted Touby's wives and small children and went to inform Fay Dang, who delayed the pursuit for several days. As soon as Touby learned that his family's location had been revealed, he had them escorted out of the region to join him at Phou Dou. When Fay Dang sent Japanese soldiers to arrest Touby's women and children, a tragic encounter drew the Lys of Nong Khiaw onto Touby's side.[32] Mao Song continued:

Then Tsai Saykao Thao went and told Uncle Fay Dang, "Elder Fay, if you were not informed, you might say I was involved in hiding them. I should tell you that Tasseng [Tou]By's wives and children are taking shelter at the edge of my field. I'm here to inform you." So Uncle Fay Dang ordered Kao Saychao of the Lo clan to guide the Japanese to attack them near the fields. Uncle By's wives and children were living only in makeshift shelters made of leaves in the jungle near the fields, but those [Ly women] who were working in the fields, they have chickens, pigs, maize, and all sorts of things by their field houses. When the Japanese arrived, the Ly bodyguards had already guided Uncle By's wives and children to safety, so the Japanese attacked those in the field, forced them to be dogs and pigs [i.e., they raped them]. The Hmong say [the Japanese] raped the women—old, young, maiden, daughters-in-law—raped them all. They cried and cried. [Ly] Nao Yeng [the only man in the field] was beaten by the Japanese. That Kao Saychao, he did not speak Japanese either! He tried and tried to communicate, saying that these were not the wives and children of Tasseng By; they were just cultivators who had come to farm their fields. It was not until daylight arrived that this message was finally understood. Then they [the victims] were ordered to slaughter their chickens and pigs and use their cows and horses to transport these [goods] to the Japanese [at Nong Het]. This was what happened to draw the Lys [of Nong Khiaw] into the feud [against Fay Dang].[33]

During an interview in 1995, Nhia Vu denied that he or Fay Dang had ever assisted the Japanese in hunting down Touby and the French. When Touby left for the jungle, he said, they also went into hiding.[34] Perhaps from Fay Dang's and Nhia Vu's perspective, they were forced to do the bidding of the Japanese just as Touby was coerced by circumstances, as he explained above, to aid the French. Just as Touby was unable to resist the French, Fay Dang may have found himself in the difficult position of not being able to say no to the Japanese who legitimated him. Like Touby, he had to project an image of cooperation with his own colonial masters. This may be the reason why he delayed for several days before sending the Japanese to the area where Touby's family was hiding.

Whatever the case, the damage was done when Fay Dang's escorts took the Japanese to the fields. Rape was an unspeakable humiliation for the Hmong. The victims endured social stigma while their family members—particularly the men of the clan—suffered shame for failing to protect their women. If the men did not avenge the women, which was impossible in this case, the humiliation was complete. This incident was considered a terrible embarrassment for the Ly clan—a loss of their manhood. After they had raped the Ly women, the Japanese took Ly Mao Nao, a young girl of eleven, to Nong Het to be used as a comfort woman. For decades the Ly men, out of shame and fear of being stigmatized, kept what had happened to their women a secret. They only spoke of the rape of Mao Nao because, on account of her youth, that act was felt to be so egregious that no Hmong would dare to place the blame on anyone.[35] Tougeu Lyfoung stated, "We said nothing. No matter whose wives got forced as dogs and pigs, we said nothing out of shame. We only spoke about the little girl that they took to Nong Het."[36]

Until this time, the Lys of Nong Khiaw had quietly watched as Fay Dang spearheaded the hunt for Touby and his wives. Since Fay Dang was married to one of their daughters, the Ly clan was determined not to pick a side, according to Ly Na. They considered what had happened to their women unforgivable, however. Fay Dang and Nhia Vu had ordered their clansmen to lead the Japanese to the area. Whether it occurred by accident or design, the Lys held the brothers directly responsible.[37]

If the rape had occurred by accident, Fay Dang's subsequent actions left no doubt in the minds of the Lys that he was out to get them. Just two and a half decades earlier, Blia Yao had acquired a massive fortune extorting bribes from people who had sympathized with Vue Pa Chay and joined in the anti-French struggle. Now Fay Dang found it convenient to employ his father's practices against the Ly clan. After their women were raped, Fay Dang extorted silver from the Lys of Nong Khiaw. Before the Japanese *coup de force*, Fay Dang had seen the Lys take loads of French silver into hiding. He wanted a portion of this wealth. In exchange for ten thousand kip, the equivalent of forty silver bars, he promised not to harass them anymore. Afraid for their safety because Fay Dang had the might of the Japanese army behind him, the Lys grudgingly paid off the extortion. Next Fay Dang led the Japanese on a raid at Ly Tong Pao's house in Tha Khu.[38] Tong Pao's family suffered because he had escorted the French into hiding. If lineage boundaries and personal and/or regional interests had separated members of the Ly clan before, they now had a reason to unite. Months later, when members of the Ly clan caught Fay Dang's brother, Nhia Vu, at Phou Tha, they beat him unconscious.

Lowland Political Split Exacerbates Highland Factionalism

The political split in the royal family of Luang Prabang, reminiscent of that between Fay Dang and Touby, exacerbated Hmong political factionalism in the highlands, and lent a nationalist voice to what was primarily a personal feud between the Lobliayaos and the Lyfoungs. The lowland political divide that plagued Laos for the next three decades originated with the French and intensified during the Japanese Occupation between King Sisavangvong and Prince Phetsarath, the viceroy of Luang Prabang. Some argue that Phetsarath, much like Fay Dang, despised the French, who had deprived his family of its royal prerogatives. Phetsarath's father, Boun Kong, was the former *maha ouparat* (viceroy) of Luang Prabang. Following the Siamese system of succession dating back to the Ayutthaya period, he should have succeeded as king, but the French imposed a western system of primogeniture. In 1904 they installed Crown Prince Sisavangvong as king, permanently depriving Phetsarath's family of the opportunity to ever ascend the throne.

Grant Evans disputes this argument. The prince, he says, was loyal and had no kingly pretensions. In effect Phetsarath's distaste for the French stemmed from their arrogant treatment of the Lao monarch. Evans writes:

> There is no evidence that he ever wished to displace the king, as some French tried to say after 1945 in order to discredit him. To these claims the prince replied: "I have never asked for recognition from anyone, and I am happy to have been useful to my country. And it is not now, when I only have a small number of years to live, that I would dream of dirtying all my past honor, probity, and devotion to the service of my country, by working to challenge the place of my king, to usurp the throne of a legitimate and venerated sovereign of his people."[39]

Evans concludes, however, that King Sisavangvong and Phetsarath were wrapped up in the political chaos after 1945 in a manner that got the better of their egos. He writes, "The dismissal of Phetsarath by the king [in September 1945] and then the dethroning of the king by the Lao Issara [in November 1945] was a deep blow to the pride of both men. . . . It was something not easily forgiven by either of them, and their bitterness was no doubt given voice behind closed doors, further warping memories of these tumultuous events."[40]

By early 1945, with the tide in the Pacific turning against the Japanese, they scrambled to grant independence to emerging Southeast Asian nations in the hopes of attracting them to their side. Similarly, the French also maneuvered for political loyalty in Laos. They had lost Lao confidence when strips of land on the west bank of the Mekong were handed over to Thailand in May 1941.[41] The French aimed to win back the royal family, promising to restore Luang Prabang's lost land following liberation. Crown Prince Savang Vatthana was encouraged to stage a coup, after which he decreed a death sentence for anyone who worked against France. The authority of the crown prince was immediately compromised, however, for the Japanese forced the king to declare Laos an independent nation on April 8, 1945.[42] Savang Vatthana's decree, though quickly undermined by the Japanese, allowed Touby to proclaim his collaboration with the French as an extension of his duty to the king. "The French are friends of Laos and the king. I am a friend of France and a subject of the king. For me, you [Frenchmen] are not strangers," he said.[43] Touby was a keen political player. The Luang Prabang king was a legitimate sovereign, the descendant of a lineage stretching back to the ancient King Fa Ngum, the founder of the Lanxang Kingdom in the thirteenth century. Whether or not Touby anticipated France's defeat a decade later, he had found an important patron in the lowland monarch. Touby used the French to pressure the king for political advantages, obtaining the legitimation of both authorities against Fay Dang.

On September 1, just weeks after the bombing of Hiroshima and Nagasaki, Prince Phetsarath declared Laos a single independent kingdom that included Luang Prabang and Champassak. Several weeks after the formal surrender of Japan, however, King Sisavangvong announced that the French protectorate was still in force. Phetsarath was stripped of his title, viceroy. Seeing that the king was now willing to accommodate France's return, Phetsarath began to work actively for independence. He organized a Defense Committee to vote on a Provisional Constitution, forming a Provisional People's Assembly. The assembly later evolved into Phetsarath's emerging government, known as the Lao Issara (Lao Independence Movement).[44]

The Highland Feud Continues in Laos

Meanwhile, in the hills of Laos, the personal war between Touby and Fay Dang was culminating in an explosion of violence and counterviolence. On September 2, the day after Phetsarath declared Laos independent, Fay Dang's half brother Nhia Vu was spotted on CR7. He was traveling with several kinsmen, heading toward Tasseng Moua Nao Tou's house. Nao Tou, the leader of the Moua clan, lived in Phou Tha, another village in the Phou San mountain range. A man of considerable influence, he ranked among the few Hmong leaders of the period who were wealthy enough to obtain five wives. Nhia Vu was married to one of the daughters of Nao Tou's most senior wife.[45] Informants on Touby's side believed Nhia Vu was returning from Xieng Khouang, where he had gone to confer with the Lao Issara and to gather intelligence for the Viet Minh. Nhia Vu said, however, that he and Fay Dang had been summoned by the provisional governor to answer Touby's charges that they had staged the rape of the Ly women. The brothers denied being involved, and the governor promised to urge Touby to drop these accusations and end the feud between the Ly and Lo clans.[46] Fay Dang remained at Xieng Khouang while Nhia Vu went to visit his father-in-law at Phou Tha.

Nhia Vu entered Nao Tou's village at dusk. According to his sister-in-law, Tsia Moua, who heard Nhia Vu's account firsthand when he returned to Laos during the short period of collaboration between the royal Lao government and the Pathet Lao in 1958–59, he knew he had been recognized. As he walked into the village, he saw a shadowy figure running away. Still he marched undeterred to his father-in-law's house. Nao Tou was surprised by his son-in-law's sudden appearance and immediately warned him that Touby and members of the Ly clan were nearby at Phou Dou. Nhia Vu shrugged off the warning. He acted as if he aimed to stay, so Nao Tou's family prepared to host him for the evening.[47]

Hmong informants had spotted Nhia Vu on CR7, but much earlier in the day than he thought. These informants had already reported to the French and Touby. Tougeu Lyfoung was the translator for these Hmong informants. Much like Fay Dang did, he later recast these events in terms of the French versus the Viet Minh, with himself and Touby playing the role of interpreters. Tougeu stated:

> Just as the Japanese left, the French came out of hiding to find that Nhia Vu and Lo Tou had been spotted by people on their way back from Xieng [Khouang]. They had gone there to contact the Japanese and the [anti-French] Lao leaders. After the Japanese lost, they left [Xieng Khouang], and then they [Nhia Vu and Lo Tou] also left. The French ordered [Ly] Tong Va, [Ly] Tong Pao, and [Ly] Neng Tong, too, I believe—I can't recall clearly anymore—and [Moua] Chia Sa to lead a group of soldiers to go and capture Nhia Vu and Lo Tou. Two people had come to inform the French [earlier]. We were the interpreters. These two said, "Oh, we met two people down by the road who said they were going to go spend the night at Nao Tou's house in the evening. They asked the way there and were told where to go." The French investigated quickly, and Uncle By and I interpreted what was said. Then the French ordered people to go arrest [them]—going six or seven kilometers from Phou Dou.[48]

Before Nhia Vu could sit down for dinner, Touby's men surrounded Nao Tou's house. Angry about the rape of their women just months earlier, the men stormed through the door and began beating Nhia Vu with their rifles. Ly Tong Pao, whose house in Tha Khu had been pillaged, led the brutal thrashing.

Nao Tou could do nothing to stop the men. Nhia Vu was beaten to within an inch of his life, suffering cuts on his face, mouth, and nose and multiple broken ribs. Nhia Vu carried these physical and emotional scars for the rest of his life.[49] Realizing that Touby's men would not stop until he was dead, Nao Tou told them that if Nhia Vu died in his house these men would, in accordance with Hmong customary law, have to pay compensation and perform expensive ritual sacrifices to appease his domestic spirits. The Hmong have strict taboos against letting members of another clan die in their houses. Not wanting that kind of financial burden, Tong Pao ordered the men to stop and tie Nhia Vu up. They marched him in the dark back to Phou Dou to let Touby decide his fate.[50]

At Phou Dou, Chong Toua, the village chief, waited anxiously. He was Nao Tou's adopted nephew and, by clan extension, also an in-law of Nhia Vu. Soon enough Chong Toua saw Nhia Vu being ushered into his house, his hands tied behind his back. Having bled profusely for several hours, Nhia Vu was barely able to stand. His face was swollen "like a beehive," and he was unrecognizable. Chong Toua averted his eyes, horrified at the sight. Touby entered behind Nhia Vu and said, "Chong Toua, find food for him to eat his fill. Tomorrow, we'll have him killed and tossed away."[51] Chong Toua said nothing.

Once Touby and his men had left, Chong Toua quietly sent word for his Moua relatives to convene and make a decision. The Moua clansmen decided that if Nhia Vu were killed in their village, they would not only be blamed, but they would also be dragged into a personal feud between the Lyfoungs and the Lobliayaos that had been going on for several generations. Although they had supported Touby and the French in the larger political struggle against the Japanese and the Viet Minh, the Moua clan wanted nothing to do with a personal feud. On the other hand, they did not want to displease Touby either. They had elected to struggle beside Touby, and they respected Touby's prestige and influence with the colonial authorities. Caught in a dilemma, Chong Toua and his clansmen devised a plan. Nhia Vu's escape would have to look like an accident and not the result of a conspiracy on the part of the Moua clan.[52]

When Nhia Vu asked to go to the bathroom, the Moua clansmen saw their chance. They bound Nhia Vu's wrists behind his back loosely and sent only a teenage youth to watch over him. With the full moon lighting their way, the youth held one end of the rope as Nhia Vu walked ahead to a conveniently bushy area. He told the boy that he was too shy to do his business in front of him, so if the youth would release more rope he could walk behind the bush out of sight. After some urging, the naive youth relented, giving Nhia Vu as much rope as possible. As it turned out, Nhia Vu was planning his own escape and using the bathroom ruse to get away. Tsia, Nhia Vu's sister-in-law, related what she heard from Nhia Vu: "He said he prayed to his ancestors, promising a cow sacrifice if they would help him escape the ordeal alive. Then he pulled his wrists hard apart. To his surprise, the rope that bound his wrists came off easily."[53]

Once freed, Nhia Vu sprinted north of the village in effort to confuse Touby's men. Discovering that Nhia Vu had fled, the boy ran back to inform Touby. Touby demanded that Nhia Vu be found immediately. Two search parties went to look for Nhia Vu. Starting at opposite ends of the village, they met in the middle. The group coming from the north found the rope that had bound Nhia Vu's wrists. Touby was sure that Nhia Vu would make for CR7, and then head east to Nong Het. He and his men went in that direction, pursuing Nhia Vu all night with torches. At sunrise they approached Lak 10, a village. A family of Hmong had just been to its fields and was returning with baskets full of freshly harvested maize. Touby asked if they had seen anyone, and they said they had met Nhia Vu at the waterfall, Dej Tsaws Tsag, miles away. Touby ordered his men to return to Phou Dou. It was useless to pursue Nhia Vu; he was out of reach.[54]

Fay Dang had been a source of pain for Touby throughout the Japanese Occupation, so he decided to settle matters once and for all. Touby had received letters from Lokhamthi Nakaya and General Le Thiep Hong, leaders of the Viet Minh in Nong Het, demanding that he joined them in liberating Indochina and allowed their agents to operate back and forth through the Plain of Jars. Lokhamthi was a personal friend of Touby. The two had met while in school in Vinh during the mid-1930s. After convening a meeting in Xieng Khouang, Touby and his good friend, Saykham, the newly appointed provincial governor, decided not to work with Lokhamthi and the Viet Minh. Instead they sent fifty men to reinforce Tougeu at Nong Het.[55] Realizing the strategic importance of uniting the Hmong behind him now, Touby sent the retired deputy governor, Phya Anong, to ask Fay Dang to switch sides. Fay Dang maintained that he had been wronged and refused to declare his loyalty to the French. Touby attempted to negotiate with Fay Dang three more times, but Fay Dang remained adamant. Touby writes, "He only sent back elusive proverbs predicting that in the future, someone would come to establish peace in the land so that all could exist side by side."[56]

Touby acted decisively. He ordered his clansmen Ly Shoua Toua and Ly Tong Pao to lead thirty men in an attack of Fay Dang's village, Hua Pha Noi. They charged the village only to discover that Fay Dang had already relocated

across the Vietnamese border. Years later, inculcated with Communist anticolonial jargon, Fay Dang recast this family feud in nationalist terms to the leftist
scholar Wilfred G. Burchett. The personal battles between Fay Dang and
Touby became, in Fay Dang's historical memory, a struggle between Lao nationalists and French colonialists. Nowhere did he mention that his nephew
was the one who gave the order to attack him. He stated, "The French sent
troops to encircle us. With four of my friends and two boys, I slipped through
the encirclement at night into the jungle. We took our guns and cross-bows
with us, but did not shoot at the French. They shot at us."[57] Two of Fay Dang's
followers, Youachi Lor and Xiachue Yang, lay dead in the village after the
sound of the rifles had dissipated. The villagers returned to bury the men
quickly without the proper rituals. After a second attack on his village, Fay
Dang relocated permanently across the border in Vietnam. According to Lo
family members, this harassment drove Fay Dang into the arms of the Communists. Nhia Vu stated, "If Touby had not killed Youachi Lor, Xiachue Yang,
and had not tortured me near death, then my family and followers would not
have joined the Communists."[58] Just as the rape of the Ly women had drawn
the Lys of Nong Khiaw onto Touby's side, so the death of Xiachue Yang may
have solidified the Yangs' alliance with Fay Dang. Thao Tou Yang, Fay Dang's
first cousin, emerged shortly afterward as the Hmong military commander on
the Communist side. Eight of the first nine members of his Pa Chay Company
were his brothers and Yang cousins, all close relatives of Xiachue.[59]

Just as Fay Dang recast a family feud in anticolonial terms, those on
Touby's side depicted these incidents as a struggle against Vietnamese Communist invasions into Laos. In October and November 1945, they said, Fay Dang
and his Lo clansmen began leading columns of Viet Minh in repeated attacks
on Nong Het. Applying the guerrilla tactics of striking and running away,
Tougeu's men inflicted huge casualties, repulsing the Viet Minh. During an
attack on Touby's house at Nam Kuang, snipers waiting in a clump of elephant
grass killed Ly Tsai, the brother of Colonel Ly Joua Vang. Tsai was fleeing
with Touby's infant son when he was shot. Tsai's relatives threw grenades into
the clump of grass. When the smoke cleared, members of the Ly clan found
their cousin Lo Vang, the son of Blia Yao and Jer, lying dead next to a Viet
Minh cadre. Tsai and Vang were first cousins, born to a brother and sister.[60]
The nationalist struggle was entangled in a blood feud among family members —
again a reminder of what sometimes happened when marriage alliances went
awry.

The violence and counterviolence resulted in another unforgivable incident
considered highly shameful to the Ly clan. During another raid, Fay Dang's

group captured Ly Shoua Toua and a group of Ly women, wives of the Ly clan. The prisoners were marched on foot to Fay Dang's base camp. After torturing Shoua Toua for a time, Fay Dang let him go, but kept the Ly women behind as bounties for his troops. These women were returned only after 1958/59 when the opposing groups attempted to reach a reconciliation. By that time, some of these women had born children to Fay Dang's men. Colonel Nao Kao Lyfoung refused to talk about the event in detail, but he said one of these returned women was still alive in St. Paul, Minnesota, and she had a child from the other side. In 2008, Ger Lo confirmed: "Yes, my father [Lo Tsia Chue, the half brother of Fay Dang] took one of the women as a minor wife. When she was returned to the other side, he missed her so much that he defected to the other side briefly in pursuit of her. She wouldn't come back, so he came back home alone."[61] The incident was reminiscent of the 1920 feud between Lo Blia Yao and Lo Shong Ger, with Shong Ger aiming to capture Pa Hang, Blia Yao's beautiful fifth wife, as a trophy. In the case of Fay Dang's men taking the Ly women, it was not merely wishful thinking, but a reality.

Wary of more attacks, Tougeu decided to invade Muang Sen. On the way there, the weather intervened in favor of the Viet Minh. Near the village of Ha Noi, a sudden rainstorm washed away the bridge that led to Muang Sen. Tougeu's men had to wade through the high water. The man carrying a B-60 long-range machine gun dropped one of its parts in the river, depriving the group of a powerful weapon. Tougeu's men could not take Muang Sen without the machine gun. After an intense exchange of fire, they retreated back to the river. The French officer in charge was frustrated by the loss. When he saw Ly Nhia Long and another man carrying a small bucket of sugar and a copper canteen they had taken during the attack, he grabbed these objects and threw them in the river. He rebuked the two men for taking these items. Tougeu translated his verbal barrage. The men told Tougeu they would not endure such disrespect. Tong Pao, Nhia Long, and their relatives immediately abandoned Tougeu with the French officer.[62] These men demonstrated to the officer the terms of their cooperation.

What remained of Tougeu's group attempted to dig into a nearby hill, but the rocky site made the task impossible. By nightfall each of the men had succeeded in excavating only a waist-high foxhole. Sitting inside, their heads were left exposed. Tougeu's group was dislodged from the hill by a heavy counterattack the next day. After several rounds of fire were exchanged, Sithaovong, the older brother of Saykham, lay dead in his foxhole. The French officer asked Tougeu to find his clansmen and persuade them to return. Tougeu told the officer it would be impossible for him to catch up with them now. If he went all the way to Nong Het, it would take at least seven days to gather reinforcements from nearby villages. There was no way the officer and his small group could hold their ground until he returned. He recommended that they retreat. They left Muang Sen highly demoralized.[63]

Back at Nong Het, Tougeu faced a verbal reprimand from Tong Pao, who was angry that he had remained with the bossy Frenchman instead of supporting his own clansmen. The argument between them forced Tougeu to abandon Nong Het, leaving this crucial pass unguarded. Without his Ly clansmen, Tougeu felt he would have been ineffective in preventing the advance of the Communists. He recalled: "When I arrived back at Nam Kuang, Chaomuang Tong Pao said to me, 'Why didn't you die at Muang Sen instead of Sithaovong?' I had to control myself in order to bear the rebuke silently. I spent the night, then the next day I took three guards and left for Xieng [Khouang], never to return to Nong Het."[64]

While Tougeu had been guarding the pass of Nong Het, Touby was in the town of Xieng Khouang. On September 3, 1945, Touby and his Hmong partisans had left the village of Phou Dou to reoccupy the provincial capital. The main figures of the rudimentary militia posed for a historic victory photo (see fig. 18).[65] The Lao Issara dominated the political situation in Luang Prabang, however. Because of his allegiance to France, the aged monarch had been ordered by Phetsarath's Lao Issara government to abdicate. On November 10, Prince Sisoumang Saleumsak and Prince Bougnavat placed the king and the royal family under house arrest. After Touby liberated Xieng Khouang in late January 1946, he sent a contingent of six hundred men, led by Toulia, toward Luang Prabang. At Sala Phou Khoun, the men split up. Toulia led three hundred men along CR7 to recapture Luang Prabang and rescue King Sisavangvong. Ly Pa Cha of Nong Khiaw took the rest south down CR13 to help liberate Vientiane.[66]

Toulia's interest in the royal family's affairs may have become personal. While studying law in Vientiane in 1942, he had met and married a royal princess, becoming a member of the inner circle of the royal family.[67] When news of Toulia's approach reached Luang Prabang, the Lao Issara abandoned the city. Toulia occupied the city and found King Sisavangvong unharmed in a nearby cave. Fear of an assassination attempt against the king prevented the Hmong from transporting the monarch back to the royal palace right away, but they had to demonstrate the royal seizure of power to the people. Toulia ordered some of his men to guard the king while he devised a plan to show that the king, backed by Hmong soldiers, now controlled the city. As part of this plan, Vang Say Pao, who was deemed to be the handsomest and tallest of the bunch, was dressed up in the king's clothes, placed on a horse, and marched back into the palace.[68] Vang Geu related the incident, which was told to him

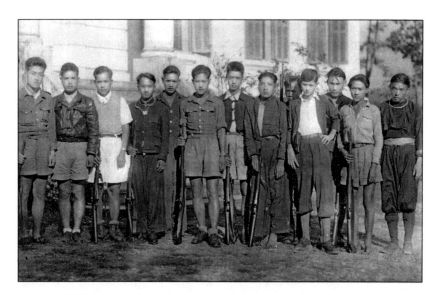

Figure 18. Touby's rudimentary militia, composed mostly of his Ly kinsmen, occupied Xieng Khouang on September 9, 1945. *Left to right*: Toulia Lyfoung, Touby Lyfoung, Moua Chia Sa, Ly Blia Chue, Ly Mai, Lo Bee Chou, Ly Neng Tong, Ly Joua Va, unidentified, Jean Sakarek, Ly Nao Lue (?), unidentified, and Ly Chue "Tuam Phom." (Courtesy of Maurice Gauthier, digitized by Vang Tsoua Yang)

many times by Say Pao when they were back in Laos: "My brother, Say Pao, was reluctant to pretend to be the king. He feared that the people would know he was only an imposter once they saw his face, but he was encouraged when Toulia told him Lao peasants were not allowed to look directly at the king. Instead they would be cowering alongside the road with their heads bowed down low. Say Pao did not have to worry about anything."[69] Capturing the city and successfully staging his return to power probably impressed on the king for the first time the strategic importance of the Hmong in the national struggle.

By January 1946, the French commandos and Touby's Hmong partisans had routed the Viet Minh and loyal followers of the Lao Issara out of Xieng Khouang, Luang Prabang, and Sam Neua. In the south, Prince Boun Oum na Champassak also brokered a deal that strengthened France's efforts to reclaim Laos. French forces recaptured Vientiane on March 6, 1946, and declared Laos a free state within the Indochinese Federation and the French Union. On April 24, after a major battle, the Lao Issara was forced to seek sanctuary across the Mekong in Thailand. For the moment, Touby was on the side of the winners of the revolution.

Hmong Competition Finds Revolutionary Voices in the Kingdom of Laos (1946–1960)

Competition between communist and noncommunist nationalists in the post–World War II period allowed Touby Lyfoung and Lo Fay Dang to maintain their bargaining positions, changing dramatically the Hmong's political status within the Lao state. As in former periods, Touby's and Fay Dang's legitimacy during this time rested on their abilities to mediate between Hmong desires and the demands of the state. Lowland factionalism complicated the state's relation with the Hmong, however. Touby and Fay Dang were no longer mere servants. In the midst of lowland division and competition, they were leaders who had to be courted. As such, both were in a position to negotiate for political concessions. As communists and noncommunists struggled to capture the state, both men found advantages as minority leaders that commanded manpower. The revolution allowed Fay Dang and Touby to thrust their personal feud onto the nationalist stage. As the two men offered their services and conscripted Hmong soldiers in defense of competing ideologies, they obtained recognition for their people, but only at the expense of Hmong blood.

Touby Lyfoung:
"King of the Hmong"

If ever there was a Hmong political broker who came close to being crowned, it was undoubtedly Touby Lyfoung. Dubbed the "King of the Hmong," Touby was, according to Captain Serres Ayrolles, the French officer who recruited him for guerrilla warfare against the Japanese, "received as a prince."[1] Tall, handsome, fair skinned, and portly, Touby had the physique of a lowland aristocrat. Often dressed impeccably in a white suit, he exuded the confidence of someone who always had more than enough to eat—an impression that is crucial in a society of rampant want. His size allowed him to move with a unique kind of command. Wherever he went highlanders and lowlanders alike presumed he was a dignitary. "Once I was driving Touby to Vientiane and our car broke down on the road," said his nephew Yangsao. "Touby said we should walk to get help in the Lao village nearby. As soon as the Lao villagers saw him approaching, they saluted him like a lord. By his looks alone they presumed he was important. Because of his physique, Touby never had to exert himself in order to get noticed."[2] When Touby spoke, his voice reverberated flawlessly in Lao, French, or Hmong. He had the charisma, the oratorical power, and the physical attributes to carry a crowd. He was a combination of the Weberian definition of a charismatic and legal-rational authority.

When Touby emerged as both a visionary Hmong leader and an educated bureaucrat of the state in the 1940s, his influence was paramount. Acutely aware that his position as a leader depended on outside and state legitimation, however, Touby dismissed any notion that he had royal pretensions. When French journalists asked if he was the king of the Hmong, he replied with humor, "Tell me where my kingdom is so I can run there quickly."[3] Therein lay the secret of his success. Touby was perceived like a prophet, but he made no apparent gesture toward sovereignty. Often addressed only by his title, *phya* (lord), he was a king to the Hmong but a loyal servant to the state. As early as 1946, Touby obtained political autonomy for the Hmong while also professing to be a subject of the Lao monarch. The ability to balance Hmong aspirations for independence and Lao interest in their own political hegemony in the nation-state distinguished Touby as the great Hmong diplomat of the twentieth century.

Upon returning to Laos in 1946, the French focused immediately on nation building. A large of part of that effort involved recognizing Touby and integrating the Hmong, and, for the first time, including them in national politics. During the Japanese Occupation, the French had lured Touby to their side with promises of political opportunity and equality. According to him, at their historic meeting on March 3, 1945, Captain Ayrolles promised, "At this time, we have no money to pay the young men [guides provided by Touby], but in the future we Frenchmen will not leave anyone behind."[4] Captain Bichelot, who replaced Ayrolles later, made the additional vow to introduce Touby to the lowland authorities: "Not long from now, I will take Touby to the south to meet Prince Boum Oum Na Champassak and to Luang Prabang to meet Crown Prince Savang Vatthana, the oldest son of King Sisavangvong. The new French government wants the leaders in Laos who still respect the French to meet, to know one another, and to work together to build an independent nation. We would like those who are pro-French to govern Laos after this World War has ended."[5] Bichelot was offering Touby the opportunity to obtain further legitimation from the lowland rulers along the Mekong, which would solidify his position as a paramount Hmong leader and demolish once and for all the challenges of Fay Dang. In light of the intense competition between the two, this promise was no small matter. Before the Japanese arrived, Fay Dang's strength lay in the fact that he had Phetsarath's support.[6] By way of the French, Touby could also obtain an alliance with the Lao aristocracy, particularly the powerful opponents of Phetsarath.

The French dangled more extensive political rights in front of other Hmong leaders to get them to join their cause. Moua Chong Toua, the first to work with the Free French commandos, provides another testimony of French promises:

> Why did I fight alongside them? . . . Because these two officers [Ayrolles and Bichelot] were authorized to promise that which we most desired. They said to us . . . if you want change, if you want us to recognize your rights, if you want to become equal to the Lao of the plain, you must help us, struggle next to us against the Japanese occupation, and defend the independence of this country as well as your own. In exchange for your participation, we will help you obtain posts in the administration and in education, build schools for your children, and dispensaries and hospitals for your sick. We will obtain a statute that will make you real Laotians [i.e., grant you citizenship]; you will have your own administrators, your own representatives who work in collaboration with Lao administrators and leaders.[7]

As Chong Toua understood it, the French promised political autonomy: "You will have your own administrators, your own representatives." This was as close to the Hmong dream of a kingdom as could be hoped for.

The French promise to grant the Hmong equality was also attractive to Touby. According to Maurice Gauthier, "Touby saw collaboration as a means of obtaining more rights for his people."[8] Touby's success in bargaining for political rights was facilitated by the additional pain to the French caused by Fay Dang's defection to the Viet Minh. With Fay Dang now actively competing for legitimacy on the Communist side, Touby's prestige became an indisputable issue. Accordingly, the French pressured the Lao king to anoint Touby as the supreme ethnic representative so as to draw the Hmong population to their side. This meant granting Touby a title greater than those Hmong leaders before him had received, giving him authority over all the Hmong of Laos. It also meant rewarding Touby's clients, the major clan leaders through whom Touby galvanized the population at large for political action. The court of Luang Prabang was induced to distribute functionary titles to Hmong leaders and to award the Hmong that which they most desired—autonomy!

Following their return to power in Laos, the French worked on the king. The Hmong were crucial to the creation of Laos. They had kept French commandos safe during the Japanese Occupation and they had guarded Xieng Khouang from danger during the Chinese invasion, said Raymond, the French official in charge of negotiations with King Sisavangvong. At the moment, in August 1946, only the Hmong guarded the strategic pass of Nong Het, keeping the Viet Minh contained at Muang Sen. Alluding to his rescue by Toulia Lyfoung the previous November, and reminding the king that the Hmong could still be drawn to the Lao Issara, Raymond writes: "The armed support of the Meos [Hmong] to the Franco-Lao cause has been spontaneous and the loyalty which they have demonstrated even in the worst of times, both toward your person and your House, constitute a fact all the more remarkable in so far as the populations of the high regions are generally passive towards the masters of the occasion, except, when out of treason, they have followed those functionaries in authority who have thrown in their lot with the Issara."[9] In short, Touby could no longer be ignored. Raymond continues: "Now that the country has returned to order, I suggest to your Majesty that it would be politic and equitable for the Kingdom and your House to officially consecrate and acknowledge the titles that the Meo populations have acquired."[10] The French had handed out titles to the Hmong. Now Raymond wanted the king to recognize these titles and co-opt the Hmong into the newly created kingdom.

Finally, Raymond asked the king to offer the Hmong direct access to Luang Prabang without going through the provincial authorities, who had not always been kind. As the French had done for the Tai of Tonkin, Raymond was asking the king to grant the Hmong of Laos political autonomy: "The surest way to succeed will be to favourably welcome the pledge to allow the Meo population to have the privilege, at least, of administrative and judicial relations through the intermediary of notables and functionaries belonging to their own race."[11]

According to Touby's brother, Nao Kao Lyfoung, King Sisavangvong did more than what Raymond requested. His majesty placed a most cherished opportunity before Touby. In May 1941, the French had given Xieng Khouang to the king as recompense for the loss of the west bank of the Mekong to Thailand. He now gave this fief to Touby as a reward. Xieng Khouang was to be an Autonomous Hmong Zone with Touby as ruler, governing over the Hmong, the Phuan, and other ethnic minorities. Touby knew this was an incredible but serious opportunity. For days he considered the offer in his head and conferred with his brothers. He made a realistic assessment of the Hmong's ability to rule Xieng Khouang. Touby could count the number of literate Hmong administrators on a single hand. These men, including Touby himself, were individuals of extremely limited bureaucratic experience. As Touby assessed the situation, he saw the Hmong dream slipping away. Colonel Nao Kao Lyfoung, Touby's younger brother, explained why Touby did not seize this historic offer made by the king and the French:

> Uncle By [Touby] turned to assessing those who could read and write Lao. There were only eight. Would you have accepted? [Touby] said, "We do not want this"—said it to [the Lao and the French]. Only eight familiar with written Lao, but only three were really literate. As for the rest, it's like what the Hmong often say [sarcastically], the letter would have to be the size of a water buffalo in order for them to be able to read it, you know? The size of a water buffalo! That is, they could only read and write minimally. I ask you, with only eight, would you have accepted? You would not because your own people cannot help you. You may have the manpower, but there was no other quality to support you.[12]

No matter how willing, Touby's people simply lacked individuals with sufficient bureaucratic experience and literacy to take over a multiethnic province and run it as an autonomous zone. After agonizing, Touby opted for the second-best thing. He would retain the essence of Hmong autonomy by having himself named paramount chief of the Hmong. In addition, he would ask for the inclusion of the Hmong at the provincial and national levels, but he would leave the administration of Xieng Khouang to Saykham's family. Nao Kao continued: "So the king and the French said, if that's the case then we'll make you [Touby] *chaomuang* of the Hmong. *Chaomuang* of the Hmong, but with authority over all—in Sam Neua, in Luang Prabang, in Sayabury. All the Hmong in the land of the Lao would be placed under your authority. This [the offer of Xieng Khouang to Touby] really did exist. The reason why our Lyfoung family could not abandon the royal family is because of this [show of generosity]."[13]

Touby's decision may also have been stimulated by his own consideration for his good friend and former schoolmate, Saykham. The offer of Hmong autonomy had occurred without the prince's knowledge. Touby, Toulia, and Tougeu had a friendship with the prince that stretched back to their early days in the colonial school of Xieng Khouang in the mid-1920s. Toulia was also Saykham's roommate while the two attended school in Vientiane. A year after this confidential discussion, in December 1947, Tougeu presided as Saykham's best man at his wedding.[14] Loyalty to Saykham may have played a significant factor in Touby's decision. He may have calculated that during this time of upheaval it would be unwise to offend the traditional rulers of the land. Saykham commanded a force of three hundred soldiers, composed of Phuan and Khmu, and he had been essential to the liberation of Xieng Khouang from the Lao Issara the previous January.[15] Fay Dang, meanwhile, was also on the opposing side, eager to win legitimation from such a figure. Touby's break with Fay Dang had stemmed from their struggle over the canton of Keng Khoai, which Fay Dang felt was his family's personal fief. Displacing Saykham would generate similar sentiments that may lead to another feud. Saykham could turn to Fay Dang and the Lao Issara, drawing a substantial section of the Hmong, Phuan, and other minorities to that side. The division between Fay Dang and Touby may have been the tipping point in Touby's decision to decline the offer of Xieng Khouang as an autonomous Hmong zone. Disunity cost the Hmong an incredible opportunity.

More important, Touby also may have gauged the heavy price of autonomy by assessing the political circumstances of the time. The French and the king were offering Xieng Khouang to him only because of the impending struggle for Laos. Accepting their offer would have meant committing the Hmong to a bloody struggle against Viet Minh incursions from the east. Although he wanted equality with the lowland Lao and was willing to cooperate just enough to obtain it, Touby did not want his people to shoulder this huge responsibility alone. One of his major criticisms of Vang Pao in the late 1960s was that he was too willing to sacrifice Hmong lives and had turned the war into a Hmong struggle.[16] Touby may have also foreseen a precarious future in which promises could be made and retracted easily on either side of the political divide. The case of the Hmong in Tonkin who struggled with the Viet Minh, the victors in the First Indochina War, sheds light on Touby's situation. To gain their loyalty, the Viet Minh had offered the Hmong of northwestern Vietnam autonomy during the period of nationalist struggle with the French. These Hmong contributed to the victory of the revolution only to see the offer of autonomy withdrawn when the Viet Minh consolidated its power in 1957.[17] After much sacrifice, the Hmong of Tonkin found themselves back to prewar conditions. Was Touby perceptive enough to have anticipated this circumstance in Laos in 1946?

Raymond also recognized Touby's rejection in terms of the Hmong's perception of autonomy. Geoffrey C. Gunn writes, "On the one hand, he [Raymond] noted, the desire of the Hmong of Tran Ninh for emancipation was very different from that expressed by the Tai peoples, insofar as the former had not hitherto asserted any claim to (political) independence. But, on the other hand, he acknowledged, they sought to escape from the constraints of political and administrative organization."[18] Unlike the river valley Tai, who had a stricter tradition of land control by feudal lords, the tribal Hmong did not seem to connect land possession with political power.[19] Touby may not have awakened fully to the idea of land claims, hence his decision not to accept Xieng Khouang as a Hmong zone. His lack of consciousness, if true, is not surprising given that the concept of territorial boundaries had emerged quite recently even among the lowlanders of Southeast Asia.[20]

In September 1946, Touby accepted an appointment as *chaomuang* of the Hmong. Ever the cautious diplomat, he asked Saykham to express his gratitude to King Sisavangvong:

> I have the honor of requesting you to transmit to the Government of his Majesty the King of Laos the respectful sentiments of deep gratitude of the Meo [Hmong] population which I represent and for the generous policy that his Majesty has come to take vis-à-vis the Meo minority.
>
> In the name of the Meo of the province I take the oath to always serve his Majesty and his government loyally as in the past and I request that his Majesty condescends to have confidence in the Meo who will always profoundly recognize his generosity and paternal good will.[21]

The following month, the position of *chaokhoueng* (provincial governor) came into question. As before, the French offered the position to Touby first, but in light of his earlier refusal they "counted on him to refuse nomination for the *Chaokhoueng* slot."[22] Ultimately, Touby opted only to become the deputy governor. Was he, again, also thinking of his good friend Saykham and the political complications that could result from displacing the traditional Phuan rulers? Whatever the case, Touby's appointment gave the Hmong direct representation at the national level for the first time. The French and the king legitimated him as the supreme chief, the political broker of the Hmong. Two new Hmong subdistricts were also created as rewards for Touby's clients, increasing his loyal following.[23]

The French government also extended its appreciation to Touby with a medal of commendation. For his assistance during the Japanese Occupation and for driving the Viet Minh from Xieng Khouang, they inducted Touby as a

Chevalier de la Légion d'honneur on November 9, 1946. Touby was the first Hmong to be accorded such an honor. A second medal was offered to Tougeu, who had blocked Viet Minh incursions from Muang Sen, but Touby, in his highly diplomatic fashion, asked him to relinquish the medal to Saykham because the prince had lost an elder and a younger brother to the war effort.[24] Dissatisfied that Tougeu did not receive his due honor, Lieutenant Colonel André Chenivess, a former commando in Laos, continued to petition the French government until Tougeu was also inducted as a Chevalier de la Légion d'honneur in 1998, twenty-two years after he went into exile in France and fifty-two after he had deferred the honor to Saykham.[25] Tougeu was the fourth Hmong to receive the medal.[26]

The efforts of the French placed pressure on King Sisavangvong to honor Touby with equal splendor. In 1947 the king invited Touby to Luang Prabang and knighted him as a *phya* (lord), giving him the name "Phya Damrong Ritthikay" (The Lord Whose Name Is Heard from Afar). Such a tribute was rarely given to those not descended from the Lao aristocracy. To extend the honor to a member of an ethnic minority that was often looked down on with contempt was, therefore, unprecedented. Touby also came away with the Croix des Million d'Elephants et du Parasol Blanc.[27]

Sisavangvong also invited Touby's brother, Tougeu Lyfoung, one of the most highly educated persons in Laos at that time, to sit on the King's Council, the quasi-legislative upper house of the two-part National Assembly. Touby describes how he came to request this favor from the king: "That same year [1947], when I went to receive the title *phya* from the Luang Prabang Court, King Sisavangvong jokingly asked me what else I could possibly want. I said that I would like him to appoint a Hmong to serve as an adviser on the King's Council. I had only been back in Xieng Khouang for about a month when I received a letter from the king announcing, 'The king gladly appoints Tougeu Lyfoung to serve as an adviser on the King's Council in Vientiane.'"[28]

The king had awakened to the strategic importance of the Hmong in the Lao revolutionary struggle and wanted to encourage them to his side. More significantly, the Hmong were also a potential threat. By liberating Xieng Khouang, they had proven their command of weaponry and tactics. "The Hmong child carries a rifle from the moment he knows how to walk," Henri Roux writes. "There are, therefore, rifles of all sizes in the Hmong home, and it's believed that the rifle grows with the child."[29] During the Japanese Occupation, the French had exacerbated the situation by equipping Hmong men with modern firearms. The royal authorities therefore appeased Touby with rewards while demanding the disarmament of his men. After the king lavished titles on

Touby, Crown Prince Savang Vatthana ordered him to surrender the weapons of his emerging militia to the provincial authorities. The prince found a pretext to write to Touby: "His Majesty is grateful that the Hmong brothers have exercised justice toward him and have been diligent in defending the Lao kingdom during a time of great upheaval, but now the kingdom is in need of weapons to be used in the two northern regions of Hua Khong and Phongsaly, so he would like to request that the Hmong brothers turn in their weapons to this purpose."[30] Touby surrendered four thousand rifles to the lowland authorities on the Plain of Jars.

By 1947, Laos was a free state within the French Union. Touby was the officially sanctioned supreme Hmong leader of the kingdom. His brothers also occupied positions of prestige. Tougeu sat on the King's Council while Toulia was one of the two deputies from Xieng Khouang, having been chosen during the first national election. Presiding as a member of the Constitutional Assembly in 1947, Toulia pressed hard for clauses to ensure minority rights. He requested that ethnic leaders be assigned to govern their own groups, and expressed the hope that ethnic minorities affairs offices would be set up wherever there was a sizable minority population. Toulia's requests were partially granted in the form of administrative decentralization, stipulated in the Constitution.[31] As a means of phasing out the use of derogatory names for highland groups, Toulia recommended more embracive terms—"Lao Soung" for the Hmong and Yao hilltop dwellers, "Lao Theung" for those who lived on the midlevel slopes, and "Lao Loum" for the lowland Lao. Before 1972, the Hmong were called "Meo" (pronounced with a long *a* and a high tone), a word that is close in pronunciation to the Lao word for "cat" or "meow" (pronounced with a short *a* and a high tone). Many Hmong children who attended school in the lowlands learned to resent the name "Meo" because their Lao classmates would abuse them by calling them "Meow." The more progressive Pathet Lao, which vied for minority subjects, quickly popularized the use of Toulia's terms in their areas.[32] With a flick of the tongue, the Hmong had become, at least in theory, the "Lao of the highlands" (Lao Soung). In reality they continued to suffer discrimination across political lines, right down to the present day in the Communist Lao PDR. The terms advocated by Toulia never really stuck in practice. Meanwhile, the conflict in Laos was moving in a direction that heightened Hmong ethnic consciousness. By war's end in 1969, General Vang Pao and his then closest adviser, Yang Dao, the first Hmong to obtain a doctorate in France, openly promoted the name "Hmong." Yang ingeniously launched the term into popular practice after 1972 by claiming that "Hmong" means "freemen."[33]

The success of the Lyfoung brothers percolated down into Hmong society slightly. Before World War II, there were seventeen Hmong *tasseng* in Laos. That number rose to twenty-four under a policy of administrative decentralization. On the royalist side, the increased number of *tasseng* boosted Touby's support network. Touby personally distributed these titles to the clan leaders, gaining their loyalty. Minority participation in the political process was, however, an exclusive preserve of the Hmong who had French backing. Other ethnic groups remained largely on the margins of Lao society. In 1948, when the Khmu notables of Luang Prabang went to the royal capital to demand that they be governed by their own leaders, they were thrown in jail. Touby persuaded the court to release the victims, whose demands went unheard.[34] The court's action makes clear how it felt about ethnic equality and also allows us insight into how it perceived the Hmong as an exception, perhaps because of French support. Understandably, many minorities turned to the Pathet Lao, which seized the vanguard of the revolution by promising fundamental changes.

Touby Lyfoung:
Revolutionary Commander in the GCMA

Although Alfred W. McCoy argues that opium may have made Touby essential to the French, forcing them to legitimate him as a supreme Hmong leader, Linwood G. Barney contends that Touby's popularity among the Hmong during the revolutionary period may have been due largely to his military role.[35] This argument is quite valid in the context of the Hmong's oral memory of a martial king. "[Hmong] tradition tells of a powerful king . . . [who] was at the same time the supreme war-lord," Hugo Adolf Bernatzik writes.[36] Touby's role as a military leader certainly impressed the Hmong, and his influence with the French during the period of nationalist struggle can be attributed to his ability to provide the manpower needed by the French in their recolonizing efforts. During the power vacuum that followed the withdrawal of the Japanese, Touby's role shifted from bureaucrat/political/opium broker to military commander. Fay Dang played the same martial role on the Communist side as a supplier of soldiers for the nationalist cause. As emerging Hmong leaders on the right and left, Touby and Fay Dang took on the additional role of requisitioning Hmong men for war. Their effectiveness in this effort and their valor on the battlefield were requisites for obtaining the legitimation of competing lowland factions.

Touby was the first commander of the *maquis*, the local resistance groups in Xieng Khouang, earning him the rank of lieutenant under the French.

He formed the first Hmong militia during the Japanese coup de grâce in March 1945. When Captain Doussineau dismissed his Vietnamese and Lao soldiers and left Nong Het, he charged Touby with keeping the peace. Touby writes, "Mr. Kamuv [Louis Doussineau] gave me fifteen rifles and ten cases of ammunition. He requested that I keep watch over the fort and look after the citizens from that day on. I agreed to do as he asked."[37] Touby also describes his authority to form a Hmong militia as stemming from an order sent by King Sisavangvong:

> Around the same time the king of Luang Prabang, Sisavangvong, sent an announcement to us Hmong in Nong Het. He said that the twelve provinces had been formed into a single kingdom. The French had agreed to give the Kingdom of Laos independence, to allow Laos to be governed by the Lao as they saw fit. . . . The king also said he was extremely concerned about the emerging political chaos. He wanted the citizens to stand united behind him as a single faction so he can consolidate his rule over the country. He also would like the citizens to be watchful and form village militias in every village and town, including Ban Ban and Xieng Khouang. Once I received this order, I convened a meeting with the Hmong leaders and elders in Nong Het. Everyone agreed that I should form a village militia in our town of Nong Het. I equipped them with the fifteen rifles and assigned Tougeu Lyfoung to be their commander.[38]

Touby exploited Hmong social organization to rally a militia. The first armed members of his group were his brothers, Tougeu and Toulia, and close kin of the Ly clan: Joua Va, Nhia Long, Tong Pao, Neng Tong, and others. Touby also drew his cousin Lo Bee Chou, the son of Tsong Tou and grandson of Blia Yao, into the movement. Tsong Tou's break with his brothers, Fay Dang and Nhia Vu, in the 1930s had never healed. Tsong Tou sided with Ly Foung. Now, a decade later, Bee Chou was still aligned with Touby. Members of the Moua clan, drawn on to the French side through Moua Chong Toua, also became the first important military players on Touby's team (see Lee and Moua clan members in fig. 18).

As noted earlier, this rudimentary militia initially served the purpose of avenging the wrongs committed by Fay Dang during the Japanese Occupation. Later it patrolled CR7 and contained a Communist offensive east of the Plain of Jars. As Fay Dang became the supreme Hmong leader on the left and Touby commanded his troops on the royalist side, the personal feud and nationalist struggle had fused into one by early September 1945. The political split in the lowlands fueled the bloody violence between Touby and Fay Dang, entangling other clans in the dispute.

As the revolution turned against the French, they expended serious efforts to build an anti–Viet Minh resistance army in Laos and in the north and central highlands of Vietnam. Efforts toward this end resulted in the creation of the Groupement de Commandos Mixtes Aéroportés (GCMA), which was nominally under the authority of the French Expeditionary Corps but run by the Service de Documentation Exterieure et du Contre-Espionnage (SDEC), the French equivalent of the American CIA. Colonel Grall headed the GCMA in 1950, but McCoy notes that it was really Major Roger Trinquier, operations commander in Laos and Tonkin, who developed most of the GCMA's counter-insurgency tactics. The financial aspects of the GCMA had to be kept secret because the organization involved the complicity and participation of senior French officers in the illegal trade of opium. The clandestine maneuver known officially as Operation X involved the recruitment of montagnards as *maquis* soldiers while keeping close ties with the Binh Xuyen bandits who served as Saigon's local militia and monitored communist activities on the Mekong Delta, but who also controlled the distribution of opium, which had been made illegal by the French in 1946. Money from the illicit trade financed the military activities of the GCMA.[39]

According to the scheme described by McCoy, what this meant for the Hmong is a double squeeze where the French milked Hmong sweat to pay for Hmong blood and soul lost to the war efforts against the Viet Minh. By imposing a higher head tax the French forced the Hmong to focus more labor into opium production. Then, the French, in conjunction with the criminal syndicates in Saigon, converted Hmong opium into cash to pay Hmong men enrolled as soldiers in the GCMA. Touby played a major role at the center of these illicit activities in Xieng Khouang. "Until the Geneva truce in 1954 the French military continued to pay Touby an excellent price for the Xieng Khouang opium harvest, thus ensuring his followers' loyalty and providing him with sufficient funds to influence the course of Hmong politics. . . . Touby [became] extremely wealthy . . . [and] remained the most loyal and active of the hill tribe commanders in Indochina."[40]

In 1947, Touby had been told by the crown prince to surrender his weapons, but now he was ordered by the French to step up Hmong recruitments once again. They pressured Touby to use his prestige to requisition Hmong men to battle Viet Minh incursions into Laos. He worked alongside Colonel Jean Sassi, head of the GCMA in Xieng Khouang in 1951, to build a Hmong army. Five hundred Hmong soldiers received training at Cap Saint Jacques, in south

Vietnam, by 1954.[41] Those who were formally enrolled as soldiers became members of the GCMA, eligible to receive French military insignias. Others who were not part of the GCMA but were also paid by the French were referred to as "partisan" soldiers.[42] Those in the GCMA fought at the front while the partisans served as village guards. Partisan soldiers also went into battle as substitutes for GCMA members on leave. The distinction between the two was often blurred, according to Ly Na Jalao. Partisan soldiers battled beside GCMA troops, suffering fatalities and wounds without recognition because as substitutes their names were never on the official troop roster. "When a partisan soldier went into battle, he was forced to report under the name of an absent GCMA soldier. His own name was never recorded," said Ly Na, a former partisan. For this reason, living as an exile in France nearly a half century later, Ly Na was unable to obtain veterans' benefits from the French government like those Hmong who had GCMA certification. When I met him in 2002, Ly Na felt he had finally come to understand the reason why the French did not officially enroll him as a soldier. What irked him the most was that he was not just an ordinary partisan. Literate in Lao and fluent in French, he was a member of the *royale*, the elite group of telegraph operators who maintained communications from the battlefield. "Others were ordered to protect me with their lives," he said.[43] Among only a handful of Hmong telegraph operators in high demand, Ly Na saw constant combat without recognition. When he learned I had just interviewed his former GCMA commander, Colonel Jean Sassi, he asked that I compose a letter to Sassi on his behalf to ask for help in obtaining veterans' benefits before he would sit down for an interview with me.

Requisitioning soldiers in defense of the French empire was not an easy task. Touby used social ties to draw the first recruits from the Ly clan. Moua Chong Toua enlisted members of the Moua clan who came under Touby's leadership. When the lowland authorities tried to conscript Hmong men directly, they met with resistance, as evident in several short exchanges between the Lao *chaomuang* (county leader) of Khoune and a Hmong *tasseng* named Chia Cha of Phakha. When the *chaomuang* ordered Chia Cha to send Hmong men to be civic guards, Chia Cha replied via telegram: "I have received your orders to recruit young Meos [Hmong] to be civic guards. All the Meos tell me they have never performed service as soldiers. You can impose other requisitions (animals, money), but as for the recruitment of soldiers, that's impossible. It's regrettable, and it's up to you to reflect on punishing or pardoning.—Tasseng of Phakha, Chia Cha."[44]

When the *chaomuang* demanded that Chia Cha appear in person at the provincial capital to answer for his refusal to send men, Chia Cha feigned illness. He wrote on December 6, 1945: "I have received your letter of summons, ordering me to present myself at Xieng Khouang. As I am sick every day, I cannot comply. I will come when I am well. I ask for your pardon."[45] Chia Cha's aptitude for employing the "weapons of the weak" highlights Touby's importance in the recruitment of Hmong men.[46] The Hmong did not submit easily to the orders of lowland authorities. They dragged their feet when ordered to do something. As the lowlanders also detested climbing the heights, their demands that Hmong leaders come down to the town were easily rebuffed. Hmong leaders would not be able to say no to Touby, though, as he used kin connections to pressure them and often appeared in person in their villages.

Meanwhile, assassination attempts by the Viet Minh had forced Touby to relocate from Nong Het to Xieng Khouang. He built a house near that of the governor and maintained his militia in the town. When the Viet Minh invaded in 1953–54, Touby was given field command beside French and Lao officers. The Hmong militia furnished government troops with intelligence and guerrilla support.[47] Making the transition from field commander to politician, Touby urged Hmong men to undergo military training, enticing many with promises of pay and insignias of rank. Among those he personally recruited in the 1950s were men who rose to the rank of colonel during the Secret War: Ly Pao, Ly Nao Cha, Shoua Yang, Ly Na, Nao Kao Lyfoung, and others.[48] Vang Pao, who had joined the *gendarmerie*, or national police, on Touby's recommendation in 1946, achieved a unique distinction. The *gendarmerie* of Xieng Khouang was merged into the national army the following year. When Vang Pao demonstrated talent in the field by dislodging thirteen Viet Minh cadres from the Plain of Jars area in the early 1950s, he was selected to attend officer training school in southern Laos. He later became the only Hmong to attain the rank of major general in Laos and was given command of Military Region II in 1964.[49] Touby's first military recruits became the foundation for Vang Pao's Secret War Army, formed under the aegis of the American CIA in 1961.

Dien Bien Phu (Vietnam):
The Empire's Last Stand

Touby's influence reached its apogee in the early 1950s, but the time of his French patrons was also approaching its end. By early 1953, the Viet Minh armies had swept through the Tai highlands. General Vo Nguyen Giap also launched a two-pronged invasion into Laos with three divisions—one along the northern route and two more heading into Sam Neua with the aim of taking Luang Prabang. Panic ensued in the royal capital, but the king refused to leave since a blind monk had assured him that the Viet Minh would never enter the city.[50] Under strict orders to hold out until reinforcements arrived, a lone Lao battalion stood its ground at Muang Khua for thirty-six days. Only three survivors emerged from the Lao side when Giap's troops withdrew.[51] The event foreshadowed a tragic ending for the royal family and the Kingdom of Laos.

The invasion of Tonkin and Laos was a brilliant campaign of distraction. The French bought into it and quickly gathered their forces at Dien Bien Phu in an effort to protect the Tai country and prevent further incursions into Laos. According to Major General Cogny, the towering figure behind the grand design, the Tai and Hmong in the vicinity could be persuaded or paid to fight the Viet Minh.[52] The situation was more complicated than the general had perceived, however. The mountainous regions of Tonkin were ethnically complex. As evidenced by Pa Chay's War, the Hmong had struggled long and hard against exploitation by White Tai feudal lords. French reaffirmation of White Tai dominance in the region in 1948 forced numerous Hmong, as well as the Black Tai in the area, to side with the Viet Minh. Ethnic minority support was crucial to the success of the Vietnamese revolution.[53]

The French were able to obtain some support among the Hmong of Tonkin, which probably prolonged their foothold in the region. One tragic story involved the group in the region of Muang Khuong, Pha Long, and Pakha, near Lao Cai, under the leadership of Chao Quang Lo, a valiant man who became known to his communist opponents as the "Terrestrial Dragon." According to Lo Wen Teu, a survivor who went into exile in France after 1975, inhabitants in the area found themselves against the Japanese during the occupation period because of unreasonably harsh policies. Like the French, the Japanese made demands on the population, said Wen Teu, but "in contrast to the French who generally accorded a certain delay in the provisioning of porters, food, horses, the Japanese wanted everything and at once. If the chiefs did not satisfy them straight away, they would be mistreated and thrown in prison. They would be accused of being dishonest and being lackeys of the French colonialists."[54] Unwilling to suffer the many injustices, Chao Quang Lo and Lo Wen Teu attacked the Japanese troops stationed at Pha Long.

Although Ho Chi Minh's Viet Minh were also against fascism, the Hmong of Pha Long did not warm up to them. Following the Occupation, the two Hmong leaders found themselves against the Viet Minh when they refused to surrender their weapons. "We do not seek to dispute you for political power," Chao Quang Lo said to the communist agents sent to his village. "The weapons we possessed currently were bought with our own money for our protection against bandits and pirates that crisscrossed the borders." There was no room for neutralism in the hills, however. Viet Minh troops attacked shortly after this conversation. Chao Quang Lo was forced onto the side of the French. When the Viet Minh captured Lao Cai on October 26, 1950, Lo Wen Teu evacuated to Hanoi, leaving Chao Quang Lo in charge of the population. For the next few years, Chao Quang Lo bravely defended his area from combined attacks by Viet Minh and Chinese troops that crossed the frontier to aid their communist comrades in the revolutionary struggle. Chao Quang Lo decimated the Vietnamese 148th regiment in Lao Cai by early 1951, but the Chinese dislodged him from his home village and forced him into the jungle for a time. Chao Quang Lo fought back, regaining control over a sixty-mile area.

When Roger Trinquier, the head of the GCMA in Tonkin, learned that Chao Quang Lo was still alive, he encouraged the Hmong leader to continue the fight by air-dropping weapons and supplies for the troops and the Croix de Chevalier for the Hmong chief. Chao Quang Lo held out for another year, devastating three more regiments of the 302nd Chinese division that were sent as reinforcements. As more and more Chinese crossed the border with heavy artillery in 1953, however, Chao Quang Lo anticipated the consequences for his people. Now in flight, he divided his troops into small groups so as to evade capture. By August 1953, a combined Chinese and Viet Minh attack forced Chao Quang Lo and a small group of his men into hiding in a deep grotto. Completely surrounded, they prayed they would not be found. When his adopted son was captured and tortured into revealing his position, Chao Quang Lo chose to end his own life with a suicidal charge on the enemy. The Chinese shot him down and paraded his body in Tonkin as well as across the border in China as proof that the "Terrestrial Dragon" was a mere mortal. Trinquier posthumously bestowed upon Chao Quang Lo the Chevalier de la Légion d'honneur. He was the third Hmong to obtain the honor from the French empire.[55]

Another Hmong group in the vicinity of Dien Bien Phu (Muang Thaeng) was tossed to the side of the French as well. The French had favored the Tai, but during the period of the Japanese Occupation they began cultivating relations with important Hmong leaders in the region. Among them was Vang Chong, the father of Major Nao Chue, the first secretary of Vang Pao's clandestine army, whose family relocated from Dien Bien Phu, Vietnam, to Laos in 1947.[56] Vang Chong was born in August 1919 in Ban Houei Xane, in the subdistrict of Dien Bien Phu in Lai Chau Province. His uncle was a canton chief in the region. The Vangs' connection to the valley-dwelling Tai allowed Vang Chong to obtain some education while boarding with a Black Tai family. By 1936 he had acquired enough literacy to help his uncle with the administrative work.

During the Japanese Occupation in 1944, the French officer in Dien Bien Phu, a Monsieur Imfeld, selected Vang Chong to be the deputy *chaomuang* of Dien Bien Phu, giving him administrative control over a population of eighteen thousand individuals, including Black and White Tai, Lao Theung, and Hmong. For his alliance with the French, Vang Chong was imprisoned by the Japanese for five months, from March to August 1945.[57]

After his release, Vang Chong led a Hmong militia group to rescue French soldiers who had escaped to southern China during the Japanese seizure of power. These French officers aided Vang Chong in organizing and training the first Hmong militia at the colonial garrison in Lai Chau. Although the White Tai were on the side of the French as well, they saw the emerging militia as a threat. In 1947 White Tai troops attacked Hmong villages under Vang Chong's command. The situation was quite tense. The French did not want an ethnic war to ignite in the hills alongside the complex nationalist struggle occurring in the lowlands. The Hmong wanted vengeance, but the French intervened by relocating Vang Chong's group to Muang Khua in Phongsaly, Laos.[58]

At Muang Khua in 1950, Vang Chong was promoted to the rank of sergeant and given orders to secure the Lao border in the Nam Bark–Muang Ngoi region against Viet Minh incursions. Vang Geu describes Vang Chong's military prowess: "Sergeant Vang Chong was a very well-disciplined commander who knew how to fight, judging from the hundreds of enemy troops he put out of action and the sizeable amount of arms and ammunitions he was able to collect. He got a citation from the Muang Khoua [*sic*] French commander and, based on his outstanding achievements, was promoted to the rank of lieutenant and deployed to the Muang Khoua garrison to clear the Vietminh from the banks of the Nam [River] Ou."[59] In August 1953, Touby Lyfoung was invited to inspect Vang Chong's troops at Muang Say as they prepared to aid the French at Dien Bien Phu. Thirty of Vang Chong's men were selected for paratrooper training in Saigon. They were to be air-dropped as reinforcements at Dien Bien Phu.

Meanwhile, on the hillsides surrounding Dien Bien Phu in early 1954, General Vo Nguyen Giap patiently planned his final attack, concentrating four divisions on the French position and using thousands of coolies who expended "more than three million work days" dragging supplies and heavy artillery by the piece up the surrounding mountains.[60] It took the Viet Minh over three months to prepare for the final battle, which began on March 12, 1954. Two days after the attack commenced, the top French gunnery expert on the site, Colonel Charles Piroth, committed suicide. "I am completely dishonored," he

Figure 19. Hmong *maquis* volunteers lined up in Xieng Khouang in April 1954, ready to reinforce the besieged French troops at Dien Bien Phu. These ragtag troops were not given official army uniforms. Many were shoeless. They were inspected by their leaders (*left to right*): Colonel Sang Rattanasamay, Major Vang Pao, Prince Saykham, and Touby Lyfoung. (Courtesy of Jean Sassi)

Figure 20. Jean Sassi (*third from left in the white shirt*), head of the GCMA in Xieng Khouang–Sam Neau, and some French officers converse in the foreground as Hmong *maquis* soldiers are assembled in the background, ready to go rescue the besieged French troops at Dien Bien Phu. (Courtesy of Jean Sassi)

said.[61] The French Expeditionary Force was under siege for fifty-six days and completely dependent on air-dropped supplies. From Phongsaly, Laos, Vang Chong marched his men toward Dien Bien Phu in late February, harassed by Viet Minh forces at every turn. Thirty kilometers from the site, they also were forced to lay up and defend themselves until they ran out of supplies and ammunition. Vang Chong's group retreated to Muang Say to wait for supplies to be air-dropped by the French. When the Viet Minh attack began in March, the thirty men of Vang Chong's group who were training in Saigon were called to Dien Bien Phu. They had not completed their training, but were ordered to parachute into the site. All thirty were decimated by heavy artillery strategically placed on the high ground above the French bunkers.[62]

By April the French commanders at Dien Bien Phu were calling desperately for reinforcements. Colonel Jean Sassi, the GCMA commander of Xieng Khouang–Sam Neua, the "Malo" group, consulted with Touby Lyfoung to see if he could persuade the Hmong to send volunteers. As one of the commandos who had parachuted into Indochina during the Japanese Occupation in 1945, Sassi had befriended Touby. Sassi was summoned back in July 1953 as a replacement for Captain De Brazin at Khang Khay. On April 6, Touby informed him that the Hmong had agreed to go and reinforce Dien Bien Phu. Operation D (for Desperado) commenced on April 28 with thousands of Hmong men reporting for duty on the Plain of Jars (see figs. 19 and 20). Sassi guided two thousand of these *maquis* for the long march on foot to Dien Bien Phu.[63]

According to Vang Geu, one of the Hmong commandos on the trip, a total of one division, or ten thousand soldiers, embarked on the rescue mission from Laos. Among the ten thousand were two to three battalions of Frenchmen, three battalions of Hmong commandos, and two battalions of paratroopers commanded by Neng Chue Thao, the brother-in-law of Vang Pao, and a Lao colonel named Duane. "Vo Nguyen Giap knew one division was coming from Laos to rescue Dien Bien Phu. That's why he pushed so hard for victory before we arrived on scene."[64] Major Vang Pao, who inspected the troops with Touby Lyfoung, also marched with the troops. On May 7, 1954, just days before the group arrived at the besieged site, the Viet Minh flag flew over the French command bunkers. The rescuer returned to Laos.

The surrender of seventeen French battalions numbering more than ten thousand soldiers was considered the most humiliating defeat in French colonial history. Within the year, agreements were reached between Ho Chi Minh, the leader of the Viet Minh, and the French at Geneva. The French agreed to relinquish their Indochinese possessions. Ho agreed to a temporary division of Vietnam at the seventeenth parallel until a national election could be held in 1956. The separation opened the door to another war with the Americans.

After 1954 the Hmong of Tonkin who had sided with the French, including those under Vang Chong in Dien Bien Phu and Yang Minou, Yang Dao's father, of Ha Giang, relocated across the border to Laos.[65] These Vietnamese Hmong brought their fighting spirit to the subsequent chapter of the Secret War under the command of Vang Pao and his American patrons. As memories of their days under the white colonial masters faded during the next five years, Touby's hold on the Hmong declined as well. With the French gone, Touby had lost an external source of legitimation.

The Rewards of the Revolution: Vice President Lo Fay Dang and Colonel Thao Tou Yang

While Touby basked in the glory of an alliance with the French and the king, Fay Dang was enjoying similar prestige on the opposing side of the nationalist divide. During the Japanese Occupation, he had won over sectors of the Hmong that were dissatisfied with French rule. Resenting the French for betraying his father's many years of loyal service by appointing Touby as the *tasseng* of Keng Khoai, Fay Dang helped the Japanese hunt down French commandos. After the Japanese surrendered and following his escape from the attack on Hua Pha Noi in 1945, Fay Dang sought the legitimation of the Communists. He began organizing the Hmong Resistance League around the time the French reoccupied Thakhek in March 1946. Fay Dang spoke of his alignment with "Red Prince" Souphanouvong in an interview with Wilfred G. Burchett in 1957:

> I heard there had been a great battle and that the townspeople had fought very bravely against the French. I thought it would be very good if we could fight together against the same enemy. I went down to the plains myself and tried to find this prince. He had already left and was in Thailand. I sent him a message and the reply came back: "Arouse the people. Create a strong organization. Later we will fight together." So I returned to the mountains and began to organize all the villages from our own base. . . . Every village appointed organizers and formed scout and defense corps.[66]

Fay Dang had found a new patron in Souphanouvong. The Communists promised political concessions similar to those offered to Touby by the French and King Sisavangvong. Fay Dang articulated the reasons why he aligned himself with the Pathet Lao:

> When the program of the Front was distributed among our people, they saw it answered their deepest wishes. Equality for all races. Nobody had ever spoken

of this before. . . . Abolition of unjust taxes. The French had burned and plundered our villages, massacred our people, taken our women. . . . The opium tax was abolished and other taxes lightened. We formed women's associations and a youth movement. . . . After a few months people saw this was a very good thing and they joined up with great enthusiasm. From the self-defense corps we set guerrilla bases, first of all in our own province of Xieng Khouang and then in the neighboring ones. We have 40,000 [Hmong] in our province alone and later on we were able to form whole [Hmong] companies from our guerrilla bases and attach them to the regular Pathet Lao forces formed by Souphanouvong.[67]

The figure cited above by Fay Dang is significant. There are no statistics from 1945, but a 1953 census shows that Xieng Khouang contained a population of 93,609, of which Hmong and Yao comprised 39.89 percent, or 37,341 of the total.[68] Fay Dang's figure may be exaggerated, but his statement reveals a Hmong antipathy toward the French that had lingered since Pa Chay's rebellion in 1920. Paradoxically, Fay Dang had assumed the anticolonial role of Pa Chay while Touby was now portrayed in the guise of Fay Dang's father, Blia Yao, a French ally.

While Touby was civilian leader and military commander combined, on the Communist side these roles were divided between Fay Dang and Thao Tou Yang, respectively. In the summer of 1950, Fay Dang was nominated as a minister without portfolio in the Pathet Lao's First Resistance Congress.[69] Fay Dang's brother, Nhia Vu, and his cousin, Lo Fong, also played important political roles in the patriotic front. Meanwhile, Thao Tou, Fay Dang's first cousin, was a field commander on the Plain of Jars. Born in May 1916 at Ban Nong Sam Che in the district of Nong Het, Thao Tou was the fifth of seven sons by Sai Chou Yang and the sister of Blia Yao.[70] Thao Tou had four sisters, whom he used to make marriage alliances with other clans and Vietnamese cadres sent to ensure Hmong loyalty.

While the official record of Fay Dang's political role in the founding of the Lao state has yet to be penned, a government-sanctioned biography of Thao Tou, peppered with anticolonial jargon and published in 2004, recasts the revolutionary nationalist's military efforts in Marxist terms. For now, we will have to rely on Thao Tou's biography to analyze the Hmong participation on the left. As a child, Thao Tou often visited his uncle, Blia Yao, according to the book. The biographer, Sutdālā, a nephew of Thao Tou, presents a classic historical memory reconstruction of how Thao Tou was first awakened to the concept of social class differences in highland Hmong society.

Tou Yang frequented the household of Phya Kaitong Lo Blia Yao, who was the subdistrict chief of Nong Het, which was an administrative post under the French during 1913–1934. Phaya Kaitong was a brother of Tou Yang's mother. Every time Tou Yang saw people coming with their money, gold, chickens, ducks, and opium in large quantities to offer to Phaya Kaitong Lo Blia Yao, Tou Yang asked Phaya Kaitong, "Uncle, why do you collect lots of money from the people?" Phaya Kaitong answered, "People came to pay their taxes." Tou Yang, realizing that taxes collected from the people were destined to be shared with the French, started to observe that there were social classes in society.[71]

Thao Tou sided with Fay Dang during the dispute with Touby. In September 1945, following the attack of Hua Pha Noi that resulted in the deaths of his two Yang kinsmen, Thao Tou formed the first company of Hmong soldiers, the Pa Chay Company, named after the anticolonial rebel leader who was consecrated as a revolutionary nationalist hero by the Communists. It is quite the contradiction that while some Hmong have pinpointed Lo Blia Yao as a traitor who had informed on Pa Chay in 1921, now his nephew was co-opting Pa Chay's name to rally a following. As with Touby's army, Thao Tou and his closest kinsmen were the very first recruits. The original nine men in the Pa Chay Company were Thao Tou and his five brothers, Tong Tsee, Chia Kua, Sao Chai, Ger, and Tong; his Yang cousins Yia and Fay Cheng; and his brother-in-law, Lo Vang, the half brother of Fay Dang and the elder son of Jer Jalao Ly, Blia Yao's favorite fourth wife.[72] Throughout the First Indochina War (1946–54), members of the Pa Chay Company led the Viet Minh in attacks along CR7 all the way to Xieng Khouang town and made incursions north into Sam Neua and south as far as the town of Thavieng, just north of Vientiane. As they demonstrated valor in the field, more recruits joined the Pa Chay Company. Thao Tou's government-sanctioned biography states:

> Wherever Tou Yang's relatives attacked the enemy they were successful, making him known to the citizens of Xieng Khouang as "The Swallow Bird of Muang Phuan." . . . Everywhere, stories about Tou Yang's triumphs over the French were subjects of conversation, encouraging citizens of different areas to voluntarily send their sons to Tou Yang to fight the French. Tou Yang's forces found new strength daily, with a constant increase in the enrollment of soldiers. Other units under Nhia Nou Moua, Blia Sa Moua, and Kao Saychao, with nationalist devotion, merged into Tou Yang's company as well.[73]

The Hmong in the Pa Chay Company and their commander, Thao Tou, were given priority recognition by the Communists. In October 1946, the Pa Chay Company was incorporated into the armed forces of the Lao Issara, being the first company that had originated in Xieng Khouang.[74] Sometime later, in the 1950s, it became the Fifth Company of the Second Battalion of the Pathet Lao's revolutionary army. In 1958 Thao Tou was promoted to the rank of colonel and given command of the Second Battalion, located on the Plain of Jars. He was probably the very first Lao Hmong colonel, having been promoted before Vang Pao. Pa Chay Company is an officially sanctioned "hero" company of the Lao PDR today.

Considered highly charismatic, Thao Tou also possessed the political acumen to form marriage alliances that increased his influence with lowland patrons. He readily offered his own sisters, Yer and Mao, to political cadres sent from China and Vietnam. Yer was given in marriage to Lo Lue, the political cadre from the People's Republic of China, and Mao was given in marriage to Viet Xeun Hung, a Viet ethnic soldier sent by Ho Chi Minh to be the Communist liaison in Xieng Khouang.[75] The marriage to Hung was particularly notable in view of communist disciplinary practices. "Ho Chi Minh strictly prohibited cadres from fraternizing with the local population. Fraternization was punishable by death, but this marriage was allowed to go forward," said Ger Lo.[76] Ho clearly had insight into Hmong social organization and understood that marriage alliances were essential to their politics. Viet Xern Hung, who served as special adviser to the Pa Chay Company, married Thao Tou's sister, became fluent in Hmong, and, in death, is buried as a nationalist hero next to Thao Tou in Nong Het (see Hung's monument in fig. 4).

In the late 1950s Thao Tou also coerced his niece into marrying a soldier of the Pa Chay Company "in order to keep morale high." According to his biographer: "Tou Yang wrote a letter to his niece, Xia Yang of Muang Long, Vietnam, which read: 'Niece Xia Yang, when you see Chue Thao Noi, a soldier of the Second Battalion, arrive at Muang Long you must marry him. Otherwise, I will no longer consider us as father and daughter.' This was an order. Receiving the letter, Xia Yang married Chue Thao Noi whom she had never met before."[77]

Where marriage alliances were not possible, Thao Tou engaged in sworn brotherhoods with lowlanders, a practice reminiscent of the oaths of brotherhood taken by Blia Yao and Henri Roux in 1914 and 1920. In 1967 Thao Tou's children, who were studying in Vietnam, learned of an oath of brotherhood he had taken in 1946 with a Lao and a Vietnamese national. The children recalled in his biography how they came to meet one of his sworn brothers, Ngo The Xern. The incident is worth quoting at length.

> One day in the middle of August 1967, a state car with a military plate came from Hanoi. . . . The next morning school management employees went to each group of students who were boarding in different villages and said, "Anyone

who is a son, daughter, or descendent of Thao Tou Yang, please go quickly to the principal's office because their father has come for a visit." Everyone was surprised because their father had been long gone from them [he died in 1961] . . . so how come there was a father coming to pay them a visit? . . . When they arrived at the reception room, they saw a few military officers. . . . The senior one stood up . . . [and said], "'Father' is Ngo The Xern. I just came from the battle fronts of southern Laos. . . . I heard news that the American air bandits dropped bombs on the Viet Chi Plant, very close to your school. I was so concerned that I took emergency time to come visit all of you. . . . I remember the battle against the French in Muang Sen in 1946 along the mountains of Nam Kuang on the Lao-Viet border, where Father Tou Yang, Father Phia Hom Sombat, and myself swore together before the sky, earth, mountain forest, and rivers that 'All three of us are taking the oath to become brothers; Father Phia Hom, who was the older one of Lao Loum ethnicity, became big brother; Father Tou Yang, a Hmong ethnic of lesser age, became middle brother; and I, the youngest one, a Viet national, became little brother.' . . . We promised each other, 'The struggle might be long, and there will have to be sacrifices. If someone should die, the others who remain must look after his children, making sure they grow up and follow the ideals of the father's generation and maintain the heartfelt relationship between Laos and Vietnam forever.'"[78]

Ngo The Xern treated Thao Tou's children like his own. When they were young, he came to take them home during summer vacations, holidays, and special events. The Yang children and he maintained close contact until Xern passed away in 1995.

Thao Tou also used his family's wealth to obtain the support of followers. According to Sutdālā, he paid the brideprices of soldiers under his command: "Tou Yang loved relatives of all clans as if they were of the same family. . . . When his brother soldiers without money reached the age of marriage, Tou Yang used his own family's money to help with their marriages. Some examples include individuals like Cher Thao, Palee Yang, Cha Yang, Chai Du, Nengchue Kue, and many others. Tou Yang was responsible for brother soldiers who he considered to be of his own clan. (Marriage at the time cost four silver bars and up)."[79]

Another method of rallying support is reminiscent of that employed by Touby. Thao Tou distributed bounties of military and civilian titles that were legitimated by the Pathet Lao. He handed out promotions strategically so as to attract recruits into his militia. In one case, he combined a marriage alliance with a promotion: "Tou Yang arranged marriages between his family and brother soldiers from different regions. His niece, Yua Yang (a daughter of his eldest brother), was married to Pangkao Lo with no charge. Then Pangkao was promoted as the leading officer of a company." Pangkao's son, Yakua, enjoyed special privileges, becoming the first Hmong Mig 21 fighter pilot in the Lao PDR. Thao Tou promoted others, like Nhia Nou Moua and Nao Tou Lo, who commanded the Pa Chay Company in succession. Nao Tou and a contingent of the Pa Chay Company were later integrated into the coalition's First Battalion in Luang Prabang in 1958, but when the coalition failed, he broke away and led the thirty-five men of the company back to join the Communists. Perhaps Thao Tou's most important act was to entice other commanders into the Pa Chay Company by giving them military titles: "Tou Yang convinced Nhia Nou Thao's company, which fought the French at Tham Thao in 1946, to join the Pa Chay Company. Nhia Nou was promoted to the rank of a company commander."[80]

Thao Tou's politics aided Fay Dang's climb to power on the left. Having obtained lowland legitimation from Souphanouvong and Ho Chi Minh, Fay Dang garnered strong support from the Hmong who had become disenchanted with colonial rule. French policies designed to win over the Tai who occupied the strategic mountain regions around Dien Bien Phu exacerbated ethnic tensions, driving more Hmong in the region to the Communists. The establishment of the Tai Federation under Deo Van Long in 1946 revoked the autonomy achieved after the Pa Chay revolt in 1921. Once again Hmong were placed under Tai overlords. The fifty thousand Hmong in the northwestern highlands under Tai hegemony turned to the Viet Minh, playing a crucial role in the struggle against the French.[81] Many of these Hmong became the coolies who served Vo Nguyen Giap's army. The 1954 French surrender at Dien Bien Phu was in some ways karmic justice for Vue Pa Chay and the Hmong of the region who had attempted to end French authority over the highland zone.

When the Americans intervened in Indochina to create South Vietnam, Laos became a key element in President Dwight D. Eisenhower's domino theory. For this reason, the United Stated also maneuvered for rightist control in Laos between 1955 and 1960 by withholding aid to force the hands of key political figures and, after Souphanouvong and Souvanna reached an agreement to form the first coalition government in November 1958, by pumping money into the countryside to buy votes for candidates of the rightist faction.[82] Meanwhile, each of the three kinsmen, Fay Dang and Thao Tou on the left and Touby on the royal Lao government side, was adamant in supporting the lowland faction that legitimated his position. The three men posed for a final

Figure 21. A rare portrait of the three kinsmen and political rivals together on the Plain of Jars in early 1959. They wanted to demonstrate that a Hmong reconciliation had occurred in the highlands just as a coalition government was formed in the lowland capital of Vientiane. *Front row, left to right*: Touby Lyfoung, Lo Fay Dang (in black suit), and Thao Tou Yang (in gray suit). (Courtesy of Mao Song Lyfoung)

portrait together in Xieng Khouang when the lowlanders formed a coalition government (see fig. 21). They wanted to show the Hmong population that a reconciliation had taken place among the Hmong as well. Within weeks of the photo, under cloak of darkness, Thao Tou had defected with his troops across the border to Vietnam.

Thao Tou was not happy that his battalion had been integrated into the Royal Lao Army in December 1957. Once the coalition government was in place, the rightists strategized to weaken the military position of the Neo Lao Hak Xat, the political wing of the Pathet Lao, by dividing the soldiers under Thao Tou's command. Sutdālā writes, "In March 1958, aiming to weaken the forces of the Neo Lao Hak Xat, the Vientiane side designed a clever plan to divide the Second Battalion into two different battalions stationed at two different locations. The First Battalion was sent to Muang Ngeun in Luang Prabang, [and] the Second Battalion [left under Thao Tou] remained in Military Region II in Xieng Khouang, at the center of the Plain of Jars, surrounded by the soldiers of the Vientiane [rightist] side."[83]

Sensing trouble for the Communists, Thao Tou feigned illness in order to delay the formal integration ceremonies where he and his soldiers would have to accept rank decorations from the royal government. Meanwhile, he strategized an escape plan, hoping to keep what was left of his troops intact. His men had families consisting of women, children, and elderly, so he knew it would not be easy to evade capture. When he kept coming up with demands in order to buy time, Vang Pao showed up to investigate. They were childhood friends. They each had relatives caught on the other side of the political divide. Vang Pao urged him to think of Hmong unity and contemplate the potential consequences if the Hmong kept fighting on opposing sides. Sutdālā writes: "Major Vang Pao said, 'Even if the Second Battalion does not accept the rank awards, in order to avoid bloodshed I request that the Hmong company [Pa Chay Company] be authorized to integrate into the national armed forces, because I don't want the Hmong relatives to suffer again in the jungle. If you agree, I'll ask for airplanes to transport the Pa Chay Company, under the command of Nao Tou Lo in Xieng Ngeun, Luang Prabang, back to the Plain of Jars. I'll take responsibility for everything [i.e., guarantee their safety].'"[84]

The two men talked for a long time, but Thao Tou was not persuaded. He would accept integration provided that Vang Pao supplied his people with food and removed the rightist troops now encircling his encampment. Thao Tou said nothing about Hmong unity. Vang Pao sent food and had his soldiers retreat a few hundred meters from Thao Tou's camp. That was enough for Thao Tou to escape. On the evening of May 18, 1959, restocked with fresh supplies, Thao Tou ordered his men to play music and make boisterous noises as if they were celebrating their integration. In the midst of the noise, men, women, children, and the elderly escaped in the dark, using mountainous foot trails rather than the main road, CR7. When the Royal Lao Army commander came to investigate the silence that followed the next morning, the Pathet Lao Second Battalion had vanished.

By December 1960, the coalition government in Vientiane had failed and Thao Tou was back commanding his battalion on the Plain of Jars in support of Kong Le's neutralist troops. Frustrated with the political breakdown of the first coalition government, Kong Le, a captain who led the elite paratrooper company in the Royal Lao Army, staged a coup d'état in August 1960. He demanded that a genuine neutralist government be installed and that the Soviets and Americans stop interfering in Laos. Unable to hold Vientiane, however, he was forced to flee to the Plain of Jars when the rightist general Phoumi Nosavan, backed by the United States, attacked from Savannakhet.

Kong Le, who many perceived to be politically naive, was forced to run to the arms of the Communists.

On the evening of January 13, 1961, Thao Tou was riding on CR7 in a jeep on his way to the battle site of Muang Khoun. As they approached the bridge of Samxon, Thao Tou ordered his driver not to take the bridge, fearing that it might have been mined. Unfamiliar with the terrain, his Vietnamese driver veered left of the bridge going down and then accelerated as he went up the slight incline. The engine stalled as he hit a rock. Thao Tou reacted like everyone else by jumping out of the jeep. Tragically, he landed behind the vehicle. The jeep, lacking the power to go up the incline, lurched backward, running over him.[85] Thao Tou died at Samxon just north of Lat Houang. To bestow on him the full honor of a revolutionary nationalist hero, Ho Chi Minh ordered Thao Tou's body to be flown to Hanoi for a state ceremony before it was taken by motorcade back to Nong Het for the final rites in accordance with Hmong tradition.[86] Thao Tou's death ended a chapter of Hmong history.

On the rightist side, Kong Le's coup also had ramifications for the Hmong. Frustrated with the events in Laos, the CIA operative stationed in Thailand, Bill Lair, took matters into his own hands. Bypassing the Lao government in Vientiane, he flew out to seek Vang Pao, meeting him for the first time in Thavieng, just north of the capital. Vang Pao was on the retreat from a combined communist-neutralist attack. His men had not been paid for months and the families of his soldiers were on the verge of starvation. Bill Lair offered food and ammunition in exchange for recruits. Vang Pao told him to drop supplies at Padong, where he planned to make a stand.[87] The Americans had hand-picked a new Hmong leader.

Touby and Fay Dang:
Two Legitimate Hmong Leaders

Competing lowland nationalist groups fueled the struggle between Touby and Fay Dang, allowing both to acquire political concessions that made them legitimate in the eyes of the Hmong. On the right, Touby reigned supreme, backed by the French and by the Lao monarch who promoted him as the "King of the Hmong." On the left, Fay Dang was appointed a minister without portfolio while his brother Nhia Vu became a high-ranking member of the Central Committee. For years, Fay Dang dominated as the Hmong Communist leader, becoming a recognizable presence at important state events, appearing alongside revolutionary leaders like Souphanouvong, Kaysone, and Sithon Komadan. The feud between Touby and Fay Dang lasted until Touby's arrest following the Communist seizure of power in Laos in 1975. Legend has it that Fay Dang accompanied Touby to the plane headed for the seminar camp at Sam Neua. As Touby turned to wave a final farewell to the crowd that had gathered, Fay Dang was heard to have said, "Finally, the rhinoceros has been captured!"[88] The century before, Hmong men had descended the heights to offer rhinoceros horns in exchange for titles of authority. Fay Dang was alluding to that tradition as he handed his nephew, Touby, to the Communists.

According to Zong Blong, the son of Nhia Vu, Touby wrote letters asking Fay Dang and Nhia Vu to visit him at the seminar camp. Fay Dang sent only his wife, who carried a basket of food to give to Touby. Zong Blong did not know what message, if any, was conveyed to Fay Dang. "However," said Zong Blong, "to the end of his days, my father bemoaned the fact that he never made the effort to go see Touby. He often commented with nostalgia, 'Why didn't I go and see what he had to say? After all, he was my own kinsman.'"[89] For the next two decades, Fay Dang and Nhia Vu were the looming Hmong figures in the Lao PDR. Fay Dang held the position of vice president of the Lao Front for National Reconstruction until his death in 1986, a reward for his part in the revolutionary struggle.

Epilogue

The Continuity of the Two Strands of Leadership

Hmong aspiration for autonomy inspired the rebellions against the Qing in the centuries before their mass migration into Southeast Asia, where they continued to nurture this dream. The longing for autonomy was hindered by the lack of a broad political consciousness across time and space, however. As back in China, clan division, cultural group disparities, and regional rifts in Southeast Asia have prevented Hmong unity under a central figure. The quest for legitimation since the mid-nineteenth century has forced Hmong leaders to interact with the state, resulting in the emergence of two types of leaders: the prophet who rejects the state as a legitimating force and proclaims the Mandate of Heaven; and the secular political broker who, with state backing, succeeds in becoming a supreme chief or ethnic representative.

The initial phase of interaction between the Hmong and the state in Southeast Asia resulted in rebellions, both secular and messianic in nature. Violent conflicts were the consequences of Hmong attempts to renegotiate an ethnic hierarchy that placed them at the bottom. During this period, without state-sanctioned paramount figures to define an ethnic agenda for the group, prophets like Xiong Mi Chang and Vue Pa Chay emerged to struggle for the Mandate of Heaven. Appealing to this cultural heritage to establish legitimacy, they rallied sectors of Hmong society to political action, thereby achieving supraclan authority. Their claim to divine inspiration gave them, at least to an extent, an influence that surpassed the bounds of the traditional clan chief who largely affected his own kinsmen. Although their movements suffered crushing defeats, Mi Chang and Pa Chay attracted the notice of the colonial government, forcing it to reassess its governing policies.

The Hmong attributed the defeat of their prophets and the loss of divine mandate to their own moral decadence, assuming ethnic responsibility for the fall. Pa Chay and Mi Chang's defeats signified more than mundane conquests; they were perceived as the Hmong's loss of the mandate to be a sovereign people. Since Pa Chay had aimed to establish a just kingdom—the antithesis of the oppressive colonial state—once his men proved to be no better than the system they had fought against, surrender and subjection to the state became the logical path. "Cruel beings who do not follow the ways of Heaven and Earth cannot wear Heaven's crown," said Pa Chay. "Go surrender your weapons immediately before the French."[1]

According to Hmong messianic rationale, since they had failed to maintain a moral movement, they would have to wait to achieve sovereignty. The defeat of the messianic revolt, while devastating for the Hmong, was also a sign that the French had captured the Mandate of Heaven, thereby becoming an important source of legitimation for Hmong leaders. Following their defeat, then, the Hmong were forced to seek a mandate by proxy from the state. The prophet's defeat allowed for the emergence of the secular political broker, although we cannot say that it caused his emergence since both types of leaders can exist side by side, with the messianic leader having gone latent but ready to reappear should the broker fail to negotiate for autonomy. For this reason, the two kinds of leaders weave in and out of one another, depending on the political circumstances.

With the prophet defeated, the broker becomes prominent in colonial society as the agent for advancing Hmong aspiration. As a client of the state, however, the broker has the difficult task of balancing the Hmong desire for autonomy against the colonial patron's need for domination, which inevitably necessitates the subjection of the Hmong. Although he managed to obtain the legitimation of the state, the first Hmong leader in Laos, Lo Blia Yao, failed to maintain this delicate balance once he was perceived as an instrument of the French. The Hmong dealt with him in several ways. Some turned to the messianic leader, Vue Pa Chay, while others strategized to wrest away Blia Yao's paramount position. In Xieng Khouang, Laos, the former followed Lo Shong Ger, who, under Pa Chay's umbrella, stood up to Blia Yao. It made sense for Shong Ger to rally to Pa Chay. As a nephew of Blia Yao, he had no way to challenge Blia Yao's supreme position as both Lo clan leader and paramount Hmong chief. With some exceptions, the Lo clan stood behind Blia Yao, who also had French military support. Ly Foung, on the other hand, had another option. As a member of the Ly clan, he could use the power of his large kin group to challenge Blia Yao. He was also well known to the French. The successful exploitation of Hmong kinship system and outside connection led to Ly Foung's ultimate triumph in the mid-1930s. He was, of course, also aided by Blia Yao's mortality.

The final manifestation of Blia Yao's instrumental role was when he helped spearhead the defeat of Shong Ger in 1920. In addition, some Hmong believe Blia Yao was the one who revealed the secret of Pa Chay's vulnerability, allowing the French to defeat the movement. According to Keith Quincy's informants, Blia Yao told the French that the wicks of the Hmong's homemade cannons could not be lit in the rain, and he advised the French to remain in their garrisons until the rainy season.[2] The French heeded Blia Yao's advice and vanquished Pa Chay's rebellion in 1921, a year after Shong Ger's defeat in Xieng Khouang. The story of Blia Yao's betrayal seems plausible, but it is not historically accurate. As noted in chapters 2 and 3, the French carried out heavy military campaigns mostly during the milder, dry season, which lasted from October to the end of April. The French, in effect, avoided doing battle during the monsoon season. Both Shong Ger and Pa Chay suffered defeat in the month of March, just before the arrival of the rain. Nonetheless, that the Hmong blamed Blia Yao for orchestrating Pa Chay's defeat is significant, reflecting their view of Blia Yao as a betrayer of the Hmong dream. The repressive measures Blia Yao took against the rebels following the uprising, executing and extorting money from them, probably reinforced the perception of him as a traitor in the oral memory of Hmong Americans, who also fought his communist sons in the First and Second Indochina Wars.

Although Pa Chay was defeated, the Hmong withdrew their support from Blia Yao and gravitated toward a new kind of political broker, Touby Lyfoung—a hybrid between the radical messianic leader represented by Pa Chay and the instrumental broker, Blia Yao. Touby was a visionary who harkened toward the Hmong's deepest yearnings for sovereignty while being a client of the state. Admittedly, Touby operated in a very different political situation than had Blia Yao or Pa Chay. Rising during a transitional period of imperialist struggles for geopolitical control of Southeast Asia and Laos, he had bargaining powers that leaders before him did not. He was also the first Hmong leader in Southeast Asia to have a unique educational background, possessing fluency in both speaking and writing French, Lao, and other languages. Touby was the prime candidate to capitalize on the chaos caused by the Japanese Occupation. Because of his background, he had the esteem of the Hmong, the lowland Lao, and the French.

Touby's bargaining advantage was also increased by the French decision to push Fay Dang aside before the arrival of the Japanese. Fay Dang quickly obtained Japanese support, forcing Touby and the French into the jungle. After the Japanese retreat, Fay Dang continued his opposition to the French, now seeking the support of the Communist Viet Minh and Pathet Lao. Had the Hmong not been split into contending camps in the years before the Occupation, it is not certain that Touby and Fay Dang would have had such powerful bargaining positions. On the other hand, Touby could not capitalize on the advantages placed before him by the French and King Sisavangvong in 1946 precisely because the Hmong had been factionalized into two camps. When offered the province of Xieng Khouang as an Autonomous Hmong Zone, Touby was forced to opt only for being appointed *chaomuang* of the Hmong and deputy governor. He chose symbolic autonomy to retain the loyalty of the Hmong on his side of the political divide. He did not want to alienate the indigenous rulers, the Phuan, who could have easily turned to his rival, Fay Dang. Political division, while advantageous to Touby and Fay Dang on a personal level, was a costly obstacle to the broader Hmong aspiration. The split between Touby and Fay Dang had complex consequences for the ethnic group. The fact that Hmong shouldered much of the fighting of the revolution on both sides compounded the tragedy.

The Secret War (1960–75): Messianism Reemerges to Challenge Vang Pao's Authority

A Hmong political broker's legitimacy is largely dependent on external support, rendering Touby's tenure as paramount chief on the political right highly unstable. New Hmong leaders emerged when new patrons with different agendas arrived. In 1960 the Americans bypassed Touby because he had advanced Hmong aspirations too much and was not the ideal leader during a contentious time of revolutionary conflict when blood sacrifice was needed from the Hmong. The American CIA was cognizant of Touby's politics during the time of the French. "Always the politician," Alfred W. McCoy writes, "Touby had gotten the best of the bargain from the French and had never committed his troops to a head-on fight . . . [but] the CIA wanted a real battler who would take casualties, and in a young Hmong officer named Vang Pao they found him."[3]

William Colby, former director of the CIA, also articulates that choice in a memoir: "[Vang Pao] had not only the courage but also the political acumen necessary for leadership in such a conflict. He represented a new approach, sharing the dangers of the front instead of sending orders from the rear . . . and he was dedicated to the defense of his people and their homeland. . . . He knew how to say no as well as yes to Americans."[4]

Touby's authority declined when his French patron suffered defeat and disengaged from Indochina in 1954. American support and financial largesse gave Vang Pao the prestige he needed to effect political unity among the Hmong. By 1962 he had become the undisputed Hmong leader in the northeastern hills of Laos. His position was reinforced by Touby's absence from the highlands. Opting to immerse himself in Lao national politics, Touby had relocated to Vientiane after World War II to serve in ministry positions, leaving Vang Pao to create a military headquarters at Long Cheng, the "Dragon Capital." Although Touby remained prominent, his authority dwindled during the American era. Whereas immediately following Kong Le's coup in August 1960 Vang Pao had said "no one dares to make a decision without Touby," just a few years later he had stopped listening to Touby.[5] Touby urged Vang Pao to maintain small guerrilla units and not engage the much larger North Vietnamese army in a conventional war that would place the Hmong at a disadvantage. Against Touby's recommendation, Vang Pao committed the Hmong to head-on clashes that resulted in massive casualties.[6] Disagreements over how to handle the war wore down their relationship, subsequently generating the rumor that Touby was attempting to lead the Ly senior officers in a coup against Vang Pao in 1966.[7]

Vang Pao had reason to be concerned about a Ly coup. The overwhelming majority of his battalion officers were from the Ly clan.[8] "Vang Pao," said Colonel Shoua Yang, who rose to prominence as Vang Pao's right-hand man following the alleged Ly coup, "feared none but the Lys."[9] After the rumors surfaced, Vang Pao removed many Ly battalion officers from his inner circle, keeping them out of the loop. "Vang Pao kept only Colonel Ly Pao in his confidence because Ly Pao had risked getting shot by sniper bullets and climbed down to rescue him at Na Khang," said Ly Tsia Tou. "Vang Pao also gave Ly Pao a jeep as a reward."[10] The other individual whom Vang Pao kept close was Colonel Ly Tou Pao, the brother of Vang's second wife, True. Tou Pao was the chief of staff of Vang Pao's Secret Army who remained publicly loyal to him until shortly before Vang Pao's death in 2011.[11]

Furthermore, Vang Pao began promoting members of his own Vang clan and drawing other clans to his side. Colonel Shoua Yang became Vang Pao's most trusted right-hand man and his commander in the field.[12] When I asked about the allegations of a Ly coup, Vang Pao chose to remain silent. "Go ask your own Ly clan," he said to me finally.[13] Was the allegation a preemptive strike by Vang Pao, meant to snatch the last vestiges of authority from Touby and the Ly clan? Or was it simply a misunderstanding? Whatever the case, the influential Ly clan members, both civilian and military, were forced to swear an oath of loyalty to Vang Pao, neutralizing their position as potential competitors into the exile period.[14]

Perhaps the allegation was also a manifestation of Vang Pao's own doubts about his authority. Rising under the patronage of Touby and always in the shadow of the educated Lyfoung brothers, Vang Pao, who had only a third-grade education, had reasons to be doubtful. Because his command in the field was dependent on battalion leaders from the Ly clan even at the height of his career, he may have felt all the more vulnerable. Literate and conscious of his role in history, Touby denied the allegations made against him in an official confidential report to the French and American authorities. His son Touxoua possessed a carbon copy and read it aloud to me when I visited him in France in 2002. Tougeu Lyfoung, on the other hand, dismissed the charge as ridiculous. "Why would we lead a coup against Vang Pao? We held higher positions than Vang Pao," he said.[15]

Following the allegations, Touby attempted to establish deeper trust between himself and Vang Pao by arranging multiple marriages between their children. His efforts did not dispel Vang Pao's concerns about the Ly clan wanting to subvert his authority, however. Referring to these marriages and how they had failed to alleviate Vang Pao's distrust, Tougeu Lyfoung said, "Yus qab twb nyob luag cooj luag os twb nyob yus nkuaj lawm los tseem tsis ntseeg siab qees thiab tiag!" (Our hens were in his coop and his ducks were in our pen, but there was still no trust).[16] It is doubtful that the Ly clan, though a threatening presence, would have thought to challenge Vang Pao's authority without the backing of a powerful patron. Touby's patrons, the French, were long gone. Being a savvy politician, Touby would not have so foolishly orchestrated a coup. It is true, however, that Touby was disappointed with Vang Pao's efforts to drag the Hmong into a head-on conventional war with the vastly superior forces of the Vietnamese. Touby believed such a confrontation to be suicidal. Because his own Ly clansmen were in the vanguard, he was especially against it. When his brother, Colonel Nao Kao Lyfoung, was shot during the battle for Nang Khang in 1966, a deeply concerned Vang Pao went to investigate.[17] Vang Pao was shot by a sniper as he landed on the enemy-controlled airstrip. Immediately he saw a Ly conspiracy to take his life. "When I went to pick him up and carry him to safety," said Colonel Ly Pao, one of the battalion commanders on site, "he said, 'Why did you guys shoot me?' Vang Pao believed all his life that members of the Ly clan shot him, but it's not true."[18]

Although Vang Pao's fears were largely displaced, he was not wrong about Hmong wanting to subvert his authority. The Ly clan may have lacked the strong patron that would have allowed it to challenge Vang Pao's legitimacy, but there were ominous signs of a messianic movement looming in the background during the Secret War. The Hmong had retained the legend of Pa Chay's heroic struggles against the French in their oral memory, harboring the aspiration for sovereignty deep in their hearts.[19] When it became apparent that the delicate balance between what the Hmong desired and what they would have to pay to obtain it had shifted in favor of an external patron, the Americans, Vang Pao's position was seriously threatened. By 1967 it was evident that the Hmong were being asked to bear too much in the struggle against communism. As the Hmong male population died off, boys as young as fourteen were being called to the battleground.[20]

Not surprisingly, frogs and squirrels suddenly began to speak to villagers in the surrounding hills of Long Cheng, Vang Pao's military headquarters.[21] In a nearby village, a man named Yang Shong Lue had already gathered a huge following. While living across the border in Vietnam in the 1950s, Shong Lue had invented a unique writing system, claiming that it came directly from Heaven. When he became a popular figure and Hmong began to want to crown him king, the Communists threatened to arrest him, so he joined Vang Pao at Long Cheng in 1966. Colonel Shoua Yang personally orchestrated Shong Lue's transportation to the military headquarters and welcomed him into his home as a clanmate.[22] For a time, Shong Lue lived under the colonel's protection. Unlike the legends of other prophets, Shong Lue's writing system proved to be real. Men, women, and children gathered around him to learn it. Even Vang Pao's soldiers became believers. Soon letters in the divine script were being exchanged across the land, promoting the writing system. People anointed Shong Lue with the coveted title "Mother of Writing," a powerful designation in a society that has a long history of reverence for literacy.[23] For some, Shong Lue's appearance was a fulfillment of a prophecy. Now that Vang Pao's exploitation had surpassed even that of Blia Yao in 1910, Hmong expressed the desire for sovereignty once again. Shong Lue became a symbol of the struggle for the Mandate of Heaven. He was a threat to Vang Pao's legitimacy, which depended on the Lao royal family and the Americans.

When he first arrived, Shong Lue was a valuable asset to Vang Pao. Reputedly endowed with the divine gift of foretelling events like Xiong Mi Chang, he was able to tell Vang Pao where and when the Communists would attack.[24] As he became more and more popular, however, Shong Lue's abilities became liabilities. Before long, charges that he was a Communist spy surfaced. Vang Pao loyalists claimed that Shong Lue was in constant radio contact with the Communists — the reason he knew about impending attacks. These allegations led finally to Shong Lue's arrest and imprisonment as a prisoner of war in Pha Khao in September 1969.[25] Several years later he was rescued by his followers and taken to the small village of Na Chia, located at the base of Phou Bia. In February 1971, "soldiers in General Vang Pao's army" assassinated Yang Shong Lue, the Mother of Writing.[26] When Vang Pao's American patrons pulled out of Vietnam in 1975, Vang Pao was forced into exile, but the Mother of Writing's movement persisted in Laos and northern Thailand into the twenty-first century. In the United States, believers who were born in America and had never set eyes on Shong Lue established nonprofit organizations to promote his writing system as the one true Hmong script. His birthday, September 15, has become a special day of commemoration for his followers. The dream of the Hmong kingdom is alive in their hearts.

Meanwhile, Vang Pao spent three decades trying to recapture the Homeland, drawing controversies and allegations of financial corruption.[27] According to Vang Pao, when Boun Oum na Champassak died in 1981, he left Vang Pao in charge of the struggle for Laos. Vang Pao recognized Boun Oum as the final authority in the exile government. He claimed that the hierarchy of authority in the Kingdom of Laos was King Sisavang Vatthana first and Boun Oum, the inspector general, second. "The King has died," he said, "and the crown prince has died. So that leaves only Boun Oum, and he placed me in charge of recapturing Laos."[28] Vang Pao supposedly enjoyed the support of many conservatives in the United States, including American millionaires who wanted first dibs on exploring and exploiting natural resources should he succeed in retaking Laos.[29]

The global situation had been changing for Vang Pao since the collapse of the Soviet Union and the end of the Cold War in 1989, however. Thailand began to reach out to the Lao PDR by closing down the largest refugee camp, Ban Vinai, in 1992. Vang Pao had been using the camp to stage his war in Laos.[30] Vang Pao had also been officially banned from entering Thailand the year before. As the millennium approached, Vang Pao became more and more physically disconnected from Southeast Asia, which stimulated even more the rumors of financial misbehavior. The attack on the World Trade Center in New York on September 11, 2001, changed everything for Vang Pao. Although it ranked as one of the poorest third-world countries in the world, the Lao PDR was a voting member of the United Nations. The United States needed all the votes it could muster to legitimate its war on terror. The savvy Lao government capitalized on the situation by changing its label for the resistance. For years, unwilling to legitimate any antigovernment acts in the nation, the Lao PDR had labeled attacks on roads and government installations as the actions of "bandits."[31] Now the resisters were "terrorists." The Lao PDR obtained Normalized Trade Relations status with the United States in 2004.[32]

On June 7, 2007, Vang Pao and eleven others, including Lieutenant Colonel Jack Harrison, a West Point graduate and decorated officer of the Vietnam War, were arrested for attempting to buy weapons from an American ATF agent to take over Laos. The general endured months in the jails of his American patrons before massive demonstrations by his loyal followers across America pressured officials for his release due to his failing health. Vang Pao was placed under house arrest and cleared of all charges in 2009, at which time he immediately announced his return to Laos. The publicity stunt came to nothing as Hmong anxiously waited for the general to fulfill his promise. On January 6, 2011, the general succumbed to pneumonia. His loyal followers asked for, but never obtained, permission to have his body interred as an ally at Arlington National Cemetery. They buried "the King of the Hmong" in Garden Grove Cemetery, just outside of Los Angeles, in the same graveyard where Michael Jackson, the "king of pop," and other Hollywood legends rest eternally.

Notes

Preface

1. I'm borrowing Hjorleifur Jonsson's usage of the adjective in his *Slow Anthropology: Negotiating Difference with the Iu Mien* (Ithaca, NY: Cornell University Press, 2014).

2. Paul Richard Thompson, *The Voice of the Past: Oral History* (New York: Oxford University Press, 1978), 19.

3. Ibid., 23–24.

4. Ibid., 27.

5. Ibid., 46–48.

6. Karl Marx, "Speech at the Anniversary of the *People's Paper*," in *Karl Marx and Frederick Engels: Selected Works*, vol. 1 (Moscow: Progress Publishers, 1969), 500.

7. E. P. Thompson, *The Making of the English Working Class* (London: Penguin, 1991), 12. For a concise introduction into postcolonial theories, see Patrick Williams and Laura Chrisman, *Colonial Discourse and Post-colonial Theory: A Reader* (New York: Columbia University Press, 1994).

8. Maurice Halbwachs, *The Collective Memory* (New York: Harper & Row, 1980).

9. Joan Tumblety, *Memory and History: Understanding Memory as Source and Subject* (New York: Routledge, 2013), 4.

10. Sidonie Smith and Julia Watson, *Reading Autobiography: A Guide for Interpreting Life Narratives* (Minneapolis: University of Minnesota Press, 2001), 16.

11. Matt Matsuda, *The Memory of the Modern* (Oxford: Oxford University Press, 1996), 9.

12. Tumblety, *Memory and History*, 7.

13. Jeffrey K. Olick, Vered Vinitzky-Seroussi, and Daniel Levy, "Introduction," in *The Collective Memory Reader*, ed. Jeffrey K. Olick, Vered Vinitzky-Seroussi, and Daniel Levy (Oxford: Oxford University Press, 2011), 6.

14. Ibid.

15. See Alfred W. McCoy, review of *Tragic Mountains: The Hmong, the Americans, and the Secret Wars for Laos, 1942–1992*, by Jane Hamilton-Merritt, *Journal of Asian Studies* 52, no. 3 (1993); and Frank Proschan, "Rumor, Innuendo, Propaganda, and Disinformation," review essay, *Bulletin of Concerned Asian Scholars* 28, no. 1 (1996).

16. See Jane Hamilton-Merritt, *Tragic Mountains: The Hmong, the Americans, and the Secret Wars for Laos, 1942–1992* (Bloomington: Indiana University Press, 1993), chapter 2. For her aim to capture the "Hmong voice," see p. xviii.

17. Tongeu Thao, interview with author, Phonsavan, Laos, March 6, 2008.

18. I recognized two of the photos as having come from me, in fact. In summer 2006 I taught a Hmong history course at the University of Wisconsin–Madison. Eric Yang, a student from California, was in my class. The following year, he went to Vietnam for a study abroad program and met Nou Lo, a granddaughter of Nhia Vu, who was also studying at Hanoi University. He told her about me and my photo collection from Mao Song Lyfoung, and she wanted them, so I e-mailed several copies to her (see figs. 8 and 9).

19. Zong Blong Lo, interview with author, Vientiane, Lao PDR, March 3, 2008.

20. Dr. Michael Cullinane, the associate director of the Center for Southeast Asian Studies at the University of Wisconsin–Madison, first made this observation, which was confirmed by my interviews with Ger and Zong Blong Lo.

21. Paul Thompson, "Family Myths, Models, and Denials in the Shaping of Individual Life Paths," in *Between Generations: Family Models, Myths, and Memories*, ed. Daniel Bertaux and Paul Thompson (New York: Oxford University Press, 1993), 14–15.

22. Thompson, *Voice of the Past*, 116.

23. See Hamilton-Merritt, *Tragic Mountains*, 146. After my conversations with Vang Pao, I came to value Hamilton-Merritt's book as a work that expresses Vang Pao's feelings and viewpoints about various historical events. The general also told me that Hamilton-Merritt was his official biographer, although he was perplexed that she had not published his biography yet. "If she does not do it soon, I might have to find someone else," he said.

24. Jan Vansina, *Oral Tradition as History* (Madison: University of Wisconsin Press, 1985), 60.

25. Thompson, *Voice of the Past*, x.

Introduction

1. A *wai* is a classic Lao way of greeting by holding both palms together in prayer position on the chest and then tilting the head down until the nose meets the middle fingers of the palm.

2. I address Vang Pao's marriage politics in a forthcoming article, "The Women of Dragon Capital (Long Cheng): Marriage Alliances and the Rise of Vang Pao," in *Claiming Place: Hmong Women, Power, and Knowledge Production*, ed. Chia Vang, Faith Nibbs, and Ma Vang (Minneapolis: University of Minnesota Press, forthcoming).

3. According to Colonel Vang Chou, Vang Pao did divorce his Lao wife, Mae La, in 1978. Vang Chou, personal communication, August 7, 2013.

4. Roger Warner, *Back Fire: The CIA's Secret War in Laos and Its Link to the War in Vietnam* (New York: Simon and Schuster, 1995), 64.

5. See Jane Hamilton-Merritt, *Tragic Mountains: The Hmong, the Americans, and the Secret Wars for Laos, 1942–1992* (Bloomington: Indiana University Press, 1993), 201–6.

6. Madame Song told her story to Jane Hamilton-Merritt (ibid., 302–3), but she fingered a foreigner as the source of her desire, not Vang Pao, who, she said, just

happened to take an interest in her case and kept in contact until she divorced Lo Ma, after which he proposed. Following her death, however, family members confirmed in her obituary that it was "love at first sight" for her and Vang Pao. See "May Song Vang Dies from Cancer," *Asian American Press*, August 11, 2013.

7. After Vang Pao passed away on January 6, 2011, Madame Song became his public spokesperson and appeared on his behalf at national events such as the Hmong New Year's Festival and the Fourth of July Soccer Tournament in Saint Paul, Minnesota. See Sao Sue Jurewitsch, "33rd Hmong Freedom Celebration Brings Thousands to St. Paul's Como Park," *Hmong Pages*, August 1, 2013.

8. This was my second meeting with Vang Pao. I had interviewed him the week before at his home in Maplewood, Minnesota, which was destroyed by a bomb one week after our meeting in California. A male relative of mine had arranged the first meeting, which turned out to be a formal, awkward event. The general dressed impeccably in a suit and tie, and he maintained a stoic demeanor in front of his male entourage, which surrounded us in silent salute in the living room throughout the interview. For this second interview, I had asked Colonel Ly Tou Pao to help make arrangements with the general. I did not know at the time that the colonel had broken with the general politically in 2001. Tou Pao did not lead me to the general. In 2002 I had asked Tougeu Lyfoung, while in France, if he would broker a meeting with Vang Pao for me. Tougeu promised to take me to Vang Pao when he came back to California, but he passed away in February 2004, just when I had obtained the funding to go to California. When Tou Pao failed to arrange a meeting on my behalf, May Joua fulfilled her father's promise to me by calling Madame Song to ask if we could come over. Vang Pao was surprised that I had arrived at his doorstep again. Nevertheless, he was extremely polite and relaxed and exuded great charisma during our one-on-one conversation after we had eaten *pho*. The efficiency with which the women of Vang Pao's family orchestrated this interview—quite the contrast to going through the powerful men!—struck me as humorous, so I reported back to my advisory committee that I had gotten to Vang Pao "through the kitchen door."

9. Vang Pao's aunt, Nao Vang, was the fourth wife of Ly Foung, the father of Touby and Tougeu. In addition, two of Touby's sisters, Mao Song and Mao Nao, had married into the Vang clan. Mao Nao was married to Vang Pao's elder brother, Nao Tou, and she was the mother of Geu Vang and the mother-in-law of May Joua Lyfoung.

10. According to Hmong belief, the dragon is a powerful but temperamental creature. Lee Nao Mai, a renowned cultural expert who served as an assistant to Tasseng Lee Blia Tria in the 1940s, explained to me that when seeking a burial place for a deceased elder so as to ensure the prosperity of his or her descendants, the Hmong desire to inter the deceased in landscapes imbued with dragon essence. To truly harness the power of the dragon, however, one has to correctly identify and place the deceased at the site that represents the dragon's mouth or its tail, the most powerful parts of its body. Hmong who do not possess this geomantic knowledge or those who misidentify the landscape

and place the deceased in the wrong spot only harness calamity for the descendants, who may be born with dragon essence but cannot bear the dragon's power. This geomantic rule applies to the other animals of the zodiac as well. Hence, for the horse one has to place the deceased on its back, for the tiger on its head, for the boar on its snout where the tusk is located, and so forth. Lee Nao Mai, personal communication, May 2005.

11. Nao Kao Lyfoung, personal communication, April 2010.

12. Jean Lartéguy and Yang Dao, *La Fabuleuse Aventure du Peuple de l'Opium* (Paris: Presses de la Cité, 1979), 92.

13. Ger Lo, interview with author, Vientiane, Lao PDR, March 15, 2008.

14. For a biography of Suharto, see R. E. Elson, *Suharto: A Political Biography* (Cambridge: Cambridge University Press, 2001). For Vang Pao's educational background and military training, see Lartéguy and Yang, *Fabuleuse Aventure.* As one of my blind reviewers notes, Vang Pao may not have been as exposed to literacy as Suharto, who had additional formal education in the Indonesian army, so the comparison has to be viewed with some caution. Vang Pao, however, was brilliant at gathering the most educated men of his generation, such as Yang Dao and Ly Teck, into his most trusted circle in order to garner the power of literacy. Yang Dao was the first Lao Hmong to obtain a doctorate in France, in 1972, and Ly Teck preceded Yang to France and graduated with the equivalent of a bachelor's degree in the late 1960s. Ly Teck also obtained a master's degree in England. Both men subsequently broke away from Vang Pao, however.

15. For Vang Pao's military climb, see Lartéguy and Yang, *Fabuleuse Aventure,* 197–213. According to Vang Pao, he had only a rudimentary command of French, so his superior officer, Captain Fret, who urged him to take the entrance exam for the officer training school at Dong Hene, dictated the answers to him. In Vientiane, Vang was allowed to pass the exam orally (203–4).

16. Vang Pao, interview with author, Westminster, California, April 15, 2004.

17. Geoffrey C. Gunn, *Rebellion in Laos: Peasants and Politics in a Colonial Backwater* (Boulder, CO: Westview Press, 1990); Christian Culas, *Le Messianisme Hmong aux XIXe et XXe Siècles: La Dynamique Religieuse comme Instrument Politique* (Paris: Éditions du Centre National de le Recherche Scientifique, 2005).

18. There is a documentary about this arrest titled "Operation Popcorn," produced by David Grabias, that will be released as a PBS special in April 2015.

19. See, for example, Nicholas Tapp, *The Impossibility of Self: An Essay on the Hmong Diaspora* (Berlin: Lit, 2010).

20. Paul Hillmer, *A People's History of the Hmong* (Saint Paul: Minnesota Historical Society Press, 2010).

21. For example, the Lao-Hmong Coalition, a veterans' group that has successfully raised a memorial for veterans of the Secret War in Sheboygan, Wisconsin, has thus far not placed a plaque dedicated to Vang Pao at the site. It has chosen instead to promote Touby Lyfoung as the central figure of the memorial by according him a plaque in 2011

even though Touby's military role occurred during the previous French era. The break with Vang Pao dates to 1995 when the Lao-Hmong Coalition organized its first veterans' recognition ceremony in Denver, Colorado. Vang Pao agreed to appear but changed his mind at the last minute. Yang Chee, the founder and former executive director of the coalition, had a very thorough discussion about Vang's absence with me when we attended the Hmong Leadership Conference at Otterbein College in Westerville, Ohio, in March 1997. General Heine Aderholt, an event co-organizer and a proponent of the coalition, confirmed the break with Vang in a subsequent interview. Heine Aderholt, interview with author, Menomonee Falls, Wisconsin, July 27, 2003.

22. For example, Steve Schofield's video presentation, which raised funds for the Sheboygan monument, makes this argument. See Steven R. Schofield, *A Brief History of the Hmong and the Secret War in Laos* (Milwaukee: Hmong American Friendship Association, 2004), DVD.

23. See Fredrerick Melo, "St. Paul: Hmong Vets Memorial Could Soon Be Realized," *St. Paul Pioneer Press*, March 29, 2014, http://www.twincities.com/ci_22897501 /st-paul-hmong-vets-memorial-could-soon-be.

24. For over two decades, Vang Pao was consumed with the effort to recapture Laos by force of arms, but the 1996 Welfare Reform Act finally forced him and Hmong veterans' groups to focus on the economic well-being of Hmong in America. The act aimed to cut benefits for noncitizen immigrants. After Hmong elders who had delayed becoming naturalized in the hope of returning to Laos with Vang had their benefits scheduled to be discontinued, a wave of protest suicides occurred across the United States. In response, Hmong veterans' groups scrambled to persuade policy makers to delay implementing the reforms while they lobbied for passage of the 2000 Hmong Veterans' Naturalization Act, which smoothed the way for Hmong elders to obtain US citizenship and retain their benefits.

25. Mee Moua, talk presented at the forum Hmong Diaspora, Gender, and Public Policy, University of Minnesota, October 2010. For a discussion of Moua's election, see Taeko Yoshikawa, "From a Refugee Camp to the Minnesota State Senate: A Case Study of a Hmong American Woman's Challenge," *Hmong Studies Journal* 7 (2006). The Hmong influence in Minnesota's District 67 has been evident since Moua's election. She served multiple terms before deciding not to run for reelection in 2010. Three Hmong individuals stepped up to compete for her position, splitting the Hmong vote and resulting in a Hmong loss in the district. One candidate, Foung Hawj, ran again in 2012 as the lone Hmong candidate and became the second Hmong to serve in the Minnesota State Senate.

26. Yang Lor, "Hmong Political Involvement in St. Paul, Minnesota, and Fresno, California," *Hmong Studies Journal* 10 (2009).

27. Strangely, the city with the heaviest Hmong concentration, Saint Paul, has been slower to erect a Secret War memorial. It may be that the social, economic, and political complexity of this large group of Hmong makes it more challenging for them to unite for such a project. It might also be that, unlike the Hmong in the small towns

of Wisconsin or California, who experience overt racism on a daily basis, the Hmong who live in the liberally progressive bubble of the Twin Cities feel less racial tension and so have less need to justify their presence to mainstream America. Nevertheless, when Cy Thao was elected to the Minnesota legislature in 2002, he made an attempt to obtain funds from the state for a memorial. The state agreed to provide half of the five hundred thousand dollars needed for the project, but community efforts to raise more money fell short. Thao left office in 2010, and the project languished during the interim when Minnesota had no Hmong in the legislature. After his election in 2012, Foung Hawj reinvigorated the monument project, aiming to have it completed in 2015 in order to commemorate the fortieth anniversary of the Hmong exodus from Laos. See Melo, "St. Paul."

28. The official website of the monument is http://www.laohmongusmemorial .com/.

29. Schofield, *A Brief History of the Hmong and the Secret War in Laos.*

30. "Memorializing Lao Hmong Veterans and Their Quest for Freedom," National Public Radio Newswire Services, January 5, 2006, http://www.prnewswire.com/news-releases/memorializing-lao-hmong-veterans-and-their-quest-for-freedom-53154847 .html.

31. F. M. Savina, *Histoire des Miao* (Hong Kong: Imprimerie de la Société des Missions-Étrangères, 1924), 258–59.

32. For a biography of F. M. Savina, see Jean Michaud, *"Incidental" Ethnographers: French Catholic Missions on the Tonkin-Yunnan Frontier, 1880–1930* (Boston: Brill, 2007), 168–85.

33. F. M. Savina, *Dictionnaire Miao-Tseu-Français* (Hanoi: Imprimerie d'Extrême-Orient, 1917); Savina, *Histoire des Miao.*

34. Anthony Smith, *The Ethnic Revival* (Cambridge: Cambridge University Press, 1981), 63.

35. For the Karen, see Smith, *Nationalist Movements*, 9–10; for the Chin, see Lian Hmung Sakhong, *In Search of Chin Identity*, NIAS Monograph 91 (Copenhagen: NIAS Press, 2002).

36. Anthony Smith, ed., *Nationalist Movements* (London: MacMillan, 1976).

37. See Yuepheng Xiong, *Taug Txoj Lw Ntshav: Keeb Kwm Hmoob Nyob Suav Teb* (Saint Paul, MN: Hmong ABC, 2000), DVD; and Vwj Zoov Tsheej [Wu Rong Zhen], Yaj Ntxoov Yias, and Txiv Plig Nyiav Pov [Yves Bertrais], *Haiv Hmoob Liv Xwm* [Hmong history] (Quezon City, Philippines: Patrimonie Culturel Hmong, 1997).

38. Savina, *Histoire des Miao*, 183–84.

39. Tapp, *Impossibility of Self.*

40. Teev Lis, "Virtual Hmong Nation," Social Culture Hmong Discussion Forum, https://groups.google.com/forum/?fromgroups#!topic/soc.culture.hmong /gUb2MTohvwY.

41. Nicholas Tapp, *Sovereignty and Rebellion: The White Hmong of Northern Thailand* (Singapore: Oxford University Press, 1989), 131–44. For this reason, messianic groups in the modern era worship the boar as an important symbol in their movements.

42. Gary Yia Lee, "Cultural Identity in Post-modern Society: Reflections," *Hmong Studies Journal* 1, no. 1 (1996): 3.

43. This woman warrior is also referred to as Nkauj Mog Mim (The Virgin Mee). The appellation is not so much a personal name as a description of her supernatural powers. While Nkauj Ntxuam refers to her ability to protect, Nkauj Mog Mim refers to her youth and purity. In modern messianic traditions, this virgin girl leads the battle bearing a standard. Her violation by some unscrupulous man often serves as an explanation for the loss of the Mandate of Heaven and the defeat of the movement. See Yaj Txooj Tsawb, *Rog Paj Cai* (Vientiane: Y. Bertrais, 1972), 25–27.

44. The original curse is a typical Hmong cultural trope. According to the "Qhuab Ke" (Teachings of the Way) song, humans were created to be immortal. Death befell humanity when the sons of Nkauj Ntsuab and Nraug Nab killed the Toad. Before the Toad entered the realm of Ntxwg Nyoog, he cursed humans: just as he had died so would humankind also die. See Yves Bertrais, *Kab Ke Pam Tuag: Cov Zaj* (Guyane, France: Association Communauté Hmong, 1986).

45. As a child, I lived among the messianic groups in the jungles of Laos from 1975 to 1978 and heard this version of the story from the messianic leader Ly Pa Yia, who lived in my home village of Tiaj Nyuj Qus. Pa Yia was from Kia Boua, Vietnam, and a follower of Yang Shong Lue, the Mother of Writing, who led a literacy movement in the 1960s that threatened Vang Pao. Pa Yia was assassinated in my home village in 1977 by unknown assailants. Keith Quincy was the first to render this tale of a divine female avatar in English. He calls this woman warrior Ngao Shing (Nkauj See) and claims that she was a historical figure during the Tang dynasty. See Keith Quincy, *Hmong: History of a People* (Cheney: Eastern Washington University Press, 1988), 41–42.

46. For eyewitness accounts of young virgins leading battles, see Yaj, *Rog Paj Cai*, 25–27; Savina, *Histoire des Miao*, 258; and Hamilton-Merritt, *Tragic Mountains*, 384.

47. Tapp, *Sovereignty and Rebellion*, 122.

48. On December 2, 2012, Shong Ger Thao, the top ritual expert in exile from Laos, and representatives from the Hmong Cultural Center and the 18 Clan Council of Saint Paul, Minnesota, publicly conferred upon Yang Cheng Vang the title "tshaj lij," which Shong Ger explained was equivalent to a western PhD. Shong Ger also proclaimed Yang Cheng, who had just completed his training with him, as his successor and the top Hmong ritual expert globally. Shong Ger said he did not know of another Hmong with comparable knowledge and training. Shong Ger also articulated his authority to confer the title on his student in a speech where he explained that back at Long Cheng, Laos, in the mid-1960s, Vang Pao had organized a national Hmong ritual knowledge contest that was judged by the top experts of the period, including individuals like Lis Txawj Sua of Muang Pha and Yang Minou, Yang Dao's father. All the Hmong ritual experts of Shong Ger's generation were summoned to come participate in the contest. Shong Ger won by proving he possessed ritual knowledge beyond others, and was conferred the title "tshaj lij" and awarded 50,000 kip. The late Colonel Wa Seng Vang of Madison, Wisconsin, won second place and got 40,000 kip, while a man of the Xiong clan, whose name Shong Ger could not recall, placed third and collected 30,000 kip as a reward.

Following the contest, Shong Ger sat as a ritual and custom law expert at the Hmong custom law court of Long Cheng from 1966 to 1974. Shong Ger further legitimated Yang Cheng as the top expert by designating him to be the *txiv coj xaiv* (master of the ritual blessings), the most prestigious position of a funeral event, following his passing. Yang Cheng, sadly, had to assume this role at Shong Ger's funeral in September 2014. Shong Ger Thao, speech made at Yang Cheng Vang's initiation as a master ritualist, Hmong Village Complex, December 2, 2012, Saint Paul, Minnesota.

49. The Hmong worship Xwm Kav or Xwm Kab as a household spirit today, perhaps in the hope of accessing his awesome power. This act of worship may also reflect an aspect of the Han Chinese conquest and cultural imposition. Hmong people recognize that Xwm Kab is a foreign spirit that originates outside the home. When a Hmong man comes of age and establishes his own house, for example, the ceremony to set up the shrine dedicated to the household guardian includes going to the forest to cut a small branch—representing the guardian—and taking it into the house. Once established, the man must sacrifice a rooster to the guardian annually during the time of the New Year. To ensure the prosperity of the patriarchal clan, only the sons, who will not marry outside the clan, are allowed to feast on the meat of the rooster. See chapters 4 and 7 in Ya Po Cha, *An Introduction to Hmong Culture* (Jefferson, NC: McFarland, 2010).

50. Yang Cheng Vang, "Origin of the Loss of Hmong Writing," talk and *zaj qeeg* performed for History 3483: Hmong History Across the Globe, University of Minnesota, October 2011, and at the conference Hmong Across Borders, University of Minnesota, October 4, 2013. This song also explains why every Hmong funeral requires at minimum a pig and a cow sacrifice and why the deceased must be dressed in funeral clothes containing special embroideries. Only those who possess writing are allowed to pass through the gates of Ntxwg Nyoog to reincarnate, said Yang Cheng. For the Hmong who have lost their writing, the animals that ate their Book, the pig and cow, have to bear witness, so they are sacrificed. Their souls accompany that of the deceased to testify before Ntxwg Nyoog that their kind had devoured some portions of the Hmong's writing. The deceased must also wear funeral clothes that contain the remaining characters as evidence of a writing tradition.

51. See Christian Culas's definition of the messiah as a divine being in "Innovation and Tradition in Rituals and Cosmology: Hmong Messianism and Shamanism in Southeast Asia," in *Hmong/Miao in Asia*, ed. Nicholas Tapp, Jean Michaud, Christian Culas, and Gary Yia Lee (Chiangmai, Thailand: Silkworm Books, 2004).

52. For example, the Hmong refer to Pa Kao Her's messianic group who engaged in anticommunist activities after 1975 as the "Hmong Chao Fa." Pa Kao Her, interview with author, Chiangrai, Thailand, August 15, 2001.

53. Max Weber, *Economy and Society* (Berkeley: University of California Press, 1978), 215–16. For full details, see part 1, chapter 3, and parts 10–16.

54. See, for example, John Potts, *A History of Charisma* (New York: Palgrave Macmillan, 2009).

55. Len Oakes, *Prophetic Charisma: The Psychology of Revolutionary Religious Personalities* (Syracuse: Syracuse University Press, 1997).

56. Weber, *Economy and Society*, 241.

57. Ibid., 215–16.

58. Studies of Hmong women include Nancy D. Donnelly, *Changing Lives of Refugee Hmong Women* (Seattle: University of Washington Press, 1994); Carol Ireson-Doolittle, *Field, Forest, and Family: Women's Work and Power in Rural Laos* (Boulder, CO: Westview Press, 1996); Patricia Symonds, *Calling in the Soul: Gender and the Cycle of Life in a Hmong Village* (Seattle: University of Washington Press, 2004); and Pranee Liamputtong, *Hmong Women and Reproduction* (Westport, CT: Bergin and Garvey, 2000). There is one dissertation on young Hmong American males in the metropolitan United States, Pao Lee Vue, "Racial Assimilation and Popular Culture: Hmong Youth (Sub)Cultures and the Persistence of the Color Line" (PhD diss., University of Minnesota, 2009).

59. I have ventured an opinion on the origin and dangers of this warlike characterization in Mai Na M. Lee, "The Thousand-Year Myth: Construction and Characterization of Hmong," *Hmong Studies Journal* 2, no. 1 (1997).

60. See Louisa Schein and Bee Vang, "*Gran Torino*'s Hmong Lead Bee Vang on Film, Race, and Masculinity: Conversations with Louisa Schein," *Hmong Studies Journal* 11 (Spring 2010).

61. See Mark Tang and Lu Lippold, *Open Season* (Minneapolis: Passionfruit Films, 2011), DVD.

62. See the many versions of this story recorded in Charles Johnson and Se Yang, *Dab Neeg Hmoob: Myths, Legends, and Folk Tales from the Hmong of Laos*, 2nd ed. (Saint Paul, MN: Linguistics Department, Macalester College, 1992), 127–99.

63. Nicholas Tapp recorded another story of the Orphan Boy and the princess from the Hmong of China in *The Hmong of China: Context, Agency, and the Imaginary* (Leiden: Brill, 2001), 439–43.

64. The tale of Maum Nyab Lwj is among my favorite folktales told by my mother, Lia Vue, when I was a child. To my knowledge, this story has not been published or translated into English anywhere.

65. My grandfather, Lee Nao Mai, loved to tell me this very popular story when I was a child in Laos. Also a renowned master of the bamboo reed, in his storytelling my grandfather also included recitations of the *qeej* songs that Nuj Nplhaib supposedly played for Ntxawm at her funeral.

66. Oratorical skills are also esteemed in women. Patricia Symonds writes, "The degree of skill and grace with which girls sing love songs is highly valued." Symonds, *Calling in the Soul*, 56.

67. The late Shong Ger Thao of Saint Paul, Minnesota, for example, was considered the top ritual expert of his generation (see note 48). In the Nong Het region of Laos, Touby Lyfoung noted that Lo Nhia Ma and his father, Ly Foung, were the most renowned ritual experts during the early twentieth century. See Touxa Lyfoung, *Tub*

Npis Lisfoom Tej Lus Tseg Cia [Words left by Touby Lyfoung] (Minneapolis, MN: Burgess Publishing, 1996), 29.

68. There have been some exceptions to keeping knowledge only within a family, according to Yang Cheng Vang, who has sought out masters in Southeast Asia as well as the United States. When a master deems a student as incredibly worthy or when he does not have a male heir but wants the knowledge to survive, he will pass on everything he knows. Yang Cheng Vang, personal communication, October 2011. Nicholas Tapp notes, however, that Hmong masters would hold back bits and pieces so that the oral knowledge is gradually lost to successive generations. See Tapp, *Sovereignty and Rebellion*.

69. Potts says the term "charisma" is often characterized in the modern era as an "X-factor." See Potts, *History of Charisma*, 3.

70. Vang Pao, interview with author, Maplewood, Minnesota, April 8, 2004.

71. Nusit Chindarsi, *The Religion of the Hmong Njua* (Bangkok: Siam Society, 1976), 7. William R. Geddes also notes that the Hmong perceive strength and security through the size of their clans. One ritual performance by the Tang clan includes the words "Let the Tang clan be so numerous that when they walk the sound will be like thunder. Other clans will then say that the Tang are so many that they make a great commotion walking. Our clan will grow and spread like the forest, and none will die like the trees in it." William R. Geddes, *Migrants of the Mountains: The Cultural Ecology of the Blue Miao (Hmong Njua) of Thailand* (Oxford: Clarendon Press, 1976), 57.

72. Don A. Schanche, *Mister Pop* (New York: McKay, 1970), 287.

73. Hamilton-Merritt, *Tragic Mountains*, 203.

74. James William Lair, interview with author, Menomonee Falls, Wisconsin, July 27, 2003. I discuss how Vang Pao's wives contributed to his political climb by providing material bounty and manpower in "Women of Dragon Capital."

75. Mao Song Lyfoung, interview with author, Maplewood, Minnesota, October 24, 2002.

76. Yan was commissioned to study and strategize against the rebellion led by Wu Bayue. See Daniel McMahon, "Identity and Conflict on a Chinese Borderland: Yan Ruyi and the Recruitment of the Gelao during the 1795–97 Miao Revolt," *Late Imperial China* 23, no. 2 (2002): 57.

77. Quoted in Robert Darrah Jenks, *Insurgency and Social Disorder in Guizhou: The "Miao" Rebellion, 1854–1873* (Honolulu: University of Hawai'i Press, 1994), 34.

78. See Yaj, *Rog Paj Cai*; Pa Kao Her, interview with author, Chiangrai, Thailand, August 15, 2001.

79. Michael Adas, *Prophets of Rebellion: Millenarian Protest Movements against the European Colonial Order* (Chapel Hill: University of North Carolina Press, 1979), xx.

80. Culas, "Innovation and Tradition in Rituals and Cosmology," 114.

81. James C. Scott, *The Art of Not Being Governed: An Anarchist History of Upland Southeast Asia* (New Haven, CT: Yale University Press, 2009).

82. Geddes, *Migrants of the Mountains*, 10.

83. Ibid., 45.

84. Savina, *Histoire des Miao*, 232.

85. Ibid.

86. Gary Yia Lee, "Cultural Identity in Post-modern Society," 9. The phrase *Hmoob yuav tsum hlub Hmoob* translates as "Hmong should love Hmong."

87. Pao Saykao Thao, "Hmong Leadership: The Traditional Model," 1997, http://www.hmongnet.org/hmong-au/leader.htm.

88. Jean Michaud and Christian Culas, "The Hmong of the Southeast Asian Massif: Their Recent History of Migration," in *Where China Meets Southeast Asia: Social and Cultural Change in the Border Regions*, ed. Grant Evans, Christopher Hutton, and Khun Eng Kuah (New York: St. Martin's Press, 2000), 114.

89. Long Yu-xiao, "The Origin of the Hmong in China," talk given at Concordia University, Saint Paul, Minnesota, December 18, 2009.

90. For example, a major Hmong controversy erupted into the American mainstream in 2002 when Paoze Thao claimed that the Mong Leng (Blue/Green Hmong) and Hmong are two separate groups. He wanted the US government to recognize the two groups by using both spellings (Hmong/Mong) in legal documents. Prasit Leepreecha also talked about emerging tensions between Hmong Christians and non-Christians of Thailand, where converted Hmong perceive themselves as more modern than their traditional counterparts. Prasit Leepreecha, keynote address at the conference Hmong Across Borders, University of Minnesota, October 5, 2013.

91. Norma Diamond, "Miao as a Category," in *Cultural Encounters on China's Ethnic Frontiers*, ed. Stevan Harrell (Seattle: University of Washington Press, 1995), 100–102.

92. Frank M. Lebar, Gerald C. Hickey, and John K. Musgrave, *Ethnic Groups of Mainland Southeast Asia* (New Haven, CT: Human Relations Area Files, 1964), 64–65.

93. Jacques Lemoine, *Un Village Hmong Vert du Haut Laos* (Paris: Éditions du Centre National de la Recherche Scientifique, 1972), 16.

94. Robert G. Cooper, *Resource Scarcity and the Hmong Response: Patterns of Settlement and Economy in Transition* (Singapore: National University of Singapore Press, 1984), 30; Chindarsi, *Religion of the Hmong Njua*, 4.

95. Charles Johnson and Se Yang, "The Flood and the World's Second Beginning," in *Dab Neeg Hmoob: Myths, Legends, and Folk Tales from the Hmong of Laos*, 2nd ed. (Saint Paul, MN: Linguistics Department, Macalester College, 1992), 113–20.

96. Yang Dao, *Hmong at the Turning Point*, ed. Jeanne L. Blake (Minneapolis: WorldBridge Associates, 1993), 23; Kao-Ly Yang, "Problems in the Interpretation of Hmong Clan Surnames," in *Hmong/Miao in Asia*, ed. Nicholas Tapp, Jean Michaud, Christian Culas, and Gary Yia Lee (Chiangmai, Thailand: Silkworm Books, 2004).

97. Although it is rare, some Hmong of Laos have been known to practice intra-clan marriage in the past. These groups bore social stigmas, as Keith Quincy notes about the Vang clan in *Harvesting Pa Chay's Wheat: The Hmong and America's Secret War*

in Laos (Cheney: Eastern Washington University Press, 2000), 162. See also Cooper, *Resource Scarcity and the Hmong Response*, 34. I note Vang Say Pao's explanation of why the Vang Chinese marry the Vang Hmong in chapter 1.

98. William H. Hudspeth, "The Cult of the Door amongst the Miao," *Folk-Lore* 33, no. 4 (1922).

99. For details about the Door and Ox Ceremonies, see Chindarsi, *Religion of the Hmong Njua*, 113–30.

100. Gary Yia Lee, "The Religious Presentation of Social Relationships: Hmong World View and Social Structure," *Lao Studies Review* 2 (1994–95).

101. Lee Cha Yia, personal communication, June 2007. Cha Yia is one of the remaining Lee clan elders in Minnesota.

102. Yang Cheng Vang, for example, says his clan myth stipulates that there are three wives whose sons founded the Vang nine, seven, and five *txim* lineages. Personal communication, July 2007.

103. The Moua and Her clans, for example, have myths about elder and younger brothers.

104. On funeral and burial practices, see Bertrais, *Kab Ke Pam Tuag: Cov Zaj*, and *Kab Ke Pam Tuag: Cov Txheej Txheem*.

105. This was the case with Ly Dra Pao, the grandfather of Touby Lyfoung, when Ly Nhia Vu refused to invite Dra Pao into his lineage even though ritual similarities were discovered. See Touxa Lyfoung, trans., *Touby Lyfoung: An Authentic Account of the Life of a Hmong Man in the Troubled Land of Laos* (Minneapolis, MN: Burgess Publishing, 1996), 17.

106. Geddes, *Migrants of the Mountains*, 71.

107. This is despite Savina's desire to link the Hmong to the Judeo-Christian traditions. See Savina, *Histoire des Miao*, xiii and 234–44. Creation myths do exist among the Hmong, as articulated in the "Qhuab Ke" (Teachings of the Way) and the "Zaj Tshoob Ntuj Tsim Teb Raug" (Marriage Song of the Creation), but this knowledge is relegated largely to the realm of the ritual experts and kept secret from ordinary Hmong.

108. Some versions of the flood myth exclude the role of Saub. For a brief description of Saub, see Robert Cooper et al., *The Hmong* (Bangkok: Artasia Press, 1991), 54. "It was Saub who, after the mighty floods receded from the Earth, told the surviving brother and sister to carve up the shapeless flesh of their incestuous child. From the pieces of flesh grew the original twelve Hmong clans," Cooper writes in *Resource Scarcity*, 51. For other versions, see Hugo Adolf Bernatzik, *Akha and Miao: Problems of Applied Ethnography in Farther India* (New Haven, CT: Human Relations Area Files, 1970), 302; Johnson and Yang, *Dab Neeg Hmoob*, 113–20; Jean Mottin, *Contes et Légendes Hmong Blanc* (Bangkok: Don Bosco Press, 1980), 28–59; and Savina, *Histoire des Miao*, 245–46.

109. Cooper, *Resource Scarcity*, 34.

110. Dang Nghiem Van, "The Flood Myth and the Origin of Ethnic Groups in Southeast Asia," *Journal of American Folklore* 106, no. 421 (1993): 305.

111. David Crockett Graham, "The Customs of the Ch'uan Miao," *Journal of the West China Border Research Society* 9 (1937): 27. See also Gary Yia Lee, "Household and Marriage in a Thai Highland Society," *Journal of the Siam Society* 76 (1988): 164.

112. Thao, "Hmong Leadership."

113. Tougeu Lyfoung, interview with author, Champlin, Minnesota, July 3, 2003.

114. Vang Pao, interview with author, Maplewood, Minnesota, April 8, 2004.

115. Ibid.

116. Edmund R. Leach, *Political Systems of Highland Burma: A Study of Kachin Social Structure* (Boston: Beacon Press, 1965).

117. Willem van Schendel, "Geographies of Knowing, Geographies of Ignorance: Jumping Scale in Southeast Asia," *Environment and Planning D: Society and Space* 20, no. 6 (2002).

118. Jean Michaud, "Zomia and Beyond," editorial, *Journal of Global History* 5 (2010).

119. Scott, *Art of Not Being Governed*, ix.

120. Ibid., 16; Michaud, "Zomia and Beyond," 194.

121. Scott, *Art of Not Being Governed*, 13.

122. Victor Lieberman, "A Zone of Refuge in Southeast Asia? Reconceptualizing Interior Spaces," *Journal of Global History* 5 (2010): 343.

123. Scott, *Art of Not Being Governed*, 22.

124. Hjorleifur Jonsson, *Slow Anthropology: Negotiating Difference with the Iu Mien* (Ithaca, NY: Cornell University Press, 2014), 2, 16.

125. Ibid., 22.

126. Ibid., 18, my emphasis.

127. Ibid., 19.

128. Ibid., 22.

129. Ibid., 25.

130. Michaud, "Zomia and Beyond," 191.

131. Jonsson, *Slow Anthropology*, 32.

132. Hjorleifur Jonsson, *Mien Relations: Mountain People and State Control in Thailand* (Ithaca, NY: Cornell University Press, 2005), 20.

133. Ibid., 28.

134. Bernard Formoso, "Zomian or Zombies? What Future Exists for the Peoples of the Southeast Asian Massif?," *Journal of Global History* 5 (2010): 315.

135. Jean Michaud, *Moving Mountains: Ethnicity and Livelihoods in Highland China, Vietnam, and Laos* (Vancouver, BC: University of British Columbia Press, 2011).

136. C. Patterson Giersch, "Across Zomia with Merchants, Monks, and Musk: Process Geographies, Trade Networks, and the Inner-East-Southeast Asian Borderlands," *Journal of Global History* 5 (2010): 217, 215.

137. Arjun Appadurai, *Modernity at Large: Cultural Dimensions of Globalization* (Minneapolis: University of Minnesota Press, 1996).

138. Jenks, *Insurgency and Social Disorder in Guizhou*, 34.

Chapter 1. Hmong Alliance and Rebellion within the State

1. Vwj Zoov Tsheej (Wu Rong Zhen) constructs a history of violent struggles between the Hmong and the Han that date back over five thousand years to the time of Chiyou, the mythical Hmong king. See Vwj Zoov Tsheej [Wu Rong Zhen], with Yaj Ntxoov Yias and Txiv Plig Nyiav Pov [Yves Bertrais], *Haiv Hmoob Liv Xwm* [Hmong History] (Quezon City, Philippines: Patrimonie Culturel Hmong, 1997).

2. The English word *Chinese* is derived from *Qin* or *Chin*.

3. Long Yu-xiao, "The Origin of the Hmong in China," talk presented at Concordia University, Saint Paul, Minnesota, December 18, 2009.

4. Nicholas Tapp, *Sovereignty and Rebellion: The White Hmong of Northern Thailand* (Singapore: Oxford University Press, 1989). According to Vwj Zoov Tsheej, however, both the Hmong and the Han concede that the Hmong is the elder brother, the aboriginals of the land. Vwj, *Haiv Hmoob Liv Xwm*, 58. The disagreement about who is the elder brother serves to explain several issues here. Tapp's version supports my contention that the Hmong concede to Han Chinese material superiority—hence, the Han is the "elder" brother in the cultural/material realm—while Wu's version correlates with the historical belief that the Hmong are the aboriginals of China and thus are the "elder" brother or first peoples. The syntactic uses of *elder*, rather than appearing inconsistent, can both thus be perceived as true here.

5. Nicholas Tapp, *The Hmong of China: Context, Agency, and the Imaginary* (Leiden: Brill, 2001), 15.

6. For cultural and historical influences, see ibid., 11-17. For Chinese influence on Hmong language, see Gordon Downer, "Chinese, Thai, and Miao-Yao," in *Linguistic Comparison in South East Asia*, ed. H. L. Shorto (London: School of Oriental and African Studies, University of London, 1963), and "Tone-Change and Tone-Shift in White Miao," *Bulletin of the School of Oriental and African Studies* 30, no. 3 (1967); see also Jacques Lemoine, *Parlons (H)mong* (Paris: L'Harmattan, 2013), 37-39.

7. Ka Houa Yang ranked among the last of the masters who could recite the "Txiv Xaiv" in Chinese. He passed away in Saint Paul on March 24, 2002. Ka Houa said that among Hmong Americans only Yang Minou, the father of Yang Dao, who had preceded him in death, could also recite "Txiv Xaiv" in Chinese. Ka Houa played some of his recorded songs in "Chinese" for me in 2001, but I was unable to confirm the specific dialect.

8. I often encounter Hmong American-born students of both sexes at the University of Minnesota who are named Suav. These new Americans have no idea why they were given such names and listen intently as we discuss their names in my classes.

9. Lee Cha Yia, interview with author, Saint Paul, Minnesota, January 3, 2002.

10. Tapp, *Hmong of China*, 15.

11. David G. Atwill, *The Chinese Sultanate: Islam, Ethnicity, and the Panthay Rebellion in Southwest China, 1856-1873* (Stanford, CA: Stanford University Press, 2005), 26.

12. Quoted in Richard D. Cushman, "Rebel Haunts and Lotus Huts: Problems in the Ethnohistory of the Yao" (PhD diss., Cornell University, 1970), 36.

13. My mother, Lia Vue, who is of the same clan as Vue Pa Chay, loved to tell stories like this when we discussed politics and Hmong civilization.

14. For multiple versions of the "Qhuab Ke" and Hmong funeral practices, see Yves Bertrais, *Kab Ke Pam Tuag: Cov Zaj* (Guyane, France: Association Communauté Hmong, 1986), and *Kab Ke Pam Tuag: Cov Txheej Txheem* (Guyane, France: Association Communauté Hmong, 1985); Jacques Lemoine, *L'Initiation du Mort Chez les Hmong* (Bangkok: Pandora, 1983); and Nicholas Tapp, *The Impossibility of Self: An Essay on the Hmong Diaspora* (Berlin: Lit, 2010), 139–46. Tapp translates the title "Qhuab Ke" as "Opening the Way" while Jacques Lemoine translates it as "Showing the Way." See Jacques Lemoine with Kenneth White, *Kr'ua Ke/Showing the Way: A Hmong Initiation of the Dead* (Bangkok: Pandora, 1983). I have chosen to stick to the meaning conveyed in the Hmong word *Qhuab*, which means "Teaching." The "Qhuab Ke" is sometimes referred to as "Zaj Taw Kev," which would translate as "The Showing of the Way" or "The Pointing of the Way." By translating "Qhuab Ke" as "The Teachings of the Way," I am guided by my East Asian background, especially with the translation of the works of Lao Tzu, such as the *Tao Te Ching*, into English.

15. See, for example, Catherine Falk, "Upon Meeting the Ancestors: The Hmong Funeral Ritual in Asia and Australia," *Hmong Studies Journal* 1, no. 1 (1996).

16. The versions of the "Qhuab Ke" in Yves Bertrais's *Kab Ke Pam Tuag: Cov Zaj* describe only a journey through the spiritual world without much reference to the historical world I have heard about from my grandfathers in the Lee clan. Since my grandfathers have all passed on, I asked a highly regarded Hmong cultural expert and shaman, Yang Cheng Vang, of Madison, Wisconsin, why this was the case, and he explained to me that he believes the versions recorded by Bertrais show influence from shamanism. The version passed down in his Vang family also resembles the ones I heard from my grandfathers. His family's version stresses the historical return trip to China after the retrieval of the placenta and amniotic sac at the deceased's natal village. The instructions include details of mountains and passes in Tonkin, including mentions of the Red and Black Rivers, and descriptions of the Yangtze River in China; it ends at the Yellow River, where the ancestors live. Yang Cheng Vang, personal communication, November 2011.

17. Bertrais, *Kab Ke Pam Tuag: Cov Zaj*, 53, 93.

18. Tapp, *Impossibility of Self*, 146.

19. Edward Schafer, *The Vermillion Bird* (Berkeley: University of California Press, 1967), 71; Cushman, "Rebel Haunts and Lotus Huts," 49, 153–54; Atwill, *Chinese Sultanate*, 25–26; and Jennifer Took, *A Native Chieftaincy in Southwest China: Franchising a Tai Chieftaincy under the Tusi System of Late Imperial China* (Leiden: Brill, 2005), 27.

20. For Han portrayal of "Miao," see Norma Diamond, "Miao as a Category," in *Cultural Encounters on China's Ethnic Frontiers*, ed. Stevan Harrell (Seattle: University of Washington Press, 1995); Louisa Schein, *Minority Rules: The Miao and the Feminine in China's Cultural Politics* (Durham, NC: Duke University Press, 2000); Zhiqiang Yang, "From *Miao* to *Miaozu*: Alterity in the Formation of Modern Ethnic Groups," *Hmong Studies Journal* 10 (2009).

21. Kou Yang makes precisely this point about being cautious in highlighting historical hatreds between the Hmong and the Han. See Kou Yang, "Challenges and Complexity in the Re-construction of Hmong History," *Hmong Studies Journal* 10 (2009).

22. On Vang Say Pao as one of the first Hmong leaders to convert to Christianity, see G. Linwood Barney, "The Meo: An Incipient Church," *Practical Anthropology* 4, no. 2 (1957).

23. Vang Say Pao, interview with author, Roseville, Minnesota, May 2004.

24. Ly Na Jalao, interview with author, Toulouse, France, July 13, 2002.

25. Cushman, "Rebel Haunts and Lotus Huts," 171.

26. Madame Ly Na Jalao, interview with author, Toulouse, France, July 13, 2002. Ly Na was an "uncle" to me because he and my father belong to the same generation of the Ly clan.

27. Vwj, *Haiv Hmoob Liv Xwm*, 21–27.

28. Yuepheng Xiong, personal communication, November 2010.

29. Xinzhong Yao, *An Introduction to Confucianism* (Cambridge: Cambridge University Press, 2000), 149.

30. F. M. Savina, *Histoire des Miao* (Hong Kong: Imprimerie de la Société des Missions-Étrangères, 1924), 252.

31. Yao, *Introduction to Confucianism*, 186–87.

32. Michael Loewe and Edward L. Shaughnessy, eds., *The Cambridge History of Ancient China: From the Origins of Civilization to 221 B.C.* (Cambridge: Cambridge University Press, 1999), 314–15.

33. Yao, *Introduction to Confucianism*, 166.

34. Yu-Lan Fung, *A History of Chinese Philosophy*, vol. 2, trans. Derk Bodde (Princeton, NJ: Princeton University Press, 1953), 47.

35. Yao, *Introduction to Confucianism*, 187.

36. Frederick Wakeman Jr., *The Fall of Imperial China* (New York: Free Press, 1975), 55–56.

37. James Legge, trans., *The Four Books*, in *The Chinese Classics*, vols. 1–2 (Taipei: Culture Book Co., 1992), 383–85.

38. Ibid., 286, 288.

39. Yao, *Introduction to Confucianism*, 184.

40. Ibid., 167.

41. Some of these case studies of ethnic minorities appropriating lowland philosophical and religious symbols for larger political action include such works as Cushman, "Rebel Haunts and Lotus Huts"; and Anthony R. Walker, *Merit and the Millennium: Routine and Crisis in the Ritual Lives of the Lahu People* (New Delhi: Hindustan Publishing Corporation, 2003).

42. See Kimber Charles Pearce's study of radical feminist writers' appropriation of patriarchal ideologies, "The Radical Feminist Manifesto as Generic Appropriation: Gender, Genre, and Second Wave Resistance," *The Southern Communication Journal* 64, no. 4 (1999): 307–15.

43. William R. Geddes, *Migrants of the Mountains: The Cultural Ecology of the Blue Miao (Hmong Njua) of Thailand* (Oxford: Clarendon Press, 1976), 3; Yeuh-Hwa Lin, "The Miao-Man Peoples of Kweichow," *Harvard Journal of Asiatic Studies* 5, no. 3/4 (1940); F. M. Savina, *Histoire des Miao* (Farnborough: Gregg, 1924), 127-29; Yuepheng Xiong, *Taug Txoj Lw Ntshav: Keeb Kwm Hmoob Nyob Suav Teb* (Saint Paul, MN: Hmong ABC, 2000), DVD. Xiong uses the word *Hmoob* and does not make a distinction between "Miao" and Hmong in his video documentary.

44. Vwj, *Haiv Hmoob Liv Xwm*. Vwj uses the word *Hmoob* in this text and does not make a distinction between "Miao" and Hmong.

45. Ibid., 57.

46. Ibid., 58.

47. Yang Dao, "The Hmong: Enduring Traditions," in *Minority Cultures of Laos: Kammu, Lua,' Lahu, Hmong, and Mien*, ed. Judy Lewis and Damrong Tayanin (Rancho Cordova, CA: Southeast Asia Community Resource Center, Folsom Cordova Unified School District, 1992), 258-59.

48. Xiong, *Taug Txoj Lw Ntshav*.

49. Kaiyi Yang, "Hmong-Mongolian?," *Hmong Forum*, January 1996, 50.

50. Keith Quincy, *Harvesting Pa Chay's Wheat: The Hmong and America's Secret War in Laos* (Cheney: Eastern Washington University Press, 2000), 23-24.

51. Guy Moréchand, "Le Chamanisme des Hmong," *Bulletin de l'École Française d'Extrême Orient* 54 (1968): 77.

52. Yang, "Hmong-Mongolian?," 51.

53. Moréchand, "Le Chamanisme des Hmong," 77.

54. Jennifer Took, *A Native Chieftaincy in Southwest China: Franchising a Tai Chieftaincy under the Tusi System of Late Imperial China* (Leiden: Brill, 2005), 24.

55. Ibid., 227-28.

56. Daniel McMahon, "Identity and Conflict on a Chinese Borderland: Yan Ruyi and the Recruitment of the Gelao during the 1795-97 Miao Revolt," *Late Imperial China* 23, no. 2 (2002); Donald S. Sutton, "Myth Making on an Ethnic Frontier: The Cult of the Heavenly Kings of West Hunan, 1715-1996," *Modern China* 26, no. 4 (2000); Donald S. Sutton, "Violence and Ethnicity on a Qing Colonial Frontier: Customary and Statutory Law in the Eighteenth-Century Miao Pale," *Modern Asian Studies* 37, no. 1 (2003); Tapp, *Sovereignty and Rebellion*, 18.

57. Robert D. Jenks, *Insurgency and Social Disorder in Guizhou: The "Miao" Rebellion, 1854-1873* (Honolulu: University of Hawai'i Press, 1994); Yuepheng Xiong, *Taug Txoj Lw Ntshaw Daim 3: Tsab Xyooj Mem Sawv Tua Suav, 1855-1873* (Saint Paul, MN: Hmongland Publishing, 2005), DVD.

58. Harold J. Wiens, *Han Chinese Expansion in South China* (Hamden, CT: Shoe String Press, 1967), 202.

59. Jenks, *Insurgency and Social Disorder in Guizhou*, 50.

60. In his seminal study of American Indians in the Great Lakes region, Richard White defines *upstreaming* as "a technique of using ethnologies of present-day or nineteenth-century Indian groups to interpret Indian societies of the past." Richard

White, *The Middle Ground: Indians, Empires, and Republics in the Great Lakes Region, 1650–1815* (Cambridge: Cambridge University Press, 1991), xiv.

61. Jean Michaud and Christian Culas, "The Hmong of the Southeast Asian Massif: Their Recent History of Migration," in *Where China Meets Southeast Asia: Social and Cultural Change in the Border Regions*, edited by Grant Evans, Christopher Hutton, and Khun Eng Kuah (New York: St. Martin's Press, 2000).

62. Intriguingly, and also to lend some credit to Culas and Michaud's theory, the Hmong phrase for freedom is "thaj yeeb" which literally translates as "opium field" or "tilling opium."

63. See Wiens, *Han Chinese Expansion in South China*; and Jenks, *Insurgency and Social Disorder in Guizhou*.

64. Jeremy Hein, *Ethnic Origins: The Adaptation of Cambodian and Hmong Refugees in Four American Cities* (New York: Russell Sage Foundation, 2006), 60–63.

65. Wiens, *Han Chinese Expansion in South China*, 90.

66. Hmong and American Indians' experiences are highlighted annually at the University of Wisconsin–La Crosse in the Indians' Widening the Circle symposium. During this annual fall event, Hmong experts from the community are invited to speak about their shared experience of being an oppressed, dispossessed, landless, and stateless people. For Hmong struggles with whites in the urban and rural Midwest, see Hein, *Ethnic Origins*, 79–124; and Cathleen Jo Faruque, *Migration of Hmong to the Midwestern United States* (Lanham, MD: University Press of America, 2002).

67. The migration to the West, the result of war and revolution caused by French and American imperialism, has gradually been characterized as economic. In the early 1990s, the United Nations and United States began categorizing Hmong who fled from Laos as "economic refugees." The label stuck as the United States and Thailand began to negotiate with the Lao PDR to close the Thai refugee camps by 1992. This shift in label allowed the United States and other countries to shirk their responsibility for what happened in Southeast Asia. Paul Hillmer demonstrates in his latest research, for example, that the United States has turned a blind eye to Hmong refugees at Houey Nam Khao, Thailand, who came out of the jungles of Laos in 2004 after thirty years of struggle against the Lao PDR. These individuals were forcibly repatriated to an unknown fate. See Paul Hillmer, *A People's History of the Hmong* (Saint Paul: Minnesota Historical Society Press, 2010), 293–99.

68. Joakim Enwall, *Hmong Writing Systems in Vietnam: A Case Study of Vietnam's Minority Language Policy* (Stockholm, Sweden: Center for Pacific Asian Studies, Stockholm University, 1995), 1–2.

69. For Wu Bayue's rebellion, see McMahon, "Identity and Conflict on a Chinese Borderland."

70. Jonathan D. Spence, *God's Chinese Son: The Taiping Heavenly Kingdom of Hong Xiuquan* (New York: W. W. Norton, 1996); Jenks, *Insurgency and Social Disorder in Guizhou*; Atwill, *Chinese Sultanate*.

71. Jean Mottin, *History of the Hmong* (Bangkok: Odeon Store, 1980), 42.

72. Being an aunt in this case meant that Jer belonged to the same generation as Mao Song's father, Ly Foung, and hence was a "sister" (cousin) to him. Direct blood relations cannot be maintained, but all Hmong of the same clan are perceived to be relatives, and their places are carefully established in the generational tree by the elders of the clan.

73. Mao Song Lyfoung, interview with author, Maplewood, Minnesota, October 18, 2002; Tougeu Lyfoung, interview with author, Champlin, Minnesota, July 3, 2003.

74. Ly Na Jalao, interview with author, Toulouse, France, July 13, 2002. Alfred W. McCoy also interviewed members of this Ly family in 1971. See Alfred W. McCoy, Cathleen B. Read, and Leonard P. Adams, *The Politics of Heroin* (New York: Harper and Row, 1972), 80.

75. Lee Cha Yia, interview with author, Saint Paul, Minnesota, January 3, 2002.

76. Ly Na Jalao, interview with author, Toulouse, France, July 13, 2002.

77. Tsia Long Thao, interview with author, Sun Prairie, Wisconsin, August 6, 2006.

78. Touxa Lyfoung, *Tub Npis Lisfoom Tej Lus Tseg Cia* [Words left by Touby Lyfoung] (Minneapolis, MN: Burgess Publishing, 1996), 14–15.

79. Chai Charles Moua, *Roars of Traditional Leaders: Mong (Miao) American Cultural Practices in a Conventional Society* (Lanham, MD: University Press of America, 2012), 33–34.

80. Nicholas Tapp, "The Impact of Missionary Christianity upon Marginalized Ethnic Minorities: The Case of the Hmong," *Journal of Southeast Asian Studies* 20, no. 1 (1989): 78.

81. William H. Hudspeth, *Stone-Gateway and the Flowery Miao* (London: Cargate Press, 1970).

82. Jacques Lemoine reports that descendants of these A Hmao converts who no longer wish to remain Christians have become atheists since they no longer know their own traditions. See Jacques Lemoine, "Ethnicity, Culture, and Development among Some Minorities of the People's Republic of China," in *Ethnicity and Ethnic Groups in China*, ed. Chien Chiao and Nicholas Tapp (Hong Kong: New Asia Academic Bulletin, 1989), 7.

83. Stanley Tambiah, "The Galactic Polity in Southeast Asia," in *Culture, Thought, and Social Action* (Cambridge, MA: Harvard University Press, 1985). For additional discussions of the traditional Southeast Asian state, see R. Heine-Geldern, "Conceptions of State and Kingship in Southeast Asia," *Far Eastern Quarterly* 2, no. 1 (1942); R. Heine-Geldern, *Conceptions of State and Kingship in Southeast Asia*, Data Papers, no. 18 (Ithaca, NY: Southeast Asia Program, Cornell University, 1956); Georges Condominas, "A Few Remarks about Thai Political Systems," in *Natural Symbols in South East Asia*, ed. G. B. Milner (London: School of Oriental and African Studies, 1978); Georges Condominas, "Essai sur l'Evolution des Systemes Politiques Thais," in *L'Espace Social à Propos de l'Asie du Sud-Est* (Paris: Flammarion, 1980); Clifford Geertz, *Negara: The Theatre State in Nineteenth-Century Bali* (Princeton, NJ: Princeton

University Press, 1980); Shelley Errington, *Meaning and Power in a Southeast Asian Realm* (Princeton, NJ: Princeton University Press, 1989); and O. W. Wolters, *History, Culture, and Region in Southeast Asian Perspectives* (Singapore: Institute of Southeast Asian Studies, 1982). For a comparative discussion of Vietnam's Confucian mandarinate as different from the governments of the Hindu-Buddhist states, see Charles Keyes, *The Golden Peninsula: Culture and Adaptation in Mainland Southeast Asia* (New York: Macmillan, 1977), 181–94.

84. Tambiah, "Galactic Polity in Southeast Asia," 260.

85. For a broad overview of western colonialism in Southeast Asia, see Norman G. Owen, *The Emergence of Modern Southeast Asia: A New History* (Honolulu: University of Hawai'i Press, 2005).

86. David K. Wyatt, *Thailand: A Short History* (New Haven, CT: Yale University Press, 1984); Thongchai Winichakul, *Siam Mapped: A History of the Geo-body of a Nation* (Honolulu: University of Hawai'i Press, 1994).

87. Philippe Le Failler calls this region the Twelve Tai Counties, but the Thai/Tai refer to these areas as *muang*, a word that is often translated as "state," as in Muang Thai for Thailand and Muang Lao for Laos. Snit Smuckarn and Kennon Breazeale refer to these areas as the Twelve Chuthai State. See Philippe Le Failler, "The Đèo Family of Lai Châu: Traditional Power and Unconventional Practices," *Journal of Vietnamese Studies* 6, no. 2 (Summer 2011): 48; and Snit Smuckarn and Kennon Breazeale, *A Culture in Search of Survival: The Phuan of Thailand and Laos* (New Haven, CT: Council on Southeast Asia Studies, Yale University, 1988), 36–37.

88. Failler, "Đèo Family of Lai Châu," 42.

89. Smuckarn and Breazeale, *Culture in Search of Survival*, 82.

90. Jean Michaud, "The Montagnards and the State in Northern Vietnam from 1802 to 1975: A Historical Overview," *Ethnohistory* 47, no. 2 (Spring 2000): 337. Michaud defines *chau* and *huyen* as "district," and Failler defines *chau* as "county." See Failler, "Đèo Family of Lai Châu," 42.

91. Failler, "Đèo Family of Lai Châu," 49–50.

92. Smuckarn and Breazeale, *A Culture in Search of Survival*, 82.

93. Failler, "Đèo Family of Lai Châu," 45.

94. Smuckarn and Breazeale, *A Culture in Search of Survival*, 82.

95. Quoted in Michaud, "Montagnards," 338. Jean Michaud identifies the "Tho" as the contemporary "Tay" who is linguistically related to the Tai. He further warns that the "Tho" in these colonial sources should not be confused with the officially recognized Viet-speaking Tho ethnic group of Nghe An and Thanh Hao provinces in the current Socialist Republic of Vietnam. See Jean Michaud, *Historical Dictionary of the Peoples of the Southeast Asian Massif* (Lanham, MD: Scarecrow Press, 2006), 232.

96. Failler, "Đèo Family of Lai Châu," 49.

97. Ibid., 58–62.

98. Grant Evans, *The Last Century of Lao Royalty: A Documentary History* (Chiangmai, Thailand: Silkworm Books, 2009), 260.

99. This complex political situation is articulated in Smuckarn and Breazeale, *A Culture in Search of Survival.*

100. Ibid., 47–52.

101. See Saykham's memoir, translated in Evans, *Last Century of Lao Royalty*, 260.

102. For a description of Anouvong's rebellion and his torture by the Thai, see Ngaosīvat Mayurī and Ngaosyvathn Pheuiphanh, *Paths to Conflagration: Fifty Years of Diplomacy and Warfare in Laos, Thailand, and Vietnam, 1778–1828* (Ithaca, NY: Southeast Asia Program, Cornell University, 1998).

103. Smuckarn and Breazeale, *A Culture in Search of Survival*, 9–11.

104. Ibid., 47–52.

105. Evans, *Last Century of Lao Royalty*, 260.

106. Mao Song Lyfoung, interview with author, Maplewood, Minnesota, June 18, 2002. The Hmong believe that mountains have veins (*mem toj*) that, when found and destroyed, shift the feng shui energy of locales so that good luck and prosperity dissipates from them. In this case, Mao Song is saying that the Chinese had to destroy the protective mountain veins before they could destroy Vaj Ncuab Lauj's kingdom.

107. Tougeu Lyfoung, interview with author, Champlin, Minnesota, July 3, 2003.

108. Nengher Vang, e-mail to author, December 15, 2014. Vang also talks about some of these politics in "Dreaming of Home, Dreaming of Land: Displacements and Hmong Transnational Politics, 1975–2010" (PhD diss., University of Minnesota, 2010).

109. Sure enough, I have witnessed individuals belonging to certain Hmong messianic groups in the United States now going around showing a map of Laos with a clearly delineated area that encompasses the ancient territory of Vaj Ncuab Laug, Xieng Khouang, which they claim as their autonomous state.

110. For a reference, see Edward Hull, *The Wall Chart of World History* (London: Bracken Books, 1988).

111. Vang Pao, interview with author, Westminster, California, April 15, 2004.

112. Prince Saykham notes this unstated tension in his memoir, describing how he snubbed King Sisavangvong and Prince Souvannarath when they attempted to match him up with a princess of their royal line in 1947. See Evans, *Last Century of Lao Royalty*, 264.

113. See, Smuckarn and Breazeale, *A Culture in Search of Survival.*

114. Ibid., 47–52.

115. Ibid., 57.

116. Evans, *Last Century of Lao Royalty*, 262.

117. Frank M. Lebar, Gerald C. Hickey, John K. Musgrave, *Ethnic Groups of Mainland Southeast Asia* (New Haven, CT: Human Relations Area Files Press, 1964), 73.

118. Geoffrey C. Gunn, "Shamans and Rebels: The Batchai (Meo) Rebellion of Northern Laos and North-West Vietnam (1918–21)," *Journal of the Siam Society* 74 (1986): 111.

119. Michaud, "Montagnards," 338.

120. Failler, "Đèo Family of Lai Châu," 48.

121. Ibid., 52–53.

122. Auguste Louise M. Bonifacy, "L'interrogatoire de Hung Me Giang (Siung Mi Tchang)," May 31–June 2, 1912 (Centres des Archives d'Outre Mer in Aix-en-Province [hereafter CAOM] Tonkin 56485).

123. Yang, "The Hmong," 264.

124. Keith Quincy, *Hmong: History of a People*, 2nd ed. (Cheney: Eastern Washington University, 1995), 60–61.

125. McCoy, Read, and Adams, *Politics of Heroin*, 116.

126. Yang, "The Hmong," 264–65.

127. Smuckarn and Breazeale, *A Culture in Search of Survival*, 3.

128. Lyfoung, *Tub Npis Lisfoom Tej Lus Tseg Cia*, 6.

129. According to Touby and Tougeu Lyfoung, the word *kaitong* originated from the Vietnamese. McCoy states, however, that Ly Nhia Vu's family claims that the word means "little king" or "prince" and was imported from China. A relative, Youa Xa, already had this title before the Ly clan arrived in Laos. My informant, Ly Na Jalao, a living member of Ly clan, confirmed McCoy's finding to me in 2004. Dr. Bruce Thowpaou Bliatout, a Hmong health care provider in Oregon, in a Hmong e-mail discussion forum in 2003, speculated that the word *kaitong* is much more recent, being derived from the French word *canton*, as in the phrase "chief of canton." This argument seems logical as there is close pronunciation between the two words. Moreover, Tai leaders in Tonkin also carried this title. As stated to McCoy and to me by Ly Na Jalao, the Lys may have applied the word retrospectively to their clan leader in China. If so, the fact only highlights how prestigious the title was perceived to be by the Hmong—so much so that it was even applied retroactively to a prior historical period. For Touby's view, see Lyfoung, *Tub Npis Lisfoom Tej Lus Tseg Cia*, 6–7. For McCoy's findings, see McCoy, Read, and Adams, *Politics of Heroin*, 121–22. I have also drawn on Tougeu Lyfoung, interviews with author, Herblay, France, July 10, 2002, and Champlin, Minnesota, July 3, 2003; and Ly Na Jalao, interview with author, Toulouse, France, July 13, 2002.

130. Yang Dao, *Hmong at the Turning Point*, ed. Jeanne L. Blake (Minneapolis: WorldBridge Associates, 1993), 25, 33n32.

131. Ly Na Jalao, interview with author, Toulouse, France, July 13, 2002. Touby also confirms the exchange of rhinoceros horns, talismans, and silver for titles in Lyfoung, *Tub Npis Lisfoom Tej Lus Tseg Cia*, 7.

132. The origins and meanings of these honorific titles are as vague as those of the word *kaitong*.

133. Yang, *Hmong at the Turning Point*, 25.

134. For works on opium cultivation among the Hmong, see McCoy, Read, and Adams, *Politics of Heroin*; Alfred W. McCoy, *The Politics of Heroin: CIA Complicity in the Global Drug Trade* (Brooklyn, NY: Lawrence Hill Books, 1991); Geddes, *Migrants of the Mountains*; and Joseph Westermeyer, *Poppies, Pipes, and People: Opium and Its Use in Laos* (Berkeley: University of California Press, 1983).

135. Westermeyer, *Poppies, Pipes, and People*, 43.

136. For a discussion of the debates around adoption of the *quoc ngu* system, see Hue-Tam Ho Tai, *Radicalism and the Origins of the Vietnamese Revolution* (Cambridge, MA: Harvard University Press, 1992), 10–56.

137. Milton Osborne, *River Road to China: The Mekong River Expedition, 1866–1873* (New York: Liveright, 1975), 99.

138. Milton Osborne, *The Mekong: Turbulent Past, Uncertain Future* (New York: Grove Press, 2000), 108.

139. See the accounts of Auguste Pavie and Prince Henri d'Orleans, translated in Evans, *Last Century of Lao Royalty*, 45–51; and Failler, "The Đèo Family of Lai Châu," 45–46.

140. Martin Stuart-Fox, *A History of Laos* (Cambridge: Cambridge University Press, 1997), 22.

141. According to Jean Michaud the French did establish relations with several "Hmong Kings" in Tonkin. The one "king" in Ha Giang built a huge mansion that still stands today as a tourist attraction. Jean Michaud, e-mail to author, May 1, 2014. See also the official Vietnamese government website about the Hmong king's palace, http://www.vietnamspirittravel.vn/guide/hmong_king_palace_ha_giang.htm, and http://vi.wikipedia.org/wiki/Vua_M%C3%A8o.

142. George Condominas, "Aspects of a Minority Problem in Indochina," *Pacific Affairs* 24, no. 1 (1951): 80.

143. John T. McAlister Jr., "Mountain Minorities and the Viet Minh: A Key to the Indochina War," in *Southeast Asian Tribes, Minorities, and Nations*, 2 vols., ed. Peter Kunstadter (Princeton, NJ: Princeton University Press, 1967), 2:808.

144. Ibid.

145. Claes Corlin, "Hmong and the Land Question in Vietnam: National Policy and Local Concepts of the Environment," in *Hmong/Miao in Asia*, ed. Nicholas Tapp, Jean Michaud, Christian Culas, and Gary Y. Lee (Chiangmai, Thailand: Silkworm Books, 2004), 299–300.

146. Alfred W. McCoy, "French Colonialism in Laos, 1893–1945," in *Laos: War and Revolution*, ed. Nina S. Adams and Alfred W. McCoy (New York: Harper and Row, 1970), 80.

147. Auguste Louise M. Bonifacy, "Rapport sur les Faits Reprochés au Nommé Hung Me Giang (Prononciation Meo, Siung Me Chang)," June 13, 1912 (CAOM Tonkin 56485); and Dorey, "Rapport d'Ensemble du Chef de Bataillon Dorey sur les Opérations du Détachement du Laos pendant l'Hiver 1920–21 et sur la Pacification de la Region Nord de la Province de Luang Prabang," 1921 (Service Historique de l'Armée de Terre [hereafter SHAT] Vincennes).

148. McCoy, *Politics of Heroin*, 110.

149. Ibid., 111.

150. Westermeyer, *Pipes, Poppies, and People*, 45.

151. James C. Scott, *The Art of Not Being Governed: An Anarchist History of Upland Southeast Asia* (New Haven, CT: Yale University Press, 2009).

152. McCoy, *Politics of Heroin*; Yang, *Hmong at the Turning Point*, 36.

153. Ly Na Jalao, interview with author, Toulouse, France, July 13, 2002. According to Ly Na, before she passed away at an advanced age of eighty-two in France in 1980 his mother left a cassette recording detailing the events that he recalled to me. His mother heard the accounts of these events directly from her father-in-law, Ja Lao, and Nhia Vu. Nhia Vu and Ja Lao both lived to be about a hundred years old, dying in 1930 and 1932, respectively. When Ly Na's mother married into the Ly family in the late 1920s, both men were still alive but physically debilitated due to age. Ly Na's father, the son of Ja Lao, was an opium addict, so he often spent time smoking opium with the two old men who could no longer work in the fields. In 1927 Ly Na's mother heard the two old men reminiscing about these events many times after she gave birth to her second-eldest son and was confined to the house for thirty days in accordance with Hmong custom. During her confinement month, she slept near the hearth and cared for her newborn, as her two in-laws, who were puffing opium with her husband nearby, recounted these tales and bemoaned how their Ly clan had lost power to the Lo and Moua clans. "Lam paub li xub laus" (If we had only known then), they sighed to one another nostalgically between puffs of smoke, wishing they could redo history. For another description of the 1896 rebellion, see Yang, *Hmong at the Turning Point*, 36. For Hmong childbirth practices and the confinement of women for thirty days after giving birth, see Patricia V. Symonds, *Calling in the Soul: Gender and the Cycle of Life in a Hmong Village* (Seattle: University of Washington Press, 2004); and Pranee Liamputtong, *Hmong Women and Reproduction* (Westport, CT: Bergin and Garvey, 2000).

154. Charles Achaimbault, "Les Annales de l'Ancien Royaume de S'ieng Khwang," *Bulletin de l'École Française d'Extrême Orient* 53, no. 2 (1967): 595–96; Yang, *Hmong at the Turning Point*, 36.

155. Ly Na Jalao, interview with author, Toulouse, France, July 13, 2002.

156. Lyfoung, *Tub Npis Lisfoom Tej Lus Cia*, 10.

157. The impetus for the Hmong conversion to Christianity, for example, included the prediction that they would then gain the protection of a more powerful god, who would ward off the Lao's black magic, allowing the Hmong to live in the lowlands. See Paoze Thao, *Keebkwm Hmoob Ntseeg Yexus: Hmong Christian History, 1950–2000* (Thornton, CO: Hmong District, 2000), 57.

158. Ly Na Jalao, interview with author, Toulouse, France, July 13, 2002.

Chapter 2. A Chronology of Two Rebellions
(1910–1912 and 1918–1921)

1. Yang Dao, a native of Ha Giang, has told me on several occasions that the village of Meo Vac, the locale of Mi Chang's rebellion, was founded by his great-grandfather in the nineteenth century. Yang's ancestral home, a large dwelling made of granite, still stands in the village as a national historic site. Yang said further that Num Suav Hawj, a Hmong elder from Ha Giang who now lives in the United States, told him that the

name Meo Vac, or Meo Vang (Hmong King), came into existence because lowland merchants called Yang's great-grandfather a wealthy and influential man, the "Hmong king." By extension, these traders who rested at the Yang domicile referred to the site as the "Village of the Hmong King." Yang Dao, however, did not seem to be familiar with the intricacies of Mi Chang's rebellion. Yang Dao's family, whose members found themselves on the side of the French during the First Indochina War, moved to Laos in 1954. In May 2013, he obtained permission from the Vietnamese government to visit his native home. He has shown me videos of his tour through Ha Giang, accompanied by guards; state officials; Vuong Duy Quang, a Hmong researcher at the Academy of Social Sciences in Hanoi; and a Vietnamese television crew, which documented his return.

2. The Vietnamese historian Lam Tam records Hmong rebellions in 1904, 1911 [1910?], 1917 [1918?], 1925, 1936, and 1943, but the two of interest here are the major ones recorded by the French, which have messianic overtones characterized by the emergence of a prophet leader. See Lam Tam, "A Survey of the Meo," *Vietnamese Studies* 9, no. 36 (1974).

3. Auguste Louise M. Bonifacy, "Rapport sur les Faits Reprochés au Nommé Hung Me Giang (Prononciation Meo, Siung Me Chang)," June 13, 1912 (CAOM Tonkin 56485).

4. French colonial reports inconsistently refer to this 1860 rebel leader as Hung Dai, Chiong Ta, or Chiong Tai. I chose to Anglicize his name as Xiong Tai.

5. French reports inconsistently refer to this man as Hung Me Giang (Hung being the Vietnamese pronunciation of Xiong), Chiong Mi Tchang, Siung Mi Chang, Soung My Tchang, or Sou Mi Tchang. The name Hung Me Giang appears most often in the colonial reports. For consistency I use Xiong as the clan name and keep Mi Chang as his personal name. Christian Culas also employs this convention in his works. See Christian Culas, "Le Messianisme Hmong" (PhD diss., Université de Provence-Aix-Marseille I, 1998); "Innovation and Tradition in Rituals and Cosmology: Hmong Messianism and Shamanism in Southeast Asia," in *Hmong/Miao in Asia*, edited by Nicholas Tapp, Jean Michaud, Christian Culas, and Gary Yia Lee (Chiangmai, Thailand: Silkworm Books, 2004); and *Le Messianisme Hmong aux XIXe et XXe Siècles: La Dynamique Religieuse comme Instrument Politique* (Paris: Éditions du Centre National de le Recherche Scientifique, 2005).

6. Colonial sources co-opt the titles given here (*tri phu, ma phai, binh dao, chanh quan, chung cha*). I presume these words are native in origin, but as they were written without Vietnamese diacritics, I could not find anyone I know who was familiar with them, so have left them without translation. Jean Michaud thinks these may be local indigenous terms that may combine Vietnamese, Tai (multiple dialects), and even Chinese languages. Jeans Michaud, e-mail to author, May 1, 2014.

7. Auguste Louise M. Bonifacy, "L'Interrogatoire de Hung Me Giang (Siung Mi Tchang)," May 31–June 2, 1912 (CAOM Tonkin 56485).

8. Ibid.

9. Mortreuil, "Lieutenant-Colonel Mortreuil Commandant de 3e Territoire Militaire à Monsieur le Résident Supérieur au Tonkin," February 26, 1911 (CAOM Indochine 37850).

10. Hair has long been a symbol of political protest for Hmong messianic groups. Pa Kao Her, the messianic leader who has led the Hmong against the Lao PDR from 1975 to 2002, said his men leave their hair long to express their deep disillusionment with the state. Pa Kao Her, interview with author, Chiangrai, Thailand, August 15, 2000. The Chinese state often dictated male hairstyles, so Hmong men may have picked up this form of protest from Chinese tradition. Dorothy Ko discusses this issue in *Cinderella's Sisters: A Revisionist History of Footbinding* (Berkeley: University of California Press, 2005), 51.

11. Mortreuil, "Lieutenant-Colonel Mortreuil," February 26, 1911.

12. The detail about the women being "equipped with fans" is important and evokes the imagery of the legendary Nkauj Ntxuam (Lady of the Fan), whose appearance portends the reconsolidation of the ancient Hmong kingdom, discussed in chapter 1.

13. Mortreuil, "Lieutenant-Colonel Mortreuil," February 26, 1911.

14. Ibid.

15. Ibid.

16. Bonifacy, "Rapport sur les Faits Reprochés."

17. Ibid.

18. Ibid.

19. Bonifacy, "L'Interrogatoire de Hung Me Giang."

20. Mortreuil, "A. S. des Renseignements Recueillis sur les Agissements des Meos," August 28, 1911 (CAOM Indochine 56484).

21. Colonna Report, August 4, 1911 (CAOM Indochine 56484).

22. Bonifacy, "L'Interrogatoire de Hung Me Giang."

23. Bonifacy, "Rapport sur les Faits Reprochés."

24. Auguste Louise M. Bonifacy, "Lettre au Résident Supérieur au Tonkin," May 26, 1913 (COAM Indochine 56485); Governor General, "Decree of Governor General of Indochina," May 2, 1913 (CAOM Indochine 56485).

25. Perriex, "Lettre de Quang Yen au Résident Supérieur au Tonkin," January 22, 1914 (COAM Indochine 56485); Perriex, "Lettre de Quang Yen au Résident Supérieur au Tonkin," February 26, 1914 (CAOM Indochine 56485).

26. Governor General, "Decree on Behalf of Governor General by Van Vollenhoven," February 28, 1914 (COAM Indochine 56485); Perriex, "Note Postale de Quang-Yen au Résident Supérieur au Tonkin," April 30, 1914 (COAM Indochine 56485).

27. Geoffrey C. Gunn, "Shamans and Rebels: The Batchai (Meo) Rebellion of Northern Laos and North-West Vietnam (1918–21)," *Journal of the Siam Society* 74 (1986).

28. Robert Darrah Jenks, *Insurgency and Social Disorder in Guizhou: The "Miao" Rebellion, 1854–1873* (Honolulu: University of Hawai'i Press, 1994); David G. Atwill, *The Chinese Sultanate: Islam, Ethnicity, and the Panthay Rebellion in Southwest China, 1856–1873* (Stanford, CA: Stanford University Press, 2005).

29. Saint-Chaffray, "Rapport à Monsieur le Governeur Général 'A. S. du Movement Meo de Lai Chau et Sonla (1919),'" February 10, 1919 (SHAT Vincennes). Geoffrey C. Gunn also lays out some of the chronology of this revolt in *Rebellion in Laos: Peasants and Politics in a Colonial Backwater* (Boulder, CO: Westview Press, 1990), 153-57; and "Shamans and Rebels."

30. Jonathan D. Spence, *God's Chinese Son: The Taiping Heavenly Kingdom of Hong Xiuquan* (New York: W. W. Norton, 1996).

31. Saint-Chaffray, "Rapport à Monsieur le Governeur Général."

32. Yang Zhiqiang, "From *Miao* to *Miaozu*: Alterity in the Formation of Modern Ethnic Groups," *Hmong Studies Journal* 10 (2009): 8.

33. Saint-Chaffray, "Rapport à Monsieur le Governeur Général."

34. Ibid.

35. Ibid.

36. Ibid.

37. Ibid.

38. Ibid.

39. Michael Adas, *Prophets of Rebellion: Millenarian Protest Movements against the European Colonial Order* (Chapel Hill: University of North Carolina Press, 1979).

40. Saint-Chaffray, "Rapport à Monsieur le Governeur Général."

41. Ibid.

42. Angeli, "Rapport du Colonel Angeli, Directeur des Opérations du Haut-Laos, au Général Commandant Supérieur des Troupes de l'Indochine, au Sujet des Opération Entreprises dans le Haut-Laos contre les Meos," May 25, 1920 (SHAT Vincennes).

43. Saint-Chaffray, "Rapport à Monsieur le Governeur Général."

44. Ibid.

45. Txooj Tsawb Yaj, *Rog Paj Cai* (Vientiane: Y. Bertrais, 1972), 32.

46. At the end of World War II, this rugged landscape still remained uncharted. When Maurice Gauthier and his Free French commandos parachuted into Laos in 1945, their cover story was that they were geological surveyors sent to map this impenetrable region. See Jane Hamilton-Merritt, *Tragic Mountains: The Hmong, the Americans, and the Secret Wars for Laos, 1942-1992* (Bloomington: Indiana University Press, 1993), 25.

47. Dorey, "Rapport d'Ensemble du Chef de Bataillon Dorey sur les Opérations du Détachement du Laos pendant l'Hiver, 1920-21, et sur la Pacification de la Region Nord de la Province de Luang Prabang," 1921 (SHAT Vincennes).

48. Ibid.

49. See Nicholas Tapp, "The Impact of Missionary Christianity upon Marginalized Ethnic Minorities: The Case of the Hmong," *Journal of Southeast Asian Studies* 20, no. 1 (1989).

50. The campaign against Hmong rebels in Tran Ninh (Xieng Khouang) in the winter of 1919-20 will be addressed separately in a later section due to its unique nature, which involved violence against Lo Blia Yao, a close friend of Colonel Henri Roux and an ally of the colonial administration.

51. Angeli, "Rapport du Colonel Angeli."

52. Dorey, "Rapport d'Ensemble du Chef de Bataillon Dorey." Unless otherwise noted, the following description of the campaigns against Pa Chay is derived from this report. To avoid a clutter of notes, I will cite only specific quotes from Dorey's report and other sources.

53. Ibid.

54. Ibid.

55. Ibid.

56. Ibid.

57. Ibid.

58. Ibid.

59. Ibid.

60. Ibid.

61. Gunn, *Rebellion in Laos*, 156–57.

62. Images of these gruesomely decapitated heads can be viewed in the documentary by Richard Ellison, Andrew Pearson, Martin Smith, and Will Lyman, "Roots of a War," in *Vietnam, a Television History*, disc 1 (Boston: WGBH Boston Video, 2004), DVD.

Chapter 3. Messianism as a Quest for the Mandate of Heaven

1. Franz Michael, *The Taiping Rebellion: History and Documents* (Seattle: University of Washington Press, 1966); Jonathan D. Spence, *God's Chinese Son: The Taiping Heavenly Kingdom of Hong Xiuquan* (New York: W. W. Norton, 1996); Thomas H. Reilly, *The Taiping Heavenly Kingdom: Rebellion and the Blasphemy of Empire* (Seattle: University of Washington Press, 2004).

2. Jean Lartéguy and Yang Dao, *La Fabuleuse Aventure du Peuple de l'Opium* (Paris: Presses de la Cité, 1979).

3. Auguste Louise M. Bonifacy, "L'Interrogatoire de Hung Me Giang (Siung Mi Tchang)," May 31–June 2, 1912 (CAOM Tonkin 56485). Unless otherwise noted, the information on Mi Chang's revolt is derived from this report. I cite this report again only when there is a direct quotation.

4. Mortreuil, "Le Lieutenant-Colonel Mortreuil Commandant de 3e Territoire Militaire à Monsieur le Résident Supérieur au Tonkin," February 26, 1911 (CAOM Indochine 37850).

5. Bonifacy, "L'Interrogatoire de Hung Me Giang."

6. See Yves Bertrais, *Kab Ke Pam Tuag: Cov Zaj* (Guyane, France: Association Communauté Hmong, 1986).

7. Christian Culas, "Le Messianisme Hmong" (PhD diss., Université de Provence-Aix-Marseille I, 1998).

8. Bonifacy, "L'Interrogatoire de Hung Me Giang."

9. Peter Zinoman notes that the high number of prisoner deaths resulted from "a combination of poor food, inadequate sanitation, unresponsive medical services, overcrowding, and overwork." Peter Zinoman, *The Colonial Bastille: A History of Imprisonment in Vietnam, 1862–1940* (Berkeley: University of California Press, 2001), 96.

10. Governor General, "Decree on Behalf of Governor General by Van Vollenhoven," February 28, 1914 (CAOM Indochine 56485).

11. Robert G. Cooper, *Resource Scarcity and the Hmong Response: Patterns of Settlement and Economy in Transition* (Singapore: National University of Singapore Press, 1984), 137.

12. Ritual masters are highly respected in Hmong society. When people ask them to perform services, they must kowtow and offer them payments in money and cigars to show respect, and they must formally declare that they will be indebted to the masters for life. For protocols on how to ask a ritual master to perform marriage, death, and healing ceremonies, see Yves Bertrais, *Kab Ke Pam Tuag: Cov Txheej Txheem* (Guyane, France: Association Communauté Hmong, 1985), and *Kab Tshoob Kev Kos: Liaj Lwg Tus Cag Txuj, Rhwv Mws Tus Cag Peev* (Guyane, France: Association Communauté Hmong, 1985).

13. Michael Adas, *Prophets of Rebellion: Millenarian Protest Movements against the European Colonial Order* (Chapel Hill: University of North Carolina Press, 1979); Spence, *God's Chinese Son*.

14. Bonifacy, "L'Interrogatoire de Hung Me Giang."

15. Christian Culas, "Innovation and Tradition in Rituals and Cosmology: Hmong Messianism and Shamanism in Southeast Asia," in *Hmong/Miao in Asia*, ed. Nicholas Tapp, Jean Michaud, Christian Culas, and Gary Yia Lee (Chiangmai: Silkworm Books, 2004).

16. For details about Hmong healing beliefs and practices, see Dia Cha, *Hmong American Concepts of Health, Healing, and Conventional Medicine* (New York: Routledge, 2003); Anne Fadiman, *The Spirit Catches You and You Fall Down: A Hmong Child, Her American Doctors, and the Collision of Two Cultures* (New York: Farrar, Straus and Giroux, 1997); Paja Thao, Dwight Conquergood, and Xa Thao, *I Am a Shaman: A Hmong Life Story with Ethnographic Commentary*, Southeast Asian Refugee Studies Occasional Papers, no. 8 (Minneapolis: Southeast Asian Refugee Studies Project, Center for Urban and Regional Affairs, University of Minnesota, 1989); and Jacques Lemoine, "The (H)mong Shamans' Power of Healing: Sharing the Esoteric Knowledge of a Great (H)mong Shaman," *Hmong Studies Journal* 12 (2011): 1–36.

17. Thao, Conquergood, and Thao, *I Am a Shaman*, 47.

18. Bonifacy, "L'Interrogatoire de Hung Me Giang."

19. Ibid.

20. Savina, *Histoire des Miao* (Hong Kong: Imprimerie de la Société des Missions-Étrangères, 1924), 259.

21. Mortreuil, "Le Lieutenant-Colonel Mortreuil," February 26, 1911.

22. Bonifacy, "Rapport sur les Faits Reprochés au Nommé Hung Me Giang (Prononciation Meo, Siung Me Chang)," June 13, 1912 (CAOM Tonkin 56485).

23. Bonifacy, "L'Interrogatoire de Hung Me Giang."

24. Bonifacy, "Rapport sur les Faits Reprochés."

25. Dorothy Ko, *Cinderella's Sisters: A Revisionist History of Footbinding* (Berkeley: University of California Press, 2005), 51.

26. Manchu hair fashions were so enduring among the Hmong that men such as Lo Blia Yao, who was several generations removed from China, continued to shave their crowns and wear a queue in the back.

27. Pa Kao Her, interview with author, Chiangrai, Thailand, August 15, 2001.

28. Lee Cha Yia was a *chao fa* (lord of the sky) military leader in the mountains of Laos during those years. He wore his hair long, he said, because when he served in Vang Pao's army he observed that the Lao soldiers under his command left their hair long so that they would be invulnerable to bullets. The Hmong *chao fa* emulated these Lao, keeping their hair long for the same reason. Evidently the political symbolism of long hair has now conveniently merged with Lao beliefs of invulnerability. Lee Cha Yia, interview with author, Saint Paul, Minnesota, January 3, 2002.

29. Yan Riyu's statement is quoted in Robert Jenks, *Insurgency and Social Disorder in Guizhou: The "Miao" Rebellion, 1854–1873* (Honolulu: University of Hawai'i Press, 1994), 34.

30. Adas, *Prophets of Rebellion.*

31. Emile Lunet de Lajonquiere, *Ethnographie du Tonkin Septentrionale (Rédigé sur l'Ordre de M. P. Beau, Gouverneur Général de l'Indo-Chine Française, d'après les Études des Administrateurs Civils et Militaire des Provinces Septentrionales)* (Hanoi: E. Leroux, 1906), 299–300. See also Culas, "Le Messianisme Hmong," 219; and Nicholas Tapp, *Sovereignty and Rebellion: The White Hmong of Northern Thailand* (Singapore: Oxford University Press, 1989), 139–40.

32. Maurice Abadie, *Les Races du Haut-Tonkin de Phong-Tho à Lang-Son* (Paris: Société d'éditions géographiques, maritimes et coloniales, 1924), 150; Édouard Jacques Joseph Diguet, *Les Montagnards du Tonkin* (New York: AMS Press, 1981), 129–30.

33. Mortreuil, "Le Lieutenant-Colonel Mortreuil," February 26, 1911.

34. Bonifacy, "L'Interrogatoire de Hung Me Giang."

35. Ibid.

36. Ibid.

37. Ibid.

38. Ibid.

39. See, for example, Geoffrey C. Gunn, *Rebellion in Laos: Peasants and Politics in a Colonial Backwater* (Boulder, CO: Westview Press, 1990).

40. Christian Culas addresses the cultural elements of five messianic movements in the twentieth century, but he does not deal specifically with the issue of how the Hmong remember Pa Chay's rebellion either. See Culas, "Le Messianisme Hmong."

41. Txooj Tsawb Yaj, *Rog Paj Cai* (Vientiane: Y. Bertrais, 1972).

42. For Yang Shong Lue's assassination by contingents loyal to Vang Pao in February 1971, see William A. Smalley, Chia Koua Vang, and Gnia Yee Yang, *Mother of Writing: The Origin and Development of a Hmong Messianic Script* (Chicago: University of Chicago Press, 1990).

43. Culas, "Le Messianisme Hmong," 108; Smalley, Vang, and Yang, *Mother of Writing.* See also the legend of Tswb Tshoj in Tapp, *Sovereignty and Rebellion,* 131–34.

44. Tsia Long Thao, talk given to a Southeast Asian Studies Summer Institute Hmong language class, University of Wisconsin–Madison, July 27, 2004. Information was also supplied by Ka Houa Yang, personal communication, May 22, 2000.

45. Yang Dao, *Hmong at the Turning Point,* ed. Jeanne L. Blake (Minneapolis: WorldBridge Associates, 1993), 38.

46. Jean Lartéguy and Yang Dao, *La Fabuleuse Aventure du Peuple de l'Opium* (Paris: Presses de la Cité, 1979), 99.

47. Keith Quincy, *Hmong: History of a People* (Cheney: Eastern Washington University Press, 1988), 122.

48. Isabelle Alleton, "Les Hmong aux Confins de la Chine et du Vietnam: La Revolte du 'Fou' (1918-1921)," in *Histoire de l'Asie du Sud-Est: Révoltes, Réformes, Révolutions,* ed. Robert Aarsse and Pierre Brocheux (Lille, France: Presses Universitaires de Lille, 1981), 35.

49. Geoffrey C. Gunn, "Shamans and Rebels: The Batchai (Meo) Rebellion of Northern Laos and North-West Vietnam (1918-21)," *Journal of the Siam Society* 74 (1986): 114.

50. Angeli, "Rapport du Colonel Angeli, Directeur des Opérations du Haut-Laos, au Général Commandant Supérieur des Troupes de l'Indochine, au Sujet des Opération Entreprises dans le Haut-Laos contre les Meos," May 25, 1920 (SHAT Vincennes).

51. Both the French and Chinese summarily executed the rebels. See Angeli, "Rapport du Colonel Angeli"; Dorey, "Rapport d'Ensemble du Chef de Bataillon Dorey sur les Opérations du Détachement du Laos pendant l'Hiver 1920–21 et sur la Pacification de la Region Nord de la Province de Luang Prabang," 1921 (SHAT Vincennes); and Lartéguy and Yang, *Fabuleuse Aventure,* 103. For French reports of executions of Hmong by Chinese authorities, see Alleton, "Les Hmong aux Confins de la Chine," 33.

52. Dorey, "Rapport d'Ensemble du Chef de Bataillon Dorey."

53. Angeli, "Rapport du Colonel Angeli."

54. Alleton, "Les Hmong aux Confins de la Chine," 36; Lartéguy and Yang, *Fabuleuse Aventure,* 102–3.

55. For examples of these legends, see Charles Johnson and Se Yang, *Dab Neeg Hmoob: Myths, Legends, and Folk Tales from the Hmong of Laos,* 2nd ed. (Saint Paul, MN: Linguistics Department, Macalester College, 1992), 127–99; and Nicholas Tapp, *The Hmong of China: Context, Agency, and the Imaginary* (Leiden: Brill, 2001), 439–43.

56. Tapp, *Sovereignty and Rebellion,* 131–35.

57. Ibid., 141.

58. McCoy, *Politics of Heroin*, 117; Touxa Lyfoung, *Tub Npis Lisfoom Tes Lus Tseg Cia* [Words left by Touby Lyfoung] (Minneapolis, MN: Burgess Publishing, 1996), 14–15.

59. Tapp, *Sovereignty and Rebellion*, 142.

60. Yaj, *Rog Paj Cai*, 5.

61. Savina, *Histoire des Miao*.

62. The similar roles of the shaman and the messianic figure are the main focus of Culas, "Innovation and Tradition."

63. Yaj, *Rog Paj Cai*, 5.

64. The word *niag*, or *niam*, translates as "main" or "big," but it also carries the literal connotation of "mother," such as in the term *niam dej*, "mother/main river," and also *niam ntawv*, "mother of writing," the appellation used to refer to Yang Shong Lue, the inventor of the *phaj hauj* messianic script of the Hmong language.

65. Yaj, *Rog Paj Cai*, 6.

66. For details on the way shamans are chosen, see Thao, Conquergood, and Thao, *I Am a Shaman*. Messianic leaders are also chosen without their say. For the most prominent case, see Smalley, Vang, and Yang, *Mother of Writing*.

67. Colonel Henri Roux was struck by how much the Hmong loved their animals. See Henri Roux and Tran Van Chu, "Quelques Minorités Ethniques du Nord-Indochine," *France-Asie*, nos. 92–93 (1954).

68. Yang Shong Lue was also purported to be one of the seven Sons of God. See Smalley, Vang, and Yang, *Mother of Writing*.

69. Xinzhong Yao, *An Introduction to Confucianism* (New York: Cambridge University Press, 2000), 167.

70. The Hmong consider patience a necessary virtue in a leader. In a story recorded by Tapp, Heaven granted a certain leader seventy years in which to rule, but "he was unable to reign very long because of his impatience." Tapp, *Sovereignty and Rebellion*, 132. As will be demonstrated later in this chapter, Hmong impatience led to the ultimate failure of Pa Chay.

71. Yaj, *Rog Paj Cai*, 11.

72. Ibid., 7.

73. Ibid., 7–8.

74. R. Alison Lewis, "The A Hmao in Northeast Yunnan and Northwest Guizhou Provinces: Perspectives on the Encounter with the A Hmao from Some Western Protestant Missionaries (Initial Commentary on Diaries Written by Reverend Samuel Pollard, 1910–14)," in *Hmong/Miao in Asia*, ed. Nicholas Tapp, Jean Michaud, Christian Culas, and Gary Yia Lee (Chiangmai, Thailand: Silkworm Books, 2004), 229.

75. Xiong Mi Chang's incorporation of Buddhist elements into his movement is revealed in his responses during his interrogation in 1912. See Bonifacy, "L'Interrogatoire de Hung Me Giang."

76. For Hmong healing practices, see Cha, *Hmong American Concepts of Health*.

77. An inconsistency emerges later on in the story, as the narrator describes Pa Chay's firearm, which was presented to the French along with his head, as being a fifteen-shot rifle. See Yaj, *Rog Paj Cai*, 24.

78. See Bertrais, *Kab Ke Pam Tuag: Cov Zaj*.

79. See Nicholas Tapp, "The Impact of Missionary Christianity upon Marginalized Ethnic Minorities: The Case of the Hmong," *Journal of Southeast Asian Studies* 20, no. 1 (1989): 75, and *Sovereignty and Rebellion*, 121–30.

80. Dorey, "Rapport d'Ensemble du Chef de Bataillon Dorey."

81. Smalley, Vang, and Yang, *Mother of Writing*.

82. Pa Kao Her, interview with author, Chiangrai, Thailand, August 15, 2001.

83. Yaj, *Rog Paj Cai*, 9.

84. Ibid.

85. Ibid., 10.

86. Vang Pao, interview with author, Maplewood, Minnesota, April 8, 2004.

87. Yaj, *Rog Paj Cai*, 12.

88. Tapp, "Impact of Missionary Christianity," 121–30; Tapp, *Sovereignty and Rebellion*, 75; Pa Kao Her, interview with author, Chiangrai, Thailand, August 15, 2001.

89. Culas argues that messianism can exist in peaceful times, during which there is no rebellion. See Culas, "Le Messianisme Hmong." Tapp calls this stage the "latent, or passive state." See Tapp, *Sovereignty and Rebellion*, 136.

90. Yaj, *Rog Paj Cai*, 16.

91. For Hmong weights and measurements, see Kao-Ly Yang, "Mesurer et Peser Chez les Hmong du Laos: Aspects Techniques et Notions de Précision," *Bulletin de l'École Française d'Extrême Orient* 90-91 (2004).

92. Yaj, *Rog Paj Cai*, 14.

93. Ibid.

94. Patricia V. Symonds, *Calling in the Soul: Gender and the Cycle of Life in a Hmong Village* (Seattle: University of Washington Press, 2004), x. See also Cha, *Hmong American Concepts of Health*.

95. Savina, *Histoire des Miao*, 252.

96. Yaj, *Rog Paj Cai*, 16–17.

97. Ibid., 17–18.

98. Ibid., 16–18.

99. Ibid., 11.

100. Ibid., 12.

101. Ibid., 12–14.

102. A French source cited by Geoffrey Gunn says the assassins were "Kha." See Gunn, *Rebellion in Laos*, 156–57. Yaj corroborates and says they were "Mab Daum" (Khmu).

103. Yaj, *Rog Paj Cai*, 21.

104. Dorey, "Rapport d'Ensemble du Chef de Bataillon Dorey."

105. It is believed that Lo Blia Yao, the Hmong chief in Xieng Khouang who was a target of the rebels, actively aided the French in hunting down Pa Chay's followers. Blia Yao is reputedly the one who divulged the secret that Pa Chay's powerful cannon was ineffective in the rain because its wick could not be lit. As a result, the French attacked in the rain, rendering Pa Chay's followers helpless. See Quincy, *Hmong*, 131.

106. Yaj, *Rog Paj Cai*, 23.

107. Ibid., 25.

108. Although it is not easy to guess the Hmong words from the French transliterations, Chin Minh seems to be "Tsim Meej," a name for Hmong males, which means "endowed with clarity."

109. Ibid.

Chapter 4. The Creation of a Supreme Hmong Chief (1900–1935)

1. For a description of marriage alliances among the Lao aristocracy, see Grant Evans, *The Last Century of Lao Royalty: A Documentary History* (Chiangmai, Thailand: Silkworm Books, 2009).

2. The title *kaitong* is equivalent to *tasseng*, a subdistrict chief, but according to Yang Dao, the title *kaitong* was no longer used for Hmong leaders after Pa Chay's War in 1921, having been replaced with *tasseng*. As Blia Yao was a leader during this transitional period, he retained the title *kaitong* and was referred to as Lo Kaitong until he died. He was perhaps the last Hmong *kaitong*. See Yang Dao, *Hmong at the Turning Point*, ed. Jeanne L. Blake (Minneapolis, MN: WorldBridge Associates, 1993).

3. Touxa Lyfoung, *Tub Npis Lisfoom Tej Lus Tseg Cia* [Words left by Touby Lyfoung] (Minneapolis, MN: Burgess Publishing, 1996), 147.

4. See Yan Riyu as quoted in Robert Darrah Jenks, *Insurgency and Social Disorder in Guizhou: The "Miao" Rebellion, 1854–1873* (Honolulu: University of Hawai'i Press, 1994), 34.

5. Mai Na M. Lee, "The Women of Dragon Capital (Long Cheng): Marriage Alliances and the Rise of Vang Pao," in *Claiming Place: Hmong Women, Power, and Knowledge Production*, ed. Chia Vang, Faith Nibbs, and Ma Vang (Minneapolis: University of Minnesota Press, forthcoming).

6. For a history of this system, see Jennifer Took, *A Native Chieftaincy in Southwest China: Franchising a Tai Chieftaincy under the Tusi System of Late Imperial China* (Leiden: Brill, 2005).

7. Mao Song Lyfoung, interview with author, Maplewood, Minnesota, October 18, 2002.

8. Ly Na Jalao, interview with author, Toulouse, France, July 13, 2002.

9. Ibid.; Mao Song Lyfoung, interview with author, Maplewood, Minnesota, October 18, 2002; Ger, interview with author, Vientiane, Lao PDR, March 15, 2008. I have no information about Pa Tsi's first wife or her clan affiliation.

10. Mao Song Lyfoung, interview with author, Maplewood, Minnesota, October 18, 2002.

11. Following the Paris Peace Accords in 1973, according to Yang Dao, Lo Fong, as the most educated Hmong on the left, sat on the National Political Consultative Council, a forty-two-member advisory body of the Provisional Government of National Union. Lo represented the Hmong communists while Yang represented the Hmong on the right. Yang Dao, personal communication, Brooklyn Park, Minnesota, 2007.

12. *Thao* is the Lao word for "mister," but over the years the Hmong have corrupted the Lao pronunciation to make it sound like the surname Thoj, hence they call him Thoj Tub Yaj instead of Thaub Tub Yaj. Sayasith L. Yangsao, personal communication, May 2003.

13. Thao Tou's relatives included Tasseng Cha Ger Yang, who was married to Touby Lyfoung's sister, and Po Zoua, who fled with Touby to Long Cheng. Sayasith L. Yangsao, interview with author, Brooklyn Park, Minnesota, October 25, 2002.

14. Sutdālā Yāthọ̄tū, *Tū Yā Saichū: Viraburut hǣng dǣn Lān Sāng* (Vianchian: Hōngphim Num Lāo, 2004). Because of these sacrifices, the Yang family is indisputably the most influential political family in the Lao PDR today. Thao Tou's daughter, Pany, a longtime member of the Central Committee, was twice elected (2006 and 2012) president of the Lao National Assembly. Moreover, when I traveled through Nong Het in 2008, the commander in charge of the region, CR7's latest guardian, was Colonel Chong Yang, a nephew of Thao Tou.

15. Sutdālā Yāthọ̄tū, *Tū Yā Saichū*, 16.

16. Keith Quincy, *Hmong: History of a People* (Cheney: Eastern Washington University Press, 1988), 57.

17. Ly Na Jalao, interview with author, Toulouse, France, July 13, 2002; Mao Song Lyfoung, interview with author, Maplewood, Minnesota, October 18, 2002.

18. Ly Na Jalao, interview with author, Toulouse, France, July 13, 2002.

19. Ibid.

20. Ly Tou Pao, interview with author, Fountain Valley, California, April 13, 2004.

21. Dia Yang, personal communication, November 24, 2005.

22. Mao Song Lyfoung, interview with author, Maplewood, Minnesota, October 18, 2002. It is customary for loyal Hmong followers to call their leaders "father," as I found out when I interviewed General Vang Pao. Members of his entourage, which surrounded us, called him *txiv* (father) while I called him *naiphon* (general). For this reason also, the legendary Chiyou's name is actually the word *txiv yawg* (grandfather) in Hmong rather than a personal name.

23. See Daniel McMahon, "Identity and Conflict on a Chinese Borderland: Yan Ruyi and the Recruitment of the Gelao during the 1795–97 Miao Revolt," *Late Imperial China* 23, no. 2 (2002).

24. See, for example, Robert Darrah Jenks, *Insurgency and Social Disorder in Guizhou: The "Miao" Rebellion, 1854–1873* (Honolulu: University of Hawai'i Press, 1994). This observation should not blur the serious grudge the Hmong of this period held

against the Chinese, however. As noted in chapter 1, Madame Ly Na kept her Han identity from her husband because she feared being ostracized. Ly Dra Pao, the father of Ly Foung, also suffered the stigma of affiliating with a Chinese merchant on his way down to Southeast Asia, as I will discuss in the following chapter.

25. Mao Song Lyfoung, interview with author, Maplewood, Minnesota, October 18, 2002.

26. Mao Song Lyfoung, interview with author, Maplewood, Minnesota, October 18, 2002; Tougeu Lyfoung, interview with author, Champlin, Minnesota, July 3, 2003; Yia S. Lor, "Power Struggle between the Lor and Ly Clans, 1900–2000" (undergraduate thesis, California State University, Chico, 2001), 8.

27. The husband of Pa Tsi's daughter revealed to her following Pa Tsi's assassination that his elder brother was the thief who had dug up the buried silver. Aggrieved that she had unwittingly married into the family that had played a role in her father's death but being unable to reveal the secret to anyone due to her divided loyalty, Pa Tsi's daughter determined to die. She believed like Hmong of the time did that if she buried a lock of her hair with her father's corpse he would take her soul and she would die. When she came to mourn her father, she secretly stuffed a lock of hair beneath his clothing. She did not die but, later, after her Moua husband had passed away and she had remarried into the Yang clan, she became debilitatingly ill. The shamans discerned that the lock of buried hair was the cause of the illness, and that the Yangs had to retrieve it. Once caught as the culprits who dug up Pa Tsi's grave, the Yangs had to explain their action, revealing finally the truth of the tragedy and exonerating Zong Cher. For a fuller description of this event, see Mai Na M. Lee, "The Dream of the Hmong Kingdom: Resistance, Collaboration, and Legitimacy under French Colonial Rule (1893–1954)" (PhD diss., University of Wisconsin–Madison, 2005), 145–51.

28. Tougeu Lyfoung, interview with author, Champlin, Minnesota, July 3, 2003.

29. See Lor, "Power Struggle," 40.

30. Mao Song Lyfoung, interview with author, Maplewood, Minnesota, October 18, 2002.

31. Lor, "Power Struggle," 12.

32. See Mai Na M. Lee, "The Thousand-Year Myth: Characterization of Hmong," *Journal of Hmong Studies* 2, no. 1 (1997).

33. Mao Song Lyfoung, interview with author, Maplewood, Minnesota, October 18, 2002.

34. Henri Roux and Tran Van Chu, "Quelques Minorités Ethniques du Nord-Indochine," *France-Asie*, nos. 92–93 (1954): 406.

35. Keith Quincy, *Harvesting Pa Chay's Wheat: The Hmong and America's Secret War in Laos* (Cheney: Eastern Washington University Press, 2000), 45; Keith Quincy, *Hmong: History of a People*, 2nd ed. (Cheney: Eastern Washington University, 1995) 125–26.

36. Mao Song Lyfoung, interview with author, Maplewood, Minnesota, October 18, 2002.

37. Roux and Chu, "Quelques Minorités Ethniques," 392.

38. Ibid., 397.

39. Ibid., 393.

40. The famous story of the woman who killed her husband's rooster to feed an official demonstrates how one woman's ingenuity brought her husband political recognition. See Nancy D. Donnelly, *Changing Lives of Refugee Hmong Women* (Seattle: University of Washington Press, 1994); and Charles Johnson and Se Yang, *Dab Neeg Hmoob: Myths, Legends, and Folk Tales from the Hmong of Laos*, 2nd ed. (Saint Paul, MN: Linguistics Department, Macalester College, 1992), 257–66.

41. Nkauj Nog is the Hmong equivalent of Cinderella, but the tale includes the life story of her mother, whose diligence makes her father a rich man, whereupon he takes a second wife. Eventually, the manipulative second wife maneuvers to have the hardworking first wife killed by having the husband turn the first wife into a sacrificial cow, thus bringing destitution to the man's household. Nkauj Nog, who is just as diligent as her mother, finds a suitable marriage to a young man, to the chagrin of her stepmother and stepsister. The story of Niam Nkauj Zuag Paj, on the other hand, tells of an orphan whose luck brings him to a dragon princess. She also makes him rich, but he takes a second wife who brings him only poverty. For the story of Nkauj Nog, see Jewell Reinhart Coburn, Tzexa Cherta Lee, and Anne Sibley O'Brien, *Jouanah, a Hmong Cinderella* (Arcadia, CA: Shen's Books, 1996). For the many different versions of the Niam Nkauj Zuag Paj story, see Johnson and Yang, *Dab Neeg Hmoob*, 127–228.

42. Colonel Ly Tou Pao, a direct descendent of Ly Nhia Vu, says that the village of Nong Khiaw had over two hundred households, all belonging to the Ly clan. This statistic is crucial when one considers that most Hmong villages of the period, which consisted mainly of one clan, had only twenty to thirty households. Ly Tou Pao, interview with author, Fountain Valley, California, April 13, 2004.

43. McCoy, *Politics of Heroin*, 117.

44. Mao Song Lyfoung, interview with author, Maplewood, Minnesota, October 18, 2002. In Hmong society, after a brother and sister are married and have children of their own, they show respect by addressing one another with the terms their children would use. Thus, Jer addressed Ly Foung as "dear uncle." Going by the Hmong's classificatory system, Ly Foung and Jer were a "brother" and "sister" from the same Ly clan.

45. Ibid. According to Mao Song, Hmong people of the period commonly addressed Jer as "Niam Npliaj Ntxawm" (Madame Blia Jer) because they combined the first part of Blia Yao's name, Blia, with her name, Jer. The fact that none of the other wives was called by Blia Yao's name further reflects the favoritism displayed by her husband.

46. Ibid.

47. Lor, "Power Struggle," 17; Ly Na Jalao, interview with author, Toulouse, France, July 13, 2002.

48. Lyfoung, *Tub Npis Lisfoom Tej Lus Tseg Cia*, 44. Touby Lyfoung, ever the cautious politician, did not specify in his memoir the reason why the French awarded

medals of commendation to Blia Yao and other Hmong leaders in 1921, but it is evident that it was a direct result of their roles in helping to put down Shong Ger's rebellion in 1920, bringing an end to Pa Chay's War in Laos. Moreover, according to Touby, Blia Yao ordered Ly Foung to go to Sam Neua when it came time to meet with the colonial administrators so that he would not be present at Xieng Khouang to receive the medal due him, and this became one of the many incidents that led to the eventual break between the two men.

49. Jane Hamilton-Merritt, *Tragic Mountains: The Hmong, the Americans, and the Secret Wars for Laos, 1942–1992* (Bloomington: Indiana University Press, 1993), 146; William James Lair (Colonel), interview with author, Menomonee Falls, Wisconsin, July 27, 2003.

50. Geoffrey C. Gunn, "Shamans and Rebels: The Batchai (Meo) Rebellion of Northern Laos and North-West Vietnam (1918–21)," *Journal of the Siam Society* 74 (1986): 113.

51. Jean Lartéguy and Yang Dao, *La Fabuleuse Aventure du Peuple de l'Opium* (Paris: Presses de la Cité, 1979), 99.

52. Lor, "Power Struggle," 13.

53. Roux and Chu, "Quelques Minorités Ethniques," 406.

54. Hugo Adolf Bernatzik, *Akha and Miao: Problems of Applied Ethnography in Farther India* (New Haven, CT: Human Relations Area Files, 1970), 47.

55. Shoua Yang, personal communication, Madison, Wisconsin, April 2005.

56. Mao Song Lyfoung, interview with author, Maplewood, Minnesota, October 18, 2002.

57. Quincy, *Hmong*, 2nd ed., 125–26.

58. Angeli, "Rapport du Colonel Angeli."

59. Snit Smuckarn and Kennon Breazeale, *A Culture in Search of Survival: The Phuan of Thailand and Laos* (New Haven, CT: Council on Southeast Asia Studies, Yale University, 1988), 3.

60. Roux and Chu, "Quelques Minorités Ethniques," 397.

61. Angeli, "Rapport du Colonel Angeli."

62. Ibid.

63. Ibid.

64. Ly Na Jalao, interview with author, Toulouse, France, July 13, 2002; Mao Song Lyfoung, interview with author, Saint Paul, Minnesota, October 2, 2004.

65. Frank M. Lebar, Gerald C. Hickey, and John K. Musgrave, *Ethnic Groups of Mainland Southeast Asia* (New Haven, CT: Human Relations Area Files, 1964), 74.

66. Quincy, *Hmong*, 2nd ed., 123.

67. Ibid., 126. This figure of three kip per day seems a bit too high for the period. Mao Song Lyfoung, whose father also engaged in road construction work, said the workers were paid *tsib npib*, or five centimes (half a piaster or half a silver kip), per day in the 1930s. As a teenager, Mao Song helped her father, Ly Foung, with the roadwork. She was in charge of measuring out an equivalent of the pay in opium to Hmong

workers. Mao Song Lyfoung, interview with author, Maplewood, Minnesota, June 18, 2003.

68. Lartéguy and Yang, *Fabuleuse Aventure*, 98; Mao Song Lyfoung, interview with author, Maplewood, Minnesota, June 18, 2003.

69. Lartéguy and Yang, *Fabuleuse Aventure*, 103.

70. Nao Kao Lyfoung, interview with author, Vadnais Heights, Minnesota, July 24, 2003.

71. Ger Lo, interview with author, Vientiane, Lao PDR, March 15, 2008; Mao Song Lyfoung, interview with author, Maplewood, Minnesota, June 18, 2003.

72. Ly Na Jalao, interview with author, Toulouse, France, July 13, 2002.

73. Mao Song Lyfoung, interview with author, Maplewood, Minnesota, June 18, 2003.

74. Ibid.

75. Ibid.

76. Tougeu Lyfoung, interview with author, Herblay, France, July 10, 2002.

77. Ly Na Jalao, interview with author, Toulouse, France, July 13, 2002.

78. Lor, "Power Struggle," 17.

79. Pa Hang was so young when Blia Yao kidnapped her that she survived him by nearly seventy years, dying in the Lao PDR in 2001. Pa related to her grand-daughter, Maia, that Blia Yao sent his army of men to kidnap her for marriage. They chased her on horseback until she fell into a sinkhole, breaking a leg, then retrieved and carried her on a stretcher to Blia Yao's house. Pa slept with the senior wives like she was one of their daughters until several years later, when she "became a woman," then consummated her marriage to Blia Yao. Maia Lee, personal communication, July 4, 2003.

80. Roux and Chu, "Quelques Minorités Ethniques," 406.

81. Lor, "Power Struggle," 17.

82. Mao Song Lyfoung, interview with author, Maplewood, Minnesota, June 18, 2003.

83. Lor, "Power Struggle," 17.

84. Roux and Chu, "Quelques Minorités Ethniques," 405.

85. Ibid., 406.

86. Mao Song Lyfoung, interview with author, Maplewood, Minnesota, June 18, 2003.

87. F. M. Savina, *Histoire des Miao* (Hong Kong: Imprimerie de la Société des Missions-Étrangères, 1924), 258.

88. Ibid., 233.

89. Nao Mai Lee, interview with author, Saint Paul, Minnesota, May 18, 2002.

90. Telegram, Xieng Khouang à Vientiane, February 29, 1920 (CAOM Laos F5).

91. Mao Song Lyfoung, interview with author, Maplewood, Minnesota, June 18, 2003.

92. Telegram no. 389 RD, November 17, 1920 (CAOM Laos F5).

93. Ly Na Jalao, interview with author, Toulouse, France, July 13, 2002.

94. Larteguy and Yang, *Fabuleuse Aventure*, 103.

95. Ly Na Jalao, interview with author, Toulouse, France, July 13, 2002.

96. Lor, "Power Struggle," 18.

97. Mao Song Lyfoung, interview with author, Maplewood, Minnesota, June 18, 2003.

98. Ly Na Jalao, interview with author, Toulouse, France, July 13, 2002.

99. Mao Song Lyfoung, interview with author, Maplewood, Minnesota, June 18, 2003.

Chapter 5. The Struggle for Paramountcy (1921–1935)

1. See James C. Scott's discussions about the "social structures of escape" in *The Art of Not Being Governed: An Anarchist History of Upland Southeast Asia* (New Haven, CT: Yale University Press, 2009), 207-19.

2. On the orphan boy who rises from a humble background to achieve great things, see Charles Johnson and Se Yang, *Dab Neeg Hmoob: Myths, Legends, and Folk Tales from the Hmong of Laos*, 2nd ed. (Saint Paul, MN: Linguistics Department, Macalester College, 1992).

3. Hmong often explain success (and failure) in terms of geomancy. See Nicholas Tapp, *Sovereignty and Rebellion: The White Hmong of Northern Thailand* (Singapore: Oxford University Press, 1989), 147-66.

4. For a description of Johnson's early years and his rise in the Senate, see Robert A. Caro, *The Years of Lyndon Johnson*, vol. 1, *The Path to Power* (New York: Alfred A. Knopf, 1982); and *The Years of Lyndon Johnson*, vol. 3, *Master of the Senate* (New York: Alfred A. Knopf, 1982).

5. Keith Quincy, *Harvesting Pa Chay's Wheat: The Hmong and America's Secret War in Laos* (Cheney: Eastern Washington University Press, 2000).

6. For discussions of literacy and its impact on the Hmong ethnic identity and leadership structure, see Jacques Lemoine, "Les Ecritures du Hmong," *Bulletin des Amis du Royaume Lao* 7-8 (1972); William A Smalley, Chia Koua Vang, and Gnia Yee Yang, *Mother of Writing: The Origin and Development of a Hmong Messianic Script* (Chicago: University of Chicago Press, 1990); and Nicholas Tapp, "The Impact of Missionary Christianity upon Marginalized Ethnic Minorities: The Case of the Hmong," *Journal of Southeast Asian Studies* 20, no. 1 (1989).

7. Mao Song Lyfoung, interview with author, Saint Paul, Minnesota, October 2, 2004.

8. Henri Roux and Tran Van Chu, "Quelques Minorités Ethniques du Nord-Indochine," *France-Asie*, nos. 92-93 (1954): 397.

9. A Hmong can be quite adept at estimating his age by taking into account the number of years he cultivated specific plots of land or dwelled in a certain village. For example, he would be able to remember that he was born during the third year after his

parents began planting a certain field. If he knew his parents remained on that specific plot of land for seven years before moving, he would guess he was about four years old by then. By recalling how many times his family relocated, and how long they remained at each place, he could approximate his age. According to William Geddes, the Hmong migrate every ten to fifteen years. Thus, an individual probably would move no more than four or five times during his lifetime and would be expected to remember how long he remained at each location. Moreover, his parents could tell him the season, and even the date and month, of his birth according to the lunar calendar, but one is hard pressed to match these dates with the Buddhist or Christian calendar. For Hmong shifting cultivation practices, see W. R. Geddes, *Miao Year* (Del Ray, CA: Contemporary Films and McGraw-Hill, 1970), 2 film reels, 61 min.; and *Migrants of the Mountains: The Cultural Ecology of the Blue Miao (Hmong Njua) of Thailand* (Oxford: Clarendon Press, 1976).

10. Tougeu Lyfoung, interview with author, Herblay, France, July 10, 2002; Tougeu Lyfoung, interview with author, Champlin, Minnesota, July 3, 2003; Touxa Lyfoung, *Tub Npis Lisfoom Tej Lus Tseg Cia* [Words left by Touby Lyfoung] (Minneapolis, MN: Burgess Publishing, 1996), 23.

11. Regarding the Hmong's perception of time, F. M. Savina writes, "Don't go ask a Miao to cite you a fixed date. He knows of none, not even that of his birth." Savina, however, is wrong in his claim that a Hmong "has never counted, he is completely ignorant of calculations." In addition to their ability to calculate their age, they are knowledgeable about weights and measures, skills required for sustaining an opium economy. See F. M. Savina, *Histoire des Miao* (Hong Kong: Imprimerie de la Société des Missions-Étrangères, 1924), 176. For a discussion of Hmong systems of weights and measures, see Kao-Ly Yang, "Mesurer et Peser Chez les Hmong du Laos: Aspects Techniques et Notions de Précision," *Bulletin de l'École Française d'Extrême Orient* 90–91 (2004).

12. The Hmong in this period viewed going to the lowlands as a death sentence. See Maurice Abadie, *Les Races du Haut-Tonkin de Phong-Tho à Lang-Son* (Paris: Société d'éditions géographiques, maritimes et coloniales, 1924), 164; and Savina, *Histoire des Miao*, 173.

13. Savina, *Histoire des Miao*, 178.

14. Henceforth I use the name De Mua Tha. See Lyfoung, *Tub Npis Lisfoom Tej Lus Tseg Cia*, 61–62.

15. The Ly [Lee] clan has three lineages, known as the Ly 9, 7, and 5 *txim*, as discussed in the introduction. Ly Dra Pao belonged to the Ly 5 txim, but his cow sacrifice ritual resembled that of the Ly 9 *txim* led by Kaitong Ly Nhia Vu. For details about Dra Pao's ritual practices and how they compared with those of other Ly lineages in Nong Het, see ibid., 16–17. For an anthropological explanation of the clan and lineages, see Gary Yia Lee, "Household and Marriage in a Thai Highland Society," *Journal of the Siam Society* 76 (1988).

16. Lyfoung, *Tub Npis Lisfoom Tej Lus Tseg Cia*, 17–18.

17. Alfred W. McCoy, *The Politics of Heroin: CIA Complicity in the Global Drug Trade* (Brooklyn, NY: Lawrence Hill Books, 1991), 117.

18. For a discussion of the Hmong preference for residing with the paternal clan, see Lee, "Household and Marriage."

19. Lyfoung, *Tub Npis Lisfoom Tej Lus Tseg Cia*, 23.

20. As recently as the 1970s, Hmong women did not have much opportunity to obtain an education in lowland schools. Hmong men, on the other hand, could acquire literacy in Lao in the army. See John Michael Duffy, "Writing from These Roots: Literacy, Rhetoric, and History in a Hmong-American Community" (PhD diss., University of Wisconsin–Madison, 2000), and *Writing from These Roots: Literacy in a Hmong-American Community* (Honolulu: University of Hawai'i Press, 2007).

21. Mao Song Lyfoung, interviews with author, Maplewood, Minnesota, October 24, 2002, and June 18, 2003, and Saint Paul, Minnesota, October 2, 2004. Tougeu confirmed Mao Song's claim that she knew her father's life history better. When I first met him in France in 2002, Tougeu declined to provide details about his father, referring me instead to Mao Song. Touby also said he did not return until 1939. Tougeu Lyfoung, interview with author, Herblay, France, July 10, 2002; Lyfoung, *Tub Npis Lisfoom Tej Lus Tseg Cia*, 54–55.

22. Lyfoung, *Tub Npis Lisfoom Tej Lus Tseg Cia*, 52–53.

23. Caro, *The Years of Lyndon Johnson: The Path to Power*, 132.

24. Tougeu Lyfoung, interview with author, Herblay, France, July 10, 2002; Tougeu Lyfoung, interview with author, Champlin, Minnesota, July 3, 2003.

25. Mao Song Lyfoung, interview with author, Maplewood, Minnesota, October 24, 2002.

26. Robert G. Cooper, *Resource Scarcity and the Hmong Response: Patterns of Settlement and Economy in Transition* (Singapore: National University of Singapore Press, 1984), 137.

27. Smalley, Vang, and Yang, *Mother of Writing*.

28. Keith Quincy, *Hmong: History of a People*, 2nd ed. (Cheney: Eastern Washington University Press, 1995), 57.

29. Mao Song's use of "loj leeb" or "indigent" to characterize these merchants can be traced to Confucian values that juxtaposed honorable agrarian undertakings against the corrupting influences of trading. Nicholas Tapp sheds light on the Hmong's Confucian values in his study of the Hmong of present-day Thailand. These Hmong, he notes, see trading as a dishonest career since it involves exaggeration, a skill necessary for generating profit. Business activity is therefore perceived as the main contributing factor to the erosion of traditional morality in Hmong Thai society. See Nicholas Tapp, "Hmong Confucian Ethics and Constructions of the Past," in *Cultural Crisis and Social Memory: Modernity and Identity in Thailand and Laos*, ed. Shigeharu Tanabe and Charles F. Keyes (Honolulu: University of Hawai'i Press, 2002), 102.

30. Mao Song Lyfoung, interview with author, Maplewood, Minnesota, October 24, 2002.

31. Lyfoung, *Tub Npis Lisfoom Tej Lus Tseg Cia*, 24–25.

32. Ibid., 29.

33. Mao Song Lyfoung, interview with author, Maplewood, Minnesota, June 18, 2003.

34. Roux and Chu, "Quelques Minorités Ethniques," 406.

35. Mao Song Lyfoung, interview with author, Maplewood, Minnesota, October 24, 2002.

36. Ibid.

37. Ibid.

38. Dorey, "Rapport d'Ensemble du Chef de Bataillon Dorey sur les Opérations du Détachement du Laos pendant l'Hiver 1920–21 et sur la Pacification de la Region Nord de la Province de Luang Prabang," 1921 (SHAT Vincennes).

39. Mao Song Lyfoung, interview with author, Maplewood, Minnesota, October 24, 2002.

40. Savina, *Histoire des Miao*, 173–74.

41. Abadie, *Races du Haut-Tonkin*, 164.

42. Roux and Chu, "Quelques Minorités Ethniques," 394.

43. Savina, *Histoire des Miao*, 173.

44. Jean Lartéguy and Yang Dao, *La Fabuleuse Aventure du Peuple de l'Opium* (Paris: Presses de la Cité, 1979), 97.

45. Geddes, *Migrants of the Mountains*, 31.

46. Lyfoung, *Tub Npis Lisfoom Tej Lus Tseg Cia*, 32.

47. Mao Song Lyfoung, interview with author, Maplewood, Minnesota, October 24, 2002.

48. According to Mao Song, who witnessed some events, the annual oath of allegiance ceremony involved the leaders standing before the Buddha statue in the *wat* at Xieng Khouang and, with hands raised, swearing their allegiance to the French and Lao authorities. The leaders also declared that they have not been corrupt, have not extorted money or bribes from the inhabitants, and have not cheated on their taxes by deflating the number of heads under their charge that year. They then promised to continue this moral behavior in the future. As a testament to their words, they drank water offered by a monk. The ceremony was also accompanied by a curse, which promised misfortune to those who violate the oath and prosperity to those who keep their vows.

49. Mao Song Lyfoung, interview with author, Maplewood, Minnesota, October 24, 2002.

50. Lyfoung, *Tub Npis Lisfoom Tej Lus Tseg Cia*, 32.

51. Ibid., 36.

52. Mao Song Lyfoung, interview with author, Maplewood, Minnesota, October 24, 2002; Lyfoung, *Tub Npis Lisfoom Tej Lus Tseg Cia*, 17–18.

53. Prasit Leepreecha, "Kinship and Identity among Hmong in Thailand" (PhD diss., University of Washington, 2001), 80–81.

54. Ger Lo, interview with author, Vientiane, Lao PDR, March 15, 2008.

55. Lyfoung, *Tub Npis Lisfoom Tej Lus Tseg Cia*, 28–29.

56. Mao Song Lyfoung, interview with author, Saint Paul, Minnesota, October 2, 2004.

57. Lyfoung, *Tub Npis Lisfoom Tej Lus Tseg Cia*, 68.

58. Mao Song Lyfoung, interview with author, Saint Paul, Minnesota, October 2, 2004.

59. McCoy, *Politics of Heroin*, 82.

60. Mao Song Lyfoung, interviews with author, Maplewood, Minnesota, October 24, 2002, and Saint Paul, Minnesota, October 2, 2004.

61. Lyfoung, *Tub Npis Lisfoom Tej Lus Tseg Cia*, 68.

62. This belief about the favoritism shown to minor wives is expressed in a folktale about the orphan girl. See Jewell Reinhart Coburn, Tzexa Cherta Lee, and Anne Sibley O'Brien, *Jouanah, a Hmong Cinderella* (Arcadia, CA: Shen's Books, 1996).

63. Later, in 1920, Blia Yao married Pa Hang as his fifth and most minor wife.

64. Ly Foung's mother was against the marriage because Va was a petite woman, according to Mao Song. Ly Foung's mother feared Va would be incapable of bearing heavy loads or farm for a living. He married her anyway since he was stricken with love. Mao Song Lyfoung, interview with author, Maplewood, Minnesota, October 24, 2002.

65. Ibid.

66. Roux and Chu, "Quelques Minorités Ethniques," 404.

67. Quoted in Lartéguy and Yang, *Fabuleuse Aventure*, 96–97.

68. Ibid., 94–95.

69. Angeli, "Rapport du Colonel Angeli, Directeur des Opérations du Haut-Laos, au Général Commandant Supérieur des Troupes de l'Indochine, au Sujet des Opération Entreprises dans le Haut-Laos contre les Meos," May 25, 1920 (SHAT Vincennes).

70. Savina, *Histoire des Miao*, 238.

71. Dorey, "Rapport du Chef de Bataillon Dorey."

72. Lartéguy and Yang, *Fabuleuse Aventure*, 99.

73. Dorey, "Rapport du Chef de Bataillon Dorey."

74. Txooj Tsawb Yaj, *Rog Paj Cai* (Vientiane: Y. Bertrais, 1972), 23–24.

75. Lyfoung, *Tub Npis Lisfoom Tej Lus Tseg Cia*, 43.

76. Ibid.

77. Ger Lo, interview with author, Vientiane, Lao PDR, March 15, 2008.

78. Lyfoung, *Tub Npis Lisfoom Tej Lus Tseg Cia*, 43. See also Quincy, *Harvesting Pa Chay's Wheat*, 45.

79. Mao Song Lyfoung, interview with author, Maplewood, Minnesota, October 24, 2002.

80. Ibid.

81. Ibid.

82. Ibid.

83. Bo Lua died shortly after Mai's suicide.

84. Mao Song Lyfoung, interview with author, Maplewood, Minnesota, October 24, 2002. According to Mao Song, the beating of her mother was witnessed and relayed to her by a sister-in-law who had recently been kidnapped by Ly Va Khue as a second wife. This sister-in-law, being a new bride, had to observe a three-day ritual confinement within the house. She was therefore able to witness the whole event firsthand. Not surprisingly, the story of Mai's suicide differed within the Lyfoung household according to the gender of the teller. The Lyfoung males denied that a beating had occurred, perhaps fearing that admitting it would affect their own reputations. Touby, who also denied the beating, described how people judged him harshly because he was the son of Ly Foung, fearing that he would be like his father and mistreat their daughters. As a result, Touby had a hard time finding a wife and had to settle for a "spinster." Mao Song Lyfoung's account of the beating of Mai is consistent with other versions provided in McCoy, *Politics of Heroin*, 82. For Touby's account of his mother's death, see Lyfoung, *Tub Npis Lisfoom Tej Lus Tseg Cia*, 69. On how his father's behavior affected his ability to find a wife, see pages 98–105.

85. Mao Song Lyfoung, interview with author, Maplewood, Minnesota, June 18, 2003.

86. "Kas tom hu dab!" Mao Song Lyfoung, interview with author, Maplewood, Minnesota, October 24, 2002.

87. Mao Song got the description of the last moments of her mother's life from this aunt.

88. Mao Song Lyfoung, interview with author, Maplewood, Minnesota, October 24, 2002. One *lag* is a unit of measure equal to 38 grams. A fatal dose of raw opium is .38 grams (one *fiab*), about the size of two small kernels of corn. Here Ly Foung was urging that Mai be fed two more *lag* of opium, two hundred times a fatal dose, to finish her off. For a discussion of Hmong weights and measures, see Yang, "Mesurer et Peser."

89. Mao Song Lyfoung, interview with author, Maplewood, Minnesota, October 24, 2002.

90. Twenty-four *lag* is the equivalent of two silver bars and four silver piasters, or two silver bars and twenty centimes.

91. Mao Song Lyfoung, interview with author, Saint Paul, Minnesota, March 21, 2005.

92. See McCoy, *Politics of Heroin*, 118.

93. Mao Song Lyfoung, interview with author, Maplewood, Minnesota, October 24, 2002.

94. Mao Song Lyfoung laughed heartily as she told me that her new stepmother, Choua, the one who raised her, was the only one in the family who dared to talk back to her father defiantly. Mao Song Lyfoung, interviews with author, Maplewood, Minnesota, October 24, 2002, and Saint Paul, Minnesota, March 21, 2005.

95. This ceremony, perhaps adopted from the Lao, involves a sacrificial feast, with well-wishers tying white strings on the wrists of the person for whom the ceremony is being conducted.

96. Mao Song Lyfoung, interview with author, Maplewood, Minnesota, October 24, 2002.

97. Ibid.

98. Lyfoung, *Tub Npis Lisfoom Tej Lus Tseg Cia*, 46.

99. Ibid.

100. Mao Song Lyfoung, interview with author, Maplewood, Minnesota, October 24, 2002.

101. For more information about death taboos among clans, see Lee, "Household and Marriage."

102. Tougeu Lyfoung, interview with author, Herblay, France, July 10, 2002.

103. Lyfoung, *Tub Npis Lisfoom Tej Lus Tseg Cia*, 47.

104. Mao Song Lyfoung, interview with author, Maplewood, Minnesota, October 24, 2002.

105. Ibid.

106. Tougeu Lyfoung, interview with author, Herblay, France, July 10, 2002.

107. Mao Song Lyfoung, interview with author, Maplewood, Minnesota, October 24, 2002.

108. Lyfoung, *Tub Npis Lisfoom Tej Lus Tseg Cia*, 66.

109. Mao Song Lyfoung, interview with author, Maplewood, Minnesota, October 24, 2002.

110. Ibid.

111. Ibid.

112. Of the claim that Ly Foung made up the tax shortfall for Tsong Tou in 1936, see McCoy, *Politics of Heroin*, 118. Keith Quincy reiterates McCoy but does not cite his sources in *Harvesting Pa Chay's Wheat*, 47, and in *Hmong*, 2nd ed., 139-40.

113. Mao Song Lyfoung, interview with author, Maplewood, Minnesota, October 24, 2002.

114. Mao Song Lyfoung, interview with author, Saint Paul, Minnesota, October 2, 2004.

115. Tougeu Lyfoung, interview with author, Champlin, Minnesota, July 3, 2003.

Chapter 6. The Emergence of an Educated Hmong Broker (1936–1940)

1. Nao Kao Lyfoung, interview with author, Vadnais Heights, Minnesota, July 24, 2003.

2. Mao Song Lyfoung, interview with author, Maplewood, Minnesota, October 24, 2002; Nao Kao Lyfoung, interview with author, Vadnais Height, Minnesota, July 24, 2003; Tougeu Lyfoung, interview with author, Herblay, France, July 10, 2002.

3. Touxa Lyfoung, *Tub Npis Lisfoom Tes Lus Tseg Cia* [Words left by Touby Lyfoung] (Minneapolis, MN: Burgess Publishing, 1996), 79-81.

4. Mao Song Lyfoung, interview with author, Maplewood, Minnesota, October 24, 2002.

5. Tougeu Lyfoung, interview with author, Herblay, France, July 10, 2002.

6. Lyfoung, *Tub Npis Lisfoom Tej Lus Tseg Cia*, 81.

7. Resident Superior of Laos, "Report Au Conseil de Governmount, 1926" (CAOM Laos F5).

8. Tougeu Lyfoung, interview with author, Herblay, France, July 10, 2002.

9. Ibid. Lo Blia Yao was often called only by his title, *kaitong*. It was also customary for Hmong to add Blia Yao's title to his sons' names, as Tougeu did here.

10. Ger Lo, interview with author, Vientiane, Lao PDR, March 15, 2008.

11. Zong Blong Lo, interview with author, Vientiane, Lao PDR, March 3, 2008.

12. Tougeu Lyfoung, interview with author, Herblay, France, July 10, 2002.

13. Mao Song Lyfoung, interview with author, Maplewood, Minnesota, October 24, 2002.

14. Lyfoung, *Tub Npis Lisfoom Tej Lus Tseg Cia*, 85.

15. Ibid., 87.

16. Ibid., 87-88.

17. Tougeu Lyfoung, interview with author, Herblay, France, July 10, 2002.

18. See chapter 5.

19. See, for example, Yia S. Lor, "Power Struggle between the Lor and Ly Clans, 1900-2000" (undergraduate thesis, California State University, Chico, 2001).

20. Sutdālā Yāthọtū, *Tū Yā Saichū: Viraburut hæng dæn Lān Sāng* (Vianchan: Hōngphim Num Lāo, 2004), 22.

21. Mao Song Lyfoung says that Fay Dang's mother was the second wife and Nhia Vu's mother the third, but Kou Yang says Nhia Vu's mother was the second wife. Kou Yang, "The Passing of a Hmong Pioneer: Nhiavu Lobliayao (Nyiaj Vws Lauj Npliaj Yob), 1915-1999," *Hmong Studies Journal* 3 (2000): 2.

22. Ly Na Jalao, interview with author, Toulouse, France, July 13, 2002; Zong Blong Lo, interview with author, Vientiane, Lao PDR, March 3, 2008; Ger Lo, interview with author, Vientiane, Lao PDR, March 15, 2008.

23. Mao Song Lyfoung, interview with author, Maplewood, Minnesota, October 24, 2002.

24. Mao Song Lyfoung, interview with author, Maplewood, Minnesota, June 18, 2003. It is unlikely that Tsong Tou built this huge fence alone. He probably hired workers to help him, but I think what Mao Song is conveying here is that he felt alone and abandoned by his brothers in this endeavor.

25. Ly Na Jalao, interview with author, Toulouse, France, July 13, 2002.

26. Mao Song Lyfoung, interview with author, Maplewood, Minnesota, October 24, 2002.

27. Ly Na Jalao, interview with author, Toulouse, France, July 13, 2002.

28. Ibid.

29. Ger Lo, interview with author, Vientiane, Lao PDR, March 15, 2008.

30. Mao Song Lyfoung, interview with author, Maplewood, Minnesota, October 24, 2002. Hmong informants who were not directly involved often mix up this 1936 resignation of Tsong Tou with that of Tasseng Kue Cha Tsia of Phak Boun in 1929, as discussed in chapter 5.

31. Mao Song Lyfoung, interview with author, Maplewood, Minnesota, June 18, 2003.

32. Mee Kue, personal communication, June 2010.

33. Mao Song Lyfoung, interview with author, Maplewood, Minnesota, October 24, 2002.

34. Ibid.

35. Ibid.; Tougeu Lyfoung, interview with author, Herblay, France, July 10, 2002; Lyfoung, *Tub Npis Lisfoom Tej Lus Tseg Cia*, 48.

36. Grant Evans, *The Last Century of Lao Royalty: A Documentary History* (Chiangmai, Thailand: Silkworm Books, 2009), 262.

37. Ly Na Jalao, interview with author, Toulouse, France, July 13, 2002.

38. Mao Song Lyfoung, interview with author, Maplewood, Minnesota, June 18, 2003.

39. Lyfoung, *Tub Npis Lisfoom Tej Lus Tseg Cia*, 48–49.

40. Alfred W. McCoy, *The Politics of Heroin: CIA Complicity in the Global Drug Trade* (Brooklyn, NY: Lawrence Hill Books, 1991), 83.

41. Mao Song Lyfoung, interview with author, Maplewood, Minnesota, June 18, 2003.

42. See Lyfoung, *Tub Npis Lisfoom Tej Lus Tseg Cia*, 6.

43. G. Linwood Barney, "The Meo of Xieng Khouang Province," in *Southeast Asian Tribes, Minorities, and Nations*, 2 vols., ed. Peter Kunstadter (Princeton, NJ: Princeton University Press, 1967), 1:275.

44. Mao Song Lyfoung, interview with author, Maplewood, Minnesota, June 18, 2003; Tougeu Lyfoung, interview with author, Herblay, France, July 10, 2002.

45. Mao Song Lyfoung, interview with author, Maplewood, Minnesota, June 18, 2003.

46. Ibid. Mao Song Lyfoung was married to Tong Ger Vang but widowed later on, and then was remarried to his younger brother, Ka Ge Vang, as a second wife in accordance to Hmong levirate practices. She's referring to her second husband here.

47. Ly Na Jalao, interview with author, Toulouse, France, July 13, 2002.

48. Lyfoung, *Tub Npis Lisfoom Tej Lus Tseg Cia*, 49.

49. Mao Song Lyfoung, interview with author, Maplewood, Minnesota, June 18, 2003.

50. Keith Quincy, *Hmong: History of a People* (Cheney: Eastern Washington University Press, 1988), 139.

51. Tong Pao Moua, interview with author, Madison, Wisconsin, August 1, 2006.

52. Touby's Buddhist belief comes out in the stories he relates about his life experiences. He attributes his contraction of beriberi, for example, to his having been forced

to drown a cat, thus acquiring bad karma. See Lyfoung, *Tub Npis Lisfoom Tej Lus Tseg Cia*, 92–94.

53. Mao Song Lyfoung, interview with author, Maplewood, Minnesota, June 18, 2003. Touby's adult name is Nhia By. When a Hmong male comes of age through marriage and the birth of a first child, a new syllable is added to his given boyhood name to form an adult name.

54. Ibid.

55. According to Hugh Toye, there were only fifty-two Lao graduates from the Lycée Pavie in the 1930s. See Hugh Toye, *Laos: Buffer State or Battleground* (London: Oxford University Press, 1968), 45.

56. Alfred W. McCoy, Cathleen B. Read, and Leonard P. Adams, *The Politics of Heroin* (New York: Harper and Row, 1972), 83.

57. Lor, "Power Struggle," 23–24.

58. Ly Na Jalao, interview with author, Toulouse, France, July 13, 2002.

59. Mao Song Lyfoung, interview with author, Maplewood, Minnesota, October 24, 2002.

60. Lyfoung, *Tub Npis Lisfoom Tej Lus Tseg Cia*, 146.

61. Gary Yia Lee, "Ethnic Minorities and Nation Building in Laos: The Hmong in the Lao State," *Péninsule* 11/12 (1985–86).

62. McCoy, Read, and Adams, *Politics of Heroin*, 83.

63. Zong Blong Lo, interview with author, Vientiane, Lao PDR, March 2, 2008.

Chapter 7. The Impact of the Japanese Occupation on the Highlands (1941–1945)

1. Jean Sassi, interview with author, Taverny, France, July 10, 2002.

2. Anne Fadiman, *The Spirit Catches You and You Fall Down: A Hmong Child, Her American Doctors, and the Collision of Two Cultures* (New York: Farrar, Straus and Giroux, 1997).

3. Lynellyn D. Long, *Ban Vinai, the Refugee Camp* (New York: Columbia University Press, 1993).

4. Tougeu Lyfoung, interview with author, Herblay, France, July 10, 2002.

5. Jean Michaud, e-mail to author, May 1, 2014. See also the official Vietnamese government website about the Hmong king's palace, http://www.vietnamspirittravel .vn/guide/hmong_king_palace_ha_giang.htm, and http://vi.wikipedia.org/wiki /Vua_M%C3%A8o.

6. Alfred W. McCoy, *The Politics of Heroin: CIA Complicity in the Global Drug Trade* (Brooklyn, NY: Lawrence Hill Books, 1991), 119.

7. Harry I. Marshall, *The Karen People of Burma: A Study in Anthropology and Ethnology* (Columbus, OH: The University, 1922); Jonathan Falla, *True Love and Bartholomew: Rebels on the Burmese Border* (Cambridge: Cambridge University Press,

1991); Martin Smith, *Burma: Insurgency and the Politics of Ethnicity* (Dhaka, Bangladesh: Dhaka University Press, 1999).

8. For the recruitment of the Hmong in Vietnam, see Jean Lartéguy and Yang Dao, *La Fabuleuse Aventure du Peuple de l'Opium* (Paris: Presses de la Cité, 1979), chapter 9; and Roger Trinquier, *Les Maquis d'Indochine: 1952–1954* (Paris: Éditions Albatros, 1976).

9. L. H. Ayrolles, *L'Indochine ne Repond Plus* (Saint-Brieuc: Armand Prud'homme, 1948), 27.

10. Maurice Gauthier, interview with author, Les Chesnaye, France, July 9, 2002.

11. Toulu Chongtoua Moua, cassette recording sent to author from Denver, Colorado, March 2004 (date received); Mao Song Lyfoung, interview with author, Maplewood, Minnesota, October 24, 2002.

12. Toulu Chongtoua Moua, cassette recording sent to author from Denver, Colorado, March 2004 (date received).

13. Ibid.

14. Maurice Gauthier, interview with author, Les Chesnaye, France, July 9, 2002.

15. Touxa Lyfoung, *Tub Npis Lisfoom Tej Lus Tseg Cia* [Words left by Touby Lyfoung] (Minneapolis, MN: Burgess Publishing, 1996), 116.

16. Ibid., 117.

17. Lyfoung, *Tub Npis Lisfoom Tej Lus Tseg Cia*, 118–19.

18. Charles Rochet, *Pays Laos, Le Laos Dan le Tourmente, 1939–1945* (Paris: Jean Vigneau, 1946), 163. Quoted in Geoffrey C. Gunn, *Political Struggles in Laos (1930–1954): Vietnamese Communist Power and the Lao Struggle for National Independence* (Bangkok: Duang Kamol, 1988), 109.

19. Mao Song Lyfoung, interview with author, Maplewood, Minnesota, June 18, 2003; Lyfoung, *Tub Npis Lisfoom Tej Lus Tseg Cia*, 119–20.

20. Lyfoung, *Tub Npis Lisfoom Tej Lus Tseg Cia*, 121.

21. Mao Song Lyfoung, interview with author, Maplewood, Minnesota, October 24, 2002.

22. Lyfoung, *Tub Npis Lisfoom Tej Lus Tseg Cia*, 121–22.

23. Mao Song Lyfoung, interview with author, Maplewood, Minnesota, October 24, 2002.

24. Lyfoung, *Tub Npis Lisfoom Tej Lus Tseg Cia*, 123.

25. Lartéguy and Yang, *Fabuleuse Aventure*, 148.

26. Mao Song Lyfoung, interview with author, Maplewood, Minnesota, October 24, 2002.

27. Tougeu Lyfoung, interview with author, Herblay, France, July 10, 2002.

28. Vang Pao, interview with author, Maplewood, Minnesota, April 8, 2004.

29. Lyfoung, *Tub Npis Lisfoom Tej Lus Tseg Cia*, 123.

30. Mao Song Lyfoung, interview with author, Maplewood, Minnesota, June 18, 2003.

31. Ly Na Jalao, interview with author, Toulouse, France, July 13, 2002.

32. Ibid.; Tougeu Lyfoung, interview with author, Herblay, France, July 10, 2002.

33. Mao Song Lyfoung, interview with author, Maplewood, Minnesota, October 24, 2002.

34. Yia S. Lor, "Power Struggle between the Lor and Ly Clans, 1900–2000" (undergraduate thesis, California State University, Chico, 2001), 25.

35. Ly Na Jalao, interview with author, Toulouse, France, July 13, 2002; Shoua Yang, interview with author, Nimes, France, July 8, 2002.

36. Tougeu Lyfoung, interview with author, Herblay, France, July 10, 2002.

37. Ly Na Jalao, interview with author, Toulouse, France, July 13, 2002; Tougeu Lyfoung, interview with author, Herblay, France, July 10, 2002.

38. Ly Na Jalao, interview with author, Toulouse, France, July 13, 2002; Tougeu Lyfoung, interview with author, Herblay, France, July 10, 2002.

39. Grant Evans, *The Last Century of Lao Royalty: A Documentary History* (Chiangmai, Thailand: Silkworm Books, 2009), 19.

40. Ibid.

41. Arthur J. Dommen, *Conflict in Laos: The Politics of Neutralization* (New York: Praeger, 1964), 18–19; Martin Stuart-Fox, *A History of Laos* (Cambridge: Cambridge University Press, 1997), 54.

42. Dommen, *Conflict in Laos*, 19; Gunn, *Political Struggles in Laos*, 112–14.

43. Lartéguy and Yang, *Fabuleuse Aventure*, 149.

44. Dommen, *Conflict in Laos*, 22–29.

45. Tsia Naotou Moua, interview with author, Alençon, France, July 27, 2002.

46. Lor, "Political Struggles," 28.

47. Tsia Naotou Moua, interview with author, Alençon, France, July 27, 2002.

48. Tougeu Lyfoung, interview with author, Herblay, France, July 10, 2002.

49. In July 2002, when I visited Colonel and Mrs. Ly Pao in Alençon, France, they showed me a video of Lo Nhia Vu, filmed several years before his death on June 16, 1999. The scars from the brutal beating were still visible on his face. Nhia Vu cried in the film as he reflected on the incident, but did not say much about it.

50. Toulu Chongtoua Moua, cassette recording sent to author from Denver, Colorado, March 2004 (date received).

51. Ibid.

52. Ibid.

53. Tsia Naotou Moua, interview with author, Alençon, France, July 27, 2002.

54. Toulu Chongtoua Moua, cassette recording sent to author from Denver, Colorado, March 2004 (date received).

55. Lyfoung, *Tub Npis Lisfoom Tej Lus Tseg Cia*, 130–32.

56. Ibid., 133.

57. Wilfred G. Burchett, *Mekong Upstream* (Hanoi: Red River Publishing House, 1957), 228.

58. Lor, "Political Struggles," 30.

59. Sutdālā Yāthǭtū, *Tū Yā Saichū: Viraburut hǣng dǣn Lān Sāng* (Vianchan: Hōngphim Num Lāo, 2004), 43.

60. Ly Na Jalao, interview with author, Toulouse, France, July 13, 2002; Lyfoung, *Tub Npis Lisfoom Tej Lus Tseg Cia*, 134.

61. Ger Lo, interview with author, Vientiane, Lao PDR, March 15, 2008.

62. Tougeu Lyfoung, interview with author, Herblay, France, July 10, 2002.

63. Ibid.

64. Ibid.

65. Alfred W. McCoy, *The Politics of Heroin: CIA Complicity in the Global Drug Trade* (Brooklyn, NY: Lawrence Hill Books, 1991), 120.

66. Tougeu Lyfoung, interview with author, Herblay, France, July 10, 2002; Vang Geu, "Unforgettable Laos," http://www.unforgettable-laos.com/historical-of-events/part-1/; Grant Evans, *A Short History of Laos* (Crows Nest, NSW, Australia: Allen and Unwin, 2002), 84; Gary Yia Lee, "Minority Policies and the Hmong," in *Contemporary Laos*, ed. Martin Stuart-Fox (New York: St. Martin's Press, 1982), 217n11.

67. Mao Song Lyfoung, interview with author, Maplewood, Minnesota, October 24, 2002; Tougeu Lyfoung, interview with author, Champlin, Minnesota, July 3, 2003.

68. Vang, "Unforgettable Laos."

69. Vang Geu, telephone conversation with author, November 5, 2012. Vang says further that Say Pao was never proud of having been forced to dress up as the king. As he got older, he considered what he had done to be a blasphemous act, so he refused to talk about it to anyone except his closest family members. Say Pao, for example, refused to talk to me about this incident when I interviewed him in 2004.

Chapter 8. Hmong Competition Finds Revolutionary Voices in the Kingdom of Laos (1946–1960)

1. Jean Lartéguy and Yang Dao, *La Fabuleuse Aventure du Peuple de l'Opium* (Paris: Presses de la Cité, 1979), 145.

2. Sayasith L. Yangsao, personal communication, May 2003.

3. Lartéguy and Yang, *Fabuleuse Aventure*, 92.

4. Touxa Lyfoung, *Tub Npis Lisfoom Tej Lus Tseg Cia* [Words left by Touby Lyfoung] (Minneapolis, MN: Burgess Publishing, 1996), 117.

5. Ibid., 129.

6. Ibid., 48–49; Grant Evans, *The Last Century of Lao Royalty: A Documentary History* (Chiangmai, Thailand: Silkworm Books, 2009), 262.

7. Lartéguy and Yang, *Fabuleuse Aventure*, 154–55.

8. Maurice Gauthier, interview with author, Les Chesnaye, France, July 9, 2002.

9. Geoffrey C. Gunn, *Political Struggles in Laos (1930–1954): Vietnamese Communist Power and the Lao Struggle for National Independence* (Bangkok: Duang Kamol, 1988), 226.

10. Ibid.

11. Ibid.

12. Nao Kao Lyfoung, interview with author, Vadnais Heights, Minnesota, July 24, 2003.

13. Ibid.

14. Evans, *Last Century of Lao Royalty*, 262, 264.

15. Lyfoung, *Tub Npis Lisfoom Tej Lus Tseg Cia*, 140–41.

16. Nao Kao Lyfoung, interview with author, Vadnais Heights, Minnesota, July 24, 2003; Alfred W. McCoy, *The Politics of Heroin: CIA Complicity in the Global Drug Trade* (Brooklyn, NY: Lawrence Hill Books, 1991), 268.

17. John T. McAlister Jr., "Mountain Minorities and the Viet Minh: A Key to the Indochina War," in *Southeast Asian Tribes, Minorities, and Nations*, 2 vols., ed. Peter Kunstadter (Princeton, NJ: Princeton University Press, 1967), 2:833.

18. Gunn, *Political Struggles in Laos*, 227.

19. The Hmong have become very aware of geographic boundaries in recent times, however. The Chao Fa group, for example, aims to create an autonomous Hmong zone around the region of Phou Bia in Xieng Khouang Province. For a discussion of the Tai feudal system, see McAlister, "Mountain Minorities and the Viet Minh," 779.

20. Thongchai Winichakul, *Siam Mapped: A History of the Geo-body of a Nation* (Honolulu: University of Hawai'i Press, 1994).

21. Gunn, *Political Struggles in Laos*, 227.

22. Ibid.

23. Geoffrey C. Gunn, *Rebellion in Laos: Peasants and Politics in a Colonial Backwater* (Boulder, CO: Westview Press, 1990), 227; Yang Dao, *Hmong at the Turning Point*, ed. Jeanne L. Blake (Minneapolis: WorldBridge Associates, 1993), 29.

24. Mao Song Lyfoung, interview with author, Saint Paul, Minnesota, March 21, 2005; Tougeu Lyfoung, interview with author, Champlin, Minnesota, July 3, 2003.

25. André Chenivesse, interview with author, Rouen, France, July 10, 2002.

26. Vang Pao got this medal in the 1950s and is the second Hmong to have received it. As discussed below, Chao Quang Lo was the third Hmong to be awarded the medal, albeit posthumously.

27. Lyfoung, *Tub Npis Lisfoom Tej Lus Tseg Cia*, 143.

28. Ibid., 151.

29. Henri Roux and Tran Van Chu, "Quelques Minorités Ethniques du Nord-Indochine," *France-Asie*, nos. 92–93 (1954): 400.

30. Lyfoung, *Tub Npis Lisfoom Tej Lus Tseg Cia*, 144.

31. Yang, *Hmong at the Turning Point*, 29, 38–39.

32. Gary Yia Lee, "Minority Policies and the Hmong," in *Contemporary Laos*, ed. Martin Stuart-Fox (New York: St. Martin's Press, 1982), 217–18n14.

33. Jane Hamilton-Merritt claims that Vang Pao was the first to introduce the term "Hmong" into usage in 1969. See Jane Hamilton-Merritt, *Tragic Mountains: The Hmong, the Americans, and the Secret Wars for Laos, 1942–1992* (Bloomington: Indiana University Press, 1993), 207. Jean Mottin says that Yang Dao was the first to define the

Hmong as freemen. See Jean Mottin, *History of the Hmong* (Bangkok: Odeon Store, 1980), 5. I discussed my conversation with Yang and his reasons for defining the Hmong in this manner and then changing his mind in Mai Na M. Lee, "The Thousand-Year Myth: Characterization of Hmong," *Journal of Hmong Studies* 2, no. 1 (1997). Despite Yang's changed position, the term *free* continues to be popularized in the United States by scholars who co-opt it in the titles of their works. See, for example, Suchang Chan, *Hmong Means Free: Life in Laos and America* (Philadelphia: Temple University Press, 1994); Larry Long, Lia Vang, and Eileen Littig, *Being Hmong Means Being Free: A Video Portrait of Hmong Life and Culture in Today's America* (Green Bay, WI: NEWIST/CESA, 2000), DVD; Kristel L. Hawley, *Being Hmong Means Being Free: Guide* (Green Bay, WI: Northeastern Wisconsin In-School Telecommunications (NEWIST/CESA 7), University of Wisconsin–Green Bay, 2000); and Sukalaya Kenworthy, *Hmong Means Free* (Baltimore: Publish America, 2004).

34. Yang, *Hmong at the Turning Point*, 29–30.

35. G. Linwood Barney, "The Meo of Xieng Khouang Province," in *Southeast Asian Tribes, Minorities, and Nations*, 2 vols., ed. Peter Kunstadter (Princeton, NJ: Princeton University Press, 1967), 1:280.

36. Hugo Adolf Bernatzik, *Akha and Miao: Problems of Applied Ethnography in Farther India* (New Haven, CT: Human Relations Area Files, 1970), 66.

37. Lyfoung, *Tub Npis Lisfoom Tej Lus Tseg Cia*, 120.

38. Ibid., 120–21.

39. McCoy, *Politics of Heroin*, 120, 131–46.

40. Ibid., 138–39.

41. Ibid., 139.

42. Ly Na Jalao, interview with author, Toulouse, France, July 13, 2002; Ly Pao, interview with author, Alençon, France, July 27, 2002; Jean Sassi, interview with author, Taverny, France, July 10, 2002; Shoua Yang, interview with author, Nimes, France, July 8, 2002.

43. Ly Na Jalao, interview with author, Toulouse, France, July 13, 2002.

44. "Tasseng Meo de PhaKha a M. le Chao Muong Khoune," December 4, 1945 (CAOM Laos F12).

45. Ibid.

46. James C. Scott, *Weapons of the Weak: Everyday Forms of Peasant Resistance* (New Haven, CT: Yale University Press, 1985).

47. Barney, "Meo of Xieng Khouang Province," 1:281.

48. Ly Nao Cha, interview with author, Nimes, France, July 12, 2002; Ly Pao, interview with author, Alençon, France, July 27, 2002; Nao Kao Lyfoung, interview with author, Vadnais Heights, Minnesota, July 24, 2003; Shoua Yang, interview with author, Nimes, France, July 8, 2002; and Lyfoung, *Tub Npis Lisfoom Tej Lus Tseg Cia*, 144.

49. Vang Pao, interview with author, Maplewood, Minnesota, April 8, 2004.

50. Hugh Toye, *Laos: Buffer State or Battleground* (London: Oxford University Press, 1968), 86.

51. Martin Stuart-Fox, *A History of Laos* (Cambridge: Cambridge University Press, 1997), 82.

52. Stanley Karnow, *Vietnam: A History* (New York: Penguin Books, 1984), 204–5.

53. For an articulate discussion of this ethnic dimension in the struggle, see McAlister, "Mountain Minorities and the Viet Minh."

54. Lartéguy and Yang, *Fabuleuse Aventure*, 161.

55. For a full description of Chao Quang Lo's heroic exploits as told by Lo Wen Teu, see Lartéguy and Yang, *Fabuleuse Aventure*, 160–88. As noted earlier, the first two Hmong to obtain the Légion d'honneur were Touby Lyfoung (1946) and Vang Pao (1951/52). Lartéguy and Yang also said Lo Wen Teu was awarded the Légion d'honneur, but he declined it (*Fabuleuse Aventure*, 188).

56. Nao Chue Vang, interview with author, Saint Paul, Minnesota, September 23, 2007.

57. Ibid. See also Vang Geu, "Unforgettable Laos," http://www.unforgettable-laos .com/historical-of-events/part-1/.

58. Vang, "Unforgettable Laos."

59. Ibid.

60. Vo Nguyen Giap describes his determined efforts to open roads and haul heavy artillery up the mountains in his book *Dien Bien Phu* (Hanoi: Éditions en Langues Étrangères, 1964), 104–7. Other works that detail this final stand of the French include Bernard B. Fall, *Hell in a Very Small Place* (New York: J. B. Lippincott, 1967); and Howard R. Simpson, *Dien Bien Phu: The Epic Battle America Forgot* (Washington, DC: Brassey's, 1994).

61. Karnow, *Vietnam*, 195.

62. Vang, "Unforgettable Laos."

63. Jean Sassi, interview with author, Taverny, France, July 10, 2002.

64. Vang Geu, telephone conversation with author, December 10, 2014.

65. Nao Chue Vang, interview with author, Saint Paul, Minnesota, September 23, 2007; Vang Geu, telephone conversation with author, November 5, 2012; Vang, "Unforgettable Laos."

66. Wilfred G. Burchett, *Mekong Upstream* (Hanoi: Red River Publishing House, 1957), 264.

67. Ibid., 267.

68. See tables 3 and 4 in Frank M. Lebar and Adrienne Suddard, *Laos* (New Haven, CT: Human Relations Area Files, 1960), 239–40.

69. McCoy, *Politics of Heroin*, 120; Keith Quincy, *Hmong: History of a People*, 2nd ed. (Cheney: Eastern Washington University, 1995), 147–48.

70. Sutdālā Yāthōtū, *Tū Yā Saichū: Viraburut hæng dæn Lān Sāng* (Vianchan: Hōngphim Num Lāo, 2004), 16.

71. Ibid., 18–20.

72. Ibid., 43.

73. Ibid., 44.

74. Ibid., 32.

75. Ibid., 17, 52–53.

76. Ger Lo, interview with author, Vientiane, Lao PDR, March 15, 2008.

77. Sutdālā Yāthǫtū, *Tü Yā Saichü*, 51.

78. Ibid., 83–86.

79. Ibid., 49–50.

80. Ibid., 51.

81. McAlister, "Mountain Minorities and the Viet Minh," 819. McAlister further notes that the thirty thousand Hmong east of the Red River opposed the Viet Minh because it had cultivated relations with their enemies, the Tho. Ethnicity and regionalism clearly came into play during the Indochina wars.

82. Stuart-Fox, *History of Laos*, 101.

83. Sutdālā Yāthǫtū, *Tü Yā Saichü*, 70.

84. Ibid., 77.

85. Mee Yang, personal communication, Phonsavan, Lao PDR, March 7, 2008.

86. Sutdālā Yāthǫtū, *Tü Yā Saichü*, 93–94.

87. Vang Pao, interview with author, Westminster, California, April 15, 2004; James William Lair, interview with author, Menomonee Falls, Wisconsin, July 27, 2003; see also Paul Hillmer, *A People's History of the Hmong* (Saint Paul: Minnesota Historical Society Press, 2010), 84–86.

88. Toulu Chongtoua Moua, cassette recording sent to author from Denver, Colorado, March 2004 (date received).

89. Zong Blong Lo, interview with author, Vientiane, Lao PDR, March 3, 2008.

Epilogue

1. Txooj Tsawb Yaj, *Rog Paj Cai* (Vientiane: Y. Bertrais, 1972), 17.

2. Keith Quincy, *Hmong: History of a People*, 2nd ed. (Cheney: Eastern Washington University Press, 1995), 126.

3. Alfred W. McCoy, *The Politics of Heroin: CIA Complicity in the Global Drug Trade* (Brooklyn, NY: Lawrence Hill Books, 1991), 308.

4. William Egan Colby and Peter Forbath, *Honorable Men: My Life in the CIA* (New York: Simon and Schuster, 1978), 197.

5. For Vang Pao's remark about Touby, see Jean Lartéguy and Yang Dao, *La Fabuleuse Aventure du Peuple de l'Opium* (Paris: Presses de la Cité, 1979), 216. The observation that Vang Pao had stopped listening to Touby by the mid-1960s came from Colonel Nao Kao Lyfoung, interview with author, Vadnais Heights, Minnesota, July 24, 2003.

6. Nao Kao Lyfoung, interview with author, Vadnais Heights, Minnesota, July 24, 2003.

7. Jane Hamilton-Merritt, *Tragic Mountains: The Hmong, the Americans, and the Secret Wars for Laos, 1942–1992* (Bloomington: Indiana University Press, 1993), 145–46.

8. According to the Ly senior battalion commanders, this supposed "Ly coup d'état" was only a rumor that came about because members of the Ly clan had expressed disapproval of Vang Pao; it never occurred. Nao Kao Lyfoung, interview with author, Vadnais Heights, Minnesota, July 24, 2003; Ly Nao Cha, interview with author, Nimes, France, July 12, 2002; Ly Pao, interview with author, Alençon, France, July 27, 2002. Former CIA operative Colonel William Lair, who recruited Vang Pao in 1961, also said that this coup was merely "paranoia" on the part of Vang Pao, who, during this period, often complained that certain political sectors were attempting to eliminate him. James William Lair, interview with author, Menomonee Falls, Wisconsin, July 27, 2003.

9. Shoua Yang, interview with author, Nimes, France, July 8, 2002.

10. Ly Tsia Tou, interview with author, Saint-Germain les Corbeil, France, August 16, 2002.

11. Ly Tou Pao, interview with author, Fountain Valley, California, April 13, 2004. Tou Pao and Vang Pao presented a united front to me in 2004, but I learned from Kaitong Vang later that Tou Pao had broken with Vang Pao after an incident in 2001. Kaitong Vang, interview with author, Saint Paul, Minnesota, October 2, 2004. The break did not play out publicly until the New Year's Festival of 2010, a few months before Vang Pao's death.

12. Ly Pao, interview with author, Alençon, France, July 27, 2002; Ly Tsia Tou, interview with author, Saint-Germain les Corbeil, France, August 16, 2002; Shoua Yang, interview with author, Nimes, France, July 8, 2002.

13. Vang Pao, interview with author, Saint Paul, Minnesota, April 8, 2004.

14. I had long heard the legend of the Ly clan's oath of allegiance to Vang Pao, but I had not found confirmation of it until 2009. In July 2002, when I visited Touxoua Lyfoung at his home outside Paris, he said that after Vang Pao went into exile he came to France to also extract an oath of loyalty from him, making him promise never to found any opposing political parties. When Gary Yia Lee was in Saint Paul as a professor at Concordia University in 2009, the Ly clan organized a leadership-training session for clan members at the Hmong Cultural Center. Gary and I were among the presenters. After I told the story of how Touby and the Ly clan used to lead the Hmong, Chu Pheng Ly, now president of the Lao Family Community, challenged me. If what I said was true, he said, then why was the Ly clan so weak in exile and why did it no longer engage in politics? Since some of the most important Ly clan leaders were in the room, I saw my opportunity to confirm once and for all the legend of the Ly clan oath of allegiance to Vang Pao, so I told him that the Ly clan members had taken an oath to never play politics against Vang Pao, hence their silence in exile no matter what Vang Pao did. I got my confirmation from Naikong Ly Xiong Pao, who immediately stood up to say it was true that he and others of the Ly clan had taken the oath of loyalty to Vang Pao back in Long Cheng, but only so that they would live. He then told Chu Pheng that the oath did not extend to his generation, and if he and his fellow clan members wanted to play politics, they should be encouraged to do so.

15. Tougeu Lyfoung, interview with author, Champlin, Minnesota, July 3, 2003.

16. Tougeu Lyfoung, interview with author, Herblay, France, July 10, 2002.

17. Nao Kao Lyfoung, interview with author, Vadnais Heights, Minnesota, July 24, 2003.

18. Ly Pao, interview with author, Alençon, France, July 27, 2002.

19. This is evident in the oral testimony about Pa Chay's movement by Yaj Txooj Tsawb in 1972. See Yaj, *Rog Paj Cai.*

20. Christopher Robbins, *The Ravens: The Men Who Flew in America's Secret War in Laos* (New York: Crown, 1987).

21. Chia Koua Vang, Gnia Yee Yang, and William Allen Smalley, *The Life of Shong Lue Yang: Hmong "Mother of Writing" Keeb Kwm Soob Lwj Yaj — Hmoob "Niam Ntawv,"* trans. Mitt Moua and See Yang (Minneapolis: Southeast Asian Refugee Studies, University of Minnesota, 1990), 152–54.

22. Tsia Long Thao, interview with author, Sun Prairie, Wisconsin, August 6, 2006; Shoua Yang, interview with author, Nimes, France, July 8, 2002. See also William A. Smalley, Chia Koua Vang, and Gnia Yee Yang, *Mother of Writing: The Origin and Development of a Hmong Messianic Script* (Chicago: University of Chicago Press, 1990).

23. Smalley, Vang, and Yang, *Mother of Writing*, 32.

24. Ibid., 31; Vang, Yang, and Smalley, *Life of Shong Lue Yang*, 155.

25. Yong Va Yang, interview with author, Fresno, California, February 22, 2004.

26. Smalley, Vang, and Yang, *Mother of Writing*, 38.

27. Shoua Yang traces the allegations of financial corruption using interviews with individuals in the movement. See Shoua Yang, "Hmong Social and Political Capital: The Formation and Maintenance of Hmong-American Organizations" (PhD diss., Northern Illinois University, 2006).

28. Vang Pao, interview with author, Westminster, California, April 15, 2004. Colonel Ly Tou Pao also said the same thing about Boun Oum passing his authority to Vang Pao. Ly Tou Pao, interview with author, Fountain Valley, California, April 13, 2004.

29. Kaitong Vang, interview with author, Saint Paul, Minnesota, October 2, 2004.

30. Lynellyn D. Long, *Ban Vinai, the Refugee Camp* (New York: Columbia University Press, 1993).

31. Gary Yia Lee, "Bandits or Rebels? Hmong Resistance in the New Lao State," *Indigenous Affairs* 4 (October–December 2000): 6–15, extended 2005 version available at http://www.garyyialee.com/.

32. The United States established diplomatic relations with Vietnam in 1995.

Bibliography

Primary Sources

Archives Nationales d'Outre-Mer (ANOM)*

A Official Acts
B General Correspondence
C General Administration
E Provincial Administration
F Political Affairs
G Justice
H Public Works
I Mines
J Transport
K Posts and Telegraph
L Commerce, Industry, and Tourism
M Labor, Settlement, and Land Regulation
N Agriculture
O Navigation
Q Military Affairs
R Education
S Health Services
T Customs Services
U Documents Related to the History of Indochina

Service Historique de l'Armée de Terre (SHAT), Vincennes

Angeli. "Rapport du Colonel Angeli, Directeur des Opérations du Haut-Laos, au Général Commandant Supérieur des Troupes de l'Indochine, au Sujet des Opération Entreprises dans le Haut-Laos contre les Meos." May 25, 1920 (SHAT Vincennes).

Bonifacy, Auguste Louise M. "Lettre au Résident Supérieur au Tonkin." May 26, 1913 (CAOM Indochine 56485).

---

* The holdings of the resident superior of Laos are housed at the Centres des Archives d'Outre Mer in Aix-en-Province (CAOM), now renamed the Archives Nationales d'Outre-Mer (ANOM).

———. "L'Interrogatoire de Hung Me Giang (Siung Mi Tchang)." May 31–June 2, 1912 (CAOM Tonkin 56485).

———. "Rapport sur les Faits Reprochés au Nommé Hung Me Giang (Prononciation Meo, Siung Me Chang)." June 13, 1912 (CAOM Tonkin 56485).

Colonna Report. August 4, 1911 (CAOM Indochine 56484).

Dorey. "Rapport d'Ensemble du Chef de Bataillon Dorey sur les Opérations du Détachement du Laos pendant l'Hiver 1920–21 et sur la Pacification de la Region Nord de la Province de Luang Prabang." 1921 (SHAT Vincennes).

Governor General. "Decree of Governor General of Indochina." May 2, 1913 (CAOM Indochine 56485).

———. "Decree on Behalf of Governor General by Van Vollenhoven." February 28, 1914 (CAOM Indochine 56485).

Mortreuil. "A. S. des Renseignements Recueillis sur les Agissements des Meos." August 28, 1911 (CAOM Indochine 56484).

———. "Le Lieutenant-Colonel Mortreuil Commandant de 3ᵉ Territoire Militaire à Monsieur le Résident Supérieur au Tonkin." February 26, 1911 (CAOM Indochine 37850).

———. "Le Lieutenant-Colonel Mortreuil Commandant de 3ᵉ Territoire Militaire à Monsieur le Résident Supérieur au Tonkin." February 27, 1911 (CAOM Indochine 37850).

Perriex. "Lettre de Quang Yen au Résident Supérieur au Tonkin." January 22, 1914 (CAOM Indochine 56485).

———. "Lettre de Quang Yen au Résident Supérieur au Tonkin." February 26, 1914 (CAOM Indochine 56485).

———. "Note Postale de Quang-Yen au Résident Supérieur au Tonkin." April 30, 1914 (CAOM Indochine 56485).

Resident Superior of Laos. "Report Au Conseil de Governmount, 1926." (CAOM, Laos F5).

Saint-Chaffray. "Rapport à Monsieur le Governeur Général 'A. S. du Movement Meo de Lai Chau et Sonla (1919).'" February 10, 1919 (SHAT Vincennes).

"Tasseng Meo de PhaKha a M. le Chao Muong Khoune." December 4, 1945 (CAOM Laos F12).

Telegram. Xieng Khouang à Vientiane. February 29, 1920 (CAOM Laos F5).

Oral and Personal Communications

Aderholt, Heine (General). Interview with author, Menomonee Falls, Wisconsin, July 27, 2003.

Chenivesse, André (Lieutenant Colonel). Interview with author, Rouen, France, July 10, 2002.

Coindat, Albert (MD). Interview with author, Brunoy, France, July 11, 2002.

Gauthier, Maurice (Colonel). Interview with author, Les Chesnaye, France, July 9, 2002.

Her, Pa Kao. Interview with author, Chiangrai, Thailand, August 15, 2001.

Kue, Mee. Interview with author, Vadnais Heights, Minnesota, July 24, 2003.

———. Personal communication, June 2010.

Lair, James William (Colonel). Interview with author, Menomonee Falls, Wisconsin, July 27, 2003.

Lee, Maia. Personal communication, July 4, 2003.

Lee Cha Yia (Captain). Interview with author, Saint Paul, Minnesota, January 3, 2002.

———. Personal communication, June 2007.

Lee Nao Mai. Interview with author, Saint Paul, Minnesota, May 18, 2002.

———. Personal communication, May 2005.

Lo, Ger. Interview with author, Vientiane, Lao PDR, March 15, 2008.

Lo, Zong Blong. Interview with author, Vientiane, Lao PDR, March 3, 2008.

Lyfoung, Mao Song. Interview with author, Maplewood, Minnesota, October 18, 2002.

———. Interview with author, Maplewood, Minnesota, October 24, 2002.

———. Interview with author, Maplewood, Minnesota, June 18, 2003.

———. Interview with author, Saint Paul, Minnesota, October 2, 2004.

———. Interview with author, Saint Paul, Minnesota, March 21, 2005.

Lyfoung, Nao Kao (Colonel). Interview with author, Vadnais Heights, Minnesota, July 24, 2003.

———. Personal communication, April 2010.

Lyfoung, Tougeu. Interview with author, Herblay, France, July 10, 2002.

———. Interview with author, Champlin, Minnesota, July 3, 2003.

Ly Na Jalao (Lieutenant Colonel). Interview with author, Toulouse, France, July 13, 2002.

Ly Na Jalao, Madame. Personal communication, July 13, 2002.

Ly Nao Cha (Colonel). Interview with author, Nimes, France, July 12, 2002.

Ly Pao (Colonel). Interview with author, Alençon, France, July 27, 2002.

Ly Tou Pao (Colonel). Interview with author, Fountain Valley, California, April 13, 2004.

Ly Tsia Tou (Captain). Interview with author, Saint-Germain les Corbeil, France, August 16, 2002.

Michaud, Jean. E-mail to author, May 1, 2014.

Moua, Tong Pao. Interview with author, Madison, Wisconsin, August 1, 2007.

Moua, Toulu Chongtoua (Colonel). Cassette recording sent to author from Denver, Colorado, March 2004 (date received).

Moua, Tsia Naotou. Interview with author, Alençon, France, July 27, 2002.

Sassi, Jean (Colonel). Interview with author, Taverny, France, July 10, 2002.

Thao, Tongeu. Interview with author, Phonsavan, Laos, March 6, 2008.

Thao, Tsia Long. Interview with author, Sun Prairie, Wisconsin, August 6, 2006.

Vang, Kaitong. Interview with author, Saint Paul, Minnesota, October 2, 2004.

Vang, Nao Chue (Major). Interview with author, Saint Paul, Minnesota, September 23, 2007.

Vang, Nengher. E-mail to author, December 15, 2014.

Vang, Yang Cheng. Personal communication, October 2011.

Vang Chou (Colonel). Interview with author, Saint Paul, Minnesota, August 8, 2013.

———. Personal communication, August 7, 2013.

Vang Geu (Lieutenant Colonel). Telephone conversation with author, November 5, 2012.

———. Telephone conversation with author, December 10, 2014.

Vang Pao (General). Interview with author, Maplewood, Minnesota, April 8, 2004.

———. Interview with author, Westminster, California, April 15, 2004.

Vang Say Pao. Interview with author, Roseville, Minnesota, May 2004.

Vannier, Charles (Major). Interview with author, Maplewood, Minnesota, September 18, 2002.

Vue, Lia. Interview with author, Saint Paul, Minnesota, January 5, 2002.

Xiong, Yuepheng. Personal communication, November 2010.

Yang Dao. Personal communication, Brooklyn Park, Minnesota, 2007.

Yang, Dia. Personal communication, November 24, 2005.

Yang, Ka Houa. Personal communication, May 22, 2000.

Yang, Mee. Personal communication, Phonsavan, Lao PDR, March 7, 2008.

Yang, Shoua (Colonel). Interview with author, Nimes, France, July 8, 2002.

Yang, Yong Va. Interview with author, Fresno, California, February 22, 2004.

Yangsao, Sayasith L. Interview with author, Brooklyn Park, Minnesota, October 25, 2002.

———. Personal communication, May 2003.

Secondary Sources

Abadie, Maurice. *Les Races du Haut-Tonkin de Phong-Tho à Lang-Son*. Paris: Société d'éditions géographiques, maritimes et coloniales, 1924.

Achaimbault, Charles. "Les Annales de l'Ancien Royaume de S'ieng Khwang." *Bulletin de l'École Française d'Extrême Orient* 53, no. 2 (1967): 557–674.

Adas, Michael. *Prophets of Rebellion: Millenarian Protest Movements against the European Colonial Order*. Chapel Hill: University of North Carolina Press, 1979.

Alleton, Isabelle. "Les Hmong aux Confins de la Chine et du Vietnam: La Revolte du 'Fou' (1918–1921)." In *Histoire de l'Asie du Sud-Est: Révoltes, Réformes, Révolutions*, edited by Robert Aarsse and Pierre Brocheux, 31–46. Lille, France: Presses Universitaires de Lille, 1981.

Appadurai, Arjun. *Modernity at Large: Cultural Dimensions of Globalization*. Minneapolis: University of Minnesota Press, 1996.

Atwill, David G. *The Chinese Sultanate: Islam, Ethnicity, and the Panthay Rebellion in Southwest China, 1856–1873*. Stanford, CA: Stanford University Press, 2005.

Ayrolles, L. H. *L'Indochine ne Repond Plus*. Saint-Brieuc: Armand Prud'homme, 1948.

Barney, G. Linwood. "The Meo: An Incipient Church." *Practical Anthropology* 4, no. 2 (1957): 31–50.

———. "The Meo of Xieng Khouang Province." In *Southeast Asian Tribes, Minorities, and Nations*, 2 vols., edited by Peter Kunstadter, 1:271–94. Princeton, NJ: Princeton University Press, 1967.

Bernatzik, Hugo Adolf. *Akha and Miao: Problems of Applied Ethnography in Farther India*. New Haven, CT: Human Relations Area Files, 1970.

Bertrais, Yves. *Kab Ke Pam Tuag: Cov Txheej Txheem*. Guyane, France: Association Communauté Hmong, 1985.

———. *Kab Ke Pam Tuag: Cov Zaj*. Guyane, France: Association Communauté Hmong, 1986.

———. *Kab Tshoob Kev Kos: Liaj Lwg Tus Cag Txuj, Rhwv Mws Tus Cag Peev*. Guyane, France: Association Communaute´ Hmong, 1985.

Burchett, Wilfred G. *Mekong Upstream*. Hanoi: Red River Publishing House, 1957.

Caro, Robert A. *The Years of Lyndon Johnson*. Vol. 1, *The Path to Power*. New York: Alfred A. Knopf, 1982.

———. *The Years of Lyndon Johnson*. Vol. 3, *Master of the Senate*. New York: Alfred A. Knopf, 1982.

Cha, Dia. *Hmong American Concepts of Health, Healing, and Conventional Medicine*. New York: Routledge, 2003.

Cha, Ya Po. *An Introduction to Hmong Culture*. Jefferson, NC: McFarland, 2010.

Chan, Sucheng. *Hmong Means Free: Life in Laos and America*. Philadelphia: Temple University Press, 1994.

Chiao, Chien, and Nicholas Tapp. *Ethnicity and Ethnic Groups in China*. Hong Kong: New Asia Academic Bulletin, 1989.

Chindarsi, Nusit. *The Religion of the Hmong Njua*. Bangkok: Siam Society, 1976.

Coburn, Jewell Reinhart, Tzexa Cherta Lee, and Anne Sibley O'Brien. *Jouanah, a Hmong Cinderella*. Arcadia, CA: Shen's Books, 1996.

Colby, William Egan, and Peter Forbath. *Honorable Men: My Life in the CIA*. New York: Simon and Schuster, 1978.

Condominas, Georges. "Aspects of a Minority Problem in Indochina." *Pacific Affairs* 24, no. 1 (1951): 77–82.

———. "Essai Sur l'Evolution des Systemes Politiques Thais." In *L'Espace Social à Propos de L'Asie du Sud-Est*, 259–316. Paris: Flammarion 1980.

———. "A Few Remarks about Thai Political Systems." In *Natural Symbols in South East Asia*, edited by G. B. Milner, 105–12. London: School of Oriental and African Studies, 1978.

Cooper, Robert G. *The Hmong: A Guide to Traditional Lifestyles*. Singapore: Times Editions, 1998.

———. *Resource Scarcity and the Hmong Response: Patterns of Settlement and Economy in Transition*. Singapore: National University of Singapore Press, 1984.

Cooper, Robert, Nicholas Tapp, Gary Yia Lee, and Gretel Schwoer-Kohl. *The Hmong*. Bangkok: Artasia Press, 1991.

Corlin, Claes. "Hmong and the Land Question in Vietnam: National Policy and Local Concepts of the Environment." In *Hmong/Miao in Asia*, edited by Nicholas Tapp, Jean Michaud, Christian Culas, and Gary Y. Lee, 295-320. Chiangmai, Thailand: Silkworm Books, 2004.

Culas, Christian. "Innovation and Tradition in Rituals and Cosmology: Hmong Messianism and Shamanism in Southeast Asia." In *Hmong/Miao in Asia*, edited by Nicholas Tapp, Jean Michaud, Christian Culas, and Gary Yia Lee, 97-126. Chiangmai, Thailand: Silkworm Books, 2004.

———. "Le Messianisme Hmong." PhD diss., Université de Provence-Aix-Marseille I, 1998.

———. *Le Messianisme Hmong aux XIXᵉ et XXᵉ Siècles: La Dynamique Religieuse comme Instrument Politique*. Paris: Éditions du Centre National de le Recherche Scientifique, 2005.

Diamond, Norma. "Miao as a Category." In *Cultural Encounters on China's Ethnic Frontiers*, edited by Stevan Harrell, 92-116. Seattle: University of Washington Press, 1995.

Diguet, Édouard Jacques Joseph. *Les Montagnards du Tonkin*. New York: AMS Press, 1981.

Dommen, Arthur J. *Conflict in Laos: The Politics of Neutralization*. New York: Praeger, 1964.

Donnelly, Nancy D. *Changing Lives of Refugee Hmong Women*. Seattle: University of Washington Press, 1994.

Downer, Gordon, "Chinese, Thai, and Miao-Yao." In *Linguistic Comparison in South East Asia*, edited by H. L. Shorto, 133-39. London: School of Oriental and African Studies, University of London, 1963.

———. "Tone-Change and Tone-Shift in White Miao." *Bulletin of the School of Oriental and African Studies* 30, no. 3 (1967): 589-99.

Duffy, John Michael. *Writing from These Roots: Literacy in a Hmong-American Community*. Honolulu: University of Hawai'i Press, 2007.

———. "Writing from These Roots: Literacy, Rhetoric, and History in a Hmong-American Community." PhD diss., University of Wisconsin-Madison, 2000.

Elson, R. E. *Suharto: A Political Biography*. Cambridge: Cambridge University Press, 2001.

Enwall, Joakim. *Hmong Writing Systems in Vietnam: A Case Study of Vietnam's Minority Language Policy*. Stockholm, Sweden: Center for Pacific Asian Studies, Stockholm University, 1995.

Errington, Shelley. *Meaning and Power in a Southeast Asian Realm*. Princeton, NJ: Princeton University Press, 1989.

Evans, Grant. *The Last Century of Lao Royalty: A Documentary History*. Chiangmai, Thailand: Silkworm Books, 2009.

———. *The Politics of Ritual and Remembrance: Laos Since 1975*. Honolulu: University of Hawai'i Press, 1998.

———. *A Short History of Laos*. Crows Nest, NSW, Australia: Allen and Unwin, 2002.

Fadiman, Anne. *The Spirit Catches You and You Fall Down: A Hmong Child, Her American Doctors, and the Collision of Two Cultures*. New York: Farrar, Straus and Giroux, 1997.

Failler, Philippe Le. "The Đèo Family of Lai Châu: Traditional Power and Unconventional Practices." *Journal of Vietnamese Studies* 6, no. 2 (Summer 2011): 42-67.

Falk, Catherine. "Upon Meeting the Ancestors: The Hmong Funeral Ritual in Asia and Australia." *Hmong Studies Journal* 1, no. 1 (1996): 1-15.

Fall, Bernard B. *Hell in a Very Small Place.* New York: J. B. Lippincott, 1967.

Falla, Jonathan. *True Love and Bartholomew: Rebels on the Burmese Border.* Cambridge: Cambridge University Press, 1991.

Faruque, Cathleen Jo. *Migration of Hmong to the Midwestern United States.* Lanham, MD: University Press of America, 2002.

Ferguson, R. Brian, and Neil L. Whitehead. *War in the Tribal Zone: Expanding States and Indigenous Warfare.* School of American Research Advanced Seminar Series. Santa Fe, NM: School of American Research Press, 1992.

Formoso, Bernard. "Zomian or Zombies? What Future Exists for the Peoples of the Southeast Asian Massif?" *Journal of Global History* 5 (2010): 313-32.

Fung, Yu-Lan. *A History of Chinese Philosophy.* Vol. 2. Translated by Derk Bodde. Princeton, NJ: Princeton University Press, 1953.

Geddes, William R. *Migrants of the Mountains: The Cultural Ecology of the Blue Miao (Hmong Njua) of Thailand.* Oxford: Clarendon Press, 1976.

Geertz, Clifford. *Negara: The Theatre State in Nineteenth-Century Bali.* Princeton, NJ: Princeton University Press, 1980.

Giap, Vo Nguyen. *Dien Bien Phu.* Hanoi: Édition en Langues Étrangères, 1964.

Giersch, C. Patterson. "Across Zomia with Merchants, Monks, and Musk: Process Geographies, Trade Networks, and the Inner-East-Southeast Asian Borderlands." *Journal of Global History* 5 (2010): 215-39.

Girard, Henry. *Les Tribus Sauvages du Haut-Tonkin: Mans et Méos—Notes Anthropométriques et Ethnographiques.* Paris: Imprimerie Nationale, 1904.

Graham, David Crockett. "The Customs of the Ch'uan Miao." *Journal of the West China Border Research Society* 9 (1937): 13-71.

Gunn, Geoffrey C. *Political Struggles in Laos (1930-1954): Vietnamese Communist Power and the Lao Struggle for National Independence.* Bangkok: Duang Kamol, 1988.

———. *Rebellion in Laos: Peasants and Politics in a Colonial Backwater.* Boulder, CO: Westview Press, 1990.

———. "Shamans and Rebels: The Batchai (Meo) Rebellion of Northern Laos and North-West Vietnam (1918-21)." *Journal of the Siam Society* 74 (1986): 107-21.

Halbwachs, Maurice. *The Collective Memory.* New York: Harper & Row, 1980.

Hamilton-Merritt, Jane. *Tragic Mountains: The Hmong, the Americans, and the Secret Wars for Laos, 1942-1992.* Bloomington: Indiana University Press, 1993.

Hawley, Kristel L. *Being Hmong Means Being Free: Guide.* Green Bay: Northeastern Wisconsin in-School Telecommunications (NEWIST/CESA 7), University of Wisconsin-Green Bay, 2000.

Hein, Jeremy. *Ethnic Origins: The Adaptation of Cambodian and Hmong Refugees in Four American Cities.* New York: Russell Sage Foundation, 2006.

Heine-Geldern, R. "Conceptions of State and Kingship in Southeast Asia." *Far Eastern Quarterly* 2, no. 1 (1942): 15-30.

———. *Conceptions of State and Kingship in Southeast Asia*. Data Papers, no. 18. Ithaca, NY: Southeast Asia Program, Cornell University, 1956.

Herman, John E. "Empire in the Southwest: Early Qing Reforms to the Native Chieftain System." *Journal of Asian Studies* 56, no. 1 (1997): 47-74.

Hillmer, Paul. *A People's History of the Hmong*. Saint Paul: Minnesota Historical Society Press, 2010.

Hobsbawm, E. J. *Primitive Rebels; Studies in Archaic Forms of Social Movement in the 19th and 20th Centuries*. Manchester: Manchester University Press, 1959.

Hudspeth, William H. "The Cult of the Door amongst the Miao." *Folk-Lore* 33, no. 4 (1922): 406-10.

———. *Stone-Gateway and the Flowery Miao*. London: Cargate Press, 1970.

Hull, Edward. *The Wall Chart of World History*. London: Bracken Books, 1988.

Ileto, Reynaldo Clemeña. *Pasyon and Revolution: Popular Movements in the Philippines, 1840-1910*. Quezon City, Philippines: Ateneo de Manila University Press, 1979.

Ireson-Doolittle, Carol. *Field, Forest, and Family: Women's Work and Power in Rural Laos*. Boulder, CO: Westview Press, 1996.

Jenks, Robert Darrah. *Insurgency and Social Disorder in Guizhou: The "Miao" Rebellion, 1854-1873*. Honolulu: University of Hawai'i Press, 1994.

Johnson, Charles, and Se Yang. *Dab Neeg Hmoob: Myths, Legends, and Folk Tales from the Hmong of Laos*. 2nd ed. Saint Paul, MN: Linguistics Department, Macalester College, 1992.

Jonsson, Hjorleifur. *Mien Relations: Mountain People and State Control in Thailand*. Ithaca, NY: Cornell University Press, 2005.

———. *Slow Anthropology: Negotiating Difference with the Iu Mien*. Ithaca, NY: Cornell University Press, 2014.

Jurewitsch, Sao Sue. "33rd Hmong Freedom Celebration Brings Thousands to St. Paul's Como Park." *Hmong Pages*, August 1, 2013.

Karnow, Stanley. *Vietnam: A History*. New York: Penguin Books, 1984.

Kenworthy, Sukalaya. *Hmong Means Free*. Baltimore: Publish America, 2004.

Kerkvliet, Benedict J. *The Huk Rebellion: A Study of Peasant Revolt in the Philippines*. Berkeley: University of California Press, 1977.

Keyes, Charles. *The Golden Peninsula: Culture and Adaptation in Mainland Southeast Asia*. New York: Macmillan, 1977.

Ko, Dorothy. *Cinderella's Sisters: A Revisionist History of Footbinding*. Berkeley: University of California Press, 2005.

Lam Tam. "A Survey of the Meo." *Vietnamese Studies* 9, no. 36 (1974): 7-61.

Lartéguy, Jean, and Yang Dao. *La Fabuleuse Aventure du Peuple de l'Opium*. Paris: Presses de la Cité, 1979.

Leach, Edmund R. *Political Systems of Highland Burma: A Study of Kachin Social Structure*. Boston: Beacon Press, 1965.

Lebar, Frank M., Gerald C. Hickey, and John K. Musgrave. *Ethnic Groups of Mainland Southeast Asia*. New Haven, CT: Human Relations Area Files, 1964.

Lebar, Frank M., and Adrienne Suddard. *Laos*. New Haven, CT: Human Relations Area Files, 1960.

Lee, Gary Yia. "Bandits or Rebels? Hmong Resistance in the New Lao State." *Indigenous Affairs* 4 (October–December 2000): 6–15. Extended 2005 version available at http://www.garyyialee.com/.

———. "Cultural Identity in Post-modern Society: Reflections on What Is a Hmong." *Hmong Studies Journal* 1, no. 1 (1996): 1–15.

———. "Ethnic Minorities and Nation Building in Laos: The Hmong in the Lao State." *Péninsule* 11/12 (1985–86): 215–32.

———. "Household and Marriage in a Thai Highland Society." *Journal of the Siam Society* 76 (1988): 162–73.

———. "Minority Policies and the Hmong." In *Contemporary Laos*, edited by Martin Stuart-Fox, 199–219. New York: St. Martin's Press, 1982.

———. "The Religious Presentation of Social Relationships: Hmong World View and Social Structure." *Lao Studies Review* 2 (1994–95): 44–60.

Lee, Mai Na M. "The Thousand-Year Myth: Construction and Characterization of Hmong." *Hmong Studies Journal* 2, no. 1 (1997): 1–15.

———. "The Women of Dragon Capital (Long Cheng): Marriage Alliances and the Rise of Vang Pao." In *Claiming Place: Hmong Women, Power, and Knowledge Production*, edited by Chia Vang, Faith Nibbs, and Ma Vang. Minneapolis: University of Minnesota Press, forthcoming.

Legge, James, trans. *The Four Books*. In *The Chinese Classics*, vols. 1–2. Taipei: Culture Book Co., 1992.

Lemoine, Jacques. "Ethnicity, Culture, and Development among Some Minorities of the People's Republic of China." In *Ethnicity and Ethnic Groups in China*, edited by Chien Chiao and Nicholas Tapp, 1–9. Hong Kong: New Asia Academic Bulletin, 1989.

———. "The (H)mong Shamans' Power of Healing: Sharing the Esoteric Knowledge of a Great (H)mong Shaman." *Hmong Studies Journal* 12 (2011): 1–36.

———. "Les Ecritures du Hmong." *Bulletin des Amis du Royaume Lao* 7–8 (1972): 123–65.

———. *L'Initiation du Mort Chez les Hmong*. Bangkok: Pandora, 1983.

———. *Parlons (H)mong*. Paris: L'Harmattan, 2013.

———. *Un Village Hmong Vert du Haut Laos*. Paris: Éditions du Centre National de le Recherche Scientifique, 1972.

Lemoine, Jacques, with Kenneth White. *Kr'ua Ke/Showing the Way: A Hmong Initiation of the Dead*. Bangkok: Pandora, 1983.

Lewis, Alison. "The A Hmao in Northeast Yunnan and Northwest Guizhou Provinces: Perspectives on the Encounter with the A Hmao from Some Western Protestant Missionaries (Initial Commentary on Diaries Written by Reverend Samuel Pollard,

1910-14)." In *Hmong/Miao in Asia*, edited by Nicholas Tapp, Jean Michaud, Christian Culas, and Gary Y. Lee, 219-36. Chiangmai, Thailand: Silkworm Books, 2004.

Liamputtong, Pranee. *Hmong Women and Reproduction*. Westport, CT: Bergin and Garvey, 2000.

Lieberman, Victor. "A Zone of Refuge in Southeast Asia? Reconceptualizing Interior Spaces." *Journal of Global History* 5 (2010): 333-46.

Lin, Yeuh-Hwa. "The Miao-Man Peoples of Kweichow." *Harvard Journal of Asiatic Studies* 5, no. 3/4 (1940): 261-345.

Lis, Teev. "Virtual Hmong Nation." Social Culture Hmong Discussion Forum. https://groups.google.com/forum/?fromgroups#!topic/soc.culture.hmong/gUb2MTohvwY.

Lo, Fungchatou T. *The Promised Land: Socioeconomic Reality of the Hmong People in Urban America, 1976-2000*. Bristol, IN: Wyndham Hall Press, 2001.

Loewe, Michael, and Edward L. Shaughnessy, eds. *The Cambridge History of Ancient China: From the Origins of Civilization to 221 B.C.* Cambridge: Cambridge University Press, 1999.

Long, Lynellyn D. *Ban Vinai, the Refugee Camp*. New York: Columbia University Press, 1993.

Lor, Yang. "Hmong Political Involvement in St. Paul, Minnesota, and Fresno, California." *Hmong Studies Journal* 10 (2009): 1-53.

Lunet de Lajonquiere, Emile. *Ethnographie du Tonkin Septentrionale (Rédigé sur l'Ordre de M. P. Beau, Gouverneur Général de l'Indo-Chine Française, d'après les Études des Administrateurs Civils et Militaire des Provinces Septentrionales)*. Hanoi: E. Leroux, 1906.

Lyfoung, Touxa, trans. *Touby Lyfoung: An Authentic Account of the Life of a Hmong Man in the Troubled Land of Laos*. Minneapolis, MN: Burgess Publishing, 1996.

———. *Tub Npis Lisfoom Tej Lus Tseg Cia* [Words left by Touby Lyfoung]. Minneapolis, MN: Burgess Publishing, 1996.

Marshall, Harry I. *The Karen People of Burma: A Study in Anthropology and Ethnology*. Columbus, OH: The University, 1922.

Marx, Karl. "Speech at the Anniversary of the *People's Paper*." In *Karl Marx and Frederick Engels: Selected Works*, vol. 1, 500. Moscow: Progress Publishers, 1969.

Matsuda, Matt. *The Memory of the Modern*. Oxford: Oxford University Press, 1996.

"May Song Vang Dies from Cancer." *Asian American Press*, August 11, 2013. http://aapress.com/ethnicity/hmong/may-song-vang-dies-from-cancer/.

Mayurī, Ngaosīvat, and Ngaosyvathn Pheuiphanh. *Paths to Conflagration: Fifty Years of Diplomacy and Warfare in Laos, Thailand, and Vietnam, 1778-1828*. Ithaca, NY: Southeast Asia Program, Cornell University, 1998.

McAlister, John T., Jr. "Mountain Minorities and the Viet Minh: A Key to the Indochina War." In *Southeast Asian Tribes, Minorities, and Nations*, 2 vols., edited by Peter Kunstadter, 2:771-844. Princeton, NJ: Princeton University Press, 1967.

McCoy, Alfred W. "French Colonialism in Laos, 1893–1945." In *Laos: War and Revolution*, edited by Nina S. Adams and Alfred W. McCoy, 67–99. New York: Harper and Row, 1970.

———. *The Politics of Heroin: CIA Complicity in the Global Drug Trade.* Brooklyn, NY: Lawrence Hill Books, 1991.

———. "The Politics of the Poppy in Indochina: A Comparative Study of Patron-Client Relations under French and American Administrations." In *Drugs, Politics, and Diplomacy*, edited by Luiz R. S. Simmons Abdul and A. Said, 122–29. Beverly Hills, CA: Sage Publications, 1974.

———. Review of *Tragic Mountains: The Hmong, the Americans, and the Secret Wars for Laos, 1942–1992*, by Jane Hamilton-Merritt. *Journal of Asian Studies* 52, no. 3 (1993): 777–80.

McCoy, Alfred W., Cathleen B. Read, and Leonard P. Adams. *The Politics of Heroin.* New York: Harper and Row, 1972.

McMahon, Daniel. "Identity and Conflict on a Chinese Borderland: Yan Ruyi and the Recruitment of the Gelao during the 1795–97 Miao Revolt." *Late Imperial China* 23, no. 2 (2002): 53–86.

Melo, Frederick. "St. Paul: Hmong Vets Memorial Could Soon Be Realized." *St. Paul Pioneer Press*, March 29, 2014. http://www.twincities.com/ci_22897501/st-paul-hmong-vets-memorial-could-soon-be.

"Memorializing Lao Hmong Veterans and Their Quest for Freedom." National Public Radio Newswire Services, January 5, 2006. http://www.prnewswire.com/news-releases/memorializing-lao-hmong-veterans-and-their-quest-for-freedom-53154847tml.

Michael, Franz. *The Taiping Rebellion: History and Documents.* Seattle: University of Washington Press, 1966.

Michaud, Jean. *Historical Dictionary of the Peoples of the Southeast Asian Massif.* Lanham, MD: Scarecrow Press, 2006.

———. *"Incidental" Ethnographers: French Catholic Missions on the Tonkin-Yunnan Frontier, 1880–1930* (Boston: Brill, 2007).

———. "The Montagnards and the State in Northern Vietnam from 1802 to 1975: A Historical Overview." *Ethnohistory* 47, no. 2 (Spring 2000): 333–68.

———. *Moving Mountains: Ethnicity and Livelihoods in Highland China, Vietnam, and Laos.* Vancouver, BC: UBC Press, 2011.

———. "Zomia and Beyond." Editorial, *Journal of Global History* 5 (2010): 187–214.

Michaud, Jean, and Christian Culas. "The Hmong of the Southeast Asian Massif: Their Recent History of Migration." In *Where China Meets Southeast Asia: Social and Cultural Change in the Border Regions*, edited by Grant Evans, Christopher Hutton, and Khun Eng Kuah, 98–121. New York: St. Martin's Press, 2000.

Moréchand, G. "Le Chamanisme des Hmong." *Bulletin de l'École Française d'Extrême Orient* 54 (1968): 77–81.

Mottin, Jean. *Contes et Légendes Hmong Blanc*. Bangkok: Don Bosco Press, 1980.
———. *History of the Hmong*. Bangkok: Odeon Store, 1980.
Moua, Chai Charles. *Roars of Traditional Leaders: Mong (Miao) American Cultural Practices in a Conventional Society*. Lanham, MD: University Press of America, 2012.
Nusit, Chindarsi. *The Religion of the Hmong Njua*. Bangkok: Siam Society, 1976.
Oakes, Len. *Prophetic Charisma: The Psychology of Revolutionary Religious Personalities*. Syracuse: Syracuse University Press, 1997.
Olick, Jeffrey K., Vered Vinitzky-Seroussi, and Daniel Levy. "Introduction." In *The Collective Memory Reader*, edited by Jeffrey K. Olick, Vered Vinitzky-Seroussi, and Daniel Levy, 3-62. Oxford: Oxford University Press, 2011.
Osborne, Milton. *Mekong: Turbulent Past, Uncertain Future*. New York: Grove Press, 2000.
———. *River Road to China: The Mekong River Expedition, 1866-1873*. New York: Liveright, 1975.
Owen, Norman G. *The Emergence of Modern Southeast Asia: A New History*. Honolulu: University of Hawai'i Press, 2005.
Pearce, Kimber Charles. "The Radical Feminist Manifesto as Generic Appropriation: Gender, Genre, and Second Wave Resistance." *Southern Communication Journal* 64, no. 4 (1999): 307-15.
Potts, John. *A History of Charisma*. New York: Palgrave Macmillan, 2009.
Proschan, Frank. "Peoples of the Gourd: Imagined Ethnicities in Highland Southeast Asia." *Journal of Asian Studies* 60, no. 4 (2001): 999-1032.
———. "Rumor, Innuendo, Propaganda, and Disinformation." Review essay, *Bulletin of Concerned Asian Scholars* 28, no. 1 (1996): 52-64.
Quang, Vuong Duy. "The Hmong and Forest Management in Northern Vietnam's Mountainous Areas." In *Hmong/Miao in Asia*, edited by Nicholas Tapp, Jean Michaud, Christian Culas, and Gary Y. Lee, 321-31. Chiangmai, Thailand: Silkworm Books, 2004.
Quincy, Keith. *Harvesting Pa Chay's Wheat: The Hmong and America's Secret War in Laos*. Cheney: Eastern Washington University Press, 2000.
———. *Hmong: History of a People*. Cheney: Eastern Washington University Press, 1988.
———. *Hmong: History of a People*. 2nd ed. Cheney: Eastern Washington University Press, 1995.
Rapin, Ami-Jacques. "La guerre de Pachay: Le Grand Soulèvement des Hmong du Tonkin et du Laos, 1918-1921." *Péninsule* 51 (2005): 103-47.
Reilly, Thomas H. *The Taiping Heavenly Kingdom: Rebellion and the Blasphemy of Empire*. Seattle: University of Washington Press, 2004.
Robbins, Christopher. *The Ravens: The Men Who Flew in America's Secret War in Laos*. New York: Crown, 1987.
Rochet, Charles. *Pays Laos, le Laos dans le Tourmente, 1939-1945*. Paris: Jean Vigneau, 1946.

Roux, Henri, and Tran Van Chu. "Quelques Minorités Ethniques du Nord-Indochine." *France-Asie*, nos. 92–93 (1954): 132–419.

Sakhong, Liam Hmung. *In Search of Chin Identity*. NIAS Monography 91. Copenhagen: NIAS Press, 2002.

Savina, F. M. *Dictionnaire Miao-Tseu-Français*. Hanoi: Imprimerie d'Extrême-Orient, 1917.

———. *Histoire des Miao*. Hong Kong: Imprimerie de la Société des Missions-Étrangères, 1924.

Schafer, Edward. *The Vermillion Bird*. Berkeley: University of California Press, 1967.

Schanche, Don A. *Mister Pop*. New York: McKay, 1970.

Schein, Louisa. *Minority Rules: The Miao and the Feminine in China's Cultural Politics*. Durham: Duke University Press, 2000.

Schein, Louisa, and Bee Vang. "*Gran Torino*'s Hmong Lead Bee Vang on Film, Race, and Masculinity: Conversations with Louisa Schein." *Hmong Studies Journal* 11 (Spring 2010): 1–11.

Schendel, Willem van. "Geographies of Knowing, Geographies of Ignorance: Jumping Scale in Southeast Asia." *Environment and Planning D: Society and Space* 20, no. 6 (2002): 647–68.

Scott, James C. *The Art of Not Being Governed: An Anarchist History of Upland Southeast Asia*. New Haven, CT: Yale University Press, 2009.

———. "The Erosion of Patron-Client Bonds and Social Change in Rural Southeast Asia." *Journal of Asian Studies* 31, no. 1 (1972): 3–37.

———. "Patron-Client Politics and Political Change in Southeast Asia." *American Political Science Review* 66, no. 1 (1972): 91–113.

———. *Weapons of the Weak: Everyday Forms of Peasant Resistance*. New Haven, CT: Yale University Press, 1985.

Simpson, Howard R. *Dien Bien Phu: The Epic Battle America Forgot*. Washington, DC: Brassey's, 1994.

Smalley, William A., Chia Koua Vang, and Gnia Yee Yang. *Mother of Writing: The Origin and Development of a Hmong Messianic Script*. Chicago: University of Chicago Press, 1990.

Smith, Anthony. *The Ethnic Revival*. Cambridge: Cambridge University Press, 1981.

———, ed. *Nationalist Movements*. London: MacMillan, 1976.

Smith, Martin. *Burma: Insurgency and the Politics of Ethnicity*. Dhaka, Bangladesh: Dhaka University Press, 1999.

Smith, Sidonie, and Julia Watson. *Reading Autobiography: A Guide for Interpreting Life Narratives*. Minneapolis: University of Minnesota Press, 2001.

Smuckarn, Snit, and Kennon Breazeale. *A Culture in Search of Survival: The Phuan of Thailand and Laos*. New Haven, CT: Council on Southeast Asia Studies, Yale University, 1988.

Spence, Jonathan D. *God's Chinese Son: The Taiping Heavenly Kingdom of Hong Xiuquan*. New York: W. W. Norton, 1996.

Stuart-Fox, Martin. *A History of Laos.* Cambridge: Cambridge University Press, 1997.

Stuart-Fox, Martin, and Mary Kooyman. *Historical Dictionary of Laos.* Metuchen, NJ: Scarecrow Press, 1992.

Sutton, Donald S. "Myth Making on an Ethnic Frontier: The Cult of the Heavenly Kings of West Hunan, 1715–1996." *Modern China* 26, no. 4 (2000): 448–500.

——. "Violence and Ethnicity on a Qing Colonial Frontier: Customary and Statutory Law in the Eighteenth-Century Miao Pale." *Modern Asian Studies* 37, no. 1 (2003): 41–80.

Symonds, Patricia V. *Calling in the Soul: Gender and the Cycle of Life in a Hmong Village.* Seattle: University of Washington Press, 2004.

Tai, Hue-Tam Ho. *Radicalism and the Origins of the Vietnamese Revolution.* Cambridge, MA: Harvard University Press, 1992.

Tambiah, Stanley. "The Galactic Polity in Southeast Asia." In *Culture, Thought, and Social Action,* 252–86. Cambridge, MA: Harvard University Press, 1985.

Tapp, Nicholas. "Hmong Confucian Ethics and Constructions of the Past." In *Cultural Crisis and Social Memory: Modernity and Identity in Thailand and Laos,* edited by Shigeharu Tanabe and Charles F. Keyes, 95–110. Honolulu: University of Hawai'i Press, 2002.

——. *The Hmong of China: Context, Agency, and the Imaginary.* Leiden: Brill, 2001.

——. "The Impact of Missionary Christianity upon Marginalized Ethnic Minorities: The Case of the Hmong." *Journal of Southeast Asian Studies* 20, no. 1 (1989): 70–95.

——. *The Impossibility of Self: An Essay on the Hmong Diaspora.* Berlin: Lit, 2010.

——. *Sovereignty and Rebellion: The White Hmong of Northern Thailand.* Singapore: Oxford University Press, 1989.

Thao, Paja, Dwight Conquergood, and Xa Thao. *I Am a Shaman: A Hmong Life Story with Ethnographic Commentary.* Southeast Asian Refugee Studies Occasional Papers, no. 8. Minneapolis: Southeast Asian Refugee Studies Project, Center for Urban and Regional Affairs, University of Minnesota, 1989.

Thao, Pao Saykao. "Hmong Leadership: The Traditional Model." 1997. http://www .hmongnet.org/hmong-au/leader.htm.

Thao, Paoze. *Keebkwm Hmoob Ntseeg Yexus: Hmong Christian History, 1950–2000.* Thornton, CO: Hmong District, 2000.

Thompson, E. P. *The Making of the English Working Class.* London: Penguin, 1991.

Thompson, Paul. "Family Myths, Models, and Denials in the Shaping of Individual Life Paths." In *Between Generations: Family Models, Myths, and Memories,* edited by Daniel Bertaux and Paul Thompson, 13–38. New York: Oxford University Press, 1993.

——. *The Voice of the Past: Oral History.* New York: Oxford University Press, 1978.

Took, Jennifer. *A Native Chieftaincy in Southwest China: Franchising a Tai Chieftaincy under the Tusi System of Late Imperial China.* Leiden: Brill, 2005.

Tooker, Deborah E. "Putting the Mandala in Its Place: A Practice-Based Approach to the Spatialization of Power on the Southeast Asian 'Periphery'—the Case of the Akha." *Journal of Asian Studies* 55, no. 2 (1996): 323–58.

Toye, Hugh. *Laos: Buffer State or Battleground.* London: Oxford University Press, 1968.

Trinquier, Roger. *Les Maquis d'Indochine: 1952–1954.* Paris: Éditions Albatros, 1976.

Van, Dang Nghiem. "The Flood Myth and the Origin of Ethnic Groups in Southeast Asia." *Journal of American Folklore* 106, no. 421 (1993): 304–37.

Tumblety, Joan. *Memory and History: Understanding Memory as Source and Subject.* New York: Routledge, 2013.

Vang, Chia Koua, Gnia Yee Yang, and William Allen Smalley. *The Life of Shong Lue Yang: Hmong "Mother of Writing" Keeb Kwm Soob Lwj Yaj—Hmoob "Niam Ntawv."* Translated by Mitt Moua and See Yang. Minneapolis: Southeast Asian Refugee Studies, University of Minnesota, 1990.

Vang, Thomas S. *A History of the Hmong: From Ancient Times to the Modern Diaspora.* [Raleigh, NC: Lulu Enterprises], 2008.

Vang Geu. "Unforgettable Laos." n.d. http://www.unforgettable-laos.com/historical-of-events/part-1/.

Vansina, Jan. *Oral Tradition as History.* Madison: University of Wisconsin Press, 1985.

Vwj Zoov Tsheej [Wu Rong Zhen], with Yaj Ntxoov Yias and Txiv Plig Nyiav Pov [Yves Bertrais]. *Haiv Hmoob Liv Xwm* [Hmong history]. Quezon City, Philippines: Patrimonie Culturel Hmong, 1997.

Wakeman, Frederick, Jr. *The Fall of Imperial China.* New York: Free Press, 1975.

Walker, Anthony R. *Merit and the Millennium: Routine and Crisis in the Ritual Lives of the Lahu People.* New Delhi: Hindustan Publishing Corporation, 2003.

Wallace, Anthony F. C. "Acculturation: Revitalization Movements." *American Anthropologist* 58, no. 2 (1956): 264–81.

Warner, Roger. *Back Fire: The CIA's Secret War in Laos and Its Link to the War in Vietnam.* New York: Simon and Schuster, 1995.

Weber, Max. *Economy and Society.* Berkeley: University of California Press, 1978.

Westermeyer, Joseph. *Poppies, Pipes, and People: Opium and Its Use in Laos.* Berkeley: University of California Press, 1983.

White, Kenneth, and Jacques Lemoine. *Kr'ua Ke/Showing the Way: A Hmong Initiation of the Dead.* Bangkok: Pandora, 1983.

White, Richard. *The Middle Ground: Indians, Empires, and Republics in the Great Lakes Region, 1650–1815.* Cambridge: Cambridge University Press, 1991.

Wiens, Harold J. *Han Chinese Expansion in South China.* Hamden, CT: Shoe String Press, 1967.

Williams, Patrick, and Laura Chrisman. *Colonial Discourse and Post-colonial Theory: A Reader.* New York: Columbia University Press, 1994.

Winichakul, Thongchai. *Siam Mapped: A History of the Geo-body of a Nation.* Honolulu: University of Hawai'i Press, 1994.

Wolters, O. W. *History, Culture, and Region in Southeast Asian Perspectives.* Singapore: Institute of Southeast Asian Studies, 1982.

Wyatt, David K. *Thailand: A Short History.* New Haven, CT: Yale University Press, 1984.

Yaj, Txooj Tsawb. *Rog Paj Cai.* Vientiane: Y. Bertrais, 1972.

Yang, Kaiyi. "Hmong-Mongolian?" *Hmong Forum*, January 1996, 48-62.

Yang, Kao-Ly. "Mesurer et Peser Chez les Hmong du Laos: Aspects Techniques et Notions de Précision." *Bulletin de l'École Française d'Extrême Orient* 90-91 (2004).

———. "Problems in the Interpretation of Hmong Clan Surnames." In *Hmong/Miao in Asia*, edited by Nicholas Tapp, Jean Michaud, Christian Culas, and Gary Y. Lee, 179-215. Chiangmai, Thailand: Silkworm Books, 2004.

Yang, Kou. "Challenges and Complexity in the Re-construction of Hmong History." *Hmong Studies Journal* 10 (2009): 1-17.

———. "The Passing of a Hmong Pioneer: Nhiavu Lobliayao (Nyiaj Vws Lauj Npliaj Yob), 1915-1999." *Hmong Studies Journal* 3 (2000): 1-3.

Yang, Zhiqiang. "From *Miao* to *Miaozu*: Alterity in the Formation of Modern Ethnic Groups." *Hmong Studies Journal* 10 (2009): 1-28.

Yang Dao. "The Hmong: Enduring Traditions." In *Minority Cultures of Laos: Kammu, Lua', Lahu, Hmong, and Mien*, edited by Judy Lewis and Damrong Tayanin, 249-315. Rancho Cordova, CA: Southeast Asia Community Resource Center, Folsom Cordova Unified School District, 1992.

———. *Hmong at the Turning Point.* Edited by Jeanne L. Blake. Minneapolis: World-Bridge Associates, 1993.

Yao, Xinzhong. *An Introduction to Confucianism.* New York: Cambridge University Press, 2000.

Yāthộtū, Sutdālā. *Tū Yā Saichū: Viraburut hæng dæn Lān Sāng.* Vianchan: Hōngphim Num Lāo, 2004.

Yoshikawa, Taeko. "From a Refugee Camp to the Minnesota State Senate: A Case Study of a Hmong American Woman's Challenge." *Hmong Studies Journal* 7 (2006): 1-23.

Zinoman, Peter. *The Colonial Bastille: A History of Imprisonment in Vietnam, 1862-1940.* Berkeley: University of California Press, 2001.

Unpublished Theses, Dissertations, Talks, and Performances

Cushman, Richard D. "Rebel Haunts and Lotus Huts: Problems in the Ethnohistory of the Yao." PhD diss., Cornell University, 1970.

Lee, Mai Na M. "The Dream of the Hmong Kingdom: Resistance, Collaboration, and Legitimacy under French Colonial Rule (1893-1954)." PhD diss., University of Wisconsin-Madison, 2005.

Leepreecha, Prasit. Keynote Address at the conference Hmong Across Borders, University of Minnesota, October 5, 2013.

———. "Kinship and Identity among Hmong in Thailand." PhD diss., University of Washington, 2001.

Long Yu-xiao. "The Origin of the Hmong in China." Talk given at Concordia University, Saint Paul, Minnesota, December 18, 2009.

Lor, Yia S. "Power Struggle between the Lor and Ly Clans, 1900–2000." Undergraduate thesis, California State University, Chico, 2001.

Moua, Mee. Talk given at the forum Hmong Diaspora, Gender, and Public Policy, University of Minnesota, October 2010.

Thao, Shong Ger. Speech given at Yang Cheng Vang's initiation as a master ritualist, Hmong Village Complex in Saint Paul, Minnesota, December 2, 2012.

Thao, Tsia Long. Speech given to a Southeast Asian Studies Summer Institute Hmong language class, University of Wisconsin–Madison, July 27, 2004.

Vang, Her. "Dreaming of Home, Dreaming of Land: Displacements and Hmong Transnational Politics, 1975–2010." PhD diss., University of Minnesota, 2010.

Vang, Yang Cheng. "Origin of the Loss of Hmong Writing." Talk and *zaj qeeg* performed for History 3483: Hmong History Across the Globe, University of Minnesota, October 2011. Also performed at the opening ceremony of the conference Hmong Across Borders, University of Minnesota, October 4, 2013.

Vue, Pao Lee. "Racial Assimilation and Popular Culture: Hmong Youth (Sub)Cultures and the Persistence of the Color Line." PhD diss., University of Minnesota, 2009.

Yang, Shoua. "Hmong Social and Political Capital: The Formation and Maintenance of Hmong-American Organizations." PhD diss., Northern Illinois University, 2006.

Videos

Ellison, Richard, Andrew Pearson, Martin Smith, and Will Lyman. "Roots of a War." In *Vietnam, a Television History*. Disc 1. Boston: WGBH Boston Video, 2004. DVD.

Geddes, W. R. *Miao Year*. Del Ray, CA: Contemporary Films and McGraw-Hill, 1970. 2 film reels, 61 min.

Long, Larry, Lia Vang, and Eileen Littig. *Being Hmong Means Being Free: A Video Portrait of Hmong Life and Culture in Today's America*. Green Bay, WI: NEWIST/CESA, 2000. DVD.

Schofield, Steven R. *A Brief History of the Hmong and the Secret War in Laos*. Milwaukee: Hmong American Friendship Association, 2004. DVD.

Tang, Mark, and Lu Lippold. *Open Season*. Minneapolis: Passionfruit Films, 2011. DVD.

Xiong, Yuepheng. *Taug Txoj Lw Ntshav: Keeb Kwm Hmoob Nyob Suav Teb*. Saint Paul, MN: Hmong ABC, 2000. DVD.

———. *Taug Txoj Lw Ntshaw Daim 3: Tsab Xyooj Mem Sawv Tua Suav, 1855–1873*. Saint Paul, MN: Hmongland Publishing, 2005. DVD.

Index

Page numbers in italics refer to illustrations.

age estimating, 195, 352–53n9, 353n11
alliance and rebellion within the state (1850–1900), 50–92; autonomy granted to Hmong after rebellion, 79; French colonial advances and Hmong, 84–88; Han Chinese influences on Hmong identity, 50–58; historical chronology constructed from Chinese records, 61–64; Hmong-Phuan relations in Muang Phuan (Xieng Khouang) to 1893, 80–84; introduction, 12–13; Kaitong Rebellion (1896) and Hmong-French alliance in Muang Phuan, 89–92; Mandate of Heaven as Hmong political ideology, 58–61; migrations into Southeast Asia, 64–69; political landscape of nineteenth-century mainland Southeast Asia, 70–78; relations with Tai in Tonkin, early, 78–80; renegotiating ethnic hierarchy (1858–93), 84–88; taxes plus rent, 80. *See also* French colonial advances and Hmong; Han Chinese influences on Hmong identity; migrations into Southeast Asia; political landscape of nineteenth-century mainland Southeast Asia
American Indians and Hmong, 65, 330n66
Anouvong as last king of Vientiane, 74–75, 77

Blia Yao. *See* Lo Blia Yao
boar as symbol of worship, 23. *See also* Tswb Tshoj, legend as king
Boun Oum (na Champassak), 74, 311, 370n28
bureaucratic solidarity quest and segmentation of Hmong society, 35–40; bonding of all Hmong, 36–37; branching of Hmong vs. Han, 37, 323n90; countries classification of Hmong, 38; cultural groups, clans, and

lineages, 38–40; establishing lineage rituals, 38–39; ethnic identity and limitations, 35–37; funeral practices, 39; kinship-based society, 36–37
burial beliefs, 315–16n10

Central Intelligence Agency (CIA) and Vang Pao, 9, 31
ceremonial households (lineages), 38, 39
Chao Quang Lo (Terrestrial Dragon), 289–90
China as originally Hmong, 62
China vs. Laos, confusion about homeland, 21
Chiyou (Txiv Yawg), 62, 326n1
Chong Toua. *See* Moua Chong Toua
Christianity conversion, 69, 331n82, 336n157
Chulalongkorn as king of Siam, 70, 72
clan(s): as barrier to political unity, 40–42; divisions, 36–37; Hmong-hood and, 40; incest taboo, 38, 40; leader vs. king, 12; marriage not permitted within, 38, 323–24n97; membership in, 38; number of, 38; respect for your own, 41; size importance, 31, 322n71; social unit importance, 39; without a, 39–40
Colonial Route 7 (CR7): completion of, 221; conscription of Hmong for construction of, 84; as consolidation of French rule essential, 95; construction start, 179; as defining moment in Hmong leader's career, 5–6, 9; Hmong resistance to aid building of, 172–73, 177, 179–80; Lo Blia Yao as project supervisor for, 6, 9, 14, 155, 164; Lo Blia Yao skimming from budget for, 178; Ly Foung overseeing maintenance of, 225; as physical reminder of Hmong and French alliance, 9; route of, 6; workers pay for

389

Pathet Lao Party, 244; joining Communists, 271, 277; losing support by siding
with Japanese, 263-64; neglecting his education, 233; photograph of, *300*; rebuking
Touby Lyfoung publically, 242; as seeker
of legitimacy from Communists, 294; as
seeker of legitimacy from Japanese, 252;
side-switching ease of, 8; struggles with
Touby Lyfoung, 15, 242, 253-65, 267-74;
supplied soldiers on communist side, 284;
as vice president as reward of revolution,
294-302; as vice president of Lao Front for
National Reconstruction, 303; as youngest
son of Lo Blia Yao, 227

Lo Fong, 159, 347n12

Lo Mai: death of, 215-18; enticement by Ly
Foung of, 200; kidnapping of, 206-10;
photograph of, *207*

Lo Nhia Vu: election for *tasseng* of Keng Khoai
and, 250, 251; escape of, 269-70; forced to
do bidding of Japanese, 264, 265; gambling
addiction of, 233, 237; grave monument of,
10; as high-ranking member of Central
Committee, 302; lack of help to Tsong
Tou, 237, 238; as looming Hmong figure
with Lo Fay Dang of Lao PDR, 303; Ly
clan beating him unconscious, 265, 267-
69; as main Communist Hmong leader,
xv; marriages of, 267; marriage to daughter
of Tasseng Naotou Moua, 247; mother of,
359n21; as nationalist hero, 8; on reasons
why family joined Communists, 271; scars
visible in video of, 363n39; as son of Lo
Blia Yao, 159, 237; Tsong Tou break with,
285

Lo Pa Tsi: army maintained by, small, 162; assassination of, 163; brokering opium deals,
162; China legacy and, 156-63; family tree,
158; as father of Lo Blia Yao, 157; marriage
alliances, 157, 158, 159, 161; move to Nong
Het, 160, 162; as rebel leader against Qing,
157; receiving *kaitong* title, 161; theft of his
silver, 162-63, 348n27; wealth of, 162-63

Lo Shong Ger: against Lo Blia Yao (his uncle),
178; corrupt practice of, 182; coveting Lo
Blia Yao's position, 180; daily gatherings at
house of, 181; defeat of, 185-91; ethics of Lo

Blia Yao partly reason for revolt, 179; final
break from Lo Blia Yao, 183; joined Pa
Chay's War, 180; as literate, 180; as Lo Blia
Yao's secretary, 180; loss of rifles, 181; male
lines fate, 211; position on Lo family tree,
158; recruiting Hmong for Vue Pa Chay,
181; renounced lineage and planned assassination of Lo Blia Yao, 184; resentment of
Hmong to lure him to his death, 246; revolt in Xieng Khouang (1919-20), 178-84;
sons hidden to save them, 181, 189, 190;
suicide of, 190; supervised construction of
CR7, 180; surrender of, 189

Lo Tsong Nou, 158, *158*, 159

Lo Tsong Tou: awarded rhinoceros horn by
father, 242; credibility undermined by father, 227; dispute over father's estate, 237-
38, 359n24; dispute with Fay Dang, 236,
237; fate after father's death, 221, 236, 237-
38, 238, 240, 241; Lo Blia Yao as father of,
206, 215; as Lo Blia Yao's replacement,
221-27; as opium addict, 227; photograph
of, *239*; position on Lo family tree, *158*; relinquished subdistrict of Keng Khoai to
French, 226; supporting Touby Lyfoung
as *tasseng* of Keng Khoai, 250; theft of
taxes from, 238, *239*, 240; viewed as traitor
by his family, 240, 285; wedding feast of,
208. *See also* Lo Bee Chou

Lo Wen Teu, 289, 290, 367n55

lowlands prejudiced view of Hmong, 203

Ly, Jer Jalao, xvi; as fairy-tale dragon princess,
169; as fourth wife of Lo Blia Yao, 66, 160;
Lo Vang as son of, 296; marriage alliance
for Lo Blia Yao, 168; photograph of, *170*

Ly (Lee) clan: family tree, *195*; importance of,
168-69; Ly Nhia Vu as clan leader, 157;
three lineages of, 353n15; title from Phuan
princes, 155

Ly Dra Pao: as adult returned to and rejected
by relatives, 137, 196, 201, 246, 324n105,
347-48n24; death of, 196; displaced and
left China (1870), 68, 69; family tree, *195*;
as learned arrogant man with loose mouth,
196; Ly Foung as third son of, 194; oral
history of Ly clan passed down to son of,
68; as orphan raised by Chinese family, 68,

NEW PERSPECTIVES
IN SOUTHEAST ASIAN STUDIES

The Burma Delta: Economic Development and Social Change
on an Asian Rice Frontier, 1852–1941
Michael Adas

Voices from the Plain of Jars: Life under an Air War, second edition
Edited by Fred Branfman with essays and drawings by Laotian villagers

From Rebellion to Riots: Collective Violence on Indonesian Borneo
Jamie S. Davidson

The Floracrats: State-Sponsored Science and the Failure
of the Enlightenment in Indonesia
Andrew Goss

Revolution Interrupted: Farmers, Students, Law, and Violence
in Northern Thailand
Tyrell Haberkorn

Amazons of the Huk Rebellion: Gender, Sex, and Revolution
in the Philippines
Vina A. Lanzona

Dreams of the Hmong Kingdom: The Quest for Legitimation
in French Indochina, 1850–1960
Mai Na M. Lee

The Government of Mistrust: Illegibility and Bureaucratic Power
in Socialist Vietnam
Ken MacLean

CPSIA information can be obtained at www.ICGtesting.com
Printed in the USA
LVOW10s1821150715

446355LV00003B/464/P